BLANDFORD FORUM PARISH CHURCH, from S.W. *c.* 1735

AN INVENTORY OF HISTORICAL MONUMENTS IN THE

COUNTY OF DORSET

VOLUME THREE
CENTRAL DORSET

Part I

ROYAL COMMISSION ON
HISTORICAL MONUMENTS (ENGLAND)
MCMLXX

SBN 11 700458 8*

Printed in Scotland by Her Majesty's Stationery Office
at HMSO Press, Edinburgh

TABLE OF CONTENTS

PART I

CORRECTIONS

HISTORICAL MONUMENTS IN THE COUNTY OF DORSET, VOLUME III

Part 1, p. 127, under Fittings, for *Helm* read *Helmet*, and in the entry, after 'ridge', read—and with shaped reinforce over brow, visor in two parts and lower bevor all pivoted at sides to open, the foregoing mid 16th-century, gorget plates 17th-century replacements, the whole probably English; with Freke crest, a bull's head collared or, carved in wood, added for funerary purposes.

Part 2, p. 368, for *Helm, Tilting,* read *Helmet, Close.*

ROYAL COMMISSION ON HISTORICAL MONUMENTS
APRIL 1971
LONDON: HER MAJESTY'S STATIONERY OFFICE

PARISHES DESCRIBED IN THE INVENTORY

(*see* map in pocket at end of Part 2)

PART 1

1 ALTON PANCRAS
2 ANDERSON
3 ATHELHAMPTON
4 BISHOP'S CAUNDLE
5 BLANDFORD FORUM
6 BLANDFORD ST. MARY
7 BRYANSTON
8 BUCKLAND NEWTON
9 BURLESTON
10 CAUNDLE MARSH
11 CHARLTON MARSHALL
12 CHARMINSTER
13 CHESELBOURNE
14 CHILD OKEFORD
15 DEWLISH
16 DURWESTON
17 FIFEHEAD NEVILLE
18 GLANVILLE'S WOOTTON
19 HAMMOON
20 HANFORD
21 HAZELBURY BRYAN
22 HILTON
23 HINTON ST. MARY
24 HOLWELL
25 IBBERTON
26 IWERNE COURTNEY or SHROTON
27 IWERNE STEPELTON
28 LYDLINCH

PART 2

29 MANSTON
30 MAPPOWDER
31 MARNHULL
32 MELCOMBE HORSEY
33 MILBORNE ST. ANDREW
34 MILTON ABBAS
35 OKEFORD FITZPAINE
36 PIDDLEHINTON
37 PIDDLETRENTHIDE
38 PUDDLETOWN
39 PULHAM
40 PURSE CAUNDLE
41 SHILLINGSTONE
42 SPETISBURY
43 STALBRIDGE
44 STINSFORD
45 STOKE WAKE
46 STOURPAINE
47 STOURTON CAUNDLE
48 STURMINSTER NEWTON
49 TINCLETON
50 TOLPUDDLE
51 TURNWORTH
52 WINTERBORNE CLENSTON
53 WINTERBORNE HOUGHTON
54 WINTERBORNE KINGSTON
55 WINTERBORNE STICKLAND
56 WINTERBORNE WHITECHURCH
57 WINTERBORNE ZELSTON
58 WOOLLAND

LIST OF ILLUSTRATIONS

PART 1, pp. i–lxii, 1–142; Pls., Frontis., 1–149

PART 2, pp. 143–356; Pls. 150–216

(The prefixed numerals in brackets refer to the monument numbers of the Inventory)

Glanville's Wootton Church: 14th-century floor tiles.

PREFACE

THE third Dorset Inventory covers fifty-eight parishes in the central part of the County; in it the policy regarding size and scope set out in the preface of the second volume has been continued.

Apart from 'Celtic' Field Groups and Roman Roads, the Monuments (dating from before 1850) in Central Dorset are listed, in the following order, under the names of the Civil Parishes in which they occur:

(1) Architecture
  (*a*) Ecclesiastical Buildings
  (*b*) Secular Buildings
(2) Mediaeval and later Earthworks
(3) Roman and Prehistoric Monuments
(4) Undated Earthworks etc.

Each parish has a short introductory note briefly summarising its aspect and history.

Since 'Celtic' Field Groups bear no relation to the boundaries of the parishes it has been necessary to describe them extra-parochially in a special division of the Inventory. For the same reason the description of the Roman Roads of the whole County has been reserved until the last Inventory of the Dorset series.

As in former Inventories, it has been thought best to conform with the Ordnance Survey maps (without prejudice as to accuracy) in the orthography of proper names. Where, occasionally, two versions of the same name appear on the same map we have adopted the more recent usage. In recording funerary monuments, aberrantly spelt surnames have been copied, whereas the normal spelling of the same name may be followed elsewhere in the text. The latinisation of Christian names on funeral monuments is ignored.

The entries in the Inventory are necessarily much compressed. Those for churches and other important buildings begin with a brief description of the fabric and an historical summary; this is followed by a detailed architectural description and, finally, by a catalogue of the fittings. The entries for less important buildings are more rigorously compressed from the records made in the field. For many houses and cottages, space can be found for little more than a bare record of their location and the materials used in their construction; some minor 19th-century dwellings are represented by no more than a map-reference, a restriction which is regrettable, but unavoidable in view of our desire to include all Monuments dating from before 1850.

Many plans are included in the text, and the conventions described on p. xxi of *Dorset* II have been followed.

Except for certain air photographs, the photographs for all the half-tone and coloured plates in the volume have been taken by the Commission's photographers. Copies of them, and of many others which remain in our files, may be obtained on application to the National Monuments Record. For many valuable air photographs we are indebted to Dr. J. K. S. St. Joseph, Director in Aerial Photography at Cambridge University; other air photographs have been provided by J. R. Boyden, Esq., by the Royal Naval Air Service at Yeovilton, and by the School of Army Aviation at Middle Wallop, to all of whom the Commission's indebtedness is gratefully acknowledged.

We are also grateful to the Air Surveyors of the Ordnance Survey for much invaluable assistance in our investigation of 'Celtic' Field Groups in Dorset and other areas.

Every Monument in the Inventory has been inspected by one or more of our Investigators, and every one of major importance, or which has proved difficult of analysis, has been re-examined, a process often demanding weeks rather than hours of work. The longest entry, of Milton Abbey, is the result of numerous visits and of two seasons of excavations. After being set up in print, the proofs of the whole Inventory have been circulated among my fellow Commissioners and carefully considered by them.

A number of Monuments have been destroyed since the time of investigation; for buildings, the word *Demolished* is added to the relevant entry, but no attempt has been made to recast the description in the past tense. The Inventory was checked in the field during 1967 and variations that have occurred since that date are not described.

No work of this nature can escape the intrusion of some mistakes, but I believe that they are neither numerous nor serious. Any correction that may be sent to the Secretary with a view to amendment in some future edition will be welcomed. Meanwhile these corrections will be added to our records, which are open for consultation by any accredited person after due notice has been given to the Secretary. These records really constitute the Inventory which we have been commissioned to make; the present volume is no more than a digest of them.

SALISBURY

THE ROYAL WARRANTS

WHITEHALL,
2ND OCTOBER, 1963

The QUEEN has been pleased to issue a Commission under Her Majesty's Royal Sign Manual to the following effect:

ELIZABETH R.

ELIZABETH THE SECOND, by the Grace of God of the United Kingdom of Great Britain and Northern Ireland and of Our other Realms and Territories, QUEEN, Head of the Commonwealth, Defender of the Faith,

To

Our Right Trusty and Entirely-beloved Cousin and Counsellor Robert Arthur James, Marquess of Salisbury, Knight of Our Most Noble Order of the Garter;

Our Trusty and Well-beloved:

Sir Albert Edward Richardson, Knight Commander of the Royal Victorian Order;
Sir John Newenham Summerson, Knight, Commander of Our Most Excellent Order of the British Empire;
Nikolaus Pevsner, Esquire, Commander of Our Most Excellent Order of the British Empire;
Christopher Edward Clive Hussey, Esquire, Commander of Our Most Excellent Order of the British Empire;
Ian Archibald Richmond, Esquire, Commander of Our Most Excellent Order of the British Empire;
Henry Clifford Darby, Esquire, Officer of Our Most Excellent Order of the British Empire;
Donald Benjamin Harden, Esquire, Officer of Our Most Excellent Order of the British Empire;
John Grahame Douglas Clark, Esquire;
Howard Montagu Colvin, Esquire;
Vivian Hunter Galbraith, Esquire;
William Abel Pantin, Esquire;
Stuart Piggott, Esquire;
Courtenay Arthur Ralegh Radford, Esquire;
Arnold Joseph Taylor, Esquire;
Francis Wormald, Esquire.

GREETING!

Whereas We have deemed it expedient that the Commissioners appointed to the Royal Commission on the Ancient and Historical Monuments and Constructions of England shall serve for such periods as We by the hand of Our First Lord of the Treasury may specify and that the said Commissioners shall, if The National Buildings Record is liquidated, assume the control and management of such part of The

National Buildings Record's collection as does not solely relate to Our Principality of Wales and to Monmouthshire, and that a new Commission should issue for these purposes:

Now Know Ye that We have revoked and determined, and do by these Presents revoke and determine, all the Warrants whereby Commissioners were appointed on the twenty-ninth day of March one thousand nine hundred and forty six and on any subsequent date:

And We do by these Presents authorize and appoint you, the said Robert Arthur James, Marquess of Salisbury (Chairman), Sir Albert Edward Richardson, Sir John Newenham Summerson, Nikolaus Pevsner, Christopher Edward Clive Hussey, Ian Archibald Richmond, Henry Clifford Darby, Donald Benjamin Harden, John Grahame Douglas Clark, Howard Montagu Colvin, Vivian Hunter Galbraith, William Abel Pantin, Stuart Piggott, Courtenay Arthur Ralegh Radford, Arnold Joseph Taylor and Francis Wormald to be Our Commissioners for such periods as We may specify in respect of each of you to make an inventory of the Ancient and Historical Monuments and Constructions connected with or illustrative of the contemporary culture, civilisation and conditions of life of the people in England, excluding Monmouthshire, from the earliest times to the year 1714, and such further Monuments and Constructions subsequent to that year as may seem in your discretion to be worthy of mention therein, and to specify those which seem most worthy of preservation.

And Whereas We have deemed it expedient that Our Lieutenants of Counties in England should be appointed ex-officio Members of the said Commission for the purposes of that part of the Commission's inquiry which relates to ancient and historical monuments and constructions within their respective counties:

Now Know Ye that We do by these Presents authorize and appoint Our Lieutenant for the time being of each and every County in England, other than Our County of Monmouth, to be a Member of the said Commission for the purposes of that part of the Commission's inquiry which relates to ancient and historical monuments and constructions within the area of his jurisdiction as Our Lieutenant of such County:

And for the better enabling you to carry out the purposes of this Our Commission, We do by these Presents authorize you to call in the aid and co-operation of owners of ancient monuments, inviting them to assist you in furthering the objects of the Commission; and to invite the possessors of such papers as you may deem it desirable to inspect to produce them before you:

And We do further authorize and empower you to confer with the Council of The National Buildings Record from time to time as may seem expedient to you in order that your deliberations may be assisted by the reports and records in the possession of the Council: and to make such arrangements for the furtherance of objectives of common interest to yourselves and the Council as may be mutually agreeable:

And We do further authorize and empower you to assume the general control and management (whether as Administering Trustees under a Scheme established under the Charities Act 1960 or otherwise) of that part of the collection of The National Buildings Record which does not solely relate to our Principality of Wales or to Monmouthshire and (subject, in relation to the said part of that collection, to the provisions of any such Scheme as may be established affecting the same) to make such arrangements for the continuance and furtherance of the work of The National Buildings Record as you may deem to be necessary both generally and for the creation of any wider record or collection containing or including architectural, archaeological and historical information concerning important sites and buildings throughout England:

And We do further give and grant unto you, or any three or more of you, full power to call before you such persons as you shall judge likely to afford you any information upon the subject of this Our Commission; and also to call for, have access to and examine all such books, documents, registers and records as may afford you the fullest information on the subject and to inquire of and concerning the premises by all other lawful ways and means whatsoever:

And We do by these Presents authorize and empower you, or any three or more of you, to visit and personally inspect such places as you may deem it expedient so to inspect for the more effectual carrying out of the purposes aforesaid:

And We do by these Presents will and ordain that this Our Commission shall continue in full force and virtue, and that you, Our said Commissioners, or any three or more of you, may from time to time proceed in the execution thereof, and of every matter and thing therein contained, although the same be not continued from time to time by adjournment:

And We do further ordain that you, or any three or more of you, have liberty to report your proceedings under this Our Commission from time to time if you shall judge it expedient so to do:

And Our further Will and Pleasure is that you do, with as little delay as possible, report to Us, under your hands and seals, or under the hands and seals of any three or more of you, your opinion upon the matters herein submitted for your consideration.

Given at Our Court at Saint James's the Twenty-eighth day of September, 1963, in The Twelfth Year of Our Reign.

By Her Majesty's Command,

HENRY BROOKE

By Royal Warrant dated 23rd October, 1964, William Francis Grimes, Esquire, C.B.E., and by Royal Warrant dated 21st March, 1966, both Maurice Willmore Barley, Esquire, and Sheppard Sunderland Frere, Esquire, were appointed Members of the Royal Commission on Historical Monuments (England).

By Royal Warrant dated 2nd April, 1968, Richard John Copland Atkinson, Esquire, and Arthur Oswald, Esquire, were appointed Members of the Royal Commission on Historical Monuments (England), and Henry Clifford Darby, Esquire, having completed his term of office, was reappointed a Member of the Commission.

LIST OF COMMISSIONERS

The Most Honourable the Marquess of Salisbury, K.G. (*Chairman*)
Her Majesty's Lieutenant of the County of Dorset (*ex officio*)
Courtenay Arthur Ralegh Radford, Esq.
Sir John Newenham Summerson, C.B.E.
John Grahame Douglas Clark, Esq.
Francis Wormald, Esq.
Howard Montagu Colvin, Esq., C.B.E.
Donald Benjamin Harden, Esq., O.B.E.
William Abel Pantin, Esq.
Arnold Joseph Taylor, Esq.
The above were appointed September 28th, 1963

William Francis Grimes, Esq., C.B.E.,	appointed	October 23rd, 1964
Maurice Willmore Barley, Esq.,	,,	March 21st, 1966
Sheppard Sunderland Frere, Esq.,	,,	,,
Richard John Copland Atkinson, Esq.,	,,	April 2nd, 1968
Henry Clifford Darby, Esq., O.B.E.,	,,	,,
Arthur Stanley Oswald, Esq.,	,,	,,

Secretary
Arthur Richard Dufty, Esq.

ROYAL COMMISSION ON THE ANCIENT AND HISTORICAL MONUMENTS AND CONSTRUCTIONS OF ENGLAND

REPORT to the Queen's Most Excellent Majesty

MAY IT PLEASE YOUR MAJESTY

We, the undersigned Commissioners, appointed to make an Inventory of the Ancient and Historical Monuments and Constructions connected with or illustrative of the contemporary culture, civilisation and conditions of life of the people of England, excluding Monmouthshire, from the earliest times to the year 1714, and of such further Monuments and Constructions subsequent to that year as may seem in our discretion to be worthy of mention therein, and to specify those which seem most worthy of preservation, do humbly submit to Your Majesty the following Report, being the twenty-fifth Report on the work of the Commission since its first appointment.

2. We have pleasure in reporting the completion of our recording of the Monuments in the central part of the County of Dorset, an area comprising fifty-eight parishes, containing 1,418 Monuments of sufficient significance to demand separate enumeration, and some 300 minor Monuments.

3. Following our usual practice we have prepared a full, illustrated Inventory of the Monuments in Central Dorset, which will be issued as a non-Parliamentary publication (*Dorset* III). As in the Inventory of south-east Dorset (*Dorset* II) accompanying the twenty-fourth Report, the Commissioners have adopted the terminal date 1850 for the Monuments included in the Inventory.

4. The methods adopted in previous Inventories have in general been adhered to, and, as in south-east Dorset, attention has been paid to topography and to the form and development of the man-made landscape in which the Monuments are set. It is hoped that the introductory notes to each parish will suggest the visual attributes and indicate the history of settlement of the area.

5. The method of presenting 'Celtic' Field Groups and associated Monuments follows the precedent of *Dorset* II. Since many of these Monuments extend beyond the boundaries of a single parish they are described extra-parochially in a section of the Inventory following the inventory by parishes.

6. Important entries in the Inventory of Central Dorset have been submitted in draft to the incumbents of churches and to the owners of houses, as appropriate, and we are satisfied that no significant Monument dating from before the year 1850 has been omitted.

7. Our special thanks are due to incumbents and churchwardens and to owners and occupiers who have allowed access by our staff to the Monuments in their charge or ownership. We are indebted to the Directors and Curators of many institutions for their ready assistance to us, and particularly to the Curators of the Dorset County Museum in Dorchester, the late Lieut.-Col. C. D. Drew, and Mr. R. N. R. Peers; also to Miss M. Holmes, the County Archivist, and to Miss P. K. Stewart, the Assistant Archivist in the Diocese of Salisbury, who have helped us over many points of detail. To M. J. W. Craig Esq. of the Inspectorate of Ancient Monuments we owe the identification of the Riding House at Wolfeton, Charminster. We have to record our indebtedness to the Director General of the Ordnance Survey for access to his archaeological records, for assistance in the preparation and printing of maps, and for valuable work done by the Air Surveyors of his Department. We wish to record our gratitude to Dr. J. K. S. St. Joseph, Director in Aerial Photography in the University of Cambridge, for many air photographs taken

specially for us, and we are also grateful for air photographs supplied by J. R. Boyden, Esq., by the Royal Naval Air Service at Yeovilton, and by the School of Army Aviation at Middle Wallop. To Peter Ferrey, Esq. we are indebted for permission to reproduce a drawing of Athelhampton Hall by Benjamin Ferrey.

8. We humbly recommend to Your Majesty's notice the following Monuments in Central Dorset, as being Most Worthy of Preservation:

ECCLESIASTICAL:

ANDERSON

(2) THE CHURCH OF ST. ANDREW, of the first half of the 12th century, with an apsidal E. end and interesting 18th-century fittings.

BISHOP'S CAUNDLE

(1) THE PARISH CHURCH, mainly of the 15th century.

BLANDFORD FORUM

(1) THE PARISH CHURCH, dating from *c.* 1735.

(2) ST. LEONARD'S CHAPEL, a 15th-century building now used as a barn.

BLANDFORD ST. MARY

(1) WALL MONUMENT of Francis Cartwright, 1758, in the Parish Church.

BUCKLAND NEWTON

(1) THE PARISH CHURCH, dating from the 13th and 15th centuries.

CHARLTON MARSHALL

(1) THE PARISH CHURCH, a graceful building of 1713, with a 15th-century west tower.

CHARMINSTER

(1) THE PARISH CHURCH, dating from the early 12th century, and with a fine 16th-century west tower.

CHESELBOURNE

(1) THE PARISH CHURCH, of late 13th-century origin, with 14th and 15th-century additions.

(2) LYSCOMBE CHAPEL, a late 12th-century monument now much in need of repair; also the remains of a 15th-century priest's house adjacent.

CHILD OKEFORD

(1) THE CHURCH TOWER, of the late 15th century.

DEWLISH

(1) THE PARISH CHURCH, of the 12th century and later.

DURWESTON

(1) THE CHURCH TOWER, of the late 15th century; also an inscription of 1455 reset in the south porch.

FIFEHEAD NEVILLE

(1) THE PARISH CHURCH, of 14th-century origin, with 18th-century enlargements.

GLANVILLE'S WOOTTON

(1) THE PARISH CHURCH, with a Chantry Chapel of 1344, a west tower of *c.* 1400, a 13th-century recumbent effigy, and important 17th-century wall monuments.

HAMMOON

(1) THE PARISH CHURCH, of late 12th or early 13th-century origin.

HANFORD

(1) THE PARISH CHURCH, largely of the mid 17th century.

HAZELBURY BRYAN

(1) THE PARISH CHURCH, a fine example of late 15th-century architecture, retaining interesting contemporary glass.

HILTON

(1) THE PARISH CHURCH, largely of the 15th and 16th centuries, with traces of an earlier fabric.

HINTON ST. MARY

(1) THE PARISH CHURCH, of the mid 19th century, with a 15th-century west tower.

HOLWELL

(1) THE PARISH CHURCH, largely of the late 15th century, with carved stonework of good quality.

IBBERTON

(1) THE PARISH CHURCH, of the mid 15th and early 16th centuries.

IWERNE COURTNEY

(1) THE PARISH CHURCH, of the 14th century, with important 17th-century additions.

IWERNE STEPLETON

(1) THE PARISH CHURCH, of the late 11th or early 12th century.

LYDLINCH

(1) THE PARISH CHURCH, of the 15th century.

(2) THE CHURCH at Stock Gaylard, with a 13th-century recumbent effigy.

MANSTON

(1) THE PARISH CHURCH, of 13th-century origin, with a 15th-century west tower.

MAPPOWDER

(1) THE PARISH CHURCH, mainly of the 15th century, but with a fine 12th-century font and a small 13th-century effigy for a heart burial.

MARNHULL

(1) THE PARISH CHURCH, of 12th-century origin, with 14th and 15th-century additions including a fine 15th-century west tower, partly rebuilt in the 18th century, a tomb with three recumbent effiges of *c.* 1470, and a richly decorated nave roof of *c.* 1520.

MELCOMBE HORSEY

(1) THE PARISH CHURCH, of the 14th and 15th centuries.

MILBORNE ST. ANDREW

(1) THE PARISH CHURCH, of the 12th century, with a fine original south doorway and font, and with a 15th-century west tower.

Milton Abbas

(1) The Abbey Church, of the 14th and 15th centuries, the most important ecclesiastical monument in the area.

(2) The Parish Church, of *c.* 1786, an example of the revived Gothic style.

(3) St. Catherine's Chapel, of the 12th century, with an interesting original inscription relating to indulgences.

Okeford Fitzpaine

(1) The Parish Church, with a 15th-century west tower and an unusual tower arch.

(2) The Church at Belchalwell, with a notable 12th-century south doorway.

Piddlehinton

(1) The Parish Church, of the 15th and 16th centuries, with a noteworthy south tower.

Piddletrenthide

(1) The Parish Church, of 12th-century origin, with an especially notable west tower dated 1487.

Puddletown

(1) The Parish Church, of 12th-century origin, with an original font and with 14th-century and notable 15th-century additions; containing a remarkable group of tombs of the Martyn family, and fine 17th-century woodwork.

Pulham

(1) The Parish Church, of the 15th and 16th centuries.

Purse Caundle

(1) The Parish Church, of the 15th and 16th centuries, with a noteworthy canopied table-tomb.

Shillingstone

(1) The Parish Church, of the early 12th century.

Spetisbury

(1) The Parish Church, of *c.* 1200, but much restored, and with an altar-tomb of 1599 and a fine 17th-century pulpit.

Stalbridge

(1) The Parish Church, largely of the 19th century, but with a north chapel of *c.* 1500.

Stinsford

(1) The Parish Church, of the 13th to 16th centuries, incorporating a notable relief of the late 10th or early 11th century.

Stourpaine

(1) The Church Tower, of the late 15th century.

Stourton Caundle

(1) The Parish Church, of the 13th to 15th centuries, with a noteworthy 16th-century pulpit.

(2) Chapel, of the 13th century, now used as a barn.

Sturminster Newton

(1) The Parish Church, of the late 14th or early 15th century, with a fine nave roof of *c.* 1500.

Tolpuddle

(1) The Parish Church, of 12th-century origin with 13th and 14th-century additions, having a well preserved 14th-century roof and containing an important 12th-century tomb.

Turnworth

(1) The Church Tower, of *c.* 1500.

Winterborne Clenston

(1) The Parish Church, by Lewis Vulliamy, built in 1840.

Winterborne Kingston

(1) The Church, of 14th-century origin.

Winterborne Stickland

(1) The Parish Church, of 13th-century origin, with a west tower of *c.* 1500 and with 18th-century alterations.

Winterborne Whitechurch

(1) The Parish Church, with a chancel of *c.* 1200 and a central tower of the 15th century; also with a good 15th-century font.

Winterborne Zelston

(1) The Parish Church, largely of 1866, but with a 15th-century west tower.

SECULAR:

Anderson

(3) Anderson Manor House, dating from 1622, with walls of brick with stone dressings and with interior fittings of good quality.

(4) Tomson Farmhouse, of *c.* 1620, with interesting fragments of original plasterwork and panelling.

Athelhampton

(2) Athelhampton Hall, of late 15th-century origin with a well-preserved great hall and oriel window, and with 16th-century additions of high quality.

Bishop's Caundle

(2) Cornford Bridge, incorporating 15th-century and 18th-century masonry.

Blandford Forum

(4) Town Hall, façade, dated 1734.

(5) Fire Monument, dated 1760.

(7) Ryves's Almshouses, built in 1682.

(8) Coupar House, of the mid 18th century, with rich interior fittings.

(9) Lime Tree House, of *c.* 1735, a well-preserved example of a well-to-do citizen's dwelling.

(12) The Old House, of *c.* 1660, with a façade of rusticated brickwork.

(31) Eastway House, of *c.* 1735, with an elegant street front, and interior plasterwork of *c.* 1750.

(45) Houses in the Market Place, built *c.* 1735, by the architect John Bastard, partly for his own use.

(47) The Red Lion Inn, N. front, of *c.* 1735.

(52) The Old Greyhound Inn, N. front, of *c.* 1735.

(89) No. 81 Salisbury Street, a well-proportioned late 18th-century house.

(101) No. 10 West Street, comprising the S. fronts of two fine 18th-century town houses (first and second floors).

Blandford St. Mary

(2) The Manor House, of the 17th and 18th centuries.

(3) The Old Rectory, built in 1732.

(11) Brook House, of the second quarter of the 18th century and probably designed by Francis Cartwright.

Charminster

(4) Wolfeton House, incorporating an interesting gatehouse of *c.* 1500 and the remains of a richly decorated mansion of the later 16th century.

(5) Riding House, of the last quarter of the 16th century, probably the earliest riding school to survive in England.

(6) Forston House, of the early 18th century.

Child Okeford

(2) Fontmell Parva House, incorporating parts of a mid 17th-century manor house.

Dewlish

(2) Dewlish House, of 1702, with a well-proportioned N.E. front and interior fittings of good quality.

(3) Manor Farm House, of the early 17th century.

Glanville's Wootton

(6) Round Chimneys Farm House, of the late 16th century, comprising the remains of a larger house with stonework of good quality.

Hammoon

(2) The Manor House, dating from the first half of the 16th century, with additions, including stonework of good quality, of *c.* 1560.

Hanford

(2) Hanford House, an early 17th-century mansion of considerable architectural interest.

Hinton St. Mary

(2) The Manor House, a 17th-century house incorporating vestiges of a great hall which may be of the 13th century.

Holwell

(14) Naish Farm, an interesting 15th-century hall-type farmhouse with many original features.

Iwerne Courtney

(3) Ranston, a modern house incorporating a dignified 18th-century W. front; also an ornamental Bridge of the same period.

Iwerne Stepleton

(2) Stepleton House, a 17th-century mansion with 18th-century additions, and with interior fittings of good quality.

Mappowder

(3) Mappowder Court, incorporating the remains of the 17th-century seat of the Coker family.

Marnhull

(4) Senior's Farm, a late 15th-century house with internal fittings of good quality.

(5) Pope's Farm, incorporating an early 17th-century farmhouse and an adjacent stable range of about the same date.

Melcombe Horsey

(2) Bingham's Melcombe, a 16th-century mansion noted for its beauty, with 17th and 18th-century additions.

(3) Higher Melcombe, a manor house of the 16th century with 17th-century additions including a chapel, and with decorated plaster ceilings.

Milton Abbas

(4) Milton Abbey House, a late 18th-century mansion designed by Sir William Chambers and James Wyatt, incorporating a great hall of 1498 with a fine roof and richly carved screens. The 18th-century rooms have plasterwork, joinery and marble chimneypieces of high quality.

(7) 'Model Village', of *c.* 1780.

(8) Almshouses, of *c.* 1674, transferred to the new village in 1779.

(9) The Vicarage, of *c.* 1780.

Piddletrenthide

(3) The School Gates, of the 16th century and probably from the tomb of Lady Margaret Beaufort in Westminster Abbey.

(10) Pear Tree Cottage, a 16th-century dwelling.

Puddletown

(3) Waterston House, mainly modern, but retaining two noteworthy façades, one of 1586, the other of the mid 17th century.

(4) The Vicarage, largely of the early 18th century.

(15) Tudor Cottage, probably of 1573, with original interior fittings.

Pulham

(4) The Rectory, an example of the 18th-century revived Gothic style.

Purse Caundle

(2) The Manor House, of the 15th-century and later, a notable example of a medium-sized country house.

Spetisbury

(2) Crawford Bridge, incorporating some mediaeval masonry.

(3) Johns House, formerly the Rectory, a distinguished house, built in 1716.

Stalbridge

(2) Market Cross, of the late 15th century.

(3) Thornhill, of the 18th century, the house of Sir James Thornhill.

(4) Gate Piers, 17th-century, of the demolished Manor House.

Stinsford

(3) Stinsford House, partly of the 17th century.

(4) Kingston Maurward House, a dignified mansion, mainly of 1794.

(5) The Manor House, incorporating the shell of an important 16th-century house, but extensively modernised inside.

Stourpaine

(2) Lazerton Farm House, of the first half of the 17th century.

Sturminster Newton

(3) Bridge, of *c.* 1500, with 17th-century alterations.

(4) Fiddleford Mill, incorporating a mid 14th-century dwelling house with a great hall and solar, with original timber roofs of outstanding importance.

(7) House, in the market place, with a late mediaeval roof.

(27) HOUSE, close to the church, of the late 15th or early 16th century.
(29) VINE HOUSE, a small 17th-century town house.
(47) THE 'CASTLE', probably an Iron Age fort, with a late mediaeval building superimposed.

TOLPUDDLE
(2) THE MANOR HOUSE, dated 1656.

WINTERBORNE CLENSTON
(2) THE MANOR HOUSE, of the early 16th century, with a first-floor hall and with carved stonework and woodwork of good quality.
(3) BARN, of the 16th century, with a reused 15th-century hammer-beam roof of high quality.

WINTERBORNE STICKLAND
(2) THE RECTORY, dating from 1685.
(3) QUARLESTON FARM HOUSE, incorporating the remains of a 15th-century hall.

WINTERBORNE WHITECHURCH
(3) WHATCOMBE HOUSE, an early 19th-century mansion incorporating a smaller house of 1750.

MEDIAEVAL AND LATER EARTHWORKS:

CHARMINSTER
(25) SETTLEMENT REMAINS, formerly part of the hamlet of Charlton.

DEWLISH
(7) SETTLEMENT REMAINS known as 'Court Close'.

HILTON
(29) CULTIVATION REMAINS (a).

MELCOMBE HORSEY
(9) SETTLEMENT REMAINS of Bingham's Melcombe.

MILBORNE ST. ANDREW
(13) SETTLEMENT REMAINS.

MILTON ABBAS
(20) REMAINS of the TOWN which was demolished *c.* 1780.
(23) REMAINS of a PARK PALE in Milton Park Wood.

PUDDLETOWN
(21) SETTLEMENT REMAINS of Bardolfeston.

ROMAN, PREHISTORIC AND UNDATED MONUMENTS:

N.B. Destruction of field monuments continues to be rapid and widespread, and it is desirable that all monuments listed in this Inventory should be preserved, both because of the increasing rarity of such monuments and because extent and impressiveness of surface remains are not alone indicative of archaeological importance. This can be revealed only by excavation; therefore destruction should never be allowed without archaeological investigation.

ALTON PANCRAS
(18) ENCLOSURES in Tenant's Bottom.

CHESELBOURNE
(22), (23) CROSS-DYKES on Lyscombe Hill.

CHILD OKEFORD
(22) IRON AGE HILL-FORT on Hambledon Hill.
(23) NEOLITHIC LONG BARROW.

IBBERTON
(13) DYKE on Bell Hill.

MELCOMBE HORSEY
(11) ROMANO-BRITISH SETTLEMENT, with tracks and fields, on Bowden's Hill.
(12) NETTLECOMBE TOUT, Iron Age hill-fort.
(13–17) DYKES on Bowden's Hill.

MILBORNE ST. ANDREW
(18) WEATHERBY CASTLE, Iron Age hill-fort.
(30–37) ROUND BARROWS on Deverel Down.

OKEFORD FITZPAINE
(41) CROSS-DYKE on Okeford Hill.

PIDDLETRENTHIDE
(43) SETTLEMENT on West Hill, Plush, with associated track, and fields.
(45, 46, 47) DYKES on Lyscombe Hill.
(63) ENCLOSURE on Lower Down.

PUDDLETOWN
(30) ROUND BARROW near Duck Dairy House.

SPETISBURY
(30) SPETISBURY RINGS, Iron Age hill-fort.

STOKE WAKE
(6) RAWLSBURY CAMP, Iron Age hill-fort.

STOURPAINE
(11) HOD HILL, Iron Age hill-fort and Roman fort.

STURMINSTER NEWTON
(47) *see SECULAR*, above.

TURNWORTH
(7) SETTLEMENT on Ringmoor, with associated tracks and fields.

WINTERBORNE HOUGHTON
(9) SETTLEMENT near Meriden Wood, with associated tracks and fields.
(10) SETTLEMENT near Bully Wood, with associated tracks and fields.

WINTERBORNE WHITECHURCH
(19) COMBS DITCH, linear dyke.

'CELTIC' FIELD GROUP:

(42) FIELDS, STRIP LYNCHETS AND OTHER CULTIVATION REMAINS, Watcombe Plain, Alton Pancras.

9. In compiling the foregoing lists our criteria have been architectural or archaeological importance (the latter subject to the reservation expressed in the note to *Roman, Prehistoric and Undated Monuments* above), rarity, not only in the national but in the local field, and the degree of loss to the nation that would result from destruction, always bearing in mind the extent to which the Monuments are connected with or illustrative of the contemporary culture, civilisation and conditions of life of the people of England, as required by Your Majesty's Warrant. The lists have thus an entirely scholarly basis; we have taken no account of such attendant circumstances as cost of maintenance, usefulness for present-day purposes, or problems of preservation.

10. We desire to express our acknowledgment of the good work accomplished by our executive staff in the preparation and production of this Inventory; particularly by the editor, Mr. G. U. S. Corbett, and our investigators Messrs. R. W. McDowall, N. Drinkwater, H. C. Bowen, E. A. Gee, S. T. D. Spittle, T. W. French, R. A. H. Farrar, W. E. Barbour-Mercer, J. E. Williams, J. T. Smith, C. F. Stell, D. J. Bonney, R. M. Butler, P. J. Fowler, C. C. Taylor, and Miss M. Meek; by our illustrators, Messrs. B. Marriott, A. L. Pope, and Mrs. G. M. Lardner-Dennys; and by our photographers, Messrs. F. T. Power, W. C. Light, R. E. W. Parsons and C. J. Bassham.

11. We desire to add that, as well as affording constant general assistance to us, our Secretary and General Editor Mr. A. R. Dufty has contributed important entries in this Inventory.

12. The Survey of Central Dorset was started many years ago, before the outbreak of the Second World War and the diversion of our staff to work in other areas; hence the present Inventory includes valuable contributions by the late Sir Alfred Clapham, the late Mr. G. E. Chambers and the late Mr. A. T. Phillips.

13. The next Inventory in the Dorset series will record the Monuments of thirty-four parishes in the North of the County, extending eastwards to include the parishes in the Tarrant Valley. The final volume will deal with the East part of the County and will also contain a general survey of Roman Roads in Dorset.

Signed:

SALISBURY (*Chairman*)
J. W. WELD
C. A. RALEGH RADFORD
JOHN SUMMERSON
J. G. D. CLARK
FRANCIS WORMALD
H. M. COLVIN
D. B. HARDEN
W. A. PANTIN
A. J. TAYLOR
W. F. GRIMES
M. W. BARLEY
S. S. FRERE
R. J. C. ATKINSON
H. C. DARBY
A. S. OSWALD

A. R. DUFTY (*Secretary*)

ABBREVIATIONS USED IN THE VOLUME

Ant. J.	*The Antiquaries Journal.*
Arch.	*Archaeologia.*
Arch. J.	*The Archaeological Journal.*
Arch. Rev.	*The Architectural Review.*
B.A.P.	Abercromby, J., *Bronze Age Pottery* (1912).
Barrow Diggers	Woolls, C., *The Barrow Diggers* (1839).
B.M.	The British Museum.
Cambridgeshire I	R.C.H.M., *Inventory of Cambridgeshire*, Vol. I (1968).
Coker	Coker, John (or Gerard, T.), *Survey of Dorset* (1732).
C.T.D.	Warne, C., *Celtic Tumuli of Dorset* (1866), in three parts, each separately paged: Pt. 1, *My own Personal Researches;* Pt. 2, *Communications from Personal Friends;* Pt. 3, *Tumuli Opened at Various Periods.*
Cunnington MS.	Notes by E. Cunnington, *c.* 1890, in D.C.M.; published in part in Dorset *Procs.*, XXXVII (1916).
D.B.	*The Domesday Book*, P.R.O. Passages relating to Dorset are printed in Hutchins; also *V. C. H., Dorset, III.*
D.C.M.	Dorset County Museum, Dorchester.
D.C.R.O.	Dorset Record Office, Dorchester.
Dorset I, II etc.	Other volumes of the present work.
Dorset Barrows	Grinsell, L. V., *Dorset Barrows* (Dorchester, 1959).
Dorset *Procs.*	*Proceedings of the Dorset Natural History and Archaeological Society* (Dorchester, 1879–).
Durden Catalogue	Payne, G., *Catalogue of the Museum of Local Antiquities Collected by Mr. Henry Durden* (Lewes, 1892).
Eyton	Eyton, R. W., *A Key to Domesday* (1878).
Fägersten	Fägersten, A., *Place Names of Dorset* (Upsala, 1933).
Feudal Aids	*Feudal Aids*, 1284–1431 (H.M.S.O.).
Hutchins	Hutchins, John, *History and Antiquities of the County of Dorset*, 3rd edition (Westminster, 1861–70). When reference is necessary to the 1st and 2nd editions (1773 and 1803) this is specified, otherwise the 3rd edition is to be understood.
J.R.S.	*The Journal of Roman Studies.*
I.P.M.	*Inquisitions Post Mortem*, P.R.O.; published in *S. & D.N. &* Q., VIII–XXII.
L. & P.	*Letters and Papers, Foreign and Domestic* (H.M.S.O.).
Meekings	Meekings, C. A. F., *Dorset Hearth Tax Assessments* (Dorchester, 1951).
Nightingale	Nightingale, J. E., *Church Plate of Dorset* (Salisbury, 1889).
N.M.R.	The National Monuments Record.
O.D.	Ordnance Datum; mean sea-level.
O.S., 1811	Ordnance Survey, *Map of Dorset*, scale 1 inch to 1 mile, edition of 1811. (A copy with valuable MS. additions is in Salisbury Museum.)
Oswald	Oswald, A., *Country Houses of Dorset* (1959).
P.P.S.	*Proceedings of the Prehistoric Society.*
P.R.O.	The Public Record Office, London.
P.S.A.	*Proceedings of the Society of Antiquaries of London.*
Raven	Raven, Canon, *Church Bells of Dorset* (Dorchester, 1906); see also Walters, H. B., Dorset *Procs.*, LX, 97–120.
R.C.H.M.	The Royal Commission on Historical Monuments (England).
S. & D.N. & Q.	*Notes and Queries for Somerset and Dorset* (Sherborne, 1890–).
Subsidy Rolls	*Lay Subsidy Rolls*, 1327, 1333; P.R.O., E/179/103/4 and E/179/103/5; MS. copy in D.C.M. Generally, in this Inventory, the dates 1327 and 1333 may be taken to refer to these sources without further indication.
U.L.I.A.	University of London, Institute of Archaeology.
V.C.H.	*The Victoria History of the Counties of England.*
W.A.M.	*The Wiltshire Archaeological and Natural History Magazine* (Devizes, 1854–).

3

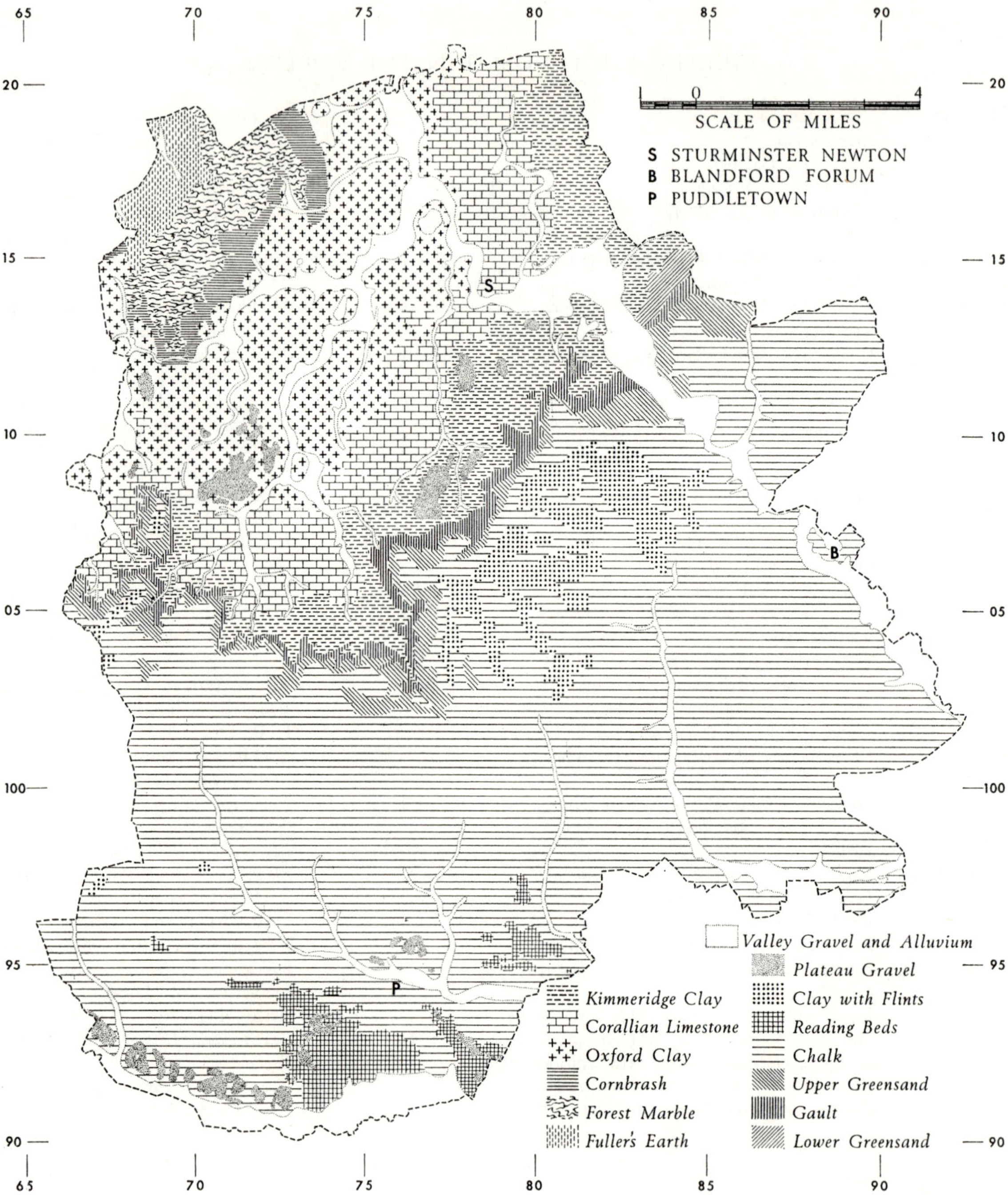

The Geology (Drift) of Central Dorset

DORSET III

SECTIONAL PREFACE

In the preface, numbers in square brackets refer to the plates; those in round brackets denote monuments in the Inventory.

TOPOGRAPHY AND GEOLOGY

THE PART OF DORSET which is described in this volume has an area of some 260 square miles and is divided into two distinct and almost equal parts by the Chalk escarpment of the Downs, which traverses it from S.W. to N.E. The scarp varies in height between 200 ft. and 500 ft., reaching its maximum altitude on Bulbarrow Hill, over 900 ft. above sea-level. The dip-slope of the escarpment falls S.E. to little more than 100 ft. at Tincleton in the S. and at Spetisbury in the E.; it is dissected by a series of streams which produce a rolling landscape with deep valleys and narrow interfluves. Erosion at the head of some valleys has resulted in large combes or basins, as at Lyscombe and Delcombe Bottom; similar erosion at Melcombe Horsey has cut through the scarp. In the extreme S., small outcrops of Reading Beds, the fringe of the S. Dorset Eocene deposits, overlie the Chalk and give rise to areas of heathland in the parishes of Tincleton and Puddletown.

To the N. of the escarpment the Vale of Blackmoor is almost entirely composed of bands of clays, sands and limestones of the Jurassic Beds, at altitudes between 150 ft. and 450 ft. above sea-level. At the foot of the escarpment is found the usual outcrop of Gault and Greensand; beyond this lies a band of heavy Kimmeridge Clay and this is succeeded by a narrow strip of Corallian Limestone and Sand which, especially in the N., gives rise to a low but prominent ridge. Further N.W. the Corallian belt gives way to a broad band of the underlying Oxford Clay, beyond which a narrow zone of Cornbrash Beds rises gently to the Fuller's Earth escarpment. The whole area is drained by small streams, mostly flowing N. from the foot of the Chalk escarpment to the River Stour; the latter flows generally south-eastwards, close to the N.E. boundary of the area under review and passes through the Chalk escarpment in a narrow gorge at Blandford Forum.

Building Materials

The varied geology of Central Dorset provides a multiplicity of building materials; among them, Corallian Limestone, common Greensand, Forest Marble, Flint, Chalk and Clay. Also within easy reach are Ham Hill stone, Greensand of superior quality, Heathstone, and Purbeck and Portland stones.

Choice of material in building naturally depends on the combination of such factors as local availability, the quality of the intended structure and ease of communication at the time of building. Before the 18th century, small domestic buildings were made of the materials that lay nearest to hand; cottages in Chalk districts were of chalk cob or, where the chalk was good enough, of clunch rubble banded with flint; cottages near the foot of the escarpment were of Greensand rubble, sometimes with flint banding; those of the Limestone area were of rubble and ashlar. On the other hand, the builders of churches and larger houses, with money to spend on appearance and solidity, brought materials of higher quality such as Ham Hill stone and Heathstone from further afield.

Although *Corallian Limestone* occurs in a broad outcrop running S.W.–N.E. across the N. part of the area, good building stone is confined to the vicinity of Marnhull and further north. In the mediaeval period it was not generally used in churches, except in the immediate vicinity of the quarries; Milton Abbey, however, is an exception to this rule. With the improved communications of the 19th century the material was used at much greater distance from the quarries, as in the rebuilt nave of Okeford Fitzpaine church. In secular architecture, where stone of poorer quality is acceptable, limestone rubble was more widely used and it is found in mediaeval buildings over the whole limestone outcrop, and even in the adjacent clay region.

Greensand in Central Dorset is not of very good quality and the local material is mainly used as rubble and squared rubble in lesser buildings. When good quality Greensand ashlar is found, as in the 15-century church towers of Child Okeford, Okeford Fitzpaine and Durweston, the material is probably from the Shaftesbury region.

Forest Marble, a rather rubbly, flaggy limestone, occurs in the extreme N.W. of the area; it is used locally for rubble walls at Stalbridge. In stone-slated roofs its use is more widespread.

Flint occurs only in conjunction with Chalk; it may be used in rough nodules, or split to give a fairly smooth face, or knapped to allow close jointing. Flint walling must be consolidated with quoins and dressings of other materials. Before the development of brick, Chalk clunch or Greensand was used for this purpose in minor buildings. In larger houses and in churches imported stones were used for the binding of flint walls; for instance in the 14th-century tower of Blandford St. Mary church the flintwork is banded with Heathstone from S. Dorset; in the 18th-century church at Charlton Marshall the flintwork is chequered with Greensand.

Chalk is used in squared blocks, as clunch, to provide an ashlar finish albeit of a weak kind; it is rarely used externally except when banded with flint, and then only in cottages. Clunch is sometimes used for the inner face of barn walls, as at Iwerne Courtney, where the outer face is of Greensand; it is also used for the web of the vaulting at Milton Abbey. Lesser secular buildings of the Chalk area commonly have walls of cob, a kind of concrete made from chalk. Since such walls rapidly deteriorate when damp they are provided with waterproof plinths, generally of flint, and waterproof rendering; occasionally, in 18th-century work, an outer skin of 'mathematical tiles' simulating brickwork is used. At Caundle Marsh cob is made from the argillaceous limestone of the local Forest Marble.

Clay occurs widely N.W. of the Chalk escarpment and in the extreme S. of the area and beyond. Since early in the 17th century it has been used for bricks; previously it was practically unused as a building material except for floor and roof tiles.

Of the imported stones, *Heathstone* is a coarse brown ferruginous material from the Bagshot Beds of S.E. Dorset (*see Dorset* II, xxxix); its distribution in Central Dorset is generally confined to the churches of the Winterborne valley and of the Stour valley S.E. of the escarpment. *Ham Hill* stone from Somerset is found in buildings of high quality all over the area. *Portland Stone* is found in 18th-century buildings in Blandford Forum and elsewhere. *Purbeck Marble* is used for decoration, in small quantities, in all parts of the area; it was much used for fonts in the 12th century and for altar-tombs in the 15th century (*see Dorset* II, xl).

Roof coverings. Until the 19th century *Thatch* was the normal roofing material of all but the most important buildings in Central Dorset, except perhaps in the Forest Marble district where material suitable for stone-slates is abundant; the great fires of Blandford Forum in 1713 and 1731 are attributable to the prevalence of thatched roofs. On the other hand, large churches and mansions all over Central Dorset were roofed with *Stone-slates* from the Forest Marble and Purbeck areas, or with slates from Devon and Cornwall. *Lead* was used for the roof of a chantry at Glanville's Wootton in the 14th century, and in the 15th century it was widely used.

ROMAN AND PREHISTORIC MONUMENTS

Most of the Roman and prehistoric monuments in Central Dorset lie on the Chalk, particularly those which have survived, until recently at least, as earthworks. A few, chiefly of the Roman period, lie on the Jurassic Beds N.W. of the escarpment. Most of the earthworks are in areas well away from mediaeval and later settlements, generally on the higher ground where arable activity has been limited if not negligible during the past 1,500 years. On lower ground, especially around modern settlements, persistent cultivation from the early mediaeval period onwards has largely destroyed the remains of earlier occupation. The distribution of the surviving monuments coincides to a remarkable degree with the commons, downlands and other uncultivated areas shown on the O.S. map of 1811.

Roads

Although the Roman road from Badbury Rings to Dorchester traverses several parishes in the S. of the area covered by this volume, it is convenient to reserve it to the last volume of the Dorset series, where Roman Roads will be treated integrally.

Roman Fort

At Hod Hill an unusually well-preserved fort of the Roman army, dating from the earliest years of the occupation, exists in one corner of the native *oppidum*. It was garrisoned by a legionary detachment with auxiliary cavalry, and appears to have been held for about a decade.

Settlements

Apart from hill-forts (*see* p. xxxviii) and the Neolithic causewayed camp on Hambledon Hill, some twenty-seven occupation sites, including villas and other buildings, are identifiable in Central Dorset (*see* distribution map at end of volume). Most of the sites are now flat, but a few survive as earthworks; except for some of the latter, from which no dating material has been obtained, all the sites are known to have been occupied in the Roman period and some were occupied in the Iron Age also. In addition, a number of settlements may possibly be detected within areas of 'Celtic' fields, chiefly as crop-marks or soil-marks rather than as earthworks; these are described in the relevant 'Celtic' Field Groups (*see* pp. 318–321).

Although most of the settlements are on the Chalk, the Iron Age and Roman sites at Marnhull, the Roman villa at Fifehead Neville and the Roman villa at Hinton St. Mary lie on the Corallian ridge. The Roman sites at Holwell and Stalbridge are on Oxford Clay and Cornbrash Beds respectively. Some differences of siting are noticeable between settlements in which occupation began in the Iron Age and those wherein the earliest occupation is of Roman date; the Iron Age sites appear to be restricted to higher ground, locally, whereas at least six of the twenty-one sites occupied only in the Roman period are low-lying, mostly in valley bottoms.

An extensive Roman villa at Fifehead Neville has mosaic pavements of high quality [*133*]. The design of one of them, and two rings with Christian symbols, link this villa with the mosaics that have recently been found at Hinton St. Mary, presumably the floors of the principal rooms of another villa [*145–7*]. At Hinton, the representation of a male head backed by a *Chi-Rho* monogram, together with figures of Bellerophon and the Chimaera surrounded by hunting scenes, raises questions about the extension of Christianity in rural Britain, and the possible Christian significance of ostensibly pagan symbols. The Frampton pavements (*Dorset* I, 150) and some of the pavements in Dorchester (*Dorset* II, 536) have many features in common with those of Fifehead Neville and Hinton St. Mary, indicating a 'Durnovarian' school of mosaicists. Other Roman sites include buildings at Milton Abbas, which were probably industrial although unlikely to have been a pottery as is usually claimed, and a well in Winterborne Kingston, the contents of which provide the best evidence for a rural shrine in the area; unfortunately the excavator of both these sites gave insufficient details for precise location.

As in *Dorset* II, few prehistoric and Roman settlements have survived to be recorded as earthworks. Most of those that do survive are Romano-British, at least in their final phase, but since none has been excavated the structural and cultural development remains unknown. The best preserved sites are at Melcombe Horsey, Piddletrenthide [*192*], Turnworth [*192*] and Winterborne Houghton; all are associated with trackways and 'Celtic' fields. The Turnworth site is unusual in that it consists of two small circular enclosures with internal occupation features. One of the Winterborne Houghton sites (10) comprises a series of poorly defined platforms in an incomplete rectangular enclosure; all the other sites consist of level platforms and closes defined by banks and scarps. At Winterborne Houghton (9), where the main occupation area covers at least $3\frac{1}{2}$ acres, the shape of some platforms is suggestive of rectangular buildings, a feature not observed on any other site.

Hill-Forts

There are eight Iron Age hill-forts in Central Dorset: one of them, Dungeon Hill, has already been described in *Dorset* I (Minterne Magna (6)) but boundary changes have now brought it into Buckland Newton parish; Nettlecombe Tout at Melcombe Horsey is probably an unfinished hill-fort and is therefore included in the number; the others are Hod Hill in Stourpaine, Hambledon Hill in Child Okeford, Rawlsbury in Stoke Wake, Spetisbury Rings, Weatherby Castle in Milborne St. Andrew and Banbury in Okeford Fitzpaine (*see* distribution map at end of volume). Only Hod Hill has been scientifically excavated, and datable material from the other hill-forts is almost entirely the product of chance.

All but one of the hill-forts lie on the Chalk: Hambledon, Hod, Rawlsbury and Nettlecombe Tout are on the high ground of the N.W.-facing escarpment; Dungeon Hill is on an outlier of the escarpment; Spetisbury and Weatherby are on the dip-slope, overlooking valleys draining S.E. On the other hand Banbury lies N. of and below the escarpment, on a patch of Plateau Gravel surrounded by an extensive area of Kimmeridge Clay, generally shunned by prehistoric peoples. With the exception of Spetisbury and possibly Banbury, the forts occupy sites obviously suited for defence.

The hill-forts vary in internal area from 3 acres (Banbury) [*182*] to 54 acres (Hod Hill) [*198*]. The defences vary in size and complexity from the comparatively insignificant bank and ditch at Banbury to the massive multiple ramparts and elaborate entrances of Hod and Hambledon. Spetisbury and Dungeon Hill, like Banbury, are univallate enclosures and there is no evidence that Nettlecombe Tout was otherwise; the other hill-forts are multivallate, but they probably all began as simple enclosures with one main bank and ditch. That this is true of Hod has been proved by excavation, while at Hambledon, which developed in at least three major structural phases, there is evidence that the first and probably the second phases were univallate. The wide spacing of the ramparts at Weatherby [*182*] suggests that the outer rampart is an addition to an original univallate enclosure. Except for Dungeon Hill, all the hill-forts had entrances with outworks, sometimes of more than one phase. The S.W. entrance at Hambledon is very similar in size and design to the Stepleton Gate at Hod Hill, albeit reversed. Details of rampart construction are available only from Hod Hill, where an initial boxed rampart of the Iron Age 'A' phase was superseded by ramparts of *glacis* construction.

Occupation earthworks are clearly visible within the defences at Hod Hill [*198*] and Hambledon [*129*], and there are traces at Rawlsbury, but they are not recognisable in the other hill-forts. At Hod these earthworks consist largely of hut-circles (at least two hundred are recorded) and storage pits; they once covered the whole of the interior, but the construction of the Roman fort, and recent ploughing, have

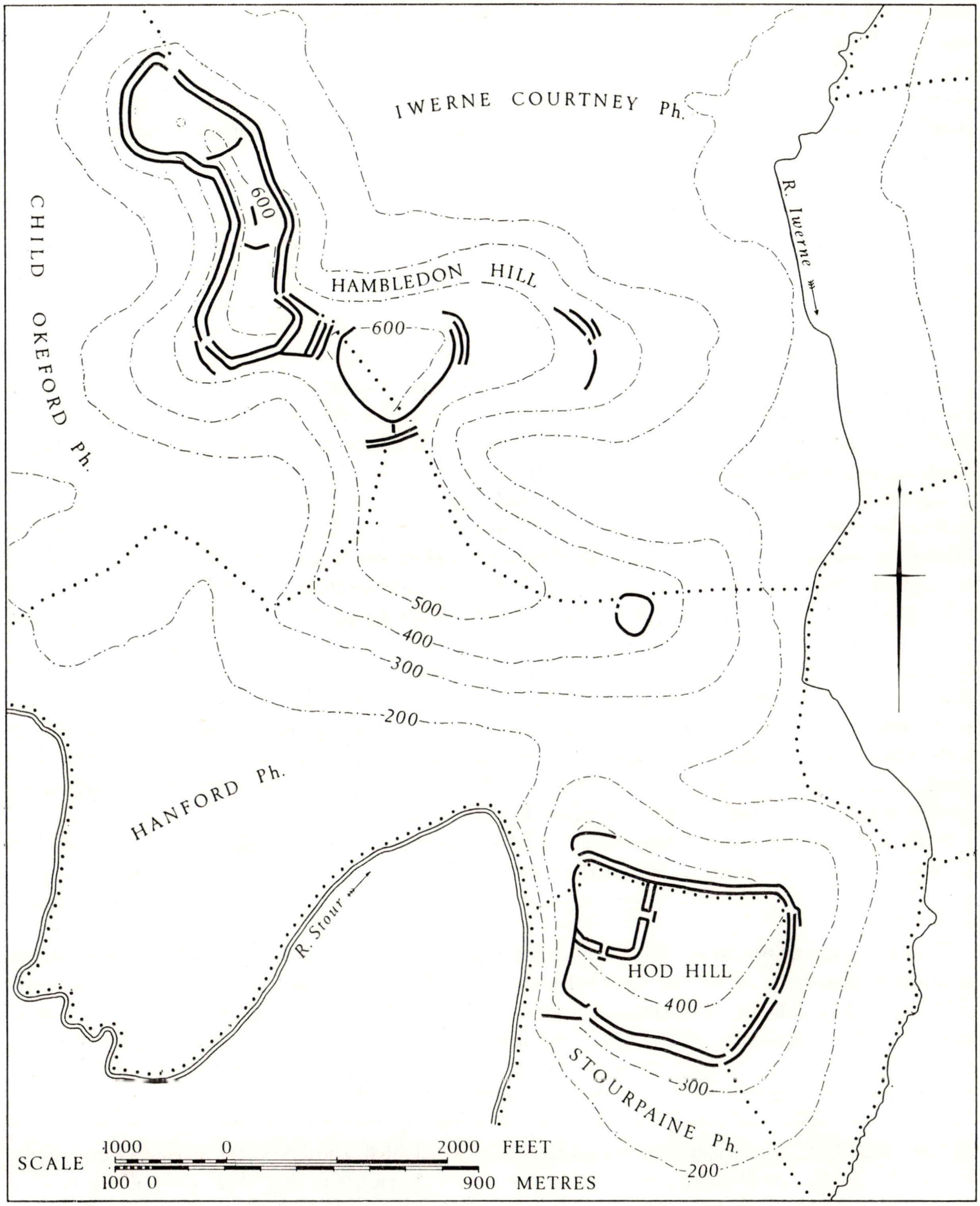

Hill-forts and other earthworks on Hod and Hambledon Hills

removed all but $7\frac{1}{2}$ acres in the S.E. corner of the site. At Hambledon the occupation earthworks are widespread and largely undisturbed; they consist almost entirely of platforms (over two hundred are recorded) levelled into the sloping interior. The contrast between Hambledon and Hod, especially in view of their proximity, could hardly be more marked; in part this is due to the more steeply sloping interior of Hambledon, necessitating the construction of platforms, but even on the gentler slopes there are no remains comparable with those of Hod.

In few cases are adjacent earthworks demonstrably associated with the hill-forts. Nettlecombe Tout, however, is surely related to the extensive area of 'Celtic' fields with cross-dykes ('Celtic' Field Group (44)) which lies immediately S. of it. Probably the same is true of Rawlsbury and the cross-dykes and 'Celtic' fields to the E. At the N. end of Hambledon traces of 'Celtic' fields are partly overlaid by the outermost rampart.

Evidence for the date of construction and length of occupation of the hill-forts is scanty, except at Hod where excavation has shown that it was continuously and intensively occupied from a late Iron Age 'A' cultural phase until the Roman Conquest. A similar length of occupation is probably attributable to Hambledon, where Iron Age 'A' pottery has been found within the earliest line of fortifications. At Rawlsbury, pottery of both Iron Age 'A' and 'C' types has been found and this, together with the multiple defences, suggests a lengthy period of occupation.

The hill-forts lie within the tribal area of the Durotriges who, on the scanty evidence available, appear to have been strongly opposed to Roman rule. That the Roman Conquest ended the occupation of the hill-forts as defensive centres is dramatically illustrated at Hod, where excavation has produced evidence of an assault by the Roman army, probably the II Augusta Legion under Vespasian; it is recorded[1] that this legion reduced twenty *oppida* in southern Britain in A.D. 43–44. A Roman fort was subsequently built within the ramparts and additional entrances were inserted. An unfinished outwork on the N. side of Hod was probably an attempt to strengthen the fortifications against the Roman attack. That a similar fate overtook Spetisbury is indicated by the discovery, within the main ditch, of a mass grave that belongs to the time of the Roman Conquest; it is almost certainly the burial place of those who fell victim to a Roman attack. Spetisbury is interesting as an example of a univallate hill-fort of the 1st century A.D. when, in Dorset at least, multiple defences were common; it would appear that the single rampart was in process of being strengthened in the face of the Roman advance [*200*].

Finds of the Roman period, including coins, have been made at Hambledon and Dungeon Hill, and Roman pottery is recorded from Weatherby Castle.

Dykes

Twenty-six dykes, or earthworks that probably represent dykes, occur in Central Dorset (*see* folding map at end of volume). All but one, Combs Ditch, are short lengths of bank and ditch, mostly of the cross-ridge type. They all lie on the Chalk, the majority of them being on or near the head of the escarpment, and they fall into two main groups: one group around the natural bowl of Lyscombe Bottom (735020), and the other group to the N.E., between Bulbarrow Hill and Shillingstone Hill. Several of the second group lie wholly or in part on 'Clay-with-flints', capping the Chalk.

Nearly every dyke consists of a single bank and ditch, but Blandford St. Mary (27), Cheselbourne (22) and Woolland (9) each comprise two banks with a medial ditch. The dykes vary in length from 70 yds. to 470 yds., and in overall width from 20 ft. to 60 ft.; the majority are from 30 ft. to 50 ft. across. In their present state, the banks rarely exceed 3 ft. in height and the ditches 3 ft. in depth.

[1] Suetonius, *Vespasian*, iv.

Although most of the dykes are of cross-ridge type not all of them are sited across ridges. A few (Milton Abbas (26), Okeford Fitzpaine (39) and (41), Shillingstone (26) and Woolland (7)) cut across and isolate spurs of ground, chiefly the short spurs that jut N. from the Chalk escarpment; they all have the ditch on the up-hill side, facing the higher ground, and they have some of the characteristics of the 'spur dykes' that have been distinguished in Sussex and Wiltshire.[1] Only at Okeford Fitzpaine (41) is there any indication of an original entrance. The dykes frequently end at or near the shoulder of the ridge or spur, but in a few instances, such as Melcombe Horsey (14) and Woolland (7), they drop right down the slope. Excavation at the W. end of the Melcombe Horsey dyke showed that the ditch ended abruptly and that the bank was probably retained by a light wooden revetment.

The date and purpose of the dykes is largely conjectural, but it is likely that they served primarily as boundaries between units of land; whether between separate estates or between parts within an estate is unknown. Many dykes probably served also to control movement along the spurs and ridges. Each of the two main groups of dykes occurs near an Iron Age hill-fort; six lie E. of Rawlsbury and ten lie S. of Nettlecombe Tout; both these groups are in areas of Iron Age and Romano-British rural settlements and their associated 'Celtic' fields, and in several instances they appear to be integrated with field lynchets. The only direct evidence of date is from Melcombe Horsey (14), where excavation revealed sherds of the Late Bronze Age or Early Iron Age in the secondary silting of the ditch. From the evidence at present available it thus appears that the dykes are a feature of the later prehistoric period, perhaps reaching their maximum development in the Iron Age. That they continued to be used in the Roman period is suggested by their relationship to nearby Romano-British settlements (*see* folding map at end of volume). Combs Ditch, a linear dyke nearly 3 miles long, began as a boundary bank and ditch, probably of Iron Age date; later it was successively enlarged to become the present formidable defensive work of the Roman period.

'Celtic' Fields

For general remarks on 'Celtic' Fields in Central Dorset, *see* pp. 318–321.

Flat Burials

Inhumation burials, unmarked above ground, have been found in ten places in Central Dorset. All are presumed to be of Roman date except for two Iron Age burials at Allard's Quarry, Marnhull. With two exceptions the sites have produced multiple burials suggesting cemeteries, but since they have usually been found by accident, and often some time ago, numbers are rarely available. At Great Down Quarry, Marnhull, over twenty burials were recorded. The sites at Marnhull are on the Corallian Limestone ridge and those at Holwell are on Oxford Clay; the others are on the Chalk.

Barrows

As in *Dorset* II, barrows are described in topographical order from S.W.-N.E. in each parish, and barrow groups are given names of local derivation (*see* distribution map at end of volume). Information from barrow excavations, which mostly took place during the 19th century and are poorly recorded, often cannot be associated with individual barrows because of difficulty of identification; in these cases the information is set out in a preliminary paragraph before the inventory of barrows. J. B. Calkin's terminology has been followed wherever applicable (*Arch. J.*, CXIX (1962), 1–65).

Two neolithic *Long Barrows*, Child Okeford (23) and (24), lie on Hambledon Hill near the causewayed camp with which they are almost certainly associated. Orientation, almost due N.-S., is unusual, although in one case (23) it is conditioned by the narrow spur top on which the barrow lies. Both mounds are

[1] *Aspects of Archaeology in Britain and Beyond*, ed. W. F. Grimes (1951), 93–107; *W.A.M.*, 59 (1964), 46–57.

parallel-sided with ditches extending the full length of the mound; one is 240 ft. long, the other 85 ft. long [*132*].

The number of *Round Barrows* in Central Dorset—just over 200—is very small in comparison with South Dorset. Most of them lie on the dip-slope of the Chalk escarpment and some of them are on the 'Clay-with-flints', which in places caps the higher levels of the Chalk. In the S., a few barrows are found on the heathland of the Reading Beds.

The barrows are well scattered over the Chalk area although, with very few exceptions, they avoid the highest parts of the escarpment. Nearly two-thirds of the total number lie between 200 ft. and 400 ft. above sea-level, the others are higher. They occupy the higher ground between the rivers; some are in prominent positions on the highest local points, *e.g.* Piddletrenthide (12–15), but many are sited on slopes and false crests and are prominent only when viewed from a particular direction, usually from below.

All the barrows are bowls except for two possible bell-barrows, Milborne St. Andrew (33) and Stinsford (13), and a possible saucer-barrow, Piddletrenthide (59). At least two-thirds of them have been damaged by ploughing, some very severely. Ditches are visible around comparatively few barrows but it is almost certain that the majority originally had ditches which now are filled in, whether by ploughing or by other agencies. Ploughing has affected the size of the barrows, reducing the height and increasing the diameter of the mounds; even so, three-quarters of the measurable mounds are small, 50 ft. across or less. Only one barrow, Puddletown (30), exceeds 100 ft. in diameter; it is unusual not only for its size but also for its situation on the broad, level flood-plain of the River Frome.

In further contrast to South Dorset there are only eight barrow groups, none with many barrows. The largest group is on Deverel Down, Milborne St. Andrew, where the group of eight barrows includes the celebrated Deverel Barrow. All are 'scattered groups' except for the group on North Down, Winterborne Kingston, which is a 'linear group'.[1]

No barrow has been excavated in recent years but many have been dug into in the past; holes are still visible in about forty mounds. Much of this activity has gone unrecorded, but records were kept of some excavations, chiefly of those carried out during the 19th century. For the most part the records are very brief and it is seldom possible to relate an excavation record with certainty to an existing barrow. The summary nature of many early excavations, together with inadequate recording and publication, means that much information about the structure and contents of barrows has been lost; often it is not even possible to establish the approximate date of the monument. The primary burial is not always to be determined from the records, and sometimes it certainly remained undiscovered; in the few instances where primary burials can be determined with certainty, the lack of associated objects makes some of them undatable.

The earliest datable barrow, one of the Lord's Down group, Dewlish (13), covered a long-necked beaker in a primary position, and it may therefore be dated to the Late Neolithic period; a series of secondary burials, including biconical urns, indicate that the barrow continued in use well into the Early Bronze Age. Of the Early Bronze Age are two other barrows in the same group, with 'Wessex Culture' primary burials, and also the two-phase barrow at Hilton (30), with its primary crouched interment and ridged food-vessel urns in the inner ditch. All the other datable barrows are of the Middle Bronze Age or later, the majority of the primary burials being associated with globular urns. The inverted collared urn which was found, possibly in a primary position, in the Deverel Barrow is unlikely to be earlier than the numerous globular and bucket urns that were found under the mound [*132*].

[1]For a definition of group types see *Dorset* II, 422.

MEDIAEVAL AND LATER SETTLEMENT

The pattern, siting and morphology of mediaeval and later settlements in Central Dorset are largely determined by the two very different physical landscapes present in the area: the Chalk land of the Downs, and the Jurassic Clays and Limestones of the Blackmoor Vale (*see* distribution map at end of volume).

The Chalk Downs

Until very recently, settlement on the Chalk Downs was almost completely governed by the availability of water. Even today settlement is rare outside the valleys, and such settlement as there is is usually of the 19th century or later. Hence mediaeval settlement was largely confined to the deeply-cut narrow valleys which drain S.E. across the Chalk dip-slope. From some of the earthwork remains it appears that the original settlements were small hamlets or farmsteads, set in the valley bottoms and spaced at distances which range from 100 yds. to a mile. Subsequent expansion was along the valley, with the result that the normal form of settlement is a long linear village; such villages sometimes grew to a considerable size, as at Cheselbourne and Piddletrenthide; indeed Piddletrenthide results from the coalescence of several settlements, each of which developed in this way [*1*]. Where villages are now partly deserted, earthwork remains indicate the same linear morphology, as at Winterborne Clenston [*214*]. The buildings of these villages were normally strung out along a single street, parallel to the watercourse, as in Winterborne Stickland and Spetisbury, or along two parallel streets on either side of a stream, as in Piddletrenthide and in the old town of Milton Abbas, now deserted (*see* plan facing p. 199).

Variations on this basic linear pattern occur only where the valleys are wider. The result is a more compact village with an irregular street plan, as at Puddletown, Winterborne Kingston, Hilton and the two deserted villages in Melcombe Horsey. Certain alterations in the pattern of narrow valley villages are evidently of late date and are probably due to changes in lines of communication. For example, Milborne St. Andrew and Winterborne Whitechurch have ceased to be linear valley settlements and have become linear road settlements; leaving the valley layout to survive in the form of earthworks, the present villages are now aligned upon the main road from Dorchester to Blandford Forum. Nearly all the Chalk-land settlements were associated with narrow strips of land running back from the river, usually on one side of the valley but sometimes on both; the boundaries of such land-blocks are often preserved as continuous hedge-lines. Evidence from charters and from Domesday Book indicates that these land-blocks and their settlements composed economic units that were already in existence in the late Saxon period. Each ecclesiastical parish appears to be composed of one or more of such land-blocks (*see* C. D. Drew, Dorset *Procs.*, LXIX (1948), 45–50).

The Blackmoor Vale

N.W. of the escarpment, in the Vale of Blackmoor, the settlement pattern is very different from that of the Chalk land. The low-lying land has large nucleated villages with outlying farmsteads and hamlets, a pattern that is superficially like that of the Midlands. Again, the surface geology controls the siting of the major settlements. The spring-line at the foot of the Chalk scarp gives rise to a line of nucleated villages from Buckland Newton in the W. to Child Okeford in the N.E. The broad Kimmeridge Clay area to the N.W. is devoid of major settlements, except where the R. Stour crosses the outcrop; here on the river terraces are Manston and Hammoon. The Corallian Limestone outcrop, further N.E., is the basis of another line of villages, extending from Glanville's Wootton in the W. to Marnhull in the N. Beyond this the wide Oxford Clay belt has no nucleated settlement except Pulham and Lydlinch, which both stand on dry gravel patches. Further N.W. the lighter Cornbrash and Forest Marble outcrops give rise to a line of villages from Bishop's Caundle to Stalbridge. The nucleated settlements do not have a common plan; they vary from long street villages such as Stourton Caundle to compact villages like Hinton St. Mary [*2*].

The outlying farmsteads and hamlets of the area are not, as in the Midlands, late settlement consequent upon enclosure of former open fields; they are the result of a long process of secondary settlement in the waste, developing beyond the open fields of the original nucleated villages. The process started certainly before the Conquest and it continued until the 19th century and later, as the map of Holwell (p. 118) shows.

Secondary settlements like Plumber Manor in Lydlinch and Colber in Sturminster Newton were in existence by 1086, and although others are not recorded in documents until the 13th and 14th centuries many of them are probably much older. There is evidence from Forest Eyres that much assarting was taking place in the area in the 13th century (P.R.O., E 32/10 and 11) and many outlying farms are likely to have been established at that time (*see* Dorset *Procs.*, 87 (1965), 251–4). The moat at Holwell Manor House probably represents one such outlying farmstead.

Some of the earliest of these farmsteads and hamlets are associated with commons or 'greens', often roughly triangular [*3*], which probably represent land left for pasture when the surrounding territory was enclosed from the waste into small irregular fields. Outlying farmsteads of 18th and 19th-century origin are associated with fields laid out geometrically, such as Lydlinch (18) and Marnhull (63). Another typical 18th and 19th-century form of settlement has cottages built on the wide verges of roads; these result from Parliamentary enclosure of waste lands, as at Bagber Common in Sturminster Newton, and at Holwell [*3*].

MEDIAEVAL AND LATER EARTHWORKS[1]

These monuments fall into three groups: (*a*) settlement remains, such as deserted villages, farmsteads and moats; (*b*) cultivation remains, principally strip lynchets and traces of ridge-and-furrow; (*c*) miscellaneous earthworks, including deer parks and gardens.

Settlement Remains

No mediaeval settlement site in the area has yet been systematically excavated and little can be said about the buildings and other features which the earthworks represent. On the other hand, careful use of the documents that survive, in conjunction with study of the earthworks, often throws light on the pattern of settlement; this is especially true in the Chalk area where the abundance of the remains helps materially to build up a picture of the mediaeval settlement pattern. Linear settlements and small compact hamlets and farmsteads all survive in the form of earthworks. The best example of the first type is in the Winterborne valley, where earthworks occur continuously over a length of 4½ miles from Winterborne Houghton in the N. to Winterborne Whitechurch in the S., showing that where now there are four parishes made up of three villages and a scatter of farms, originally there were nine separate settlements, each probably with its own open fields. Examples of separate small settlements are seen in Charminster (22) to (27), where there were once at least ten hamlets or farmsteads within the parish, as well as Charminster itself, strung out along the R. Cerne.

Off the Chalk there are no large deserted settlements since the great majority of the outlying farmsteads

[1] In compiling the inventory of these monuments, published sources principally have been consulted and documentary research has necessarily been restricted; nevertheless the Lay Subsidy Rolls for 1327 and 1333 (P.R.O. E179/103/4 and E179/103/5) and all available Tithe, Enclosure and Estate Maps have been examined. Much material in the D.C.R.O. and in the County Museum has been used, especially C.D. Drew's card-index of Dorset records. The general object has been to establish the historical context of settlement and cultivation remains.

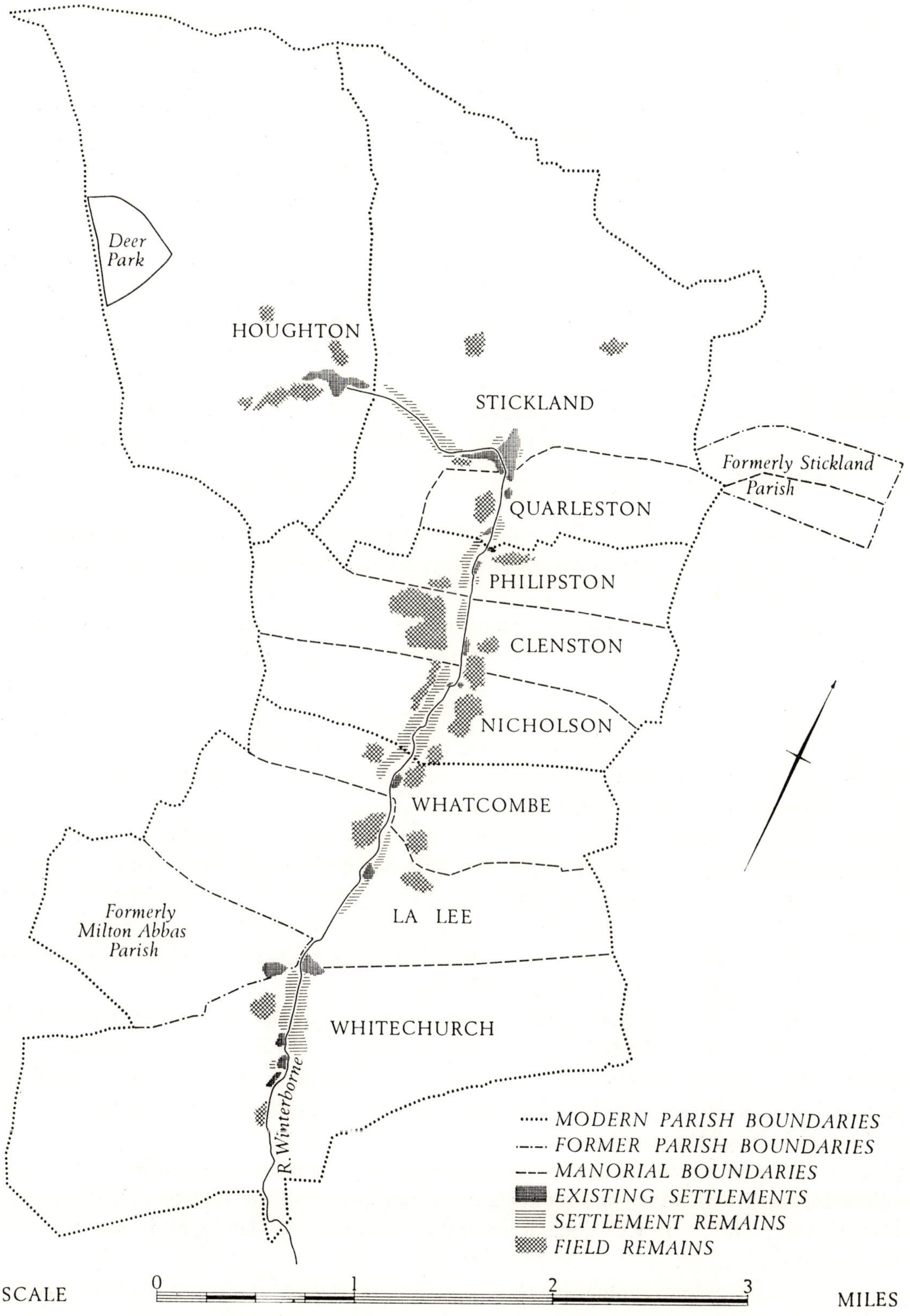

Mediaeval Settlements and Associated Lands in the Upper Winterborne Valley

and hamlets are still occupied. Only at Colber in Sturminster Newton parish are there earthworks of a deserted farmstead, and slight remains of larger deserted settlements occur at Stock Gaylard in Lydlinch and at Thorton in Marnhull.

The remains of more than fifty settlements are noted in this volume but only six of them can be said to be entirely deserted: one of the Cernes (Charminster (23)), part of Pulston (Charminster (22b)), Bardolfeston (Puddletown (21)), Cheselborne Ford (Puddletown (23)), Lazerton (Stourpaine (7)) and Colber (Sturminster Newton (69)); the others are all associated with existing villages, hamlets and farms. In a few places a large house succeeds the former settlement.

The reason for the abandonment of settlements is difficult to determine without excavation. Most of the settlements were very small, even in 1086, and the abandoned remains may be the result not of sudden desertion but of a slow decline in prosperity and population over many years. The process can rarely be proved, but Lazerton in Stourpaine may be taken as an example; in 1428 the hamlet certainly had fewer than ten inhabitants, but 250 years earlier it appears to have been almost deserted. It is clear from the Lay Subsidy Rolls that many settlements were almost deserted by the 14th century; Winterborne Clenston (5) is an example, and the pottery found at Hewish in Milton Abbas also indicates abandonment by this date. In contrast Quarleston in Winterborne Stickland was a flourishing community in the early 14th century.

Certain variations are discernible in the forms of the settlement remains. The continuous lines of settlements in the narrow Winterborne and Milborne valleys are remarkably consistent. They have long closes bounded by low banks and are set at right-angles to the stream; house sites, where preserved, are at the lower ends of the closes while other building platforms sometimes occur higher up the valley sides. Roads apparently were adjacent to the streams or were actually in the stream beds, which were often dry. Where settlements are not continuous the same forms recur, as in the Piddle valley and at Pulston and Lazerton. In wider valleys the isolated settlements often comprise square or rectangular closes set on either side of a track or a hollow-way which runs down to and crosses a river, as at Puddletown, Hanford and Blandford St. Mary village. Elsewhere less determinate patterns of closes occur, as at Littleton in Blandford St. Mary and in the two deserted villages of Melcombe Horsey.

Few house sites are well preserved. In most settlements they are merely platforms, either freestanding or cut back into slopes, up to 20 ft. wide and 60 ft. long. Good building sites are found in only two places. Milborne St. Andrew (13) has embanked rectangular building sites within an enclosure, but they are not necessarily the sites of dwellings. On the other hand the earthworks at Bardolfeston in Puddletown include the best preserved house sites in the county [*183*]; they comprise at least eleven embanked rectangular areas with opposed entrances and traces of internal subdivisions.

Another type of earthwork consists of an enclosure bounded by banks and ditches and subdivided by banks at right-angles to the perimeter. The enclosures vary considerably in size but are similarly situated on the sides of valleys. Examples occur at Charminster (25), Dewlish (7) and Milborne St. Andrew (13); their purpose is not clear; they may have been some kind of farmyard. A similar site has been noted in Wiltshire (*Antiquity* XXXVII (1963), 290).

The largest settlement remains in the area are at Milton Abbas; they comprise at least three-quarters of the mediaeval market town which was removed in the last quarter of the 18th century to make way for Lord Milton's park. The town, well documented by an 18th-century plan [*176*], is now represented by some 25 acres of earthworks.

The so-called 'Castle' at Sturminster Newton is a prehistoric earthwork, reused as a manorial site in the mediaeval period.

Cultivation Remains

Almost all major settlements in Central Dorset appear to have been associated during the mediaeval period with some form of communal or open-field farming. Off the Chalk this usually consisted of a single open field system for each parish. In the Chalk areas, by contrast, many parishes had several open field systems, each system belonging to a separate settlement; for instance Winterborne Whitechurch and Winterborne Kingston probably had three systems each. Thus the 58 modern parishes of Central Dorset contain the remains of over 100 separate open field systems. Most of the open fields were enclosed by the 18th century; there are only twelve parishes with Parliamentary Acts of Enclosure for open fields, and in eight of them the Acts are for the final enclosure of fields which had been partly enclosed earlier.

The field evidence for mediaeval agriculture is of four kinds:

(i) *Strip Lynchets* are fairly widespread in parishes on the Chalk, but they are unknown on the flatter country of the Blackmoor Vale. The remains are of the usual types and are largely identical with those discussed at length in the preceding volume (*Dorset* II, lxix). An interesting feature are 'flights' of strip lynchets, such as occur in Hilton, Ibberton and Milton Abbas. Enclosure and reploughing has sometimes resulted in unusual forms. The extremely wide terraces near St. Catherine's Chapel at Milton Abbas (24) are not strip lynchets; they appear to be special cultivation terraces and are almost certainly earlier than the 12th century.

(ii) *Ridge-and-Furrow of Open Field type* (discussed in *Cambridgeshire* I, lxvi) was formerly widespread in Dorset in parishes off the Chalk, where the pattern of curving and interlocking furlongs is identical with that well known in the Midlands. The feature is less common in the Chalk areas, probably because subsequent ploughing has destroyed the slighter remains there.

(iii) *Ridge-and-Furrow of Old Enclosure type* has been discussed at length elsewhere (*Cambridgeshire* I, lxviii) and little more need be said about it. The type occurs in almost all parishes on the Jurassic Beds and is in most instances confined to irregularly shaped fields, lying beyond the limits of the former open fields. These irregular fields were apparently enclosed direct from the waste; they are associated with small hamlets and isolated farms, secondary to the main parish settlement.

(iv) *Ridge-and-Furrow lying over 'Celtic' fields*, together with the modification of 'Celtic' fields in the mediaeval period, are discussed on p. 318 (*see* also *Dorset* II, lxix). As a rule, such remains represent a temporary, and usually undated, extension of the permanent arable into marginal land.

Miscellaneous Earthworks

The most important of these earthworks are the mediaeval *Deer Pales*. Five deer parks are known in Central Dorset but only those of Milton Abbas and Winterborne Houghton are recorded in the Inventory; those of Buckland Newton, Melcombe Horsey and Athelhampton have been omitted because the remains are too fragmentary; detailed accounts will be found in Dorset *Procs.* LXXXIV, (1962), 147; LXXXV, (1963), 145; and LXXXVIII (1966), 177. An earthwork described in Buckland Newton (21) probably represents yet another deer park.

MEDIAEVAL AND LATER BUILDINGS

Ecclesiastical Buildings

Apart from the Roman pavement with a *Chi-Rho* monogram at Hinton St. Mary, which is unlikely to be ecclesiastical (*see* p. xxxvii), no pre-Conquest church monument remains *in situ* in Central Dorset.

Minor fragments of 10th or 11th-century interlace carving are preserved at Milton Abbey [*12*], in the parish church at Puddletown, and in a house at Melcombe Horsey.

The earliest church buildings in the area are the apsed chapel of St. Andrew at Winterborne Tomson in Anderson parish [*96*], and the parish church of Iwerne Stepleton, which has a fine round-headed chancel arch; both buildings are of the late 11th or early 12th century. The S. wall of the church at Shillingstone, with round-headed loops, is of the early 12th century. Charminster retains the clerestorey walls of a large church of about the same date, but the arcades were rebuilt later in the 12th century [*6*]. St. Catherine's chapel at Milton Abbas is of the late 12th century and has a fine chancel arch [*179*], and a S. doorway with a contemporary inscription [*49*] and a round outer head enclosing a segmental tympanum arch [*10*]; this kind of doorway is apparently a local peculiarity, other doorways of comparable date and form occurring in the churches at Milborne St. Andrew, Belchalwell in Okeford Fitzpaine, Dewlish and Piddletrenthide [*11*]. A small deserted chapel in Lyscombe Bottom, midway between Cerne and Milton Abbeys, is of the late 12th century; it is urgently in need of repair.

The most notable 13th-century building is the chancel of Buckland Newton church [*120*] which, though restored, is sophisticated work for a village church, but unfortunately deprived of the original E. window. Stinsford has nave arcades and a chancel arch [*201*] of the same period. At Cheselbourne a 13th-century S. aisle or S. chapel was entered through a pair of archways with pointed heads resting on a central column with matching responds, but the original arrangement has been greatly modified. The chancels at Hammoon, Manston, Milborne St. Andrew and Winterborne Whitechurch were all rebuilt or remodelled at this time, and all of them retain well-proportioned E. windows of gradated triple lancets. Spetisbury church has a restored 13th-century N. arcade.

The predominant work of the 14th century was the rebuilding of Milton Abbey church [*161–8*] after the fire of 1309; an indulgence to assist the rebuilding was granted by the Bishop of Salisbury and the work continued throughout the century. Of comparable quality but very much smaller in scale is the chantry [*138*] at Glanville's Wooton, *c.* 1344. Later in the 14th century Marnhull church appears to have been enlarged to include a chantry chapel with a priest's cell above it. Other 14th-century works include church towers at Blandford St. Mary, Dewlish, Iwerne Courtney and Stinsford. At Okeford Fitzpaine the base of the 15th-century tower incorporates, on the E. side, a wide central archway flanked by two narrower openings [*180*]; this feature is probably of the late 14th century.

The prolific building activity of the 15th century is well represented in Central Dorset. Of the fifty-eight parishes in the area at least twenty-four rebuilt or heightened their church towers; the finest of these is Piddletrenthide [*186*], dated 1487, and good examples are found at Okeford Fitzpaine, Child Okeford and Durweston [*9*]. Handsome and spacious naves with arcaded aisles were built at Buckland Newton [*120*], Hazelbury Bryan [*138*], Holwell [*7*], Puddletown [*185*] and Mappowder, to name only the most impressive. Chantries were provided at Puddletown, Melcombe Horsey and Purse Caundle. The rebuilding of the great church at Milton Abbas was resumed; the tower over the crossing was completed and the N. transept was added. Provision had already been made in the 14th century for the addition of nave and aisles on the W. of the crossing, but the Dissolution of the Monasteries supervened and the church still remains incomplete.

Perhaps the best 16th-century church building in Central Dorset is the noble tower of Charminster [*121*], and other work of good quality is seen in the naves and aisles at Piddlehinton and Piddletrenthide. The ecclesiastical buildings of Sir Thomas Freke at Iwerne Courtney and Melcombe Horsey [*159*] are interesting examples of 17th-century 'Gothic'; pointed windows in Hanford and Manston churches represent the same style, the E. window at Hanford [*141*] being particularly noteworthy.

PIDDLETRENTHIDE. Air view from S. showing settlement along a valley bottom.

STALBRIDGE.

HINTON ST. MARY.

LYDLINCH. Triangular common resulting from mediaeval enclosure (p. xliv).

HOLWELL. Roadside development at Pleck resulting from 19th-century enclosure (p. xliv).

CHARMINSTER CHURCH. Exterior, from S.E. 12th-century and later

HOLWELL CHURCH. Exterior, from S. Late 15th-century

MELCOMBE HORSEY CHURCH. Exterior, from S.W. 14th and 15th-century

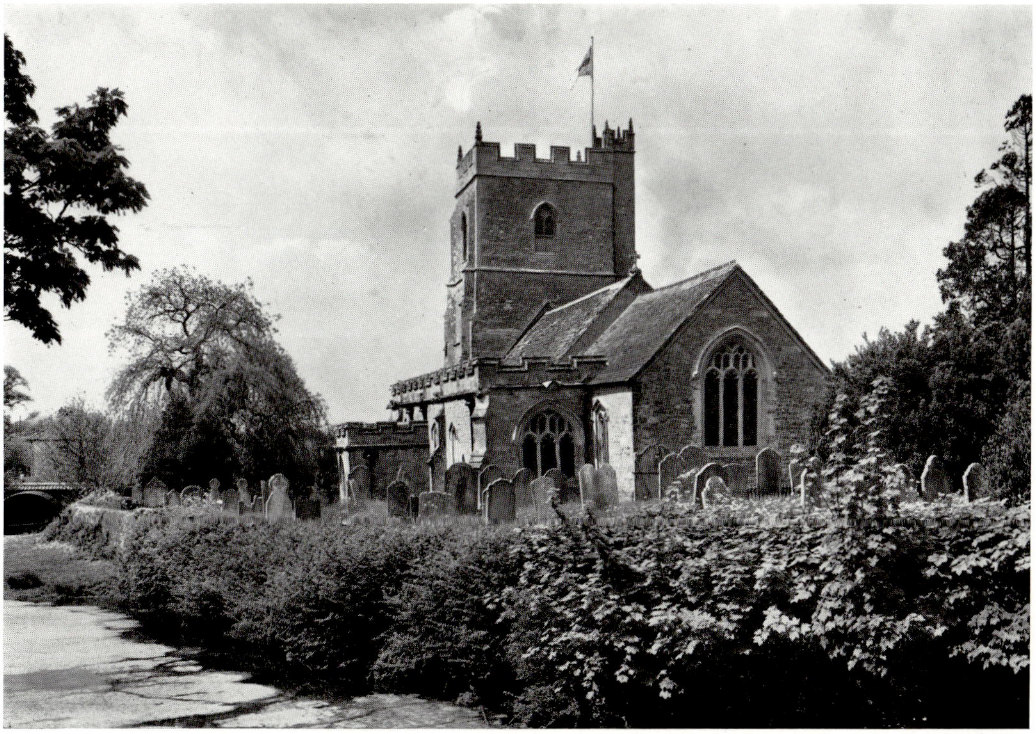

HAZELBURY BRYAN CHURCH. Exterior, from E. 15th-century

CHARMINSTER. Nave, looking E. 12th-century and later

HOLWELL. Nave, looking W. 15th century

CHARLTON MARSHALL. Nave, looking E. 1713

CHURCH TOWERS

DURWESTON CHURCH. Tower, from S.W. 15th-century

BISHOP'S CAUNDLE CHURCH. Tower, from N.W. 15th-century

TWELFTH-CENTURY DOORWAYS

MILBORNE ST. ANDREW CHURCH. Mid 12th-century

MILTON ABBAS (3) St. Catherine's Chapel. Late 12th-century

TWELFTH-CENTURY DOORWAYS

PIDDLETRENTHIDE CHURCH. 12th-century

DEWLISH CHURCH. 12th-century

OKEFORD FITZPAINE. (2) Belchalwell Church. *c.* 1190

MILTON ABBEY CHURCH. Fragment. Pre-conquest

BUCKLAND NEWTON CHURCH. Christ-in-majesty. 12th-century

STINSFORD CHURCH. Angel. Late 10th or early 11th-century

BUCKLAND NEWTON CHURCH. Warrior. 8th-century (?)

DURWESTON CHURCH. St. Eloi. 15th-century

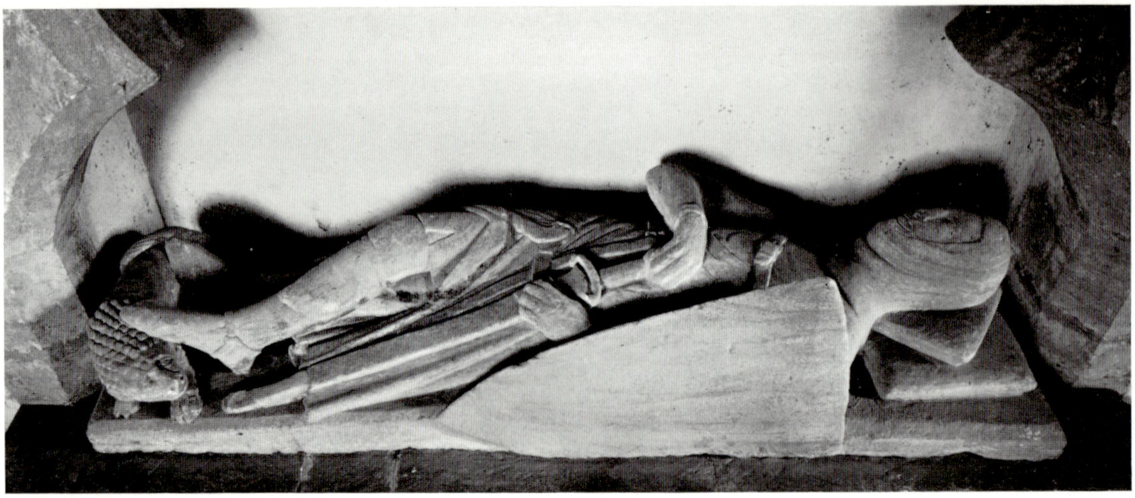

LYDLINCH: STOCK GAYLARD CHURCH. Monument (1). 13th-century, second half

HAMMOON CHURCH. 14th-century

MAPPOWDER CHURCH. Monument (1). 13th-century

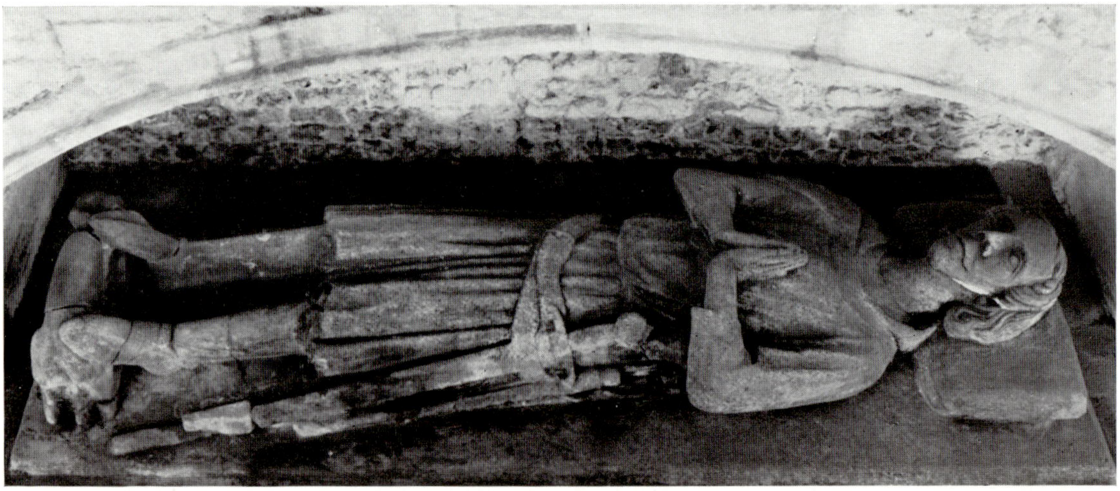

GLANVILLE'S WOOTTON CHURCH. Monument (3). Late 13th-century

PUDDLETOWN CHURCH. Monument (6) of a member of the Martyn family. *c.* 1460

MARNHULL CHURCH. Monument (6) probably of John Carent. *c.* 1470

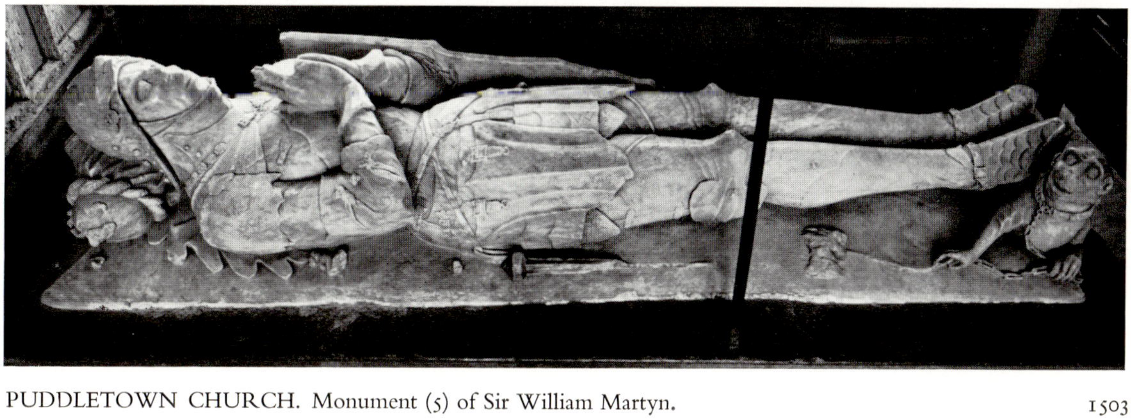

PUDDLETOWN CHURCH. Monument (5) of Sir William Martyn. 1503

MARNHULL CHURCH. 12th-century

STINSFORD CHURCH. 13th-century

HAZELBURY BRYAN CHURCH 14th-century

CHESELBOURNE. 15th-century

MAPPOWDER. 15th-century

MARNHULL CHURCH. 15th-century, second half

STALBRIDGE CHURCH. *c.* 1500

STALBRIDGE CHURCH. *c.* 1500

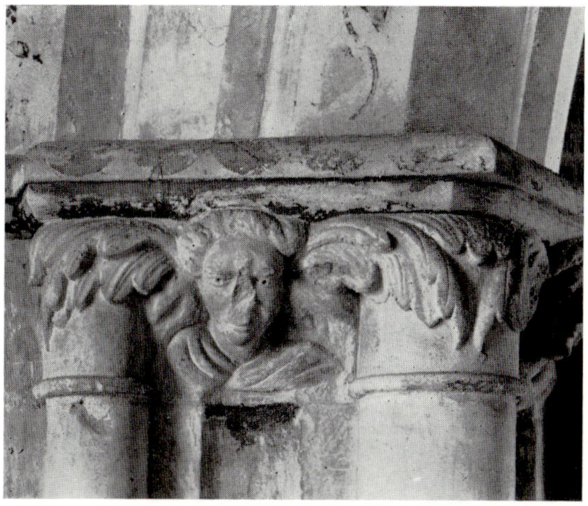

WINTERBORNE WHITECHURCH. 16th-century

PULHAM CHURCH. 16th-century

MILTON ABBAS. (4) Abbot's Hall. 1498 (restored)

STINSFORD CHURCH. 15th-century

STINSFORD CHURCH. 15th-century

MELCOMBE HORSEY. 15th-cent.

PULHAM CHURCH. 16th-cent.

PULHAM CHURCH. 16th-cent.

STINSFORD CHURCH. 15th-century

PIDDLETRENTHIDE CHURCH. *c.* 1500

MILTON ABBAS. (4) Abbot's Hall, hammerbeams in roof.

PUDDLETOWN CHURCH. Early 16th-century

HAZELBURY BRYAN CHURCH. S. Aisle. 15th-century

HOLWELL CHURCH. N. Aisle. 15th-century

MELCOMBE HORSEY CHURCH. Screen of Horsey Chapel. 1619

HAMMOON CHURCH. Panelling reset in choir stalls. Early 16th-century

BUCKLAND NEWTON. Poor-box. 16th-cent.

PUDDLETOWN CHURCH. *c.* 1635

STOURTON CAUNDLE CHURCH. 17th-century

CHARLTON MARSHALL CHURCH. 1713

MARNHULL CHURCH. 14th-century

GLANVILLE'S WOOTTON CHURCH. *c.* 1344

MILTON ABBEY CHURCH. Early 16th-century

HILTON CHURCH. Paintings of apostles, formerly in Milton Abbey. Late 15th-century

IWERNE COURTNEY. (2) Farrington Church. 12th-century

LYDLINCH CHURCH. Late 12th century

MAPPOWDER CHURCH. Late 12th-century

STOKE WAKE CHURCH. 15th-century

BLANDFORD FORUM.

CHARLTON MARSHALL.

WINTERBORNE STICKLAND.

STOURTON CAUNDLE.

MEDIAEVAL FONTS

PUDDLETOWN CHURCH. 12th-century

WINTERBORNE WHITECHURCH CHURCH. Mid 15th-century

CANOPIED TABLE-TOMBS

MILTON ABBEY CHURCH.
Monument (3) of Sir John Tregonwell. 1565

PUDDLETOWN CHURCH.
Monument (5) of Sir William Martyn. 1503

CANOPIED TABLE-TOMBS

STOURTON CAUNDLE CHURCH.
Monument (1), with extraneous effigy. 15th-century

PURSE CAUNDLE CHURCH.
Monument (1) of William Long. 1524

PUDDLETOWN CHURCH.
Monument (8) of Nicholas Martyn. 1595

SPETISBURY CHURCH.
Monument (2) of John Bowyer. 1599

HAZELBURY BRYAN. Monument (2). 1714

PIDDLEHINTON. Monument (12). 1747

MAPPOWDER. Monument (7). 1713

MAPPOWDER. Monument (12). 1726

FIFEHEAD NEVILLE. Monument (3). *c.* 1672

STOURPAINE. Monument (3). 1670

WINTERBORNE STICKLAND. Monument (1). 1653

HINTON ST. MARY. Monument (1). 1655

MANSTON. Monument (1). 1689

CHARMINSTER CHURCH. Monument (1) of Grace Pole. 1636

GLANVILLE'S WOOTTON CHURCH. Monument (5) of John Every. 1670

IWERNE COURTNEY CHURCH. Monument (1) of Sir Thomas Freke. 1654

MILTON ABBEY CHURCH. Monument (2) of Mary Bancks. 1704

WALL MONUMENTS

WINTERBORNE STICKLAND CHURCH.
Monument (2) of Honor and Robert Clavering. 1708

To the Memory of
CHARLES SLOPER D:D late
Fellow of Pembroke College
in OXFORD
Who
In 1695 was made Chancellor
Of Bristoll by Dr. HALL Bishop
of that Diocese.
In 1697 was Senior Proctor
of that University.
In 1705 was Rector of Spetisbury
with Charlton annex'd.
At SPETISBURY
He REBUILT
The Parsonage House and Outhouses,
At CHARLTON
The Parish Church, and Chancell,
Wholy at his own Expence.
And by his Will Gave Fivehundred Pound
For Instructing the Poor Children
Of these Parishes.
And left
The greatest part of his Estate
To other Charitable Uses.

CHARLTON MARSHALL CHURCH.
Monument (1) of Dr. Sloper. 1727

BISHOP'S CAUNDLE CHURCH.
Monument (1) of the D'Aubeny and Herbert families. 1815

BUCKLAND NEWTON CHURCH.
Monument (2) of Fitzwalter Foy. Probably 1806

PUDDLETOWN CHURCH. Monument (5) of Nicholas Martyn. 1595

PURSE CAUNDLE CHURCH.
Brass of Elizabeth Longe. 1527

PUDDLETOWN CHURCH. Monument (4) of Christopher Martyn. 1524

WOOLLAND CHURCH. Brass of Mary Argenton. 1616

MILTON ABBEY CHURCH. Monument (2) of Sir John Tregonwell. 1565

PIDDLEHINTON CHURCH.
Brass (4) of Thomas Browne. 1617

BUCKLAND NEWTON CHURCH.
Brass (2) of Thomas Barnes. 1624

MARNHULL. *c.* 1575

MAPPOWDER. 1570

SHILLINGSTONE. 1574

IWERNE STEPLETON. 1649

WINTERBORNE WHITECHURCH. 1653

CHARLTON MARSHALL. 1714

DURWESTON. 1764

DURWESTON. 1764

LYDLINCH PARISH CHURCH.
Hatchment (1). *c.* 1650

MARNHULL CHURCH.
Royal Arms. 17th-century; altered 1732

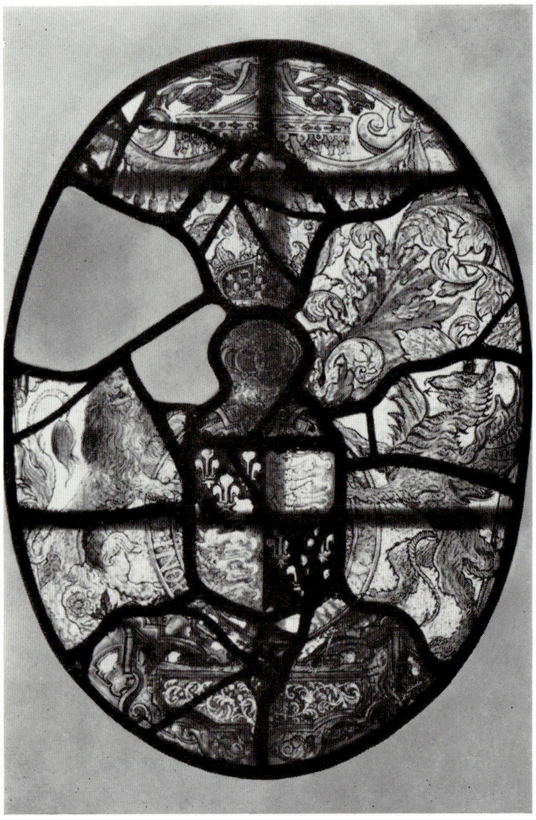

IBBERTON CHURCH. Arms of Queen Elizabeth I, in glass. Late 16th-century

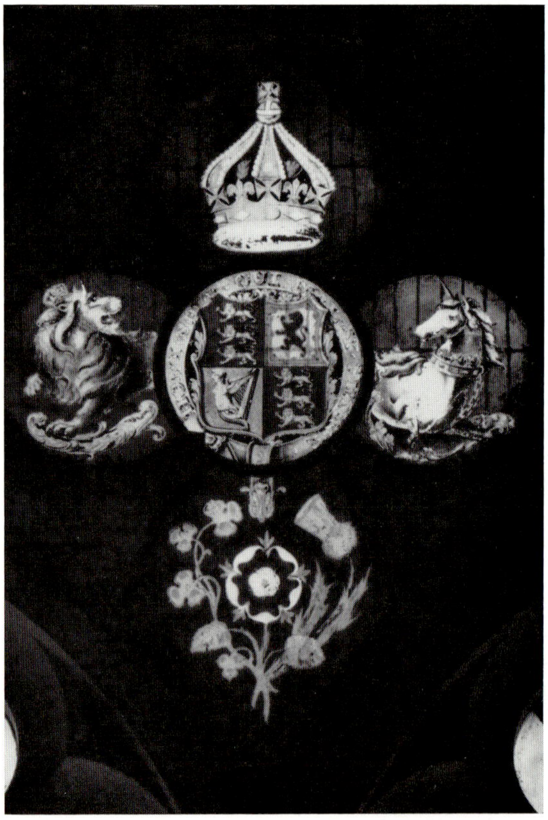

WINTERBORNE CLENSTON CHURCH. Arms of Queen Victoria, in glass. 1840

BLANDFORD FORUM CHURCH. *c.* 1735

OKEFORD FITZPAINE CHURCH. 18th-century

OKEFORD FITZPAINE. 15th-century

WINTERBORNE WHITECHURCH. 15th-century

STOURTON CAUNDLE. Early 16th-century

SPETISBURY. Early 17th-century

MILTON ABBAS. Parish Church. *c.* 1785

PUDDLETOWN. *c.* 1635

CHARLTON MARSHALL. 1713

STONE ACHIEVEMENTS-OF-ARMS

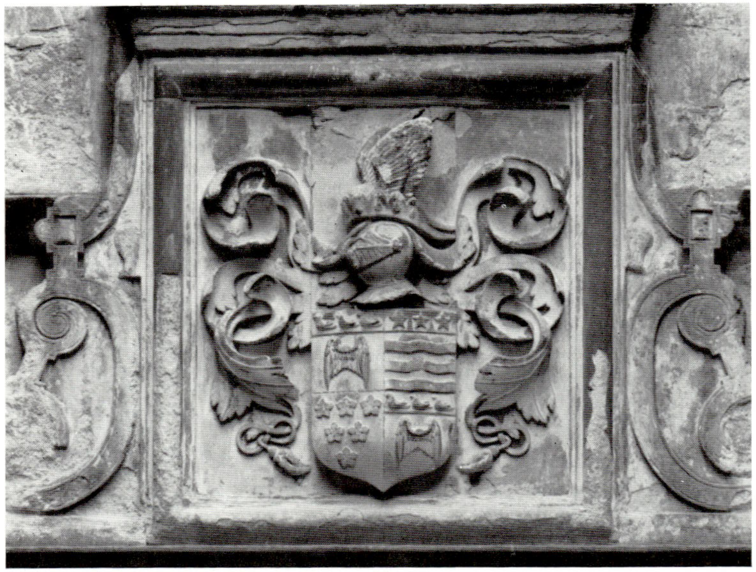

HANFORD. (2) Hanford House. Early 17th-century

STURMINSTER NEWTON. (65) Bagber Manor. 17th-century

STINSFORD.
(5) Kingston Maurward Old Manor. *c.* 1630

LYDLINCH. (5) Stock Gaylard House. 17th-century

WINTERBORNE STICKLAND.
(2) The Rectory. 1685

Blandford Parish Church [*frontispiece*], built by the brothers John and William Bastard in 1733, is doubtless the most important of the few 18th-century churches of Central Dorset, but the interior of Charlton Marshall church [*8*], remodelled in 1713, is perhaps a more distinguished work. At about the same time alterations were made to the naves of Winterborne Stickland and Fifehead Neville churches. At Bryanston a small but elegant chapel, the burial place of the Berkeley–Portman family, was built in 1745.

The earliest 18th-century 'Gothic Revival' church in Central Dorset is the parish church at Milton Abbas, consecrated in 1786. Sturminster Newton parish church was extensively rebuilt in 1827, and at Winterborne Clenston in 1839 the old parish church was pulled down and a new one by Lewis Vulliamy was built [*215*]. The parish church of Hinton St. Mary is largely of 1846. New churches were built at Plush and Tincleton in 1848 and 1849, the architect for both being Benjamin Ferrey.

Church Roofs

Milton Abbey is the only stone-vaulted church in Central Dorset. The towers of Marnhull and Piddletrenthide retain the springings of stone vaults, that of Marnhull being completed in timber. The porches of Buckland Newton and Hilton churches have small 15th-century ribbed vaults, possibly reset.

Of timber roofs, the earliest is at Tolpuddle, dating from the 14th century [*210*]; the handsomest is the late 15th or early 16th-century wagon roof of the nave at Sturminster Newton [*209*]. Winterborne Tomson chapel in Anderson parish, the nave and N. aisle at Hazelbury Bryan and the nave at Holwell have less elaborate 15th-century wagon roofs. At Puddletown the nave has an arch-braced collar truss of low pitch carrying moulded longitudinal and transverse members, forming coffers [*20*]. At Marnhull the nave is spanned by heavily-moulded, cambered beams which support a coffered ceiling with rich fretted decoration in each panel [*151*]. The aisles of Holwell, Hazelbury Bryan [*21*] and Hilton have handsome coffered oak ceilings, that at Hilton being dated 1569. The fine 15th-century hammer-beam roof which now covers a barn in Winterborne Clenston [*216*] was probably taken from a monastic building.

Church Fittings etc.

Altars: Mediaeval stone altar slabs survive in the churches of Glanville's Wootton and Mappowder. Another altar slab has been reused as the lintel of a fireplace in a house at Piddletrenthide (10).

Bells: The two oldest bells in the area, and probably the oldest in Dorset, are at Hanford and Stock Gaylard (Lydlinch); they may be of the 13th century. Numerous 15th and 16th-century bells come from the Salisbury foundry and the earliest known bell from the foundry of John Wallis of that city, dated 1581, is at Buckland Newton; the same foundry was still producing bells in 1636. William Purdue supplied a bell at Holwell in 1604, and he and others of his family are well represented in the belfries of Central Dorset. Several churches have 18th-century bells by one or other of the Bilbies.[1]

Brasses: The area is not rich in mediaeval brasses. The earliest, in Pulham church, consists of three lines of black-letter dated 1433; a somewhat similar brass at Tincleton is dated 1434. Puddletown church has three 16th-century brasses; Roger Cheverall's, 1517, Christopher Martyn's, 1524 [*40*], and the third, more elaborate and with four separate plates, of Nicholas Martyn, 1595 [*40*]; the last is mounted on the rear wall of a canopied table-tomb. Christopher Martyn's brass is the earliest in the area to have an English as opposed to a Latin inscription. At Milton Abbey the monument of Sir John Tregonwell, 1565, is a canopied table-tomb with six brasses, one depicting the knight wearing a tabard [*41*]. Purse Caundle has small brasses

[1] In listing the church bells of Central Dorset the contents of each belfry have been checked against the lists published in Raven's *Church Bells of Dorset* and in doing so the Commission has been much helped by a copy of Raven's work with MS. additions by H. B. Walters. The volume will in due course be deposited in the library of the Society of Antiquaries of London.

7

with figures and black-letter inscriptions of 1527 and 1536, that of 1527 being in English [*40*]. Piddletrenthide has a Latin black-letter inscription of 1564; henceforth there are no more black-letter brasses. At Cheselbourne are three finely engraved rectangular brass plates with shields-of-arms and a verse inscription in Roman lettering dated 1589; Marnhull has a boldly engraved inscription dated 1596. At Woolland a pleasing poem is inscribed on brass in memory of Mary Argenton, 1616; above it on a separate plate is depicted a lady at prayer [*40*]. Piddlehinton church contains a rustic brass with Latin verses and a crude portrait commemorating Thomas Browne, parson, 1617 [*41*]. Buckland Newton has a brass plate with Latin verses in memory of Thomas Barnes, 1624; Purse Caundle has one, delicately engraved, commemorating Peter Hoskyns, 1682, mounted in an original aedicule of carved oak. Reset in the 19th-century church at Athelhampton is a small plate to George Masterman, 1744.

Indents for brasses include a floor-slab at Milton Abbey outlining a recumbent figure in vestments, under a canopy; the brass probably represented Abbot Walter de Sideling (*d.* 1315). At Milborne St. Andrew the canopied table-tomb of John Morton, 1526, retains the inscription-plate, but the brasses of kneeling figures, shields and other devices have gone.

Candelabra: Hanging brass candelabra of the 17th or early 18th century are found in Milborne St. Andrew and Winterborne Stickland churches; the former is dated 1712.

Capitals, Bosses, Head-corbels etc.: A small freestanding shaft capital with four canted volutes and a chamfered abacus, found among detached fragments at Milton Abbey, is probably of the 12th century. The label of the chancel arch in St. Catherine's chapel at Milton ends in grotesque beasts of the late 12th century and Marnhull church has a four-shafted pier with head-capitals of about the same date [*16*]. At Mappowder church are some reset 12th-century head-corbels, probably from an eaves corbel-table. Head-corbels at Holwell resemble 12th-century work but their correspondence with 15th-century mouldings *in situ* shows them to be archaistic. Stinsford is the only church in the area with 13th-century stiff-leaf decoration [*16*]. Hazelbury Bryan church contains two 14th-century shaft capitals with naturalistic foliage [*16*], and Milton Abbey has many 14-century vaulting bosses of high quality [*165*]. Of the 15th century are a number of capitals carved to represent angels holding scrolls and shields; good examples are seen at Holwell, Marnhull and Stalbridge [*17*]. Mappowder has a skilfully carved 15th-century head-corbel with foliage issuing from the nostrils, and Cheselbourne has a capital representing a grotesque woman in a monstrous head-dress [*16*]. Many 15th and 16th-century church towers and parapets in the area have gargoyles of fantastic form; Pulham and Piddletrenthide are notable in this respect. At the W. end of the nave arcades Pulham also has a pair of Italianate corbels of the 16th century [*17*].

Communion Tables and Communion Rails: A table and rails were installed in Puddletown parish church *c.* 1635; the table has the usual heavy turned legs of the period and the communion rails, which enclose the sanctuary on three sides, have stout turned balusters, and corner-posts with ball finials supporting brass candlesticks [*23*]. Melcombe Horsey church has a table and rails of about the same date, but the chancel is narrow and the rail extends from side to side. A 17th-century communion table with legs in the form of stout Tuscan columns is at Charlton Marshall church, and well preserved 17-century communion rails with turned balusters are found at Purse and Stourton Caundles [*23*] and at Hammoon.

Although Charlton Marshall's present communion table is of the 17th century, the table designed for the building of 1713 is probably a smaller piece that now stands in the vestry; it is of oak and has deep arcuated top-rails, turned legs with octagonal tapering shafts, and scrolled diagonal stretchers. The tapered legs are repeated in the balusters of the communion rail [*23*]. Winterborne Stickland church has a table very similar to that of Charlton Marshall.

The communion table made, no doubt by the Bastard brothers, for the chancel of Blandford Forum church, *c.* 1733, now stands at the E. end of the S. aisle [*45*]; it is of oak with enriched cabriole legs and delicately carved top-rails. A smaller table of the same kind is found at Okeford Fitzpaine. Winterborne Tomson chapel in Anderson has communion table, rails, pulpit and seating, all probably of the second or third decade of the 18th century [*96*].

Fonts: The earliest and most interesting font in Central Dorset is at Puddletown [*28*]; it is a tapering cylinder covered externally with a reticulate pattern enclosing palmettes; Milborne St. Andrew has a tub-shaped font with cable mouldings at the top and scallops at the base; Farrington in Iwerne Courtney [*26*] and Plush in Piddletrenthide have crude stone tub fonts with horizontal roll-mouldings at about half height and vertical fluting above; all these are of the 12th century. Several churches have square or octagonal Purbeck marble bowls of the late 12th or early 13th century with recessed arcading on the sides; they usually rest on a central stem surrounded by four or eight thinner shafts and have a chamfered octagonal plinth below; Lydlinch provides a good example [*26*]. The late 12th-century font at Mappowder [*26*] elaborates the same theme, having a square bowl with shallow reliefs on each side and the underside shaped to form capitals for five supporting shafts; the shafts stand on a plinth with intersecting base mouldings. A 13th-century octagonal bowl with trefoil-headed sides, and capital mouldings below each corner, is now in the garden at Hanford Farm, Child Okeford; it probably belongs to Hanford church. The plain spherical bowl on a squat moulded stem at Stalbridge is perhaps also of the 13th century. The fonts at Hammoon and Fifehead Neville have plain octagonal bowls converted to square bases by means of broach stops; they are probably of the 14th century. Most 15th-century fonts are octagonal and have cusped panelling on stem and sides; typical examples are at Ibberton and Stoke Wake [*26*]. Winterborne Whitechurch has an elaborate 15th-century font [*28*] with an octagonal bowl decorated with rich vine-scroll carving; the stem is surrounded by three free standing shafts decorated with pinnacles; the heads of the shafts are masked by shields-of-arms.

Several churches have 18th-century fonts. Those with baluster stems, square on plan, at Blandford Forum, Charlton Marshall and Winterborne Stickland are of Portland stone and presumably come from one workshop [*27*]. Stourton Caundle has a circular version of the same theme, and a similar example has recently been taken from Melcombe Horsey and is now at Swanage (*see Dorset* II, 292). Several of the 18th-century fonts have contemporary dome-shaped oak covers with enriched finials.

Galleries: The oak gallery on bulbous Doric columns at the W. end of Puddletown church is dated 1635 and is the earliest W. gallery to survive in Central Dorset. The timbers of a W. gallery at Tomson church, Anderson, are mediaeval but reset; they probably come from a former rood-loft. At Cheselbourne the oak stairs to a former gallery are preserved but they too are now reset. In Blandford Forum church an elegant W. gallery was inserted in 1794 to accommodate the organ; the side galleries were added in 1837.

Glass: Little mediaeval window glass of merit survives in the area; the best is the 15th-century glass in the tracery lights in Hazelbury Bryan church [*139*]. Other fragments of mediaeval glass are found at Melcombe Horsey and Lydlinch [*144*]. Milton Abbey has some 14th-century grisaille, numerous 15th and 16th-century shields-of-arms, and a large mid 19th-century window by A. W. Pugin. Ibberton has one panel of 15th-century heraldic glazing [*144*] and two heraldic panels of 16th-century date [*44*].

Among secular buildings the most notable collections of heraldic glass are in the halls at Milton Abbey, at Athelhampton and at Bingham's Melcombe [*160*]. Lovell's Court, Marnhull, contains some 16th-century heraldic glass recently brought from Lancashire.

Helmet: A 16th-century close helmet with Cromwellian modifications is preserved in Iwerne Courtney parish church.

Hour-Glass Stands: of wrought iron occur in the churches at Hammoon, Manston, Holwell and Spetisbury; the latter is probably dated 1700. *Hour-glasses* are preserved at Holwell and Spetisbury.

Images: There are not many examples in the area and the most important is the earliest, namely the late 10th or early 11th-century relief of an angel, reset in Stinsford church tower [*12*]. Buckland Newton has a small Christ-in-Majesty of the 12th century [*12*]. The reredos in Hammoon church, depicting the Crucifixion and six flanking figures in niches, is of the late 14th or early 15th century, but it is a recent acquisition and of unknown provenance. Durweston has an odd clunch relief [*13*] thought to represent St. Eloi, and Winterborne Stickland has a small semicircular relief of the Crucifixion; both these are of the 15th century. Milton Abbey has part of a 15th or early 16th-century figure of St. James the Great. A small mica-schist relief of a warrior [*13*], now reset in Buckland Newton church, was discovered in a nearby garden in 1913; it probably is of the 8th or 9th century, but it can scarcely be of local origin.

Monuments: Mediaeval funeral monuments in Central Dorset include eleven with recumbent effigies. The earliest is the 12th-century relief of Philip, priest of Tolpuddle [*193*]. Effigies of an armoured man and his wife at Puddletown, and a miniature effigy from a heart-burial at Mappowder [*14*] are of the mid 13th century; of the late 13th century are effigies of a bare-headed man with a sword in Glanville's Wootton church and of an armoured figure in Stock Gaylard church [*14*]. Of the 14th century is an armoured figure at Puddletown [*189*]; it lies on an arcaded altar-tomb in a cusped ogee-headed wall-recess. Adjacent is a tomb of *c.* 1460, with figures of an armoured man and his wife, with angels in niches around the sides of the tomb-chest [*188*]; Marnhull church contains a tomb of about the same date, representing a man in armour flanked by two ladies [*15*]. Also of the mid 15th century is a small effigy of a lady at Stourton Caundle [*193*]; she now lies in a niche which was formerly part of another tomb. The splendid alabaster effigy on the tomb of Sir William Martyn (*d.* 1503) at Puddletown [*15*] is probably of the late 15th century; it lies in a rich canopied table-tomb of Purbeck marble. Stalbridge has a late 15th or early 16th-century cadaver effigy [*193*].

Late mediaeval canopied table-tombs with brasses (q.v.) instead of effigies are found at Charminster, Milton Abbey and Milborne St. Andrew. Tombs of similar form but with Renaissance instead of Gothic detail occur at Puddletown and Spetisbury; both date from the end of the 16th century [*31*].

Of numerous 17th-century monuments the most notable are those of Sir Thomas Freke at Iwerne Courtney [*36*] and of Grace Pole at Charminster [*34*], dated respectively 1633 and 1636. Glanville's Wootton church contains a large wall-monument [*35*] of 1679 and several lesser examples of about the same date. Noteworthy among the later 17th-century wall-monuments are those of John Straight at Stourpaine [*33*] and of Grace Morris at Manston [*33*].

The most impressive 18th-century monument in the area is that of Mary Bancks (*d.* 1734) in Milton Abbey [*37*]; the same church enshrines a remarkable tomb erected in 1775 by Joseph Damer, Earl of Dorchester, in memory of his wife [*169*]; it comprises a marble table-tomb in the Gothic style by Robert Adam with effigies of the deceased lady and her sorrowing lord by Carlini. Among many admirable 18th-century wall-tablets, that of Francis Cartwright at Blandford St. Mary is outstanding for sensitive design and skilful workmanship [*119*]. Of 19th-century monuments, two examples [*39*] by King of Bath are notable, one at Bishop's Caundle and one at Buckland Newton, both dated 1815. Characteristic of the mid 19th century is a monument in the chancel of Piddletrenthide church by C. R. Cockerell.

Paintings: Twelve 15th-century oak panels, each depicting an Apostle, were transferred in the 18th century from Milton Abbey to Hilton church where they still remain [*25*, *137*]. Another 15th or early 16th-century panel, possibly from the same source, is preserved at Stock Gaylard church in Lydlinch. Incorporated in the choir-stalls at Milton Abbey are two crude and much restored panels representing a king and a queen. The earliest wall-painting on plaster exposed in a Central Dorset church is the stencilled overall pattern of strawberries and leaves at Charminster; it is probably early 16th-century work. Crude 16th-century outlines of human figures are preserved on the W. wall of Marnhull church. Painted prayers and texts of 16th and 17th-century date have been exposed in several churches, notably at Charminster, Marnhull and Puddletown.

Many churches retain painted hatchments of the 17th, 18th and 19th centuries. At Marnhull one is dated 1631 and another 1663; Lydlinch parish church has one of *c.* 1650 [*44*].

Plate: The earliest dated communion cup in Central Dorset is at Mappowder [*42*]; it has hallmark and date-letter for 1570 and an undecipherable maker's mark. The cup at Charminster is probably of the same date but the letter is badly stamped. Both vessels are of the usual Elizabethan pattern in which the conical bowl is deep, slightly flared and decorated externally with a belt of engraved foliate strapwork; the stem has a central knop and the foot is domed. Between 1570 and 1573 nine Central Dorset parishes obtained similar cups, but no two have the same maker's mark.[1] On the other hand, one silversmith, Lawrence Stratford of Dorchester, supplied cups and cover-patens in 1574 for Cheselbourne, Dewlish, Okeford Fitzpaine, Shillingstone [*42*] and Winterborne Houghton; in 1575 he made one for Burleston and in 1577 he made one for Tolpuddle. None of these has a hallmark or a date-letter but they all bear Stratford's mark 'LS' and they have the date engraved on the cover-paten.

Of about the same date but of slightly different form are cups and cover-patens at Hammoon, Hinton St. Mary and Marnhull [*42*]; they are undated and without hallmarks but they all bear the mark of another local maker, the so-called 'Gillingham' silversmith.[2] These cups have trumpet-shaped stems with knops near the bowl and strapwork engraving somewhat plainer than that of Lawrence Stratford.

The taste of the 17th century is exemplified in the cup of 1649 at Iwerne Stepleton [*42*] and that of 1663 at Sturminster Newton; on the other hand a typical Elizabethan cup hallmarked as late as 1633 is found at Stoke Wake. The parish church at Milton Abbas has a cup and cover-paten of 1636, another paten given in 1678, and a flagon of 1663 presented by 'Maddam Jane Tregonwell . . . 1675'; these vessels have now been transferred from the abbey to the parish church.

At Winterborne Whitechurch a silver two-handled bowl of 1653 is used as a communion cup [*43*]. Turnworth church has a similar vessel, hallmarked in 1764; presumably it is a replica of the first.

In 1714 a silver cup and flagon were acquired by Charlton Marshall church under the will of Catherine Sloper; the cup [*43*] is of pleasing form with an unusually stout stem. The cup and flagon of 1731 and 1732 in Blandford Forum church have profiles similar to those of Charlton Marshall, but are of slenderer proportions. The handsomest set of 18th-century church plate in Central Dorset is the silver-gilt cup, cover-paten and flagon which Mrs. Strangways Horner gave to Stinsford church in 1737 [*202*]; the vessels were made by Paul Lamerie and have the date-letter of 1736; in 1755 the same donor presented a bread-knife and sheath. A similar set of church plate is at Abbotsbury (*Dorset* I, 3). Another fine set of cup, paten and flagon [*43*], with hallmarks of 1764, given to Bryanston church by the Berkeley–Portman family, is now at Durweston. An unusual cup and cover at Tincleton is probably German 16th-century work; the same parish

[1] The cups at Purse Caundle, Pulham, Fifehead Neville, Buckland Newton and Plush (Piddletrenthide) were all hallmarked in 1571; the cups at Lydlinch and Child Okeford have no hallmarks but are dated 1573 by inscription.

[2] A cup by this silversmith is engraved 'Gilyngham, 1574' and for want of better identification the maker is called by this name: *see* Nightingale, *Church Plate of Dorset*, 14 ff.

has an English flagon, apparently designed to match the cup, presented in 1718; the flagon was repaired in 1900 and new hallmarks were applied in that year.

The Congregational Chapel at Blandford Forum has two two-handled silver communion cups of 1714, each with a gadrooned base, enriched necking, and the inscription 'B.M.H.', for Blandford Meeting House.

Pulpits: of 15th-century date survive at Okeford Fitzpaine and Winterborne Whitechurch [*46*]. The former is of stone and the latter is of wood, but both pulpits are polygonal, with a canopied niche in each side; the drum walls alone are original, plinths, pedestals, top mouldings and much of the detail being 19th-century restoration. Stourton Caundle has a polygonal oak pulpit of the early 16th century in a good state of preservation [*46*]; its sides have two heights of panelling, the lower panels with linenfold decoration, the upper panels with blind tracery. The richly carved early 17th-century pulpit in Spetisbury church is also polygonal and of oak. Of similar form to the Spetisbury pulpit but simpler in detail is one at Charminster, dated 1635. Also of about 1635 is a polygonal oak pulpit at Puddletown, with arcaded sides and coupled Roman Doric columns at the corners [*47*].

Oak pulpits of the late 17th and early 18th century occur in many churches; they are polygonal and are often decorated with carving or marquetry. At Holwell the panels have reeded decoration recalling linenfold; at Hazelbury Bryan the pulpit has a wooden sounding board, formerly with a tent-shaped superstructure which has now become the font cover. Charlton Marshall has a handsome pulpit of carved oak and marquetry, crowned with a domed sounding board on top of which stands a carved pelican [*47*]; presumably this pulpit dates from the restoration of the church in 1713 and it is likely to have been made in the Bastard workshop at Blandford Forum. The same workshop supplied the pulpit at Melcombe Horsey in 1723.

Reredoses: Apart from the recently acquired stone reredos at Hammoon (see *Images*) the only mediaeval reredos to survive in Central Dorset is at Milton Abbey [*166*]; an inscription upon it is dated 1492, and although the upper parts of the masonry are largely late 18th-century work much of the lower storey, including some painted decoration, is original. Blandford Forum, Charlton Marshall and Bryanston have carved and gilded 18th-century reredoses inscribed with the Ten Commandments.

Screens: Part of a 15th-century stone screen with niches [*24*] is reset in the S. transept of Milton Abbey, and the reset beams of a timber rood-screen are preserved at Tomson chapel, Anderson. The 17th-century carved oak screen at the E. end of the N. aisle of Iwerne Courtney church [*143*] is the most notable piece of woodwork in the area; it encloses the monument to Sir Thomas Freke, 1654, but the style of decoration is earlier and the screen may have originally enclosed the Freke family pew; hence it is probably of 1610, when the church was rebuilt. In 1619 Sir Thomas Freke also erected an oak screen [*22*] in the church at Melcombe Horsey.

Seating: Very little remains of the mediaeval seating in Central Dorset churches. Milton Abbey has a notable set of painted stone sedilia [*166*] and fragments of a few oak choir stalls with plain misericordes. Many churches were provided with new seating in the 19th century, often by dismantling and reassembling earlier woodwork, whereby original bench-ends were occasionally preserved; some at Buckland Newton are perhaps of the late 15th century. Puddletown retains a noteworthy set of 17th-century panelled oak box pews [*185*], and Winterborne Tomson chapel at Anderson retains the neat box pews [*96*] which Archbishop Wake supplied in the 18th century (Hutchins I, 196). A few 17th-century oak benches survive at Okeford Fitzpaine. The Mayor's seat in the parish church of Blandford Forum, dated 1748, is handsomely carved [*101*].

Miscellaneous Woodwork: Special mention must be made of the remarkably well-preserved 15th-century hanging pyx-shrine in Milton Abbey [*167*]; it is of three stages with a spire finial and is lavishly decorated with carved tracery. Other examples are known at Wells and Tewkesbury (*P.S.A.*, XVI (1897), 287–9) and at Dennington in Suffolk. Another interesting object is the 16th-century carved oak pedestal alms-box in Buckland Newton church [*22*]. Several churches have 17th and 18th-century armchairs and coffin-stools of carved oak; a chair at Milborne St. Andrew is dated 1670 and stools at Marnhull are dated 1683.

Public Buildings

Almshouses: A row of almshouses built in 1682 [*112*] was one of the few buildings to escape the fire of 1731 at Blandford Forum. A slightly earlier almshouse building in the old town of Milton Abbas was transferred and re-erected in the new model village in 1779, a surprisingly early and successful example of conservation [*178*]. A workhouse of 1838 by Lewis Vulliamy continues to function at Sturminster Newton, converted into a home for old people.

Assembly Rooms: of the early 19th century are found in Blandford Forum and Sturminster Newton; the first is now a garage and the second is used as a badminton court.

Bridges: Sturminster Newton [*51*], Spetisbury [*199*] and Bishop's Caundle have bridges which incorporate late 15th or early 16th-century elements; a small rubble footbridge at Fifehead Neville may also be mediaeval. Blandford Bridge is principally of the 18th and 19th century but the westernmost arch is probably late mediaeval [*114*]. Durweston Bridge [*51*] and King's Mill bridge at Marnhull were built in 1795 and 1823 respectively.

Crosses: A stone market cross of the late 15th century survives in a good state of preservation at Stalbridge [*50*]; the sculptured cross-head and finial were destroyed in a storm in 1950 but they have been renewed. Other mediaeval wayside, market or preaching crosses are represented by stepped pedestals at Sturminster Newton, Minterne Parva in Buckland Newton, Hammoon, Okeford Fitzpaine and Shillingstone; at Shillingstone a modern cross-shaft has been erected on the mediaeval steps.

Town Hall: The Town Hall of Blandford Forum was rebuilt after the fire of 1731; the ground floor is an arcaded loggia and the upper storey is occupied by courtrooms; the Portland stone façade [*106*] is dated 1734 and signed 'Bastard, Architect' [*107*].

Domestic Buildings

The earliest surviving secular building in Central Dorset is probably the 14th-century hall and solar at Fiddleford Mill in Sturminster Newton [*206–8*]. In spite of 16th-century modifications the buildings retain two very important original roofs of much elaboration; the monument is now in the care of the Ministry of Public Building and Works. Hinton St. Mary Manor House may incorporate the walls of a hall as early as the 13th century, but too little remains visible for reliable assessment.

The mid 15th-century Manor House at Winterborne Clenston has a first-floor hall and an adjoining chamber with moulded and cusped arch-braced collar-beam roofs. Access to the hall is by a stone newel staircase in a projecting tower at the centre of the W. front [*213*]. Purse Caundle Manor House [*194–6*] has a mid 15th-century ground-floor hall, open to the roof, with two-storied cross-wings to N. and S.; the S. cross-wing has a pleasing first-floor bow window. The hall at Athelhampton is an important example of late 15th-century domestic architecture; it has a beautiful oriel window [*94*] and the open roof with its enormous decorative cusps is especially noteworthy [*95*]. The abbot's great hall at Milton Abbey, finished in 1498, has a richly carved hammer-beam roof [*172*].

Of smaller 15th-century buildings the most interesting is Naish Farm, Holwell. It is a mediaeval farmstead almost in its original state, except for 16th-century chambering-over of the hall. Senior's Farm at Marnhull is a handsomely decorated dwelling of the late 15th or early 16th century and probably originated either as a chantry house or as an occasional lodging for the Abbot of Glastonbury, who was lord of the manor [*56*].

Wolfeton House, Charminster, retains an impressive gatehouse of *c.* 1500 with quasi-defensive towers [*125*]; the elaborately decorated S. range is of the mid 16th century but the greater part of the original 16th-century house has perished. Bingham's Melcombe, principally of the mid 16th century although the gatehouse is slightly earlier, is renowned as one of the loveliest of English country houses [*153–60*]. Hammoon Manor House comprises an early 16th-century timber-framed dwelling with later 16th-century additions in stone [*134*]. Kingston Maurward Old Manor House in Stinsford parish has the remarkably well-preserved outer shell of a late 16th-century house on an E-plan [*204*], but the interior has largely perished. Round Chimneys farmhouse at Glanville's Wootton, another notable late 16th-century house [*56*], is much diminished from its original size.

Of minor 16th-century dwellings, Haydon Farm at Lydlinch is a good example of a farmhouse on an L-plan; it has moulded and panelled timber ceilings and a through-passage with plank-and-muntin partitions. Pear Tree Cottage, Piddletrenthide, is notable for its well documented history. Manor Farm, Caundle Marsh, has a 15th-century nucleus with 16th and 17th-century additions.

Buildings of the 17th century include Hanford House [*135*], which dates from 1604–23 and has a square plan with a central courtyard; it was probably designed in imitation of an Italian palace but apart from a few copy-book details the elevations have little Renaissance character. The neighbouring and almost contemporary house at Iwerne Stepleton originally had a somewhat similar plan, but the original design of this house has been obscured by 18th-century alterations [*148–9*]. At Anderson Manor [*52*], built in 1622, many of the traditional English architectural forms continued to be applied, and the house has much in common with Kingston Maurward Old Manor although it is a generation later in date. The plan, however, shows an improvement on the usual mediaeval 'one-room-thick' arrangement, having two parallel ranges with a common spine wall, in which the fireplaces are set back-to-back; the innovation was introduced at Glanville's Wootton (6) at the end of the 16th century but it did not become common in Central Dorset until late in the 18th century. Anderson Manor is also an early local example of the use of brick. The nearby Tomson farmhouse [*90*] is more antiquated in design, being planned in much the same way as the 15th-century Winterborne Clenston Manor, with the main rooms on the first floor; however, the use of brick shows that it must be more or less contemporary with Anderson Manor. The Manor House at Blandford St. Mary is another early example of the use of brick [*53*]. The mid 17th-century S. front of Waterston House, Puddletown, clearly in the architectural succession of Kingston Maurward and Anderson Manors, has classical details used with understanding and discrimination [*52*]; on the other hand the Old House at Blandford Forum [*110*], probably built at the Restoration, still shows the uncertainty with which country builders approached the Renaissance.

Among smaller 17th-century houses, Tolpuddle Manor [*212*], dated 1656, Pope's Farm, Marnhull, and the Old Rectory at Cheselbourne must be noted; they are all designed in the traditional late mediaeval manner. Dale House at Blandford Forum [*112*] shows that some local builders had fully mastered the classical idiom by 1689, the date inscribed on its doorway; Fontmell Parva at Child Okeford [*54*] is of about the same date and style, and illustrates the same point.

Blandford Forum is the only town of any size in Central Dorset and the only place where urban architecture is to be found. The town was almost entirely destroyed by fires in 1713 and 1731 and, being rebuilt soon afterwards, provides a homogeneous example of a mid 18th-century country town. The most notable figures in the reconstruction of the town were John and William Bastard, local builder-architects of more than ordinary competence; they certainly designed the Church and the Town Hall and they probably were responsible for many other buildings.[1] Judging by the excellence of his own monument in the church at Blandford St. Mary, Francis Cartwright was another local builder of outstanding quality. After Cartwright's death in 1758 his practice was carried on by Martin Meatyard.[2]

The most extensive single work of the 18th century in Central Dorset was the rebuilding of Milton Abbey House [*170–1*] by Sir William Chambers for Joseph Damer, Baron Milton, subsequently Earl of Dorchester. In deference to the adjacent abbey church the exterior is enriched with 'Gothic' detail, but the general form of the exterior and every feature of the interior, which was carried on by James Wyatt after Chambers had withdrawn from the engagement, are uncompromisingly classical. 'Capability' Brown laid out the park, providing a romantic setting for the mediaeval church and the 18th-century house, and for this purpose Lord Milton pulled down the original town and established the inhabitants in a 'model village' [*177*] on a new site about half a mile away.

Chambers also designed a classical mansion at Castle Hill, Buckland Newton [*123*], and Wyatt designed one at Bryanston; both buildings have now been pulled down, but the former lasted long enough to be recorded by this Commission and is included in the present volume. No doubt Sir James Thornhill was partly responsible for the architecture of his own house at Stalbridge [*197*]. In 1753 Ranston, a 17th-century house at Iwerne Courtney (3), was provided with a graceful classical façade [*148*] and an elegant staircase [*85*]; these features survive although the house has recently been extensively rebuilt, the façade having been left *in situ* and the stairs having been reset. Kingston Maurward House at Stinsford is of early 18th-century origin but it was completely refaced in stone in 1794, traditionally to please George III; it has monumental façades with Corinthian pilasters and entablatures [*205*]; the baroque interior decorations are of the late 19th century.

English 18th-century taste is illustrated in several smaller houses. A notable example is Johns House, Spetisbury [*191*, *197*], built in 1715 by Dr. Charles Sloper, the wealthy cleric who remodelled Charlton Marshall church. Puddletown vicarage [*191*] is another fine early 18th-century house, and Stalbridge rectory is a third although it has suffered 19th-century alterations. Typical of the mid 18th century are the graceful flanking pavilions of Iwerne Stepleton House [*148*], dated 1758. Eastway House, Blandford Forum (31), is of the same period and contains interesting rococo plasterwork [*113*, *117*].

The Gothic Revival is not well represented in Central Dorset. Chambers's rebuilding of Milton Abbey is really a classical composition and the same is true of the N. front of Pulham Rectory [*55*]. Internally, 18th-century Gothic details are noted in the drawing-room of the Manor House, Alton Pancras, and at Revel's Inn farmhouse in Buckland Newton.

The area contains few large early 19th-century houses. At Whatcombe House, Winterborne Whitechurch, a mid 18th-century house is incorporated in and provides the side elevation of a larger building with a pilastered façade; this was built in 1802. Clyffe House, Tincleton, an example of the 'manorial' style, was designed by Benjamin Ferrey in 1842. Bryanston House, designed by Richard Norman Shaw *c.* 1890, is one of the largest English country houses to be built in recent times.

The general remarks on vernacular buildings in the preceding volume (*Dorset* II, lxi) apply equally to Central Dorset. Of the basic types of plan, the evolution of class F is aptly illustrated at Naish Farmhouse, Holwell (14). Developed examples of class F are Shillingstone (7), Stalbridge (9) and perhaps Sturminster

[1] H. M. Colvin, *Arch. Journ.* CIV (1947), 178 f.; A. Oswald, *Country Houses of Dorset*, 1959, 30 f.
[2] *Salisbury Journal*, Jan. 8th and March 19th, 1759.

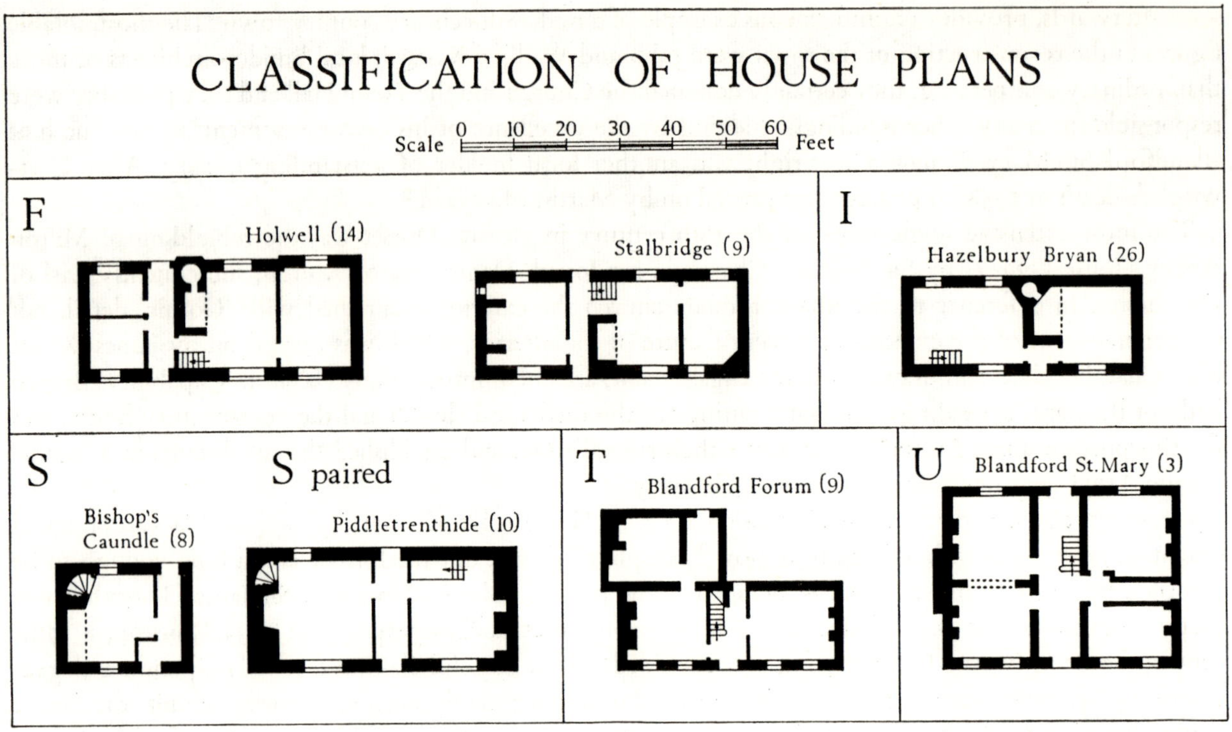

Newton (32). Class I is represented by Hazelbury Bryan (26). Class S, common in South-East Dorset, is less often noted in the central area, but a cottage in Bishop's Caundle (8) provides an example. In this connection, Pear Tree Cottage, Piddletrenthide (10) presents an interesting problem: the plan appears to show a simple two-room cottage with a central through-passage, but contemporary accounts (Winchester College Muniments, 14814) prove that as early as 1506 the building was regarded by its landlord as comprising two tenements; moreover, a map of 1771 at Winchester shows the appropriate plot of land as containing a pair of cottages. Since this simple two-room cottage is thus revealed as a pair of class S cottages, it may be asked if many other buildings, which now appear to be two-room dwellings, are really paired examples of class S? The type might often escape recognition since the clues to its existence must be either documentary or the presence of two staircases, and with later conversion to a single dwelling one staircase might well be removed. Houses of class T occur frequently in Central Dorset, especially among 18th-century buildings; they are represented by the Blandford Forum houses of *Group i*, as well as in several rural examples. Class U houses also are mainly of the 18th century. Study of the plans given in the Inventory will probably suggest additions to the plan-types thus far classified (*see* also *Cambridgeshire* I, pp. xlvi–li), and it is hoped that the accumulation of plans will finally make it possible to construct a general scheme of classified plan-types, applicable to the whole country.

Ancillary Buildings

Ornamental Buildings: Most of the larger houses described in this volume are approached through dignified *Gateways*. The 16th-century gatehouse at Athelhampton [*93*] is known only from drawings but the gatehouses of Wolfeton House [*125*] and Bingham's Melcombe [*153*] still exist, each comprising a carriageway with gate-keepers' rooms on each side and chambers above; the Wolfeton example includes quite effective fortifications although built as late as *c.* 1500. The gateway which opens into the courtyard at Hanford House is embellished with a classical frontispiece, apparently added slightly later to the early 17th-century façade. Of freestanding gateways with ornamental stone piers, good 17th-century examples are found at Mappowder and Stalbridge [*66*], both belonging to mansions that have been destroyed; two late 17th-century gate pier finials from Milborne St. Andrew, carved as military trophies, are now at Winterborne Clenston. At Bingham's Melcombe and Alton Pancras are handsome 18th-century stone piers [*66*], and late 18th-century gateways of some magnificence are found at Bryanston and Milton Abbas [*67*].

An ornamental *Bridge* of *c.* 1760 with three arches and balustraded parapets is found at Ranston in Iwerne Courtney [*64*]. Kingston Maurward House, Stinsford, has a *Garden Temple* [*64*] in the Roman Doric style, perhaps of *c.* 1780. An octagonal *Summer-house* of the early 19th century at Piddletrenthide contains plaster reliefs after Flaxman. *Obelisks* are found at Milborne St. Andrew [*67*] and at Thornhill in Stalbridge; in the same category may be included the *Fire Monument* at Blandford Forum [*102*], a small Roman Doric portico dated 1760. A '*Folly*' representing a ruined church in Milton Abbey park is probably not earlier than 1811 [*65*].

Riding House: One of the most interesting architectural survivals in the district is the Riding House or School at Wolfeton, Charminster (5). Dating from the last quarter of the 16th century the S. front and both end walls remain almost intact [*125*]. The interior arrangements have gone as, also, has the open court which appears formerly to have lain on the N. side of the roofed school. Hitherto the building has been known as Wolfeton Barn, and its true purpose has only lately been recognised.

Farm Buildings etc.: Late mediaeval *Barns* are found at Hinton St. Mary, at Lyscombe in Cheselbourne, and at Winterborne Clenston. Shroton Farm, Iwerne Courtney, has a fine stone barn of the 17th or early 18th century. *Stables* of 17th-century date are found at Pope's Farm, Marnhull, at Hinton St. Mary Manor House and at Athelhampton. Of several 18th-century examples, those of Bryanston House are the most extensive; stylistically they are closely akin to the stables at Iwerne Stepleton House [*63*] and they probably both date from about the middle of the century. The stables at Ranston, Iwerne Courtney, were built in 1782. Circular *Pigeon Cotes* of uncertain date but probably of the 17th and 18th centuries are found at Athelhampton [*92*], and Bingham's Melcombe [*158*]; in them the cylindrical inner wall-face is built with interstices to form nesting boxes, accessible to the keeper of the cote from a ladder at the end of a beam which swivels about a central pivot. An early 19th-century version of the same device at Piddletrenthide Manor House is now in ruins. Tomson Farm at Anderson and Shroton Farm at Iwerne Courtney have square pigeon cotes of the 17th century. Peter Beckford's hunt *Kennels* at Iwerne Stepleton were built about 1770 and have now been converted into cottages.

Fittings and Component Parts of Secular Buildings

Chimneys: Hanford House [*135*] and Iwerne Stepleton House have chimneystacks wherein the flues terminate in plain cylindrical shafts that are united at the top by a slab of stone with moulded edges; the shafts at Hanford are of stone while those of Stepleton are of brick; Round Chimneys Farmhouse at Glanville's Wootton has similar chimneys [*56*], and another example occurs at Rodmore Farm, Lydlinch. These houses are all of the late 16th or early 17th century and the chimneys may well have been inspired by those of Montacute. The Manor House [*52*] and Tomson Farmhouse [*90*] at Anderson, both *c.* 1620, have square brick chimneys set diagonally in groups. At the Old House, Blandford Forum, *c.* 1660, the flues are contained in heavily moulded polygonal brick stacks, embellished externally with terracotta angle shafts. At Fontmell Parva, Child Okeford, a large square stack with arcaded sides stands centrally above the symmetrical façade [*54*].

Doors and Doorways: Few secular buildings retain mediaeval doors; the most notable are those with pointed heads and traceried decoration at each end of the screens-passage in Athelhampton Hall [*80*]. Hammoon Manor House has a heavy oak door with a four-centred head. Naish Farm, Holwell, retains a massive original door of elm, hung in a chamfered oak doorway with a two-centred head.

A fine internal stone doorway of the late 16th century, with classical pilasters and pediment, is preserved at Wolfeton House [*127*]; it represents the pre-Flemish phase of the English Renaissance.

Several late 16th or early 17th-century houses in Central Dorset retain round-headed archways of classical inspiration, with moulded archivolts, often with shaped keystones, and jambs with attached shafts and moulded imposts; they form a well-defined group and may be derived from a common original. The best example is the porch archway at Hammoon Manor House [*136*]; other examples are in the porches at Hanford House, Waterston House, Puddletown and, internally, at Round Chimneys Farmhouse, Glanville's Wootton; also at Blandford St. Mary Manor House and at Stinsford Manor House.

Stone doorways with classical surrounds and pediments of various shapes add dignity to the entrances of numerous early 18th-century houses; examples are at Dewlish House [*68*], at Quarleston Farm, Winterborne Stickland [*68*], at Dalton's Farm, Hinton St. Mary, at Church Farm, Marnhull and at the Manor House, Stoke Wake. Of many mid 18th-century wooden doorcases with projecting hoods and scrolled brackets, the most noteworthy are at Lime Tree House, Blandford Forum, and at the Old Rectory and Brook House, Blandford St. Mary [*69*]; a later version of the same kind of doorcase is seen at Close House, Blandford Forum.

Fireplace Surrounds: The earliest datable fireplace surround in Central Dorset is in a bedchamber at Athelhampton; it is of stone and the heraldry implies that it is of the late 15th century. About the middle of the 16th century a stone fireplace surround was inserted in the Solar at Fiddleford Mill, Sturminster Newton; it has moulded stone jambs corbelled out to support a four-centred head. Stone chimneypieces of the later 16th and early 17th centuries with Renaissance enrichments and strapwork details are found at Wolfeton House, Charminster [*127*], and at Hanford House [*74*]. Oak overmantels of the same period occur in several houses, the majority reset although one at Melcombe Horsey (3) is probably *in situ*. Later 17th-century stone chimneypieces with more sophisticated classical details are rare in the area; Wolfeton House has one with nicely proportioned rustication and another with handsome Ionic pilasters and richly carved gadrooning [*75*]. The only other stone chimneypiece of true classical style to survive from the 17th century is in the hall of Milton Abbey House; it probably is of *c.* 1675. In spite of these examples, the late mediaeval type of chimneypiece with a shallow four-centred or 'Tudor' head remained in general favour; even as late as *c.* 1700 the fireplaces in the N.E. range of Blandford St. Mary Manor House preserved the old form in every respect except their flat lintels. Waterston House, Puddletown, has a chimneypiece of the second quarter of the 17th century with a 'Tudor' head capped by a fairly accurate classical entablature, but flanked by highly experimental pilasters [*75*].

Wooden chimneypieces in the classical style with pedimented overmantels, cornice-shaped mantelshelves and pilastered side pieces began to appear in good houses early in the 18th century; two examples of *c.* 1702 are found at Dewlish House [*78*]. The type was soon to proliferate; Blandford Forum has many examples, the most notable being in John Bastard's own house, No. 75 East Street [*116*]. An example at Thornhill House, Stalbridge [*76*], with caryatid pilasters but without an overmantel, is interesting because it is in Sir James Thornhill's own house and may well have been designed by him; the details suggest a painter's rather than an architect's hand. All the early 18th-century chimneypieces are of wood, but towards the end of the century handsome marble examples were imported; those installed by Chambers at Castle Hill, Buckland Newton, *c.* 1760, were among the first to reach the area.

Glass: The small quantity of coloured window glass to survive in secular buildings has already been mentioned together with glass in churches (above, p. li).

Panelling and Partitions: Plank-and-muntin partitions dating from the 16th to the 18th centuries are found in many houses and cottages of Central Dorset. Two early and well-preserved examples are at Senior's Farm, Marnhull, where a ground-floor partition has chamfered and moulded members with original painted decoration while a partition on the first floor, near the head of the stairs, is embellished with blind tracery [*80*]. Many houses have rooms lined with oak wainscot of the 16th and 17th centuries, with panels in several heights, but a great deal of it is reset. A good example that appears to be *in situ* is in a first-floor room at Melcombe Horsey (3); it is of the early 17th century and therefore was probably installed by Sir Thomas Freke, who also erected the fine screens [*143*] in Iwerne Courtney church. Of 18th-century rooms panelled in two heights there are numerous examples; John Bastard's own room [*116*] at 75 East Street, Blandford Forum is certainly one of the handsomest in the area. This type of panelling is usually of pine but examples in oak are also noted; that at Dewlish House [*78*] is extraordinarily well preserved, and a small oak-panelled room in an inn at Hazelbury Bryan may also be mentioned. At Fontmell Parva, Child Okeford (2), the 18th-century panelling is partly of mahogany [*79*].

Plasterwork: Plaster ceilings of the 16th and 17th centuries with moulded geometric ribs and foliate enrichments occur in many Central Dorset houses. The earliest, at Fiddleford Mill [*70*], is probably of the mid 16th century; other good examples are found at Hanford House, Bingham's Melcombe, Higher Melcombe [*71*], and at Tomson Farm in Anderson [*91*]; they are probably of the first third of the 17th century. Other houses contain fine 18th-century ceilings; one of the best, dating from *c.* 1735, is in John Bastard's own house at Blandford Forum, and another good example occurs above the staircase at Blandford St. Mary Manor House [*72*]. Rococo plaster ornament of *c.* 1750 is found at Ranston, Iwerne Courtney, and in Eastway House, Blandford Forum [*117*]. Later 18th-century plaster ceilings of very high quality by James Wyatt and others are found in the main rooms at Milton Abbey [*73, 77, 174*]; drawings for them are preserved at the Royal Institute of British Architects. Other good 18th-century ceilings, probably by Chambers, existed at Castle Hill, Buckland Newton, now demolished [*72*].

Roofs: The oldest and most interesting roofs in Central Dorset are unquestionably those of the 14th-century Hall and Solar at Fiddleford Mill, Sturminster Newton (4); they are of oak, with trusses, horizontal braces and windbraces richly moulded and cusped; the hall roof retains a small additional truss to support a smoke-louvre [*208*]. Of 15th-century open timber roofs perhaps the most noteworthy is in Abbot William Middleton's Hall [*172*] at Milton Abbey, dated 1498; other examples of about the same date are in the halls at Athelhampton [*95*], Purse Caundle Manor [*194*] and Winterborne Clenston Manor. Quarleston Farm at Winterborne Stickland has a hall roof similar to the last named, but smaller [*211*]; also noteworthy is the open timber roof at Naish Farm, Holwell.

Mediaeval wagon roofs are rare in secular buildings but two examples occur in the Manor House at Purse Caundle [*195*]. Hammoon Manor House retains a pitched roof with a boarded ceiling decorated with painted stars, probably of the 16th century. Many small late 16th or early 17th-century houses have moulded ceiling beams intersecting to form coffers; examples are at Haydon Farm, Lydlinch, and at Puddletown Rectory. The late 15th-century ceiling of the oriel recess in the Abbot's great hall at Milton has more elaborate coffering [*80*].

Several barns in the area retain roof trusses of early type. At Tomson Farm, Anderson, the barn has massive upper-cruck trusses with arch-braced collar beams; a 16th-century barn at Hazelbury Bryan has jointed crucks; Lyscombe barn in Cheselbourne had large jointed upper-cruck trusses until they collapsed in 1948. The barn at Winterborne Clenston is roofed with very impressive reused 15th-century moulded hammer-beam trusses [*216*], obviously brought from a building of some grandeur, perhaps at Milton Abbey.

Screens: The richly carved oak screen dated 1498 in the great hall at Milton Abbey [*173*] is perhaps the most notable piece of mediaeval woodwork to survive in the area. The screen at Athelhampton Hall, although mediaeval, has been brought from elsewhere. No other hall screen in the area remains *in situ*.

Staircases: The Gatehouse at Wolfeton, Charminster, has a circular stair of *c.* 1500 with solid oak treads that are integral with the newel; a similar but larger example of the same kind of stair, probably dating from the mid 16th century, is at Athelhampton [*81*]. Winterborne Clenston Manor House has a 16th-century stone newel stair in a polygonal turret, with unusual external corbelling to support a rectangular roof; Tomson Farmhouse, Anderson, has a somewhat similar circular stair in a square turret, of the early 17th century [*81*]. Lazerton Farmhouse, Stourpaine, retains part of a 17th-century staircase which appears originally to have been similar to that of Tomson Farmhouse, but with timber treads.

Hanford House has a very handsome and well-preserved oak dog-leg staircase of the early 17th century [*82*]. Vine House, Sturminster Newton, has a well staircase of about the same date, but smaller than the one at Hanford and probably reset; Pope's Farm, Marnhull, has a well staircase of the first half of the 17th century.

Of many fine 18th-century staircases, that at Dewlish House is the most impressive [*83*]; it is of mahogany and dates from early in the century. An oak staircase of *c.* 1715 at the Old Rectory, Spetisbury, has tapered octagonal balusters, Tuscan-column newel posts and a fist-shaped volute at the foot [*84*]; the latter feature appears to be characteristic local work and was possibly invented in the Bastards' workshop at Blandford Forum. The Old Rectory at Blandford St. Mary has a staircase [*84*] with a fist-shaped volute and balusters shaped like small Doric columns above vase-shaped lower sections; this staircase is dated 1732. Similar features are repeated in a richer form at Coupar House, and more modestly at Lime Tree House, Blandford Forum [*84*].

Later 18th-century staircases with stone steps, wrought-iron balustrades and mahogany or walnut handrails are found at Ranston in Iwerne Courtney, Iwerne Stepleton House, Milton Abbey, and Whatcombe House, Winterborne Whitechurch [*85*]; the balustrade at Ranston is dated 1753.

Wrought Ironwork [*62*]*:* Apart from the stair balustrades mentioned above, Central Dorset is poor in wrought ironwork and only one important piece is recorded: the village school at Piddletrenthide has a pair of early 17th-century gates which come from Westminster Abbey. Fontmell Parva House at Child Okeford has an early 18th-century garden screen with gates of scrolled iron. Also noteworthy is a garden gate at Purse Caundle Manor House.

DURWESTON CHURCH. From the tomb of William Dounton, rector. 1455

MILTON ABBAS. (3) St. Catherine's Chapel. 12th-century

TOLPUDDLE CHURCH. Tomb-slab of Philip, a priest. 12th-century

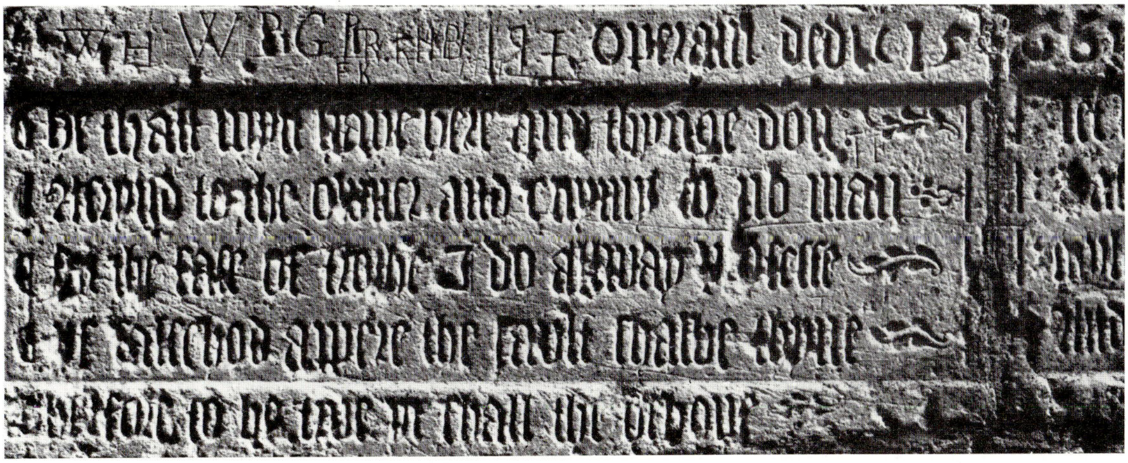

STURMINSTER NEWTON. (4) Fiddleford Mill. 1566

MARKET CROSSES

SHILLINGSTONE (2) 15th-century and modern

STALBRIDGE (2) 15th-century

STURMINSTER NEWTON. (3) Town Bridge. *c.* 1500 and 17th-century

FIFEHEAD NEVILLE. (2) Footbridge. Probably mediaeval

DURWESTON. (2) Bridge over R. Stour. 1795

BLANDFORD FORUM. (3) Blandford Bridge, E side. 1812

ANDERSON. (2) Manor House. 1622

PUDDLETOWN. (3) Waterston House. 17th-century

HINTON ST. MARY. (2) Manor House. 17th-century and later

BLANDFORD ST. MARY. (2) Manor House. 17th-century and *c.* 1700

CHILD OKEFORD. (2) Fontmell Parva House. *c.* 1665, with 19th-century additions

DEWLISH. (2) Dewlish House. 1702

MILTON ABBAS. (9) The Vicarage. c. 1780

PULHAM. (4) The Rectory. Late 18th-century

MARNHULL. (4) Senior's Farm. *c.* 1500

GLANVILLE'S WOOTTON. (6) Round Chimneys Farm. *c.* 1590

STOURPAINE. (2) Lazerton Farm. 17th-century

PIDDLEHINTON. (7) East Farm. 1622 and later

WINTERBORNE KINGSTON (5) 17th and 18th-century

LYDLINCH (10) Early 18th-century

HAZLEBURY BRYAN (26) Probably before 1607

SHILLINGSTONE (7) 16th-century

OKEFORD FITZPAINE (9) 17th-century

IWERNE COURTNEY (15) 17th-century

IWERNE COURTNEY. (11) *Cottage orné.* Early 19th-century

PUDDLETOWN (5) Range of cottages and shop. 18th-century

STURMINSTER NEWTON. (14) House and shop in Market Place. 1730

CHILD OKEFORD. (2) Fontmell Parva House, garden screen. 18th-century

PURSE CAUNDLE. (2) Manor House, gate.
Late 17th or early 18th-century

PIDDLETRENTHIDE. (3) School gates.
17th-century

IWERNE STEPLETON. (3) Stables of Stepleton House. 18th-century

IWERNE COURTNEY. (3) Ranston. Bridge. Mid 18th-century

STINSFORD. (4) Kingston Maurward House. Garden temple. *c.* 1780

STURMINSTER NEWTON. (47) The 'castle'. 14th-century

MILTON ABBAS. (6) 'Ruined chapel'. 19th-century

STALBRIDGE. (4) Manor House gateway. Late 17th-century

MAPPOWDER (2). *c.* 1700

ALTON PANCRAS. (2) Manor House gateway. *c.* 1740

BRYANSTON. (2) Gateway to Bryanston House. *c.* 1778

MILTON ABBAS. (5) Higher Lodge. Late 18th-century

MILBORNE ST. ANDREW.
(2) Obelisk. 1761

MELCOMBE HORSEY. (2) Bingham's Melcombe. Park Gateway.
Late 18th-century

DEWLISH. (2) Dewlish House. 1702

WINTERBORNE STICKLAND. (3) Quarleston Farm. Early 18th-century

BLANDFORD FORUM. (9) Lime Tree House. *c.* 1735

BLANDFORD ST. MARY. (11) Brook House. Mid 18th-century

STURMINSTER NEWTON. (4) Fiddleford Mill. 16th-century

HANFORD. (2) Hanford House. *c.* 1620

HINTON ST. MARY. (2) Manor House. 16th-century

MELCOMBE HORSEY. (3) Higher Melcombe. Early 17th-century

BLANDFORD ST. MARY. (2) Manor House. Staircase. Mid 18th-century

BUCKLAND NEWTON. (4) Castle Hill. Drawing Room. *c.* 1760

MILTON ABBAS. (4) Abbey House. Ballroom. *c.* 1775

HANFORD. (2) Hanford House. Early 17th-century

CHARMINSTER. (4) Wolfeton House. 17th-century

PUDDLETOWN. (3) Waterston House. 17th-century

STALBRIDGE. (3) Thornhill. *c.* 1730

MILTON ABBAS. (4) Abbey House. *c.* 1775

MILTON ABBAS. (4) Abbey House. *c.* 1775

N. Chamber. *c.* 1760

Oak Room. *c.* 1760

DEWLISH. (2) Dewlish House.

BLANDFORD FORUM. (45) No. 75 East Street. *c.* 1732

CHILD OKEFORD. (2) Fontmell Parva House. 18th-century

MARNHULL. (4) Senior's Farm. *c.* 1500

ATHELHAMPTON. (2) The Hall. Late 15th-century

MILTON ABBAS. (4) Abbot's Hall. Details of screens and of oriel ceiling. 1498

WINTERBORNE CLENSTON.
(2) Manor House. 16th-century

ANDERSON.
(4) Tomson Farm. 17th-century

ATHELHAMPTON. (2) The Hall. 16th-century

CHARMINSTER. (4) Wolfeton. 16th-century

HANFORD. (2) Hanford House. Early 17th-century

DEWLISH. (2) Dewlish House. *c.* 1760

SPETISBURY. (3) Johns House. 1716

BLANDFORD ST. MARY. (3) Old Rectory. 1732

BLANDFORD FORUM. (9) Lime Tree House. *c.* 1735

BLANDFORD FORUM. (8) Coupar House. *c.* 1750

IWERNE COURTNEY. (3) Ranston. 1753

MILTON ABBAS. (4) Abbey House. c. 1775

WINTERBORNE WHITECHURCH.
(3) Whatcombe House. 1750

IWERNE STEPLETON.
(2) Stepleton House. c. 1745

Group (42). Watcombe Plain, Alton Pancras, looking N.; bank 'n' in foreground. 'Celtic' fields associated with track best seen in background, *left*. (Centre of photograph: ST 712032)

Group (43). Ball Hill, Piddletrenthide, looking S.W. towards settlement area 'a', at top centre. (Centre of photograph: ST 723031)

Group (45). Puddletown. Settlement (a), air view from N.W. (ST 742966)

Group (45). Hog Leaze, Piddletrenthide. Part of area (e), air view from S.W. (Centre foreground: ST 736991)

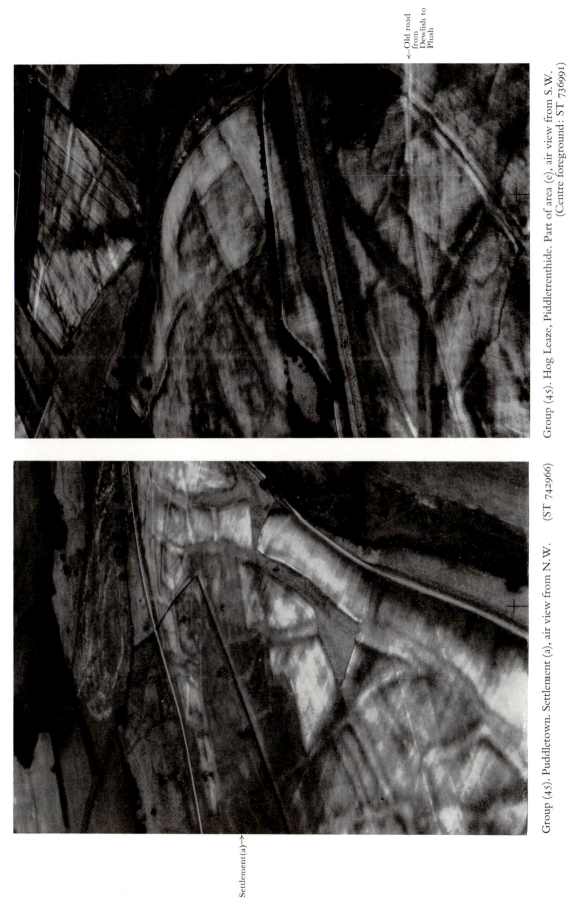

Group (41). Fields N.E. of Barcombe Farm, Alton Pancras, from S. (ST 704033)

Group (53). Fields S. of Winterborne Houghton (9), seen from (10). Arrows point to intersection of Park Pale and Road 'd'.

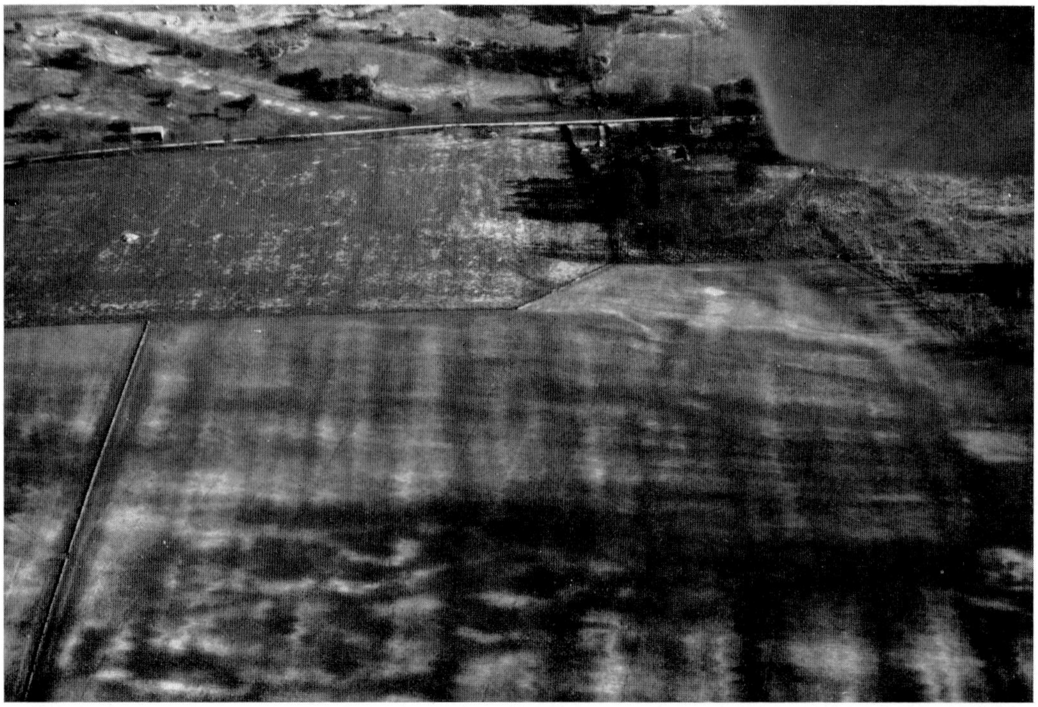

Group (58). *Left* foreground, Settlement Area, Old Park, Bryanston (N.G. 860070). *Left* background, 'Celtic' fields (ST 864066).—(*Top right*, wing of aircraft).

AN INVENTORY OF THE ANCIENT AND HISTORICAL MONUMENTS IN CENTRAL DORSET

Arranged by Parishes

The group of four figures immediately following the heading of each parish is the National Grid reference to the parish church, permitting easy location of the place on the one-inch Ordnance Survey Map at the end of the volume. The next line indicates the sheets of the six-inch O.S. (edition of 1960) covering the parish. Monuments generally are located by six or eight-figure grid references and by orientation and distance from another monument, usually the parish church.

In general, earthwork plans are given at a scale of 25 inches to one mile, but the smallest sites are shown on a larger scale and some of the biggest sites, notably the hill-forts, have been reduced to a smaller scale to avoid large folding pages. Maps of 'Celtic' fields are given at 6 inches to one mile.

Architectural plans have auni form scale of 24 ft. to the inch, except small key plans which are scaled at 48 ft. to the inch. Dimensions given in the Inventory are internal unless otherwise stated. The date given in the description of a memorial is that of the death of the person commemorated; if known the date of erection is added. Surnames in round brackets are maiden names; data enclosed in square brackets are derived from literary sources, usually Hutchins. Numbers following unidentified shields-of-arms refer to their blazons, listed on p. 346.

'Celtic' Field Groups are described extra-parochially in a separate section (*see* p. 318) and Roman roads will be dealt with as a whole in *Dorset* V; these exceptions apart, the monuments of Central Dorset are listed under the names of the fifty-eight civil parishes in which they occur.

1 ALTON PANCRAS (6902)

(O.S. 6 ins. ST 60 SE, ST 70 SW)

Alton Pancras is an irregularly shaped parish of 2,280 acres at the head of the valley of the R. Piddle and at the top of the main Chalk escarpment; the land is almost entirely Chalk and falls from altitudes over 800 ft. above sea-level in the N.E. and N.W. to about 350 ft. at the point where the river crosses the S. boundary. Several deeply cut dry valleys drain from E. and W. into the main valley. Over the escarpment, a N.E. extension of the parish lies on Greensand, Gault and Kimmeridge Clay at an altitude of about 450 ft. The village is now scattered for nearly $\frac{3}{4}$ m. along the Piddle valley but it appears originally to have been two separate settlements, Barcombe and Alton, each with its own mediaeval open field system.[1]

ECCLESIASTICAL

(1) THE PARISH CHURCH OF ST. PANCRAS was rebuilt in 1875 except for the *West Tower* which is of the 15th century. A little tracery in the W. window of the S. wall of the nave may also be of the 15th century; it is a three-light opening with cinquefoil cusping under pierced spandrels in a square head. Hutchins (IV, 461) records 12th-century mouldings on the chancel arch and over the N. and S. doorways, but nothing of that date is seen today, apart from some dubious chevron ornament reset over the N. doorway.

Architectural Description—The *Tower* (9 ft. square) is of flint and rubble, with rubble bonding courses and ashlar quoins and dressings. It has two external stages divided by a weathered string-course. The embattled parapet has crocketed corner finials which were restored in the 19th century. The two-centred tower arch has casement mouldings on the E. and W. sides and continuous jambs. The restored W. doorway has a moulded two-centred head, continuous jambs and a moulded label; the internal lintel is a reused late 13th-century coffin-lid with a double hollow-chamfered border, decorated on the upper surface with a floriate cross. The restored 15th-century W. window has a casement-moulded two-centred head and continuous jambs, with three trefoil-headed lights with vertical tracery. Just above the string-course the N. wall has a small rectangular window. Above, the E., W. and S. sides of the tower have belfry windows of two square-headed lights with chamfered surrounds; the N. window is of two trefoil-headed lights. The belfry windows are closed by stone slabs with quatrefoil perforations.

Fittings—*Bells*: four; treble, dated 1596, probably by William Warre; 2nd, perhaps late 15th century and from Salisbury foundry, inscribed 'Maria' in black-letter; 3rd, 14th century, inscribed 'ave grcia (*sic*) plena' in Lombardic letters; 4th, with

[1] Tithe Map, 1840, and O.S., 1 in., edition of 1811, Dorset, with MS. additions, in Salisbury Museum.

vine-scroll fillet below dome and foliate crosses as stops between initials, with date 1664; bell-frame carved with dates 1761,1818, 1842. *Coffin Lid:* In W. tower, reset above W. doorway, with double hollow-chamfered edge and traces of floriate cross, 13th century. *Coffin Stools:* Pair, with turned legs, 18th century. *Communion Table:* In vestry, $3\frac{1}{2}$ ft. by 2 ft., with turned legs, 18th century. *Font:* Octagonal stone bowl with quatrefoil panels, pedestal and underside of bowl with recessed round-headed panels, moulded base; late 15th or early 16th century. *Monument* and *Floor-slabs. Monument:* In churchyard, S. of nave, of Mary Barle, 1715, headstone with cherub and scroll-work. *Floor-slabs:* In chancel, under communion table, (1) of Thomas Haskett, 1744, Purbeck marble slab with arms; in middle of chancel, (2) of John Haskett, 1730, Purbeck marble slab. In tower, (3) of Edwin Tomkins, 17 . ., trimmed and partly defaced slab with arms; adjacent, (4) of Giles Tomkins, apothecary, 1784, fragmentary and worn. *Weathervane:* On W. Tower, with scrolled wrought iron standard and hollow copper cock; 19th century.

SECULAR

(2) MANOR HOUSE (69940238), 20 yds. S.E. of (1), is of two storeys; the walls are of brick in Flemish bond with stone dressings and the roofs are slate-covered.

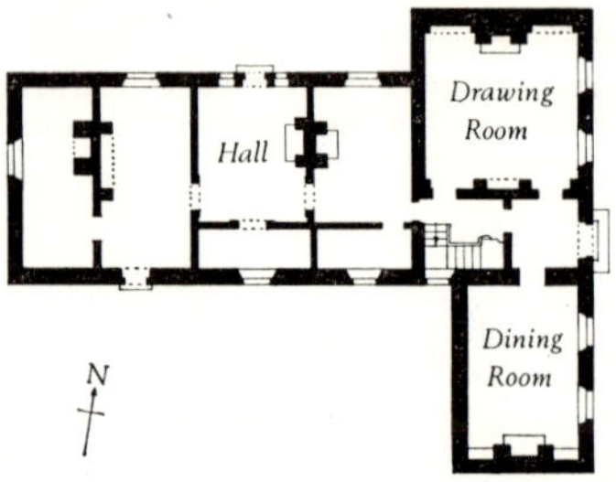

The plan is T-shaped and the principal rooms are in the cross-wing, facing E. According to Hutchins (IV, 460) the house was remodelled by Thomas Haskett (d. 1744), who inherited it from his uncle John Haskett (d. 1730), an eminent Salisbury apothecary. Further improvements were made in the decoration of the interior *c.* 1760 and the Gothic details of this date in the Drawing Room are examples of a style that is not common in Dorset.

The E. front is symmetrical; it has an ashlar plinth, a plat-band at first-floor level, rusticated quoins and a moulded eaves-cornice; plat-band and cornice are mitred around the quoins. The doorway in the centre has a moulded stone surround with a pedimented cornice supported on brackets, and the sashed window above has a stone architrave with side-scrolls and a key-block; the other eight sashed windows have flat gauged brick heads with key-stones, rubbed brick jambs, plain stone sills and shaped aprons. The ends of the cross-wing are gabled; the N. end contains a blocked round-headed opening and the S. end is hung with mathematical tiles. The W. wing contains a number of original windows, two with round heads and radiating glazing-bars in the upper sashes.

Inside, the Drawing Room has fielded panelling in two heights and a cornice with dentils. The fireplace surround has Tuscan columns and a Doric entablature with a central panel of grapes and foliage. Recesses on each side have Gothic ogee heads decorated with foliate arabesques; a third recess facing the fireplace is flanked by Tuscan pilasters. The Dining Room is similarly panelled and has a fireplace surround with Ionic pilasters and an entablature with a carved panel. Two vestibules between the Drawing and Dining Rooms are also panelled; that to the E. is entered through the central doorway of the E. front while the other contains the stairs, with turned newel posts and balusters and a moulded handrail. In the W. hall are three 18th-century doorcases with richly carved and moulded architraves; two are surmounted by foliate friezes with carved cornices. The doors have fielded and beaded panels with enriched mouldings.

The *Stables* to the S. are of the second half of the 18th century. Half-way between the house and the stables stands the *Brew-house*, a single-storied brick building of the late 18th or early 19th century containing coppers and a fireplace; a *Pigeon-cote* adjoins it to the S. To the W., another brick-built outhouse has a stone doorway with an elliptical head; this leads to a vaulted, partly underground chamber, perhaps an *Icehouse*. The road to the church and manor house passes between a pair of rusticated stone *Gate Piers* with moulded cornices surmounted by gadrooned urns with foliate finials (Plate 66). The inner face of each pier has a projecting stone check with a scroll finial; on the outside of each pier a larger scroll forms the capping of the adjacent brick wall, which sweeps up to meet it.

(3) AUSTRAL FARM, 50 yds. N.E. of the church, is of two storeys with attics. The walls are rendered and the roofs are slate-covered. The farmhouse was built in the 18th century and contains a staircase with fluted newel posts, turned balusters and a moulded handrail terminating in a scrolled knob with leaf enrichment.

MONUMENTS (4–12)

Unless otherwise described the following monuments are of the 18th century and of two storeys, with cob walls, thatched roofs, brick chimneys and casement windows.

(4) *Cottages*, four, dispersed, three on the E. side of the main road 250 to 300 yds. S.E. of the church, and one facing them across the Piddle brook. The most southerly of the three was originally a pair of cottages; the others are single dwellings, each of two bays with a central doorway. The fireplaces are in the end walls.

(5) *Post Office* (70040235), 130 yds. E. of (2), is of banded brick and flint; the symmetrical three-bay S. front is dated 1826 on a panel over the central doorway.

(6) *Cottage*, 30 yds. N. of the foregoing, is of one storey with dormer-windowed attics.

(7) *Cottages*, row of three (69950270).

(8) *Farmhouse* (69930285) is in two parts; the W. part has walls of rendered brick and rubble and may be of the 17th century; the E. part is brick and probably of the 19th century. The older part contains a plank-and-muntin partition. An adjacent *Barn* of brick and thatch is of *c.* 1800.

(9) *Cottage* (69900286) has a symmetrical three-bay S. front and chimneys in the gabled end walls.

(10) *Cottage* (69960309).

(11) *Cottage* (69950314) has been rebuilt at the S. end in flint with occasional brick courses; it has stop-chamfered ceiling beams and may be of the late 17th century.

(12) *Narn Barn* (68980360), perhaps of the 17th century, has walls of flint with rubble dressings and an iron roof; the long axis lies E. to W. and the doorways are in projecting bays to N. and S.

Early 19th-century buildings include 'Beechmead', formerly the Vicarage (69820279), and Alton Mill (70230136). The latter, a water-mill on the R. Piddle, has rendered walls of brick and rubble and a slated roof.

MEDIAEVAL AND LATER EARTHWORKS

(13) SETTLEMENT REMAINS (69950255), formerly part of Alton village, lie around Croker's Barton. They include some well-preserved closes bounded by low banks and scarps up to 2 ft. high, and other more disturbed remains.

(14) SETTLEMENT REMAINS (700032), part of the hamlet of Barcombe, lie N. of Barcombe Farm. Within an area of 4 acres are a number of small closes and platforms bounded on the N.E. and E. by a bank 16 ft. wide and up to 2 ft. high, with an outer ditch 10 ft. wide.

(15) CULTIVATION REMAINS. The open fields of *Alton Pancras* still existed in 1724 (Survey of Manors of Alton Pancras, 1724, D.C.R.O.) but were all enclosed by 1741 (Court Book of Alton Pancras, 1741–1865, D.C.R.O.), presumably by agreement as there is no Parliamentary Act of Enclosure. Remains exist in three places. To the W. of the village, on both sides of Rake Bottom (around 690022), are some 45 acres of strip lynchets arranged in end-on and interlocking furlongs; on the W. these run into 'Celtic' fields (Group (38), p. 326). E. of the village in Burnt House Bottom (702025) are three interlocked furlongs of contour and cross-contour lynchets covering some 20 acres; immediately to the S.E. strip ploughing has modified other 'Celtic' fields. In the extreme E. of the parish running N.W.–S.E. across Watcombe Bottom (713030) is a massive riser, up to 15 ft. high, which perhaps represents former strip cultivation. There are other strip fields immediately to the N.W. on Watcombe Plain, where they overlie 'Celtic' fields (Group (42), p. 327).

Nothing is known of the date of enclosure of the open fields of *Barcombe* but remains are found in a few places. E. of Barcombe Farm (705031) are slight remains of contour strip

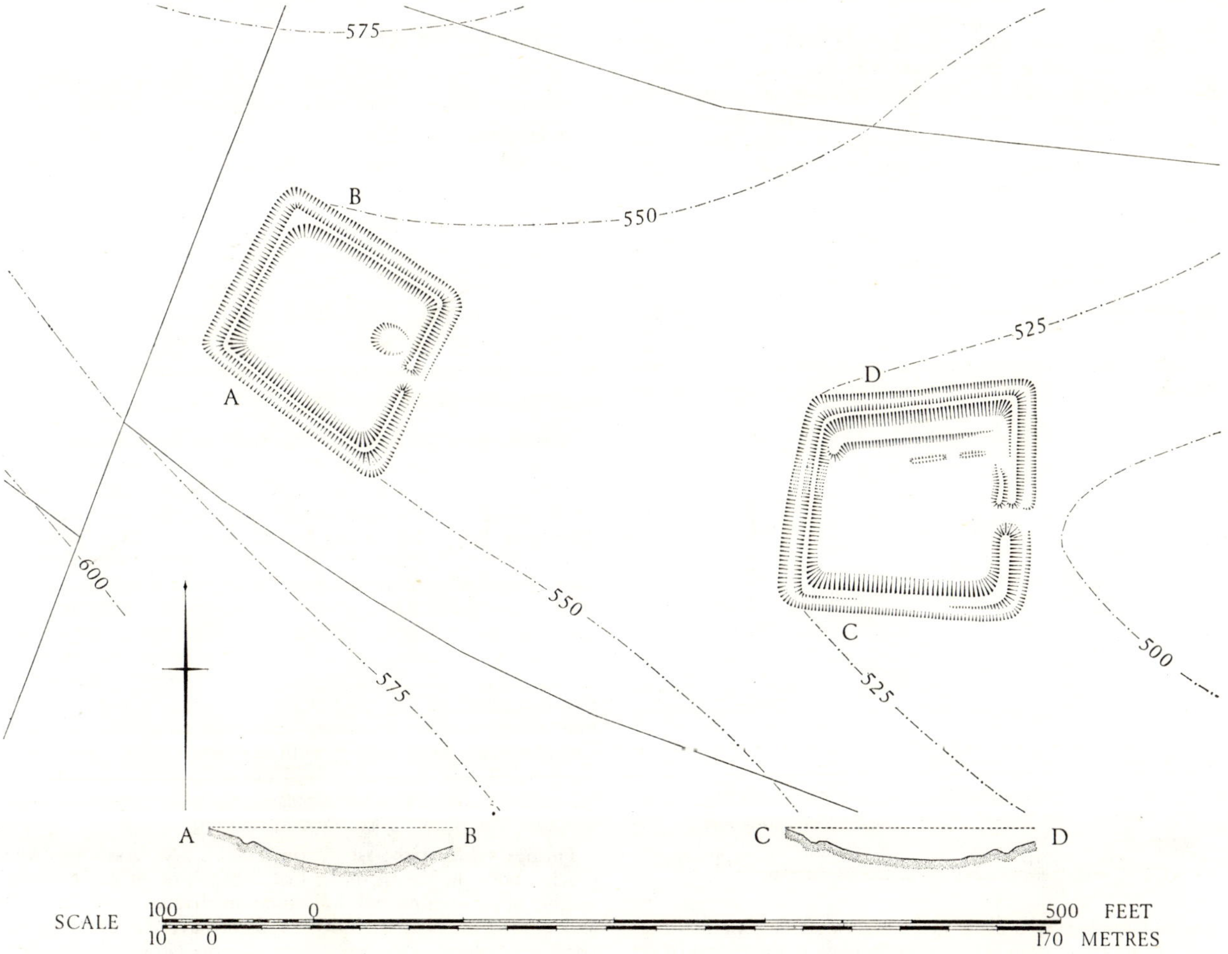

ALTON PANCRAS. (18) Rectangular Enclosures in Tenant's Bottom.

lynchets, and on the S. side of Church Hill (704034) strip fields have modified 'Celtic' fields (Group (41), p. 327). In and around Holcombe Bottom are extensive remains of contour and cross-contour strip lynchets, and ridge-and-furrow (e.g. 694032, 694035, and 687034). To the W. strip lynchets run into 'Celtic' fields (Group (39), p. 326).

ROMAN AND PREHISTORIC

Possible Settlement, *see* 'Celtic' Field Group (42).

'Celtic' Fields, *see* pp. 325f., Groups (38), (39), (41) and (42).

Monuments (16–17) Round Barrows

(16) *Bowl* (70360355) on Church Hill on a gentle S. slope at 660 ft. O.D.; centre of mound disturbed; diam. 35 ft., ht. 2 ft.

(17) *Bowl* (70620250) on West Hill at about 690 ft. O.D., covered with thick scrub; diam. about 36 ft., ht. $3\frac{1}{2}$ ft.

UNDATED

(18) Rectangular Enclosures, two, lie close together in Tenant's Bottom, spanning the floor of a dry valley in the Chalk (*see* plan on p. 3). Both are undated but are perhaps mediaeval, as they appear to be later than the surrounding 'Celtic' fields (Group 38). The more westerly of the two enclosures (69210155) covers about $\frac{1}{5}$ acre and is bounded by a bank 2 ft. high, with an outer ditch, $1\frac{1}{2}$ ft. deep. There is an entrance 8 ft. wide at the centre of the S.E. side. The interior is featureless except for a slightly irregular hollow, $1\frac{1}{2}$ ft. deep, near the entrance. The other enclosure (69340152), 70 yds. E. of the first, is approximately $\frac{1}{4}$ acre in area and is bounded by a bank and outer ditch as before, and has a comparable entrance on the E. On the inside, immediately N. of the entrance, a length of bank runs N. at first and then curves W.; this is more likely to be the remains of a structure than an inner bank of the enclosure, as has been suggested (Dorset *Procs.* XXXIII (1912), 42). On the N. side between this bank and the enclosure bank is a broad terrace 1 ft. high.

(19) Enclosure (71560358) lies on Church Hill at about 760 ft. O.D. It consists of a rhomboidal area of approximately

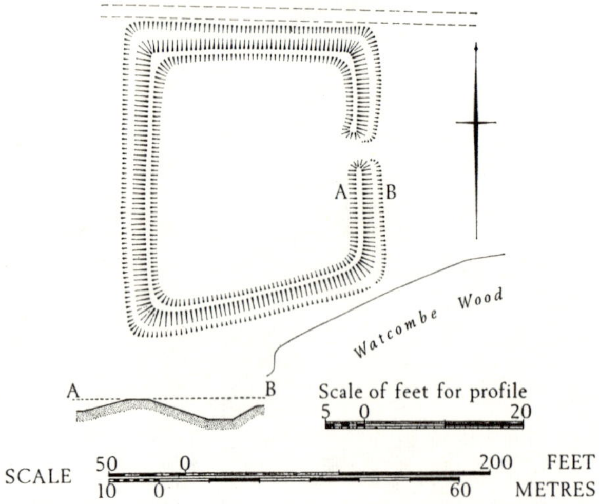

$\frac{2}{5}$ acre bounded by a bank $1\frac{1}{2}$ ft. high with an external ditch 1 ft. deep. There is an entrance 15 ft. wide in the centre of the E. side. The interior is featureless.

2 ANDERSON (8897)

(O.S. 6 ins. SY 89 NE)

In 1933 the two adjacent parishes of Anderson and Winterborne Tomson were combined under the former name, with a total area of 1074 acres. The land, mainly on the N. bank of the Winterborne River, is Chalk with altitudes from 150 ft. to 400 ft. above sea-level. Each village now consists of a manor house and a few cottages, but Tomson was formerly somewhat larger (6). Each probably had a separate mediaeval open field system. The principal monuments are an early 12th-century church and a small 17th-century manor house at Tomson, and a handsome 17th-century manor house at Anderson. The fact that Tomson church remained without enlargement from the 12th to the 16th century implies a continuously small population in the middle ages, and documentary evidence confirms this (*see* (6)). The parish church of St. Michael at Anderson was largely rebuilt at the end of the 19th century.

ECCLESIASTICAL

(1) The Parish Church of St. Michael stands in Anderson village. The nave walls are of banded flint and Heathstone ashlar, the S. chapel is of banded flint and brick, the chancel is rendered; the roofs are tiled, with stone-slate verges. Although largely rebuilt in 1889 the original plan is preserved. The S. wall of the *Chancel* is probably mediaeval, at least in its lower part; the *Nave* was rebuilt in 1889 with the W. wall approximately as before, but higher, witness an early photograph kept in the church; it appears originally to have been of the 13th century. The *South Chapel* was built in 1755 and altered in 1889.

Architectural Description—The walls of the *Chancel* (17 ft. by 9 ft.) are rendered, but the extra thickness of the S. wall and the presence of a mediaeval piscina suggest that it is mediaeval. The E. and N. walls and all three windows are of 1889. The *Nave* (28 ft. by 12 ft.) has modern N. and S. walls of banded flint and ashlar; the W. wall, of similar construction, has a central pilaster corbelled out to support a bell-cote at the apex of the gable. The corbels are roll-moulded and the apertures for the bells have chamfered trefoiled heads; the top of the cote is weathered; these features reproduce the previous arrangement, with reuse of some of the 13th-century stonework that composed it. The *South Chapel* ($12\frac{1}{2}$ ft. by $11\frac{1}{4}$ ft.) has a flint plinth with a chamfered ashlar capping; the S. gable contains a date-stone of 1755 with the initials T.T., for Thomas Tregonwell. The S. window is of the late 19th century. To the N. of the E. doorway are traces of an earlier opening, now blocked. The timber *South Porch* is modern.

Fittings—*Bells:* two; 1st inscribed M . . . M, 2nd with 'Ave gracia', both mediaeval. *Font:* In S. chapel, octagonal Purbeck marble bowl with central drain-hole, mediaeval, now detached and disused. *Monuments:* On S. wall of nave, (1) of Margaret (Baskett) Galpine, 1803 and others of same family, marble disc with moulded border and fine lettering, by J. Brine, 1807. In

ANDERSON *The parish church of St. Michael*

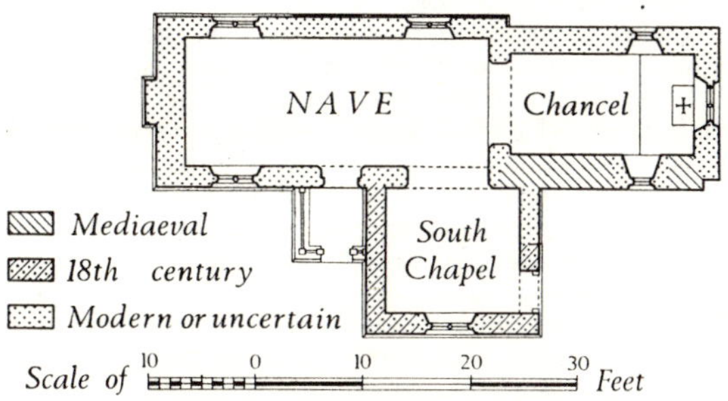

churchyard, E. of chancel (2) of John Marsh, 1763, tomb-slab. *Piscina:* In chancel, in S. wall, with chamfered ogee head and continuous jambs, basin with drain-hole, front part cut off, 14th century. *Plate:* includes silver cup of 1684 engraved with lozenge-of-arms of Tregonwell; also pewter flagon and dish, both 18th century. *Miscellanea:* In S. chapel, over S. window, plaster cartouche-of-arms of Tregonwell impaling Lister, 18th century, perhaps originally from S. chapel ceiling.

(2) THE CHURCH OF ST. ANDREW (88479742) stands near the middle of the settlement of Tomson. It is of flint and rubble with ashlar dressings and buttresses, the latter mainly of Heathstone; the roof is tiled, with stone-slate verges (Plate 96). The building, consisting only of an apsidal *Chancel* and a rectangular *Nave*, with no dividing arch, was probably built in the first half of the 12th century; in the 16th century it was repaired, heightened and given a wagon roof and new windows; further improvements were made early in the 18th century at the expense of Archbishop Wake. The building was restored in 1931 by A. R. Powys with money from the sale of Thomas Hardy's MSS. Powys is buried in the churchyard.

The church is of special interest for its apse, a unique survival in Dorset, and for the unspoiled, rustic appearance of the interior.

Architectural Description—The church is a simple rectangle with an apse at the E. end (Plate 96). The side walls are about 2½ ft. thick at the base but taper sharply towards the top. The apsidal *Chancel* (7½ ft. by 15½ ft.) has three shallow 12th-century ashlar pilaster-buttresses of two stages, with chamfered plinths, chamfered offsets at about three-quarter height, and weathered tops. Those to E. and S. appear to have been partly rebuilt but the N. buttress retains original masonry throughout. The much worn plinth of the E. buttress appears to have an ovolo moulding. A fragment of ashlar extending into the N.E. quarter of the apse from the N. buttress suggests that the original apse was wholly ashlar-faced, but the rest of the N.E. sector and all of the S.E. sector has been refaced in rubble and flint with random ashlar blocks and a few bricks; this work seems likely to have been done in the 17th century. The N. wall of the *Nave* (34 ft. by 15¾ ft.) is mainly original and of flint, but the upper 2 ft., in coursed rubble, probably indicates heightening in the 16th century. Attached to the wall are three secondary buttresses; the middle one is of stone and probably of the 15th century, the others are of brick and perhaps of the 18th century. The middle buttress blocks a narrow original doorway with ashlar jambs and a deep lintel which is barely longer than the width of the opening, indicating that behind the buttress the jambs are probably corbelled; above the lintel protrudes a rough corbel. A blocked window in the E. part of the N. wall is probably a 15th-century insertion. The S. wall has three 16th-century windows, each of two lights with segmental heads, moulded stone jambs and mullions and square labels. To the W. is a narrow original loop with an elliptical head and a chamfered and rebated surround; it is blocked internally. The square-headed W. doorway has a chamfered head and jambs with shaped stops and is probably of the 18th century. The 16th-century wagon *Roof* is segmental in cross-section and forms a shallow half-dome over the apse. Its transverse and radial wooden ribs rise from hollow-chamfered wall-plates and intersect two longitudinal ribs and a central ridge piece; in the apse these members are moulded but in the nave they are chamfered. The intersections are masked by wooden bosses, some modern and plain, others original and foliate. A blank wooden shield decorates the hollow-chamfered wall-plate at the base of each rib and plain stone corbels project from the wall-face below many of the shields.

Fittings—*Brass Indent:* In floor-slab in third pew on N. side, indent for rectangular plate, 7 ins. by 2 ins. *Communion Table:* In apse, of oak with tapering spirally turned legs, probably early 18th century; top board curved to fit apse wall. *Communion Rails:* of same period as table, with spirally turned balusters, moulded rails and rectangular posts with ball finials. *Font:* octagonal Purbeck marble bowl truncated to about half original height, each face formerly with a blank shield enclosed in a quatrefoil; octagonal stone pedestal with hollow-chamfered octagonal base; 15th century. *Gallery:* of oak, now at W. end of nave but probably originally a rood-loft; main beam with casement and roll mouldings; parapet, partly restored, with plain oak panels between chamfered uprights with traces of red and green pigment; to the W., gallery floor rests on second moulded beam with deep mortices suitable for posts of central rood-screen doorway and twelve subsidiary uprights; late 15th or early 16th century.

ANDERSON *Church of St. Andrew Winterborne Tomson*

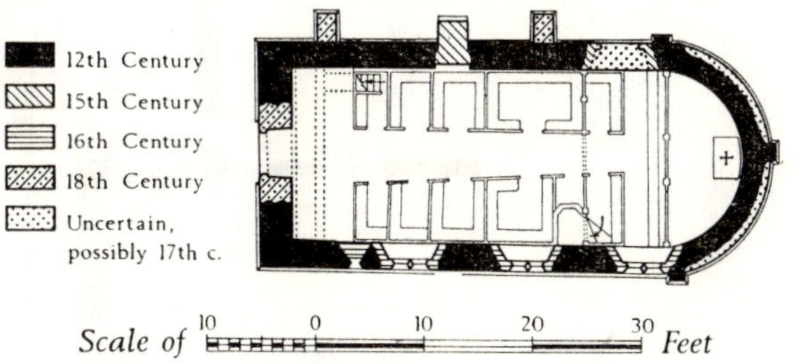

Monuments and *Floor-slabs. Monuments:* On N. wall of nave, (1) of A. R. Powys, 1936, Purbeck marble wall tablet. In churchyard, S. of nave, (2) anonymous table-tomb with brick sides and stone top. *Floor-slabs:* In nave, on S. side, in second pew from W., (1) of John Morton, 1654; in centre aisle, (2) of James Ainsworth, 1849. *Plate:* includes a silver cup and cover-paten, by I.M., with hall-mark of 1638. *Pulpit:* In S.E. corner of nave, uniform with pews (*see Seating*); with polygonal oak sounding board above. *Screen:* standing 7½ ft. W. of communion rails and dividing chancel from nave, with plain oak posts and rails and moulded cornice; top rail in S. bay arcuated to give head-room for pulpit steps; early 18th century. *Seating*: In chancel and nave, ten high-sided box pews, of oak, with panels fielded in 18th-century manner on obverse but with posts and rails with moulded edges, more typical of 17th-century panelling, on reverse; pews provided by William Wake, Archbishop of Canterbury 1716–37. (Hutchins I, 196.)

SECULAR

(3) ANDERSON MANOR (88019760) stands 80 yds. N. of (1). Above a plinth of knapped flint banded with squared rubble, the walls are of brick with Purbeck stone dressings; the roofs are tiled. The house was built by John Tregonwell in 1622 on a modified E-shaped plan and reference to it is made by Coker (*c.* 1625): 'of late Mr. Tregonwell has built him a faire house near the church'. In the third quarter of the 17th century a service wing was added at the N.W. corner of the main block, and this was extended westward, probably towards the end of the century; the principal staircase was remodelled at about the same time. At some period there appears to have been a building, now demolished, against the W. wall of the main block. In recent times minor additions have been made to the N.W. wing, and the interior of the house has been extensively reconditioned.

The house is noteworthy for its sensitive execution of a traditional architectural design in a material, brick, that was then comparatively new in Dorset (Plates 52, 89).

Architectural Description—The S. front is a symmetrical three-gabled composition of five bays; at the centre is an octagonal three-storied porch; at each end is a projecting gabled bay of two storeys with an attic. The flint and stone plinth is hollow-chamfered and the wall above is of thin bricks, four courses rising 11 ins., in bonding consisting of two courses of stretchers to one course of vitrified headers; there are stone quoins at the angles of the three projecting bays, and moulded stone strings between the storeys; the strings lie immediately above the windows and act as hood-moulds. The parapet and gables have a continuous stone coping, with modern ball-finials at the corners and on the apices. In the centre bay the entrance to the porch is a round-headed archway of one roll-moulded and hollow-chamfered order with a plain keystone, continuous jambs and shaped stops; the round-headed inner doorway has continuous ogee-moulded jambs, sunk spandrels and an ogee-moulded square surround; the mouldings end at chamfered and moulded stops. The nail-studded door with strap-hinges and a small spy-hole protected by a metal grill is of the 17th century. Above the porch on the first floor is a hollow-chamfered stone mullioned and transomed window of six square-headed lights extending across the front and the two canted sides of the bay. On the second floor is a mullioned window of the same width and, immediately above it, a moulded string course and a low parapet; from the middle of the window upwards the porch is backed by a central gable which stands in the plane of the main wall-face. The intermediate flanking bays have each a two-light transomed window on the ground and first floors; lead rain-water heads and pipes are embellished with the arms of Tregonwell, the initials I.T.

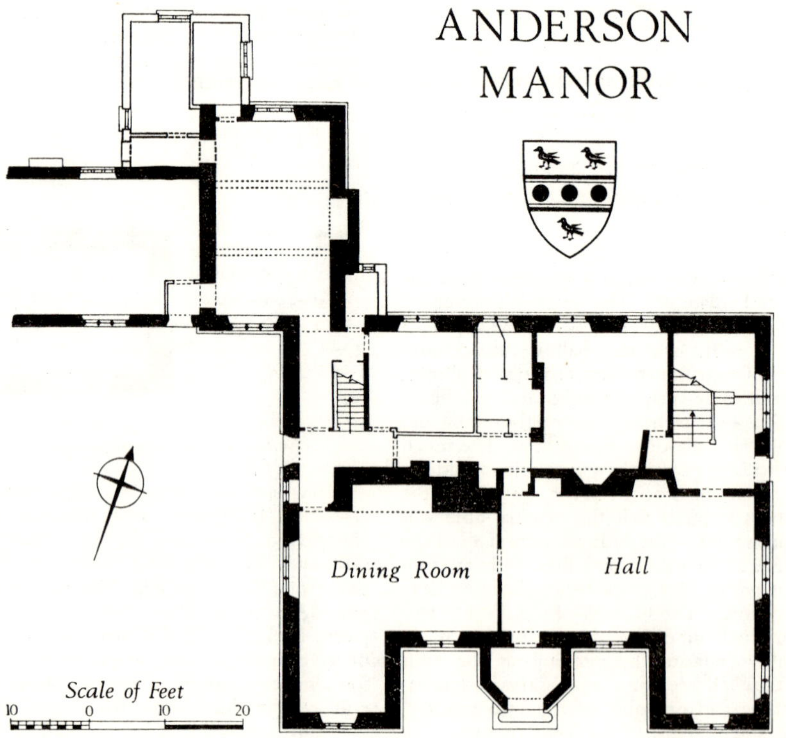

and the date 1622. Each projecting end bay has a two-light mullioned and transomed window on the ground and first floors, and a two-light attic window with a hood-mould in the gable; a blocked window occurs on the ground floor in the E. return of the western bay. Lofty chimneystacks with flues set diagonally and arranged in two groups of four are symmetrically disposed behind the intermediate bays; they are capped with projecting courses of brickwork.

The E. front is in three bays with the two northernmost gabled; the plinth and strings are carried round from the S. front. The windows, of two and three lights, and the rain-water heads are as described above. A doorway between the N. and middle bays is of the early 18th century; it has a moulded architrave and a pulvinated entablature. The N. front comprises three gabled bays, partly masked by the N.W. wing; the plinth is continued from the E. front but the strings are omitted; in their place the mullioned two-light windows have labels with returned stops. The Tregonwell crest appears on two rain-water heads, and a third is inscribed S.T. 1770. The W. front has two gables and stone-mullioned windows of one, two and three lights with labels; a doorway in the N. bay has a chamfered four-centred head and continuous jambs. Two diagonal chasings in the upper part of the wall suggest the pitched roof of some former addition, since removed. The Tregonwell crest is repeated on the lead rain-water boxes and on the lugs of one of the down-pipes; the boxes are also decorated with lead rolls at the top and have small standards with pierced decoration at the angles.

The original N.W. service wing is of three storeys; the hollow-chamfered plinth, where it occurs, is continuous with that of the main house but of brick instead of flint. In the S. front each storey has a hollow-chamfered mullioned window of three square-headed lights with a label, and there is a single attic light, now blocked. At the top of the S. wall is a half-gable, the other half being incorporated in the N. wall of the main house. The gabled N. elevation has rusticated brick quoins, formerly rendered. A first-floor window has a brick relieving arch with projecting bricks to represent rustication. The late 17th-century W. extension is two-storied; in the S. front is a doorway with a chamfered four-centred head and stop-chamfered jambs, and two and three-light stone-mullioned windows; the walls are extensively patched.

Inside, the Hall is lined with 17th-century panelling in four heights. Several doorways have moulded surrounds and panelled oak doors with wrought-iron hinges. An E. window has in stained glass the arms of Tregonwell with helmet, mantling and crest, all reset. The Hall fireplace has a stone surround with a moulded four-centred head. Between the Hall and the present Dining Room, originally the kitchen, is a 17th-century plank-and-muntin partition, made up with some modern material. The Dining Room has a wide open fireplace with a chamfered segmental stone head; the exposed ceiling-beams are stop-chamfered. The N.E. staircase is in two flights; the moulded handrail, turned and moulded balusters, and newels with acorn terminals are of the late 17th century; however an original window on the half landing shows that there was always a staircase in this position. The W. staircase is original; it is of four dog-leg flights and has close strings, moulded handrails and turned and moulded balusters. The ground-floor rooms between the two staircases have fireplaces similar to that of the Hall, and on the first floor are other fireplaces of the same kind, and also some 17th-century panelled doors. The chamber above the Hall has an original ceiling roundel of moulded plaster consisting of radiating stylised branches of roses, thistles, pears and shamrock leaves within a wreath of bay-leaves with foliate bosses at intervals.

In the present century, while the garden and forecourt were being laid out anew, the line of an early terrace to the S. of the house was uncovered. Two lead cisterns with the initials and dates, F.G.H. 1723 and I.W.W. 1764 stand in the garden.

(4) Tomson Farm (88569740), 100 yds. E. of St. Andrew's church (2), is an early 17th-century house of two storeys with attics. The walls are of coursed rubble with squared rubble dressings and with some brickwork in the upper parts; the E., S. and W. fronts are rendered; the roofs are principally of stone-slate but tiled near the ridges. Two large chimneybreasts project from the N. wall, each with three diagonally set brick flues at the top. Hutchins (I, 195) interprets foundations to the W. as evidence that the house was originally longer, having had a symmetrical plan centred on the stair tower, but this is doubtful. Many original windows survive; they are of two to five lights with recessed and hollow-chamfered stone jambs and mullions, square heads and moulded labels. The house is fairly well preserved and incorporates interesting original features. Originally, the ground-floor plan probably comprised three rooms: a central hall with a kitchen to the E. and a parlour to the W. A screens-passage between the kitchen and the hall may well have had N. and S. doorways, but the latter is obliterated. The hall appears to have had no fireplace. The spiral stairs opened off the hall and led up to a well appointed chamber over the parlour.

The S. front is of four bays, each bay with a four-light mullioned window on each storey, except where replaced by modern openings. The wall-face is interrupted by three brick buttresses, to a large extent rendered, but probably of the 18th century; one of them may mask an original S. doorway. The present entrance to the house has been formed in one of the S. windows. The W. end wall has a modern three-light window on the ground floor and an original window of five lights above; the E. end wall has original four-light openings in both storeys. The N. front has a large projecting chimney-breast near each end, and a projecting stair tower on the E. of the western breast (Plate 90). At the base of the tower, on the N. side, is a low doorway with a shallow four-centred chamfered head and continuous jambs; above it are square-headed three-light windows in two storeys. Between the stair tower and the eastern chimney-breast the lower part of the N. front is masked by an out-building but, inside this, the N. wall contains an original window and doorway; the latter has a chamfered four-centred head and is somewhat taller than the doorway in the stair tower.

Inside, an original plank-and-muntin partition forms the E. side of the W. ground-floor room. The N. and E. sides of the adjacent closet are also of plank-and-muntin, but reset. The chimney-breast on the W. side of the E. room is probably of the 19th century. There is no visible evidence for or against a S. doorway in correspondence with either of the known N. doorways.

The spiral stair is of stone and the doorway which opens from the stairs to the first floor has a shallow four-centred head, hollow-chamfered and ogee-moulded jambs and shaped stops (Plate 81); the mouldings are on the S. side of the opening and the rebate is towards the stairs. The doorway opens into

ANDERSON *Tomson Farm*

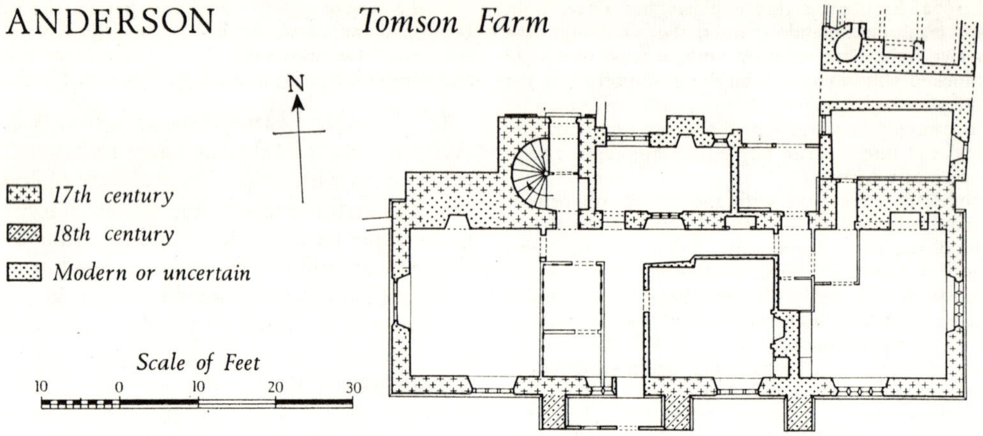

an original draught-lobby of oak, with fluted Ionic pilasters and an enriched cornice. The W. chamber, into which the draught-lobby projects, originally occupied about two-thirds of the first floor but it is now divided into two rooms and a passage. The chamber has a moulded plaster ceiling embellished with crowned Tudor roses, fleurs-de-lis, rampant lions, grotesque masks and arabesques (Plate 91); the plasterwork is intersected by the later partitions and parts of it are missing. The fireplace of the W. chamber has a moulded stone surround with a shallow four-centred head and a carved frieze of stone panels with lozenges and stylised foliage. The E. chamber has a moulded plaster ceiling with intersecting ribs forming geometrical patterns around a central pendant; the fireplace is modern. At the top of the stairs the attic landing has an oak railing of turned balusters in two heights with a moulded top rail. The doorway from the landing to the attic is of oak with chamfered jambs and a four-centred head. The principal members of the roof are original.

A range of buildings running N. from the E. end of the house is partly of the 19th century but towards the N. it incorporates a single-storied *Cottage* that is probably of 17th-century origin. A gabled wing projecting to the E. contains a wooden newel staircase with a large oven beneath it. At the N. end of the cottage is an open fireplace with a chamfered and cambered bressummer. The attic floor rests on reused deep-chamfered beams with splay stops. Reset in the W. wall of the cottage is a block of stone, 6 ins. square, cut from a carved shield-of-arms of the Hussey family (*see* Hutchins IV, 312). At the N. end of the range is an extension, perhaps of the 18th century, incorporating heavy timber-frame construction, probably reused.

A *Barn*, 50 yds. W. of the house, was partly rebuilt in the 19th century but to the S. are two original bays, of the early 17th century. It has rubble walls with squared rubble quoins and weathered coping and it retains two original raised arch-braced open cruck-trusses of very heavy scantling. A projecting wing to the W. is of two storeys and has on the ground floor a chamfered square-headed doorway with a moulded label; the upper storey is a pigeon-cote and has a small square window with chamfered reveals and a moulded label.

(5) Cottage (88469738), 30 yds. S. of (2), of two storeys with rubble and brick walls and thatch-covered roofs, is probably of the 17th century but lengthened and heightened subsequently.

A range of stone-walled *Cottages* 75 yds. to the W. of (5) is probably of the early 19th century but built of old materials.

MEDIAEVAL AND LATER EARTHWORKS

(6) Settlement Remains (884973), formerly part of Winterborne Tomson village, cover some 10 acres immediately S. and S.W. of (2).

The settlement is one of several unidentified Winterbornes in Domesday Book. Eyton (p. 122) suggests that it and Anderson together composed the manor of the Count of Mortain (D.B. Vol. 1, f. 79*b*) with a combined recorded population of only six. Tomson is not recorded in the 1327 or 1333 Subsidy Rolls, but since the parish was exempt from tax in 1428 the population must have been fewer than ten (*Feudal Aids*, 1284–1431, Vol. II, 97); it was granted a tax reduction on account of poverty in 1435 (P.R.O., E/179/103/79). The remains, which are bounded by a bank 1½ ft. high and an external ditch, have been extensively damaged by quarrying but there are at least two well-marked house platforms and fragmentary closes.

(7) Cultivation Remains. Both former parishes apparently had open fields but nothing is known of the date of enclosure. Only in *Tomson* are there any remains; 360 yds. N. of St. Andrew's Church (884977) is a block of ridge-and-furrow, 250 yds. long and 280 yds. wide, cut on the E. by the present field boundary.

ROMAN AND PREHISTORIC

Roman Road from Badbury Rings to Dorchester (*see Dorset* II, 539; also *Dorset* V).

Combs Ditch, forming the N. boundary of the parish (*see* Winterborne Whitechurch (19), p. 313).

3 ATHELHAMPTON (7794)

(O.S. 6 ins. SY 79 SE)

Athelhampton, a parish of only 480 acres, lies mainly S. of the R. Piddle on fairly level terrain between 150 ft. and 200 ft. above sea-level. The land is Chalk except for a small area of Reading Beds to the S.E. The original settlement must have been beside the river; nothing is known of its open field system, but certain lands were already enclosed by the late 15th century,

ANDERSON. (3) Manor House, from S.E. 1622

ANDERSON. (4) Tomson Farm. Exterior, from N.W. Early 17th-century

ANDERSON. (4) Tomson Farm. Ceiling in W. chamber. 17th-century

Exterior, from S.W. 15th and 16th-century

Exterior, from N.W. 16th-century and later

ATHELHAMPTON. (2) Athelhampton Hall.

ATHELHAMPTON. (2) Athelhampton Hall and Gatehouse; drawing by B. Ferrey. 1834

CHARMINSTER. (4) Wolfeton House from N.E.; artist unknown. Early 19th-century

ATHELHAMPTON. (2) Athelhampton Hall. Oriel, exterior. Late 15th-century

ATHELHAMPTON. (2) Athelhampton Hall. Great Hall, looking N.W. Late 15th-century

Exterior, from S.E.

Interior, looking E.

ANDERSON. (2) Church of St. Andrew.

12th to 18th-century

when a deer park (3) was enlarged in the southern part of the parish. Athelhampton Hall is the most important monument.

ECCLESIASTICAL

(1) The Parish Church of St. John was built in 1862 to replace an earlier church, now demolished, which stood some 80 yds. S.W. of (2).

Fittings—*Brass:* reset in N. wall of nave, to George Masterman, 1744, inscription plate. *Plate:* includes an Elizabethan silver cup and cover-paten by Lawrence Stratford, cover-paten inscribed 1575, also a stand-paten of 1717 and a 19th-century almsdish and flagon.

SECULAR

(2) Athelhampton Hall (770942) stands beside the R. Piddle ½ m. E. of Puddletown. The main part of the house has two principal storeys with attics, except the Great Hall which is open from floor to roof. The ashlar-faced external walls are mainly of limestone and Greensand, with Ham Hill stone for many of the dressings. The roofs have large stone-slates in the lower courses and tiles above. The house was started in the reign of Henry VII by Sir William Martyn, Lord Mayor of London in 1493, and was continued by his heirs throughout the 16th century. Sir William built the *Great Hall* with its oriel window, and the *Service Range* which extends N.E. from the S.E. end of the Hall. A solar at the N.W. end of the Hall, shown on Buckler's plan of 1828 (BM. Add. MS. 36361, f. 128) but subsequently pulled down, was probably original; the present solar is a modern reproduction. Robert Martyn (d. 1550) built the *West Wing*, which runs W. from the N.W. end of the Hall, forming the N. side of a forecourt in front of the house. This forecourt was originally bounded to the W. by a *Gate House* which, with connecting walls, completed the enclosure. The gate house and the connecting walls were pulled down in 1862 but many architectural fragments are preserved. The complete gatehouse is known from Buckler's plan, from a sketch by Benjamin Ferrey dated 1834 (Plate 93), from Nash's engraving (*Mansions in the Olden Time*, 1839–, III, pl. ix) and also from J. Pouncy, *Dorset Illustrated*, *c.* 1857. That the gate house was the work of Robert Martyn is proved by the arms of Martyn quartering Kelway in a stone cartouche, formerly above the gateway and now preserved in the house. Robert married Elizabeth Kelway and their daughter Katherine married Edward Knoyle of Sandford Orcas; it is curious to note that lozenge panels on the gables of the W. wing at Athelhampton are closely paralleled at Sandford Orcas (*Dorset* I, 196). Robert Martyn's wing is entered through an original doorway in the 15th-century oriel window of the Hall, proving that at least part of the wing replaces some earlier building contemporary with the Hall; possibly it was a W. extension of the solar. In the 17th century, the 15th-century service range was remodelled and heightened, masking a window in the S.E. gable of the Hall. The present *Kitchen Wing* was probably built in the later 16th century. Late in the 19th century, ranges of buildings of uncertain date which had formed the N.W. and N.E. sides of the court to the N.E. of the Hall were demolished. In 1891 the house was bought by A. C. de Lafontaine and carefully restored. The S.E. range, incorporating the original service rooms, was remodelled and extended. Later, the solar was reconstructed, together with a stair leading to it from an original archway in the N.W. side of the Hall; at the same time a new range was built on the N.E. side of the inner court.

Today Athelhampton Hall is famous for its beauty and for its fine setting among magnificent gardens, laid out at the end of the 19th century. The early parts of the house constitute an important specimen of late mediaeval domestic architecture. The Hall has a remarkable roof, a graceful oriel window and fine original doors. Some original heraldic window glass is preserved.

Architectural Description—The S.W. front incorporates the side of the 15th-century Hall, with its porch and oriel, and one end of the service wing (Plate 92). The façade has a moulded plinth and is crowned by an embattled parapet with a moulded string-course and copings. At the S. corner is a 15th-century turret, at the foot of which are traces of the demolished 16th-century forecourt wall. In the W. wall of the turret is an original doorway with moulded jambs and a four-centred head. The string-course and embattled parapet continue along the façade, crossing the end of the service wing at the base of its gable and showing that the attic storey is secondary. The two-storied porch has the front corners splayed, giving it five external sides; each angle has an attached shaft rising to the string-course from a polygonal plinth. Heraldic emblems mask the junction of the shafts with the string; to one side of the doorway is the chained ape crest of Martyn, to the other is the Faringdon unicorn, the crest of Sir William's first wife. The porch arch is two-centred and of three continuous orders; above it is a hood-mould of Ham Hill stone with the Martyn ape at the summit and large headstops at the springing, one of the latter perished. On the ground floor, each side of the porch contains a small quatrefoil light. Above the arch the porch chamber has a pair of two-centred lights under a square hood-mould with headstops.

N.W. of the porch the Hall is lit by a window of four moulded, hollow-chamfered and two-centred lights within a square-headed casement moulding under a hood-mould with headstops. The central mullion is incorporated in the upper stage of a weathered two-stage buttress which continues upwards as a faceted standard, intersecting the hood-mould and string-course and terminating in a lion finial. Beyond this window projects the oriel, a five-sided bay with lights in four faces, the place of the fifth being taken by a buttressed angle at the junction of the W. wing (Plate 94). The masonry of the oriel is not perfectly integral with that of the Hall and it appears to be an afterthought. Each corner of the oriel has a small two-stage buttress with moulded weatherings, developing at the top into a standard which intersects the parapet string-course at a grotesque head. The lower moulded copings of the oriel parapet are level with the main string-course of the Hall. Each exposed face of the oriel has a tall two-centred window of two double-transomed lights; below the lower transom the lights are ogee-headed with open spandrels; in the middle tier the lights are two-centred; in the top tier they are ogee-headed and at the apex each window has a central tracery light. Above, moulded labels die into the buttress standards.

S.E. of the porch, the S.W. end wall of the service wing has a moulded plinth uniform with that of the Hall. On the ground floor is a square-headed window of three lights with ovolo mouldings and a label with reused head stops; the first floor has a similar window of four lights and the attic has another three-light window; these openings are of the 17th century and presumably are contemporary with the attic gable which, as noted above, is superimposed on the original parapet.

The S.E. front acquired an approximately symmetrical appearance *c.* 1895, when the E. turret and the adjacent gable were built. S.W. of this modern work the rubble wall-face up to the level of the first-floor window-sills remains from the 15th-century wing, to which the S. turret also belongs. At the base of the wall the remains of the original moulded plinth, a few inches lower than the plinth of the S. turret and S.W. front, are traceable throughout the length of the original masonry. More evenly coursed stonework above the first-floor window-sills is probably refacing of the 17th century but, towards the N.E., a fragment of banded flint and rubble work is probably part of the original upper storey. A projecting bay with a two-centred archway in the middle of the façade is modern; within is reset a two-centred doorway with ovolo mouldings. Behind the modern E. turret and the adjacent gable stands the late 16th-century kitchen wing; its N.E. wall is of thin red and blue bricks with ashlar dressings; the openings are modern. At the E. corner of the kitchen is a diagonal two-stage brick buttress with ashlar weatherings. The original N.E. wall of the service wing is represented by a weathered moulding, probably part of a chimney-breast, that survives in the attic storey; it rises directly over the wall between the dining-room and the kitchen.

In the West Wing, which adjoins the oriel at the N.W. corner of the Hall, the S. front has three four-light casement windows in each of the two lower storeys, and two three-

ATHELHAMPTON HALL

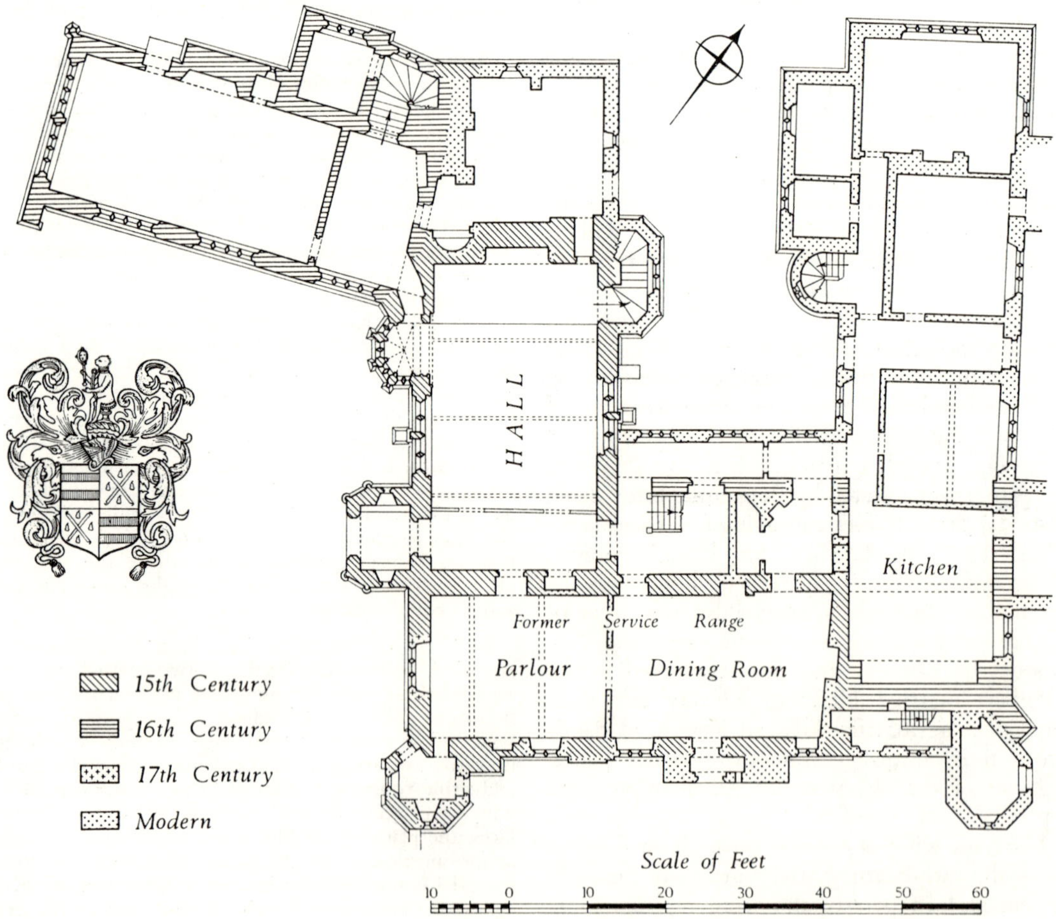

light windows in gabled stone-fronted dormers, asymmetrically disposed, in the attic. The ground and first-floor windows have casement-moulded square heads and jambs, enclosing lights with moulded and hollow-chamfered mullions and four-centred heads; the dormer windows are similar except that the mullions are only hollow-chamfered and the lights have elliptical heads. All the windows have labels with square stops, and on the ground floor the horizontal member of the label continues between the windows, forming a string-course; this turns up at the S.W. corner to avoid the capping of the former forecourt wall, part of which survives in the guise of a weathered buttress. Above eaves level each attic dormer is decorated with a moulded lozenge-shaped panel with foliate bosses at the corners.

The corners of the gabled W. end of the W. wing are defined by octagonal angle shafts with concave facets; the shaft at the N.W. corner runs down to the ground but the other is based on a moulded corbel, level with the ground-floor window heads and thus clearing the former forecourt wall. For a short length at the top of each shaft the fluting is spiral and above this the shaft terminates in a Martyn ape. A moulded string at the base of the spiral portion of the shaft is continuous with the inclined coping of the gable. At the apex the gable has a finial composed of a cluster of crockets above a moulded shaft with a ring of projecting volutes. The W. façade is pierced in the lower storey by two coupled four-light transomed windows, in the upper storey by a six-light window and in the attic by a four-light window; hood-moulds and other details, including a lozenge above the first-floor window, are similar to those of the S. front.

The N. wall of the W. wing (Plate 92) is faced with coursed rubble. To the E. of a large chimney-breast projects a gabled bay of two storeys with a cellar and an attic, with a casement-moulded window on each floor; further E. are the windows of a spiral stair, that at the lowest level being square-headed with two-centred lights under blind tracery; it is of the 15th century but probably reset. Beside the stair bay the line of the N. wall forms an obtuse re-entrant angle and to the E. of the angle a short stretch of the 15th-century solar wall survives; some 20 ft. above ground it is traversed by a fragment of weathered and moulded string-course and above this is a section of the original weathered gable.

The courtyard N.E. of the Hall incorporates some ancient features although the walls have been extensively refaced; the banded stone and flintwork of the Hall itself is seen beside the modern solar stair bay. The four-light N.E. window of the Hall is uniform with that of the S.W. front; above it the eaves of the Hall roof have neither string-course nor parapet.

Inside, the doorway from the S.W. porch to the Hall has a two-centred head with mouldings continuous on the jambs. The original oak door (Plate 80) is decorated on the outside with moulded and cusped wooden tracery. At the opposite end of the screens-passage another doorway with a similar traceried oak door now leads to the staircase hall; it formerly opened into a single-storied corridor between the old service range and the inner courtyard; however, the N.W. wall of the corridor is of the 16th century and originally there may have been no more than a wooden lean-to porch. In the W. jamb of the Hall doorway is a square mortice for a long wooden draw-bar. On the S.E. side of the screens-passage two openings with moulded four-centred heads and continuous jambs communicate with the former service wing; one is blocked. The oak screens are partly of the late 15th century but apparently not *in situ* since Nash's engraving (*op. cit.* pl. X) omits them. They have moulded base rails and muntins, and 16th-century linenfold panels between the muntins. The parapet is a recent addition.

The Hall (21¼ ft. by 38¼ ft., including the screens-passage) is lined to half its height with linenfold panelling brought from elsewhere in the 20th century (Plate 95). Near the N.W. end, the N.E. wall is pierced by a 15th-century archway with a moulded four-centred head the inner member of which is carried on three-quarter shafts with moulded and carved capitals and bases; the winding stairs from this archway to the rebuilt solar are wholly modern. At a higher level the central part of the N.E. wall contains the four-light window noted externally. The restored glazing includes some 16th-century quarries with monograms, and armorial achievements; those of Faringdon, Martyn and de Pidele noted by Hutchins (1st ed., I, 473) in the 18th century are still present; the fourth light has the crest of Brune, apparently original, above a modern shield of Mohun. The corresponding window on the S.W. side of the Hall has similar achievements representing families associated with the house, but these appear to be modern reproductions. The tall four-centred opening to the oriel has three moulded ribs springing from slender wall-shafts with moulded octagonal caps and bases. The two inner shafts of the N.W. jamb are truncated by a doorway set partly in the reveal and partly within the oriel; it has a moulded four-centred head and continuous jambs. The tracery of the four windows has already been noted; the mantled shields in the glazing of the upper pairs of lights are modern reproductions showing Martyn alliances, but the crests in the tracery lights appear to be original; however, Hutchins makes no mention of them and the openings are shown blank in Nash's engraving of 1840. The fifth side of the oriel, above the N.W. doorway, has blind tracery. The internal angles have attached shafts carrying octagonal capitals at the springing of the window-heads and, above these, hollow-chamfered and cusped vault ribs which meet at a foliate central boss. The brick-lined fireplace at the N.W. end of the Hall has a stone surround with a wide elliptical moulded stone head and continuous jambs, apparently restored. Adjacent, to the N.E., is an original doorway with a chamfered four-centred head; it is masked by the panelling. High up in the S.E. gable, a square-headed original window of three two-centred lights has recently been uncovered and restored; externally it is masked by the attic storey which was added to the original service range in the 17th century.

The 15th-century open timber roof of the Hall has been repaired from time to time but otherwise it seems to be largely original. Iron braces which strengthen the principals were probably inserted in the present century. The base of each member for about a foot above its junction with the wall has been repaired in plaster, moulded and painted to resemble wood. Possibly the roof originally rose from deep timber cornices or wall-plates, as in the Great Hall at Milton Abbey (p. 193), the decay of which may have necessitated the renewal of the lower extremities of the principals. This may have been the occasion for a modification of the original design, wherein gadrooned stone corbels were substituted for the presumed wall-plates. If the walls between the principals were then heightened, this would account for the position of the lower purlins, only a few inches above the wall-head. The date of the modification is uncertain; Hutchins (edition of 1774) may refer to it when he says 'it was lately repaired by Sir Robert Long'; alternatively the style of the gadrooned corbels suggests a date in the 17th century.

Five heavily moulded principal trusses rise from the gadrooned corbels and are collared 3 ft. below the apex. The principals and collars are strengthened with moulded archbraces which are produced to form large cusps with open spandrels, creating enormous trefoils which span the Hall from side to side. About 1 ft. below the collars the four bays are traversed by heavily

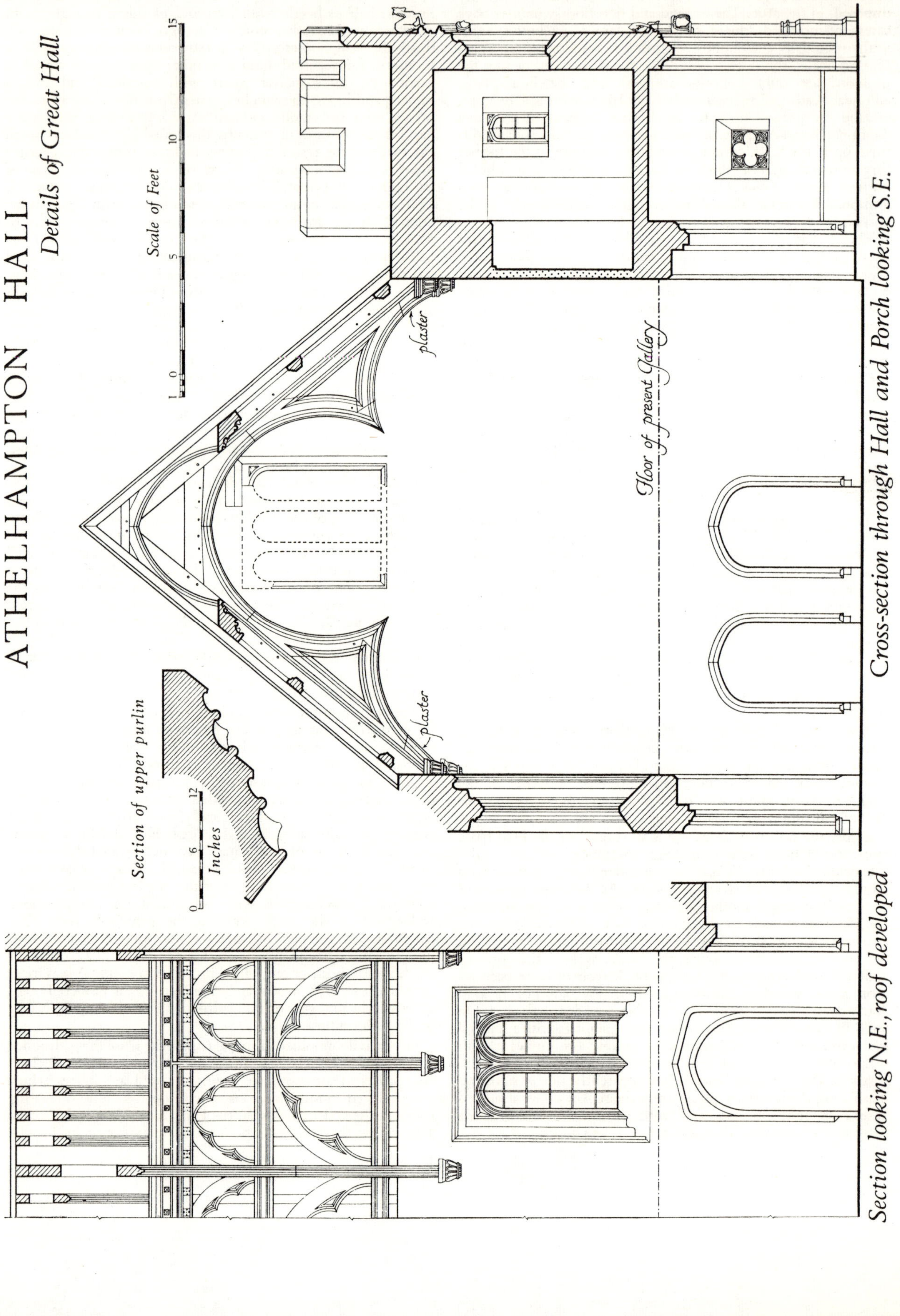
ATHELHAMPTON HALL
Details of Great Hall
Scale of Feet
0 1 5 10 15
Section of upper purlin
Inches
0 6 12
plaster
plaster
Floor of present Gallery
Cross-section through Hall and Porch looking S.E.
Section looking N.E., roof developed

moulded main purlins, of such a depth as almost to constitute cornices; they are decorated with two tiers of spaced leaf bosses. Against the purlins rest the upper ends of moulded subsidiary principals, one in the middle of each bay, its foot resting on an intermediate gadrooned corbel. The common rafters are carried on moulded secondary purlins at two levels, the lower ones, as noted above, very close to the wall-head. The rafters continue over the main purlins to the ridge, where they are trussed with curved and moulded braces. Between the purlins are two orders of curved wind-braces; above the upper subsidiary purlins they are set four to a bay, facing one another to make a small arch on either side of each subsidiary principal; between the lower purlins larger braces are set two to a bay, forming larger arches. Every wind-brace is hollow-chamfered and cusped.

The doorway with a four-centred head in the N. side of the oriel leads to an antechamber at the E. end of the W. wing. The four-light S. window contains roundels with shields of Martyn, Tregonwell and Kelway; two of them were noted by Hutchins. To the E. is a 16th-century doorway to the solar undercroft, with a moulded four-centred head and continuous jambs; adjacent is a fireplace with a similar surround. To the N. an archway with a moulded four-centred head leads to a newel staircase. The walls have late 17th-century panelling.

The large ground-floor room in the W. wing has a chamfered oak doorway with a four-centred head in an original 16th-century stud partition. The walls have 17th-century panelling brought from elsewhere. Above the wide four-centred stone arch of the fireplace are set eight carved wooden panels of *c.* 1540 depicting male and female heads in medallions with scrolls above. To the W. of the fireplace a doorway leading directly to the garden is reversed so that the moulded four-centred stone head and jambs are seen internally. To the E. of the fireplace a small concealed closet contains modern wooden stairs to the room above. The richly moulded plaster ceiling is a modern reproduction. The heraldic roundels in the windows are as reported in Hutchins's edition of 1863 (II, 587) but differ from the edition of 1774. The winding stair on the N. side of the antechamber has stone treads to first-floor level and solid oak baulks above (Plate 81); the doorways opening off the stairs have chamfered stone jambs and four-centred heads. On the first floor a single large chamber, the Library, occupies the entire W. wing; it is entered from the winding stair through a stone doorway on the jambs of which are several 17th and 18th-century *graffiti*. The glass of the most easterly window in the S. wall includes four 16th-century roundels with shields; Strangways impaling Wadham; Zouch quartering St. Maur and Cantelupe; Tregonwell impaling Kelway; Martyn impaling Wadham (Nicholas Martyn, d. 1595, married Margaret Wadham). The rich oak panelling is dated 1893; the moulded plaster ceiling is of the same period.

On the S.E. side of the screens-passage one of the arched openings to the original service rooms is blocked; the other leads to a 'Parlour' in the S.E. wing. The ceiling of this room is supported by two deep-chamfered oak beams enriched with 17th-century chip-carving. The two-light S.E. window incorporates roundels of fragmentary 16th-century glass. The Dining Room to the N.E., probably the original kitchen, has no early features. The principal Staircase, inserted where there was originally a corridor beside the kitchen, includes 16th-century carved oak balustrades that have recently been brought from the Priory at Bradford-on-Avon; these replace a staircase of the late 19th century. Underneath the lower flight is a wide 16th-century doorway with a chamfered four-centred head that originally opened into the courtyard.

On the first floor the State Bedchamber occupies the S.W. end of the Service Range. The 15th-century fireplace in the S.E. wall has a square head of Ham Hill stone, moulded on soffit and jambs, with a frieze of six quatrefoil ogee panels enclosing plain shields, a rose and foliate bosses. The spandrels between the panels are carved with conventional foliage and heraldic emblems; two have Martyn apes and three have Faringdon unicorns showing that the surround dates from the time of Sir William Martyn whose first wife was a Faringdon. The 17th-century oak panelling in four heights is surmounted by a frieze with sea monsters in low relief. A doorway beside the fireplace leads to the S. turret, originally containing a stair but now fitted on the first floor as an oratory; another doorway leads by a narrow diagonal passage to the chamber over the porch, now a bathroom. An original doorway at the N.W. end of the N.E. wall has chamfered wooden jambs and traces of a four-centred head. The adjoining bedroom, above the Dining Room, has reset bolection-moulded 17th-century panelling surmounted by a modern strap-work frieze and cornice. Other bedrooms are lined with 17th and 18th-century panelling brought from elsewhere when the house was restored at the end of the 19th century.

A circular *Pigeon-cote* about 50 ft. N.W. of the house is of the early 16th century. It is of roughly coursed rubble with occasional repairs in brick and has a coved stone eaves cornice; four ashlar buttresses of two stages are set symmetrically around the circumference. The cote is entered from the E. through a low ashlar doorway with a chamfered four-centred head. The internal wall-face has about 600 pigeon-holes accessible by a wooden ladder on a cantilevered frame which pivots on a central post. The conical timber roof is tiled, with a stone-slate verge. The timber turret at the apex is modern.

The *Stables* S.W. of the house are of the first half of the 17th century and have ashlar walls with some brickwork and cob. The E. wall has two 17th-century windows with four-centred openings below square heads; a wide doorway has a chamfered four-centred head and continuous jambs.

MEDIAEVAL AND LATER EARTHWORKS

(3) DEER PALE (771940–776933) is marked by a length of bank and ditch extending from the S.E. corner of the parish, across Park Hill, towards the parish church. The bank is 14 ft. wide and from 3 ft. to 6 ft. high; the ditch is about 10 ft. wide. Although the circuit cannot be fully traced the pale probably enclosed about 160 acres, including a small part of Burleston parish (Dorset *Procs.*, 88 (1967), 177–80).

ROMAN AND PREHISTORIC

ROMAN ROAD from Badbury Rings to Dorchester (*see Dorset* V).

4 BISHOP'S CAUNDLE (6913)

(O.S. 6 ins. ST 61 SE, ST 71 SW)

The parish, 960 acres in area, rises gently from the Caundle Brook in the S., at an altitude of some 200 ft. above sea-level, to a maximum elevation of over 400 ft. in the N.W. The N.W. third of the parish lies on Forest Marble; the rest is a combination of Oxford Clay, Cornbrash Beds and Forest Marble.

BISHOP'S CAUNDLE *The parish church of St. Peter & St. Paul*

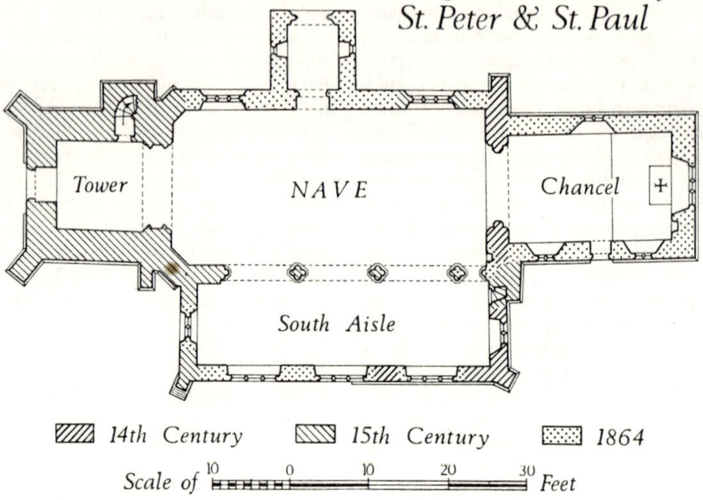

Until 1886 several outlying parts of Bishop's Caundle were wholly surrounded by the parishes of Caundle Marsh and Folke; conversely, detached lands of Caundle Marsh lay inside the bounds of this parish.[1] While a few of these 'islands' may result from early enclosure of the forest most seem to lie in the area of former open fields. The present parish contains two original settlements, Bishop's and Wake Caundle. It is not known whether each had a separate open field system. Wake Court (5) incorporates a 16th-century farmhouse and stands in an area where early enclosure is to be suspected (15). The most important monument in the parish is the church (1). Part of Cornford Bridge (2) is mediaeval.

ECCLESIASTICAL

(1) THE PARISH CHURCH OF ST. PETER AND ST. PAUL stands near the middle of the parish. The walls are of coursed rubble with ashlar quoins and dressings; the nave roof is tiled, with stone-slate verges; the chancel and S. aisle roofs are wholly stone-slated. The *Chancel* was largely rebuilt in 1864 but the faculty petition (Salisbury Diocesan Archives) shows that the original foundations and probably the lower courses of the N. and E. walls were reused; the windows are in the 14th-century style but renewed. Original 14th-century work survives in the E. wall of the nave, including the lower courses of the chancel-arch responds, and also in the E. wall of the *South Aisle* and the eastern part of its S. wall. The rest of the *Nave*, the *West Tower* and the western part of the S. aisle are largely of the second half of the 15th century; the N. wall of the nave, part of the S. wall of the S. aisle and the whole *North Porch* were rebuilt in 1864.

Architectural Description—The *Chancel* (21 ft. by 13½ ft.) has a pointed E. window of three lights with cinquefoil cusping beneath moulded external and internal labels. Similar windows of two lights open in the N. and S. walls, and the S. wall has a small two-centred doorway. The chancel-arch is two-centred and of two chamfered orders springing from chamfered imposts; the lower parts of the chamfered responds appear to be original. At the N.E. corner of the *Nave* (40 ft. by 19 ft.) is a square-set 14th-century buttress of one weathered stage. The N. side of the nave has, to the E., a 15th-century three-light window with cinquefoil cusping and vertical tracery in the two-centred head. The rest of the N. wall, the N. doorway and the N. porch are of 1864; the window to the W. of the doorway is a 19th-century replica of that to the E. On the S. side of the nave is a three-bay segmental-pointed arcade of the late 15th century. The arches, of two chamfered orders, rise from moulded capitals on chamfered shafts which repeat the orders of the arches; the bases have polygonal ogee mouldings on recessed octagonal plinths. A narrow opening, with details to match the arcade has been formed in the E. respond. The *South Aisle* (37 ft. by 10½ ft.) has, in the gabled E. wall, a two-centred 14th-century window of two lights with trefoil cusping below an ogival quatrefoil. Adjacent, to the N., is a projection containing the remains of the 15th-century rood-loft vice; it has a two-centred doorway within which the three lowest steps are preserved. The diagonal buttress at the S.E. corner of the aisle is of the 14th century, and 14th-century masonry with a chamfered plinth occurs below window-sill level in the E. half of the S. wall. The western part of the S. wall and all three S. windows are of 1864. The diagonal S.W. buttress and the W. wall of the S. aisle are of the 15th century but the W. window is a 19th-century insertion.

The *West Tower* (11 ft. square) has three principal stages defined by hollow-chamfered string-courses (Plate 9); at the base is an ogee-moulded plinth and at the top is an embattled parapet with crocketed finials at each corner and in the middle of each side; the finials are supported by shafts which rise from

[1] Tithe Map, 1841.

grotesque gargoyles in the top string-course. Each of the four corners has a diagonal buttress, diminishing in weathered stages in correspondence with the tower stages; a fifth buttress, square-set and of two stages, provides the S. abutment of the tower arch. The vice turret, to the N., is square in the two lower stages and octagonal in the top stage. Plinth and string-courses are continuous around the turret and the buttresses. The tower arch is two-centred; it is outlined to E. and W. by ogee mouldings, continuous on the responds, and has responds and soffit decorated with hollow-chamfered trefoil-headed panels. In the N. wall the vice has a small two-centred doorway. The W. doorway has a two-centred moulded head and continuous jambs; above is a two-centred W. window of three cinquefoil-headed lights with restored vertical tracery. The head of the W. window rises into the second stage, the string-course forming a hood-mould. A small two-centred two-light window in the N. wall of the second stage has incised cusping on the jambs. The third stage has, in each face, a mullioned and transomed belfry window of two cinquefoil-headed lights under a quatrefoil in a two-centred head. Below the transoms the lights are blocked; above they have perforated stone slabs.

Fittings—*Bells:* five; 2nd, 1758, 4th, 1627, others modern. *Benefactors' Table:* In tower, on N. wall, dated 1833. *Font:* Octagonal Ham Hill stone bowl and pedestal; side of bowl with quatrefoil panels enclosing blank shields and foliate bosses, splayed base of bowl with trefoil-headed arcading, pedestal with similar arcading; 15th century. *Monuments:* In nave, on N. wall, (1) of the D'Aubeny and Herbert families (Plate 39); oval panel of white marble with drapery, mounted on splayed black slate background between white side-scrolls with inverted cornucopiae; below, gadrooned white marble bracket; above, white marble cornice over which shaped slate panel forms background for white marble draped urn, standing on sarcophagus with shields-of-arms of the two families between sprays of foliage; by King of Bath, 1815. In S. aisle, (2) of William Claver, 1769, marble tablet with moulded cornice and base; (3) of Mary Fry, 1830, similar to (2), by Mitchell of Sherborne. In churchyard, close to N. wall of chancel, (4) burial vault with rusticated quoins, protruding 2 ft. above ground and surmounted by stone table-tomb with fluted corner pilasters and moulded cornice, tomb formerly enclosed in iron railings; 18th-century, inscription obliterated. *Plate:* includes silver cup and flagon, both marked BB, with hall-marks and inscriptions of 1734; also silver tray on claw feet, with date-letter of 1713, used as paten. *Royal Arms:* In tower on N. wall, painted wooden panel with arms and cypher of Charles II and date 1661.

SECULAR

(2) Cornford Bridge (69171204), of coursed rubble with ashlar dressings, carries the road to Holwell across the Caundle Brook about $\frac{3}{4}$ m. S. of the village. The bridge was extensively repaired in the 18th century and later but it incorporates 15th-century features. The three segmental-pointed arches have voussoirs laid in two orders. Between the arches are rubble piers; on the upstream or W. side these have cut-waters with ashlar facing, probably of the 18th century; on the E. side the S. pier has a coursed rubble cut-water while the N. pier retains a mediaeval weathered buttress of three stages above a rough plinth. The upstream cut-waters support refuge niches. The rubble parapets are capped with bevelled coping-stones except at one point where a hollow-chamfered mediaeval coping-stone is used.

(3) White Hart Inn, 100 yds. N.E. of the church, is of two storeys, with rendered walls and a tiled roof with stone-slate verges. It probably dates from the 18th century. Originally the doorway opened into a through-passage flanked by plank-and-muntin partitions but the plan has been changed and the partitions have been reset. The muntins have vertical reeding.

(4) Farm House (69381301), of two storeys with rendered walls and tiled roofs, has a symmetrical 18th-century S. front with a central doorway flanked by sashed windows, and three sashed windows in the upper storey. Low outbuildings to E. and W. have lean-to roofs masked by wing walls with shaped copings. A rusticated wooden porch is modern.

(5) Wake Court (69981237), $\frac{1}{2}$ m. S.E. of the church, is a farmhouse of two storeys with attics, with walls of rubble, partly rendered, and stone-slated roofs with tiling near the ridge. The main house, facing E., is probably of the first half of the 18th century; it contains several stop-chamfered ceiling beams and on the first floor there is at least one beam, evidently reused, with mouldings for a panelled ceiling. Detached and running W. from the N. end of the house is a 16th-century range of one storey with an attic; it is now used as a workshop and storehouse but it must originally have been the farmhouse itself. According to Coker (p. 96) it was in ruins in the 17th century.

BISHOP'S CAUNDLE *Wake Court*

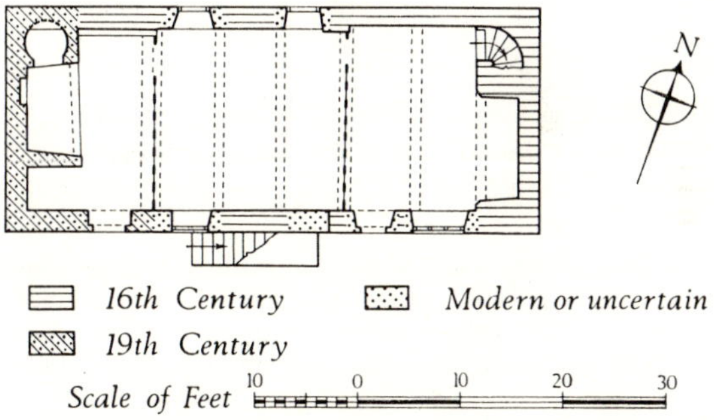

The walls of the 16th-century wing are of rubble, and all the window and door openings appear to be secondary. On the ground floor are three rooms. The E. room has an original open fireplace with chamfered ashlar jambs and a heavy timber bressummer with a continuous chamfer and a raised centre. N. of the fireplace is a spiral staircase to the attic. The ceiling has a massive chamfered beam with run-out stops. The unheated middle room is divided from the E. room by an original plank-and-muntin partition with chamfered muntins pegged to chamfered and grooved top and bottom rails; a doorway with a four-centred head at the N. end of the partition is chamfered on the E. face only. The middle room has two chamfered ceiling beams with run-out stops; in the S. wall a straight vertical joint and a timber lintel indicate the position of a former opening, now blocked. The middle room is separated from the W. room by a plank-and-muntin partition similar to the first but probably reset. The W. end of the range is probably of the 19th century; it incorporates an open fireplace with ashlar jambs, a chamfered oak bressummer and an oven in the N. jamb. The spiral stair in the E. room leads to an attic chamber ceiled at the level of the lower purlins but with a central E.-W. beam exposed. The loft over the middle and W. rooms is reached by outside steps of rubble, built against the S. wall. The partition between the E. chamber and the loft is combined with a framed truss in which the principals rise from a tie-beam at wall-plate level and are collared at half height; a king-post between the collar and the tie-beam is morticed to receive the tenon of the ceiling beam in the E. chamber; the panels of the truss are filled with wattle-and-daub to form the W. wall of the chamber. Three purlins are housed into the principals, and at the apex is a ridge piece set diagonally. While this truss and the roof to the E. of it are original, the roof to the W. is probably not older than the 19th century.

(6) RYALL'S FARM (70061268) is an 18th-century farmhouse of two storeys with a tiled roof and rendered walls. The symmetrical three-bay E. front has a coved eaves cornice. The central doorway has a moulded stone architrave with a fluted keystone but all other openings are modern.

(7) FARMHOUSE (69711283), at the S.W. end of Brown's Street, now two cottages, is of rubble in two storeys with a thatched roof. It probably dates from the 17th century and originally had a normal three-room plan, perhaps with a through-passage. A single-storied addition extends the range to the S.

(8) COTTAGES (69611318), two adjoining, now combined as a single dwelling, stand 20 yds. N. of the church; they have rubble walls and thatched roofs. The S.W. cottage is of the late 16th century; it is now two-storied but originally was single-storied with an attic. The N.E. cottage is of the 18th century and is single-storied. The 16th-century cottage retains an original stone winding staircase beside an open fireplace, now blocked.

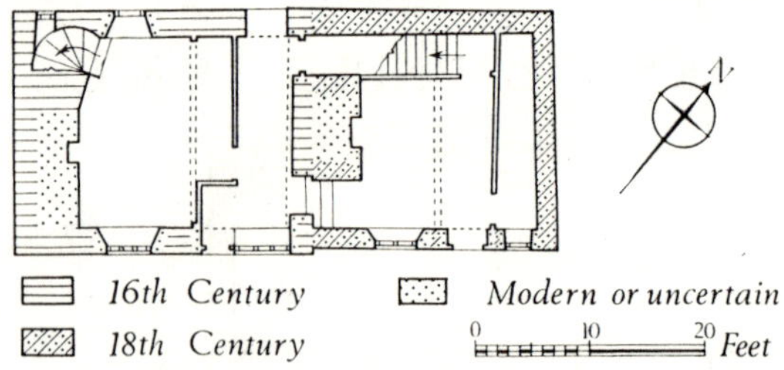

MONUMENTS (9–15)

The following late 18th or early 19th-century farmhouses and cottages are built of rubble in two storeys, or in one storey with dormer-windowed attics. Most have thatched roofs. Unless noted otherwise the buildings are simple ranges with approximately symmetrical three-bay fronts, having central doorways, casement windows on either side and three corresponding first-floor windows.

(9) *Cottage* (69411294), of two bays with a central doorway, stands on a narrow strip of land, perhaps part of a former roadway.

(10) *Farmhouse* (69641325), 100 yds. N. of the church, has a rendered S. front. The roof is tiled and has two dormer windows. Each gabled end-wall is crowned by a chimneystack.

(11) *Cottages*, two adjoining, stand 30 yds. E. of the foregoing. Both have symmetrical S. fronts; that to the E. is of three bays, that to the W. is of two bays with a central doorway.

(12) *Manor Farm* (69801325), 200 yds. N.E. of the church, repeats the characteristics of (10) but has been extended to the W. in two storeys and to the E. in one storey. Further two-storied extensions occur to the N.

(13) *Cottages* (70011308), two adjoining, have been converted to a single house and modernised.

(14) *Cottages* (69161210), pair, 50 yds. N. of Cornford Bridge, have doorways coupled at the centre of the S. front, each with one casement window beside it; the two tenements have now been converted into one dwelling.

Early 19th-century monuments include *Cottages* near the church (69591317), in Holt Lane (69201317) and (69031353), in Milburn Lane (69261280), in Giles's Lane (69481282), and in Caundle Wake (69971263).

MEDIAEVAL AND LATER EARTHWORKS

(15) CULTIVATION REMAINS. Nothing is known of the open fields of the parish or of the date of their enclosure. Field names on the Tithe Map of 1841 perhaps indicate former North and West Fields. Air Photographs (R.A.F. CPE/UK 1974: 2192–94) reveal faint traces of ridge-and-furrow in the N. and N.W. of the parish (693135 and 686127); it is arranged in curving furlongs and may be the remains of the open fields.

Ridge-and-furrow, 5 yds. to 9 yds. in width, occurs in the existing fields around Wake Court (5) and is clearly of post-enclosure date.

5 BLANDFORD FORUM (8806)

(O.S. 6 ins. ST 80 NE)

Blandford Forum, the largest town described in this volume, stands in a curve of the R. Stour which bounds it to S. and W. The land varies in altitude between 100 ft. and 200 ft. above O.D. and is of Valley Gravel and Chalk. Habitation probably originated in the vicinity of the present Market Place, at the junction of the river terrace and the Chalk declivity. The settlement prospered by reason of its position at the intersection of roads from Poole, Wimborne, Salisbury, Shaftesbury and Dorchester, and from its command of a bridge over the Stour. The parish was formerly more extensive than the present borough; until the 19th century it included the Manors of Nutford, Nutford Lokey and Damory, all of which had mediaeval open fields. Having been partly burned down in 1713 and then almost entirely consumed by a disastrous fire in 1731 Blandford was rebuilt within the space of about thirty years and consequently provides a noteworthy example of an 18th-century market town. The most important building to survive the two fires is the Old House (12), dating from *c.* 1660. The work of reconstruction was largely guided by the brothers John and

BLANDFORD FORUM. The Market Place, looking E.

Mainly 18th-century

Apse.

S. Gallery.

Interior, looking E.

BLANDFORD FORUM CHURCH. *c.* 1735; galleries 1837

Monument (14). 1752

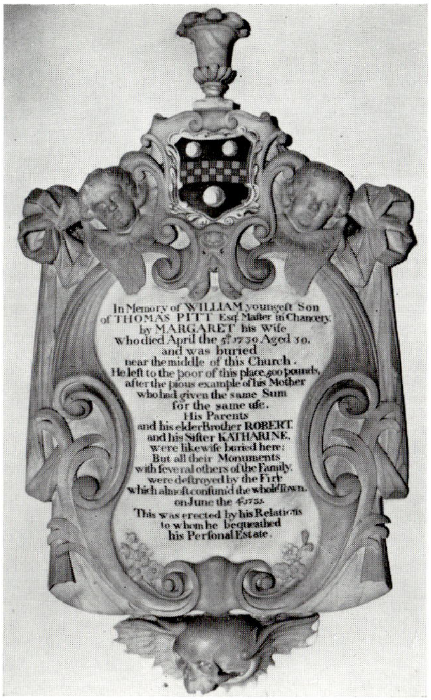

Monument (16). c. 1735

Monument (10). c. 1735

Monument (12). 1801

Monument (22). c. 1735

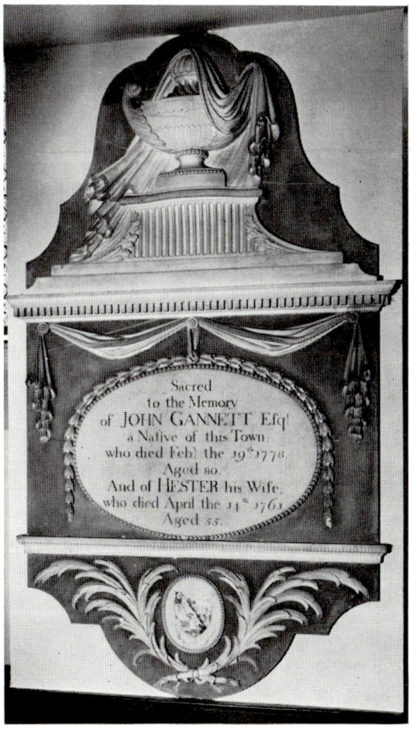

Monument (3). 1778

BLANDFORD FORUM CHURCH. Wall Monuments.

Organ. 1794

Pulpit. late 17th-century

BLANDFORD FORUM CHURCH.

General view.

Hood and cresting.

Reverse side of cresting.

BLANDFORD FORUM CHURCH. Mayor's seat.

1748

BLANDFORD FORUM. (5) Fire Monument. 1760

BLANDFORD FORUM CHURCH. (16) Bastard Monument. 1769

Great Mace. 1769

Seal. *c.* 1800

Small Mace. 1609

BLANDFORD FORUM. Civic Plate.

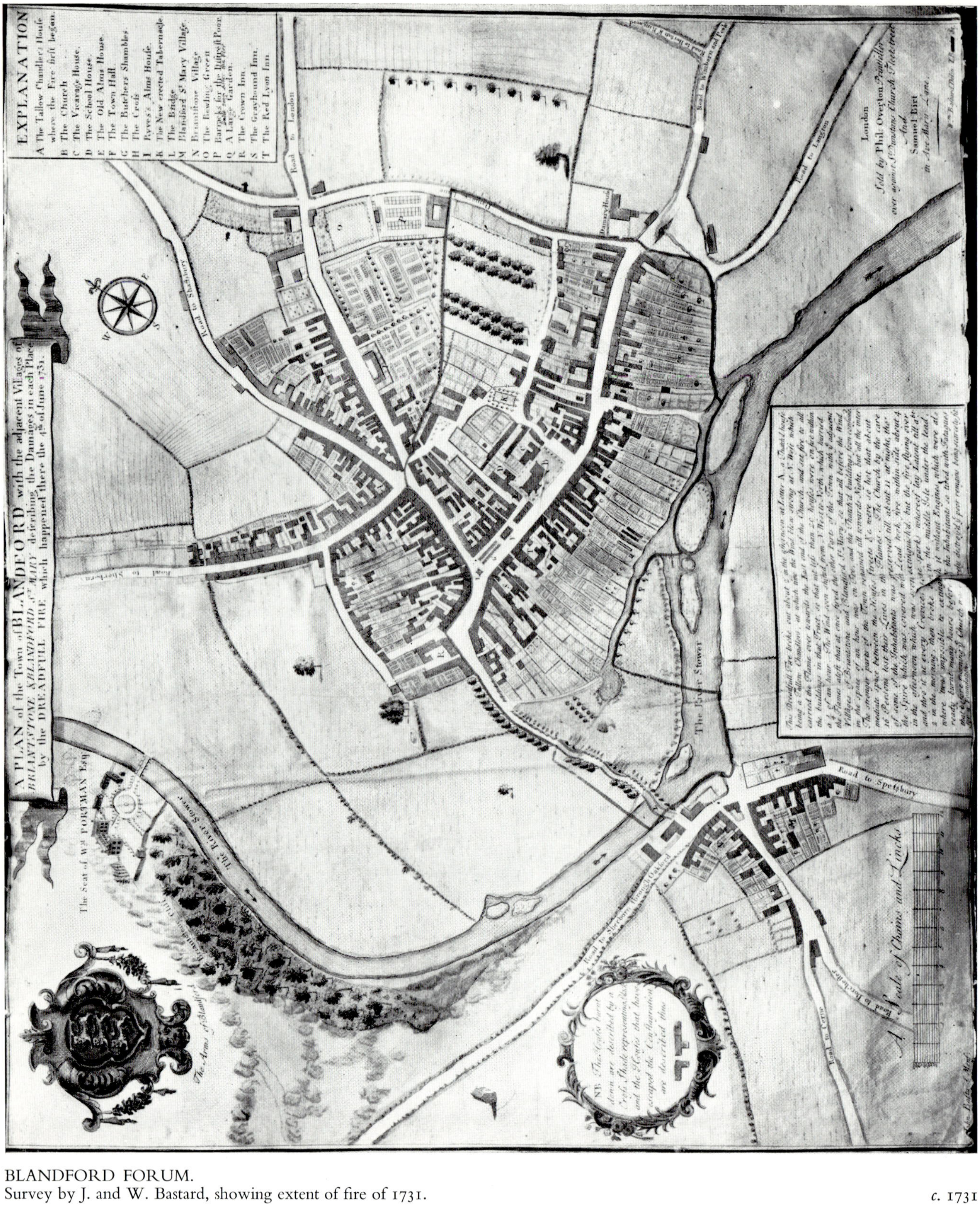

BLANDFORD FORUM.
Survey by J. and W. Bastard, showing extent of fire of 1731. *c.* 1731

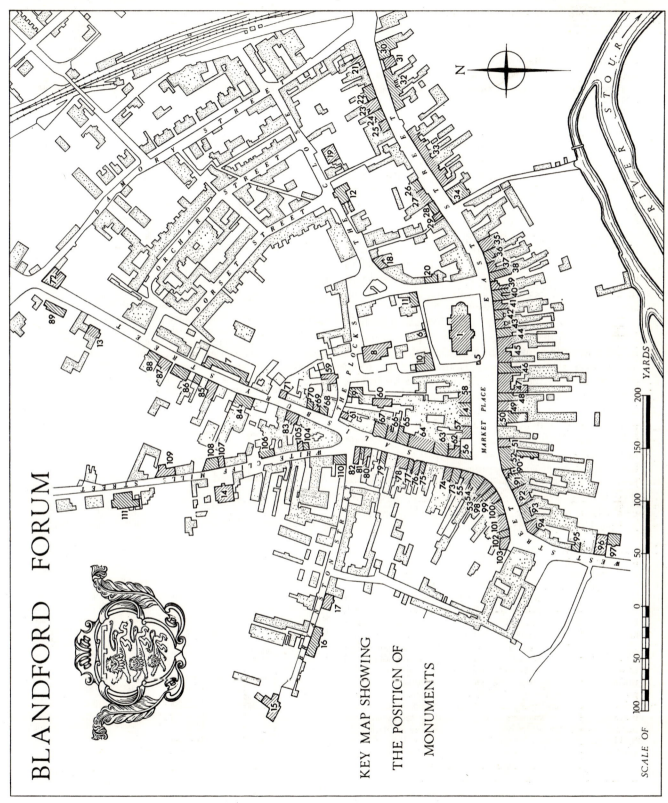

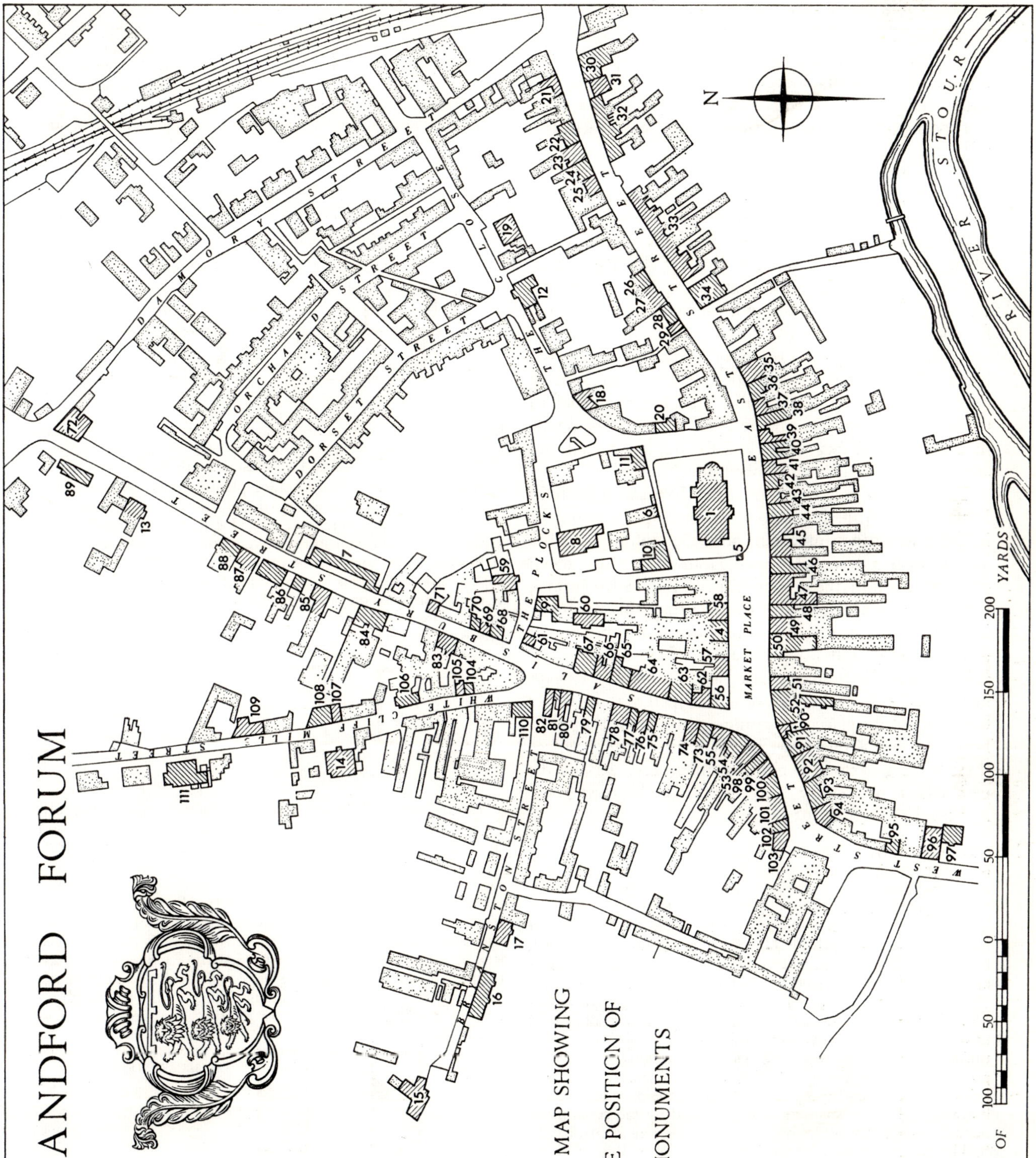
BLANDFORD FORUM
KEY MAP SHOWING
THE POSITION OF
MONUMENTS
N
RIVER STOUR
EAST STREET
MARKET PLACE
THE PLOCKS
SALISBURY STREET
WHITE CLIFF MILL STREET
DORSET STREET
ORCHARD STREET
DAMORY STREET
SHEEP MARKET HILL
CLOSE
WEST STREET
BRYANSTON STREET
SCALE OF YARDS
100 50 0 50 100 150 200

William Bastard, master-builders, who on several occasions also filled the office of bailiff or mayor of the town. For brevity we use the term 'post-fire' to denote the period of intense building activity between 1731 and 1766, many details of which are recorded in a contemporary manuscript 'Survey Book' by John Bastard; it is now preserved in D.C.R.O. The Bastards drew up an accurate map showing the extent of the destruction (Plate 104); it shows that the old street plan was retained in the rebuilding, the only important change in lay-out being the enlargement of the Market Place. The work of restoration was regulated by Act of Parliament (5 George III) and, to give effect to the Act, Parliament set up a Court of Record with power to make rules for the rebuilding of the town; a Commission was also established for the just apportionment of the losses incurred and for the distribution of the large sum of money that was publicly subscribed for the relief of the afflicted citizens. The Minutes of the Commissioners' meetings, still preserved by the Borough Council, are another useful source of information.[1]

The Parish Church, designed by John and William Bastard and finished in 1739, is the principal monument in the town; other important post-fire buildings are the Town Hall (4) and Coupar House (8). The town changed little in the second half of the 18th century, but in the first half of the 19th century the wealthier inhabitants began to build houses to the N., beside the Salisbury road and along the road which branches off it leading to Shaftesbury. Later in the century, perhaps in consequence of the provision of piped water, denser building took place on rising ground to the N.E. between the Wimborne and Salisbury roads, where there had formerly been gardens and where, as Bastard's plan shows, temporary 'Barracks for the Distrest Poor' had been erected in 1731.

Building materials. The surviving pre-fire buildings are mostly of red brick with stone dressings. In the post-fire reconstruction every building was brick-faced, except the Church and the Town Hall which are of stone and the Greyhound Hotel which has a stucco façade. Stone dressings were used only on Coupar House, the largest private house in the town; other brick buildings have quoins, cornices, doorway-surrounds, keystones and other details executed in plaster and wood. Variety was obtained by special brick bonding and by the use of bricks of various colours; for instance dark red brick was often used to outline openings, and quoins and window-heads were sometimes defined by finely-jointed pale red bricks, contrast being provided in each case by building the main wall-face in blue bricks. Flemish bond was generally used in the post-fire period, but a special effect was sometimes obtained by the economical device of using headers only; economical because it enables the builder to use broken bricks. Façades are also diversified by vertical *chaînage* of brickwork of contrasting colour which connects the openings of one storey with those of another.

[1] *See* H. M. Colvin, *Arch. Journ.* CIV (1947), pp. 178 ff.

Many façades retain traces of false brick jointing applied in white paint to the wall-face, the latter having been coloured red and blue, in correspondence with actual bricks but masking the real joints. Sometimes the painted joints do not exactly correspond with the real ones. It is uncertain if this work is of the 18th or of the early 19th century.

Classification of house-types. Ignoring minor variants, the houses that were built in the post-fire period may be classified in five main groups. The houses of *Group (i)* were designed for wealthier professional men and leading merchants. They are rectangular in plan and narrow enough to be spanned by a single roof. The ground floor has a central vestibule and staircase, with one room on each side. The vestibule is usually

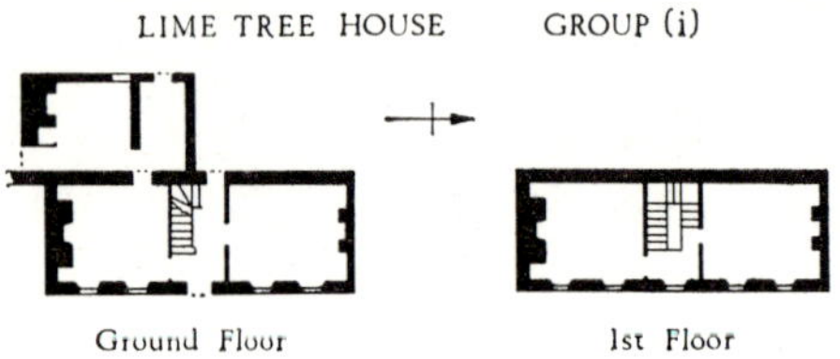

lit by a fanlight over the front door while two sashed windows light each flanking room; the fireplaces are against the end walls of the rectangle and the chimneystacks emerge at the apex of the gables. The first-floor plan is similar to that of the ground floor, with two principal bedrooms; smaller bedrooms are provided in a dormer-windowed attic. Kitchens and service rooms, with other bedrooms above them, occupy a lower wing at the rear or to one side of the main block. The symmetrical façade always has an ornate central doorway, with sashed windows disposed on each side of it and corresponding windows on the first floor. Lime Tree House (9) is an example of this group (Plate 109).

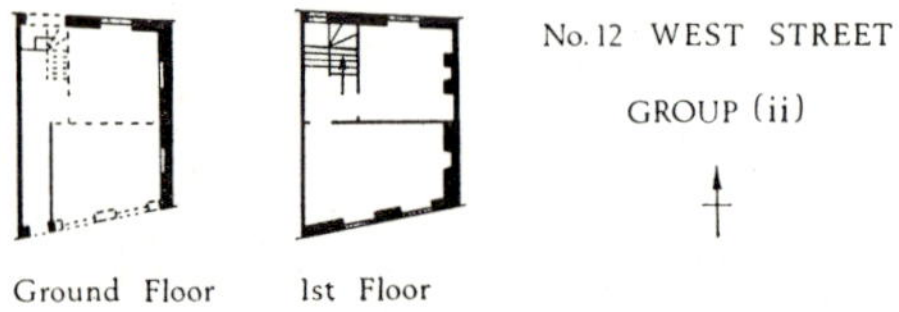

The buildings of *Groups (ii)* and *(iii)* were probably designed for occupation by shopkeepers and middle-class families and they are found at the centre of the town, in the Market Place, West Street and at the S. end of Salisbury Street. In every case the ground floor is a shop, whether in origin or by subsequent modification, and the typical plans have to be deduced from the disposition of the upper floors. Many of these houses have three storeys. In Group (ii) the entrance is placed to one side of the façade and opens into a narrow passage which leads to the staircase, set against the back wall of the house; there is one room in front beside the passage and a smaller room behind beside the stairs; on the first floor the front room extends across

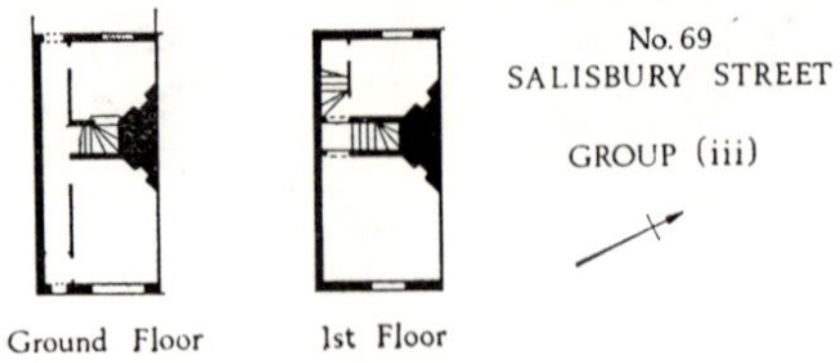

the ground-floor passage. The houses of Group (iii) have a plan similar to the preceding group except that the staircase, un-lit, rises between the front and rear rooms.

Group (iv) houses were for artisans and are mostly in the E. part of East Street, on the W. side of Salisbury Street and in White Cliff Mill Street. They are built in pairs and share a common service-passage leading through to the rear, from which both dwellings are entered (Plate 115). Each dwelling may have one or two ground-floor rooms; where there are two, the fireplaces are sometimes set corner-wise so as to be served by one chimneystack. In such pairs of houses one of the tenements is usually bigger than the other so that one wall of the service-passage may stand half-way between the end-walls, thus supporting the roof purlins with greater economy.

Nos. 15 & 17 EAST STREET GROUP (iv)

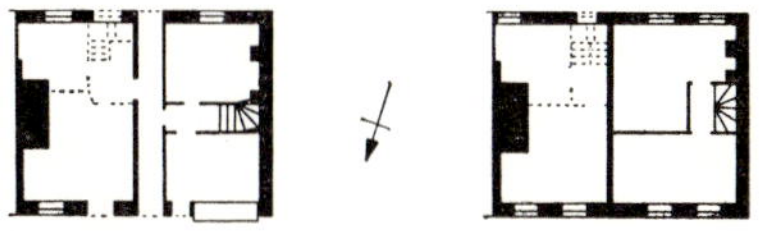

Ground Floor 1st Floor

In *Group (v)* houses the plan of the foregoing group is repeated in a single tenement, which may be with or without its own service-passage; in the latter case the front room is entered from the street. A still simpler version of the artisan's dwelling has only one room on each floor. Wherever possible the inventory will be abbreviated by means of the foregoing system of classification.

ECCLESIASTICAL

(1) THE PARISH CHURCH OF ST. PETER AND ST. PAUL (*see* Frontispiece and drawing facing p. 32) stands at the E. end of the Market Place, on the site of the mediaeval church which perished in the fire of 1731. The new church was designed and built by John and William Bastard; trustees for the rebuilding were nominated in 1733 and the new church was opened in 1739, although work went on for several years after that date. The church has walls of Greensand ashlar with dressings of Portland and Ham Hill stone; the roofs are tiled and of lead. The original design comprised *Apse*, *Nave*, *North* and *South Aisles*, and a *West Tower*. The last was originally intended to have a spire but a wooden bell turret was substituted, much to the Bastards' disgust. An organ gallery was installed at the W. end of the nave in 1794, and extended into the western part of the aisles in 1819; in 1837 both aisles were fully galleried. In 1895 the apse was taken down and the *Chancel* was inserted between the nave and the rebuilt apse; at the same time the organ was transferred to a chamber on the N. side of the chancel.

Blandford Forum parish church is a notable example of Georgian church architecture in the classical style, as interpreted by provincial builder-architects. (For plan, *see* p. 20.)

Architectural Description—Externally, the nave and aisles are combined in a rectangular structure of Greensand ashlar with Portland stone dressings, defined at the four corners by french quoins and capped by a cornice and parapet. The windows are round-headed, with moulded Portland stone architraves, impost blocks and keystones. Immediately above each window is an oblong panel of knapped flint on the N. and of Ham Hill stone on the other three sides; two panels to the S.E. are enriched with carved fleurs-de-lis. Above the cornice the parapets are interrupted at intervals by Portland stone balustrading. The *West Front* is broken at the centre by a projecting pedimented bay some 10 ft. higher than the main cornice. In the lower part of the bay is the W. doorway, a round-headed opening with Tuscan pilasters and a horizontal entablature; over this rises a tall W. window with scrolled sides and a segmental hood on scrolled brackets, all of Portland stone. The pediment of the W. front has a bold and simple cornice, the horizontal member being interrupted to make room for a clock-face. Above the central bay of the W. front rises the *Tower*, square on plan, with rusticated quoins and with a single round-headed and pedimented belfry window in each side; the triple keystones of the belfry window heads extend into the open pediments. The tower entablature is enriched with a heavy modillion frieze; over it is a parapet, lightened with balustrades in the middle of each side and thickened at each corner to form the pedestal of an urn finial. Quoins, cornices, balustrades and urns are of Portland stone. Above the balustrades is a wooden bell-cote, square at the base, with large scrolls set diagonally at the four corners; the scrolls were perhaps intended for the base of the projected spire. Over them rises an octagonal aedicule with round-headed openings on the four major sides and, above, a lead cupola with a weather-vane finial.

In the *South Front* a projecting central transept is flanked symmetrically by six bays of round-headed windows as described above. The *Transept* has colossal Portland stone pilasters at the angles and a pedimented Doric entablature with a triglyph frieze; the tympanum contains a sundial and at the apex of the pediment is an urn. The S. doorway, in the centre of the S. front of the transept, has a moulded Portland stone architrave and a horizontal stone hood on console brackets; above, an apron flanked by scrolls forms the base of a rectangular central window with an eared architrave and a keystone that touches the soffit of the Doric entablature.

The *East Front* was altered in 1895 by the addition of the chancel and the rebuilding of the apse further E. Above the chancel roof the E. wall of the nave is capped by a closed pediment, some 4 ft. higher than the balustraded parapets of the aisle walls and joined therewith by carved stone scrolls which mask the nave roof. The *Apse* now stands 25 ft. to the E. of its original position; it is flanked by the angle quoins of the modern chancel, which repeat those of the aisles. The apse windows are similar to those of the S. front but smaller.

The *North Front* repeats that to the south except for simpler treatment of the transept; instead of the Doric order the projection is capped by a return of the N. aisle cornice and parapet; the central doorway and window have relatively plain architraves and keystones; above rises a pedimented attic with a round window at the centre.

Inside, the W. doorway opens into a square *Vestibule* in the base of the tower; from it arched openings lead into the nave and aisles. The vestibule is ceiled below the level of the W. window and the latter illuminates an upper chamber, with arched recesses to N. and S. and a round-headed window to the E. through which light from the W. window finds its way to the nave.

The *Nave* (Plate 98) is flanked by Ionic colonnades raised on high pedestals above the level of the former box pews. On each side are an E. end pilaster, five columns with cylindrical stone shafts, and one with a rectangular shaft, the latter engaged in the tower. The fourth intercolumniation from the E. is wider than the others and corresponds with the N. and S. transepts which, although now partitioned off at ground level, formerly opened into the aisles and constituted a cross-axis. The column shafts, each of three stone drums as old photographs show, have capitals with canted volutes; they support entablatures with architraves of two fasciae, plain friezes and modillion cornices. At the W. end of the nave, the window to the upper tower chamber culminates in a keystone enriched with cherubs' heads. At the E. end the pilaster responds are coupled with square columns which support the wide arch at the entry to the chancel, formerly the front of the apse; the intrados is enriched with square coffers enclosing rosettes. Above the cornices of the colonnades the nave has a vaulted plaster ceiling of elliptical cross-section, each bay having a cross-vault which terminates laterally in lunettes. The vault ribs have oak-leaf wreaths and egg-and-dart mouldings, with acanthus bosses at the intersections; that of the fourth bay is larger and richer than the others.

The *Aisles* are lit by the six windows of the N. and S. walls, by the windows of the N. and S. transepts and by a window in each end wall, except that since 1895 the E. window of the N. aisle has been blocked by the organ chamber. In 1837 the aisles were divided into two storeys by galleries suspended between the colonnades and the outside walls. Below gallery level the N. and S. transepts were walled off and the cross-axis formed by the widened central intercolumniation was to a large extent nullified; however, the transepts remain open in the upper storey and the small galleries which they originally contained are now continuous with the large 19th-century galleries. The original galleries are approached by stone stairs beside the N. and S. doorways. The aisle ceilings (Plate 98) are plaster cross-vaults similar to those of the nave but of shallower elliptical cross-section; they spring from the Ionic architraves, the upper orders of the entablature being omitted on the reverse of the trabeation. The architrave mouldings continue on all four sides of each aisle and also on the E. and W. walls of the transepts but they do not return across the N. and S. sides of the transepts. The ribs of the aisle vaults have mouldings similar to those of the nave.

The *Chancel* of 1895 has, to the N., a wide opening to the organ chamber; to the S. are two round-headed windows similar to those of the aisles but slightly smaller. In general the architectural ornament of the walls is uniform with that of the apse. The barrel-vaulted roof is decorated with square coffering, each coffer having a central acanthus boss and four angle paterae.

The *Apse* (Plate 98) is lit by two round-headed windows with splayed reveals, outlined by enriched and gilded plaster architrave mouldings rising from sill fasciae with wave-spiral ornament; the impost moulding at the springing of each window-head has Greek-key decoration and the apex has a foliate spray; the window reveals are coffered, each coffer enclosing a rosette. The apse vault, moved bodily from its original position in 1895, is ornamented with octagonal coffering outlined in egg-and-dart enrichment, and filled with various ornaments such as cherubs' heads and conventional flowers; similar ornaments fill the small lozenge-shaped panels between the octagons. At the apex of the dome is a band of wave-spiral ornament and a central sunburst; the keystone of the archivolt is decorated with a trinity of cherub heads.

Fittings—*Chests:* At W. end of S. aisle, oak bible chest with

BLANDFORD FORUM *The parish church of St. Peter & St. Paul*

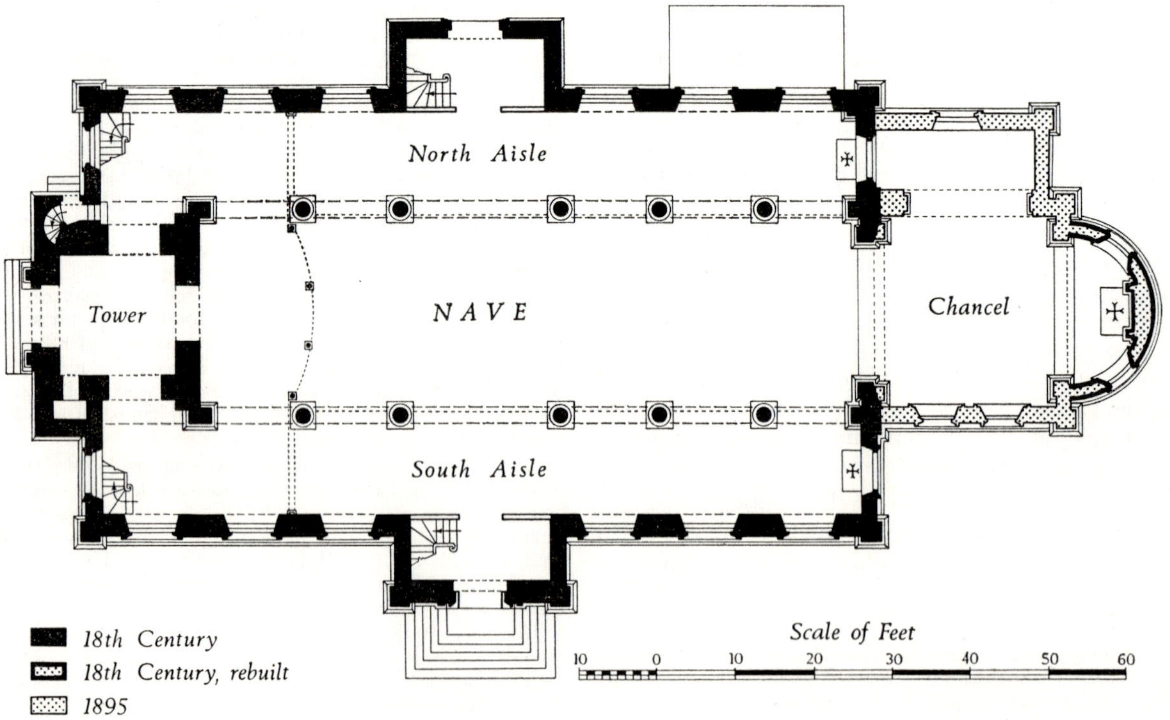

desk lid, carved front panel including initials T.G. between palms, iron lock and hinges; 17th century. At W. end of N. aisle, plain oak chest 3 ft. long, with moulded skirting and three locks; 18th century. *Communion Rail:* balusters from 18th-century communion rail, seen in an old photograph, now reset in front desks of modern choir-stalls. *Communion Tables:* At E. end of S. aisle, of oak, with cabriole legs, enriched fascia, top board moulded and enriched on three sides; *c.* 1735 and probably the original communion table (Plate 45); in vestry, table with spiral legs and plain stretchers and top; late 17th century. *Font:* (Plate 27); at W. end of S. aisle, of Portland stone, with gadrooned octagonal bowl on square baluster with flower and formal enrichment, and moulded base; octagonal domed cover, of oak, with carved pine-cone finial; *c.* 1739. *Galleries:* W. gallery, added in 1794 in W. bay of nave, with bow-fronted oak-panelled parapet, supported on small wooden Ionic columns; parapet with moulded capping set forward at centre to accommodate painted Royal Arms, *q.v.* Also N. and S. galleries, inserted in 1837 by John Tulloch of Wimborne, with panelled oak parapets and pine box-pews.

Monuments and *Floorslabs. Monuments:* In chancel, (1) of G. W. J. Chard, 1836, wall-tablet by Marshall. In N. aisle, (2) of Mary (Pitt) Whitmarsh, 1753, marble tablet with arms; (3) of John Gannett, 1778, marble tablet in slate surround with urn and arms (Plate 99); (4) of Lucy (Pitt) Baskett, 1764, John Pitt, 1757 and Dr. Christopher Pitt, 1801, marble tablet with Latin inscription and arms; (5) of Christopher Pitt, clerk, 1748, white marble tablet with arms; (6) of Nathaniel Benjafield, 1795 and his wife Ann, 1773, oval plaque with urn finial; (7) of Nicholas Humfrey, 1776, and his wife Cecilia, 1768, veined marble tablet with urn, arms and harpy crest; (8) of Mary Marsh, 1787, and George Marsh, 1713, marble tablet with urn; (9) of Robert Raynes, 1749, and his wife, Elizabeth, 1757, marble tablet with pediment, flame-finials and cartouche-of-arms; (10) of members of the Creech and Bastard families (Plate 99), stone tablet inscribed 'Near this Place Lie the remains of Thomas & Iane Creech; the latter dyed 1693; the former 1720, Leaving one Son & one Daughter. Thomas the Son was the Learned, Much admir'd, & much envied Mr Creech, Fellow of All souls Coll: in Oxford: Bridget, the Daughter, was the Wife of Thomas Bastard of this Town. (A man useful, & industrious in his generation, a peaceable, & inoffensive neighbour, and eminent for his Skill in Architecture;) By Whom she had Issue six Sons, and four Daughters; Two of which, Iohn and William, educated In the same Art, rebuilt this Church, the Town Hall, with several other Publick & Private Edifices, And, from a Pious regard for these their Ancestors, erected this monument to supply the place of one destroy'd in the General Conflagration, on the 4th of June, 1731'; (11) of Thomas Waters, 1787, and Elizabeth (Goodenough) Waters, 1807, marble tablet with arms. In S. aisle, (12) of Richard Pulteney, F.R.S., 1801, tablet with urns and arms (Plate 99); (13) of his wife Elizabeth Pulteney, 1820, tablet by Hiscock of Blandford; (14) of Robert Lewen, 1752, variegated marble tablet (Plate 99); (15) of William Milbourne, 1760, and others of same family, marble tablet with arms; (16) of William Pitt, 1730, and others of same family, baroque cartouche with arms (Plate 99); (17) of Thomas Edward Baker, 1833, tablet by Patent Works, Westminster; (18) of Robert Williams, 1757, marble tablet with painted arms of William of Herrington, now almost erased; (19) of William Sollars, 1816, oval tablet representing hand holding scroll, by Hiscock of Blandford; (20) of John Bastard, 1809, and his wife, Isabella, 1811, sarcophagus-shaped tablet with urn, by Hiscock and son; (21) of John Dennett, 1772, and others of same family, marble tablet with arms; (22) of William Wake, 1705, and Amy his wife, 1673, parents of Archbishop Wake, obelisk-shaped monument evidently erected after 1731 (Plate 99); (23) of Thomas Lacy, 1815, and his wife Alice, 1812, marble cartouche by Marshall. In churchyard, numerous 18th and early 19th-century stones, none earlier than the fire; the most important, (24) of members of the Bastard family (Plate 102); table-tomb with moulded plinth and top, extended at one end to form the base of an obelisk dated 1769, each figure, surrounded by a wreath, occupying one side of the needle; W. side inscribed 'To the memory of John Bastard aged 82, of William Bastard aged 77, whose skill in architectural and liberal benefactions to this town well deserve to be publickly recorded'; S. side of table-tomb inscribed 'This obelisk is erected by their nephews Thomas Bastard Sen'r. and Thomas Bastard Jun'r. the said John Bastard and William Bastard are the same persons mentioned on a monument erected for that family in the south aisle of this church'; on N. side 'To the memory of Thomas Bastard of this town died November the 12th 1771 aged 51'. *Floorslabs:* In nave, (1) of Mary McCombe, 1762; (2) of John Curson, 1795, white marble slab; (3) of Elizabeth Pitt, date hidden. In N. aisle, (4) of William Pitt, 1755; (5) illegible, 1755; (6) of Richard Steyner, 18th-century. In S. aisle, (7) vault of I. K. Caplin; (8) of John White, 1769; (9) of . . . . Hoare.

Hatchment: of painted canvas in moulded wooden surround with lozenge-of-arms of Ryves. *Organ:* (Plate 100) built in 1794 by England (*Salisbury Journal*, Sept. 1, 1794), moved in 1895 from W. gallery to N. side of chancel; wooden case decorated with classical mouldings and acanthus carving, with royal crown as central finial and Prince of Wales's crest on each side. *Panelling:* In apse, oak dado with fielded panels with enriched borders and enriched cornice; 18th century. *Plate:* includes silver cup, paten and flagon with hall-marks of 1731 and 1732; cup engraved with arms of Pitt; paten inscribed 'The gift of Mrs Elizabeth Pitt, relict of ye late Dr. Christopher Pitt of Blandford'; flagon inscribed 'The gift of Mr. Charles Pitt of Pimperne'. *Pulpit:* (Plate 100) of oak, formerly in St. Antholin's, London (*The Builder*, Jan. 10, 1880); hexagonal, with raised panels with acanthus enrichment on five sides; ledge similarly enriched and breaking forward at angles above foliate brackets; late 17th century, base and stairs *c.* 1895. *Reredos:* In apse, of carved and gilded oak, reset and made 2 ft. higher than formerly by adding to height of column pedestals; on each side, three-quarter Corinthian columns with gilt enrichment supporting pedimented entablature; tympanum with gilded cherub heads and corona with gilt foliage; above, on shaped and panelled pedestal with festoons at corners, free-standing Pelican-in-Piety and flanking urns; between columns, panel with gilded egg-and-dart border, and carved fruit and flower festoons above; panel now enclosing modern painting but originally with text of Lord's Prayer and Creed (Hutchins I, 224).

Royal Arms: painted on square panel at centre of W. gallery, with cypher of George III and date 1794. *Seating:* In nave and aisles, oak-panelled pews, originally box-pews rising to level of column pedestals, remodelled and cut down to present height in 1880. In third intercolumniation of S. side of nave, ordinary arrangement of pews, interrupted to make way for ornate *Mayor's Seat* (Plate 101) in which two parallel benches upholstered in red velvet face each other on either side of main chair, of oak, with seat, scrolled arm-rests and back upholstered in velvet; vertical oak posts on each side of chair back flanked by carved cheek-pieces in two orders, richly ornamented with scrolls, acanthus foliage and swags of fruit; uprights support foliate consoles enriched with flower festoons, and segmental hood, coffered on underside; space between top of chair back and hood filled with pierced and carved panel displaying town arms and, on reverse, carved date 1748.

Tables of Decalogue: At W. end of nave, two round-headed panels with moulded architraves, scrolled and foliate cheek-pieces on either side and gilt lettering on black background. In N. and S. aisles, painted Beatitudes on wood panels with rounded heads and moulded surrounds.

(2) St. Leonard's Chapel (89060647), on the E. boundary of the parish, is a half-ruined 15th-century building now used as a barn (Plate 114). The E. wall and the eastern part of the N. and S. walls survive. The masonry is partly of flint and partly of squared rubble alternating with triple courses of knapped flint, with ashlar dressings and quoins at the N.E. and S.E. corners, and with putlog holes outlined in ashlar at regular intervals. The roof is modern. Internally the walls are of coursed clunch with random flint courses. The 'chapel' is notable as the only mediaeval building to survive in the parish. It probably originated as an infirmary.

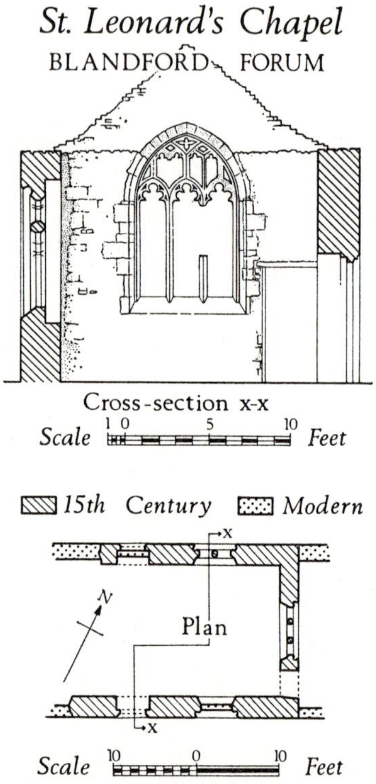

The E. wall has a casement-moulded window of three cinquefoil lights with vertical tracery in a two-centred head; to the S. is a modern doorway. The N. wall has, to the E., a window of two lights with vertical tracery in a segmental-pointed head; further W. is a doorway with a two-centred wave-moulded head and continuous jambs; both openings have timber beams in place of rear-arches; the doorway is blocked. The S. wall is uniform with the N., but the head and tracery of the window have perished; W. of the doorway is one jamb of another S. window. Drawings of 1791 and 1859 (Dorchester Museum, Shipp Album I) show that the N. and S. walls were formerly symmetrical, with central doorways flanked by uniform windows. The W. part of the building has disappeared.

SECULAR

(3) Blandford Bridge (Plate 51) carries the road from Blandford to Dorchester across the R. Stour, ½ m. S. of the town. The main bridge, with six arches, is separated from the town by a belt of water-meadow, across which the road is carried on a causeway and two other bridges respectively of two and three arches. All three bridges are of Greensand with a certain amount of brown Heathstone, especially on the W. side. The main bridge is mentioned in the Quarter Sessions records of 1631 as being in need of repair, and similar references occur throughout the 17th century. In 1726 an order was made for the bridge to be thoroughly restored and for a causeway to be built across the adjacent marsh; £115 was paid for this work in the following year. In 1783 William Moulton contracted to repair and widen 'the Blandford Bridges' for £840, and in 1812 William Bushrod undertook to rebuild the E. side of the bridge for £2,450.

In the main six-arch bridge the two central openings are slightly higher, and the two outside openings slightly lower than the intermediate ones. Triangular cut-waters with weathered pyramidal tops project from both sides. All spans have plain archivolts with projecting keystones. Above the keystones continuous ashlar plat-bands follow the rise of the arches, and above these are ashlar parapet walls with weathered copings. The intrados of each arch is divided into three zones by offsets and straight joints running in the direction of the road. The lateral zones are about 4½ ft. wide; the inner zones are about 14 ft. wide and all but one of them are constructed of smaller and less carefully jointed ashlar than the lateral zones. The central part of the N. arch (Plate 114) is supported on four chamfered ribs of Heathstone, probably a vestige of the bridge which existed before 1726, and perhaps mediaeval. The two causeway bridges resemble the main bridge except that the E. sides have been rebuilt in concrete.

(4) The Town Hall (Plate 106) stands on the N. side of the Market Place; it is signed and dated 'Bastard, Architect, 1734' in the entablature of the central window. It replaces the former Town Hall, destroyed by the fire of 1731, which stood on an island site to the south of the present building (Plate 104). The two-storied elevation is of Portland stone ashlar. On the ground floor is an open loggia of three semicircular arches, with moulded archivolts and plain keystones, on rectangular piers with lightly moulded imposts. A moulded string-course runs immediately above the arcade. The first-floor windows have moulded architraves, pulvinated friezes with foliate enrichment, and pediments, that of the centre window being curved; the sills are continued as a string across the elevation. At the top of the façade is an enriched modillion cornice of wood and a pediment with a clock in the tympanum; three stone vases complete the composition.

The ground-floor arcade opens into a stone-flagged loggia, known as the Shambles and originally part of the market; its ceiling is supported on two Doric columns, axial with the piers of the façade. An archway at the back of the Shambles leads to the staircase, which rises to the first floor against the E. wall and is lit at first-floor level by a round-headed window in the N. wall. The present stairs are of the mid 19th century; beside them is the entrance to a late 19th-century assembly hall, the Corn Exchange.

On the first floor, a courtroom extends across the front of the building and corresponds with the loggia below. Behind the courtroom lie two compartments; the staircase to the E. and the Council Chamber to the W. The latter has three windows in the N. wall, a doorway from the staircase, and another doorway leading into the W. part of the courtroom. There is a fireplace in the S. wall. The Courtroom is plainly decorated. The E. wall contains a fireplace framed by a plain eared architrave of wood; at either end of the N. wall are the doorways to the stairs and Council Chamber; between them is a blind archway with pilasters and a moulded archivolt. The principal feature is the Magistrates' Bench, filling the W. end of the room in a long shallow curve from wall to wall, with the chairman's seat in the centre, the whole being raised upon a wooden platform with a panelled front. The wooden bench rests on short Doric columns, and a high back is formed by ten fielded panels, five on each side of the chairman's seat; the latter is distinguished by its round-headed raised and fielded back-panel with a triple keystone at the top, and a pediment-canopy on scroll brackets. The seat has scrolled arm-rests supported on vase-shaped uprights.

Civic Insignia, etc: (i) Small Mace (1⅜ ft. long) silver, parcel gilt over an iron core, not hallmarked (Plate 103). A drum-shaped head embossed with fleurs-de-lis, with a tapering neck, meets the plain shaft at a raised band from which three scrolled brackets rise to support the head. The top of the head is a disc of silver with the Stuart royal arms, initials C.R. and the Garter motto. The shaft has a spherical knop with incised radial lines and a grip with wavy serrated flanges. On the lower part of the shaft is engraved DONUM LODOVICI ARGENTYNE AR: 1609 (*sic*) with shield of Argentyne, *three covered cups*. (ii) Great Mace (3¼ ft. long), silver-gilt, by WG., with London hall-mark of 1769; with a crowned head, a plain shaft with a knop decorated with embossed acanthus foliage, and a trumpet-shaped grip similarly embossed (Plate 103). Inscribed on the lower part of the shaft, 'Robert Biggs Gent Bailiff 1770'. The head meets the shaft at a circlet of bay-leaves; the bowl has embossed cornucopias and floral decoration forming two oval panels, one with the arms of George III, the other with the arms of the borough, *i.e.*, the shield of the Duchy of Lancaster. (iii) Borough Seal, silver (1½ ins. in diameter) with a turned ivory handle; probably late 18th or early 19th-century (Plate 103); the shield of the Duchy of Lancaster is flanked by ostrich plumes and is surrounded by the inscription SIGILLVM BVRGENTIVM VILLAE DE BLANDFORD FORVM. (iv) Royal Arms of George II, painted on canvas in moulded wooden frames, two panels; one on E. wall of courtroom, the other on E. wall of staircase. (v) Chest, wood, with scrolled iron reinforcement and three hasps, 17th-century. (vi) Pillory, in the Shambles, wooden cross-piece with apertures for the neck and wrists supported on a wooden Tuscan column, 18th-century.

(5) FIRE MONUMENT (Plate 102), commemorating the fire of 1731, stands at the E. end of the Market Place against the churchyard wall. It was designed by John Bastard and was erected in 1760 at a cost of £66 0s. 5d. (Bastard's Survey Book, D.C.R.O.). Two free-standing columns support a pedimented Roman Doric entablature with the date 1760 on the tympanum. The rear wall, of ashlar, with terminal pilasters to correspond with the columns, bears the following inscription: 'In REMEMBRANCE of God's dreadful Visitation by FIRE which broke out the 4th June 1731, and in few Hours reduced, not only the CHURCH, and almost this whole Town to Ashes wherein 14 Inhabitants perished, but also, two adjacent Villages. And, In grateful Acknowledgement of the DIVINE MERCY, that has raised this Town, like the PHAENIX from it's Ashes, to it's present beautiful and flourishing State, And to prevent by a timely Supply of Water, (with God's Blessing) the fatal Consequences of FIRE hereafter THIS MONUMENT of that dire Disaster and Provision against the like, is humbly erected by JOHN BASTARD, a considerable Sharer in the general Calamity. 1760'. An inscription of 1768 records an endowment of £600 by John Bastard and another inscription records the repair of the monument in 1858.

(6) THE ALMSHOUSES, on the N. side of the churchyard, which were built on land that formerly belonged to the school (Act of Parliament, 5 Geo. III refers), have now disappeared except for the gateway or S. front (Plate 114). This is a triple archway of Greensand ashlar surmounted by a pediment with a central oculus. The round-headed middle arch is larger than the side openings, which have shallow segmental heads. Above each side arch is a recessed limestone plaque; that to the W. is inscribed 'THE ALMSHOUSES AT THE WEST END OF THE CHURCH BEING DESTROYED BY THE FIRE, THE 4TH OF JUNE 1731, THIS WAS BUILT BY THE CORPORATION TO SUPPLY ITS LOSS 1736'. The E. plaque has an inscription of 1846.

(7) RYVES'S ALMSHOUSES (Plate 112) stand on the E. side of Salisbury Street. They were built in 1682 and, being situated near the outskirts of the town, escaped the fire. They are single-storied with brick walls and have tiled roofs with stone-slate verges. The main range stands parallel with but a little back from the street, and at each end a short gable-ended wing runs out at right angles as far as the roadside. Four round-headed doorways, symmetrically disposed in the W. wall of the main range, give access to what were originally ten dwellings, now five. Casement windows between the doorways have wide stone surrounds and mullions. The eaves are masked by a plaster cove which turns up at the centre of the range to form a small gable supported on wooden consoles. Beneath the gable is a stone tablet, surrounded by a moulded architrave and surmounted by an achievement-of-arms of Ryves. The tablet is inscribed 'GEORGIVS RYVES ARMIGER DE DAMARY VICE COMES DORSETENSIS GERONTOCOMIVM HOC FECIT DICAVIT ANNO DNI MDCLXXXII'.

(8) Coupar House, at the corner of Church Lane and The Plocks, is probably of *c.* 1750; in 1731 the site was an open garden with a small building at the middle of the W. side (Bastards' plan, Plate 104). The W. range has a normal Group (i) plan and is of three storeys. The E. range is differently orientated from the W. and therefore appears to be of another period; presumably it is earlier since the top floor of the W. range is accessible only from the E. range.

Coupar House is the largest and most splendidly decorated private house of the post-fire period in Blandford Forum, and the only one to have the richness of Portland stone dressings on its brick façade (Plate 105). In the front garden, handsomely carved urn finials surmount the piers which flank the gateways and occur at intervals in the wall. Despite the use of costly materials the façade is curiously amateurish in design. The various elements of the composition, adequate in themselves, are ill co-ordinated and little attention is paid to rules of proportion. The interior is richly fitted and the main staircase is the handsomest in Blandford.

The brickwork of the W. front consists only of headers, red bricks being used in the wings and blue bricks in the central feature. In the two lower storeys the central feature is flanked by Ionic pilasters carrying an entablature with a pulvinated frieze just above the first-floor window heads. The lower orders of the entablature distinguish the central feature alone but the cornice continues across the whole façade, terminating at French quoins at the extremities of the five-bay elevation. Above the cornice the second storey has at each extremity a panelled stone pilaster superimposed on the quoin below, and French quoins on each side of the centre bay superimposed on the Ionic pilasters. The façade is capped by a second cornice, returned as a pediment over the central bay. On the ground floor the central doorway is flanked by three-quarter columns carrying a full Doric entablature and pediment. Above, the middle first-floor window has an eared architrave, scrolled stone cheek pieces and shaped consoles to the window-sill. The lintel and keystone are squeezed with difficulty into the space below the main entablature, the window architrave being thinner than it should be and the keystone cutting into the fascia of the architrave; this is a serious fault of design, and strange in view of the fact that the same problem had been successfully evaded in monuments (1) and (52). The round-headed middle window of the top storey is extended by false panes into the field of the pediment and surrounded by a rusticated architrave with a triple keystone. The lateral windows are simpler than those of the central feature; they have stone architraves with plain keystones, and on the first floor they have sills with shaped consoles.

The stonework of the W. front does not extend in the N. and S. elevations beyond the returns of the corner members. On the S. side, both cornices continue across the end wall of the main range in brickwork and follow the projection of the

COUPAR HOUSE *BLANDFORD FORUM*

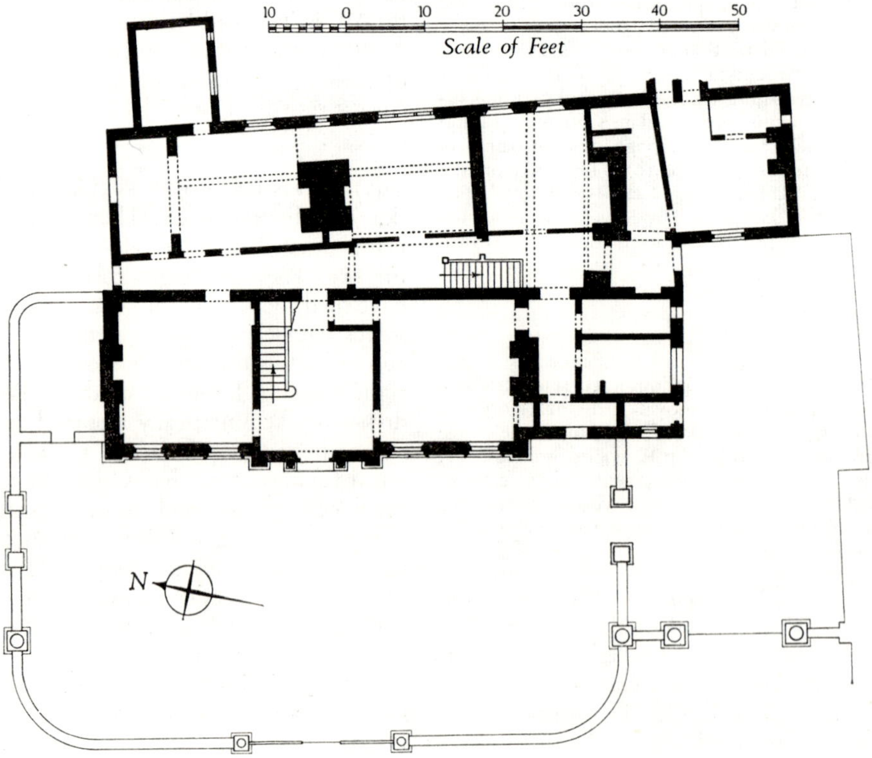

BLANDFORD FORUM. (8) Coupar House. Exterior, from S.W. *c.* 1750

BLANDFORD FORUM. (4) The Town Hall, from S.W. 1734

(4) Town Hall. Detail of centre window. 1734

(45) John Bastard's house. Plaster panel in mezzanine room. *c.* 1732

BLANDFORD FORUM.

(45) No. 75 East Street and No. 26 The Market Place. *c.* 1732

(47) The Red Lion Inn. *c.* 1732

BLANDFORD FORUM.

(9) Lime Tree House, E. front. *c.* 1735

(10) Old Bank House, S. front. Mid 18th-century

BLANDFORD FORUM.

BLANDFORD FORUM. (12) The Old House.

c. 1660

c. 1735

BLANDFORD FORUM. (52) The Old Greyhound Inn.

(7) Ryves's Almshouses. 1682

(13) Dale House. 1689

Central feature of Monument (7).

BLANDFORD FORUM.

S. chimneystack. On the N. wall of the range, the main cornice is not represented and only the upper cornice continues at the foot of the gable. There are no windows in either end wall.

Inside, the square vestibule has a dado of fielded panelling capped with a moulded rail which turns up to follow the stairs and is continued on the first-floor landing. On the ground floor, doorways to N. and S. have eared architraves and six-panel doors; the entrance doorway is similarly treated but with an eight-panel door. The carved oak stairs (Plate 84) have an open string and a rich version of the Tuscan-column balustrade that is usual in 18th-century Blandford buildings; each tread carries three balusters and the moulded handrail ends at the bottom in a fist-shaped scroll. The square end of each step is panelled and the spandrel below the panel is enriched with a foliate scroll. The S.W. room is panelled to its full height with fielded 18th-century panelling, the middle panel of each wall being accentuated by bolection mouldings; the dentil cornice is of wood. The marble fireplace surround is flanked by foliate scrolled cheek-pieces; above rests a pulvinated laurel and acanthus frieze with an oblong centre panel on which is carved a delicate swag of flowers and fruit; the overmantel has a shouldered centre panel flanked by fluted composite pilasters supporting an entablature with a broken pediment. The N.W. room (Plate 117) is decorated in much the same way, but with a cornice enriched with egg-and-dart mouldings, a tier of fluted modillions alternating with rosettes, and a fillet of leaf-and-dart below the plain corona. The door heads have flat entablatures with pulvinated leaf friezes. On each side of the fireplace is a round-headed recess. The fireplace surround is flanked by pilasters with pendant leaf festoons crowned by scrolls with scale decoration on the front; these are spanned by an architrave with wave ornament, above which a foliate scroll extends on each side of a central panel; the overmantel consists of an eared architrave with guilloche enrichment flanked by foliate scroll cheek-pieces and crowned by a pediment.

On the first floor the stair hall has a moulded plaster ceiling. The S.W. room has wall panelling of much the same style as in the room beneath, but less rich. The 19th-century fireplace has a reeded stone surround with roundels at the corners; over it rises an overmantel composed of large acanthus brackets supporting a broken pediment and flanking a flat panel with foliate cheek-pieces and a scrolled head. The N.W. first-floor chamber has no panelling; its cornice resembles that of the S.W. room on the ground floor.

The passage between the E. and W. ranges is lined with wooden panelling from the N. end to a transverse arch about half way along it. The N.E. room is wholly lined with fielded panelling above and below a moulded dado rail. The adjacent room has a plain dado rail of *c.* 1820. Towards the S. end of the passage, stairs lead up to the first floor of the W. block, which is also entered from the half-landing of the main staircase. The first-floor N.E. room has a bolection-moulded overmantel and a moulded wooden cornice around part of the ceiling.

The house is separated from the street by a forecourt 30 ft. wide, bounded by high brick walls which terminate at stone piers on either side of an iron-railed centre section. The piers have panelled sides and moulded cappings and support carved stone vases. Other vases decorate brick piers at the N. and S. ends of the court.

(9) Lime Tree House (Plate 109) faces Coupar House across Church Lane and is a small Group (i) residence; it probably was built soon after the fire (for plan, *see* p. 18). The house is of two storeys with attics; a service wing extends W. and S. at the rear and there is a further S. extension which may formerly have been for stables. The E. front is of blue header bricks with red brick dressings and red brick *chaînage* between the jambs of the ground and first-floor openings. The windows have gauged red brick flat arches with triple keystones; the tiled roof has two flat-topped dormers with sashed windows. At the eaves is a moulded cornice. The central entrance has an eared architrave and fluted Tuscan pilasters supporting two orders of scrolled foliate brackets; these support a segmental wooden hood (Plate 69).

Inside, the stair balustrade (Plate 84) is of the common Tuscan column pattern, a modest version of the one at Coupar House; the moulded handrail ends in a fist-scroll with acanthus enrichment. The hall and staircase walls have fielded dado panelling capped by a moulded rail. The N. room is lined to the ceiling with fielded panelling in two heights, with a moulded dado and a deep cornice. The fireplace has an eared stone surround enclosed in a carved wooden architrave moulding with leaf enrichment, flanked by wooden cheek-pieces with scrolls and acanthus ornament; above is a pulvinated frieze with laurel and ribbon enrichment and an oblong centre panel with a floral swag; a band of egg-and-tongue moulding supports the mantel-shelf. The overmantel is an oblong panel with bead-and-reel and leaf-and-dart mouldings. The S. room has a panelled dado, and panelled cupboard doors on each side of the fireplace. The two principal bedrooms have panelled window shutters and that to the N. has a panelled overmantel.

(10) Old Bank House, 25 yds. N.W. of the church, has a Group (i) plan with a service wing stretching out to the N. from the W. part of the main range. The lower part of the W. wall survives from before the fire of 1731 and is probably a vestige of the School House (Bastard's town plan, and Survey Book, p. 29); it is built of thin, variegated bricks and terminates to N. and S. in stone quoins. Three windows, one blocked, and a doorway with a chamfered stone surround, a segmental head and a stone hood-mould, open in this wall. The upper courses of the W. wall belong to the post-fire period like the rest of the house.

The S. front (Plate 114) has a basement, two main storeys and a dormered attic and is of five bays, the middle bay slightly wider than the others. The basement corresponds in height with the stone quoin of the School House. The tall ground-floor windows have segmental arches of half bricks, with painted keystones. The first-floor windows have flat brick heads without keystones; a few inches above them is a moulded wooden cornice which returns for a short distance on each end-wall. The front door, of six panels, is sheltered by a porch, perhaps a later addition, consisting of a segmental hood on two free-standing, square wooden columns and corresponding pilasters; the columns rest on stone podia which flank the six steps leading up to the doorway. A large scroll-shaped cast-iron lamp or sign bracket projects from the W. corner of the S. front. Inside, the stairs from ground to first floor have plain balusters, presumably in replacement of an earlier balustrade, which may be represented by the Tuscan newel-post at the foot. The flight to the second floor retains turned balusters similar to those in Lime Tree House (9). The stairs which go up to the N.W. attics retain some 18th-century lattice-work balustrades.

(11) THE RECTORY, 50 yds. N.E. of the church, faces S. across the churchyard. It was built after the fire, somewhat N. of the original vicarage site (Act of Parliament, *cit.*) and has a Group (i) plan with a five-bay, two-storied S. front of blue brick headers, with red brick quoins and dressings; the flat window heads have triple keystones. The original central doorway has been removed and a window substituted, the inserted brickwork being skilfully bonded so that little trace of the former opening remains. Wings were added to N. and W. of the original block in the 19th century. An 18th-century door frame reset in the S. wall of the W. wing may be from the original front entrance. It is flanked by pilasters which are divided into two equal panels by roundels; the lower panels are reeded, those above have pendant leaf swags; the pilasters support scrolled consoles and a segmental hood.

Internally the house has been extensively altered but the stairs seem to be original, albeit reset. They are of the familiar pattern already noted at Lime Tree House (9).

(12) THE OLD HOUSE (Plate 110), on the S. side of The Close and about 200 yds. N.E. of the church, is of brick in a free English bond wherein one header course alternates with two, three or four stretcher courses. The steep hipped roof with wide spreading eaves is of gradated stone-slates for two thirds of its height and

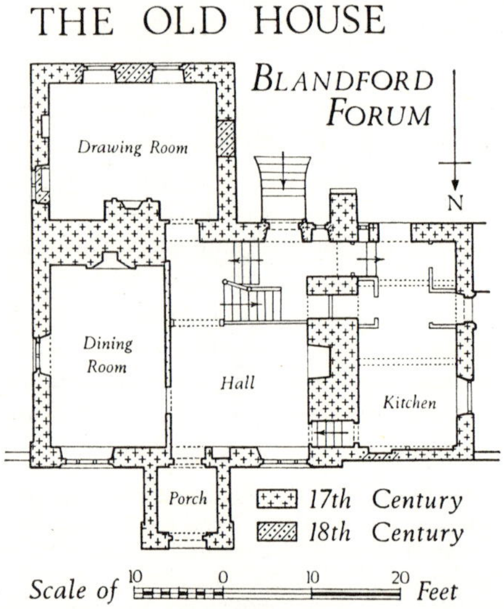

of tiles above. Although the kitchen wing appears to have been added after the walls of the main block were complete, the roofs are homogeneous and the addition must have been made while the house was still in building. The proportions of the windows, the rustication of the brickwork and the design of the roof all indicate the middle of the 17th century. In the later part of the 17th century the house belonged to Dr. Joachim Frederic Sagittary, a German, who entered Queen's College, Oxford, at the age of 17 in 1634, received his M.D. in 1661, practised medicine in Blandford and died in 1696. The house is likely to have been built by him some time between 1650 and 1670.

The house is something of an oddity and is described by Hutchins as 'an architectural graft from the "fatherland" planted by the worthy doctor on the soil of his adopted country' (I, 242). Nevertheless it has affinities with the 'artizan' style of the second half of the 17th century, exemplified in the contemporary halls of City Livery Companies, and in a number of houses of the period in the City of London and elsewhere.

The plan is L-shaped with the re-entrant angle to the S.W., and a porch of two storeys projecting from the principal front, to the N. Apart from the W. extension the porch and the rest of the N. front are symmetrical. Bold rustication is formed by recessing every fourth brick course and by setting recessed vertical bricks in the intervening courses. The rustication only occurs on N. walls; on the flanks of the porch and on the E. elevation of the main block it turns the corner and ceases in the form of a quoin. A three-course plat-band above the ground-floor window heads is continuous on all sides of the house; where rustication occurs the plat-band is surmounted by a brick roll-moulding. Above the first-floor windows is a brick cornice, with a cavetto at the bottom, a roll in the middle and a cyma at the top. Over this rests a wooden wall-plate from which project shaped eaves brackets; they are about 1½ ft. long and 4 ins. wide, except those which correspond with the main roof trusses, which are 6 ins. wide. Similar brackets form a cornice to the porch, although the porch roof is flat. The N. front of the porch has a doorway with a semicircular arch of rusticated brick voussoirs and a similar outer arch over the central portion. The central voussoir of the upper arch is truncated to leave room for a sphere, cut in brick, while the spandrels between the outer voussoirs and the plat-band are filled with cryptic emblems in cut brickwork, apparently representing a rose with three leaves (or a flaming catherine-wheel) and a heart lying on its side. Over the doorway is a niche with sill, jambs, impost and elliptical head of moulded brick; it is flanked by baluster-shaped square standards. The first-floor window immediately above the niche is of two lights with a moulded wooden surround, mullion and transom. The window-head lies immediately below the cornice, with neither arch nor lintel. The E. and W sides of the porch are of plain brick in the lower storey but they have recessed moulded panels at the level of the ornamental niche, and panels outlined with chamfered bricks at the level of the first-floor window. On each side of the porch, the N. wall of the main range has, at ground-floor level, single three-light transomed windows with details as in the two-light porch window; they are spanned immediately below the plat-band by flat brick arches, recessed at intervals to represent rusticated voussoirs. The first-floor windows are similar except that, like the porch window, their wooden surrounds support the cornice without the intervention of a lintel. Recessed aprons below the first-floor window-sills have panels corresponding with those already noted in the lateral walls of the porch.

The W. part of the N. elevation, fronting the kitchen, is set 9 ins. behind the main plane; it is traversed by a three-course plat-band in continuation of that already noted. Nevertheless this wing has three storeys in place of two and the first-floor window intersects the plat-band; it and the second-floor window are of two lights, with moulded wooden frames and mullions but without brick lintels. A corresponding opening at ground level is blocked up. At eaves level, to compensate for the set-back, the eaves brackets have an extra 9 ins. length of shank to allow one roof to cover the whole N. front. A dormer window of three lights, with a hipped roof to match the main roof, is set a little to the E. of the centre-line of the three-light windows on the W. side of the porch.

The E. front is traversed by continuations of the plat-band and cornice noted on the N. front. Near the N. end an unmoulded two-light casement window gives light to the basement. The first and second storeys have each two two-light transomed windows similar to those described, the lower pair with rusticated segmental brick heads. The S. opening in each storey is blocked up internally, but the wood surrounds and the vertical bars to which leaded glazing was formerly attached are still seen externally. On the S. front of the S. wing the plat-band and the cornice continue as before, but the original casements have been replaced on each floor by a pair of 18th-century sashed windows. A blocked window occurs on each floor in the W. wall of the S. wing. A doorway in the S. wall of the W. wing, near the re-entrant angle of the L plan, is perhaps of the 18th century but a sashed window above it appears to be modern. To the W. of these openings a stout buttress projects from the S. wall. It is of brick in four stages, with moulded and tiled weathering to the two upper stages and stone weathering to the two lower stages; it appears to be contemporary with the house. The W. part of the S. wall of the W. extension is built for a height of about 6 ft. above ground in banded brick and flint, and the same material continues in the W. elevation to within 2 ft. of the N.W. corner; above the banded masonry the W. wall is of brick with no noteworthy features. Two large chimneystacks emerge from the roof ridges; one at the intersection of the W. hips has recently been rebuilt but the other, near the middle of the S. range, appears to be original. An oblong brick flue, perhaps originally square as indicated by a vertical joint, is capped, 2 ft. above the ridge, by a bold cornice; above this rises a polygonal stack of eight unequal sides, encircled by a ring of detached terracotta shafts, one shaft at each change of plane. The shafts stand on moulded brick plinths and support rectilinear projections of the oversailing moulded brick cornice, which returns around the whole stack, breaking forward at each angle.

Inside, the house is disappointing since many original features were removed about 1900. A wooden column supporting a beam in the basement is probably of the early 19th century. The massive oak stairs to the basement are probably original; they have close strings, heavy turned balusters, square newels with ball finials and a deep rectangular handrail. The panelling of the hall is modern, and probably the chimney-piece also. The dining room has a moulded dado-rail and panelled window shutters. The wooden fireplace surround has a bolection-moulded architrave surmounted by a rococo frieze of arabesques and garlands, deeply undercut. The drawing room has fielded 18th-century panelling that probably dates from the period when the windows were altered. Two first-floor rooms have fireplaces with bolection-moulded surrounds, possibly original. The hipped roofs, visible in the attics, have massive principals running from wall-plate to ridge, with tie-beams at the base, collar-beams at attic ceiling level, and shaped king-posts rising from the collars.

(13) DALE HOUSE (Plate 112 and illustration facing p. 38), No. 79 Salisbury Street, is now the Constitutional Club. The Bastards' town plan indicates that the nucleus of the building survived the 1731 fire, and this is confirmed by the stone entrance doorway dated 1689. The original building was more than doubled in size in the first half of the 19th century by additional wings to N. and W., and it was again enlarged about 30 years later. In 1930 the entrance doorway was transferred from the E. to the S. front.

The five-bay E. front is of brick with stone dressings, and of two storeys, with a central projection comprising one bay. The lateral bays and the corners of the central bay have rusticated stone quoins. The lateral windows have flat lintels of gauged brick with stone keys; immediately over the ground-floor keystones the whole façade is traversed by a stone plat-band. The E. front is crowned by a heavy coved cornice of plaster and wood, steeply gabled over the centre bay. The central ground-floor opening originally had a stone doorway surmounted by a pulvinated frieze and a segmental pediment inscribed 1689; these now embellish the S. front. In the upper storey, the centre bay has a round-headed window with stone imposts and a keystone.

Internally the house has been entirely rearranged and no notable 17th-century feature survives. The dado and cornice of the S.E. room (the S. room of the original house) are of the 19th century. The S.W. room, *c.* 1830, has a reed-moulded plaster cornice, and the door surrounds in the entrance hall have reeded architraves with angle paterae of the same period. A wooden fireplace surround in the S.E. first-floor room is of the common late 18th-century pattern, with festoons and rosettes of *carton-pierre.*

(14) EAGLE HOUSE stands on the W. side of White Cliff Mill Street, 130 yds. from the junction with Salisbury Street. Since the architectural style suggests a date rather earlier than 1731 it seems possible that this was 'Widdow Evens dwelling house, pretty good, chimneys and part of the walls standing', as noted in Bastard's Survey Book, p. 15; but the value of £78 seems low for such a handsome Group (i) house.

The original structure consists of the usual Group (i) range with a brick E. front of five bays. Service annexes must have existed behind the main block but their extent is not known; they disappeared when the house was more than doubled in size early in the 19th century. The E. front is of vitrified blue headers with dressings of red brick; and the ends of the façade and the sides of the middle bay are accentuated by projecting pilasters outlined in red brick. The eaves have an ornate plaster cornice with modillions and leaf-and-tongue mouldings. Between the central pair of pilasters the horizontal cornice is replaced by an open pediment. The sashed windows have flat gauged red brick lintels with triple keystones. On the ground floor, the S. part of the original façade is interrupted by a late 19th-century bay window and porch. The central first-floor window has a round head with a moulded architrave and a triple keystone. The S. front has, to the E., the gabled end wall of the original block with a projecting chimneystack and, to the W., the wall of the block which was added in the first half of the 19th century and which contains the stairs, lit by a tall round-headed window. Internally the house has been much altered, first by its 19th-century remodelling and later when it was turned into offices. The former entrance hall, where the original stairs were presumably located, has been thrown into the S.E. room, which has fielded 18th-century panelling. A moulded wooden cornice follows the E., S. and W. walls but is absent from the N. wall, in the former entrance hall. The 19th-century stairs are of stone with a plain iron balustrade. Part of the original staircase connects the first floor of the E.

block with the somewhat higher first floor of the later W. wing; the wooden balusters have the usual form of Tuscan columns above vase-shaped lower sections.

The foregoing comprise the public buildings and larger private houses in the town. The descriptions of the smaller houses follow, street by street.

Bryanston Street

(15) Park House stands at the W. end of Bryanston Street, which was formerly a through road. It is of two storeys with walls that are mainly rendered; the roof is tiled, with stone-slate verges. The house represents several periods and makes no pretence at symmetry. Bastard's town plan shows it as escaping the fire of 1731, but the present outline differs greatly from that on the plan. The oldest part of the existing house is the N. wing; additions have been made to E. and S., and there is also an addition to the W. of the S. wing. The latter seems to date from the beginning of the 19th century; the E. and S. rooms are perhaps of the mid 18th century but with windows altered in the last phase; the N. wing, presumably the building shown on the Bastard plan, is of the late 17th or early 18th century but with features, such as panelling, of a later period.

(16) Bryanston Cottage, of brick in two storeys, stands on the S. side of the street with its back to the road and the S. front looking over a garden. The E. part of the S. front is symmetrical and of three bays, with a central doorway and flanking bow windows; the latter are of the mid 19th century. The central and western bays were probably built *c.* 1750 and the eastern bay seems to have been added *c.* 1820. The part of the 18th-century elevation that can be seen beside the bow window is of blue headers; in it is a flat-headed 18th-century doorway with a moulded wooden architrave. Internally, apart from the added bow windows and the E. room of *c.* 1820, the original plan is preserved. The front door opens into a square vestibule at the back of which an elliptical-headed opening leads to the staircase. To the right, a doorway with a reeded architrave opens into the E. room, passing through a thick wall which was originally external. To the left, in the staircase hall, the door to the W. room has a moulded architrave with leaf-and-tongue enrichment. The stairs have close strings, Tuscan-column newel posts and slender balusters of the usual type.

(17) House, 20 yds. E. of the foregoing, is a small two-storied building of the late 18th century with a three-bay S. front faced with mathematical tiles imitating brickwork in English bond. To the E. extends an added wing, probably of the mid 19th century but perhaps incorporating earlier service rooms. Inside, the 18th-century range contains a narrow entrance hall with a staircase and, to the W., a ground-floor room decorated with a moulded plaster cornice, with leaf-and-tongue, egg-and-dart and dentil ornament. The open-string stairs have Tuscan newel posts and three balusters to each tread, the balusters being of the column and vase pattern, but unusual in that the columns have pronounced entasis. The step spandrels are ornamented with simple scrolls.

The Close and Sheepmarket Hill

(18) House, facing N. across The Tabernacle, is planned on a difficult site with acute corners; by its style it dates from the late 18th or early 19th century. The N. front is of vitrified headers with red brick dressings and gauged red brick lintels; it is symmetrical and of three bays. The round-headed central doorway, with reeded pilasters, panelled reveals, traceried fan-light and flat hood, is flanked by square sashed windows. Three corresponding windows open in the upper storey and there are two dormer windows in the roof, which is tiled. A moulded wooden eaves cornice with modillions stops at each end against shaped brick kneelers. Inside, the plan is of Group (i), with a room on each side of the central stair hall and a third ground-floor room in a projecting wing at the back; the latter is reached through an archway beneath the upper flight of the dog-legged open-string staircase. The stairs have scroll-outlined step spandrels, Tuscan newels, two turned balusters to each step and a panelled dado. The two front ground-floor rooms have moulded dado-rails with acanthus ornament, enriched plaster cornices and reeded door cases with angle paterae. The larger room, to the W. of the entrance, has a chimneypiece with *carton-pierre* garlands. The upstairs rooms retain contemporary fireplace surrounds and decorations of more modest description.

The Rectory, *see* Monument (11).

The Old House, *see* Monument (12).

(19) Close House, on the S. side of the Close, is separated from the road by a small garden. The symmetrical five-bay two-storied N. front, with its tall windows, thin glazing bars and concealed sash-weight boxes, belongs to the end of the 18th or the beginning of the 19th century. The plan improves on the Group (i) prototype by having two back rooms as well as two front rooms on each floor, with the result that the roof has two ridges and a valley. The N. front is of red brick headers, except in the gauged brick flat window-heads, each with a white keystone. The eaves have a rich cornice with egg-and-dart mouldings, modillions and dentils; the tiled roof has three hipped dormer windows. The valley between the two roofs is concealed by a large chimneystack at the middle of each end-wall. The front door, of six fielded panels, is surrounded by a moulded architrave, above which is a frieze of *carton-pierre* garlands. Slender pilasters on each side are capped by brackets with vertical and horizontal scroll consoles, supporting an open pedimental hood. Inside, a narrow passage with a panelled dado passes between the two front rooms to the staircase hall at the rear, emerging into the hall through a semicircular archway with acanthus and leaf-and-tongue beading. The stairs have outline scroll decoration on the spandrels, two slender turned balusters to each tread and a mahogany handrail. The N.E. ground-floor room has a dado of fielded panelling with a fluted dado-rail with rosettes at intervals. The fireplace surround is very richly decorated with garlands and urns and has a highly enriched cornice in which dentils alternate with pine-cones. The plaster ceiling cornice is ornamented with swags. The N.W. room has a similar cornice, a plain dado-rail and a mid 19th-century fireplace. The S.E. room has a dado of fielded panelling and a wooden fireplace surround with a dentil frieze and a moulded cornice.

(20) Cottages, 6 and 7 Sheepmarket Hill, facing the church-yard, are a symmetrical pair of brick-fronted early 19th-century two-storied tenements, each having one room and a scullery on the ground floor, and no vestibule or service-passage. The winding staircases are beside the chimney-breasts, which are set in the side walls. A blind first-floor window recess corresponds with the coupled front doorways.

East Street

The eastern part of the street was destroyed in the fire of 1713 (Hutchins I, 216) and was spared by the fire of 1731 probably because the rebuilt houses had tiled instead of thatched roofs. Hence the houses E. of Nos. 34 and 41 (Bastard's town plan clearly marks the extent of the second fire) are potentially as early as 1713; nevertheless it is clear that many of them were rebuilt later.

North side:—

(21) Houses, Nos. 6 and 8, near the E. end of the street, are small, late 18th-century Group (iv) dwellings, of two storeys with dormer-windowed attics under tiled roofs (Plate 115). The common service-passage leads to accommodation that was originally a third dwelling. The S. front is of red and blue bricks, partly in Flemish, partly in English and partly in header bond. Internally, the stairs of No. 6 have an open string with scroll spandrels, turned balusters and square newel-posts. No. 8 has a winding stair, and a small area of fielded panelling in the back room.

(22) Houses, Nos. 14 and 16, of two storeys with a rendered S. front, are probably of the early 18th century but have been modernised internally.

(23) Houses, Nos. 18 and 20, of two storeys with a rendered S. front, have Group (iv) plans and are probably of early 18th-century origin but altered in the 19th century when an additional range of dwellings was built at the rear of No. 18. The entrance to the common service-passage has a gabled hood on scrolled brackets.

(24) Houses, Nos. 22 and 24, of two storeys, have a nearly symmetrical three-bay S. front, faced with mathematical tiles. The entrance to the common service-passage has a pedimental hood on foliate brackets. The fireplace in a ground-floor room of No. 22 has a panelled overmantel flanked by scroll-shaped cheek-pieces.

(25) House, No. 26, a two-storied dwelling with attics and cellar, is a humble version of the Group (i) plan, not isolated, and having a brick S. front of only three bays. A two-storied N. wing behind the E. part of the S. range has flush-framed sashed windows with heavy glazing bars and is probably earlier than the front range. The stairs have been renewed at ground-floor level but the upper flight has original turned balusters and moulded newels. A small passage room in the N. wing, opening off the staircase landing and lit by one of the early sashed windows, has a coved plaster ceiling with ornate rococo decoration of serpentine acanthus foliage.

(26) Lyston House, No. 32 East Street, is a five-bay two-storied Group (i) house. Bastard's town plan shows that the site was spared by the fire of 1731 but the building has the character of the post-fire period and is likely to have been rebuilt, probably before 1750. The Flemish-bond brick façade has pilasters at each end and a slightly projecting centre bay containing the doorway. A plat-band traverses the lateral parts of the façade at first-floor level, stopping against the central feature but carried across the terminal pilasters; the façade is crowned by a cornice with fluted modillions and leaf-and-tongue ornament. Over this rises the tiled roof, with two hipped dormer windows. The nine sashed windows of the S. front are uniform, each with a flat lintel of gauged bricks in which the three middle bricks project to form a key, in this case not rendered. The pedimented door hood seems to be of the 19th century, perhaps replacing one more elaborate. Internally, the hall contains a wooden open-string staircase with the usual Tuscan newel post and two balusters to each tread; the staircase wall has a dado with fielded panels and the step spandrels have outline scrolls. The front room (Plate 116) on the W. of the hall has fielded panelling from floor to ceiling, with a moulded dado-rail. Cross-beams with guilloche ornament divide the ceiling into four compartments, each with rococo enrichment. The fireplace, to the W., has an eared marble surround outlined in egg-and-dart moulding and flanked by scrolled cheek-pieces; the frieze has pendant acanthus buds flanking a flower festoon over which rises a pediment. The overmantel has a panel of Greek-key ornament culminating in a cherub head with scrolls; on each side are pendant festoons of flowers and ribbons hanging from shells.

(27) House, No. 34, now a shop, adjoins (26) and continues the plinth and cornice. The lower storey has been replaced by modern shop fittings but the S. front on the first floor retains three segmental-headed sashed windows. The E. bay is in the same plane as (26) but the two W. bays are set forward.

(28) Cottages, Nos. 36 and 38, are of Group (iv), in two storeys with brick fronts; they are of the late 18th century.

(29) House and Shop, No. 40, two-storied with a rough-cast front, is of the late 18th or early 19th century. The glazing-bars of the shop-window and door have the form of minute columns supporting elliptical arches.

South side:—

(30) Houses, Nos. 1 and 3, are an asymmetrical pair, of two storeys, with rendered walls and tiled roofs; they were built probably soon after 1713. No. 1 marks the beginning of the S. side of East Street and has its main façade facing E.; a side entrance to No. 1 and the front-door of No. 3 open side by side in the N. front. The E. front has a hipped roof with a dormer window while, to the left, a subsidiary wing extends southwards, first in two storeys and then in one. The main part of the elevation has a moulded and coved eaves cornice. The front doorway, in the S. part of the main E. front, has a moulded architrave and fluted side pilasters terminating in scrolled consoles, upon which rests a segmental hood; the tympanum is ornamented with flower wreaths. A large sashed window with exposed weight-boxes opens to the N. of the doorway and a similar window occurs to the S. in the slightly recessed subsidiary wing. Smaller openings on the first floor approximately correspond with those below. Unlike the E. front, the N. front has a plat-band; the cornice is continuous. On the ground floor, the N. front has a big sashed window to the E., then two uniform doorways followed by two more windows; the doorways have moulded architraves, panelled reveals and soffits, and flat hoods on scroll brackets. On the first floor are four uniform sashed windows, irregularly spaced, two to each house.

(31) Eastway House, No. 5, is in the part of the street which was spared by the 1731 fire, but Bastard's town plan shows a building close to the street whereas the present house is set appreciably back from the building line; hence the house is probably of the post-fire period. The main doorcase and the shaped parapet and urns of the N. front are perhaps mid 18th-century additions to a façade of *c.* 1735. The plan is two rooms deep and is covered with a double roof, but the rear drawing-room may be another addition of *c.* 1750; without it the plan would be typical of Group (i): a straight front range with a kitchen wing at the rear. The N. front (Plate 113) shows interesting rococo tendencies and the rococo plasterwork of the interior is noteworthy.

The symmetrical N. front is of five closely spaced bays and has a central doorway flanked by pairs of flat-headed sashed windows, with five similar windows on the first floor and a round-headed attic window centrally above. The ground and first-floor windows have gauged brick flat arches punctuated by projecting keystones; the central first-floor window is accentuated by a curvilinear soffit. Plat-bands are set at first and attic floor levels; a brick parapet rises above the upper plat-band and, over the three middle bays, develops into a pediment with ramped abutments and three ornamental urns. The attic window which opens in the pediment has plain impost blocks and a keystone. The central doorway, on the ground floor, has a round head with a fanlight and a lion-mask keystone; it is flanked by wooden Ionic pilasters supporting a moulded entablature and pediment. Since the first-floor plat-band has been rather carelessly hacked away to make room for the apex of this pediment it seems that the doorcase may be secondary; it is, moreover, rather cramped between the flanking windows. The S. front is rendered and asymmetrical. On the ground floor the drawing-room has a three-light Venetian window; the first floor has a similar window set between two flat-headed openings, and the attic storey has a single dormer window.

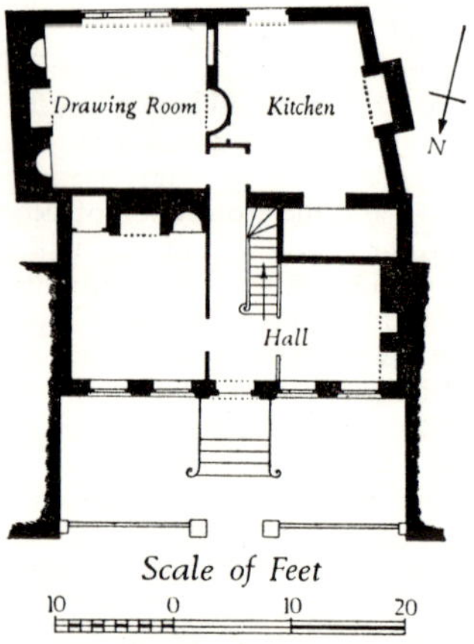

EASTWAY HOUSE
No. 5 EAST STREET

Inside, the front door opens into a passage containing the stairs, with a room on each side, but the cornice suggests that the E. room originally was not divided from the passage. The open-string stairs have fluted Tuscan newel posts and the usual balusters of small columns above vases. The step spandrels are enriched with outline scrolls. The ceiling of the W. room is decorated with a central mask surrounded by radiant beams and a foliate wreath, perhaps 19th-century work. The drawing-room, at the rear of the house, has elaborate rococo decorations of *c.* 1750. The fireplace, on the E. wall (Plate 117), has a shaped marble surround outlined with egg-and-dart and leaf mouldings, and surmounted by a roundel of *amorini* in a wreath of flowers and fruit; above is a scrolled and shaped mantelshelf and a highly enriched plaster overmantel, with C-scrolls and flower festoons enclosing an oval panel. On each side of the fireplace is a niche with a round head decorated with a mask in an aureole of acanthus leaves. The W. wall of the room has two doorways, one of them false, flanking a niche with a marble shelf on which rests a gadrooned marble vase; over the vase the niche is embellished with waterfowl and plants in relief; over the niche-head are delicate grape festoons. The coved cornice is enriched with rococo ornament and the ceiling is bordered with flower wreaths and arabesques; at the centre three flying doves bear a wreath of flowers.

(32) Houses, Nos. 7 to 17, are a row of paired Group (iv) houses. Although built individually they all date from the first quarter of the 18th century; all are of two storeys with dormer-windowed attics. Nos. 15 and 17 are higher and have larger windows than the others, and an attempt is made to equalise the two tenements of each pair by setting the service-passage walls a little to the left of the centre-line (*see* plan on p. 19). The original entrances from the service-passages have been replaced by 19th-century street doorways, and the ground-floor windows have been modernised.

(33) Houses and Shops, Nos. 21 to 39, are small early 18th-century houses of two storeys with tiled roofs, mostly with dormer windows; all are of brick but some have rendered fronts. Most of the houses were originally of Group (iv) although they have now been modified. All the shop-fronts are of the 19th century or later but the first-floor elevations have 18th-century sashed windows and some have coved eaves cornices.

(34) Stour House, No. 41, occupies the site of the most easterly building in the street to be destroyed in the 1731 fire (Bastard's town plan). The N. range has a Group (i) plan, albeit of four bays. On the E. it is separated from the next house by a narrow driveway; on the W. it is flanked by Common Lane, which goes down to the river. The two-storied N. front, of Flemish-bonded brickwork, has a plaster modillion cornice with egg-and-dart and leaf-and-tongue mouldings. On the ground floor the front doorway is placed to the W. of the centre line, with two sashed windows to the E. and one to the W.; the first floor has four openings. All windows have gauged brick lintels punctuated by keystones. The doorway has an eared architrave flanked by plain uprights which develop at the top into double console brackets with scale and foliate enrichment; these support a flat, lead-covered hood, panelled on the underside. The original range, only one room thick, is joined at the W. end to a S. wing of *c.* 1800 containing the stairs; these are lit by a tall round-headed W. window. The S. wing presumably takes the place of an earlier service wing.

The front door opens into a passage between the dining-room on the left and the study on the right. At the S. end of the passage an archway with moulded architrave and keystone leads into the early 19th-century stair hall, in which an 18th-century staircase has been reset; it has the usual Tuscan newel posts and three balusters to each step. The spandrels have carved scrolls with leaf enrichment and the moulded handrail ends at the bottom in a horizontal volute. The dining-room has a panelled dado and a rich plaster cornice; the fireplace has an eared marble surround framed in wooden leaf-and-tongue moulding and flanked by deeply fretted acanthus cheek-pieces; the mantelshelf rests on paired acanthus consoles between which is a frieze of acorn, oak and acanthus sprays, in high relief, flanking a central vase. The drawing-room, in the S. wing, has a fireplace surround recently transferred from the first floor; it is of carved wood with flowered and scrolled cheek-pieces, deeply carved foliate arabesques on the frieze and a moulded cornice of cable and stylised foliage. The late 18th-century fireplace surround in the study has recently been brought from elsewhere.

(35) House, No. 45, appears to be a mid 18th-century structure although extensively rebuilt. Apart from the gauged brick lintels with triple keystones, the three-storied N. front is entirely of header bricks. The S. elevation contains two large segmental-headed Venetian windows on the ground floor, and a wrought-iron balcony on stone brackets on the first floor.

(36) House, Nos. 47, 49, was built soon after 1731 and is

two-storied, with a five-bay N. front of blue headers with red brick dressings to the window openings. The first-floor windows have label-shaped aprons. The gauged brick lintels have triple keystones and the eaves have a coved plaster cornice that returns on itself at each end inside the width of the façade. On the ground floor the three W. bays are obliterated by a mid 19th-century shop-front. It is likely that the original entrance to the house was in the central bay and that there were two windows on each side; the two eastern openings still exist but one of them has now become a doorway.

(37) HOUSES, pair, No. 51, are exceptionally small and low Group (iv) houses, probably built soon after 1731. The N. front is rendered and the shop-fronts are modern. The first-floor windows have 19th-century sashes in original sash-boxes.

(38) THE STAR INN, although remodelled at the end of the 19th century, contains elements of an 18th-century building.

The elevations of Monuments (39) to (44) appear in the illustration facing p. 32. Unless otherwise stated, the façades are of blue brick with red brick dressings.

(39) HOUSE, No. 55, is of the mid 18th century and in its original form was probably of Group (ii); the plan has now been obliterated by a modern shop. The E. wall, flanking the entry to an adjacent yard, is of banded rubble and flint and may be a survival from before the fire of 1731.

(40) HOUSES, Nos. 57 and 59, are a pair of mid 18th-century Group (iv) houses. The first-floor bay window of No. 57 is a later addition and the shop fronts are modern.

(41) HOUSE, No. 61, now two shops, was originally a three-storied residence representing Group (iii) in a large form; it was probably built soon after 1731. Although the ground-floor shops are modern, the carriage-way to the E. is original. The main entrance of the house, in the W. wall of the carriage-way, opens into a transverse corridor behind the front room. The stairs are at the W. end of the corridor; they have open strings and foliate scrolls on the step spandrels; the newels and balusters are of the usual Tuscan pattern. On the first floor the two front rooms have moulded cornices, and one contains a late 18th-century *carton-pierre* fireplace surround.

(42) HOUSES, Nos. 63 and 65, are a pair of mid 18th-century Group (iv) houses.

(43) HOUSES, Nos. 67 and 69, are a pair of 18th-century Group (iv) houses with the unusual feature of a central chimneystack bridging the common service-passage. The doorways on each side of the passage now give access to stairs leading directly to first-floor flats but this is probably the result of 19th-century remodelling. The street front has modern shops on the ground floor, sashed windows on the first floor and gabled attic dormers in a mansard roof.

(44) HOUSE, Nos. 71, 73, is now four-storied but it was originally of two storeys. The ground floor has been completely obliterated by a modern shop; the first floor is lit by two sashed windows and a large wooden bay window. The latter must be original, otherwise the red brick jamb of a former sashed window would be seen beside it. The moulded plat-band above the first-floor windows is probably part of an original eaves cornice and the two upper storeys are 19th-century reproductions of the first floor. Internally, the remains of an 18th-century staircase on the top storey have presumably been moved up from their original position.

For No. 75 East Street, *see* Monument (45).

THE MARKET PLACE

South side:—

The following description of the Market Place (Plate 97) begins with No. 26, which is the W. half of No. 75 East Street. The elevations of Monuments (45) to (52) appear in the illustration facing p. 32. As before, façades are of blue brick with red brick dressings unless described otherwise.

(45) HOUSES, Nos. 26 The Market Place and 75 East Street (Plate 108), were originally three houses. No. 75 was John Bastard's own house, which he rebuilt for £704 10s. after the fire. No. 26 was two houses, built by Bastard for £420 and leased to Mr. Price, apothecary, and Mr. Morgan, brazier; the ground belonged to Williams's Charity. These facts are confirmed in the Survey Book: '. . . the house they lived in, which was the house belonging to Mr. Williamses charoty on the south side the street opposet the church'; and later in the same book: 'Memorandum. Before the fier we had but one of the houses on Williamses charoty land . . . that on the east side of the gate, where we lived. . . . To incurage us to build the other two houses they gave us a lease for 90 years. . . .'

The three houses almost certainly date from the 1730s. They resemble the nearby Red Lion Inn (47) in having a central carriage-way leading through to a back yard and, in the upper storeys of the N. front, two ornamental pilasters rising above the carriage-way to support an open pediment. Today there are shop fronts on each side of the archway. The W. shop is of the late 19th century; that to the E. is modern. Photographs taken before 1937 show the E. part of the N. front with a rendered ground storey with two sashed windows on the left and, next to the carriage-way, an 18th-century doorway, with pediment, pilasters and panelled reveals. In the upper part of the façade red bricks in Flemish bond are used for the lateral wings while the central feature, between the pilasters, is of blue headers. The ends of the façade have rusticated quoins of painted plaster. The Corinthian caps of the two pilasters have a single tier of acanthus leaves and up-growing corner volutes, in-turned and joined together by delicately moulded, individually designed swags of fruit and flowers. The rear of the building has no formal design; most of the window openings have segmental brick heads and the walls are capped by brick dentil cornices. The carriage-way, about 21 ft. long, leads to an irregular yard flanked by the rear wings of the building.

Inside, the disposition of the staircases confirms that the building was originally three separate houses, all of Group (iii), the E. house large and richly appointed, the others more modest. The central room on the first floor belonged to one of the W. houses while that of the second floor may have been part of the E. house. In John Bastard's house, the doorway and ground-floor windows of the N. front, which perished in 1937, opened into a vestibule and a large room, of which only the plaster ceilings remain. The ceiling of the room is divided into six compartments by one longitudinal and two transverse beams, all decorated with flower scrolls on the sides and soffits and with rosettes at the intersections. Behind this room the house is traversed from side to side by a corridor, 7 ft. wide, originally entered through a doorway from the carriage-way, now blocked. A transverse arch divides the corridor into two equal parts; the inner part contains the stairs, with balusters of the usual Tuscan column pattern, a fist-shaped lower terminal to the handrail, carved and scrolled step spandrels and a panelled dado. A doorway on the landing at the top of the first flight of stairs leads to a richly decorated mezzanine apartment (Plate 116) in the rear wing, lit by two sashed windows on the W. Above a plain dado the walls have 18th-century wooden panelling with raised fields surrounded by leaf-and-dart mouldings. Above is a plaster frieze composed of heavy swags of oak leaves and acorns, alternating with human masks on pendant drapery; the cornice is similar to that of the N. front. The modelled ceiling has an octagonal centre panel surrounded by oblong panels with acanthus *rinceaux* (Plate 107); each corner has a chaplet of foliage enclosing a bust in low relief; intervening spaces are embellished with rococo arabesques and *amorini*. The fireplace, at the N. end of the room, has a moulded and mitred architrave and a rich overmantel composed of panelled pilasters capped with scrolled brackets and flanked with pendant drapery and tassels; above is an open pediment. The door from the staircase, on the E. side of the fireplace, has fielded panels outlined with leaf-and-tongue mouldings; the two top panels are decorated with roundels. The enriched architrave is surmounted by an entablature, above which is an oblong recess. The matching doorway on the other side of the fireplace opens into a small cupboard. Facing the fireplace at the S. end of the room is another and more splendidly decorated doorway; it leads to nothing but a blank wall and appears always to have done so.

In No. 26 the ground floor is now a single office, but the plan of the upper storeys shows that it was originally two tenements, divided by a N.–S. party wall; the E. tenement seems to have been entered from the S. side, the W. from the N. Each tenement has its own staircase, with newel posts and balustrades of the common Tuscan column form. In the E. tenement, the N. first-floor room has a dado-rail on which the fascia is enriched with interlacing ornament. The door has an eared architrave with paterae in the ears, and the fireplace surround has a frieze of *rinceaux*. The rear room has a zone of fielded panelling below the dado-rail, a simple fireplace and a moulded plaster cornice. The W. tenement has a fireplace with reeded pilasters and frieze.

(46) HOUSE, Nos. 24 and 22, now two tenements but originally one, is of the late 18th century. A service-passage to the E. leads to a back yard, flanked by 19th-century outbuildings.

(47) THE RED LION INN, Nos. 20 and 18 (Plate 108), now converted into dwellings and a warehouse, appears on stylistic grounds to date from soon after the fire. It resembles (45) in having a symmetrical N. front of three storeys and five bays, with a carriage-way flanked by shops on the ground floor, and a pedimented centre bay flanked by Corinthian pilasters in the first and second storeys.

Although the arrangement of the main features is similar to that of (45) the architectural composition is more advanced. The various elements are effectively disposed and the freedom of the baroque style is exploited with restraint and ability.

Above the carriage-way the principal feature of the N. front is a pair of pilasters rising through two storeys to support an open pediment in which is displayed the inn sign, a heraldic lion in relief with a scroll in its forepaws, backed by an ornate plaster cartouche. The pilasters have Corinthian capitals with reversed volutes and pendant acanthus foliage. The open pediment and cornice are elaborately modelled, with rosettes between foliate modillions and a leaf-and-tongue moulding below the corona. The S. elevation is of English-bond brickwork and has segmental-headed sash windows, except in the W. part where a wooden bay window has been added on the first and second storeys; the wall is capped by a brick dentil cornice. Inside, the building has been greatly altered. The inn was converted into three houses before 1802 (*Salisbury Journal*, Feb. 15th) and the only remains of original decoration are a moulded plaster cornice in the N.E. first-floor room and a Tuscan-column stair balustrade in the W. part of the building.

The present *Red Lion Inn* stands at the rear of No. 20; it has a dentil cornice as on the back elevation of the main building, and gauged brick window lintels as on the N. front. The front wall, facing E., originally had in its S. part a central doorway with two windows on each side; but the doorway was widened, the two southern windows were rebuilt and one of the northern windows was obliterated in the 19th century, leaving only one original window intact. Of the five symmetrically disposed first-floor windows one is now blocked. A first-floor room contains a fireplace of about 1750.

(48) HOUSE, No. 16, has a late 18th-century N. front of two bays, with segmental-headed sashed windows. A pair of Greek Doric columns incorporated in the modern shop-front may be of the early 19th century. The interior was remodelled in the late 19th century but the staircase from the first to the second floor is probably of the 18th century.

(49) HOUSE AND SHOP, No. 14, has a mid 19th-century shop front but the two upper storeys are probably of the early post-fire period. A brick plat-band marks the second floor and the façade is capped by a moulded cornice of red brick. The eight uniform sashed windows have segmental heads with triple keystones; in each storey the E. window is set a little apart from the other three. The interior was completely remodelled in the 19th century.

(50) HOUSES, three adjoining, comprise a pair of houses, now No. 12 fronting the Market Place, and a third house, No. 10, in an alley to the S. Each tenement of No. 12 has a plan that may originally have been a simple version of Group (ii). The ground-floor shop-front is modern; above, a deep plat-band supports three Tuscan pilasters, the middle one marking the party wall between the two tenements and the outer ones standing close to the extremities of the dual façade. Framed by the pilasters each tenement has, on the first and second floors, two uniform sashed windows with heavy glazing bars and exposed weight boxes. A moulded string-course passes across each tenement at second-floor level, stopping before it reaches the pilasters. To the W. of the façade a first-floor extension of the W. tenement is built out above a carriage-way; it is lit by a wooden bow window of the early 19th century; above it is a dormer-windowed attic. Although the two houses have now been thrown into one, two staircases still exist in the upper storeys; they have rectangular newel posts and Tuscan-column balusters. The first-floor room in the E. house is lined from floor to ceiling with fielded panelling. The two houses share a central chimney-stack.

No. 10 stands in an alley at the back of No. 12 and is probably of the late 18th century. It appears originally to have been a Group (i) house with a central doorway flanked on each side

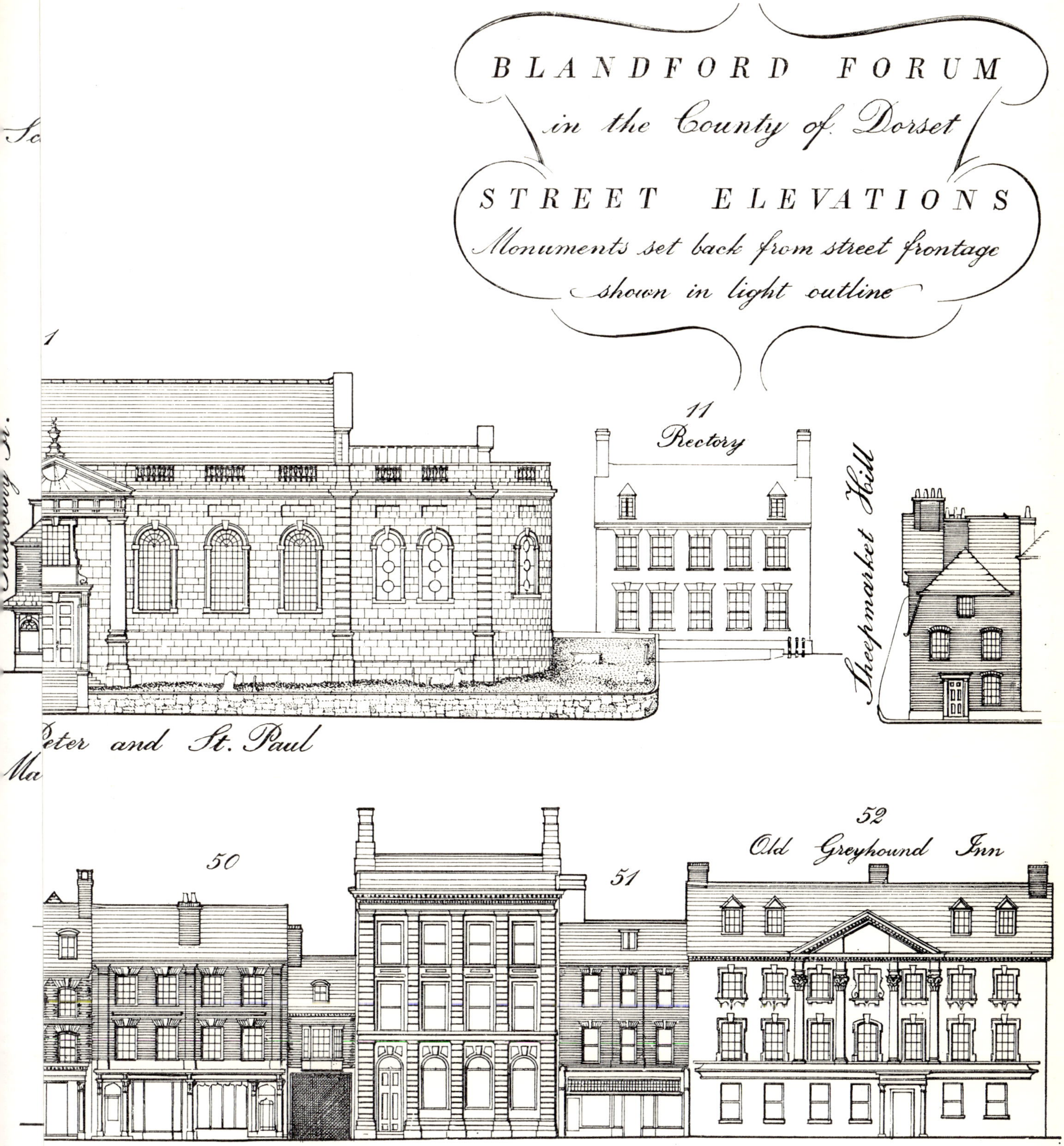

Original survey by A. T. Phillips, 1943–4, now in N.M.R., revised and redrawn by B. Marriott, 1966.

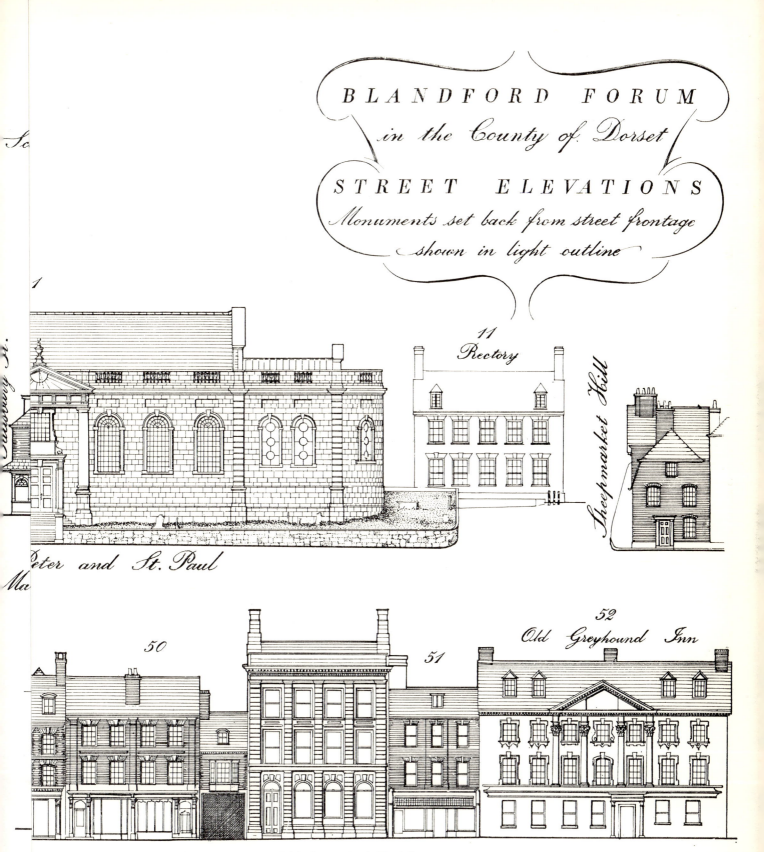

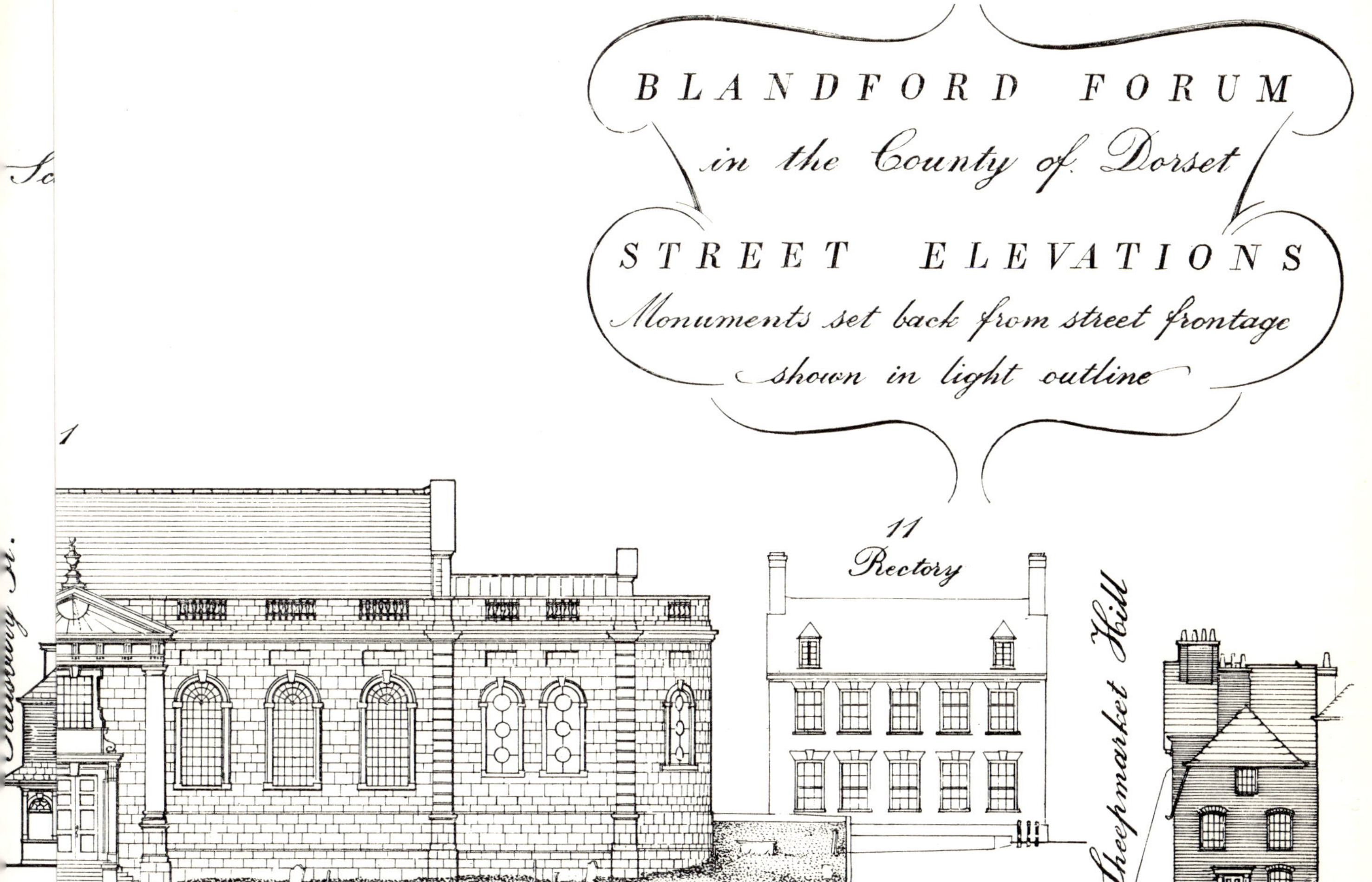

Original survey by A. T. Phillips, 1943-4, now in N.M.R., revised and redrawn by B. Marriott, 1966.

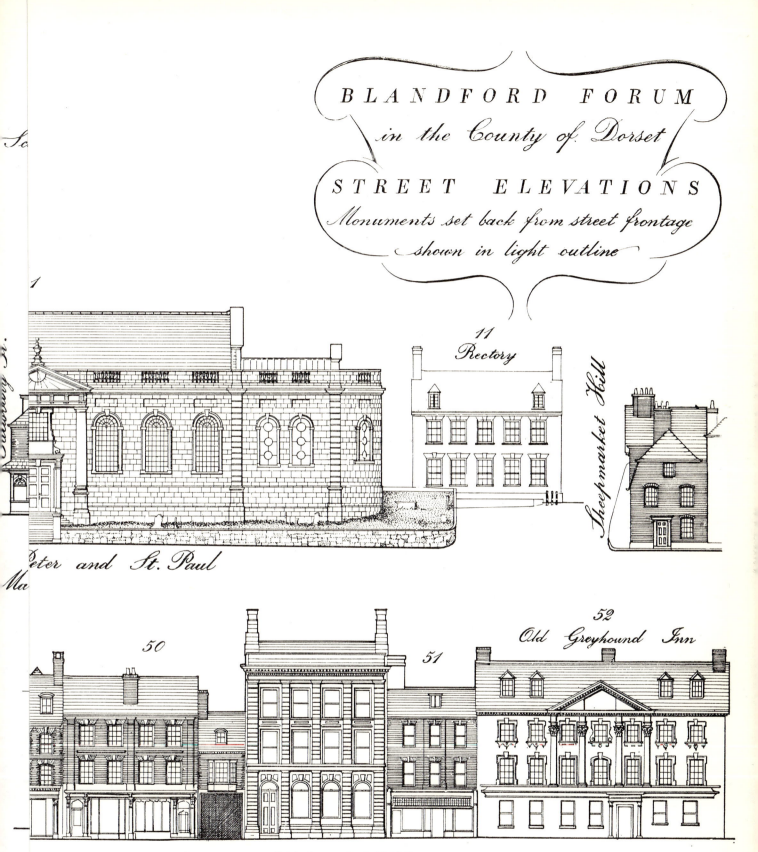

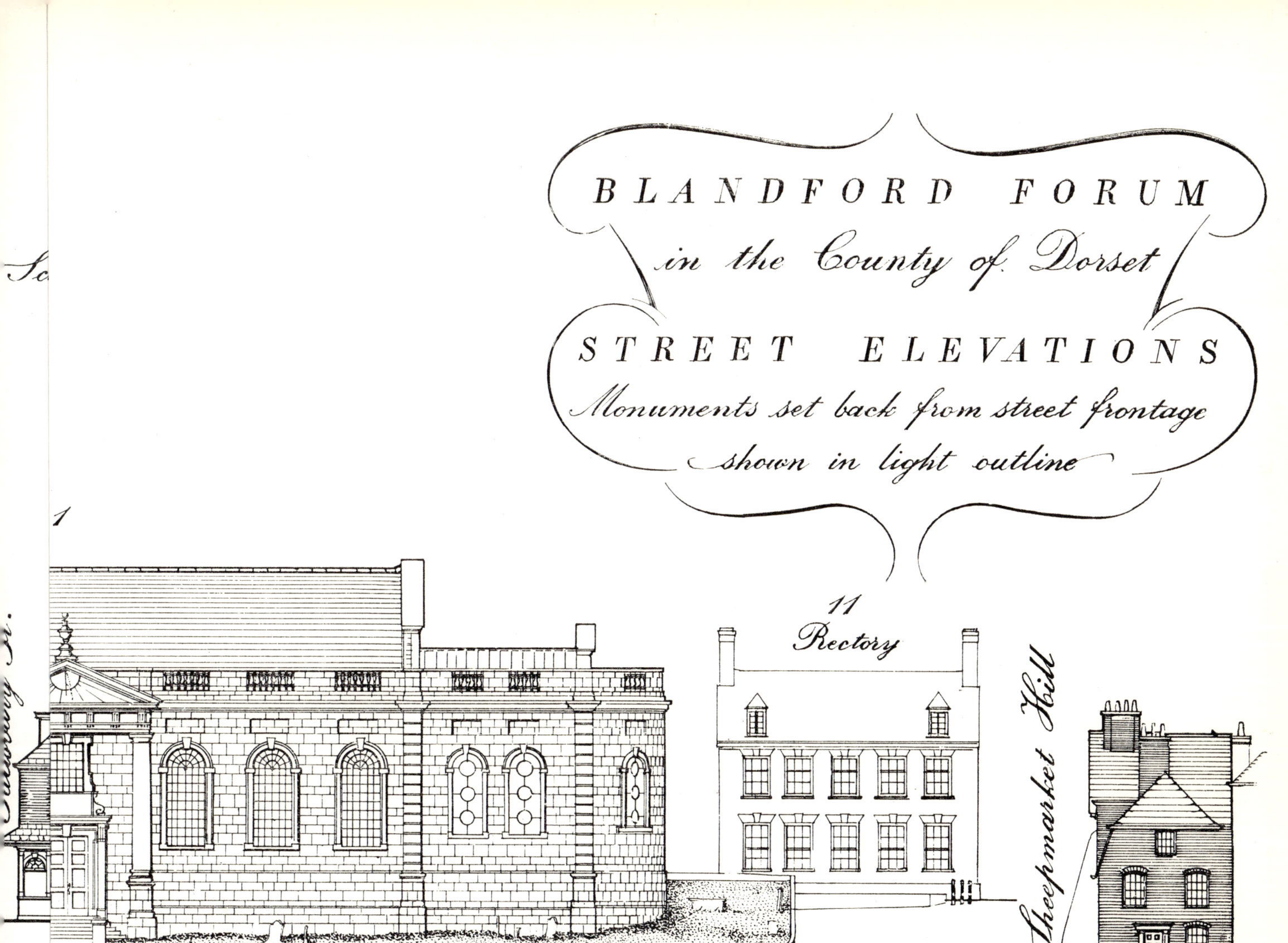

Original survey by A. T. Phillips, 1943-4, now in N.M.R., revised and redrawn by B. Marriott, 1966.

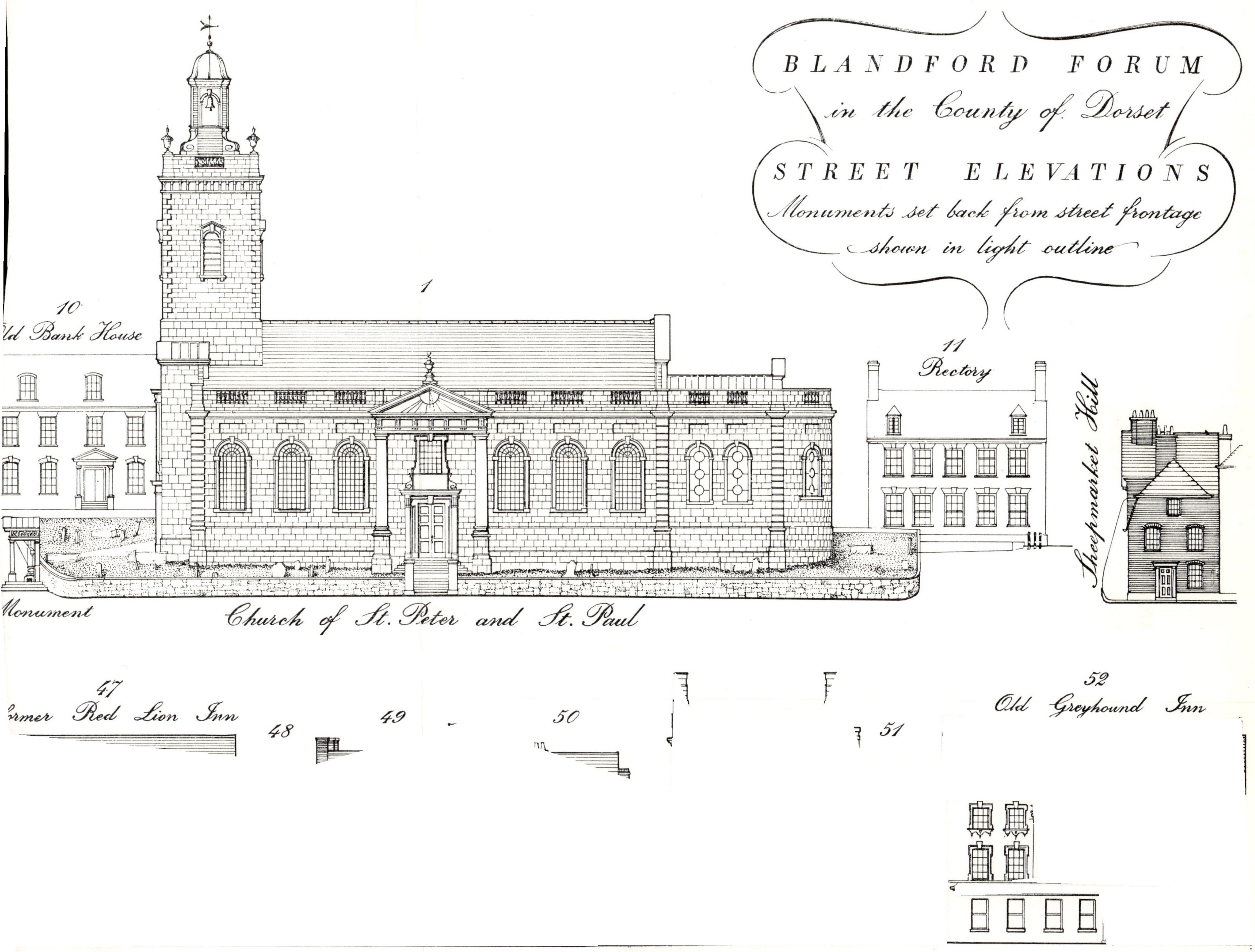

Original survey by A. T. Phillips, 1943-4, now in N.M.R., revised and redrawn by B. Marriott, 1966.

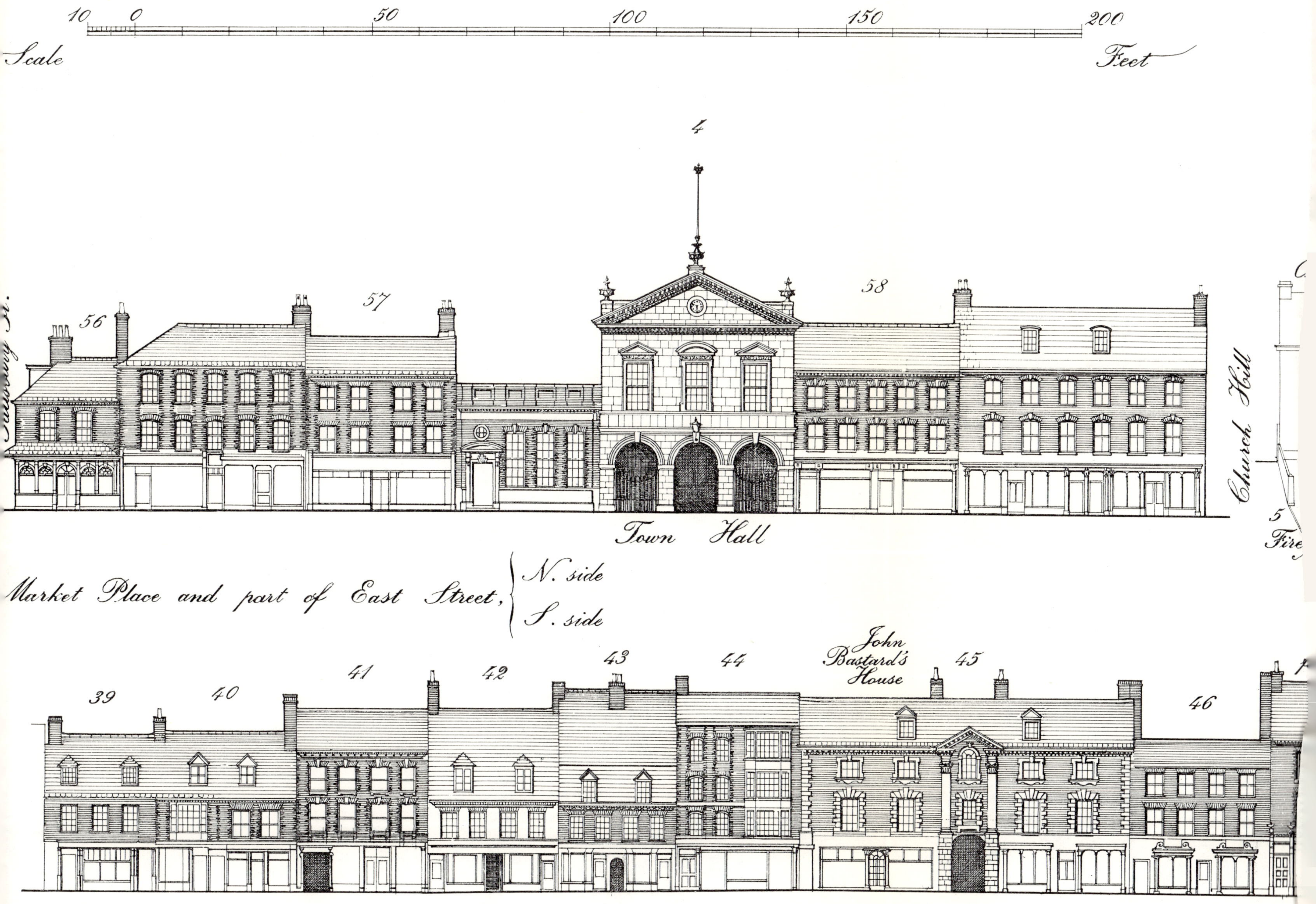
10 0 50 100 150 200
Scale
Feet
4
56
57
58
Salisbury St.
Church Hill
5
Fire
Town Hall
Market Place and part of East Street, N. side
S. side
39
40
41
42
43
44
John Bastard's House
45
46

2/33

by two sashed windows, with five sashed windows above. The doorway still exists, with a segmental hood on carved scroll consoles, and the five first-floor openings survive although only one retains the original sashes. On the ground floor, the windows N. of the doorway have been blocked up and replaced by an early 19th-century Venetian window; to the S. is a modern bay window. The interior has nothing noteworthy.

(51) HOUSE, No. 4, has a N. front of dark red brick with lighter red brick quoins; the centre bay is set a little forward of the others. The ground-floor shop is modern but the upper storeys of the façade are probably of the 18th century. The interior has been entirely altered.

(52) THE OLD GREYHOUND INN (Plate 111), now a bank, stands on the S. side of the Market Place at the beginning of West Street. It was built soon after the fire of 1731 and is of three storeys; the N. front is stuccoed, with lavish details of the Corinthian order. Internally the ground floor has been altered beyond recovery but the first and second floors retain much that is original.

As with monuments (45) and (47) the façade of the former Greyhound Inn is a noteworthy example of provincial urban street architecture in the English Baroque style. It is the only post-fire façade in Blandford to be wholly rendered in stucco. The Bastard brothers owned the inn at the time of the fire and had recently refronted it (Bastard's Survey Book, D.C.R.O.); presumably they were responsible for the rebuilding.

Although the N. front is in other respects symmetrical, the main doorway is set to the right of the centre-line with two windows to the W. and four windows, slightly lower, to the E.; only the three easternmost ground-floor openings correspond with the regularly spaced fenestration above. The doorway is sheltered by a porch carried on two free-standing Doric columns, with pilaster responds on each side of the opening. Licence to build the porch was granted in 1812 (Corporation Memorandum Book) and it is likely that the two ground-floor windows to the W. were modified at the same time, for they are asymmetrical, and without the porch the façade would be seriously out of balance. At the level of the porch entablature the façade is traversed by a coved fascia with leaded weathering which acts as a base for the symmetrical composition above; early prints show similar projections on many house fronts in the Market Place. The two upper storeys are each of seven bays, the three central bays, with plain Corinthian pilasters and a pediment, forming a tetrastyle centrepiece. The architrave and the frieze are interrupted between the columns to allow height for the second-floor windows but the modillion cornice is continuous. The pediment has a recessed panel, now empty but formerly containing the sign of the Greyhound. The six windows under the pediment have narrower and richer mouldings than those of the lateral bays; the middle first-floor window differs from the others in having a segmental head, and the window above it is enriched with scrolled cheek pieces and with a mask on the apron below the sill.

The S. elevation is rendered up to first-floor level and of English-bond brickwork above. The W. part projects about 3 ft. to the S. and contains two sashed windows on each floor, those of the ground floor being round-headed. The other windows have segmental heads.

Inside, the room to the right of the main entrance has a moulded cornice, following the walls and returning along a longitudinal centre beam. The window reveals have early 19th-century reeded architraves and the fireplace has a moulded wooden surround; segmental-headed recesses on each side of the chimney-breast probably represent former windows. The open-string stairs have wooden balustrades with Tuscan newel posts, balusters of the usual Tuscan pattern, and a moulded handrail ending in a volute. The end of each step is decorated with a simple scroll in outline. On the first floor, overlooking the Market Place, are two large rooms each with three windows, and a small E. chamber with one window. The W. room (27 ft. by 16 ft.) has a dado with fielded panelling, and a fireplace with a moulded architrave and a panelled overmantel with flat cheek-pieces. The ceiling is divided by transverse beams into four compartments each subdivided by plaster mouldings into three panels, the central one shaped, the others oblong. The adjoining room (22 ft. by 14 ft.) has a simpler panelled dado, and a wooden fireplace surround, with mantelshelf and pedimented overmantel less elaborate than those of the W. room. The small E. chamber has a reeded fireplace surround with corner roundels. The second-floor rooms have early 19th-century basket grates.

The building at the rear, which is now called the *Greyhound Inn*, was presumably an annex of the original inn; perhaps the kitchens or tap-room. It appears to be mentioned in Bastard's Survey Book; 'at the Greyhound Inn, all the long back building thats cellared and arch'd under and the front, 1734, cost £787'. The W. front has six bays and is of two storeys with a basement, and with an attic in a mansard roof. The main floor is raised six steps above ground level, allowing for a half-underground cellar that is entered through low doorways. On the main floor are two wide doorways, symmetrically set in the façade so that a segmental-headed window opens on either side of each doorway. The first floor has six uniform sashed windows, corresponding with the openings below. At the eaves is a wooden dentil cornice over a plain fascia board.

West side:—

The elevations of Monuments (53) to (55) appear in the illustration facing p. 38.

(53) HOUSE, No. 1 The Market Place, has a modern shop in the ground floor but, above, it retains the two upper storeys of a small but distinguished mid 18th-century Group (ii) town house. The N. and S. corners of the façade have French quoins of painted plaster; between these each storey has three sashed windows, the central windows being set in a slightly projecting bay which is further accentuated by finely coursed red brickwork in contrast to the blue headers of the lateral bays. The façade is crowned by a modillion cornice which breaks forward at the central bay and is capped by a pediment. Internally, the ground-floor plan has perished as completely as the lower third of the façade; the stairs have been transferred to a wing at the rear. There appears originally to have been a service-passage to the W. The front room on the first floor is panelled to the ceiling with fielded panelling, evidently not *in situ* but possibly brought up from the ground floor. The fireplace has a moulded architrave and a panelled overmantel with a volute pediment. The stairs to the second floor have an open string and Tuscan-column balusters.

(54) HOUSES, Nos. 3 and 5, seem originally to have been two uniform Group (ii) houses, each of three storeys and three bays. Although the brick coursing does not run through, the sills and lintels of each storey are at the same level in the two houses, all windows have similar triple keystones and each house has a similar but discontinuous cornice, with dentils and

modillions. Internally No. 3 has been completely gutted; in No. 5 the stairs from the ground to the first floor have been moved but the upper flights remain *in situ* and have details resembling those of (53). Two rooms retain 18th-century fireplace surrounds.

(55) House, No. 7, at the beginning of Salisbury Street, is of two storeys. The ground floor is modern but the first floor has a header-bonded brick façade with three sashed windows, and a fourth, smaller window to the N., above a carriageway. In the course of recent repairs a tile scratched with the date 1734 was discovered; this is likely to be the year when the house was built.

North side:—

The elevations of Monuments (56) to (58) appear in the illustrations facing pp. 32 and 38.

(56) Shop, No. 9, at the corner of Salisbury Street, is of two storeys with cellars and attics and was built probably in the late 18th century. The shop-front seems to be original and consists of six sturdy plaster-faced piers, rectangular in plan, standing on a low brick plinth and supporting, at first-floor level, a wide coved pentice which continues on the W. front, in Salisbury Street. The round-headed shop-window openings are traversed by horizontal architraves enriched with reeding and paterae, above which are beaded fanlights. The upper storey has two sashed windows with segmental rubbed brick arches; the wall is capped by a simple dentil cornice. The W. front is similar; it has one window on the first floor, and three shop windows below; to the N. are two lower bays, continuous with the adjoining house (62).

(57) Shops, Nos. 13 and 15, each have two flat-headed sashed windows on the first and second storeys, and a heavily moulded common cornice with egg-and-dart and acanthus ornament. The building probably dates from the end of the 18th century.

No. 19, The Town Hall, *see* Monument (4).

(58) House, No. 21, is of five bays. The sashed windows on the first and second floors have flat gauged brick heads with triple keystones; above is an elaborate cornice with modillions, egg-and-dart and leaf-and-tongue mouldings. Although extensively remodelled, the skeleton of the house seems to be an early one and a stone embedded in the E. wall of the ground floor bears the inscription 'This is a parti wall, 1732'.

The Plocks

(59) House, No. 2, now the Municipal Offices and much altered internally, was originally a Group (i) house of three bays. A lease of 1759 in the Council's possession describes it as 'new built'. The original S. front has a doorway in a boldly projecting two-storied centre bay, with one wide sashed window in each side bay, three corresponding windows on the first floor and two gabled dormer windows in the attic; the extension of the façade to E. and W. by two further bays on each side is secondary. The projecting bay may have been inspired by that of the Old House (12). The two ground-floor windows and the central window on the first floor have segmental gauged brick heads, the other first-floor windows have flat heads, and all five openings have triple keystones. The side bays and the sides of the centre bay are capped with moulded wooden cornices with modillions; in the centre bay the same cornice forms an open pediment. The central doorway is surmounted by a fanlight and a segmental hood on scrolled consoles. Internally the original plan has been changed and the stairs, which must originally have been in the central passage, have been transferred to the E. part of the house; the passage has been robbed of half its former width to enlarge the W. room. The stairs have close strings, Tuscan newels and turned balusters. The E. extension, No. 3, incorporates, at the rear, a room which was originally the service wing of No. 2. The remodelling of No. 2 probably took place when the E. and W. extensions were built, *c.* 1820.

(60) House, No. 10, stands to the S. of Monument (9) but is entered through an alley from The Plocks. It is an early post-fire building, of red brick in Flemish bond, and of two storeys and five bays. To the S. is a 19th-century one-bay extension, and the two-storied porch at the centre of the E. front may have been added at the same period. The four sashed windows on each storey of the E. front, symmetrically disposed about the porch, have flat gauged brick heads; above the ground-floor openings is a brick plat-band of three courses. The original plan consisted of two rooms divided by a central chimneystack, with a small vestibule between the stack and the central doorway. From the entrance, a passage, parallel to the front wall and lit by the two southern ground-floor windows, leads to the stairs, adjacent to the S. wall. The N. ground-floor room contains original fittings. A centrally placed chimneypiece, with fluted pilasters and a panelled overmantel with scrolled cheekpieces, is flanked by doorways with moulded and eared architraves; the E. doorway is blind and at the centre of the N. wall is another blind doorway. The windows have moulded architraves and panelled shutters; the moulded ceiling cornice is of wood. The small entrance vestibule is divided from the passage to the S. by an archway with fluted pilasters. The stairs rise in a single flight; they have closed strings and turned balusters with moulded handrails, the latter being partly set into the containing walls to form blind balustrades. (*Demolished.*)

(61) House, No. 12, near the corner of Salisbury Street, is the shell of a late 18th-century house with a header-bonded N. front. The whole ground floor has been gutted to make a shop but the first floor survives. On the N. front are three sashed windows with red brick quoins and gauged brick flat arches with keystones. The moulded stone sills continue as a string-course across the façade. The mansard roof has a panelled eaves soffit and contains two dormer windows.

Coupar House, *see* Monument (8).

Lime Tree House, *see* Monument (9).

Salisbury Street

Bastard's map shows that the whole street was burned down in 1731 except for Ryves's Almshouses (7) and a few buildings on the outskirts of the town. The post-fire houses are smaller than those in the Market Place and in the W. part of East Street. Unless otherwise described, the façades are of blue-brick headers, with openings framed in red brick and with red gauged brick window heads. Remodelling of the shops has destroyed the ground plans of most houses but many of the first-floor plans can be recovered; they usually conform to the standard Group (ii) or (iii) pattern. A common 19th-century modification was to convert the winding stairs into straight flights.

East side:—

The W. elevations of Monuments (62) to (70) appear in the illustration facing p. 38.

(62) HOUSES, Nos. 2 and 4, are two-storey post-fire buildings with shops on the ground floor. No. 2 has three unequally spaced bays capped by a moulded brick eaves cornice; to the S. are two more bays, continuous with No. 2 but belonging to Monument (56). No. 4, of four bays, has an eaves cornice of three projecting courses of unmoulded brick and two gabled dormers in the tiled roof.

(63) HOUSES, Nos. 6 and 8, probably date from the early post-fire period. They were originally united in an approximately symmetrical five-bay elevation but the two N. bays, No. 8, have been altered beyond recognition. Above the ground storey the whole W. front is hung with mathematical tiles simulating header bricks; above is a moulded wooden cornice. In No. 6, to the S., the ground storey is capped by a coved plaster pentice, tiled above; this shelters an 18th-century shop-front comprising two shallow bow windows and a central doorway. Inside No. 6 the original plan survives, the house having always contained a shop. A straight staircase, entered from the through-passage on the N. side of the shop, occurs in the N.E. corner of the plan. On the first floor are two rooms, that to the S. having two windows, the other room one window. Only the S. room has a fireplace, the sole chimney being against the S. wall. No. 8 has been altered beyond recovery.

(64) HOUSES, Nos. 10–16, are a group of three-storey two-bay houses of the post-fire period. The ground and first floors have been altered to form shops but the original disposition of the rooms is preserved on the second floor. The Group (iii) plan is common to all except No. 14, which is of Group (ii). No. 16, at the N. end, comprises two Group (iii) dwellings each of one bay with a common chimneystack. Between Nos. 12 and 14 there is a service-passage leading through to the rear. Above the mid 19th-century shop-fronts the elevation of each house differs. No. 10, to the S., is of blue brick in header bond with red brick dressings and *chaînage*. No. 12 is of red brick in Flemish bond with flat brick heads to its first-floor windows; the heads of the second-floor openings are masked by the eaves cornice. No. 14, of red brick in Flemish bond, has elliptical-headed windows with moulded stone sills and rendered architraves with impost-blocks and keystones; above the first-floor windows is a moulded brick string-course. The moulded brick eaves cornice is continuous with that of No. 12. No. 16 is in Flemish bond with red stretchers and blue headers.

(65) HOUSE, No. 18, is of the post-fire period; above a modern shop the W. front is of red brick with an occasional blue header. On the first floor, two three-light sashed windows with pilaster strips and dentil cornices replace the three original windows, of which the bricked-up centre opening remains visible. The second floor retains three windows, the middle one blind. Adjacent to the N. is a carriage-way, above which is a large room lit by a late 18th-century bow window.

(66) HOUSES, Nos. 20 and 22, are small two-storey post-fire buildings, each of two bays. The ground floors have been converted into modern shops.

(67) HOUSES, Nos. 24 and 26, possibly originally a version of Group (iv), seem to be of the mid 18th century. Originally the two houses were nearly uniform but, perhaps at the end of the 18th century, No. 26 was provided with bow windows in place of sashed windows. The gauged brick heads of the original openings are seen on each side of the bow windows.

(68) HOUSE, No. 36, is a two-storied post-fire building consisting of two dwellings, that to the S. of two bays, the other of one bay. The ground floor of the S. dwelling is now a shop and there is a service-passage leading through to the rear between it and its neighbour. The ground-floor window of the N. dwelling has a gauged brick head; on the first floor the front is of blue brick. The heads of the first-floor sashed windows are incorporated in a dentilled eaves cornice, above which rises a tiled roof with dormer windows.

(69) HOUSE, No. 38, is of the mid 18th century. On the ground floor there is a service-passage to the S. but the rest has been gutted to make a modern shop. The first and attic floors have each two rooms divided by a central chimney-stack; the middle bay of the three-bay W. front is blind. Alfred Stevens (1817–1875) was born in this house.

(70) HOUSE, No. 40, is a small Group (ii) house of the mid 18th century apparently converted into a shop during the 19th century. The ground-floor shop-front has two splayed bays flanking a central doorway with a straight hood which continues from side to side and also shelters the entrance to a service-passage on the N. On the first floor a bow window replaces the original centre window and the two outer openings are blocked; on the second floor the centre window is blocked while the outer openings remain. At the top is an enriched cornice. The rear first-floor room and the front second-floor room have 18th-century wooden chimney-pieces.

(71) HOUSE, No. 52, of two storeys with attics, has a rendered W. front of three bays. On the ground floor is a 19th-century shop-front but the first floor has three small sashed windows with thick glazing bars and exposed boxes, suggesting that the house goes back to the mid 18th century. The gabled N. elevation has no window on ground and first floors but a Venetian window in the attic. A later 18th-century house to the E. became part of No. 52 in the first half of the 19th century, when doors were cut through the party wall; its tiled mansard roof is parallel with the slated roof of the first house and is joined to it by a common gutter.

RYVES'S ALMSHOUSES, *see* Monument (7).

(72) SALISBURY HOUSE, at the corner of Salisbury Street and Damory Street, has recently been demolished. Bastard's town plan shows it as having escaped the fire of 1731 and it is likely to have been built *c.* 1700. The W. front, of dark red brickwork in Flemish bond, was of two storeys and three widely spaced bays. The central doorway had narrow pilasters supporting an open-pediment hood with a fanlight below it. The windows were sashed and the N. ground-floor window appears at one time to have been a doorway. The roof was tiled. The N. front had single sashed windows on the ground, first and attic floors, the last in a dormer. The S. elevation was in two parts; to the W., the S. end of the W. range was faced with mathematical tiles; to the E. was a two-storied early 19th-century S.E. wing, with walls of blue header bricks with red brick dressings and with two Venetian windows, one on the ground floor and one on the first floor. Inside, the plan consisted of four main rooms, three of approximately equal size in the W. range and a slightly smaller room in the S.E. wing. The middle room of the W. range contained an open-string staircase with scroll spandrels, plain balusters and Tuscan newel posts. The house seems to have evolved in three stages, the N. bay of the W. range having been originally a small cottage with one room in each storey, probably with service rooms to the E. To this cottage, some time before 1731, were added the centre and S. rooms of the W. range; the S.E. room may have been added *c.* 1830.

West side:—

(73) HOUSE, No. 1, probably dates from about the middle of the 18th century. On the E. front (*see* illustration facing p. 38) a modern shop is surmounted by two storeys each of two bays; at the top is an enriched modillion cornice. Internally, traces of a passage are seen on the N. side of the shop and the original plan seems to have been of Group (ii). The first floor consisted originally of a two-windowed front room and a smaller back room beside the stairs, but the front room is now divided into two.

(74) HOUSE, No. 3, has an E. front closely resembling (73) but independently designed, as its differently moulded and slightly lower cornice shows. Internally it has been completely rebuilt.

(75) HOUSE, No. 13, has a rendered front with a single bow window on each of the two upper storeys, but these are mid 19th-century alterations and the original 18th-century E. front was probably of brick, perhaps with two windows on each floor, like Monument (76).

(76) HOUSE, No. 15, of two bays and three storeys, has an early 19th-century shop front, and 18th-century sashed windows on the two upper floors. The first-floor windows have segmental heads; those of the second floor come directly under the cornice, in which brick-on-edge dentils are surmounted by a wooden corona. The first floor has a Group (ii) plan. The stairs and the fireplace of the first-floor room are of the 19th century.

(77) HOUSE, No. 17, is two-bayed and three-storied and probably almost contemporary with No. 15 although of taller proportions and with modernised windows. The ground-floor plan is of Group (ii), modified by a service-passage leading through to the rear on the S. side; the original winding staircase remains at the N.W. corner.

(78) HOUSES, Nos. 19 and 21, are paired and have a common chimneystack; they are two-storied and probably date from the mid 18th century. On the ground floor the party-wall has been removed but the two staircases are preserved, back-to-back, against the W. wall. To the S. of No. 19 is a service-passage. The E. front has a modern shop-front on the ground floor and on the first floor each house has a bow window, perhaps of the 19th century.

(79) HOUSE, No. 25, is of two bays and three storeys with an attic. After a period during which the first floor had a single bay window the original 18th-century design of two sashed windows has recently been restored. A second-floor string-course of gauged brick has shaped ends set in a little way from the sides of the façade. The ground floor is modern, but the typical Group (ii) plan survives on the first floor.

(80) HOUSE, No. 29, is two-bayed and of two storeys with a dormer-windowed attic. Above the sashed first-floor windows is a moulded and coved plaster eaves cornice. The service-passage which formerly passed along the S. side of the shop is said by the owner to have been removed in 1899. The first floor has the usual Group (ii) plan and the E. room contains a late 18th-century fireplace flanked by alcoves.

(81) HOUSE, No. 31, has a cornice continuous with that of the foregoing and the two houses are probably contemporary. About 1830 the E. front was rendered and a single window was put in place of the original pair. The ground floor is a shop but the Group (ii) plan, with a winding stair in the N.E. corner, is preserved on the first floor.

(82) HOUSE, No. 33, of two bays and two storeys, stands on the corner of Bryanston Street and has a hipped roof. The shop-front seems to be of the early 19th century; over it the rendered E. front has sashed windows with segmental heads. The N. front is similar to the E. front but of three bays and the first-floor windows have flat heads. The house probably dates from about the middle of the 18th century.

(83) HOUSE, No. 45, is of two storeys with attics and has an E. front of five bays. It was built probably as a private house towards the end of the 18th century. Except for a service-passage to the S. the original ground floor perished when the house became a shop, about 1830, but the first floor retains five sashed windows set symmetrically in a header-bonded brick façade; above them is a panelled brick parapet wall. The rectangular first-floor plan has four rooms, two in front and two at the back, with the staircase between the two back rooms. The open-string stairs have scroll-outlined spandrels and the usual Tuscan-column balustrades.

(84) HOUSE, No. 57, is of two storeys with an attic. The two-bay E. front has a 19th-century shop on the ground floor but the first floor retains two original sashed windows with gauged brick aprons, flat heads and triple keystones; above is a moulded brick eaves cornice. The house is probably of the mid 18th century.

(85) HOUSE, No. 63, is a two-storied, mid 18th-century building with an E. front of three bays in a mixture of blue and red header-bonded brickwork, with light red brick dressings and a modillion eaves cornice. A two-storied 19th-century bow window in the E. front has the entrance doorway to the S. and a carriage-way to the N.; above, it is flanked by sashed windows with gauged brick flat heads and triple keystones. The doorway has a flat hood on scrolled brackets.

The elevations of Monuments (86) to (89) appear in the illustration facing p. 38.

(86) HOUSES, Nos. 67, 69, 71 and 73, are small mid 18th-century houses with Group (iii) plans. The red brick front of No. 67 appears to have been rebuilt in the early 19th century; it has a small shop window on the ground floor, the doorway is spanned by an elliptical brick arch of two orders and above it is a deep round-headed niche. No. 69 (*see* plan, p. 18) has a rendered E. front with an inserted shop-window on the ground floor. The E. ground-floor room has fielded panelling above and below a moulded dado rail, and a small wooden cornice. The E. front of No. 71 is built in a mixture of blue and red bricks in Flemish bond and has a splay-sided, two-storied bow window; inside, early 19th-century embellishments include a cast-iron bucket grate in the first-floor front room. The E. front of No. 73 is rendered and a modern window has recently been inserted on the ground floor. Nos. 71 and 73 have a continuous brick dentil eaves cornice.

(87) HOUSE, No. 75, is of the mid 18th century but the E. front, up to the heads of the first-floor windows, has been refaced. The second storey of the five-bay front is in its original state, the sashed windows having gauged brick flat arches with triple keystones. The brickwork is of Flemish bond with blue headers and red stretchers; at the top is a moulded brick cornice. Permission to view the interior was refused.

(88) HOUSE, No. 77, is of the mid 18th century and was originally two dwellings, each of two bays; on the E. front a vertical straight joint is visible immediately N. of the central doorway. The S. house has a brick dentil eaves cornice but the N. house has none. Inside, as well as combining them into one house there have been considerable alterations in both parts. In the N. part the chimney is against the W. wall while that of the S. part rises on the S. gable wall; a winding stair to the

attic from the first floor is set against the latter chimney, in the S.W. corner of the house.

DALE HOUSE, No. 79 Salisbury Street, *see* Monument (13).

(89) HOUSE, No. 81 (Plate 118), is stylistically of the second half of the 18th century and must therefore be a rebuild of the house which Bastard's plan shows as surviving the 1731 fire. It is of three storeys and has a three-bay E. front of red brick, carefully coursed in Flemish bond with thin joints. The central doorway, with fluted Composite pilasters supporting a pedimented entablature, is flanked by wooden two-storied three-sided sashed bay windows, with dentil cornices at each level. The first floor has a small segmental-headed central window and the second floor is lit by three square-headed sashed windows. At the top is a moulded stone cornice and a brick parapet; the cornice continues across the N. gable but on the S. gable, which is rendered, it is only returned. A two-storied service wing of two bays adjoins the N. gable and a later range has been added along the W. side of the house and service wing. The plan is a normal specimen of Group (i) except that it is of three instead of five bays. Inside, most rooms retain original dados, plaster cornices and panelled doors. In the S. ground-floor room, round-headed niches flank the chimney breast and the door-frame has a small entablature. The staircase has two turned balusters to each tread and outline scrolls on the spandrels of the cut string.

WEST STREET

All the façades except the front of No. 13 are built in header bond with red brick dressings and quoins, and have flat rubbed-brick window heads with keystones. No. 13 has been rendered, but the 18th-century fenestration is preserved. Nos. 3 to 7 inclusive have uniform windows and a continuous cornice, with a plaster cyma above brick-on-edge dentils.

South side:—

(90) HOUSE, No. 1, has been modernised on the ground floor but the first floor retains one mid 18th-century sashed window and a 19th-century bay window. Above a moulded wooden eaves cornice is a tiled roof with two gabled dormer windows.

(91) HOUSE, No. 3, is three-storied and of five bays; it was presumably built soon after the fire. On the ground floor is a handsome mid 19th-century shop-front with fluted Corinthian columns and entablature; over this rise two storeys of sashed windows with moulded wooden sills and label-shaped brick aprons. The cornice and parapet were probably added early in the 19th century in imitation of No. 5, for a print dated 1793 shows the roof with eaves. Internally the building has been extensively remodelled, but an original, or perhaps an early 19th-century staircase occurs above the first floor; it is open-stringed and has Tuscan-column balusters and newels, the latter with ball finials.

(92) HOUSES, Nos. 5 and 7, are a uniform pair of three-storied, three-bay houses, stylistically of the late 18th century. The sashed first and second-floor windows are set at the same level as in No. 3 and have similar keystones, but the sills are unmoulded and have no aprons. The double façade has red brick quoins at either end and is capped by a brick and stone dentil cornice with a brick parapet above.

(93) HOUSES, Nos. 9 and 11, of three storeys, were probably built soon after 1731, the former with four bays and the latter with three. The ground floors now have modern shop-fronts, but seven equally spaced sashed windows open in the first and second storeys of the N. front, part of which is crowned by a moulded plaster cornice of egg-and-dart mouldings with scrolled modillions. On the first floor the W. house retains the original Group (ii) plan. The rooms were redecorated early in the 19th century but a few minor 18th-century features survive. The E. house was destroyed by fire in 1949 but the N. façade is preserved.

(94) HOUSE, now the Crown and Anchor Hotel, stands in the curve of West Street and has an irregular plan. Although faced with modern imitation half-timbering the three-storied N. front probably dates from the second half of the 18th century. The doorway, near the centre, has two segmental-headed sashed windows to the W. and a three-light sashed window to the E. On the first floor are five segmental-headed windows with sashes with thick glazing bars, apparently original; the second floor has similar openings, two of them blind. The doorway opens into a passage which passes through the house from front to back, leading to the stairs which are against the rear wall. To the E. of the passage a front and a back room have now been united into one; to the W., where is now a single large room, the original plan is not recoverable. Apart from a few Tuscan-column balusters on the first-floor landing the stairs are modern, although probably in their original position. Some bedrooms retain fragments of original cornice, dado-rail and fielded panelling.

(95) HOUSE, No. 27, is of red brick in three storeys and has a W. front of two bays; it is probably of the second half of the 18th century. The doorway has a 19th-century fluted architrave developing into scroll brackets which carry a pedimental wooden hood. The first-floor sashed windows have gauged brick heads with keystones. Above is a plat-band which terminates at each end 9 ins. from the corner; over this are two second-floor windows, equal in width to those below but squatter; their heads coincide with a brick dentil cornice. The interior was greatly altered, and some early 18th-century woodwork was probably inserted, when the house became a masonic lodge at the end of the 19th century.

(96) ASSEMBLY ROOMS, now a garage, stand on the E. side of West Street, near the N. end of the causeway which leads to Blandford Bridge (3). The building is two-storied and has walls of Flemish-bonded red brickwork, and tile-covered hipped roofs. It is possible that the adjacent house to the N. (95) was originally part of the same complex; the brickwork is similar and the façades are of equal height and until recently had similar brick cornices. The ground floor of the assembly-room building appears originally to have had open arcaded sides; on the first floor the remains of a spacious and lofty ballroom (56 ft. by 29 ft.) are now used as a store. The building appears to date from the end of the 18th century.

The W. front has been greatly altered; the ground-floor arcade has been replaced by a wide garage doorway and the first-floor fenestration has been extended into a single window, the jambs of which probably represent the outside jambs of narrower openings. The S. elevation has, in the lower storey, three segmental brick arches with stone key and impost blocks on rectangular brick piers; to the E. the arcade continues in the form of a half arch which abuts against the N.W. corner of the adjoining house (97). The archway nearest the street is now blocked and the other three openings are partly blocked and partly glazed. On the first floor are three windows, corresponding with the three arches of the lower storey; the centre window is round-headed and has a gauged brick archivolt, a stone sill, stone imposts and a keystone; the side windows are similar but square-headed, with gauged brick heads; that to the E. is blocked. The N. elevation is obscured by adjacent buildings but several of the ground-floor segmental arches can be seen internally; a chimney breast projects at the centre. The E. wall has three segmental arches at ground level and a large round-headed window on the first floor.

The interior decorations have now completely perished but parts of the plaster ceiling of the ballroom were still intact in 1953, although much damaged. A rectangular central panel, decorated at the corners and in the middle of each long side with rococo ornament, was surrounded by a double cove rising from a wall cornice of egg-and-dart mouldings, and fluted modillions alternating with paterae. Of the stairs which led up to the ballroom no trace remains.

(97) CLIFF VIEW was built soon after 1731 but has since been much altered. Originally the house was of two storeys, with a three-bay W. front and a Group (i) plan; a single-storied service wing projected to the E. At the end of the 18th century the Assembly Room (96) was built against the N.W. corner and a third storey was added to the W. front; other accretions at the rear subsequently caused the service wing to be included in an enlarged rectangular plan. A front porch and ground-floor bay windows were added late in the 19th century. The W. front, separated from West Street by a garden, is of Flemish-bonded brickwork with rusticated plaster quoins at the corners. The quoin to the N. ceases at second-floor level, where the original eaves lay, but the S. quoin was heightened to include the second storey, *c.* 1800. On the S. front the original gable can be distinguished, by different bonding, from the spandrels which were added when the second storey was built. Internally, the front ground-floor rooms have mid 18th-century joinery with enriched mouldings, and acanthus cornices. A fireplace surround has a sculptured frieze representing scenes from Aesop's fables. The lower flight of stairs is of the late 19th century, but higher up the stairs have open strings, turned balusters and Tuscan-column newels of 18th-century pattern.

North side:—

The elevations of Monuments (98) to (103) appear in the illustration facing p. 38.

(98) HOUSE, No. 2, is of the mid 18th century with a two-bay, three-storied S. front in header courses of red brick. The front terminates in a parapet wall with a stone coping, swept up at the angles. The segmental brick arches of the sashed windows have rendered keystones. The ground floor was remodelled in the 19th century to form a shop but the upper floors retain the original plan, together with some fittings and the original staircase from the first to the second floor. The plan is of Group (iii) with the stairs lit by a skylight. The original entrance seems to have been from the service-passage which passes through to the rear, in the adjacent house (53) on the E. The staircase has an open string with scroll spandrels and two turned balusters to each tread. The front rooms on the first and second floors retain original fielded panelling in two heights, and wooden ceiling cornices.

(99) HOUSE, No. 4, dates from the post-fire period and is faced with blue header bricks, red brick being used for the quoins, the window openings and their flat gauged brick heads. The elevation finishes in a parapet wall above a heavy moulded stone cornice, returned at the ends. The ground floor has been entirely remodelled to form a shop; the upper floors, while retaining the original Group (ii) plan, contain no early fittings. A service-passage passes through the building on the W. side.

(100) HOUSES, Nos. 6 and 8, are of three storeys and date from the early post-fire period; they present a unified five-bay S. front with an emphasised central bay. This façade embraces two Group (ii) houses, that to the E. of three bays, that to the W. of two. The ground floors contain modern shop fronts but above these the elevation is of blue header bricks with red brick quoins and window surrounds. At the top is a coved plaster cornice, returned at the ends. The middle windows of the first and second floors have round heads with triple keystones and moulded imposts. The other windows have shallow segmental heads and plain keystones, except for the windows beside the central second-floor opening, which have serpentine soffits. On the upper floors the original plan survives. A service-passage to the rear of the building is placed centrally below the party wall between Nos. 8 and 10.

(101) HOUSE, No. 10, built soon after the fire, was originally two houses, that to the E. of five bays, the other of two (Plate 115); their elevational details are in most respects identical and they share a common cornice and parapet, but the brickwork of the façade is not continuous. The ground floors have been combined and remodelled to form a shop with a shop-front of *c.* 1830. The S. front of the W. house is predominantly of purple brick, that of the E. house is of grey brick; red brick is used for quoins and window surrounds in both houses. The middle window on each upper floor of the E. house has a keystone with a mask; all other windows have keystones in which the upper part is decorated with scale ornament while the lower part is fluted. Label-shaped red brick aprons embellished with guttae project below the second-floor sills. The elevation terminates in a moulded dentil cornice, and a parapet wall with projecting panels of red brick. The house shares the service-passage at its E. end with No. 8. The upper storeys have been converted into modern flats and retain no noteworthy features.

(102) HOUSE, No. 12 (plan on p. 18), belongs to the early post-fire period and has a Group (ii) plan. The S. front is faced with a random mixture of header bricks; the details are similar to those of No. 10, but the storeys are lower and the cornice is simpler. The ground floor has a 19th-century shop front and the interior was altered when the shop was made, but the service-passage leading through to the rear, on the W., remains. The original staircase survives from the first quarter-landing above ground to the attic. The first-floor rooms contain fielded panelling and the front room has a wooden cornice.

(103) THE THREE CHOUGHS INN is of the mid 18th century. The two W. bays of the five-bay S. front are splayed back from the street front. The three storeys of sashed windows are linked by red brick *chaînage* and the first and second-storey windows have flush aprons of the same colour. Between the two E. ground-floor windows is a blocked opening. The N. elevation is of red brick, and three of the segmental-headed windows have leaded casements in wood surrounds. The tiled roof has a central valley which emerges on the W. The original plan consisted of four rooms set two on each side of a through-passage running from N. to S., with the staircase at the N. end. A central chimneystack is set in each E. and W. wall. The building has recently been repaired and the internal arrangements much altered. Between the first and second floors, part of an original winding staircase with Tuscan newels and balusters is

Original survey by A. T. Phillips, 1943–4, now in N.M.R., revised and redrawn by B. Marriott, 1966.

preserved. It has a small well and retains three flights with winders. The newels consist of superimposed Tuscan columns separated by square blocks, against which the handrails are stopped; each tread has two turned balusters.

White Cliff Mill Street

East side:—

(104) Cottage, No. 4, is a mid 18th-century artisan's dwelling of Group (v). The single ground-floor room is entered from the street through a doorway in the N. part of the W. front, and a large adjacent window implies that the dwelling was originally a shop. The chimneystack takes up most of the S. wall but there is space in the S.W. corner for a winding stair against the side of the stack; it leads direct to the single first-floor room, whence other steps wind up to the attic. A scullery occupies a one-storied annex at the rear. (*Demolished.*)

(105) Cottage, No. 6, is contemporary with (104). It is two-storied and has a two-bay W. front of header brickwork with red brick dressings; the gauged brick flat window heads have triple keystones. Originally the ground floor had a doorway and one small window, but the window was enlarged early in the 19th century; the two sashed first-floor windows and the attic dormer are unchanged. The doorway has a flat hood on simple scroll consoles. Inside, the plan consists of a front room with a small entrance vestibule and staircase to the N., and a back room extending across the width of the house. The first-floor plan is similar. At the back of the house is a long workshop; this and an odd collection of interior woodwork, including a fluted column-shaft, suggest that the cottage was once occupied by a joiner. (*Demolished.*)

(106) Half Moon Inn, No. 16, is composed of two cottages. The older cottage to the N. is contemporary with (104) and has much the same plan; the other is of the end of the 18th century.

(107) House, No. 26 (Plate 115), preserves many features from the early post-fire period. It is two-storied with an attic and has a W. front of two bays with regularly disposed sashed windows. The front is of header bricks with red brick quoins and dressings, and has at first-floor level a plat-band which ends short of the corners; the eaves have a moulded plastic cornice with vertical fluting. The plan is of Group (ii) with a service-passage leading through to the rear. The doorway, to the S. in the W. front, opens into the service-passage and at the E. end of the passage another doorway opens on a back yard. Internal doorways on the N. side of the service-passage open into the front and back ground-floor rooms. The front room has panelling on two sides and a fireplace in the N.E. corner. The staircase is at the N. end of the narrower back room and thus adjacent to the chimneystack. The first-floor plan repeats the ground floor except that the rooms extend over the service-passage. The attic has only one room.

(108) Cottages, Nos. 28 and 30, repeat the Group (v) plan of No. 4, but the smaller chimney-breasts suggest a somewhat later date. (*Demolished.*)

(109) White Cliff House, No. 38, is substantially a mid 18th-century Group (i) house but it was extensively altered *c.* 1850 and again at the end of the 19th century, to which periods the Venetian windows and pediment-hooded doorway of the W. front may be assigned. Traces of original openings are discernible in the W. front, and an original one-storey service annex in the S.E. quarter of the plan is betrayed by the stretcher-bonded brickwork of the lower part of this wing, the random-bonded upper storey being later. Internally, the partitions between the central vestibule and the two front rooms have been moved N. but the original plan is suggested by a length of plaster cornice at the E. end of the vestibule, which terminates some distance from the N. side wall. The close-string staircase with swelling Tuscan-column newel posts and balusters is probably a mid 19th-century version of the usual 18th-century pattern. Panelling below the window-sills in the S.E. bedroom does not correspond with the present openings and presumably represents an earlier scheme of fenestration. The blocked central first-floor window of the original W. front is seen in a closet which opens out of the N.E. bedroom. The latter has full-height panelling on the S. and E. walls; the woodwork stops short of the N.E. corner but this may be due to enlargement of the room by removal of cupboards on the N. side. A mid 18th-century fireplace surround with pulvinated frieze and scrolled cheek-pieces occurs at the centre of the N. wall in the same room.

West side:—

(110) The King's Arms Hotel, No. 1, was built probably in the mid 18th century as two-storied houses, and was converted into a single property *c.* 1840. The smaller of the two houses, on the corner of Bryanston Street and White Cliff Mill Street, probably had a S. front of three bays, but only the W. windows remain; the wall is of English-bonded brickwork for about half the height of the ground storey, and in random bond above that level. To the W. of the S. front is a covered entry to the yard at the back; a perpendicular joint running up to the eaves from the E. abutment of its segmental arch shows that the first-floor room has been extended across the entry. The E. front of the S. house is rendered and has one sashed window centrally in the ground storey and another on the first floor. The N. house fronts White Cliff Mill Street. Its E. front is aligned with that of the S. house and since both have a common plaster revetment the division between the two fronts is indistinguishable, apart from the fact that the windows are set at different levels conforming to the rise of the ground. The entrance to the hotel, at the S. end of the E. front of the N. house, has three stone steps flanked by iron handrails; panelled pilasters flanking the doorway support scrolled brackets and a flat hood. The passage inside originally ran straight through to the yard but it is now interrupted by stairs of *c.* 1840 which cross it at right angles. The stairs lead to the first-floor room of the S. house, which is now the dining-room. At the W. end this room extends across the covered entry from Bryanston Street.

Eagle House, No. 19, *see* Monument (14).

(111) Houses, Nos. 21 and 23, are suburban villas of *c.* 1830, symmetrically designed with pleasing red brick E. fronts of two storeys and three bays; the roofs are slate-covered. The doorways have flat wooden hoods, one of which is supported on slender Gothic shafted columns; on either side are broad sashed windows. The first floors have similar sashed windows on each side and slightly narrower windows over the doorways. Internally, in No. 23, a hall-passage runs from front to back of the square plan, opening half-way along the S. side to a staircase which extends to the S. wall. A doorway under the stairs gives access to the service wing which juts out from the W. part of the S. side. Four rooms open from the T-shaped hall-passage; those in the N.E., S.E. and S.W. corners of the plan are of about equal size, but the N.W. room is larger because it includes the equivalent width of the staircase. Adjacent to the N. are two similar isolated houses and two more, paired; they are probably all of *c.* 1850.

Noteworthy early 19th-century buildings in Blandford Forum also include the following.—No. 19 East Street is a large isolated house standing well back from the road; according to an inscription discovered during recent works it was built in 1832. On the E. side of Salisbury Street, near the N. end and located between Monuments (7) and (72), are seven three-storied houses of *c.* 1830–50. The southernmost, No. 76, is brick-fronted, with a symmetrical W. façade of three bays; the ground-floor openings are set in round-headed recesses. Adjacent, but set further back from the road, No. 78 has a rendered, symmetrical W. front of three bays, with a rusticated lower storey and a single order of shallow Doric pilasters embracing the two upper storeys. No. 80, adjacent, is somewhat similar to No. 78 but the pilasters are omitted, the centre bay is slightly recessed, and the doorway has a flat-topped porch supported on two Ionic columns. The other four houses of this group are paired; Nos. 82–84 have rendered fronts and each house is of two bays; in Nos. 86–88 the façade is unified by coupling the doorways and adding blind Palladian windows centrally on the first and second storeys.

The houses of Dorset Street and Orchard Street were built in the first half of the 19th century on the site of a former orchard and gardens between The Close and Salisbury Street. The land is shown on Bastard's town plan and it appears that the two streets follow the line of two former groves of trees; the alley which still cuts northwards from the S.E. corner of Dorset Street to the W. side of Orchard Street existed formerly and appears on the map as a diagonal footpath between the two groves. The short E.–W. street in the same quarter corresponds with the N. boundary of the orchard, and northwards from there the streets change direction and converge on Salisbury Street, crossing the area where Bastard found gardens. The 19th-century development is a mixed one of predominantly two-storied one-bay brick-built terrace houses, mainly with slated roofs and rendered fronts. A few groups of three-storied terraces occur, such as Nos. 28–34 Orchard Street, with a symmetrical rendered elevation, and Nos. 14–20 Dorset Street. Nos. 12 and 22 Dorset Street, and No. 24 Orchard Street are two-storied houses of three bays with central entrances. Damory Street, called Damary Lane on Bastard's map, appears to have had few buildings until the middle of the 19th century, when groups of houses were erected on the E. side; they are of two storeys, with brick walls and slated roofs with wide overhanging eaves. Among them are four groups of terraced houses with paired doorways under concave metal canopies, and two groups of semi-detached houses with similar entrances.

A cottage at 22 Bryanston Street illustrates the continued use of blue all-header brickwork in modest housing, as late as *c.* 1825.

6 BLANDFORD ST. MARY (8905)

(O.S. 6 ins. ST 80 NE, ST 80 SE)

The parish lies S. of Blandford Forum, on the S.W. bank of the R. Stour, and extends over some 2,500 acres, almost entirely on Chalk. It includes the former parish of Littleton which was part of Langton Long Blandford until 1933; Littleton House and farm are all that remain of Littleton village, but many traces of former dwellings occur as earthworks. Thorncombe, in the S.W., was a detached part of Turnworth until the 19th century. In Blandford St. Mary itself there were originally two settlements; Martel in the N. and St. Mary in the S., each with its own open fields.[1] A large expanse of downland to the W. was not enclosed until 1716, when it became Down Farm, later The Down House estate (*see* (22)).

The church tower and the Manor House are the principal monuments.

BLANDFORD ST. MARY
The parish church of St. Mary

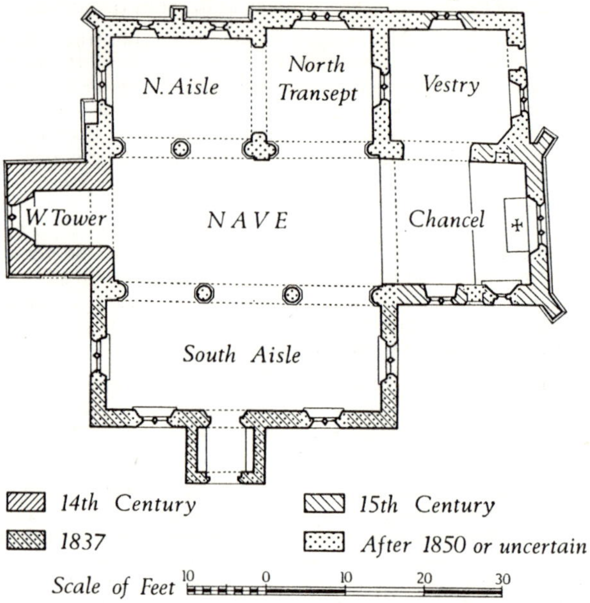

ECCLESIASTICAL

(1) THE PARISH CHURCH OF ST. MARY stands near the centre of the village in the W. part of the parish. In general the masonry is chequered flint and ashlar but the E. wall of the chancel is of banded flint and Greensand; the lower part of the tower is of Heathstone rubble alternating with courses of knapped flint; the quoins are heavy blocks of Greensand and Heathstone. The roofs are partly tiled and partly slated. The *West Tower* dates from the late 14th century; the *Chancel* is of the late 15th century but restored. The *Nave* has no early features. The church was restored and a N. aisle was added in 1711 by Governor Pitt, whose father had been rector, but Pitt's aisle disappeared in 1862 when the present *North Aisle* and *North Transept* were built. The *South Aisle* was built in 1837; originally two iron pillars took the place of the former S. wall of the nave but

[1] T. F. Almack, *A Village Heritage*, (Dorchester 1962).

BLANDFORD FORUM. (31) Eastway House. N. front. *c.* 1735

(2) St. Leonard's Chapel. Exterior, from N. 15th-century

(3) Bridge, detail. Probably mediaeval.

(6) Almshouse gateway. 1736

BLANDFORD FORUM.

(101) No. 10 West Street. *c.* 1735

(107) No. 26 White Cliff Mill Street. *c.* 1735

(21) Nos. 6 and 8 East Street. Artisans dwellings. Late 18th-century

BLANDFORD FORUM.

(26) Lyston House. Ground-floor room. *c.* 1750

(45) John Bastard's house. Mezzanine room. *c.* 1732

BLANDFORD FORUM.

(8) Coupar House. N. ground-floor room. 18th-century

(31) Eastway House. Drawing room. *c.* 1750

BLANDFORD FORUM. (89) No. 81 Salisbury Street. 18th-century

BLANDFORD ST. MARY. (3) The Old Rectory, N.E. Front. 1732

Monument (1) of Francis Cartwright. 1752

Monument (3) of John Pitt. 1672

Detail of Monument (1). 1752

BLANDFORD ST. MARY CHURCH. Monuments.

Chancel, looking S.E. 13th-century

Nave, looking S.E. 15th-century

BUCKLAND NEWTON CHURCH.

in 1919 stone columns and pointed arches were substituted. The *South Porch* was built in 1837 and restored in 1901; the *Vestry* was built in 1908.

Architectural Description—The *Chancel* (18½ ft. by 15½ ft.) has diagonal two-stage N.E. and S.E. buttresses with chamfered plinths and weathered offsets. The S. wall contains a blocked doorway with a chamfered two-centred head and, to the W., a late 15th-century square-headed window of two pointed lights without cusps. A corresponding two-light window, probably from the N. side of the chancel, is now in the N. wall of the vestry. The chancel arch was built in 1862.

The *Nave* (33½ ft. by 18 ft.) retains no visible ancient masonry; the plaster barrel-vault is probably of 1711. The 19th-century *South Aisle* (13 ft. by 35 ft.) has walls of chequered flint and stone; an old photograph shows that it originally had round-headed windows with brick surrounds but these were replaced by pointed two-light stone openings at the end of the 19th century.

The *Tower* (7½ ft. by 7 ft.) has four stages, the bottom stage very low and little more than a plinth. Moulded and hollow-chamfered string-courses mark the stages and at the top is an embattled parapet; there are no buttresses. The tower arch is two-centred and of two plain chamfered orders springing from hollow-chamfered abaci, perhaps restored; the responds are chamfered. The W. window, in the second stage, is probably of 14th-century origin although restored and perhaps altered in the 18th century; it has two two-centred lights. An 18th-century doorway with a four-centred head in the S. side of the lowest stage is now blocked. On the N. side, in the third stage, is a small chamfered square-headed loop. The top stage has in each wall a 14th-century single-light belfry window with a chamfered two-centred head and perforated wooden shutters. When the parapet was restored in 1912 traces of former angle pinnacles are said to have been found.

Fittings—*Bells:* three; treble by W. Purdue, 1660; 2nd, probably 15th century, inscribed 'Ave Maria' in Lombardic capitals; tenor, 15th century, inscribed 'Ac Cam Pana Sanc Diti Cata In Hono Re Marie' (*sic*) in black-letter. *Chests:* two; one of oak with panelled front and moulded lid, 18th century; another of cast-iron with panels and date 1813. *Coffin-stools:* pair, of oak, with trefoil-fretted board legs and turned stretchers, 18th century. *Monuments:* In S. aisle, reset on S. wall, (1) of Francis Cartwright, 1758, and his wife Ann, 1762, wall-tablet of white and variegated marbles with apron and open pediment on consoles (Plate 119); central inscription tablet with scrolled sides and head and, between tablet and pediment, convex oval, wreathed with laurel; on apron, separated from inscription tablet by gadrooned string, laurel-wreathed emblems of architect's occupation, T-square, dividers, folding-rule and two scrolls of paper showing details of Corinthian capital and façade, probably of Came House (*Dorset* II, p. 384). Adjacent to foregoing, (2) of Admiral James Brine, 1814, small marble tablet by Marshall. In S. aisle, on W. wall, (3) of Rev. John Pitt, 1672, marble wall-tablet (Plate 119) inscribed '. . . Hanc Inscriptionem, postquam Hanc Sacram Aedem instauraverat, Ornavit Honoratus Thomas Pitt, Armiger, Defuncti Filius natu Secondus . . . erexit Monumentum Anno Domini 1712; (4) of John Baskett, 1801, and his wife Rachel, 1779, marble wall monument with arms and urn finial. In tower, on N. wall, (5) of Henry Willis, 1726, and his wife Sara, 1733, marble tablet with sculptured enrichment; (6) of Alice Browne, 1704, and Robert Browne, 1710, tablet similar to (5), with arms; on S. wall, (7) of William Sutton, 1632, slate tablet in moulded stone surround; (8) of John Willis Burrough, 1799, marble tablet with sculptured enrichment. In churchyard, 10 paces S. of chancel, (9) of Admiral Brine, 1814, table-tomb with channelled Greek-key decoration; 8 paces S.W. of tower, (10) of W. North of London, 1821, headstone with mason's emblems; 12 paces S. of S. aisle, (11) of members of the Wheller family, 1731 and later, table-tomb with panelled sides, moulded cornice and shield-of-arms; also four other 18th and early 19th-century table-tombs. *Plate:* includes silver paten and dish, both hall-marked 1712. *Seating:* Oak seating in nave incorporates remains of mid or late 18th-century panelled box pews. A detached bench has details similar to those of the coffin-stools.

SECULAR

(2) THE MANOR HOUSE (89090553), some 300 yds. N. of the church, is of two storeys with attics and cellars (Plate 53). The walls are of English-bonded brickwork, with quoins and dressings of ashlar; the roofs are tiled. Apart from service rooms to N.W. and N.E., which are largely of the 19th century, the house comprises work of three main periods. The S.W. range, containing the Drawing Room, staircase and N.W. room, is probably of the first half of the 17th century. At this period there was undoubtedly a wing to the N.E., but its extent is unknown since it was replaced, probably *c.* 1700, by the present N.E. range, containing the Dining Room. Lastly, the interior was extensively refitted and the staircase was remodelled about the middle of the 18th century.

The house is a pleasing specimen of domestic architecture of the 17th and 18th centuries; the mid 18th-century staircase is perhaps the most notable feature.

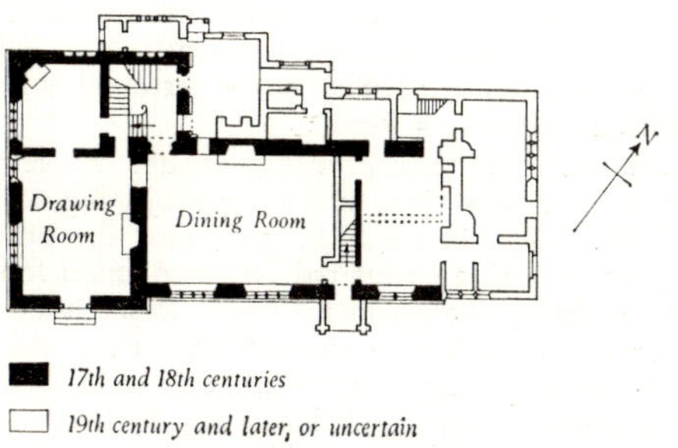

The S.E. front of the N.E. range has four bays; at the base is a low brick plinth and above the ground-floor windows is a brick plat-band. The windows are of two and of four lights with chamfered and hollow-chamfered square-headed casements; their flat heads of gauged brickwork have some bricks set forward to represent rustication. One bay contains the front doorway; before it is a single-storied wooden porch with Tuscan pilasters and an elliptical-headed archway. Above, in the brickwork, are traces of the upper storey of an earlier porch; it had a pitched roof and was entered through a doorway in place of the present first-floor window. Set slightly forward from the S.E. front, to the S.W., is the S.E. end wall of the 17th-century S.W. range. The walling is similar to that of the N.E. range except that the plinth has a moulded ashlar capping, there is no plat-band and the original windows have weathered labels with returned stops. On the ground floor is a later french window with a moulded stone architrave and an enriched keystone; the first floor has an original casement window of four square-headed lights and the attic has a similar three-light window. The gable has a moulded coping above rounded kneelers.

The S.W. front is of three bays; the central bay has two-light windows on each floor and the side bays have windows of four lights. The middle ground-floor window is a modern restoration in place of a doorway which was probably inserted in the 19th century. On either side, the moulded stone plinth is returned upwards to accommodate two cellar windows.

The N.W. gabled end of the S.W. range, with a chimney-stack at the apex, is in part masked by a modern addition; it has a mullioned three-light window centrally on the ground floor and a window E. of centre on the first floor, both blocked. The original N.W. wall extends N.E. beyond the gable, and inserted in this part of the wall, above the roof of the addition, is a large 18th-century staircase window; the opening is round-headed, with a brick arch and ashlar imposts and keystone; it has sliding sashes with radial glazing bars in the head. Below, concealed by the addition, the same wall contains a blocked ground-floor window of three mullioned lights.

Inside, the drawing-room, in the S.E. part of the S.W. range, was redecorated in the 18th century. The plaster ceiling has an octagonal field with four marginal panels and four corner roundels. The octagon is outlined by strapwork between cable-moulded borders, the margin panels have leaf enrichment, and the roundels are wreaths of laurel enclosing male and female busts in low relief. The walls are lined with panelling in two heights, the bolection mouldings more pronounced in the upper height than in the dado. At the S.E. end of the room fluted pilasters flank the french window. The fireplace has panelled pilasters supporting a mantelshelf and extending upwards to flank the overmantel; above the mantelshelf they have festoons of fruit and leaves. Within the wooden fireplace surround the remains of an earlier stone surround are seen; the mouldings of the horizontal stone head continue down the jambs and terminate at shaped stops. The N.W. room is lined to the ceiling with 17th-century oak panelling. The corner fireplace has a moulded stone surround with a four-centred head and run-out stops.

The original stairs were probably situated where the 18th-century staircase now rises, in a wing projecting to the N.E. of the S.W. range. In the N.E. wall, near the N. corner, a stone doorway with a chamfered surround and a four-centred head was probably the original entrance to the house; it has a butt-jointed oak plank door studded with nails and hung on wrought-iron strap hinges. In the S.E. side of the staircase hall is a 17th-century round-headed archway with two orders of roll-mouldings rising from moulded imposts, to a plain keystone; the roll-mouldings are repeated in the jambs and terminate on shaped pedestals about 2 ft. above the floor. The archway proves that a 17th-century wing formerly existed in the place of the present dining-room, the S.E. front of which is of *c.* 1700.

The 18th-century stairs are of oak, with open strings and with foliate scrolls at each step. Three turned balusters of vase and Tuscan-column pattern stand on each tread and support moulded handrails; the newel posts are larger Tuscan columns. The plaster soffit of the first-floor landing is decorated with acanthus sprays, two lozenge-shaped panels and a circular panel containing a shield-of-arms of Foster. The staircase window has a moulded plaster reveal with egg-and-dart ornament culminating in a shell keystone. Above, the walls of the staircase have a rich plaster entablature having a frieze of acanthus scrollwork, human mask medallions and eagles; the cornice has an ovolo moulding enriched with shells, and foliate modillions alternating with flower paterae. Above the cornice, a deep cove rises to a flat ceiling with a square border of strapwork guilloche enclosing a rococo panel of acanthus leaves, shells and volutes; these surround a displayed eagle with laurel branches in its claws (Plate 72).

The dining-room ceiling has a coved plaster cornice with wind-blown acanthus leaves. The fireplace has an eared wooden surround, inside which the inner mouldings of an earlier stone surround are seen. In the service rooms N.W. of the dining-room, the plinths of former outside walls suggest the extent of the early building. On the first floor, the bedroom over the drawing-room is lined to the ceiling with 17th-century oak panelling in four heights with a frieze. The fireplace is flanked by fluted pilasters which continue above the mantelshelf and terminate in Ionic capitals; the overmantel has a central Ionic pilaster flanked by geometric panels. The N.W. bedroom has 17th-century oak panelling. The bedroom above the dining-room has been divided by a secondary partition; the doorway from the staircase is flanked by panelled pilasters capped by scroll consoles with cornices. The fireplace, in the N.E. half of the partitioned room, has a moulded stone surround with splayed stops decorated with fleurs-de-lis.

Outbuildings include a late 18th-century brick *Coach-house* and *Stables*, some 50 yds. N.W. of the house, and a slightly earlier brick *Barn*, the same distance to the N.E.

(3) The Old Rectory (89140535), about 100 yds. N. of the church, is a two-storied building with dormer-windowed attics beneath a tiled roof. The N.E. front is of header-bonded brickwork, the S.W. front is rendered, the S.E. elevation is of Flemish-bonded brickwork and the N.W. elevation is masked by a late addition. The house is nearly square on plan and the roofs have two ridges and an intervening valley. The staircase is dated 1732 and this is probably the date of the whole house, apart from additions to the S.W. front which are probably of the first half of the 19th century, and the N.W. extension which dates from 1870.

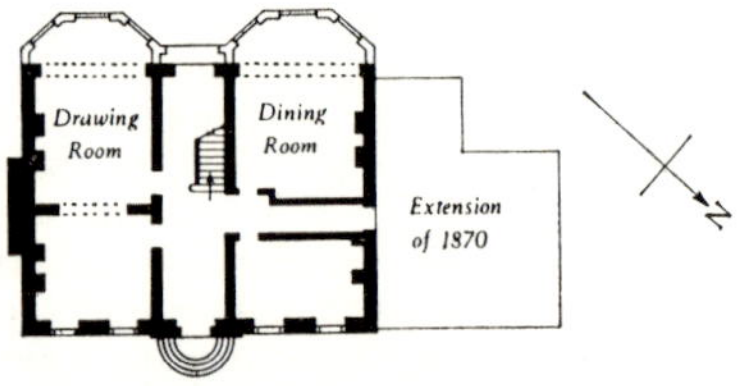

The N.E. front is symmetrical and of five bays, with a slightly projecting middle bay containing the front doorway (Plate 118). The eaves have a coved plaster and wooden cornice, returned on itself at the ends. The doorway is preceded by a flight of semicircular steps with swept wrought-iron handrails, and is flanked by wooden pilasters supporting elaborate carved consoles in the form of double scrolls decorated with acanthus leaves and scale-work; the consoles support a segmental hood. The moulded architrave of the doorway has eared corners and a keystone; the eight-panel door is of oak. The four ground-floor and five first-floor windows have stone sills with brick aprons, and flat gauged brick heads with triple keystones; the first-floor sashes retain original heavy glazing bars. In the roof are three casement dormer windows with hipped roofs and lead cheeks. The N.W. elevation is masked by the 19th-century wing but an 18th-century lead rainwater head can be seen at the end of the central roof valley; it has a moulded rim and a fluted bowl. The S.E. elevation has no openings and no rainwater outlet from the roof valley. The rendered S.W. front is largely of the 19th century, but it retains the old cornice, similar to that on the N.E. On the ground floor are two 19th-century projecting bays, each with three large sashed windows; in the upper storey the original façade has been rendered and the three sashed windows appear to be contemporary with the projecting bays below.

Inside, the Drawing-room has a reeded ceiling cornice and a fireplace with a moulded architrave with corner roundels, presumably contemporary with the bay windows. The Hall ceiling has a moulded cornice with leaf-and-dart ornament. The staircase is of oak and in two flights, extending only to the first floor. The string is open and the moulded nosing of the treads is returned at the end of each step, the spandrels below being enriched with carved scrolls (Plate 84). The turned balusters are small Tuscan columns above vase-shaped lower sections and the newel posts are larger Tuscan columns. The heavy moulded handrail is continuous, being ramped at the corners; at the foot it finishes in a fist-shaped volute. The wooden fascia of the landing is carved with flower and leaf arabesques surrounding a central medallion in which 'R.W. 1732' is incised, evidently for Robert Willis, rector from 1731 to 1748.

The *Stables* to the N. of the rectory are built in Flemish-bonded brickwork and probably date from the late 18th or early 19th century.

(4) Manor Farm, about 45 yds. N. of the church, is built of stone, brick and flint in two storeys, with dormer-windowed attics in a tiled roof. The main block, dating from the early 18th century, has a S.E. elevation of five bays with a central doorway flanked by sashed windows and five corresponding sashed windows on the first floor. This façade is of banded flint and brick, with a brick plat-band at first-floor level and a plaster eaves cove; much of the lower storey has been refaced with brickwork but some of the original banding survives at the E. end. Contiguous, to the W., is a slightly lower two-storied cottage of uncertain date but presumably later than the main block; it is of mixed brick and flint with brick quoins; further W. it is entirely of brick. The oak staircase in the main block has moulded close strings, turned balusters, moulded handrails and square newel posts.

A *Barn*, 15 yds. W. of the church, is of banded brick and flint with some weather-boarding and with a tiled roof; it is probably of the late 18th century but it has been much altered and repaired.

(5) Littleton House (89500480) is brick-built in two storeys, with cellars and attics. The main block, dating from late in the 18th century, was built in two stages, the central range being extended to N.E. and S.W. soon after it was built. In the 19th century various additions were made at the N.E. end of the range.

In the symmetrical N.W. front, which has a high proportion of header bricks, the first phase of construction comprising five bays is distinguishable, by perpendicular joints in the brick-work, from the two-bay additions at each end. The whole façade is capped by a light cornice with paterae at intervals in a band of fluting; over it the hipped roof is masked by a parapet, now partly cut away. The central doorway, at the top of a flight of stone steps, has an elliptical fanlight and a flat-roofed porch with two freestanding Ionic columns. All windows are sashed and have elliptical heads with stone impost blocks, keystones and sills. The dormer windows also have elliptical-headed sashes. The S.E. elevation is of English-bonded brickwork and is capped by a dentilled brick cornice and a parapet. The E. part of the S.E. front is hidden by later additions, which incorporate a reset 18th-century elliptical-headed door-way; the original windows are square-headed and sashed; at ground-floor level one opening has been superseded by a late 19th-century bay window.

(6) Cottages, three adjoining, 100 yds. W. of (5), have brick walls and tiled roofs. The plan is L-shaped, there being two tenements in a N.–S. range and a third tenement projecting E. at the S. end of the range. The middle cottage is two-storied with dormer-windowed attics; it was built about the end of the 18th century. The N. cottage, single-storied, and that to the E., two-storied, are of the 19th century; in the latter the N. front is entirely of blue header-bricks with red *chaînage*. A late 18th or early 19th-century brick granary with staddle-stones stands a few paces to the S.

(7) Cottages, pair (89240535), 100 yds. N.E. of (1), are single-storied with attics and have cob walls and thatched roofs; they were built about the middle of the 18th century. Each dwelling has a single ground-floor room and a lean-to scullery at the back. Large fireplaces, set back-to-back, are served by a central chimneystack. Winding stairs are fitted between the chimney-breasts and the front wall, the spaces on the other side of the fireplaces being filled by ovens. (*Demolished.*)

(8) Lower Farm, 200 yds. N. of the church, is two-storied with cob walls and thatched roofs. It was built at two periods, a straight vertical joint being visible in the N.W. wall. The N.E. part, which may be of the late 17th century, has lower eaves and floor-levels and smaller casement windows than the later and larger S.W. range. A bedroom in the later part has a bolection-moulded fireplace surround with a moulded mantel-shelf; the stairs have serpentine splat balusters.

(9) St. Mary's School (88740568) has walls of banded brick and flint with ashlar dressings, and tiled roofs; it is dated 1846. On plan the two classrooms are set at right-angles to one another to form a T, while the entrance vestibule forms the fourth arm of a cross. The doorways have four-centred heads and the windows have hollow-chamfered stone mullions in square-headed casement-moulded surrounds under hollow-chamfered labels.

(10) Old Ford House (88470592), on the N. side of the Poole road and 70 yds. E. of the junction with the Dorchester road, comprises two parts; the E. part dates from early in the 18th century and the W. part was added about a century later. Externally all walls are rendered. The older and smaller E. range has two storeys with attics under a tiled roof; in the N. front the ground floor has two three-light casement windows with wooden mullions, the first floor has corresponding sashed windows and there is a modern dormer window in the roof. The chimneystack rises above two open fireplaces set back-to-back in the wall which divides the ground floor into two rooms. One fireplace is spanned by a cambered and chamfered bressummer. The 19th-century W. range has large sashed windows in a N. front of three bays.

(11) Brook House (88450588), slightly set back from the S. side of the Poole road, 60 yds. from the Dorchester road junction, is of two storeys with attics and has brick walls and tiled roofs. It was built probably in the second quarter of the 18th century and belongs to Group (i) of the classified house-types (*see* p. 18). We cannot be

sure that this is the house built for his own use by the architect and carver Francis Cartwright (Colvin, *Biographical Dictionary*, 127), but no other building now found in the parish is more appropriate with regard to size and date.

The symmetrical five-bay N. front is of blue header brickwork with red brick dressings; it has sashed windows with stone lintels with triple keystones, a coved and moulded cornice stopped at each end against the side walls of adjacent buildings, and a central doorway (Plate 69). As usual the doorway is the most elaborate feature; on each side plain wooden pilasters carry carved double scroll consoles, the lower scrolls with scales and the larger upper scrolls with ornate undercut acanthus leaves; these support an open pedimental hood. Inside, the oak stairs have open strings and foliate scrolled spandrels; each tread has two turned balusters, vase-shaped below and with slender Tuscan columns above. The moulded oak handrail is ramped up at the corners and ends at Tuscan-column newel posts. The two main ground-floor rooms have moulded plaster cornices. The fireplace surrounds are of the 19th century.

(12) HOUSE, adjacent to the foregoing on the W., is probably of slightly earlier date. The N. front is largely rendered but a small portion of the wall displays banded brick and flint. The doorway, with a flat hood on shaped brackets, has two sashed windows to the E. and one to the W. The first floor has three three-light casement windows, the one to the W. retaining an original wrought-iron frame. Two gabled dormer windows in the tiled roof have two-light casements.

MONUMENTS (13–17)

The angle formed by the Dorchester and Poole roads contains a group of small, rendered and slate-roofed mid 19th-century dwellings, facing N. and W. To the S. of these, a row of late 18th and early 19th-century houses of two storeys with dormer-windowed attics fronts the Dorchester road.

(13) *House* (88390589) has a symmetrical W. front of Flemish-bonded brickwork in two bays with a central doorway. The ground-floor windows have projecting bays with sashed lights. The doorway has a flat hood on scrolled wooden brackets. On the first floor a sashed window occurs over each ground-floor bay window.

(14) *House and Shop*, adjacent to the foregoing on the S., has a rendered W. front; the N. end of the façade is defined by a vertical band of rustication. The ground floor has been largely rebuilt. On the W. front the first floor has two small sashed windows and there is a hip-roofed dormer with leaded casements in the roof; the latter is tiled, with stone-slate verges. The single chimneystack is at the N. end of the house and the winding staircase is placed beside the chimney breast.

(15) *The Stour Inn* continues the façade and roof of (14). It has a W. front of four bays, with a doorway flanked by bay windows similar to those of (13) and, at the S. end, a subsidiary doorway to a passage leading through to the rear of the building.

(16) *Houses* (88380586), two adjacent, originally one dwelling, have a rendered W. front set back about 3 ft. behind that of (15). The main part of the building, to the S., has a symmetrical three-bay W. front with sashed bay windows flanking the doorway on the ground floor, and three two-light casement windows above. The doorway has wooden pilasters terminating in scrolled consoles with acanthus foliage and masks; these carry an open-pediment hood. The first-floor windows have moulded wooden architraves, and casements with glazing-bars patterned in hexagons and squares. The N. house has a sashed window and a doorway on the ground floor and one first-floor window, as before.

(17) *Range* of three cottages (88360576), has walls built in a mixture of knapped flint, brick and rubble, with ashlar quoins and dressings, and a tiled roof. The gabled W. end wall has a central doorway flanked by casement windows on the ground floor, two corresponding windows and a blind central recess lined with brick headers on the first floor, and a casement window in the gable. The S. front is mainly of flint with brick dressings; the N. wall is rendered.

(18) HOUSE (88480588) is L-shaped in plan; it has rendered walls and a central brick chimneystack; the windows are sashed. It is probably of the mid 18th century.

(19) BARN (88770572) is constructed of weather-boarded timber framing on walls about 5 ft. high; the latter are of squared rubble, probably reused and perhaps taken from the church, with some brick and flint. The roof is slate-covered. Large doorways face one another in the N.W. and S.E. side walls, the S.E. doorway being in a projecting bay. The timber superstructure is of the mid 19th century but the plinth walls may be of the 18th century.

(20) TOLL HOUSE (88040519) is a mid 19th-century dwelling of one storey, with brick walls and slated roofs.

(21) THORNCOMBE FARM (85970283), house, 2½ m. S.W. of (1), is two-storied, with cob walls and a modern roof; it was built late in the 18th century. On the S. front the doorway is flanked by modern casement windows and there are three similar windows on the first floor.

(22) STABLES (86350455), of The Down House, are single-storied, with brick walls and tiled roofs. They comprise two ranges joining one another at right-angles. The older range, facing E., dates from the late 18th century and has an arched carriage-way flanked internally to N. and S. by entrances to two blocks of loose-boxes; each block is lit from the E. by a large round-headed window set between two small circular lights and, from the W., by other circular lights. The adjacent range, facing N., is of the early 19th century and contains four coach-houses and a hay-loft. A centrally placed terracotta medallion displays a helm with the crest of Smith. The Down House was destroyed by fire in 1941. It was a two-storied brick building with an E. front of seven bays, the three central bays enriched with pilasters and a pediment (*see* J. Pouncy, *Dorset Photographically Illustrated*, vol. 2). It may have incorporated late 18th-century elements, but the greater part was of *c.* 1820.

Early 19th-century monuments in the village also include Ivy Cottage (88290549), a house (88370579), and cottages at (88610580), (88740573) and (89230512).

MEDIAEVAL AND LATER EARTHWORKS

(23) SETTLEMENT REMAINS (892054), formerly part of the village of Blandford St. Mary, occur around the Manor House and immediately E. of Lower Farm. The remains, covering about 20 acres, lie on both sides of a broad hollow-way, 40 ft. wide and 3 ft. deep, running S.E.–N.W. and continuing the line of a lane in the village. Until the 19th century this hollow-way was the main road along the S.W. side of the R. Stour

(O.S., 1811). S.W. of the hollow-way are at least five rectangular closes, up to 70 yds. long and 50 yds. wide, bounded by low banks, with disturbed areas indicating the sites of former houses at their N.E. ends. N.E. of the hollow-way and N. of the Manor House, numerous small square and rectangular closes are defined by low banks and scarps. The remains are bounded on the N.W. by a shallow valley beyond which lies Monument (24).

(24) SETTLEMENT REMAINS (888057), formerly part of Blandford Martel, lie 400 yds. N.W. of the Manor House on either side of the railway. The remains, covering about 6 acres, consist of at least ten rectangular closes with sides up to 70 yds. long, bounded by low banks, scarps and slight ditches.

(25) SETTLEMENT REMAINS, part of the former village of Littleton, lie immediately E. of (5). The village, which was formerly a separate parish with its own church, had a recorded population of eight in 1086 (D.B. Vol. I., f. 79b). It is not mentioned in the 14th-century Lay Subsidy Rolls, but this is more probably because it was included under Langton Long Blandford than because it was deserted. Rectors continued to be appointed until 1427 (Hutchins I, 167). The remains cover about 12 acres and consist of fifteen rectangular closes, bounded by banks and scarps 1 ft. to 6 ft. high, lying on either side of and between two parallel embanked hollow-ways, 10 yds. wide and 4 ft. deep, orientated S.W.–N.E. There are no definite house-sites, but rectangular platforms 20 ft. by 30 ft. occur in some closes. Ridge-and-furrow 5 yds. to 6 yds. wide is superimposed on the N.E. half of the site and partly obliterates the closes. This part of the site is divided from the better-preserved S.W. half by an irregular but continuous bank and scarp, which cuts across the hollow-ways. Traces of other closes are seen on air photographs immediately S. of Littleton House (R.A.F. CPE/UK 1934: 3160).

ROMAN AND PREHISTORIC

(26) SETTLEMENT REMAINS, Romano-British, on high ground some 2 m. W. of Littleton, were noted about 1870 when the downland was converted to arable. Eight pits about 6 ft. deep and 4 ft. in diameter produced finds including pottery, oyster shells, animal bones, two brooches, and coins of Allectus and Constantine II. 'Vestiges of ancient dwellings and inclosures' were observed before ploughing, and it was noted afterwards that 'the discoloration of soil consequent on human occupation extends around for many acres' (Hutchins I, 167). Air photographs (R.A.F. CPE/UK 1934: 1092–3) show soil marks of an occupation area on Little Down (856039), with a trackway leading in from the E., and set among 'Celtic' fields (Group 68). Dykes (*see* below) are probably contemporary with the settlement.

'CELTIC' FIELDS, *see* p. 345, Group (68).

(27) CROSS-DYKE (86040460–86040396) runs N.–S. across the top of a W.–E. ridge at over 300 ft. O.D. between Little Down and Fox Ground Down. It is just over 100 yds. long but was probably somewhat longer before ploughing destroyed it at each end; it consists of a medial ditch between two banks with traces of a second ditch on the E. The W. bank is 24 ft. across and 3½ ft. high; the ditch is 12 ft. across and 1 ft. deep; the E. bank is 14 ft. across and 2½ ft. high. The dyke lies some 500 yds. E. of Monument (26) and is probably associated with it.

(28) DYKE (85390353–85690358) runs roughly W.–E. for over 300 yds. across the S. part of Little Down on an E.-facing slope. The W. portion, in Winterborne Clenston, has been destroyed by cultivation; to the E. it survives as a ditch 15 ft. across and 1½ ft. deep; there are no traces of a bank. The dyke appears to be associated with 'Celtic' fields and is possibly related to the settlement (26) which lies 400 yds. to the N.

(29) DYKE ? (86450392–87500372) is aligned W.N.W.–E.S.E. for some 1200 yds. along the axis of a low ridge, S. of Fox Ground Down; it comprises a ditch, up to 20 ft. across and 3 ft. deep, with a low bank along the S. side. The earthwork survives least damaged along the N. edge of New Plantation; cultivation has almost destroyed it E. of the Blandford–Dorchester road and has severely reduced it for some distance W. of this road. It probably was associated with 'Celtic' fields which lie to the N. It appears to have been used as a hollow-way and is shown as a track on O.S., 1811.

At the W. end, the earthwork meets another length of dyke (86440386–86500448) which extends for some 700 yds. from S.–N., across the ridge and down the N. slope, towards the bottom of the combe, S. of The Down House. Much of this dyke lies within woodland; where best preserved it comprises a scarp, 3 ft. high, falling eastwards to a shallow ditch, 4 ft. across.

(30) INHUMATION BURIALS, Romano-British, were found in 1833, ¼ m. S. of Blandford Bridge. Coins of Trajan and of the period from Maximian to Honorius, brooches, tweezers, 'spear-heads', a small glass vessel and a bronze figurine accompanied these burials and others found later (Hutchins I, 178–9; *Archaeologia* XXV (1834), 676–8).

MONUMENTS (31–38), ROUND BARROWS

Remains of eight barrows are traceable, all heavily ploughed. Nos. (33–8) comprise a compact group near Thorncombe and may represent the group of barrows, allegedly five in number, at least two of which were opened by Henry Durden in 1838. They are described as being on Little Down 'between Blandford and Thorncombe'; one barrow contained a cremation, probably primary, in a globular urn within a cist covered by a flint cairn etc., (*Barrow Diggers*, 50, 92; *C.T.D.*, *Pt. 2*, No. 3; *Arch. J.* CXIX (1962), 57); the other barrow contained an urn surrounded by a circular wall of flints (*Barrow Diggers*, 50). A 'bucket' urn that was found by Durden in a barrow on Littleton Down may be identical with the second named, or it may have been found in a third barrow (*ibid.*, 91).

(31) *Bowl* (86110404), on Little Down, on a spur at over 300 ft. O.D., is very heavily ploughed. Diam. 24 ft., ht. 6 ins.

(32) *Bowl* (86670397), on Fox Ground Down, lies further E. on the same spur as (31). Diam. 35 ft., ht. 1½ ft.

Thorncombe Group comprises six barrows at 300 ft. O.D. on a S.-facing slope near the summit of a broad E.–W. ridge. On air photographs (N.M.R.) all the barrows appear as ring ditches but on the ground only the first four are visible.

(33) *Barrow* (87280368) is now a low irregular mound about 36 ft. across surrounded by a very shallow ditch some 12 ft. wide; the whole barrow lies in a depression, set into the slope, measuring about 75 ft. across.

(34) *Barrow* (87290371), 28 yds. N.N.E. of (33), is now visible as a roughly circular, flat-bottomed depression about 75 ft. across and up to 3 ft. deep.

(35) *Bowl* (87280373), 29 yds. N. of (34), is a flat-topped mound 42 ft. in diameter and 9 ins. high, surrounded by a ditch 10 ft. wide and 1½ ft. deep.

(36) *Barrow* (87300374), 29 yds. N.E. of (35), is now an irregular hollow 66 ft. across and up to 3 ft. deep.

(37) *Barrow* (87300370), immediately E. of (34), is visible only on air photographs as a ring-ditch about 30 ft. in diameter.

(38) *Barrow* (87300372), just N. of (37), is in a similar condition. Diam. about 40 ft.

UNDATED

(39) Enclosure and Ditch, in Thorncombe Bottom, have been completely flattened by cultivation in the past and are identifiable only as soil marks brought to the surface by deep ploughing. They lie at about 250 ft. above O.D. on the S. slope of a low Chalk spur, extending E. and covered with a thin, patchy layer of Clay-with-Flints (*see* illustration, p. 345).

The enclosure (86550300) is an irregular oval, approximately 200 ft. by 140 ft. and about ⅜ acre in area; it is defined by a ditch 6 ft. to 8 ft. across, with a simple gap entrance on the S.S.E. Air photographs suggest that the bank lay outside the ditch. On the N.E. the enclosure dips into the head of a narrow gully where an oval brown earth patch represents the fill of a depression, probably a 'marl-pit' of relatively recent date. Within the enclosure are two slight E.–W. scarps, possibly lynchets; the lower scarp seems to continue outside the enclosure, suggesting that the enclosure was built over it. No 'finds' or other evidences of occupation are recorded.

The ditch (86420292, centre) comprises a shallow curve of bank and ditch, 550 ft. long, appearing in the plough on the E. side of a modern field hedge running N.–S.; there is no clear indication of it W. of the hedge. It is not known whether it is part of an enclosure or of a longer linear work. Spread chalk indicates that the bank lies on the W. of the ditch.

7 BRYANSTON (8706)

(O.S. 6 ins. ST 80 NE)

Bryanston parish extends over some 1,500 acres, rising from an altitude of 100 ft. on the S.W. bank of the R. Stour, which forms its eastern boundary, to 500 ft. above sea-level in the W. Three dry valleys cross the area from W. to E., draining into the Stour. Quarleston Down at the S.W. end of the parish was until recently divided between Winterborne Clenston and Winterborne Stickland. The original village of Bryanston lay in the vicinity of the church, now the Portman Chapel (1), at the mouth of a dry valley. In mediaeval times it was a relatively large settlement; twenty-three taxpayers are recorded in the 1333 Subsidy Rolls (P.R.O., E. 179/103/5), but in 1662 the number of households had dwindled to six (Meekings, 69). Early in the 18th century the site of the village was occupied by a large house and its dependencies, the seat of the Berkeley Portman family from the 17th century onwards. In 1778 the house was demolished and replaced by another, and in 1890 this house was in turn demolished and replaced by the great mansion which still stands some 500 yds. to the N.W. of the first site. It is now part of Bryanston School. In 1898 a new parish church was built on or very near the site of the former houses.

BRYANSTON - *Portman Chapel*

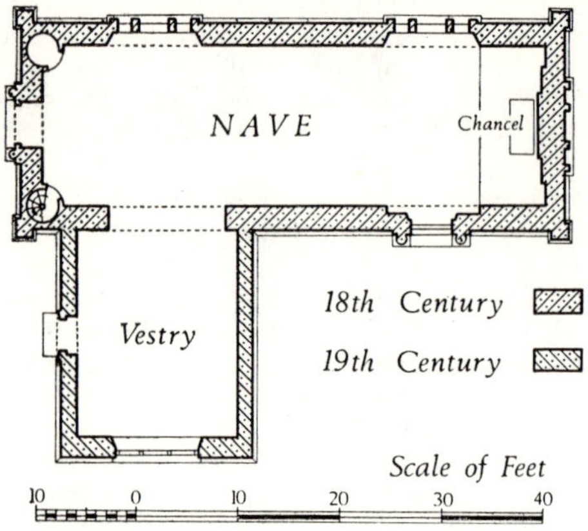

ECCLESIASTICAL

(1) The Portman Chapel (87460705) stands on the site of the mediaeval church. Hutchins (I, 263) states that the chancel of the old parish church was rebuilt in 1745, and by this he probably means that the present undivided *Nave* and *Chancel* took the place of the old chancel, the rest of the mediaeval church being demolished. The antecedent nave had been rebuilt in the 16th century but nothing visible today is earlier than the 18th century; only the flint plinths in the E. part of the chapel may incorporate earlier masonry. A *Vestry* with rendered brick walls to the S. of the chapel is of the 19th century.

The 18th-century chapel has walls of rendered flint and rubble, with ashlar dressings and rusticated stone quoins forming angle pilasters; the roofs are slate-covered, with lead ridges. The N. and S. walls have stone cornices with modillions, and the E. and W. walls have pedimented gables with moulded cornices. Above the W. gable is a wooden bell-cote with a clock and a small bell under a concave lead-covered cupola. On the outside of the E. wall is a blind Palladian window. The chapel is lit by two Venetian windows in the N. wall and by a round-headed window to the S.; the latter was originally a doorway and is flanked externally by a pair of Ionic columns supporting an entablature with a reeded frieze and paterae. The square-headed W. doorway is flanked by Ionic columns carrying a segmental pediment.

Inside, the combined *Nave* and *Chancel* form a chamber measuring 49½ ft. by 15½ ft., rectangular, except that the two W. corners are convex, making space in the S.W. corner for a wooden vice to the bell-cote and in the N.W. corner for a closet. Plaster cornices with acanthus mouldings run the length of the N. and S. walls but do not return to E. and W.; over them, coves lead up to a flat plaster ceiling with a moulded border.

Fittings—*Doorway:* At W. end of nave, with carved oak internal architrave and scroll pediment, 18th century. *Monuments:* On N. wall, at E. end, (1) of H. W. B. Portman, 1796, and others of same family, marble wall-tablet with fluted and enriched border. Opposite, on S. wall, (2) of Henry William Berkeley Portman, 1761, and his wife Ann Fitch, 1781, marble wall-monument in form of obelisk, with arms. In churchyard, reset in pavement W. of W. doorway, (3) of Henry Wills,

1741 (?); (4) of John Gaun . . ., 1715; (5) of William M. t . . ., 1753, stone slabs; (6) of Robert Kingston, 1741, Purbeck stone slab with moulded border, probably from former table-tomb. S. of vestry, (7) of John Tomson, 1765, stone slab; also several other slabs, illegible. *Panelling:* On nave walls, of oak, with two heights of fielded panels, from 18th-century box pews, recently reset and restored. *Plate:* recorded by J. E. Nightingale (*Church Plate of Dorset*, 140), now at Durweston (*see* p. 91). *Pulpit*: hexagonal, panelled oak, on hexagonal pedestal, with oak stair; 18th century, restored. *Reredos:* On E. wall, of painted plaster and wood with pedimented entablature on foliate console brackets; central panel with tables of Decalogue, side panels with festoons of flowers and various emblems in relief; 18th century. *Royal Arms:* Formerly over W. door of chapel and now transferred to modern church, arms as used 1714–1800, carved in wood.

SECULAR

(2) Bryanston House. Reference has been made in the parish introduction to the history of the site. The house demolished in 1778 is known from J. Kip's engraving (*Britannia Illustrata*, 1714, pl. 77) and from a perspective view included in Bastard's plan of Blandford Forum (Plate 104). Kip shows it as standing about 50 yds. S. of the old church (1). The house that replaced it was designed by James Wyatt; it probably stood a little S. of the first house, on the site that is now occupied by the church of 1898. Wyatt's house was pulled down in 1890, but its appearance is recorded by Hutchins (I, facing p. 263), and in photographs and paintings in possession of the Portman family. It was replaced by a mansion (870074) designed in the grand classical manner by Richard Norman Shaw, with a great central block, inspired by Coleshill in Berkshire, and lower flanking wings set well back from the S.E. or garden front and extending N.W. to flank a large forecourt; it is one of the largest English country houses to be built in modern times.

Of the two preceding houses some traces remain. Wyatt's house is represented by an *Annex*, probably part of the service range; it stands some 50 yds. S. of (1) and is single-storied, with walls of Greensand ashlar and a slated roof. The E. front has a pedimented centre bay of three arched recesses flanked by lateral wings, each of three bays. The middle recess contains a square-headed doorway, that to each side has a sashed window and all three recesses have lunette windows above. Each lateral wing originally had three round-headed sashed windows. The W. side of the structure is sunk in sharply rising ground and two massive ashlar chimneystacks rise from the W. wall. Inside, there are three large rooms with moulded plaster cornices and plain ceilings.

The *Stables*, 30 yds. W. of (1), were probably built towards the middle of the 18th century; Bastard's plan of Blandford Forum (*see* Plate 104) shows that they are later than 1731. They are single-storied with lofts and comprise three ranges on three sides of a courtyard open to the E.; each range is traversed by a central carriage-way. The walls are of brick. The hipped roofs, with lead dressings, are partly slate-covered and partly tiled; they rise from lath-and-plaster modillion cornices. The W. range is more decoratively treated than those to the N. and S.; the central archway on the E. front is outlined in rusticated ashlar and opens in a pedimented feature set a little in front of the main wall-face and defined by rusticated ashlar quoins; a round attic window in the pediment has a rusticated stone surround. On either side of the central bay are two round-headed windows. The N. and S. ranges have central carriage-ways flanked, on the courtyard side, by round-headed windows with gauged brick archivolts and white stone impost blocks and keystones. The E. ends of the N. and S. ranges have blank walls embellished with false Palladian windows. Inside, some loose-boxes retain original cast-iron fittings. To the N. of the N.W. corner of the stables is a projecting annex, now a cottage but originally a coach house. Its three wide doorways have elliptical brick heads with stone imposts and keystones; these openings have been blocked and the cottage door and windows are inserted in the blocking.

The *Gateway* (88330592), nearly 1 m. S.E. of (1), is of Greensand ashlar with Portland stone dressings; presumably it was designed by James Wyatt *c.* 1778 and it comprises, on the E. front, an archway flanked by Doric columns supporting a pedimented entablature; attached to each side of the entry are single-storied lodges, each with one tall sashed window. To right and left stone walls curve forward to the roadside, bounding a broad exedra; each wall ends at a large stone pier surmounted by a heraldic beast with a shield (Plate 67).

Earthwork Remains (875073) of gardens and outbuildings of the house which preceded that of 1778 lie N.E. of (1) on land which slopes gently E. to the R. Stour. Low banks and scarps, much obscured by later work, and rectangular platforms, appear to represent the northern third of the gardens and outbuildings of the house depicted by J. Kip (*loc. cit.*); presumably they were abandoned *c.* 1778.

(3) Bryanston Farm House (87030692) is L-shaped in plan; the main block, facing N., is of the late 18th or early 19th century while the S. wing may be an earlier 18th-century building, altered when the N. wing was added. The house is of two storeys, with attics in low-pitched slated roofs; the walls are rendered. The symmetrical N. front has a central doorway in a projecting porch, two sashed windows on each side and five in the first floor; the windows of the three middle bays are grouped together while the outer windows are set further apart and are wider than the others. Inside, the N. wing contains nothing of note, but a first-floor room in the S. wing is lined from floor to ceiling with 18th-century fielded oak panelling with moulded skirtings and oak cornices.

(4) Model Farm, immediately S. of (3), dates from the first half of the 19th century; it does not appear on the O.S. map of 1811. The extensive buildings are laid out around a narrow courtyard, at the S. end of which remains the moulded stone base of a factory chimney, now demolished. The buildings, in English-bonded brickwork, are two-storied with slated roofs. Many of the openings are spanned by elliptical gauged brick arches.

(5) Cottages, in a row, parallel with the E. range of (4) and 50 yds. to the E., are of brick in two storeys, with slated roofs. Most of the cottages are probably contemporary with the Model Farm, but the *Post Office* at the N. end may be a little earlier; it has a tiled roof.

(6) Broadley Cottage (85080628) is a two-storied dwelling with rendered walls and a tiled roof; the central part, with a symmetrical E. front of three bays, is probably of the late 18th century.

(7) Ranges of estate cottages on each side of the road (88330579), five to the N. and three to the S., have brick walls

and tiled roofs and are probably of *c.* 1825. Each tenement is two-storied with a dormer-windowed attic. The original ground plan of each cottage probably comprised a single room with stairs against the side wall, but later improvements have caused the stairs and an entrance passage to be partitioned off and a kitchen annexe to be added at the back.

(8) BERKELEY LODGE (88350583) stands on the W. side of the Dorchester road, 100 yds. S. of the gateway of (2). It is two-storied with rendered walls and slate-covered roofs and was built in the second half of the 18th century. The symmetrical E. front has a central doorway sheltered by a flat-roofed Doric porch with two free-standing fluted columns and two engaged half columns. A sashed window opens on each side of the porch and there are three corresponding windows on the first floor, each with a narrow keystone. The six openings are set in a slightly projecting central feature, to either side of which the wall-face is blank. The eaves have a coved cornice which breaks forward around the central feature and returns on the gabled end walls. The S. elevation includes the gabled end of the E. range and, to the W., the side of a two-storied rear wing, the house having an L-shaped plan. On the W. side of the E. range, to the N., is an early 19th-century wrought-iron trellis-work veranda, now glazed to form a conservatory. Inside, the close-string staircase has turned balusters, a moulded oak handrail and oak steps.

MEDIAEVAL EARTHWORKS

(9) CULTIVATION REMAINS. Nothing is known of the open fields of the parish or of the date of their enclosure. On the S. side of a dry valley, W. of Bryanston Farm (866068–869068), are three contour strip lynchets up to 500 yds. long. The very uneven nature of the risers suggests that the strip lynchets were formed by ploughing over earlier 'Celtic' fields; the latter continue, largely undamaged, immediately to the W. (Group (60), p. 341).

ROMAN AND PREHISTORIC

'CELTIC' FIELDS, *see* Group (60), p. 341.

(10) INHUMATION BURIAL and OCCUPATION DEBRIS (870075), Romano-British, were found in 1958 at Bryanston School at about 300 ft. above O.D. on a chalk ridge. The burial, an extended adult male in a shallow grave, had been deposited in a wooden coffin. Some 16 ft. to the N. a circular pit, 5½ ft. deep and 4½ ft. in diameter, contained chalk rubble, flints, 2nd-century to 4th-century pottery including a samian sherd, and a bronze brooch. There were traces of another pit to the S.E. Previously other coins and pottery had been found in the area. (Dorset *Procs.* XXVIII (1907), xxxix; LXXX (1958), 108–10.)

8 BUCKLAND NEWTON (6805)

(O.S. 6 ins. ST 60 NE, ST 60 SE, ST 70 NW, ST 70 SW)

The parish, covering about 6,000 acres, straddles the Chalk escarpment which at this point is relatively low, and extensively cut into by N.-flowing streams. The S. half of the parish rises from 500 ft. to 800 ft. above sea-level and is almost entirely Chalk; in the N. half the land undulates gently between 300 ft. and 500 ft. and is composed of Gault, Kimmeridge Clay and Corallian Beds, except for the 600 ft. Chalk outlier of Dungeon Hill.

The hill-fort on Dungeon Hill, now incorporated in Buckland Newton, has already been described in *Dorset* I (*Minterne Magna* (6)); conversely the monuments of Minterne Parva are described in this volume although they now lie within the boundaries of Minterne Magna. Plush, a detached part of Buckland Newton until 1933, is now in Piddletrenthide (*see* p. 212).

The mediaeval and later history of the parish is complex and in some respects obscure. There appear to have been five original settlements: Minterne Parva, Buckland Newton, Henley (probably identical with the Knoll of some early documents), Duntish and Brockhampton. Each settlement probably had its own open field system. Beyond the open fields, secondary settlements associated with small enclosures were established by the 13th century; for instance Chaston Farm, Revels Farm, and perhaps Bookham.[1] There are extensive areas of 'Celtic' fields in the S., and a Deer Park of about 190 acres, which was made at the latest in the 13th century, has been identified N.W. of Duntish.[2] Large parts of the parish were still uncultivated at a late date and extensive areas of Common were not enclosed until the middle of the 19th century.[3]

The principal monument is the Parish Church. Castle Hill (4), another important monument, was demolished in 1965.

ECCLESIASTICAL

(1) THE PARISH CHURCH OF THE HOLY ROOD, which stands near the centre of the parish, was extensively restored in the second half of the 19th century, and external rendering makes analysis of the architectural development difficult. The walls are probably of rubble with ashlar dressings; the roofs are lead-covered. The *Chancel* is largely of the 13th century and the *Nave* and the *North* and *South Aisles* are of the 15th century; the uniformity of the aisle windows might suggest Victorian restoration but Hutchins's early 19th-century account of the church (2nd ed., vol. iii (1813), p. 262f., and illustration on p. 254) leaves no doubt that they are original. The *West Tower* and the *South Porch* date from the 15th century; above the porch is an upper chamber. Although the chancel is the oldest standing part of the church, fragments of 12th-century sculpture

[1] Fägersten, 203.
[2] Dorset *Procs.*, 84, (1962), 147.
[3] Enclosure Map, 1849, (D.C.R.O.).

bear witness to an earlier building; they include a representation of Christ in Majesty, formerly in the tower but recently reset in the porch.

The 13th-century windows in the side walls of the chancel (Plate 120) are unusually fine work for a country church of that date, and the 15th-century nave and aisles (Plate 120) are notable for their symmetry and spaciousness.

Architectural Description—The *Chancel* (33½ ft. by 18½ ft.) was restored in 1869 but it appears to retain the original N. wall; the S. wall is 7 ins. thinner than the N. and it may have been rebuilt, the original windows being reset. In 1841 the original E. window, of three lancets, was replaced by an opening in the Perpendicular style but this was removed in 1869 and the present three-light window, of 13th-century style, was substituted. Externally, the walls have moulded ashlar plinths, hollow-chamfered plaster string-courses and embattled parapets. The N. wall has three uniform lancet windows with chamfered external reveals and plaster hood-moulds; internally, the splays are flanked by Purbeck marble shafts, with moulded bases and capitals, supporting chamfered trefoil rear-arches of Ham Hill stone; the rear-arches are restored but the shafts are original. The moulded internal sills are continuous with that of the 19th-century E. window. The S. wall has three lancet windows uniform with those to the N., and a later doorway with a chamfered two-centred head and a segmental rear-arch. On both sides of the chancel, at the W. end, are small squints from the aisles, with chamfered segmental heads. The late 15th-century chancel arch is two-centred; the responds and soffit are decorated with tiers of cusped stone panelling flanked to E. and W. by continuous mouldings. The N. respond is pierced, high up, by the rood stair passage, the chamfered half-arch of which is seen in the N. aisle. The 19th-century roof is supported on sculptured corbels that are probably of the 15th century: N. wall, (i) and (iv) an angel with folded wings bearing a shield; (ii) a mitred bishop, blessing; (iii) a king. S. wall, (i) a human face; (ii) a head flanked by hands bearing torches; (iii) a similar head and hands bearing a cross and a book; (iv) a bearded head.

The *Nave* (39 ft. by 18 ft.) is flanked to N. and S. by uniform arcades of three bays; that to the N. was extensively restored in 1877. The arches are two-centred and of two hollow-chamfered orders springing from slender piers and responds, composed of attached shafts separated by hollow-chamfers, with moulded capitals and bases. The *North Aisle* (10 ft. wide) has, externally, a chamfered and moulded plinth, a hollow-chamfered parapet string-course and an embattled parapet with a moulded coping, all rendered. The N.E. and N.W. corners have two-stage diagonal buttresses with weathered offsets; the two intermediate square-set buttresses, of ashlar and rubble, are of 1877. The E. window and the three N. windows are uniform except that the sill of the central N. window incorporates the head of the N. doorway; each window is of three transomed lights with vertical tracery in a two-centred head, and with casement-moulded outer reveals; the transoms are composed of the four-centred cinquefoil heads of the lower lights combined with inverted trefoils at the foot of the upper lights; the upper lights have cinquefoil ogee heads; the tracery lights are cinquefoiled at top and bottom. The N. doorway has a two-centred head with ogee and hollow-chamfered mouldings, continuous jambs and chamfered stops. The *South Aisle* is uniform with the N. aisle except that the middle bay, masked by the two-storied porch, has no window. The S. doorway has a moulded four-centred head with continuous jambs; beside it, in the S. aisle, is a four-centred doorway to the porch chamber vice; both openings are of *c.* 1877.

The *West Tower* (12½ ft. by 12 ft.) is set a little to the S. of the nave centre-line. It has three storeys internally and two stages externally; the N.W. and S.W. diagonal buttresses are of two weathered stages; they do not extend into the upper stage of the tower, suggesting that it may originally have been lower than at present. At the base is a chamfered plinth; the upper stage is defined by a hollow-chamfered string-course and below the parapet is a moulded string-course with gargoyles.

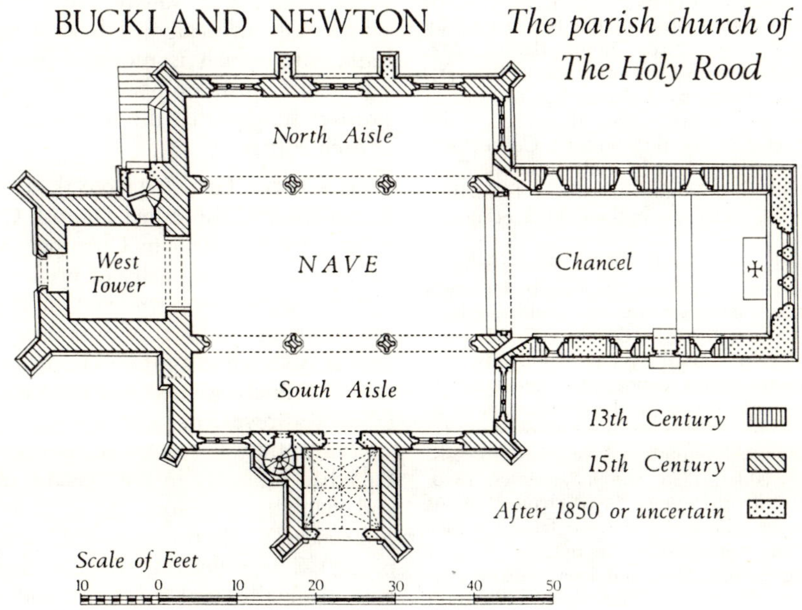

The parapet is embattled, with a crocketed finial on each corner. The two-centred tower arch is of two moulded orders, the outer order continuous and the inner order dying into the responds at springing level. The tower vice, on the N. side, has a 19th-century external doorway and an original internal doorway with a chamfered two-centred head. The 15th-century W. doorway has a two-centred head with a concentric hollow-chamfered label terminating to the N. in a lion stop and to the S. in a beast; above, the W. window has three cinquefoil-headed lights with vertical tracery in a casement-moulded two-centred outer head, with a hollow-chamfered label. The upper stage has square-headed two-light belfry windows on the E., N. and W. sides; at a lower level the N. side also has a square-headed two-light window to the clock chamber. The clock-face is to the W. and a 12th-century figure of Christ in Majesty, now in the S. porch, was formerly set in a small niche above it.

The *South Porch* (10 ft. square) has an upper chamber and at the S.E. and S.W. corners are diagonal buttresses of two weathered stages. The rendered, embattled parapet is continuous with that of the aisle; it has a hollow-chamfered parapet string with a gargoyle at each southern corner. The S. archway, probably of the 19th century, is of ashlar, with a moulded four-centred head under a square label; the spandrels are decorated with trefoils and quatrefoils. Above, the square-headed two-light window of the upper chamber is probably of the 18th century. The 15th-century lierne vault of the porch has hollow-chamfered wall, diagonal and intermediate ribs springing from moulded angle corbels; the ridge and diagonal ribs meet at a large central boss carved with a double rose; the intersections of the intermediate ribs and liernes are masked by foliate bosses while smaller leaf bosses mask the outer intersections.

Fittings—*Bells:* six; 2nd, by John Wallis, inscribed 'Iohn Phillippes Vicar Gilbert Duning John Squier' with monogram IW and date 1581; 3rd, inscribed 'Ave Maria' in Lombardic capitals; 4th, by Thomas Purdue, 1670; 5th, by T. and J. Bilbie, 1793; 6th, by John Wallis, inscribed 'John Phillipps vicar Edward Boxly Thomas Frye churchwardens', with monogram IW and date 1609. *Books:* Bible in black-letter, 8 ins. by 6 ins., 1589, rebound. *Brasses:* In chancel, on S. wall, (1) to Leonard Pount, 1829, inscription-tablet (8 ins. by 16 ins.) by J. Latten. In S. aisle, on W. wall, (2) to Thomas Barnes, 1624, brass plate (8 ins. by 14½ ins.) with Latin inscription (Plate 41). *Chair:* of mahogany, with reeded sabre-shaped legs and carved shell-shaped back, early 19th century. *Chest:* of oak, (1¼ ft. by 3¾ ft.) with three locks, mid to late 18th century. *Coffin stools:* two, with turned legs. 17th and early 18th century. *Font:* Octagonal stone bowl with vertical sides carved with formalised flowers, hollow-chamfered underside and moulded octagonal stem, 15th century.

Monuments: In chancel, on S. wall, (1) of Anna Selleck, 1680, stone cartouche, part of a monument recorded by Hutchins (III, 712). In S. aisle, (2) of Fitzwalter Foy, 1781, and Elizabeth Maria his wife, 1806, erected by their daughter E. M. Foy, grey and white marble tablet flanked by reeded pilasters, surmounted by female figure posed beside urn, fluted apron below, signed 'T. King, Bath' (Plate 39). In churchyard, E. of chancel, (3) of Ann Venables, 1817, table-tomb with arms, (4) of Richard Childes, 1627, table-tomb, (5) of Henry Lewis, 1845, Mary Caroline Venables, 1846, and J. Venables, 1850, table-tomb in form of Hellenistic altar; N. of chancel, (6) of Michael Millar, 1681, and others of the same family, table-tomb with 17th, 18th and 19th-century inscriptions; S.E. of chancel, (7) of Dunning family, 1600 and later, table-tomb; W. of porch, (8) of Rev. Timothy Collins, 1766, table-tomb with arms; E. of porch, (9) of Mary Tucksberry, 1698, head-stone.

Plate: includes silver cup of 1571 and pair of stand-patens of 1827 and 1829, also silver flagon of 1762. *Poor-box:* of oak, 3 ft. high, with chamfered post with diagonal banding on two sides supporting square coffer carved on each face with crocketed ogee ornament and decorated at corners with knopped standards; lid fastened by hinged iron cross-straps, one fixed, three with locks; 16th century (Plate 22). *Pulpit:* of oak, hexagonal, with moulded base and cornice, each face with two fielded panels with marquetry decoration; 18th century. *Seating:* In chancel and nave, twenty-two 15th-century oak bench ends with moulded edges and linenfold panels, four with foliate finials, others square-topped, many with new top rails; twelve similar panels incorporated in desks to front pews. *Sundial:* On parapet of S. porch, rectangular stone dial with initials I.H., H.E. and date 1704. *Weather-vane:* of wrought-iron, inscribed FF, 1735, now in porch chamber. *Miscellanea:* Loose in porch chamber, (1) floor-tiles, 15th or 16th century; (2) three carved stone fragments with chevron ornament and roll-mouldings, 12th century. In S. aisle, reset over S. doorway, (3) mica-schist relief (13 ins. by 10 ins.) representing warrior with bow and spear, possibly N. European, 7th or 8th century (*cf.* Böhner, *Bonner Jahrbuch* (1951), 108 f.), discovered in Vicarage garden, 1910 (Plate 13). In porch, over S. doorway, (4) sculptured limestone fragment depicting Christ in Majesty, with right hand raised in blessing and left arm across waist, perhaps holding book, 12th century (Plate 12); moved from W. side of tower, 1960.

SECULAR

(2) Brockhampton Bridge (71690622), 12 ft. wide by 21 ft. long, is of the early 19th century and has two spans and round-ended rubble piers. The rubble parapets are capped with rough stones set on edge.

(3) Wayside Cross (66430345), at Minterne Parva, is probably of the 15th century. It now consists of a stone plinth, 3 ft. square and 1 ft. 3 ins. high, upon which rests an octagonal base, 3 ft. across and 6 ins. high, into which is morticed the stump of a shaft, 1 ft. 3 ins. square on plan and 2 ft. 4 ins. high. Vertical grooves suggest that the shaft had a moulded standard at each corner.

(4) Castle Hill (69230682), 1 m. N.N.E. of the parish church, also called Duntish Court, was designed *c.* 1760 by Sir William Chambers for Fitzwalter Foy. The house was originally of brick with stone dressings but the walls were rendered in the 19th century; at the same time the roof was heightened. The house was demolished in 1965 and in the course of its destruction the finely jointed red brickwork of the original fabric was revealed.

Castle Hill was a dignified country residence showing Palladian influence in the massing of the central block and flanking pavilions. It is illustrated in *Vitruvius Britannicus*, V, pls. 61–3, and in Hutchins (1st ed., II, opp. p. 257). These illustrations show that the central block was originally without attics and that the pavilions were joined to the central block only by low screen walls, pierced by gateways. Each pavilion was surmounted by a square lantern with arched sides and a concave tent-shaped roof, probably lead-covered, supporting a weathervane. Subsequently, to enlarge the house, the roof-level of the centre block was raised and dormer-windowed attic rooms were provided; the stairs were remodelled and a vestibule was added; the N. pavilion, originally containing stables, was made into kitchens and service rooms; the pavilions were joined to the central block by converting the screen walls into ground-floor passages, and the lanterns on the pavilions were turned into chimneys by removing the tent-shaped roof and inserting a tall octagonal flue at the centre of each. These changes were made in the second half of the 19th century.

The following description, compiled while the house was still standing, is given in the present tense in the usual terms of the Commission's survey.

Architectural Description—The main part of the house is of three storeys with dormer-windowed attics. The ground floor, originally service rooms, now contains a billiard room and living rooms of secondary importance; the principal rooms are on the first floor and are approached from the garden by ornamental flights of steps; the principal bedrooms are on the second floor. The main entrance, at ground level on the W., is preceded by a 19th-century octagonal vestibule, rusticated externally and roofed with a lead dome. The vestibule and the passages on either side, leading to the N. and S. pavilions, conceal the lower part of the main block. Above them, the W. façade is symmetrical and of five bays, the three middle bays being grouped in a slightly projecting pedimented feature; the windows of the flanking bays are more isolated; the central projection is also emphasised by a subsidiary cornice at second-floor sill level. The main cornice, with modillions, is set some distance above the second-floor window heads; the same mouldings with the addition of a corona form the inclined coping of the pediment. Above the flanking bays the original cornice is surmounted by a high plaster cove decorated at intervals with acanthus scrolls in relief; the cove and the dormer windows in the heightened roof are of the 19th century.

The E. façade (Plate 123) resembles the W. in having a pedimented central projection of three bays, and single-windowed flanking bays. The ground floor has rusticated quoins at the outer angles and window lintels with heavily rusticated voussoirs. In the centre a double stone stair sweeps up to a balustraded platform in front of the central first-floor opening, which extends down to the floor and has a semicircular head, and glazed doors in place of the lower sash. The other first-floor windows have moulded stone architraves with horizontal entablatures; the second-floor windows have architraves only. The cornice, pediment and coved eaves are similar to those of the W. front. The S. façade is without a pediment, but otherwise repeats the details of the E. front; it has three openings on each floor including a doorway at the centre on the ground floor; a pedimented hood distinguishes the central window on the first floor. The N. façade has fenestration similar to that on the S. but the openings resemble those of the W. front in having no architrave mouldings.

The N. and S. pavilions are single-storied. The N. pavilion is faced on the E. side with rusticated round-headed arcading in five bays, the end bays projecting a little in front of the other three. The middle arch has a doorway with a fanlight above, the other four arches have rectangular windows. The roof is of slate with lead dressings and the eaves have coved cornices. The plan of the service rooms inside the pavilion bears no relation to the E. façade, being separated from it by a corridor. The S. pavilion is similar to the N., except that the S. bay of the arcaded E. front is replaced by a glass conservatory. The great central chimneystack on each pavilion is a prominent feature; it comprises an embattled octagonal flue rising through an open aedicule, square on plan, with a round-headed arch in each side and ball finials on canted pedestals at the corners. The aedicules appear to survive from the roof lanterns of the original design.

Inside the main block, the central doorway of the W. front leads into the octagonal vestibule and thence, by a short flight of stairs, to the Hall where are the principal staircase, a doorway to the Saloon on the E., and doorways to the Drawing Room and Boudoir on the S. The stairs and other fittings are of the 19th century. The Saloon has a panelled dado and six-panel doors with a central bead to simulate two leaves. The doorway

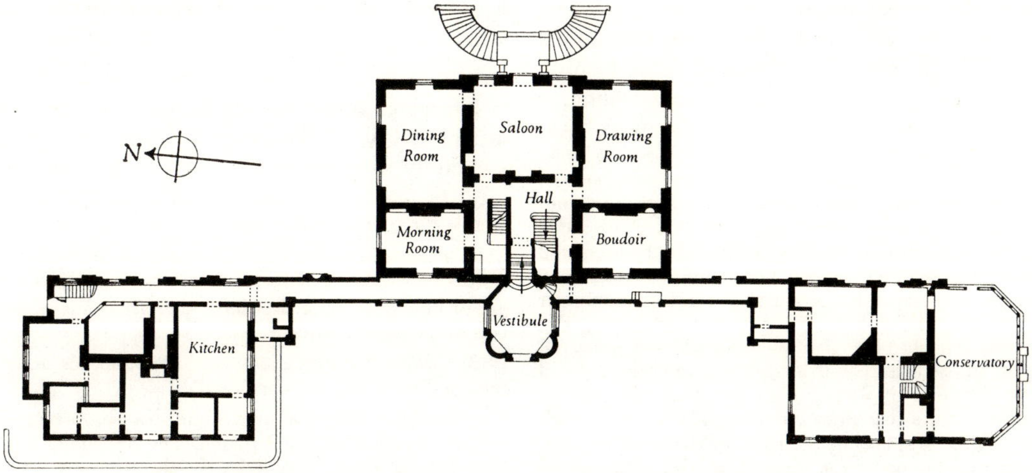

BUCKLAND NEWTON. (4) Castle Hill. Plan of principal storey.

architraves are capped by heavy entablatures with pulvinated oak-leaf friezes in gesso. The fireplace surround, of plaster in imitation of stone, is decorated with swags of drapery flanking a bull's skull below a Doric cornice. The Drawing Room doors and doorways are generally similar to those in the Saloon. The 18th-century plaster ceiling and cornices are enriched with foliate ornament, swags, reeding and trophies of musical instruments (Plate 72). In the fireplace surround, richly decorated white marble brackets support a white marble frieze and cornice, set off against a background of red marble; the middle panel of the frieze has a classical urn and sprays of foliage, the side panels, over the brackets, have paterae; below the brackets are lion masks and pendent wreaths. In the Dining Room the walls are decorated with large plaster panels. A frieze of pendent drapery between vases is surmounted by a modillion cornice, and the ceiling is enriched with a reeded oval border entwined with vine sprays; at the centre are three wreaths of ears of corn, the central wreath surrounding an urn and patera. The fireplace has an inner surround of red veined marble flanked by wooden Ionic columns which support an entablature with a centre panel depicting *putti* among vine wreaths. The Morning Room has a wooden fireplace surround enriched with acanthus leaves and a central frieze panel of leaves and wreaths. In the Boudoir, niches flanking the fireplace have glazed doors with traceried glazing bars. The variegated marble fireplace surround is flanked by wooden pilasters carved with masks from which hang wreathed leaf sprays, above is a frieze of classical urns and swags of leaves. On the ground floor, below, the Billiard Room has an ornate fireplace in which the cornice is supported on foliate scroll brackets from which pendent sprays of flowers and fruit hang down on each side; in the frieze swags of grape vine luxuriate on each side of a central urn.

The mullioned stone windows from a 16th or 17th-century building are reset in the flint wall of a *Summer House*, 100 yds. W. of the main building. They are chamfered and hollow-chamfered and have plain labels. They probably come from the earlier house, which stood to the S. of the 18th-century building (Hutchins, III, 708); Thomas Barnes repaired it in the 17th century (Coker, 95). To the S. of the S. pavilion is an 18th-century *Grotto* of rubble and flint.

Buckland Newton, Henley and Brockhampton Green

(5) The Vicarage (68810527), 30 yds. E. of (1), has two storeys and attics; the main block is of the first half of the 18th century and a S.W. wing was added about 1850. The E. front is of brickwork in Flemish bond; elsewhere the walls are rendered or tile-hung.

The symmetrical E. front is of seven bays, including a pedimented central block of three bays standing forward some 10 ft. The corners of the centre block and of the extremities have brick pilasters rising from a chamfered plinth and continuing through the parapets, which mask the roof. A moulded brick parapet string-course is returned around the pilasters and at the top is a moulded stone coping. The pediment, an inclined continuation of the parapet, has a central urn finial, rectangular on plan, with a moulded base and a gadrooned bowl. The central doorway is flanked by a pair of rusticated Doric pilasters, in wood, with an entablature with a triple keystone and a dentil cornice. The windows on each side of the doorway and the three windows on the first floor have segmental brick heads with keystones; the window to the right of the doorway and the middle one on the first floor are false, so also is the round window in the pediment; the others are sashed. The sashed windows in the four flanking bays have flat brick lintels without keystones; the ground-floor openings are taller than those above, reaching down to the floor. Inside, the hall and one bedroom contain 18th-century panelling. The open-string stairs have moulded and ramped handrails with a horizontal curtail volute on a Tuscan-column newel post. The balusters, two to a tread, consist of small Tuscan columns above vase-haped pedestals.

(6) The Manor House (68660527), 100 yds. W. of the church, has two storeys with basements and attics. The walls are of rendered rubble with ashlar dressings and the roofs are slated. Although the remains of a 17th-century building are identifiable, particularly in the basement, the greater part of the house is probably of the early 19th century. It is an unusually early but successful example of the revival of the 'Tudor' style. The overall proportions are those of an 18th-century house but most of the architectural ornament is of 16th-century inspiration.

The E. front has two gabled bays flanking a narrow, parapeted middle bay. Low casement windows in the chamfered plinth light the basement. Above, each gabled bay has a three-light mullioned and transomed window with wooden casements on ground and first floors and a smaller three-light attic window in the gable. The middle bay contains the front doorway, above which the first floor has a sashed window with glazing-bars of Gothic design. All windows have hood-moulds, and the shoulders and tops of the gables have crocketed finials. The lead rainwater head of the middle bay bears the initials E.P., the wild-man crest of the Pouletts who formerly owned the house, and the date 1803. The N. and S. fronts have details similar to those of the E. front. The W. front comprises various later additions, among them a drawing-room wing that is probably of the late 19th century. Inside, the original house is represented by a large fireplace in the basement kitchen, spanned by two four-centred arches, by two stone angle fireplaces with four-centred heads, moulded jambs and chamfered stops on the ground and first floors, and by the remains of walled-up stone-mullioned windows in the inner wall of the drawing-room. Some rooms contain reset 17th-century oak panelling.

The *Stables* to the S. are of rubble with brick dressings, and have slated roofs; a rainwater head is dated 1839.

Monuments (7–14)

Except as otherwise stated the following dwellings are probably of the latter part of the 18th century. Generally they are two-storied, or of one storey with an attic, and the walls are of cob, rubble or brick; many have thatched roofs.

(7) *Cottages* (69320532), two adjacent at right angles, are two-storied with thatched roofs. The walls facing S. and E. are of flint with brick dressings; the others are of rubble, with cob in the upper part.

(8) *Cottages* (68660520), two adjacent, 60 yds. S. of (6), have rendered walls and thatched roofs.

(9) *Cottages* (68770487), two but now comprising one house, are of coursed rubble and thatch. The S. cottage is of the 17th century; the other was added in the late 18th or early 19th century.

(10) *Henley Farm* (69600418), of two storeys with rubble walls and thatched roofs, was originally two cottages. Adjacent, to the N., is a brick *Barn*.

(11) *Cottage* (69490436), two storied, has been largely rebuilt in recent times but retains one 17th-century bay in which the wall is of banded flint and stone, with stone quoins, and in which occurs a three-light window with hollow-chamfered stone mullions and a label. An arcaded *Granary* to the S. dates from the late 18th or early 19th century.

(12) *Bookham Farm* (70660417), house, is probably of the early 18th century. Large parts have been rebuilt in brickwork but the remaining original walls are of rubble. The roof is thatched. Inside are some deeply chamfered beams with plain run-out stops, and there is an open fireplace in the S. end wall.

(13) *Brockhampton Farm* (71190559), house, is of the early 18th century and has brick and rubble walls with a brick plat-band at first-floor level; the roof is thatched. A two-storied porch has a round-headed brick doorway with moulded imposts to the S., and bull's-eye windows to E. and W.

(14) *New Inn* (68730510), now a private house, is two-storied, with rubble walls and a thatched roof, and has a ground plan of three rooms in a straight range. It was built about the end of the 17th century. The chimneystack on the S. side of the middle room serves two open fireplaces set back-to-back. The entrance is in the W. front, opposite the base of the stack. The N. room has a fireplace with a separate chimney in the N. gable wall.

Early 19th-century buildings in Buckland Newton village include the *Post Office*, 300 yds. S. of the church, of flint with brick dressings, and *Bladeley House* (68720479), a two-storied building, gracefully proportioned, with rendered walls, low-pitched slated roofs with wide eaves, and large sashed windows; it was built in 1850. Also of the early 19th century are *Millers Farm* (70590536), mainly of brick but with the N.E. front of coursed rubble with brick quoins, and a *Cottage* (70620649), with a symmetrical rendered front, end chimneys and a thatched roof.

Duntish

Castle Hill, *see* Monument (4).

(15) White House (69000676) is two-storied with rendered walls and a low-pitched slated roof. The W. wing dates from the 18th century and the E. wing was added in the 19th century.

(16) Duntish Mill (69400600) is a single-storied 18th-century dwelling house of coursed rubble with dormer-windowed attics in a thatched roof. The former water-mill has been dismantled.

(17) Cottage (69060652), of cob in one storey with attics under a thatched roof, is probably of the late 16th century; the gabled end walls have been subsequently rebuilt in brick. The ground plan comprises two rooms separated by a chimney-stack, the S. room being the larger of the two. Winding stairs to the E. of the stack give access to the N. attic. The S. room is sub-divided by a timber-framed partition with an ogee-headed doorway. A second staircase in the S.W. corner of the range suggests that the cottage was at some time divided into two tenements. The roof appears to comprise four jointed-cruck trusses.

Monuments of the 19th century in Duntish also include a house at 69520668 and a pair of cottages at 69500649. Cottages at Spring Grove (69060612) were refaced in the 19th century, but probably incorporate 18th-century walls.

Cosmore

(18) Revels Inn Farm (67540603), house, is of two storeys with rendered walls and a slated roof. It was built towards the end of the 18th century and is said to have been an inn formerly and to figure in Thomas Hardy's 'The Woodlanders'. The symmetrical W. front is of five bays, with the doorway in a slightly projecting pedimented centre bay; the windows are sashed. Inside, the room to the N. of the entrance hall-way is lined from floor to ceiling with fielded panelling in two heights, with panelled dado-rail and dentilled cornice; the door-case has details in the Gothic style comprising clustered shafts on each side and a moulded ogee arch with crockets and finials above the lintel.

(19) Revels Farm (67700524), house, is a two-storied building with walls of banded flint and rubble. The nucleus is of the 17th century and has an L-shaped plan; at the S. end is a late 18th or early 19th-century barn with walls of brick and rubble. The E. wall of the 17th-century house has a hollow-chamfered stone window of four square-headed lights with a moulded label on the ground floor and a similar three-light window on the first floor. The original N. wall, concealed by a lean-to addition, includes the remains of similar mullioned windows. The S. side of the W. wing retains stone windows with ovolo-moulded mullions and weathered hood-moulds, and a stone doorway with a chamfered four-centred head; the latter is surmounted by a small three-light stone window. There is a mullioned two-light attic window in the W. gable wall. A fireplace in the W. wing has a four-centred stone head.

Clinger Farm (66890537) is an early 19th-century farmhouse of rubble in two storeys with a tiled roof.

Minterne Parva

(20) Minterne Parva Farm (66450345) includes an early 19th-century *House* with rendered walls and a slated roof, and a *Granary* that is probably of the 18th century. The latter is a circular building raised above ground on eight arches; the lower part is of rubble with squared rubble dressings, the upper part is of brick, and the conical roof is slated.

MEDIAEVAL AND LATER EARTHWORKS

(21) Bank and Ditch (66830523–67590517), on the N. side of Little Minterne Hill in the extreme W. of the parish, encloses about 150 acres and is probably a park pale. Where best preserved, to the S.W., the bank is 20 ft. wide and 3 ft. high with an internal ditch 12 ft. wide and 2 ft. deep. The circuit is very irregular with many changes of direction, especially on the W. side.

(22) Cultivation Remains. Traces of open fields occur in three distinct areas of the parish. *Buckland Newton* had a two-field system in 1548 (Buckland Manor Court Roll, 1548, P.R.O., S.C.2, Bundle 169, No. 4); it was finally enclosed in 1734 (Enclosure Award, D.C.R.O.). On the S.E. side of Ridge Hill (677046–685052), S.W. of the village, are extensive remains of contour strip lynchets arranged in four end-on interlocking furlongs, 100 yds. to 250 yds. long. To the S.W. the strip lynchets run over 'Celtic' fields (Group (39)). In 1734 all but the S.W. furlong lay in West Field.

Henley, or *Knoll*, had five separate open fields before enclosure in 1734. Traces of ridge-and-furrow visible on air photographs (R.A.F. CPE/UK 2431: 3353–5) S.E. of Bladely House (687047) appear to have been in Arberry Field in 1734 (Enclosure Award, D.C.R.O.).

Nothing is known of the date of inclosure of the open fields of *Duntish* but there are remains in three places. Immediately N.W. of Knapp Hill Farm (686057) is a series of strip lynchets running obliquely to the contours, 170 yds. long with low risers and treads 40 yds. wide. Below and to the N. are two furlongs of ridge-and-furrow 6 yds. to 7 yds. wide. On the E. side of Dungeon Hill (691073) are four contour strip lynchets up to 330 yds. long, in poor condition.

There are no remains of the open fields of *Minterne Parva*, which had a two-field system in 1548 but was enclosed by 1734.

PREHISTORIC

PROBABLE SETTLEMENT, *see* 'Celtic' Fields.

'CELTIC' FIELDS, *see* pp. 326–7, Groups (39), (40).

(23) BOWL BARROW (67410320), on the ridge top W. of Holcombe Wood and on the boundary with Cerne Abbas and Minterne Magna, lies in a hedgerow, but ploughing has largely destroyed it on either side; diam. about 50 ft., ht. 5 ft.

(24) BARROW (67670474), at 680 ft. O.D. on Gales Hill, has had most of the top dug away; diam. 42 ft., ht. 2 ft.

(25) BARROW (67660477) 30 yds. N.N.W. of (2); diam. 27 ft., ht. 2 ft.

(26) BARROW (67030430), formerly in Buckland Newton parish and now in Minterne Magna, lies at over 800 ft. O.D. on Little Minterne Hill, in an area of 'Celtic' fields. It is very irregular, having been heavily ploughed; diam. about 50 ft., ht. 1 ft.

DUNGEON HILL hill-fort, *see Dorset* I, 169, Minterne Magna (6).

9 BURLESTON (7794)

(O.S. 6 ins. SY 79 NE, SY 79 SE)

The parish of Burleston covers only 366 acres and measures barely 500 yds. from W. to E. It stretches N. from the R. Piddle between Puddletown and Tolpuddle, the Devil's Brook forming the W. boundary. The village is at the S. end of the parish at the edge of the flood plain. The mediaeval open fields were not enclosed until the 19th century.

BURLESTON *Remains of Church*

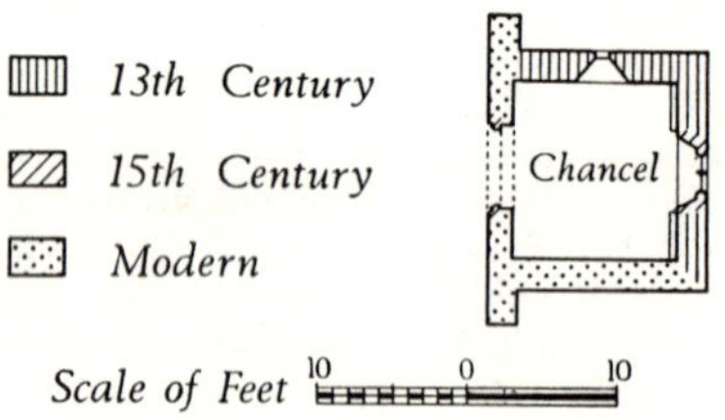

ECCLESIASTICAL

(1) THE PARISH CHURCH, now in ruins, stands N.W. of the village. The walls are of flint with ashlar dressings; the surviving roofs are slated. Only the *Chancel* remains standing; the N. and possibly the E. walls are of the 13th century; the S. and W. walls, of flint with brick bonding courses, were probably rebuilt in 1910 when the structure was repaired and reroofed.

Architectural Description—The *Chancel* (11¼ ft. square) has in the E. wall a 15th-century window of two lights with vertical tracery in a two-centred head. The N. wall retains an original chamfered lancet light. A 15th-century doorway with casement-moulded head and jambs has been reset in the modern W. wall.

Fittings—*Brackets:* Reset on each side of the E. window, plain mediaeval corbel-stones. *Font:* Stone bowl approximately 2 ft. in diameter and of uncertain date, now transferred to Broadwindsor. *Monuments* and *Floorslab. Monuments:* In churchyard, E. of chancel, (1) of Thomas Grose, 1675, and commemorating his parents and ancestors, table-tomb; S. of chancel, (2) of Richard Phillips of E. Elworth, 1644, table-tomb; (3) of Thomas Jesse, 1744, and Thomas Jesse, junior, 1746, headstone. *Floorslab:* W. of chancel, originally in nave, of Mrs. Susannah Grosse, 1693, with incised mask. *Plate:* kept at Puddletown, includes Elizabethan cup and cover-paten, the cup with mark of Lawrence Stratford and the cover-paten with '1575' engraved on foot; also silver stand-paten of 1717 and 19th-century silver-plated flagon, both given in 1843.

SECULAR

(2) THE RECTORY (77679428), 130 yds. S.E. of the church, is of two storeys, with walls of rendered brick and cob; the roofs are slated and tiled. The house consists of a late 17th or early 18th-century N. wing, much altered, and a main S. range which was added in the second half of the 18th century. The symmetrical S. front is of three bays and has a plat-band at first-floor level, a moulded brick eaves-cornice and sashed windows. The central doorway has 18th-century Gothic clustered side-pilasters and an entablature with cusped arcading. The staircase has latticed banisters and a moulded handrail.

(3) HOUSE (77559426), 40 yds. S. of the church, is of two storeys with walls of rendered rubble and cob; the roofs are modern. Built in the 18th century, with later lean-to additions, the house is now divided into three tenements. A *Barn* to the E. of the house has been altered and reduced in size; the 19th-century brick S. wall has two-stage buttresses with stepped weatherings.

MEDIAEVAL AND LATER EARTHWORKS

(4) CULTIVATION REMAINS. As late as 1843 (Tithe Map) the open fields of the parish were still unenclosed; they were named Bottom, Hill, and North Fields; the date of enclosure is unknown. A single contour strip lynchet, 130 yds. long, some 200 yds. N.E. of the village, is the only fragment that remains; in 1843 it was one of a group of strips which made up Heading Bottom Furlong in Hill Field.

ROMAN AND PREHISTORIC

MONUMENTS (5–8), ROUND BARROWS

Four barrows lie above 250 ft. O.D. on Burleston Down at the W. end of a scatter that extends into the adjacent parishes of Dewlish and Milborne; all have been heavily ploughed. An incense cup was recovered from a large barrow 'removed for agricultural operations on Burlestone Farm, near Dewlish Old Turnpike Gate' (*C.T.D.*, illustration on title-page). The barrow must have been adjacent to (7) and (8).

(5) *Bowl* (77849599), on a gentle N. slope on the summit of the down; ploughed almost flat; diam. about 45 ft.

(6) *Bowl* (77699632), immediately N. of the Puddletown–Milborne road; diam. about 45 ft., ht. 9 ins.

(7) *Bowl* (77949634), 270 yds. E. of (2) and immediately S. of the Puddletown–Milborne road; diam. about 75 ft., ht. 2 ft.

(8) *Bowl* (77989635), 50 yds. E. of (3); diam. about 90 ft., ht. 2½ ft.

10 CAUNDLE MARSH (6814)

(O.S. 6 ins. ST 61 NE, ST 61 SE)

The parish, of about 1,000 acres, lies W. of Bishop's Caundle and Stourton Caundle, in a shallow basin that drains S. to the Caundle Brook. To the E. the land is on Forest Marble and rises to 400 ft. above sea-level; to the W. it is on Oxford Clay and attains only 250 ft.; the N. part of the parish is on Forest Marble and Cornbrash Beds. Large parts of the area remained open common until finally enclosed in 1845.[1] Until 1886 five detached 'islands' of Bishop's Caundle lay inside Caundle Marsh. They were enclosed by 1727[2] but their outline still revealed that they had once been strips in the Caundle Marsh open fields. Secondary settlements, each with its own enclosed fields, developed in the waste beyond the open fields; examples are Ashcombe Farm (7) which certainly existed in the 14th century and perhaps earlier,[3] and probably Prytown Farm (3), which was one of the detached parts of Bishop's Caundle.

ECCLESIASTICAL

(1) THE PARISH CHURCH OF ST. PETER AND ST. PAUL was entirely rebuilt in 1857 to the design of R. H. Shout. Altar, communion rails, pulpit, lectern, font and other fittings are skilfully carved in Ham Hill stone. Two monuments from an older church are incorporated in the present building.

Fittings—*Monument* and *Floorslab*. *Monument:* In chancel, built into N. wall, of John Brit, 1587, recessed table-tomb spanned by low four-centred moulded arch; stone front of tomb chest stands flush with chancel wall; front divided into three panels, lateral ones oblong with lozenge infilling, middle one square with shield-of-arms, *on a chevron between three bugle-horns, two daggers and a nail*, presumably variant of Brett (Coker, 156); moulded edge of tomb with plain band inscribed HERE LIETH THE BODIE OF JOHN BRIT GENTLEMAN ANNO DOMINI 1587; the word 'gentleman' replaces another, obliterated. *Floorslab:* In S.E. part of nave, of William Gollop, 1691, Purbeck marble slab with added inscription to William Gollop, 1802, *Plate:* includes silver cup and paten with hallmarks of 1712, both inscribed 'the gift of Mrs Jane Hoare relict of Henry Hoare Esqr. late of Stourton, to ye parish of Caundlemarsh, Com. Dorset'; also stand-paten, probably 18th century, and paten of 1712, both with same inscription as cup.

[1] Enclosure Map, 1845, D.C.R.O.

[2] Map of Caundle Marsh, 1727, D.C.R.O., and Caundle Marsh Tithe Map of 1838.

[3] Fägersten, 212.

SECULAR

(2) MANOR FARM (67841323), house, immediately E. of the church, is built of roughly coursed rubble with ashlar dressings and has two storeys with attics. The roofs are tiled, with stone-slate verges, except for one slope which is wholly stone-slated. The middle part of the dog-leg plan is the oldest, dating probably from the 15th century and comprising the N. and S. walls of a hall. To W. and N. is a 16th-century wing, possibly in place of an original solar and undercroft. To the E., a 17th-century wing occupies the probable place of the eastern part of the original house and also extends S. The stone fireplace and chimneystack in the 15th-century building are of the 17th century.

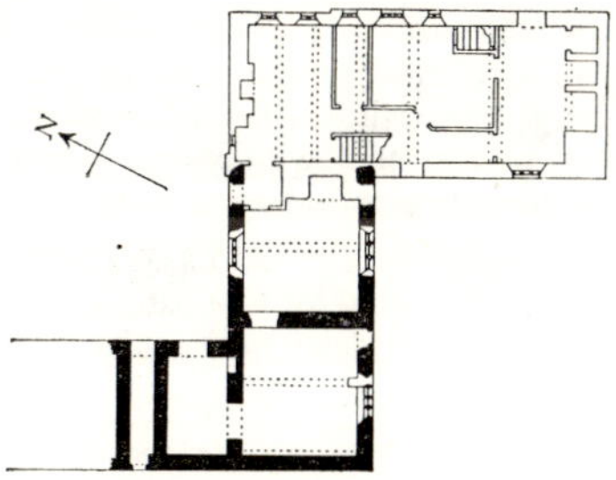

Of the original house only the W. part survives. It was entered from the N. through a doorway which is still the main entrance; its wide chamfered jambs are surmounted by a hollow-chamfered segmental-pointed door-head that seems to be secondary. Opposite this opening, in the S. wall, are traces of a second doorway now walled up. A fireplace and chimney-stack are inserted in place of the through-passage which, presumably, lay between the N. and S. doorways; it has narrow-chamfered stone jambs and a reset wide-chamfered stone head that was originally four-centred. The W. end of the 15th-century building is indicated by a vertical joint on the outside of the N. wall, near the junction of the 16th-century N.W. wing; the E. extremity is lost in the construction of the 17th-century wing. The stone mullioned three-light window in the original S. wall is of the 17th century and the window in the N. wall is of the 19th century. Doorways on each floor of the original house give access to the 16th-century W. extension.

The 16th-century extension has, in the S. wall, a narrow doorway with a chamfered four-centred head, continuous jambs and a square label; adjacent is a partly blocked window of four four-centred lights with hollow-chamfered jambs and mullions; on the first floor is a similar window. Inside, the 16th-century range contains two unheated ground-floor rooms; to the N. an unconnected through-passage, with external doorways with four-centred heads to E. and W., proves that the range formerly extended further northwards. The first floor has two rooms and there are other chambers in the attic. A window with ovolo-moulded mullions is probably a 17th-century insertion; a fireplace on the first floor is probably of the 18th century.

The 17th-century E. wing is now divided into several compartments but it originally had only two ground-floor rooms, with fireplaces in the gabled end walls. The area of the former N. room is spanned by three chamfered beams, and a chamfered half-beam marks the position of the former partition; the former S. room was spanned by a single transverse beam. The stairs retain some 17th-century turned balusters and a moulded handrail. The external walls of the E. wing have been extensively refaced and all openings appear to be of the 19th century.

(3) PRYTOWN FARM (67941441), cottage, is single-storied with dormer-windowed attics; it has rubble walls and thatched roofs and it dates from the late 17th or early 18th century. The gabled W. end has a stone coping on moulded kneelers and culminates in a brick chimney; a second chimneystack stands near the middle of the range. The S. front is of four bays; to the W. is a wooden casement window of three lights, next is the doorway with a modern round head, to the E. are two casement windows similar to the first.

(4) SANDY VIEW (67671345) is a late 17th or early 18th-century cottage of coursed rubble in two storeys with a thatched roof. The central doorway is flanked by pairs of casement windows and there are four corresponding windows on the first floor.

(5) COTTAGES, pair (67841240), of rubble and cob, partly rendered, and of two storeys with thatched roofs, are of the late 17th or early 18th century. Each tenement has a central doorway flanked by casement windows; a common chimneystack rises above the party-wall.

(6) COTTAGES, two (68471427 and 68541430), of rubble with thatched roofs, are probably of the late 17th century. The narrow plots on which they stand were evidently encroachments on the former roadway.

(7) ASHCOMBE FARM (67921506), house, is of two storeys; the walls are rendered, with some ashlar dressings, and the roofs are partly tiled and partly of stone slates. The gabled N. and S. end walls have stone copings on shaped kneelers. A stone mullioned window of four square-headed lights with chamfered jambs occurs in the W. wall but all other openings are modern. The main range, of three bays, is probably of the 17th century and there are later extensions at the N. end and against the W. side.

(8) MARSH COURT (67671383) is a two-storied house with dormer-windowed attics; it has walls of coursed and squared rubble with ashlar dressings; the roof is of stone slates. Although the greater part of the house is modern it contains an 18th-century nucleus. The central doorway of the W. front and the window above it appear to belong to the original structure. The doorway is square-headed and has a pedimental stone hood on scrolled brackets. The window is of two elliptical-headed lights with continuous ovolo-moulded jambs; it opens in an ashlar panel flanked by scrolled cheek-pieces. A rebuilt chimneystack incorporates a stone inscribed D.G.M. 1731. Two 18th-century mullioned windows are reset in the E. front and in the S. side of the N.E. wing.

MONUMENTS (9–12)

Unless described otherwise the following buildings are of the 18th century and have walls of rubble and cob in two storeys.

(9) *Poll Bridge Farm* (68131247), house, dates from the middle of the century; until recently it had thatched roofs. The plan is a half-H and the principal front, to the N., is symmetrical, with a central doorway and a stone mullioned window of three square-headed lights on either side; on the first floor are three similar windows, except that the central window is of Venetian form, the middle light having a false round head. The N. range is gabled at each end but the two wings which project to the S. have hipped roofs. The S. front of each wing has a stone mullioned three-light window on the ground floor and a modern window above. The interior has been extensively modernised, but some chamfered beams are exposed.

(10) *Holt Cottage* (69001373) has walls of rubble and brick, partly rendered, and a thatched roof. The original range was extended to E. and W. in the 19th century; the cottage is now derelict.

(11) *Tut Hill Farm* (68571435), house, was originally two cottages, that to the N.W. being probably earlier than the other. The roofs are slate-covered.

(12) *Yew Tree Farm* (67401406), house, has rubble walls and slated roofs. The S. front is symmetrical and of three bays, with a central doorway and casement windows. The house probably dates from the late 18th or early 19th century.

Monuments of the late 18th and early 19th centuries include a house at *West Hays Farm* (67791308) in which a symmetrical 19th-century E. range of three bays is added to an 18th-century nucleus; the casement windows of the E. front have geometrical lattices; also a house at *Hawkins's Farm* (68241343), a two-storied rubble building with a tiled roof and casement windows.

MEDIAEVAL AND LATER EARTHWORKS

(13) CULTIVATION REMAINS: Nothing remains of the original open fields; they were in existence in 1499 (*S. & D.N. & Q.*, XIII, (1913) (203) and had already been enclosed by 1727 (Map of Caundle Marsh, 1727, D.C.R.O.).

Ridge-and-furrow remains can be seen on air photographs at a number of places: E. and S. of Ashcombe Farm (679150 to 679148), E. of Prytown Farm (681144), formerly in Bishop's Caundle, and S.W. of West Hays Farm (676127); it is 5 yds. to 7 yds. wide with headlands of 8 yds. (R.A.F. CPE/UK 1974: 2151–2, 2193–5, 4150–2). These traces are confined to existing fields that are associated with secondary settlements beyond the original open fields of the parish.

11 CHARLTON MARSHALL (9004)

(O.S. 6 ins. ST 80 SE, ST 90 SW)

Charlton Marshall is a long strip-like parish of about 2,300 acres, rising from the S.W. bank of the R. Stour, at 200 ft., to a maximum altitude of 400 ft. in the S.W. Most of the land is on Chalk and the village is concentrated on a narrow river terrace above the flood plain. There appear to have been three early settlements beside the river, and the extended pattern of the present village reflects this origin. Each settlement had its own strip of land running up to the Chalk and the boundaries of the strips are still marked by continuous hedges.

CHARMINSTER CHURCH. W. Tower. 16th-century

CHARMINSTER. (6) Forston House. Exterior, from S.W.

Early 18th-century

BUCKLAND NEWTON. (4) Castle Hill. Central block, from S.E. *c.* 1760

CHARMINSTER. (4) Wolfeton House, from S.

16th and 17th-century

(5) Riding House, from S.W. Late 16th-century

(4) Wolfeton House. Gatehouse, from S.E. Early 16th-century

CHARMINSTER.

Doorcase in E. Drawing Room.

Chimneypiece in E. Drawing Room.

Assemblage of early 17th-century parts

CHARMINSTER. (4) Wolfeton House. Woodwork.

Chimneypiece in Gallery.

Doorway to Gallery.

CHARMINSTER. (4) Wolfeton House. Interior stonework.

Late 16th-century

DEWLISH. (2) Dewlish House. Centre of N.E. front. 1702

These lands became three manors,[1] but in 1799 the central manor was the only one to preserve open fields.[2] On the downs at the S.W. end of the parish large parts of all three manors remained unenclosed until well into the 19th century.[3] The most important monument is the parish church.

ECCLESIASTICAL

(1) THE PARISH CHURCH OF ST. MARY, standing beside the river in the N. part of the village, incorporates the remains of a late 15th-century structure, mainly in the *West Tower*, but the *Chancel*, *Nave*, *North Aisle*, *Organ Chamber* and *South Porch* were rebuilt in 1713. The W. tower is of banded flint and squared Greensand rubble with ashlar dressings. In the 18th-century parts of the church the walls are faced with knapped flint into which are set large rectangular Greensand ashlar blocks. The nave roof is tiled, with wide stone-slate verges; the roof of the S. porch is entirely stone-slated; the tower and N. aisle have flat leaded roofs concealed by parapets.

The interior of the church is a good example of graceful and sensitive 18th-century design. The original fittings, probably from the Bastard workshops at Blandford, are of high quality.

CHARLTON MARSHALL

The parish church of St. Mary

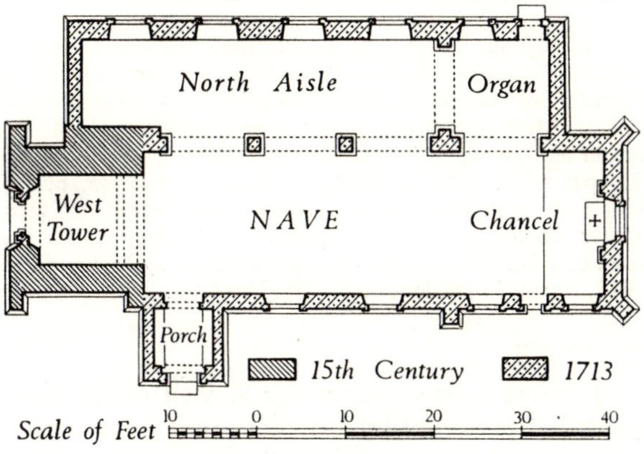

Architectural Description—Externally, vestiges of a mediaeval chancel are perhaps recognisable in three weathered ashlar three-stage buttresses, two set diagonally at the N.E. and S.E. corners of the present chancel and one, square-set, projecting from the S. wall, 18 ft. from the E. end. Since no internal feature separates the chancel from the nave, the southern buttress has no function and this also suggests that it survives from, or at least represents, a mediaeval building; nevertheless the masonry appears to have been rebuilt in 1713. On the other hand the lower part of the S.W. corner of the nave appears to be of the 15th century. The 18th-century *Nave* and *Chancel* (52 ft. by 15½ ft.) have a continuous roof terminating to the E. at a gable of flint and ashlar with an inclined ashlar coping above shaped kneelers. The round-headed E. window has a plainly moulded architrave with a keystone and impost blocks. The S. wall of the nave and chancel has four similar windows, but set at a lower level and without impost blocks; between the eastern pair of windows is a square-headed chancel doorway with a beaded stone architrave. Over the keystone of the most westerly window is an ashlar block with the date 1713 in large Arabic numerals. The *South Porch* (6½ ft. square) is a low gabled structure with details similar to those of the nave and chancel; the round-headed outer archway has a beaded architrave with imposts and keystone; at the apex of the gable is a prism-shaped stone sundial. The N. wall of the *North Aisle* (40 ft. by 10½ ft.) and *Organ Chamber* (11 ft. by 10½ ft.) has masonry and details similar to those of the S. wall of the nave, except that the stone architraves of its five round-headed windows have impost blocks as well as keystones. An ashlar plat-band immediately above the windows is surmounted by a chequered parapet with a moulded coping. At the E. end of the N. wall is a square-headed doorway with an ashlar architrave; the E. and W. walls have no openings.

The *West Tower* (9 ft. by 10 ft.) is of two stages divided by a weathered string-course. The tower arch is two-centred and of two chamfered orders which die into the responds at the springing. In the N. side of the tower, the vice turret is concealed by the W. wall of the N. aisle, except for its weathered stone roof which protrudes above the aisle parapet. The doorway to the vice, a chamfered four-centred opening, was originally set some distance above ground in the inner face of the N. wall, but it has been transferred to the outer face of the same wall and now opens at an upper level in the W. part of the N. aisle. The W. wall of the tower, in the lower stage, extends N. and S. to form two two-stage ashlar buttresses with weathered offsets. The two-centred 15th-century W. window has casement-moulded jambs extending almost down to the ground and thus flanking the W. doorway. The present doorway is an 18th-century square-headed opening flanked by plain pilaster strips and surmounted by a moulded cornice; over it, within the 15th-century window surround, is an 18th-century round-headed window with impost blocks and a triple keystone. In the upper stage, each face of the tower has a square-headed 15th-century belfry window of two two-centred lights with cinquefoil cusping on the W. side and trefoil cusping on the other three sides. On the S. side, below the belfry window, is a one-light opening, partly covered by a clockface. The tower parapet dates from 1713; above a hollow-chamfered weathered string-course the four corners of the parapet wall are shaped to form square pedestals, above which are pyramidal pinnacles with ball finials; between the pedestals each parapet wall is set slightly forward and surmounted by a plain pediment.

Inside, the *Nave* (Plate 8) opens into the N. aisle through three round-headed stone archways, with moulded and panelled archivolts springing from rectangular piers with panelled sides and moulded cornices and bases; the date 1713 is carved on the keystone of the westernmost arch. At the E. end of the arcade a wider pier, panelled and moulded as before, marks the division between nave and chancel; a cross-arch springing from the N. side of the pier divides the N. aisle from the present organ chamber, perhaps originally a vestry. A single archway, similar to those of the nave, opens from the organ chamber into the chancel. The ceilings of the N. aisle and organ chamber are flat; that of the nave and chancel is a continuous plaster

[1] Hutchins III, 522.

[2] Enclosure award, 1800, D.C.R.O. Survey of the Horlock Estate, 1726, D.C.R.O.

[3] O.S., 1811; also Hutchins III, 526.

barrel-vault of elliptical cross-section, springing from a coved and moulded wooden cornice. At the W. end the cove returns for a short span on the E. face of the tower and is interrupted to make way for the tower arch. On the E. wall of the chancel the coved cornice returns and is incorporated in the reredos.

The elaborately carved oak reredos occupies the whole E. wall. At the base is a panelled dado with a moulded capping, set forward on each side of the communion table to form pedestals for two fluted Corinthian pilasters with gilded capitals, which flank the E. window. Each capital supports a section of entablature, the cornice of which is a continuation of the coved ceiling cornice; at the arrises the cove is decorated with gilded palm leaves. In an attic storey above the cornice, short scroll-footed pilasters enriched with gilt swags support a pediment with the inscription GLORY TO GOD IN THE HIGHEST in the tympanum. On each side, the lunette of the vault-end is filled with a shaped panel in front of which stands a gilded ewer. The pediment and its pilasters enclose the semicircular head of the E. window, the intrados and jambs of which are lined with panelled oak culminating in a keystone with a gilt festoon. The window-sill is masked by a broken pediment, supported at each end on a gilded bracket; the pediment encloses a cartouche of a heart encircled by a crown of thorns, below which is a ribbon inscribed 'The sacrifice of God is a troubled spirit: a broken and contrite heart'. Under the cartouche is a pair of gilded cherub heads with a carved garland of flowers. Below are two panels with shaped tops and moulded and gilded surrounds, inscribed one with the Lord's Prayer the other with the Creed, in gilt lettering with elaborate flourishes. At a higher level, to right and left of the Corinthian pilasters, are other panels inscribed with the Ten Commandments; these also have gilded cherub heads in the spandrels above them.

Fittings—*Bells:* four; treble inscribed 'ave gratia', 3rd, inscribed 'ave Maria', both 15th century; others modern. *Chest:* of oak, with moulded edge to lid, and shaped bottom rail; 18th century. *Coffin-stool:* with turned legs and carved rails, 17th century. *Communion rails:* of oak, with moulded and shaped rail, and posts in form of fluted Roman Doric columns, and tapering octagonal balusters (Plate 23); centre bay hinged; 1713. *Communion tables:* In chancel, of oak, with massive turned legs representing Doric columns, and moulded rails, 17th century. In N. aisle, of oak with tapered octagonal legs, scrolled and shaped diagonal cross-braces, arcaded top rails and moulded edge to board, 18th century; since legs match communion-rail balusters this was presumably the original communion-table. *Doors:* In S. doorway, of oak, with round head and six moulded panels; in porch archway, with shaped top, spiked, and with six fielded panels; both 18th century. *Doorcase:* In S. doorway of chancel, internal surround with moulded wooden architrave flanked by Ionic half pilasters supporting entablature with gilded acanthus scroll-work and a central bracket; over this rises a tall bow-fronted panel with scrolled cheek-pieces and pediment, inscribed to record donation of communion plate by Catherine Sloper, 1712, and other items. *Font:* In tower, of Portland stone with octagonal bowl gadrooned at base, on square baluster with Ionic capitals at top and with band of leafwork above bulb (Plate 27); first half of 18th century and closely akin to font at Blandford Forum. *Font-cover:* of oak, with eight-sided dome surmounted by large pineapple finial, hanging from pulley with gilded metal cherub-head counterweight; 18th century.

Monuments and *Floorslabs. Monuments:* In chancel, on N. wall, (1) of Dr. Charles Sloper, rector of Spetisbury and Charlton (1705–27), wall monument of white and polychrome marbles in form of a Roman-Doric pavilion surmounted by a shield-of-arms; apron decorated with a laurel-wreathed skull; tablet inscribed '. . . At Spetisbury he rebuilt the parsonage house and outhouses, at Charlton the parish church and chancell, wholy at his own expence' (Plate 38). In nave, on S. wall, (2) of Henry Horlock, 1719, and other members of the Horlock family, polychrome marble obelisk-shaped wall-monument with white marble urns and reliefs. In N. aisle, on N. wall, (3) of Margaret Horlock Bastard, 1845, marble tablet by Marshall of Blandford; (4) of Thomas Bastard, 1791, and his wife Jane, 1798, sarcophagus-shaped tablet with obelisk and sculpture, by R. Cooke; (5) of Thomas Street, 1805, and his wife Christian, 1816, oval marble tablet with arms, by Hiscock of Poole. In churchyard, immediately E. of chancel, (6) of Dr. Charles Sloper, 1727, table-tomb surrounded by railings with fluted columnar corner posts, scroll-work and urn finials of wrought iron. Eight paces N.W. of corner of N. aisle, (7) of Elizabeth Horlock, 1729, headstone with fluted pilasters and conventional symbols. Six paces S. of chancel, (8) of Edward Wake, 1680, table-tomb. Close to N. wall (9) and (10) anonymous headstones, 1674, 1678. *Floorslabs:* In chancel, (1) of Catherine Sloper, 1712, Purbeck marble slab with fine italic lettering. In N. aisle, (2) of Thomas Bastard, 1791, and Thomas Horlock Bastard, 1849.

Plate: includes silver cup (Plate 43), paten and flagon given by Catherine Sloper, 1712, with hallmarks of 1714, cup and flagon with arms of Sloper; also paten of 1695. *Pulpit:* of oak, hexagonal, with five sides; each side with two fielded marquetry panels, moulded ledges, and cornice with central console (Plate 47); desk supported on scrolled brackets; oak back-board in two panels flanked by foliate scrolls, lower panel marquetry, upper panel carved with winged cherubs; above, sounding board, with marquetry soffit and carved cornice, surmounted by ogee cupola on pinnacle of which stands gilded pelican-in-piety. *Reredos:* See architectural description, above. *Royal Arms:* In nave, over S. doorway, painted panel with shaped, moulded head and scrolled shoulders; arms are those of George I but panel must survive from earlier period since in fourth quarter, beneath those of Hanover, the arms of England impaling Scotland as used by Queen Anne can be discerned. *Seating:* Eight oak benches of varying length but otherwise uniform, with beaded edges to boards, fretted board legs and turned stretchers; 18th century. Modern oak pews incorporate panelling probably from former box-pews; other panels reset on N. and S. walls. *Sundial:* On apex of S. porch gable, stone block on moulded pedestal, with iron gnomons; 18th century. *Miscellanea:* In vestry, pewter chamber-pot, 18th century. In N. aisle, on N. wall, panel of painted wood with moulded frame, and text of Isaiah LVIII, 13, 14, in gilt lettering, with date 1712.

SECULAR

(2) STOCKS, reset against the S. wall of the church tower and protected by a modern roof, have renewed timbers but the ironwork is perhaps of the 18th century.

(3) CHARLTON HOUSE, 100 yds. W. of the church, is an early 19th-century building with a symmetrical E. front of three storeys and five bays, with rendered walls and a slated roof. Single-storied two-bay wings extend to either side. The central doorway has a Greek Doric porch with coupled columns.

MONUMENTS (4–10)

Unless otherwise described the following are two-storied dwelling-houses of 18th-century origin.

(4) *Cottage* (89970413), 100 yds. N.W. of the church, has walls of cob with a brick and flint plinth and is two-storied with an attic under a thatched roof. It probably dates from the second half of the 18th century. The N.E. front is of three bays, with a central doorway, a modern four-light casement window to the S.E., an original two-light casement to the N.W., and three original two-light casements on the first floor. The latter have wrought-iron frames and leaded lights.

(5) *Cottage*, 10 yds. N.W. of the foregoing, is of one storey with an attic; the walls are of cob, with some banded brick and flint, and the roof is thatched.

(6) *House* (89950418), has walls of flint with brick bonding, with a little ashlar; the roof is slated. Although entirely modernised externally the house has a through-passage and contains chamfered ceiling-beams and large fireplaces which probably indicate a 17th-century date.

(7) *Cottages* (89940417), two adjacent, have cob walls and thatched roofs. The cottage to the N.W. has a symmetrical N.E. front of three bays, with a central doorway and sashed windows on the ground floor, and casement windows above; that to the S.E. is of one bay, with a doorway to one side of the ground-floor window.

(8) *Charlton Cottage*, 30 yds. S. of the foregoing, is of rendered brick in two storeys, with attics under a slated roof. The N.E. range was built *c.* 1800 but the S.W. part is probably earlier. The doorway, at the N.W. end of the earlier part, is flanked by fluted Doric pilasters with a pedimented entablature. The N.E. front is of three bays, with a central french window with a sashed window above it, and with two-storied bay windows on either side.

(9) *Little Manor* (89930444), house, of 18th-century origin, has been completely modernised.

(10) *Manor Farm* (88710315), house, 1 m. S.W. of the church, has a mid 18th-century nucleus with cob walls, and later additions to the E. and N.; the roofs are tiled.

Monuments of the first half of the 19th century include the house at *Sparrowbush Farm* (87760312), which has rendered walls and a tiled roof and dates from *c.* 1830. The *Working Man's Club House*, erected in 1854 (Hutchins III, 525), stands in the village 230 yds. S.E. of the church (90130388).

ROMAN AND PREHISTORIC

(11) ROMAN BUILDING AND OCCUPATION DEBRIS. Foundations of a 'Roman Villa' are reported (Hutchins III, 522) within ¼ m. of Charlton Barrow (904033); finds from the site included samian and coarse ware, two Kimmeridge shale 'amulets' and bronze brooches.

Numerous coins from allotments in the parish included bronze autonomous Greek coins of the 2nd century B.C. (J. G. Milne, *Finds of Greek Coins in the British Isles* (1948), 18f., 24; H. S. L. Dewar (ed.), *The Thomas Rackett Papers* (1965), 72–3, 86–7).

COMBS DITCH (*see* WINTERBORNE WHITECHURCH (19)) forms the S.W. boundary of the parish.

'CELTIC' FIELDS, *see* p. 345, Group (67).

MONUMENTS (12–20), ROUND BARROWS

Nine barrows in the S.W. of the parish form part of a barrow scatter that is continued in the adjacent parishes of Winterborne Whitechurch and Winterborne Kingston; they lie between 250 ft. and 400 ft. O.D., on the E.-facing slopes of the Chalk downland between the valleys of the Stour and the Winterborne; all have been heavily ploughed. Three barrows on Charlton Down were opened by H. White in 1811 (Warne *C.T.D., Pt. 3*, Nos. 48, 49 and 50; Hutchins III, 525); one contained, near the surface, an inhumation, probably intrusive, with the feet to the E.; the second contained a cremation in an urn; the third contained a primary cremation in a globular urn set in a circular cist 2 ft. deep and 1½ ft. wide, cut into the chalk beneath (*Barrow Diggers*, 91–2 and Pl. 8; *Arch. J.* CXIX (1962), 57). A skull (*Barrow Diggers*, 81–2 and Pl. 6) may be that of the skeleton found by White, or from a further barrow as suggested by Hutchins. The nine barrows are as follows—

(12) *Bowl* (86830082), on Charlton Down, 60 yds. N. of Combs Ditch; diam. 40 ft., ht. 1 ft.

(13) *Bowl* (87170083), on Charlton Down; top of mound disturbed by N.–S. trench; diam. of mound 40 ft., ht. 4½ ft., ditch 6 ft. across and 1½ ft. deep.

(14) *Bowl* (85960185), N.W. of Charisworth; diam. 50 ft., ht. 1 ft.

(15) *Bowl* (86020180), 80 yds. S.E. of (14); diam. 48 ft., ht. 1 ft.

(16) *Bowl* (86300251), just N. of the Blandford–Dorchester road; diam. 50 ft., ht. 1 ft.

(17) *Bowl* (86320249), 25 yds. S.E. of (16); diam. 42 ft., ht. 1½ ft.

(18) *Bowl* (87480202), 500 yds. N. of Holly Brake at 300 ft. O.D. on a spur sloping N.E.; much ploughed; diam. 57 ft., ht. 1½ ft.

(19) *Bowl* (87660206), 200 yds. E.N.E. of (18) and at a lower level on the same spur; almost completely destroyed by ploughing.

(20) *Bowl* (87790217), 185 yds. N.E. of (19) and in similar condition.

12 CHARMINSTER (6892)

(O.S. 6 ins. SY 69 SE, SY 69 NE)

The parish of Charminster, covering about 4,500 acres mainly on Chalk, extends N. from the R. Frome and is divided into two parts by the R. Cerne, the E. portion being much the larger of the two. The physical partition is reflected in the pattern of mediaeval settlements and fields. The land W. of the Cerne belonged to Charminster village and much of it was occupied by the open fields of that settlement; presumably the village originated on the W. bank. To the E. of the Cerne the land was divided between a number of small settlements all of which seem to be recorded in Domesday Book as Cernes; each had a length of river bank and a strip of land running N.E. up to the Chalk. The most northerly, Forston, is still an independent hamlet. Adjacent is Pulston and next, to the S., lies a narrow nameless strip with a settlement at the S.W. end; in 1839 this strip belonged to Cowden Farm and, like Cowden, was an isolated part of Frampton parish. After this came Herrison, Cowden, Charlton, Wolfeton and, in the S.E. corner of the parish, Burton. The last named is still an independent hamlet.

MEDIAEVAL SETTLEMENTS AND ASSOCIATED LANDS, CHARMINSTER

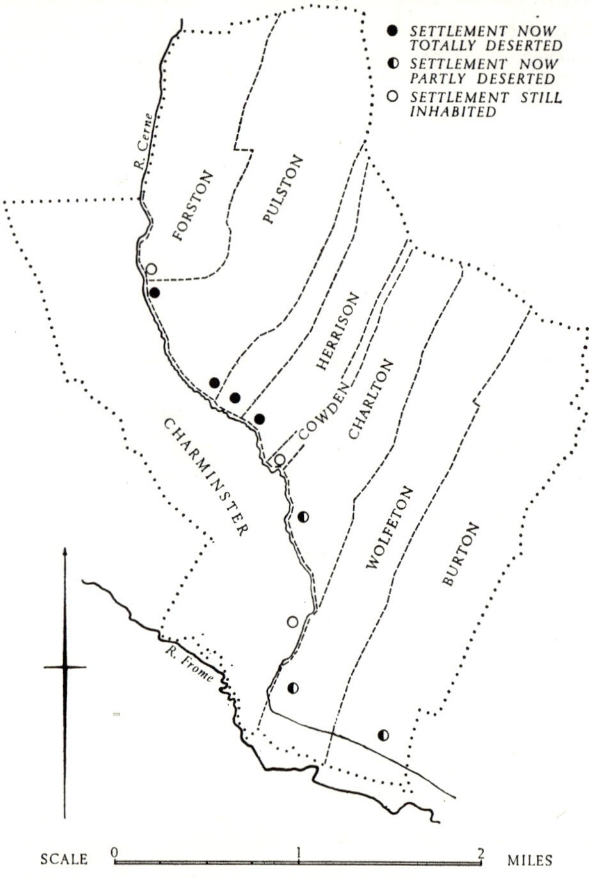

The village of Charminster stands in the S. part of the parish, astride the R. Cerne and ½ m. above its confluence with the R. Frome. The most important monuments are the Church (1), Wolfeton House (4) and the Riding House at Wolfeton (5). Up on the downs to the E. an extensive and important area of 'Celtic' Fields and associated settlement extends into Piddlehinton and Puddletown. A tesselated pavement found in Walls Field in 1891 almost certainly marks the site of a Roman villa.

ECCLESIASTICAL

(1) THE PARISH CHURCH OF ST. MARY is built of local stone rubble with some flint coursing, coursed rubble and limestone, and Ham Hill ashlar (Plate 121). The roofs are lead-covered, except those of the chancel and the N. aisle which are slate-covered. An 11th-century church is represented by parts of the E. wall of the present *Nave* and by the responds at the E. end of the arcades; the S. respond partly retains its original thickness but that to the N. has been pared down to match the thickness of the present arcade, which is later. The 11th-century building was probably cruciform, with chancel and transepts projecting from a crossing or nave, wider than themselves. Four small clearstorey lights in the present nave must be survivals from the original building since they do not correspond with the spacing of the arcades. The present N. and S. arcades and part of the *South Aisle* date from the late 12th century, and the chancel arch was inserted at the same time. The E. half of the S. aisle was widened and extended E. in the second half of the 15th century to form the *South Chapel*, and the S. doorway and an adjacent window are of about the same date. In the early 16th century, part of the S. chapel was again extended to provide space for a canopied table-tomb. The *West Tower* was built by Thomas Trenchard, probably during the second quarter of the 16th century, and the *North* and *South Vestries* are of the same date. The *Chancel* was demolished in the 17th century and rebuilt *c.* 1838, the 17th-century window which had previously been set in the blocking of the chancel-arch being reset at the new E. end. The *North Aisle* was rebuilt later in the 19th century. There were general restorations in 1838–9, and in 1895, when the roofs were renewed.

The church is of considerable interest for its 11th and 12th-century features and for its noble 16th-century tower. The early monuments are important, and surviving fragments of 16th-century stencilled wall decoration are a rarity.

Architectural Description—The *Chancel* (17½ ft. by 16½ ft.) has a 17th-century E. window reset inside-out; it is of four lights with vertical tracery in a four-centred moulded head with moulded splays and has a chamfered label, now on the inside. In the N. wall a 19th-century doorway with a three-centred head and keystone has been converted into a window. The reset window in the S. wall is of the 16th century; it has two four-centred lights in a square moulded head with moulded reveals and label. The chancel arch is round-headed and of two lightly chamfered orders; on the E. side it has a chamfered label and on the W. a label with nail-head ornament; the shafted jambs have a three-quarter shaft to each outer order and a cluster of three segmental shafts to the inner order; the middle shaft has a pronounced keel. The much restored capitals are carved with scallops, enriched with simple foliage and fluting, and the moulded abacus on each side is continued as a string across the E. and W. wall-faces. The bases are moulded and those of the three-quarter shafts have spurs, now badly worn. N. of the arch is a squint, perhaps of the 16th century, with a square head and a modern sill.

The *Nave* (51 ft. by 20 ft.) retains on the exterior face of the E. wall the weathering of the steeper roof of a slightly narrower chancel; the present parapets, copings and finial are modern. Internally (Plate 6), the 12th-century N. arcade has four bays, each with a two-centred arch. On the S. side each arch is of two plain orders with a continuous label with nail-head ornament, on the N. side it is of one order with a chamfered label. The arches spring from columns with scalloped capitals, with volutes at the corners, and moulded bases on square sub-bases, with carved chevron ornament; the E. and W. responds are square. The carving of the capitals consists of numerous shallow scallops; two have angle volutes to bring the round to a square. At clearstorey level, towards the E. end, is the upper doorway to the roodloft; it is of the 15th century with a square head and plain jambs, the rebated W. jamb being cut into by the E. splay of the adjacent clearstorey window. This window dates from the late 15th century and has two trefoil lights in a square head. A little further W. is a splayed round-headed light of *c.* 1100, decorated externally with a continuous band of chevron ornament. W. of this is another 15th-century window, taller than the first but otherwise of similar design; it is followed by a second early 12th-century light and, towards the W. end, by a third 15th-century window like the first. The westernmost 12th-century light and a similar one opposite to it in the S. wall are not central with the arcades below. The S. arcade of the nave and the S. clearstorey are similar to those on the N. except that the E. respond is notably thicker than its fellow and than the spandrel above it; the extra breadth shows that the responds are surviving parts of the antecedent nave. The column bases have spurs and the head of the easternmost window is probably a restoration. Supporting the roof ridge-piece and trusses are a number of reset 15th-century corbels: busts of angels holding shields or with clasped hands, human busts, grotesques, a king, a jester (?), and one with a head on the side and, on the front, a representation of a woman in horned head-dress standing beside a table with a cup. The W. wall of the nave includes the boldly projecting tower buttresses flanking the tower-arch; they have small plinths and weathered off-sets at two levels, one on the E. face at clearstorey sill-level, the other on the S. and N. faces just below the wall-plate.

The *North Aisle* (20 ft. wide) was rebuilt in the second half of the 19th century; the E. and W. ends are gabled and a 12th-century corbel carved with a grotesque head is reset as a kneeler in the W. gable; a similar kneeler at the E. end is perhaps a modern copy. The E. window is of 15th-century date, reset; it has two cinquefoil lights in a square head with a moulded label and head stops, one a man, the other a woman with horned head-dress. The rood-stair in the S.E. angle is a 15th-century insertion; the lower doorway has continuous hollow-chamfered jambs and a high four-centred head; the vice is lit by two chamfered rectangular loops. The four reset windows in the N. wall are all of the 15th century, with modern repairs, and similar to the window in the E. wall. In the W. wall is a modern segmental-headed opening to the N. Vestry, which abuts the N.E. side of the tower; further N. is a doorway of 1895.

The *South Chapel* (28½ ft. by 14½ ft.), occupying the widened E. half of the S. aisle, is also known as the Wolfeton Aisle. Except for the shallow early 16th-century S.W. extension it dates from *c.* 1470, but the parapets and copings are modern, like those of the rest of the aisle. The E. wall contains a 15th-century window of three cinquefoil lights in a square head below a moulded label with head-stops. N. of the window is the opening to a squint with chamfered jambs and a square head; it is probably of the 15th century and it was blocked when the original chancel was destroyed. The S. wall has, toward the E., a much restored three-light window contem-

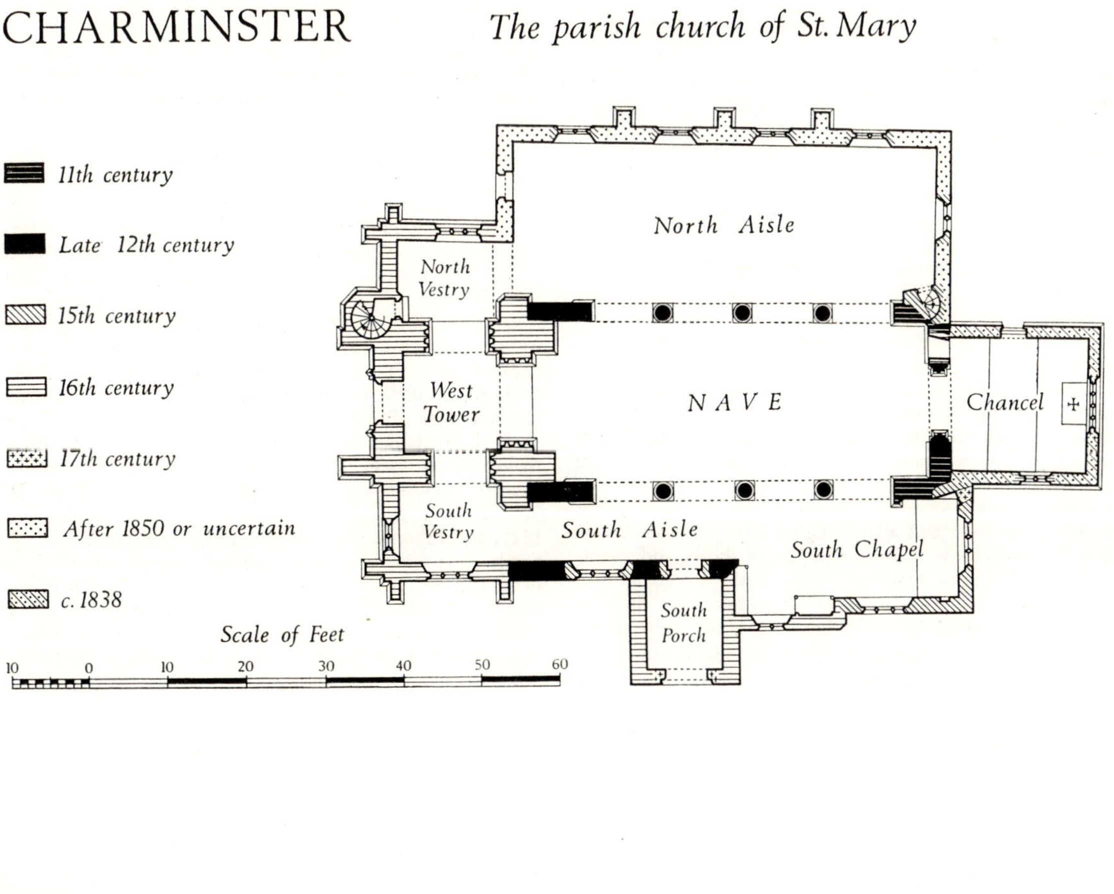

porary with and similar to that of the E. wall; further W. a crudely turned depressed arch spans the recess-like 16th-century extension. Externally the recess is capped with weathered ashlar; in its S. wall is a 16th-century window of two elliptical-headed lights in a square head with chamfered reveals. Inside, supporting the chapel roof are three reset corbels, perhaps from the later 12th-century structure, one carved with a bull's head. The rest of the S. wall of the *South Aisle* (7¼ ft. wide) is probably of 12th-century origin. The late 15th-century S. doorway has a two-centred moulded head and continuous moulded jambs with run-out stops and a triangular chamfered rear-arch. W. of the doorway is a 15th-century three-light window, uniform with the E. window of the S. chapel. The S.E. buttress of the tower projects into the N.W. angle of the aisle.

The *West Tower* (12½ ft. square) bears in many places the monogram shown below; presumably it is for Thomas Trenchard. The tower is of three stages, with a moulded plinth and moulded strings which are carried round the angle buttresses and the octagonal vice turret at the N.W. corner (Plate 121). The embattled parapet has a moulded string interrupted by seven gargoyles. Crocketed pinnacles stand at the corners and in the middle of each side and are also continued up from the tops of the buttresses; the vice turret is higher than the main parapet and has eight smaller pinnacles and a central pedestal for a weathervane. The buttresses, of four weathered stages, end at the level of the belfry window labels; those flanking the turret merge into it at the second weathering. Trenchard's monogram

is carved on each stage of the W. buttresses, those of the lowest stage being inlaid in lead. Inside, the tower arch has a two-centred head and continuous jambs with spur-stops; reveals and arch-soffit are decorated with pairs of cusped ogee-headed stone panels in two heights, the lowest panels having shields carved with the double T.; the arch is of Ham Hill stone down to stop-level; below it is of Purbeck stone. In the N. and S. walls are arched openings to the N. and S. vestries; they have panelled reveals like the tower arch and the Trenchard monogram again appears on shields in the lower tier of panels. The W. doorway has, externally, a moulded four-centred head and continuous moulded jambs with pedestal stops, all in a square surround formed by diagonal side-standards and a moulded string across the head. Each traceried spandrel includes a quatrefoil containing a shield with the double T.; the segmental rear arch of the doorway is plain. The W. window has five transomed lights with four-centred openings below and ogee cinquefoil openings above the transoms; the high four-centred head contains vertical tracery; head and jambs are casement-moulded and a moulded string is carried up over the head as a label; the rear arch is four-centred and chamfered. The W. face of the second stage of the tower is pierced by a small rectangular window with moulded head and jambs. The third stage contains in each face two two-light, double-transomed, square-headed belfry windows with square labels; the main head and jambs are casement-moulded and all the lights have elliptical heads and are filled with pierced stone panels. On the N. side some panels have the form of grotesque masks with pierced mouths and eyes. Access to the lead roof from the stair-turret is through a doorway with rebated triangular head and continuous jambs.

The *North* and *South Vestries* (respectively 12½ ft. by 10 ft. and 13 ft. by 9¾ ft.) flank the W. tower and are contemporary with it. In general they are uniform; on the free corners are two-stage angle buttresses, those to the N.W. with the Trenchard monogram on the lower stages; a similar square-set buttress marks the E. end of the 16th-century S. wall. The parapet walls and copings are modern and the walls have modern repairs. In the N. vestry, the N. wall has a window of three four-centred lights in a square head with a moulded label and a square rear-arch; at the S. end of the W. wall is a doorway to the tower vice, with a four-centred moulded head and continuous jambs above spur stops. In the S. vestry, the S. wall has a three-light window similar to that of the N. vestry, and in the W. wall is a similar window of two lights.

The *South Porch* (9½ ft. by 11½ ft.) is of the 16th century, but the porch arch was reconstructed in the 17th century; the parapet wall includes two 16th-century gargoyles and a corbel with the Trenchard monogram, now supporting a modern cross. The porch arch has a nearly round head of two chamfered orders with continuous jambs. The churchyard wall to the S. is of rubble with weathered copings and may in part be of the 16th or 17th century.

Fittings—*Bells:* six, in modern steel frame; 2nd, by Thomas Purdue, 1663; 3rd, probably by William Purdue, late 16th century; 4th, 1631; 6th, by Thomas Purdue, 1661, recast 1952. *Brackets:* In N. aisle, in N.W. angle of rood-stair turret, corbel carried on carved male head, 15th century. In S. porch, flanking doorway, two semi-octagonal capitals of Ham Hill stone, 15th century, reset. *Brasses* and *Indents: see* below, *Monument* (3). *Chair:* In chancel, with turned uprights and carved back, 17th century. *Churchyard Cross:* Loose against wall of S. aisle, portion of tapered shaft, 3¼ ft. long with chamfered angles, late mediaeval. *Clock:* In second stage of tower, wrought-iron frame with brass cogwheels, possibly of *c.* 1700, rebuilt 1896. *Font:* Circular bowl turning to octagonal below small roll moulding and tapering to roll necking, on straight octagonal stem with chamfered circular plinth and square base, traces of red painting on stem; rim with mortice and dowel-holes for fixings; probably 12th century, recut and reshaped in 15th century. *Glass:* In S. aisle, in cusping of E. window, fragments including four double roses and pieces of two more, floral patterns, black-letters reset upside-down and IHS monogram, late 15th century. *Graffito:* On S.E. respond of tower arch, carved devil's head.

Monuments and *Floorslabs. Monuments:* In S. chapel, on S. wall, (1) of Grace Pole, 1636, daughter of Thomas Trenchard, wall monument of marble, slate and plaster with effigy of woman in voluminous dress with falling lace-edged collar kneeling at prayer-desk (Plate 34); on each side freestanding Corinthian columns with side scrolls supporting entablature with broken pediment surmounted by seated cherubs and cartouche containing lozenge-of-arms of Pole impaling Trenchard; inscription tablet below with scrolled and jewelled surround flanked by lion masks; semicircular tympanum over effigy enclosing modelled cherubs and clouds, and, in spandrels, cartouches with faded painted crests of Pole and Trenchard; vertical panels behind columns modelled to represent branches from which hang shields with painted arms, now largely effaced, representing on E. side Trenchard and on W. side Pole alliances. Adjacent to the foregoing, (2) of Mary Henning, 1821, and others later, marble tablet; (3) canopied mural table-tomb of Purbeck marble, second quarter of 16th century; front and W. end of chest with moulded plinth with traces of red and purple paint, and divided into traceried panels containing cusped and sub-cusped quatrefoils enclosing blocks for brass shields, now missing; at angles, spirally-turned pedestals below octagonal columns, the latter standing on tomb-slab and supporting flat-arched canopy with moulded cornice, enriched with quatrefoils and capped with blind brattishing; soffit of canopy elaborately traceried and with central pendant; in back wall, indents of brasses, now gone, of kneeling figure with scroll issuing from hands, Trinity, shield surrounded by scrolls, and inscription plate; brass fillet from chamfered edge of tomb-slab also missing. Built into S.W. corner of S. chapel, (4) canopied mural table-tomb, not *in situ*, of Purbeck marble and of similar form to (3), but dating from rather earlier in the 16th century and more Gothic in style; fascia below canopy divided into two bays of flat four-centred arches with sunk spandrels and cusping; canopy-frieze enriched with square quatrefoil panels; reset in back wall, frieze of four diagonal quatrefoil and sub-cusped panels enclosing blank shields, much decayed. In S. aisle, on S. wall, (5) of Thomas Nicholls, 1822, and others, black and white marble tablet; (6) of Robert Devenish, 1839, sarcophagus-shaped marble tablet with arms and crest of Devenish, by Lester of Dorchester; (7) of John, 1800, and Sara Devenish, 1820, marble tablet by Lancashire and Tyley of Bath; (8) of Martha Devenish, 1836, tablet similar to (6) and by same maker. In churchyard, (9) of Robert Gray, 1656, table-tomb; (10) of Lewes Cockrum, 1660, table-tomb. *Floorslabs:* In chancel, (1) of the daughters of Thomas Hawker of Somerset, 1704, 1720, with incised architectural decoration, partly hidden; (2) of Henry Trenchard of Fulford in Devon, 1720; (3) of the daughter of Thomas and Elizabeth Trenchard, 1707, partly hidden. In N. aisle, (4) of Henry Hayward, 1705. In S. chapel, (5) of Thomas Trenchard, 1727, worn and partly hidden; (6) of Mary Henning, 1821, and others later.

Paintings: In nave, over chancel arch, faint traces now unidentifiable but when uncovered in 1897 thought to be scenes from Passion and Resurrection, 15th century. On N. wall, below doorway to rood-loft, areas of stencilled decoration depicting strawberries and strawberry-leaves in red on white ground, early 16th century; over first pier of N. arcade, traces of black-letter inscription from Matthew V, 16; over third bay, rectangular panel with black, gold and red surround containing black-letter inscription from Nahum I, 15, with traces of another painting higher up, all late 16th century; on S. wall, over E. respond, faded and fragmentary stencilled decoration corresponding with the one opposite; over second bay of arcade, fragment of the Apostles' Creed in black-letter, late 16th century; over third pier, fragment of text in rough capitals possibly from I Peter III, 7; over fourth arch, fragment of black-letter inscription possibly from Romans VI, 4 and 5, late 16th century; on W. wall, N. and S. of tower-arch, sepia paintings of trees, that on S. nearly obliterated, 16th century; at wall-plate level, initials in plain capitals. *Piscina:* In S. chapel, in S. wall, with hollow-chamfered ogee head, continuous hollow-chamfered jambs, shaped dish with boss carved as a half-rosette, and two drains, mediaeval. *Plate:* includes a cup and cover-paten of 1570 (or 1577, date-letter worn), maker's mark an orb surmounted by a crown; also stand-paten of 1836. *Pulpit:* of oak, octagonal, with moulded and jewel-ornamented plinth, on modern base; sides in two heights of panelling with enriched framing, rails carved with acanthus and guilloche ornament, stiles fluted and reeded; upper panels with round-headed arcading; cornice enriched with small console-brackets at corners and capped by modern book-rest; pulpit dated 1635 on internal panel. *Royal Arms:* In S. aisle, painted on wood, in moulded frame, 1757. *Sundials:* Scratch-dials, one on E. quoin of S. aisle, much worn and inverted, another on parapet-wall of S. porch. *Weathervane:* On tower, of wrought iron with copper vane pierced with initials T.S. and date 1744. *Miscellanea:* In S. chapel, moulded stone fragments with nail-head and chevron ornament, 12th century. In vestry, on N. wall, wood panel recording enlargements and repairs to church in 1838 and 1839. At foot of tower, outside W. wall, slab with Lombardic lettering '. . . MEN . . HI . . .'.

SECULAR

(2) BRIDGE (67649193), over a branch of the R. Frome, ½ m. S.S.W. of the church, is of two spans and of brick in English bond with ashlar dressings. The segmental arches spring from a squat centre pier with rounded and domed cut-waters at each end. The bridge is probably of the mid 19th century.

(3) BRIDGE (67959266), over the R. Cerne, 40 yds. S.E. of the church, is in three spans and has rubble walls and semi-circular arches turned in brick. It is probably of late mediaeval origin but the arches were rebuilt in the 18th or early 19th century.

(4) WOLFETON HOUSE (678921), 650 yds. S. of the church, is built in two storeys with walls of Purbeck stone rubble, squared and coursed rubble, and ashlar; the roofs are covered with stone-slates (Plate 124). On the death in 1480 of John Mohun, who had married an heiress of the Jurdains, the former owners of the property, Wolfeton passed to his grandson John Trenchard. Before the end of the century it seems that timber from Frome Whitfield was supplied for structural work (Hutchins II, 547). The reception here of the Archduke Philip of Austria and Joanna of Castile in 1506, though largely fortuitous, points to the existence of a house of some pretensions. However, nothing survives that is demonstrably of the 15th century; the *Gatehouse* alone may perhaps have been begun by the turn of the century. Fragments of an elaborately decorated 16th-century structure incorporated in the present house, which on the evidence of a date tablet are not later than 1534, show that extensive rebuilding took place during that period; Sir Thomas Trenchard was then the owner. From Hutchins's account (II, 546) it seems clear that the house was arranged around a courtyard; the present Gatehouse occupied the E. range and a chapel to the N. formed, or stood close to, the N. range; the N. part was the oldest. The chapel was in ruins in *c.* 1800 and was then demolished, and the greater parts of the *South Range* and of the *West Range* were demolished between 1822 and 1828. The appearance of the complete S. range, with a curious diagonal wing off the S.E. corner, is preserved in W. Walker's engraving of the house (Hutchins's 1st edn., 1774, opp. p. 453) and in a drawing of 1811 reproduced in *Country Life* (17th December 1953). An early 19th-century sketch of the W. range, in the owner's possession (Plate 93), shows an elaborate arched entrance more or less axial with the Gatehouse; the presumption that this was the entrance to the screens-passage of the Hall seems to be confirmed by Hutchins's statement (*loc. cit.*) that 'near it (*sc.* the hall) to the N. is a small domestic chapel', since the latter is known to have been N. of the courtyard. The westward exten-

WOLFETON HOUSE - CHARMINSTER

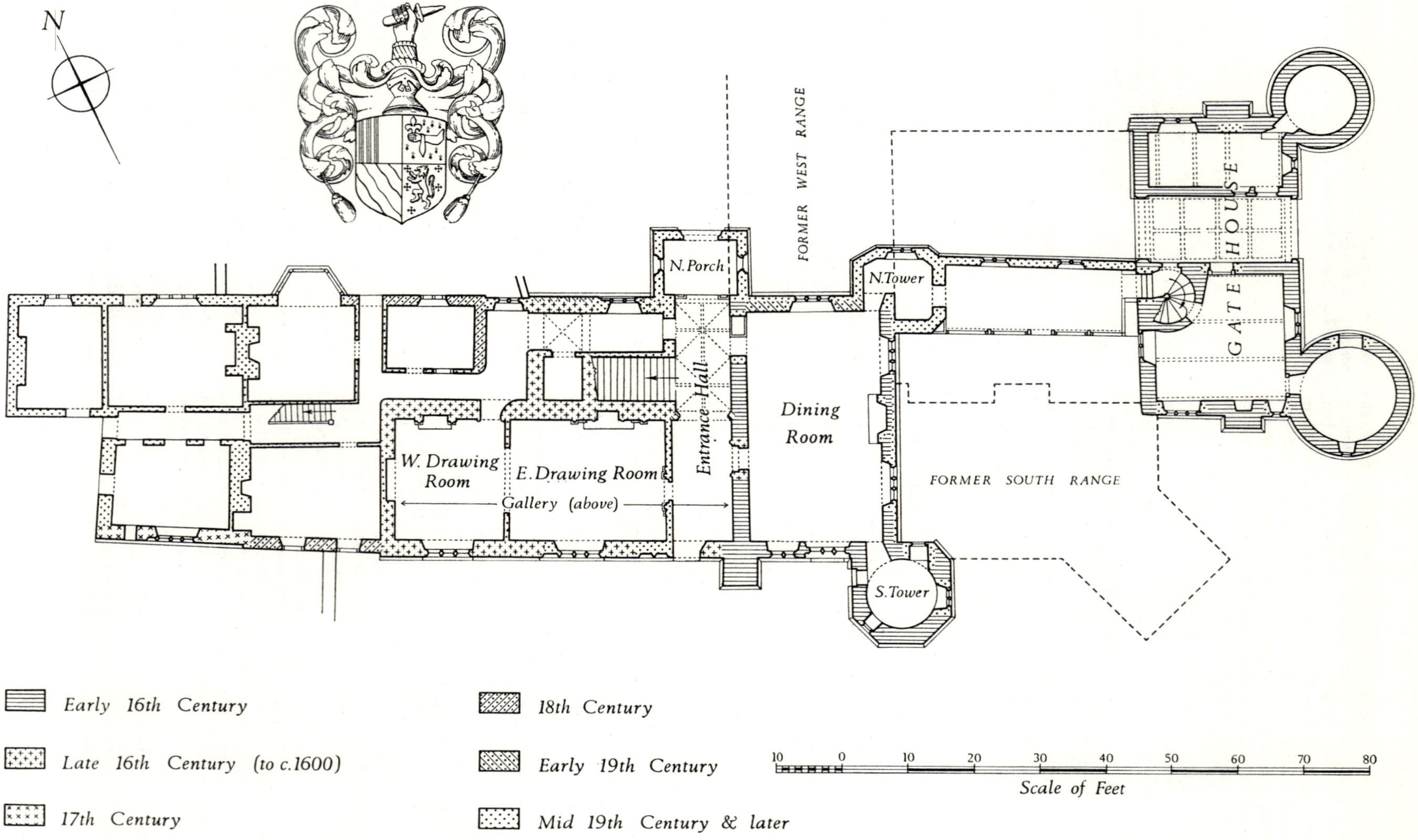
N
N. Porch
FORMER WEST RANGE
N. Tower
GATE HOUSE
Dining Room
Entrance Hall
W. Drawing Room
E. Drawing Room
Gallery (above)
FORMER SOUTH RANGE
S. Tower
Early 16th Century
Late 16th Century (to c.1600)
17th Century
18th Century
Early 19th Century
Mid 19th Century & later
10 0 10 20 30 40 50 60 70 80
Scale of Feet

sion of the S. range, containing the 'Gallery' on the first floor, was built in the last quarter of the 16th century, possibly *c.* 1580, during the ownership of Sir George Trenchard; at the same time a spacious stone stairway, now in part a 19th-century reconstruction, was built in the re-entrant angle between the S. range and the hall range.[1]

After the demolitions of the first half of the 19th century the house was practically derelict, as appears in Buckler's drawings of 1828 (British Museum, Add. MSS. 36361, ff. 197–9; 36439, f. 287). In 1862 the house was bought by W. H. P. Weston and his works of restoration and rebuilding were extensive. They included a reconstruction of the top stage of the octagonal S. tower, building a new octagonal N. tower and a new N. porch, and rebuilding or refacing the walls connecting the three. He also formed a passageway between the house and Gatehouse and made alterations to the offices to the W. The elaborate plaster ceilings in the drawing-rooms are perhaps of this period. Many windows have been altered and reset. The 'Gallery' on the first floor has been divided up, and in recent years the whole house has been divided into three units. Nothing remains of the important heraldic glass that was in the hall and other rooms (Hutchins II, 547–52); much of it was moved in 1798 and largely destroyed in transit to Lytchett Matravers.

Wolfeton when complete must have been a building of remarkable individuality and interest. The Gatehouse, provided for effect rather than real defence, and the surviving fragments of an early 16th-century house of high elaboration suggest considerable architectural ebullience, whereas the extensions of *c.* 1580 exhibit details, outside and in, suggestive of the classical sophistication that is associated with Protector Somerset and Old Somerset House; the stone carving of the 'Gallery' doorway is akin to that at Longleat, attributed to Allen Maynard, *c.* 1575.

[1] The original lay-out is difficult to determine. A list of stained glass in specified windows compiled in 1742 and annotated in 1799 is transcribed by Hutchins (II, 547–52). From it, evidently, the Hall had at least one S. and one E. window; the 'Long Parlour over the Hall' had two S. and two N. windows and an E. window. The Walker engraving and the 1811 drawing, both nearly contemporary with the 1799 revised window lists, show that there was no E. window at first-floor level in the E. end of the S. range. With the Hall in the position indicated in the text above, and having a S. extent equal at least to that of the Dining Room on the accompanying plan, the list becomes explicable if the 'Long Parlour' was an L-shaped room occupying the first floor of the S. range and returned over the Hall. Thus the Hall had a window to the S. and a window to the E., the latter being between the N. wall of the S. range and the screens entrance (all since demolished), and the Long Parlour had the requisite N. and S. windows, as the early drawings show, and an E. window over the E. window of the Hall. With the Hall and Long Parlour thus, the S. tower, which probably contained a stair, is seen to be logically placed for access from the dais end of the Hall to the Long Parlour above.

The *Gatehouse* consists of a rectangular building with round towers on the N.E. and S.E. corners and with a gate-passage (13½ ft. by 10¼ ft.) through it from E. to W. (Plate 125). On the E. side the wall between the towers has a moulded plinth, a moulded string at first-floor level and a coved stone eaves-cornice. The entrance archway is set slightly N. of centre; it has a four-centred and moulded head and continuous jambs with pedestal-bases to each moulding, graded in height to create an illusion of greater recession, and a moulded label with carved stops representing a satyr and a woodhouse, each holding a stave; reset above is a cartouche of *c.* 1720 containing the quarterly arms of Trenchard, Mohun and Jurdain, with an inescutcheon of Tuckfield quartering two other coats. The windows on ground and first floors are of one, two and three lights with hollow-chamfered four-centred heads with foliate spandrels; they are of the early 16th century and those on the ground floor have been reset. The N.E. and S.E. towers are respectively 10¾ ft. and 14½ ft. in internal diameter. The first tower incorporated a garderobe in the N.E. sector and the head of the outlet is visible above ground-level. The towers have moulded plinths, higher than that of the main front, and they are divided into two stages by moulded strings which are continuous with the string on the main front; they stand above the general eaves-level of the building and are covered with low-pitched conical roofs. In each tower, just below the string-course, an original gun-loop covering the main entrance-archway consists of a chamfered slit with a round widening in the centre; the wall-string mitres over it. The other openings below the string-course are modern or reset; the upper windows are small, of single lights and of the early 16th century with high four-centred hollow-chamfered heads and jambs and foliated spandrels; the S.E. tower has a small louvred rectangular opening below eaves-level, the entrance to a large pigeon-loft. The N. end wall is gabled and the plinth and string are similar to those on the E. front; in the centre is a projecting chimney-breast with the first-floor flue supported on hollow-chamfered corbelling at string level and weathered back above; in the stack and reset from the destroyed south range is an inscribed panel in a moulded stone frame. The inscription reads HOC OPUS FINITU[M] EST ANNO DNI MDXXXIIII. A restored 16th-century window on the ground floor has two lights with elliptical heads and foliate spandrels, and a single-light window on the first floor is similar to the windows in the towers. Although the S. end has been much patched and repaired it is evident that a wall originally projected S. from the W. angle. The arrangement is very similar to that of the N. end; the projecting chimney is in part corbelled and in part continued down to the ground; the plinth mouldings on the tower change to a chamfer and in this form are continued across the front; all the ground-floor windows are 19th-century insertions. The W. side has plinth, string and cornice mouldings similar to those of the E. front; the archway has a high four-centred double-chamfered head, continuous chamfered jambs stopping against the returned plinth-mouldings, and a moulded label rising at the apex to a finial-like pedestal on which a naked child sits carrying a shield carved with the initial S (for Strangways) or possibly a double T (for Thomas Trenchard); the stops have the form of crouching *putti* holding shields, one with the same letter in a foliated wreath, the other T E (for Thomas Trenchard and Elizabeth (Strangways) his wife) and interlacement; set in the wall-face flanking the finial are two more shields with the initials T T and T E respectively, looped together with tasselled cords. The 16th-century windows are of one, two and three lights with four-centred and round-headed openings; those on the upper floor have shallow square heads and foliated spandrels and to some extent have been altered or reset. Under the eaves towards the N. is a reset head-stop of a man. At each end of this W. side are indications of pre-existing walls projecting westward. (For interior of Gatehouse *see* p. 67.)

The bulk of the surviving *House* stands some 13 yds. W. of the Gatehouse, the two now being connected solely by a mid 19th-century covered passage. Originally the S. range of the quadrangular courtyard house continued E. to join the Gatehouse and had a small wing projecting diagonally from the free S.E. corner. On it was the date panel that is now reset in the Gatehouse.

The S. front of the house retains, to the E., the only surviving part of the early 16th-century S. range. This comprises the S. tower, a projecting garderobe and the main S. wall linking them. The S. tower, originally probably a stair-tower, is of three stages, the topmost being a rebuilding of *c.* 1862 to replace the gabled attic storey, demolished some thirty-five years earlier, shown in W. Walker's engraving of the house (Hutchins, *loc. cit.*). The tower has a moulded plinth and moulded strings, and in the W. face is an original doorway with a restored square moulded head and jambs with pedestal stops; to the S.W. is a rectangular window with hollow-chamfered head and jambs; to the E. is a 19th-century two-light window and, in the second stage, two original windows of one and two lights respectively, with four-centred openings in square heads with carved spandrels. The N.E. splay and all of the free northerly wall is refaced. To the W. of the tower the surviving part of the main S. wall has been much patched and the moulded upper members of its plinth have been cut away for the lowered sill of the easternmost window; this last is of the early 16th century, reset, and has three lights with segmental openings in the square head, moulded jambs and mullions with small discrete pedestal bases to each moulding. The bases are shortened in height in recession, as on the Gatehouse, perhaps to force the perspective. The label is moulded and embattled and the E. return, for which the W. wall of the tower has been cut back, has a carved stop of a cross-legged man wearing a hat; the W. end stops on a carved grotesque beast and is without a vertical member on account of the proximity of another window immediately W. The second window is also of the early 16th century but partly restored; it was probably originally of five lights and placed axially below the window above. It now has two transomed lights with round-headed openings and carved spandrels, below as well as above the transom. The jambs have pedestal bases. The ovolo moulding of the head and jambs is carved with a twisted garland of ribbon and fruit of Renaissance character; the label has elaborate foliage carving and stops representing the busts of a man and a woman. The five-light window on the first floor is similar in detail to the opening just described, except that it is without a transom and retains the original moulded mullions with small semi-octagonal moulded pedestal-bases with pyramidal stops bringing them out to the square; the label is carved with grapes and vine tendrils and the carved label-stops are of a man and a winged and feathered grotesque; the moulded sill is continued across the wall-face as a string. The garderobe immediately to the W. comprises a small semi-octagonal first-floor projection supported on a rectangular shaft; the shaft has a moulded plinth and capping, moulded corbelling at the sides and small broaches at the corners to bring it to the semi-octagon above. The garderobe has in the S.E. face a small restored window with wood frame, two-centred and with foliate spandrels; it has a moulded stone eaves-cornice and a roof of weathered ashlar, pyramidal and semi-octagonal, with a carved finial representing a seated man holding sword and buckler. Adjoining on the W. is the ashlar front of the late 16th-century block, which contained the former 'Gallery' on the first floor; it has a moulded plinth, a classical entablature of shallow projection carried across the front as a string-course immediately above the ground-floor windows, and an eaves entablature with dentil-like modillions, breaking forward at extended intervals over shaped and moulded consoles. Each of the three windows on ground and first floors was originally of four transomed lights with square heads and moulded jambs and mullions, with moulded pedestal-stops above transoms and sills; but a door has been cut in the E. window, the westernmost light of the W. window has been built up flush with the wall-face in ashlar, and a number of other lights have been blocked. Walker's engraving (Hutchins, *loc. cit.*) shows a bay-window where the centre windows are now; it was demolished in 1798 and there is patching and evidence of resetting in the area.

The lower W. end of the house has been much altered and rebuilt and is now largely of the late 18th or early 19th century, except towards the W. extremity, where the front has a moulded plinth, a four-light stone-mullioned window on the ground floor, with a square head and a label and, on the original first floor, traces of another blocked window. All these features are of the 17th century and perhaps are the remains of the small twin-gabled annex shown in Walker's engraving, since heightened and in part rebuilt.

The wall of the E. front, N. of the S. tower, is ostensibly of the mid 19th century; so also is the return N. wall from the N. tower as far as the N. porch. The 19th-century drawings already mentioned, and another sketch in the Dorchester Museum (Gorland 19), suggest that they are on the lines of original and early 19th-century internal and exterior walls; thus this mid 19th-century appearance may be no more than refacing. The N. tower is entirely mid 19th-century.

The N. front has, to the E., the mid 19th-century screen-wall to the passageway that joins the house to the Gatehouse. Further W., the N. wall of the stair is of the late 16th century, refaced in the early 19th century but retaining over the porch a window of three mullioned and transomed lights in a square head with moulded jambs and pedestal-stops. The gabled upper part of the W. return wall of the stair appears above the adjoining buildings; it has a parapet-wall, moulded coping and shaped kneelers and contains a blocked late 16th-century two-light window with square head and moulded label. Further W. the walls of the office buildings are of squared and coursed rubble and are, in part, of the late 18th century with some earlier material reused.

Inside, the house was extensively remodelled in the second half of the 19th century and many of the features and fittings are of that date, albeit in Elizabethan or Jacobean style. The *Entrance Hall* contains a number of reset fragments of *c.* 1600, among them a stone achievement-of-arms of Trenchard quartering Mohun, Bruer or Briwere, and Jurdain (*see* illustration on p. 64). The cartouche is now over the north doorway but it was originally over the 'great door at the east front' (Hutchins II, 547); that is to say it was on the W. range, over the entrance to the screens (*see* Plate 93). Two late 16th-century half-length figures of naked women carved in stone stand in circular recesses in the W. spandrels of the archway to the stairs. The doorway to the *Dining Room* from the S. part of the entrance hall has an elaborately carved timber surround made up in the 19th century with some early 17th-century pieces, and a frieze of reused panels, perhaps of the early 16th century, carved with Zodiac scenes and also part of an Annunciation; the doorway in the opposite wall is of similar origin, one of the incorporated pieces being dated 1642. The walls are lined with restored early 16th and 17th-century panelling, the earlier with linen-fold decoration, and the cornice includes a number of reused early 16th-century carved panels of French Renaissance character.

The *East Drawing Room*, the former 'Parlour', contains a doorcase and fireplace-surround with overmantel all comprising highly enriched assemblages of early 17th-century woodwork from other parts of the house. The doorway has a semicircular arched head on moulded imposts and reeded and fluted responds; Corinthian side pilasters on pedestals support an entablature with lions' masks in the frieze, over which is a much mitred and gadrooned panel flanked by standing figures of a king in grotesque armour and a woman; the whole is flanked by a pair of colossal attached Composite columns on pedestals and these support an entablature which meets the ceiling and has a modillion cornice, and strapwork in the frieze flanking a shield-of-arms of Trenchard quartering Mohun and Jurdain. The door is panelled in three heights, with a gadrooned centre panel and a semicircular upper panel with radiating jewel and strapwork ornament; every member of the doorcase is elaborately carved (Plate 126). The fireplace-surround is of similar character, with flanking terminal-figures supporting a frieze and, above, an overmantel with three standing male figures flanking two panels which contain figures of Hope and Justice framed in round-headed arches; on each side, colossal attached Composite columns on pedestals support an entablature with a modillion cornice and a frieze with consoles and strapwork ornament (Plate 126). The fireplace opening is reduced in size by the insertion of a timber surround comprising two small Corinthian half-columns with arabesque ornament on the shafts and twenty-three carved panels of the Labours of the Months, signs of the Zodiac, etc., mostly of the early 16th century; they came from the Smoking-room which was demolished in the 19th century.

In the *West Drawing Room* the N. door is made up of pieces of 16th and 17th-century carving. The late 16th-century overmantel is of plaster, now painted dark brown, and comprises flanking terminal figures on pedestals supporting an entablature with a deep strapwork frieze; they frame a panel depicting the Judgement of Paris in an elaborate strapwork surround with angels, fruit and foliage, all modelled in high relief; the shelf below, which has been associated, bears the date 1652. The overmantel is closely similar in general design and workmanship to one in the garden chamber at Montacute.

The great *Staircase* is of stone; it appears to have been restored in the 19th century but it no doubt follows the general form of the late 16th-century staircase. The whole stair is monumental in scale. It has a balustrade with a pierced arcade of round-headed arches supporting a continuous moulded capping, all returned along the front of the first-floor landing; here, where the balustrade meets the wall, is a carved stone caryatid, either a finial or the respond to an upper height of arcading that is now entirely missing. The doorway from the landing into the former Gallery has a stone surround of the late 16th century, with Corinthian side pilasters, a pedimented entablature with small pedestals on the slopes, and a bust of a man with a knotted cloak in the tympanum; the frieze has an unusual carved enrichment of honeysuckle, acanthus and roses, a design that occurs also at Longleat. Although somewhat gauche, the doorway has the classical purity of the pre-Flemish phase of Renaissance work in England (Plate 127).

The *Gallery*, which occupied the whole length of the late 16th-century W. extension, is known to have had a coved and enriched plaster ceiling; it may in part survive but the room has been divided up and flat inserted ceilings prevent any sight of it. The original stone chimneypiece survives (Plate 127); it rises the full height of the room and is in two stages; the lower stage has flanking coupled Composite columns on panelled pedestals supporting an entablature in which the frieze is carved with arabesques and, over the columns, reclining female figures representing Faith and Hope; a decorative apron below the architrave is carved with strapwork incorporating human masks. The fireplace opening has been reduced in size by the insertion of a later surround with half-columns and cornice-shelf. The overmantel has superimposed Composite columns on jewelled pedestals supporting a modillion cornice; they frame a large panel carved with a central reclining female figure in an elaborate strapwork frame, incorporating naked figures and heads of men and women. The whole chimneypiece is closely similar in design and workmanship to one in the great chamber at Montacute; thus the decorative apron is not a later association as might at first be supposed. The adjoining bedroom, a sub-division of the Gallery, has some reset 17th-century panelling.

The interior of the *Gatehouse* (for exterior, *see* p. 65) retains some noteworthy features. In the N. wall of the carriageway is a 16th-century doorway with a cambered chamfered head and continuous jambs with splayed stops; adjacent is a single-light window with a four-centred head and foliate spandrels; in the S. wall is an original doorway with moulded jambs with worn stops and a moulded two-centred head. The original open timber ceiling is divided into eight panels by chamfered beams and plates. Access to the N.E. tower is through a damaged stone doorway with chamfered jambs and flat head; it is fitted with a 16th or 17th-century nail-studded plank door. The ground-floor rooms retain a number of chamfered ceiling beams. The circular stair with centre newel has the first six steps of stone; above, the steps are of oak with the newel cut from the same timber balks as the steps and the soffits cut to the slope of the rise, as in a stone vice (Plate 81). On the upper floor are two stone fireplace surrounds of the first half of the 17th century; one has Ionic side pilasters supporting an architrave and, around the opening, a wide moulded frame enriched with fluting and gadrooning, with acanthus leaves at the corners (Plate 75); the other has rusticated Tuscan side pilasters supporting an entablature with a rusticated frieze below which the lintel is embellished with two courses of rustication. Two doorways have chamfered stone jambs and flat heads with rounded corners; one retains the original studded oak-plank door with strap-hinges and a latch with a fretted plate. The 16th-century doorway of the S.E. tower has a four-centred chamfered head, continuous jambs and splayed stops; it is hung with the original plank door. The stair continues up to the roof-space, where there is studded partitioning.

Walker's engraving of *c.* 1774 shows two garden walls extending S., at right angles to the S. front of the house. The one to the W. survives and is probably Tudor; it is of coursed rubble with embattled cresting and it contains a damaged doorway with a four-centred head.

The *Stables*, W. of the house, are of one storey with lofts and have coursed rubble walls and slate-covered roofs; they are of the 18th century. The W. front has a carriage entrance with round head, moulded archivolt and imposts, keystone and rusticated jambs, and three two-light stone-mullioned windows.

The *Lodge* and *Gates*, 270 yds. S.E. of the house, are of coursed rubble and ashlar. The lodge is of one storey and was probably rebuilt with older materials in the 19th century; it is connected to the W. gate-pier by a length of rubble wall containing an elliptical-headed doorway. The square ashlar gate-piers, with plain plinths and cappings and ball-finials, are perhaps of the late 18th or early 19th century. Two pairs of 18th-century gate-piers, 50 yds. E.S.E. and 125 yds. S.E. of the gatehouse, are rusticated and have ball-finials supported on shaped and moulded pedestals.

RIDING HOUSE AT WOLFETON - CHARMINSTER

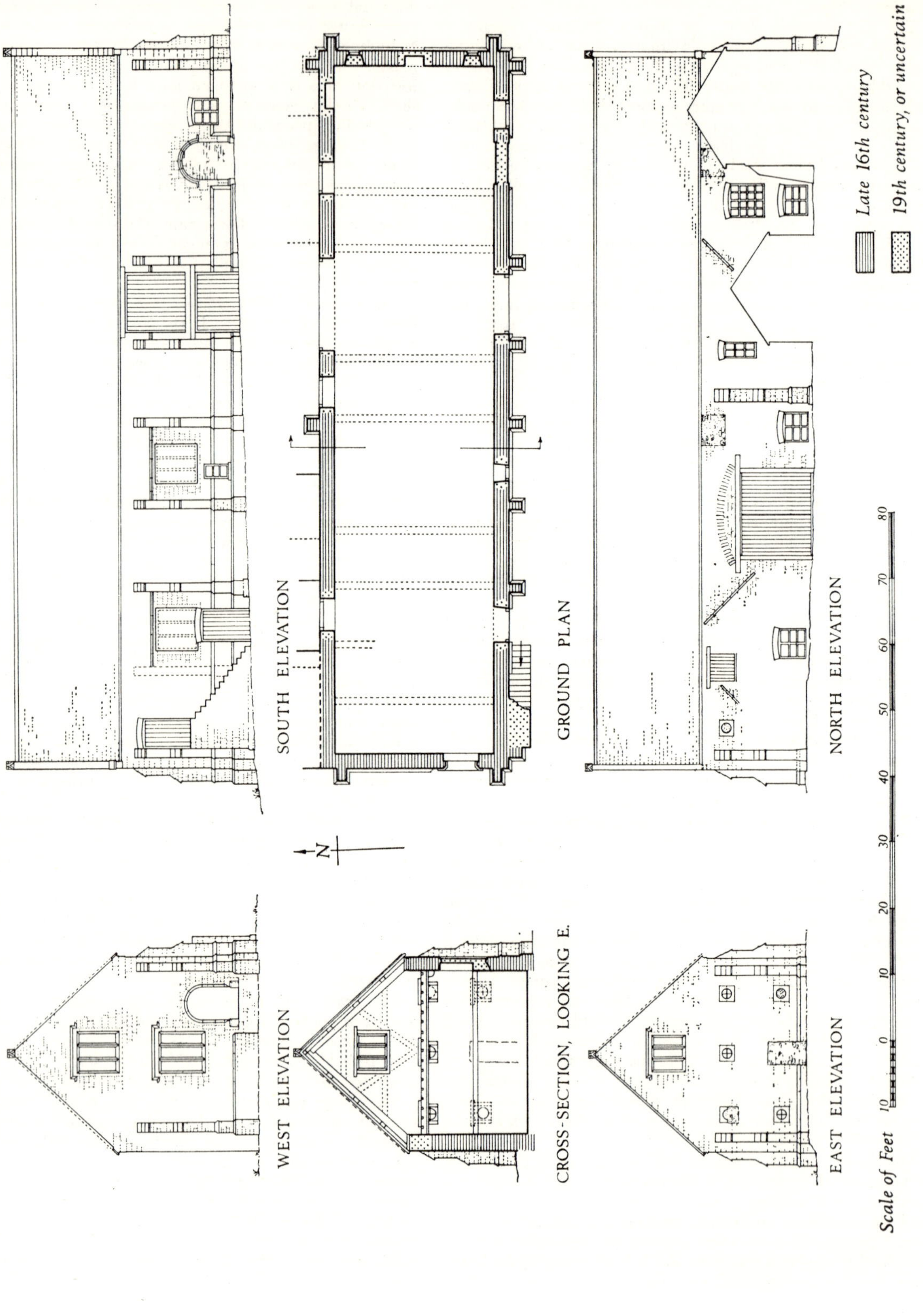

(5) RIDING HOUSE (67869225), 125 yds. N. of Wolfeton House, was originally two storied, the lower storey very high, the upper storey little more than an attic. The walls date probably from the last quarter of the 16th century and are of ashlar on the E., S. and W., and of squared and coursed rubble on the N.; later alterations are in coursed rubble of poorer quality. Traces of two subsidiary ranges at right angles to the building suggest that an open-air *manège* lay formerly on the N. of the riding house.

As the earliest surviving riding house known in England the building is of considerable architectural importance. Prince Henry's riding house at St. James's Palace, built *c.* 1604, was in many respects similar to the present building although larger; the riding houses at Welbeck Abbey and Bolsover Castle date from later in the 17th century.[1]

The S. elevation has a plinth with a chamfered footing course and an ogee moulded capping, and is divided into seven bays by buttresses of two weathered stages (Plate 125). The most easterly of the seven bays is nearly three times the normal width; the buttress between the two western bays has been removed to make way for a secondary external stone stair. At the centre of the wide E. bay is a round-headed doorway, now blocked, on each side of which the plinth mouldings are returned downwards. The opening has a moulded head, continuous jambs and an ogee-moulded label; the arch mouldings are concealed by the rubble blocking wall. Above the doorway is a small lion mask, in relief, with the locks of the mane arranged radially; a similar feature occurs at Lulworth Castle (*see Dorset* II, 148). The fourth and sixth bays from the E. have mullioned windows of three square-headed lights, now blocked, with weathered labels which continue laterally and stop against the buttresses. Remains of a similar label flanking a large secondary doorway in the second bay show that originally there was a third window in this position.

The W. wall has two weathered buttresses and moulded plinths, as before. To the S. is a round-headed doorway similar to that of the S. elevation; it has continuous ogee and hollow-chamfered mouldings ending at shaped stops. In the centre of the wall and at the same level as the windows of the S. elevation is a window of three square-headed lights with double-chamfered surrounds, under a label with returned stops; the opening is blocked with brickwork. Above, in the upper storey, is a similar window, still open. The gable has moulded kneelers and a finial with crossed gablets.

The E. wall has plinth, buttresses, upper window and gable approximately uniform with those on the W. Below the gable the wall is pierced by small round windows in two storeys, as shown on the drawing. Each window has a chamfered and rebated ashlar surround and three of the openings retain original iron cross-bars. A blocked secondary doorway in the lower storey may replace a sixth window.

In the N. elevation a weathered buttress uniform with those of the E. wall, but now without a plinth, stands near the N.E. corner. Near the middle of the elevation is another buttress, stouter than those described but otherwise similar. Some 3 ft. from the E. buttress is a blocked round window, uniform with and at the same level as the upper row of eastern round windows. Two blocked rectangular openings occur near the eaves, one adjacent to the central buttress, the other about 15 ft. from the N.W. corner; it is uncertain if these openings are original or secondary. All other openings in the N. elevation are clearly secondary; the large barn doorway, however, may well replace a narrower original doorway. Two subsidiary buildings formerly stood adjacent to the main building; large parts of the creasing courses of their roofs, undoubtedly original, are neatly bonded with the original coursed rubble masonry. These were probably stable ranges, perhaps flanking an open-air *manège* on the N. side of the riding house. Part of the W. wall of the western range may still exist, incorporated in the E. wall of an adjacent cottage.

Inside, the building now has a secondary floor, some two feet above the sill-level of the original S. windows. The original first floor has been removed, but most of the beams upon which it rested remain; they are chamfered and measure 12 ins. by 12 ins. in cross-section; in the upper part, on each side of each beam are the housings of former floor joists; below, on one side is a row of small mortices for the ends of smaller ceiling joists and on the other side is a groove to receive the ends of corresponding joists. Thus the beams evidently supported both a floor and an independent ceiling, the groove enabling the ceiling joists to be inserted after the beams were in position. To the N. the beams are housed in the wall; to the S. they rest on rounded stone corbels which project from the wall, directly above the level of timber lintels spanning the window recesses. The roof retains many original members, but they have been extensively strutted and repaired.

[1] R.I.B.A. Library, Smythson Collection, I/14 and III/15 (3–4). *See* M. Girouard, *Journal of the Society of Architectural Historians of Great Britain*, 5 (1962), 33, 57, 76, 153; also, by same author, *Robert Smythson* (1966), pl. 166, 167.

(6) FORSTON HOUSE (66589574) is of two storeys with attics. The walls are of brick in Flemish bond with ashlar dressings; the roofs are slated. Hutchins (II, 544) records that it was built by Robert Browne of Frampton (1670–1734) and in all probability it dates from the early years of the reign of George I. Some embellishments were added by Robert's son John, who died in 1750; in recent times a new wing has been built to the N. and alterations have been made internally.

The house is a graceful specimen of early 18th-century domestic architecture, interesting for an adroit solution of the problem of masking the gables of parallel roofs (Plate 122).

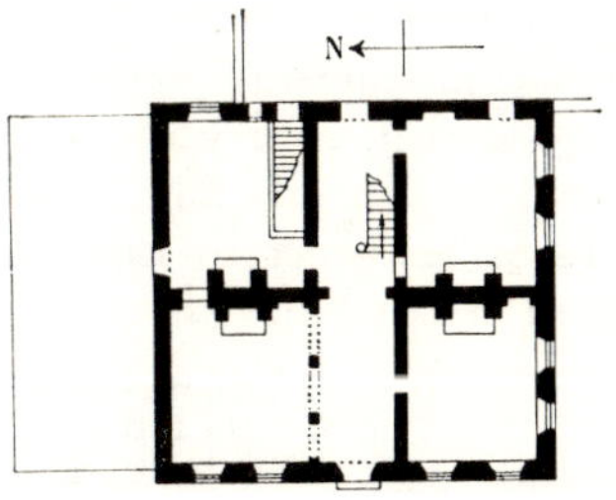

The W. façade is symmetrical and of five bays, with ashlar plinths, strings, parapet coping and flush quoins; above the second string the quoins become pilasters. The parapet wall screens the attics, but to each side it sweeps down in a bold curve to a little above eaves level; it is surmounted by decorative vases. The central doorway has been remodelled and provided with a reset early 18th-century wooden canopy on carved console brackets, and a modern architrave. The windows are rectangular, with plain stone architraves and double-hung sashes. On the E. the lower storey is concealed by later additions but otherwise it is similar in design to the W. front; many windows retain their original sashes with heavy glazing-bars. The S. front has a moulded stone eaves-cornice which returns for a short distance on the W. and E. fronts, corresponding with the upper string-course; the plinth and lower string are continued from the other fronts and the windows too are uniform. The N. side of the house is concealed by a modern wing the N. front of which has a curvilinear gable similar in style to that of the W. front. Reset over the modern doorway is a stone pediment on console brackets, with a cartouche in the tympanum carved with the arms of Browne; the pediment is of the second quarter of the 18th century and was presumably transferred from the central doorway of the W. front.

Inside, many of the rooms are panelled, some with original bolection-moulded panelling with panelled dados and moulded dado-rails. Many of the fireplace surrounds have been renewed. The original oak staircase has been very extensively repaired; it has turned and moulded newels and balusters, and a moulded handrail.

A *Cottage* 200 yds. N. of the house has a reset 17th-century stone doorway with moulded jambs and moulded four-centred head; the spandrels are carved with the date 1660 and the initials G.B. The *Terrace* W. of the house has low ashlar walls with flat copings and pedestal-piers supporting 18th-century urns.

(7) Charminster House, 50 yds. S.E. of (1), is of two storeys with attics. The brick walls are rendered and the roofs are slate covered. It was built early in the 18th century but extensive remodelling in the 19th century and alterations in more recent times have left little evidence of original work. The symmetrical S. front appears to date from the first half of the 19th century. The chimneystacks are of brick with segment-headed panels on each face, and heavy cappings; the E. stack includes a specially modelled brick with the date 1706. Inside, the responds of an archway between the entrance-hall and the stair-hall are cased with early 16th-century wooden panels, of French or N. Italian origin, carved in low relief with figures of saints in flat niches with shell-heads and side-standards. The circular staircase, of the late 18th or early 19th century, has turned balusters and newels and a moulded handrail. The Drawing Room on the first floor has a late 18th-century moulded plaster ceiling.

Monuments (8–18)

The following monuments, unless otherwise described, are two-storied, with walls of banded rubble and flint, of rough ashlar and flint, or occasionally of plain rubble. Roofs are generally thatched but in some instances modern materials have been substituted.

(8) *Cottage* (68059275), now two tenements, of one storey with attics, is of the late 17th or early 18th century but has been extensively renovated.

(9) *Mill* (68039297), now converted into a house, was built probably early in the 17th century, of banded flint and ashlar, but the walls now present a chequer-work of subsequent patching and rebuilding in clunch and brick. Two original casement windows in wood frames survive. Inside, the ceiling of the N. room is divided into four panels by deeply chamfered intersecting beams.

(10) *Cottage* (67859288), now a shop, was perhaps originally of the late 17th or early 18th century, but it has subsequently been much altered.

(11) *Cottage* (67739264) is of mid 18th-century origin and retains some original ceiling-beams.

(12) *Range* of three cottages (67849263), on the S. side of the road 100 yds. S.W. of the church, is of two dates; the centre and E. cottages have walls of banded flint and ashlar and are of the late 16th century; the W. cottage has rendered walls and is of the late 17th or early 18th century. The middle cottage retains, in the N. front, two original stone-mullioned four-light windows with labels; the N. front has been heightened and a stone corbel which supported the original wall-plate is seen towards the W. In the S. front is a blocked original window and part of a chamfered stone jamb. The staircase is of *c.* 1800. The range was altered and restored in the 19th century and again recently.

(13) *Cottage*, now a storehouse, 20 yds. N. of (12), was built late in the 16th or early 17th century and retains an original three-light stone-mullioned window with a label. A modern cement shield over the doorway, with the date 1674, may replace an original date stone.

(14) *Cottage*, 20 yds. E. of (13), is of late 17th or early 18th-century origin but has recently been extensively rebuilt.

(15) *Barn*, 55yds. S.W. of the church, now largely demolished, is of brick in Flemish bond and until recently bore the date 1704; the heavily buttressed N. wall is retained as the boundary of a garden.

(16) *Cowden Farmhouse* (67779400), has walls of banded flint and rubble with some later brick. It is of the mid 17th century with a later extension to the W. The 16th-century windows with three-centred lights which flank the doorway are recent insertions, but at the E. end of the S. side the house retains

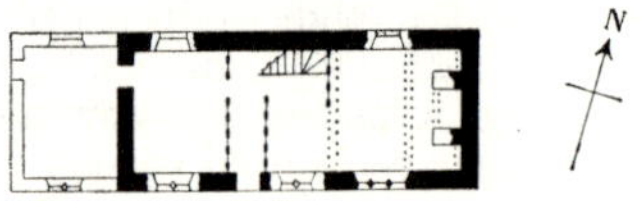

one original stone-mullioned window with three square-headed lights. Plank-and-muntin partitions stand on either side of the entrance passage; that to the E. has been partly reset to accommodate a modern staircase. The open fireplace in the E. room has recently been brought from elsewhere. There are a number of original stop-chamfered ceiling beams.

(17) *Pulston Barn* (66719530) has walls of banded flint and rubble, with ashlar quoins, subsequently repaired and heightened in brickwork; the roof is tiled. The entrance is in the centre of the N. side and a projecting exit bay occurs in the middle of the S. side. The structure appears to be of the late 16th or early 17th century, but the brick repairs and the roof are of the 19th century. Hutchins (II, 544) implies that the building originated as a chapel, but the existing fabric shows nothing to substantiate this.

(18) *Forston Barn*, 100 yds. S.W. of the foregoing, has walls of banded flint and rubble with brick quoins and a thatched roof. It is probably of the late 17th or early 18th century, with later rebuilding at the S. end and in the transeptal bays.

Monuments (19–21)

The following monuments are of the second half of the 18th and first half of the 19th century.

(19) *The Yews* (68109276), 200 yds. N.E. of the church, has walls of brick in Flemish bond with blue headers. It is of the later 18th century with a 19th-century extension to the E. The symmetrical three-bay S. front has a rendered plat-band at first-floor level and a brick dentil eaves cornice; the central doorway has an open porch of wood with free-standing Roman Doric columns supporting a flat hood with triglyphs in the frieze; the sashed windows have flat gauged brick heads.

(20) *East Hill House* (68099265), 165 yds. E.S.E. of the church, is of two storeys with rendered walls, slated roofs and sashed windows; it was probably built *c.* 1840. A rounded two-storied bow window projects on the W. side and there is an iron trellis-work verandah.

(21) *Toll-House* (67559207), on the W. side of the Dorchester road, 300 yds. W. of (4), has rendered walls and slated roofs and is of the 19th century. It is hexagonal on plan with rusticated quoins to the corners which are visible from the road. The low-pitch roof rises to a central ball-finial of copper. The porch on the E. has rusticated jambs and a segmental head; the sashed windows have slightly rounded heads.

Other 19th-century monuments include the following—The *Post Office*, 100 yds. E.S.E. of the church, is of two storeys with rendered walls and a tiled roof; it was built early in the century and has, on the S., an original shop-front with two small-paned bay-windows flanking a central doorway. *Rose Cottage*, 20 yds. S.E. of the foregoing, is in part rendered; the early 19th-century S. front probably conceals an earlier building. *Bridge Cottage*, 35 yds. S.E. of the church, was built late in the 18th or early in the 19th century and has a rendered symmetrical E. front with a projecting gabled bay in the centre, and sashed windows. A *Cottage* (67659260) is built partly of cob and is of the late 18th or early 19th century. *Forston Grange* includes a pair of cottages and a range of three cottages, all built of flint and brick; they are of the early 19th century.

MEDIAEVAL AND LATER EARTHWORKS

(22) SETTLEMENT REMAINS (667953 and 671947), originally two separate settlements but for long known as Pulston, lie on the E. side of the R. Cerne, S. of Forston.

The settlements are one or perhaps two of the Cernes in Domesday Book but they cannot be identified with certainty. Eyton (123–4) has suggested that Pulston was the Cerne belonging to the Count of Mortain (D.B. Vol. I, *f.*79a), of 2½ hides; if this is correct the recorded population was only two bordars, though six thegns had held it in the time of King Edward. The settlement is not recorded separately in the 1327 or 1333 Subsidy Rolls but it appears to be included under Forston, where eleven taxpayers are listed. A chapel dedicated to All Saints existed there, and a chaplain was officiating as late as 1411 (Hutchins II, 546). In 1403 twelve 'messuages' are recorded (Hutchins, *loc. cit.*). In 1539 ten men are listed for Pulston and Forston (L. & P., Henry VIII, Vol. 14, Pt. 1, pp. 267–9). Desertion appears to have been complete by the 17th century for there is no record of Pulston in the Hearth Tax Assessment of 1662. However, Forston Grange (formerly Pulston Farm) and a number of post-1850 cottages around it still remain as the last part of Pulston to be inhabited (*see* Map of Pulston Farm by I. Taylor, 1770, D.C.R.O.).

Around Pulston Barn (17), the alleged site of the Chapel, are about 5 acres of remains. To the N. of the barn are at least four rectangular closes, cut back into the valley side, 17 yds. to 30 yds. wide and 30 yds. long, bounded by low banks of flint rubble 6 ins. to 1½ ft. high. Irregular scoops 15 yds. across at the lower W. end of the closes, just above the river, may be the sites of former houses. S. of Pulston Barn are the fragmentary remains of at least two more closes and to the N. of Forston Grange are another three closes.

Another 5 acres of earthworks lie 700 yds. to the S.E. The remains, which were ploughed in 1964, consist of eight parallel closes at right angles to the R. Cerne, 50 yds. long and 12 yds. to 18 yds. wide, bounded by rounded banks of flint rubble 20 ft. wide and 1 ft. to 2 ft. high. Four of the closes have platforms cut into the upper ends. Extensive areas of flint rubble and fragmentary banks indicate the sites of former houses. Large quantities of pottery, 12th to 15th-century in date, have been picked up on the site.

(23) SETTLEMENT REMAINS (673945) formerly existed ¼ m. S.W. of Herrison House on the E. side of the R. Cerne.

Nothing is known of the history of this settlement, but from its position and from the fact that it lay at the S.W. end of a narrow strip of land which was a detached part of Frampton Parish (Tithe Map of Frampton, 1839), it seems likely to have been one of the many Cernes recorded in Domesday Book. It was probably never more than a single farmstead. The remains, which are now completely destroyed, consisted of a slight hollow-way running N.W. from a ford across the river and very fragmentary banks and scarps. Pottery of the 12th to 13th centuries has been found in the area.

(24) SETTLEMENT REMAINS (675943), formerly part of the hamlet of Herrison, lie on the E. side of the R. Cerne at the mouth of a small tributary valley, ¼ m. S. of Herrison House.

The settlement is one of the Cernes in Domesday Book but cannot be identified with certainty, though Eyton (123–4) suggested that it was one of the Cernes belonging to the Count of Mortain (D.B. Vol. I, f.97a) of three hides. If this is correct the recorded population is either six or eight, depending on which three-hide manor is the correct one. Only four taxpayers are listed in 1333 and the settlement is among a list of Dorset vills granted a tax reduction in 1435 (P.R.O., E.179/103/79). The remains consist of four closes, 30 yds. long and 20 yds. wide, lying on either side of a slight hollow-way, 30 ft. wide, running N.E. up the tributary valley. There are no certain building sites. Low scarps and banks all around are perhaps the remains of other closes. The field is called Rough Piece on the Tithe Map of 1839.

(25) SETTLEMENT REMAINS (679936) of the former farmstead of Charlton lie on the E. side of the Cerne valley ½ m. N. of Charminster.

The site is almost certainly one of the Cernes in Domesday Book but it cannot be identified more exactly. It is not listed in any of the 14th-century Subsidy Rolls, and indeed not until 1662 is there any recorded population (Meekings, 8); then only one household is listed 'atte Charleton Farme'. It seems likely from the records that the site was never more than a single farmstead and the remains confirm this. The earthworks, covering about 2½ acres, consist of a roughly square enclosure on a steep slope of 15° surrounded on the N., E. and S. by a bank 2 ft. to 4 ft. high with an external ditch. The interior is divided by similar banks and ditches into five roughly rectangular areas, three on the S. side and two on the N., though there may once have been another in the N.W. Two platforms

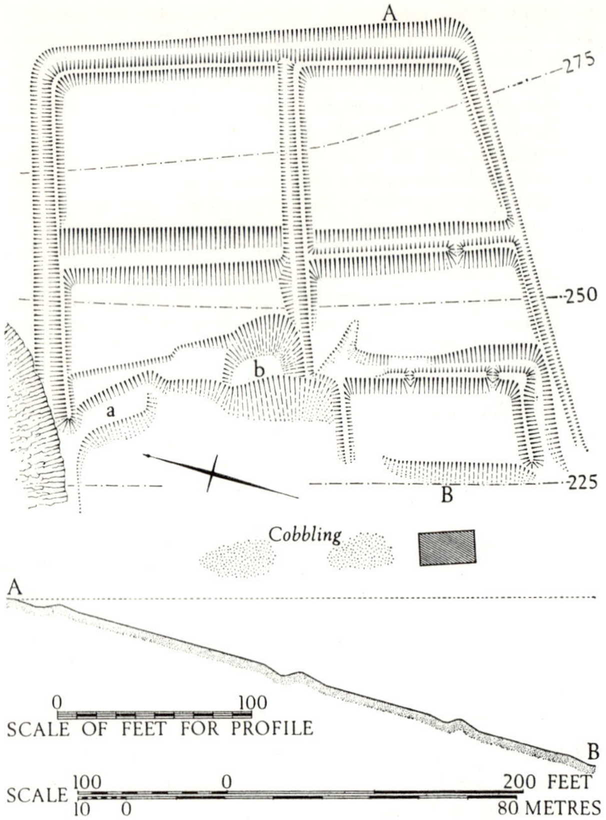

(25) Settlement Remains of Charlton

(a and b), in the N.W. corner, may be the sites of buildings. On the flat valley floor immediately below and W. of the remains recent ploughing has disclosed two areas of flint cobbles together with pottery of the 13th to 18th centuries.

(26) Settlement Remains (679923), part of the former hamlet of Wolfeton, lie on the N. side of the R. Frome immediately W. of (4).

Eyton (123–4) identified these with the 1½-hide manor of Cernel held by Hugh de Bosch Herbert in Domesday Book (Vol. I, *f.*83a). If this is correct it had a recorded population of only four. In 1327 there was a recorded population of two. The Muster Rolls for 1539 (L. & P., Henry VIII, Vol. 14, Pt. I., pp. 267–9) list nineteen men for Wolfeton, but this total almost certainly represents the household of Wolfeton House, and also possibly includes Burton, not listed in the Roll, which formerly had a chapel (Hutchins II, 547 & 544). In the 1662 Hearth Tax Assessment, only Wolfeton House is recorded (Meekings, 8). The remains, covering about 3 acres, consist of at least five long parallel closes set at right angles to the present road to Wolfeton House. The closes are 20 yds to 30 yds. wide and of indeterminate length owing to the destruction of their E. ends; the length was at least 70 yds. They are bounded by low scarps. At their W. ends are rectangular platforms, 30 ft. by 20 ft. with 5 ft. high scarps falling to the road. The site of the former chapel is covered by a modern road.

(27) Settlement Remains (686919), part of the hamlet of Burton, lie N.E. of Lower Burton Farm.

The settlement is probably listed as one of the Cernes in Domesday Book. There are no known documents giving population figures and the place was deserted by 1772 (Map of Charlton and Lower Burton Farms by B. Pryce, 1772, D.C.R.O). The remains, covering some 15 acres, are now mostly destroyed and only a few indeterminate scarps and banks remain; before 1962 they consisted of a complex series of hollow-ways, 30 ft. to 50 ft. wide and 2 ft. to 4 ft. deep, associated with closes and platforms. Another hollow-way 200 yds. long and 40 ft. wide runs W. from the settlement towards Wolfeton (26).

(28) Cultivation Remains. The open fields of *Charminster* lay N. of the R. Frome and W. of the R. Cerne. Parts of them, in the area of Haydon Hill, were enclosed by agreement in 1587 (*S. & D.N. & Q.*, XIII, 1912–13, 162–70); the rest, divided into three large open fields and two smaller ones, were finally enclosed in 1837 (Map and Award, 1837, D.C.R.O.). On Haydon Hill (671943) are some 40 acres of fragmentary contour and cross-contour strip lynchets, up to 250 yds. long and with massive risers up to 15 ft. high, arranged in end-on and butting furlongs. The N. part of these lay in Middle Field until 1837, the rest were enclosed in 1587. A further 10 acres of fragmentary contour strip lynchets lie 500 yds. to the N., W. of Forston House (6). These lay in Higher Field until 1837.

The settlement of *Forston* had open fields but nothing is known of their enclosure. Contour strip lynchets of these fields lie 700 yds. N. of Forston (667964); they are arranged in two end-on furlong blocks.

The open fields of *Pulston* were enclosed before 1770 (Map of Pulston Farm by I. Taylor, 1770, photo-copy in D.C.R.O.). Five contour strip lynchets of these fields lie on the valley side, 300 yds. S. of Pulston Barn (668950).

The date of the enclosure of the open fields of *Wolfeton* is unknown. About 40 acres of fragmentary contour and cross-contour strip lynchets cover Wolfeton Eweleaze (686933), 700 yds. N.E. of Charminster church.

ROMAN AND PREHISTORIC

(29) Roman Villa in Walls Field (66729492). A tessellated pavement was found in 1891 on Chalk at the foot of an E.-facing slope, about 260 ft. above O.D. and some 100 yds. W. of the R. Cerne.

An area of mosaic 'of very interesting design' covering 12 ft. by 4 ft. was cleared in 1891 by E. Cunnington and F. A. H. Vinon. The design, a square of small white tesserae surrounded by a border of blue and red, had apparently formed a square of 15 ft. Excavations in 1960 by H. S. L. Dewar revealed a furnace flue, three flint steps and two fragments of walling. Two reused voussoirs of Ham Hill stone, slate and tile roofing materials, hypocaust tiles, tesserae, painted wall plaster, one piece with a 'convolvulus', and window glass, indicate a major structure. Samian, green-glazed and New Forest ware, and coins of Victorinus, Tetricus II and Gratian suggest occupation in the 2nd to 4th centuries A.D. Near the building lay an inhumation burial with a bronze brooch pin. Iron Age sherds were also found. Some 19th-century finds are in D.C.M. (*Dorset County Chronicle*, 2nd April, 1891, 5; Dorset *Procs.* XIII (1891), xxii; XVII (1896), xxv; XXI (1900), 84; LXXXII (1960), 86–7; *S. & D.N. & Q.* XXVII (1961), 7–10.).

(30) Settlement, late Iron Age and Romano-British, on Charlton Higher Down (694956), is associated with trackways and an extensive area of 'Celtic' fields (Group 36); it occupies about 4 acres in the corner of a modern field adjoining the

Piddlehinton boundary and has been much reduced by ploughing. The settlement lies at 475 ft. O.D. on the ridge of a spur sloping gently E. from the high ground between the valleys of the Cerne and the Piddle. The main part consists of some seven platforms or hollows set into the slope and surrounded on all but the S. by banks confining them within about 1¼ acres. A track running S. from these platforms is bordered on the E. by a series of small, irregular, terraced areas. It joins a major through track running N.–S. along the E. side of the settlement, and between it and the 'Celtic' fields; this in turn is joined by a track from the E. Finds from the platforms and terraces, and from the area E. of the main trackway, include sherds in the Iron Age tradition, samian and coarse pottery from the 1st to 4th centuries, tile and worked stone (Dorset *Procs.* LXXIV (1952), 89–91).

For a possible ROMAN ROAD by-passing Dorchester, *see Dorset* II, p. 541.

'CELTIC' FIELDS and POSSIBLE SETTLEMENTS, *see* pp. 322–4, Groups (34–36).

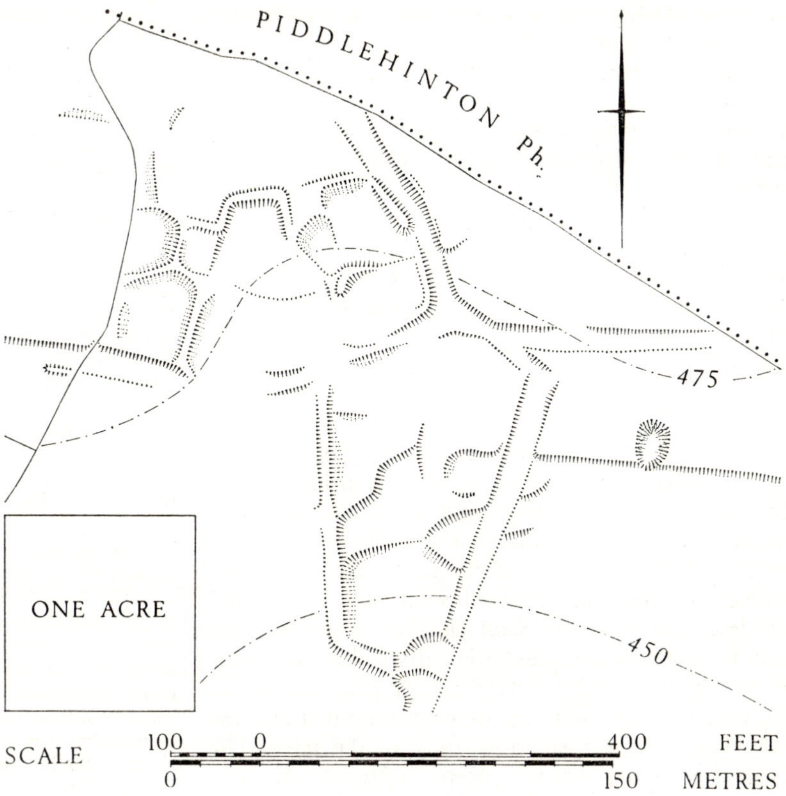

(30) Settlement on Charlton Higher Down.

MONUMENTS (31–46), ROUND BARROWS

All these monuments except (31) lie E. of the R. Cerne, on the higher ground between it and the R. Piddle; (34–40) form a scattered group on Bushy Eweleaze and (43–46) lie among the remains of 'Celtic' fields (Group (36)).

(31) *Bowl* (66589450), on Charminster Down above 400 ft. O.D.; diam. about 66 ft., ht. 2 ft.

(32) *Bowl* (67159665), just N. of Forston Barn at 500 ft. O.D. on the S. slope of Cowden Hill; ploughed; diam. about 60 ft., ht. 1½ ft.

(33) *Bowl* (67469556), near the summit of a spur E. of Forston Field Bottom; heavily ploughed; diam. about 50 ft., ht. 2½ ft.

Bushy Eweleaze Group comprises the following seven barrows. Nearly all lie above 400 ft. O.D. on the summit and E. slopes of a broad spur E. of Forston Field Bottom.

(34) *Bowl* (67599611), in arable; diam. 60 ft., ht. 2 ft.

(35) *Bowl* (67669609), 85 yds. S.E. of (34); diam. about 20 ft., ht. 2½ ft. before ploughing.

(36) *Barrow* ? (67789610), 140 yds. E. of (35) on a gentle E. slope; irregular in shape, apparently disturbed in the centre; thickly overgrown when visited, no diam. measurable, ht. about 2½ ft.

(37) *Barrow* ? (67959625), 240 yds. N.E. of (36) on a slight S.E. slope; mound irregular and much disturbed; diam. 39 ft. by 24 ft., ht. 1½ ft.

(38) *Bowl* (67999618), 80 yds. S.E. of (37) in arable; diam. about 25 ft., ht. 1½ ft. before ploughing.

(39) *Barrow* ? (68059612), 100 yds. S.E. of (38) in arable; an irregular mound, diam. 35 ft. by 27 ft., ht. 2 ft. before ploughing.

(40) *Bowl* (68049607), 53 yds. S.S.W. of (39) in arable; centre dug into; diam. 40 ft., ht. 2½ ft. before ploughing.

(41) *Barrow* ? (68039390), on Wood Hill at about 350 ft. O.D., now a flinty mound in arable; diam. about 55 ft., ht. 1½ ft.

(42) *Barrow* ? (68059414), on the summit of Wood Hill at over 400 ft. O.D., overgrown and much disturbed; diam. about 48 ft., ht. 3½ ft.

(43) *Barrow* ? (68949570), on Charlton Higher Down on a gentle N. slope at about 550 ft. O.D.; disturbed by digging immediately below it on the N. side; diam. 45 ft., ht. 4½ ft.

(44) *Bowl* (69459518), 200 yds. W. of Wolfeton Clump on the S. slope of Charlton Higher Down at just over 400 ft. O.D.; diam. 50 ft., ht. 2 ft.

(45) *Bowl* (69449497), 225 yds. S. of (44); centre slightly disturbed; a low 'Celtic' field lynchet runs up to the barrow on either side but is clearly later; diam. 36 ft., ht. 2½ ft.

(46) *Bowl* (69659484), 270 yds. S.E. of (45) on the same slope; bisected by a hedgerow and ploughed away on the E. side, diam. 46 ft., ht. 4½ ft.

13 CHESELBOURNE (7699)

(O.S. 6 ins. SY 79 NW, SY 79 NE, ST 70 SW, ST 70 SE)

Cheselbourne is a small village in a parish of 2,900 acres, lying entirely on Chalk between 250 ft. and 800 ft. above sea-level. Three nearly parallel streams flow across the parish in a S.S.E. direction: Lyscombe Brook, the Cheselbourne and the Devil's Brook. The village is scattered for over a mile along the banks of the stream from which it takes its name, the earthwork remains of former dwellings and closes occurring frequently among the existing cottages and in open land to the S. of the church. The open fields of the parish were not finally enclosed until 1845. Lyscombe, formerly a detached part of Milton, is now joined to Cheselbourne. The parish church of Cheselbourne and an abandoned chapel at Lyscombe are the principal monuments.

ECCLESIASTICAL

(1) THE PARISH CHURCH OF ST. MARTIN stands at the S. end of the village. The walls are principally of flint with ashlar dressings and occasional bonding courses of squared rubble, but the N. aisle, the N. porch and the top stage of the tower are of coursed rubble; the roofs are covered with tiles, stone-slates and lead. The *Nave* and *South Aisle* are of the late 13th century; the arcade appears originally to have consisted of two pointed arches between wide responds but in the 15th century the responds were modified and the aisle was thrown open more fully to the nave. The *Chancel* is of the first half of the 14th century. The *West Tower* dates from the middle and end of the 15th century and the chancel arch appears to have been rebuilt at that time. The *North Aisle* and the *North Porch* were added late in the 15th century. The *South Porch* was built *c.* 1500. The church was restored in 1874 and 1924.

The late 12th-century font and the remains of the 13th-century south arcade are perhaps the most important features; the church also contains interesting 16th-century brasses.

Architectural Description—The *Chancel* ($17\frac{1}{2}$ ft. by $13\frac{1}{2}$ ft.) has a widely splayed 14th-century E. window of three gradated lancet lights with trefoil cusping, with a moulded outer label and a segmental rear arch; above is a steeply pointed straight-sided rubble relieving arch. In the N. wall are two windows with a blocked 14th-century doorway between them; the doorway has a chamfered two-centred head; the more easterly window is of the late 15th century and has two cinquefoil lights in a square head below a label with square stops; the other window is a 14th-century opening of two trefoil ogee-headed lights with a transom; a rectangular cutting in the W. splay is for a squint from the N. aisle. The S. wall contains, to the E., a window similar to the corresponding opening of the N. wall and, to the W., a 14th-century two-light window with a 15th-century head similar to that of the adjacent opening; a square-headed squint from the S. aisle pierces the W. splay. The chancel arch is two-centred and of two hollow-chamfered orders springing from semi-octagonal responds with concave faces and moulded capitals and bases.

In the *Nave* ($30\frac{1}{2}$ ft. by $15\frac{1}{2}$ ft.) the N. arcade dates from the second half of the 15th century and consists of two two-centred arches, each of two hollow-chamfered orders dying into the wall at the W. and into a square respond on the E., and springing from an octagonal central pier with a moulded cap and a hollow-chamfered base; the W. bay is a little wider than that to the E. Continuing the arcade eastwards and pierced in the wall abutting the E. respond is an early 16th-century opening with a lightly chamfered triangular head. In the S. arcade, the central pier and the narrow pointed arch W. of it date from the end of the 13th century; the pier is circular, with a moulded capital and base of Purbeck marble; the adjacent respond to the W. is a similar half-pier, and the pointed arch is of two plain chamfered orders. The two-centred E. arch has much greater height and span than that just described, although the orders are uniform; presumably an original narrow arch here was enlarged at the

CHESELBOURNE *The parish church of St. Martin*

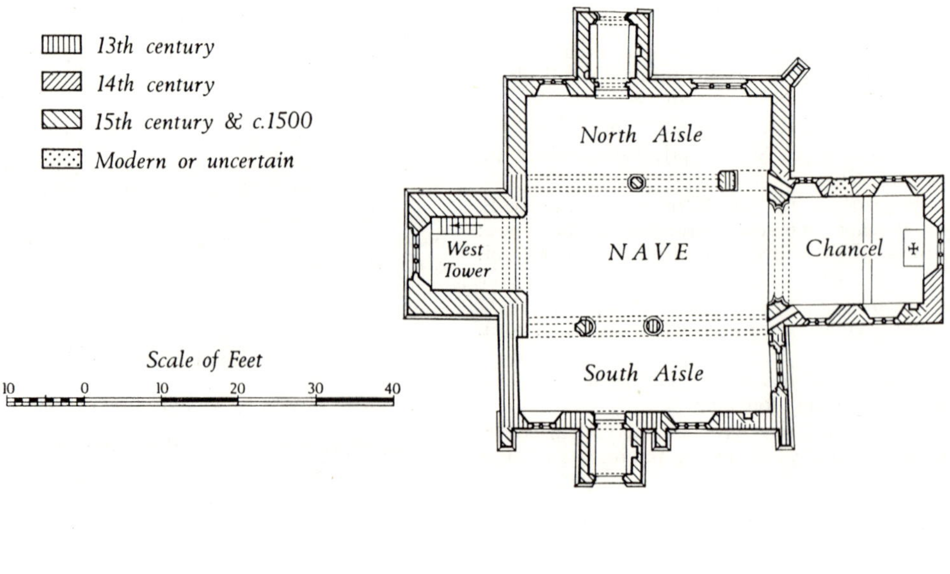

expense of the E. abutment, probably in the middle of the 15th century. The W. end of the S. arcade has been differently treated; here the original W. half-pier has been left in position and a narrow archway has been cut through the abutment behind it. The arch is two-centred and of two wave-moulded orders springing from a three-sided E. respond with moulded cap and chamfered base; to the W., the inner order rests on a grotesque corbel representing the head and shoulders of a woman in an exaggerated headdress (Plate 16); the W. opening was made probably about the middle of the 15th century.

The *North Aisle* (9½ ft. wide) has in the N. wall, towards the E. end, a large two-centred window of three cinquefoil-headed lights with vertical tracery beneath a label with square stops; the N. doorway has a moulded four-centred head, the mouldings continuing down the jambs to shaped stops; further W. is a square-headed window of two cinquefoil ogee-headed lights under vertical tracery, with a moulded label with return stops; all these openings are of the late 15th century.

The *South Aisle* (9½ ft. wide) has a late 15th-century E. window of three cinquefoil-headed lights with quatrefoil tracery in a segmental-pointed head; the rear arch is hollow-chamfered and the same moulding continues on the jambs, ending at hollow-chamfered plinths on the window sill. The easternmost window in the S. wall is also of the late 15th century; it has three cinquefoil-headed lights with squat vertical tracery below a square head and a moulded label which terminates in male headstops. The S. doorway, of the same date, has a continuous wave-moulded segmental head and jambs, with shaped stops. At the W. end of the S. wall is a late 13th-century window of two trefoil-headed lights with a round trefoil tracery light in a two-centred head; it is chamfered externally and rebated internally.

The *West Tower* (9¼ ft. by 9 ft.) was built about the middle of the 15th century and heightened at the end of the same century. It is of three stages divided by weathered string-courses. At the base is a chamfered plinth and at the top is an embattled parapet with gargoyles and crocketed pinnacles. The two lower stages are of flint with stone bonding-courses and quoins; the top stage is of squared coursed rubble. The two-centred tower-arch is of two wave-moulded orders, the inner order springing from three-sided corbels with 16th-century mouldings; in the outer order the moulding on the E. side continues down the responds, that on the W. side dies into the side walls. The W. window is of three trefoil-headed lights with large quatrefoil tracery in a casement-moulded two-centred head, with a four-centred hollow-chamfered rear arch. In the W. wall of the second stage is a plain single light with a square head, and in each wall of the third stage is a casement-moulded belfry window of two trefoil ogee-headed lights, with a quatrefoil in a two-centred head. The lower half of each belfry window is closed by a pierced stone screen decorated with quatrefoils.

The *North Porch* (6 ft. by 6½ ft.) is of the late 15th century and has an archway with a moulded two-centred head and continuous jambs with run-out stops. Stone benches, moulded underneath, flank the entry. The oak roof is original, with plain rafters and chamfered plates and ridge-piece. The *South Porch* (5½ ft. square) is of the late 15th or early 16th century; it has a four-centred archway with a moulded head and continuous jambs with shaped stops.

Fittings—*Bells:* five; 1st and 3rd by John Wallis, both dated 1618; 2nd by Thomas Roskelly, 1754; 4th, inscribed in black-letter 'Sancta Maria ora pro nobis', probably 15th century and from Salisbury foundry; 5th, with inscription 'ac non vadi via nisi dicas ave Maria', mediaeval. *Brass* and *Indent. Brass:* In N. aisle, on E. wall, reset on wood panel, three rectangular plates from memorial of Hugh Kete, 1589; the largest (11 ins. by 9 ins.) has a lengthy verse in Roman lettering and, above, a shield-of-arms of Kete quartering Coles of Somerset (with chevron engrailed), impaling Grove quartering Mansell; brass commissioned by Mat. Grove and engraved by Tho. Wittes; smaller plates (each 5½ ins. by 4 ins.) display separately the two quarterly coats of the large plate. *Indent:* In nave, on floor-slab, indent of rectangular plate (12½ ins. by 3½ ins.). *Chest:* In W. tower, with panelled front and ends, stiles and rails carved with conventional flower and acanthus patterns, two lock-plates, moulded lid, early 17th century. *Churchyard Cross:* N.E. of N. porch, lower part of 15th-century shaft with moulded angles, set diagonally on rectangular pedestal with hollow-chamfered plinth; below, two steps with hollow-chamfered nosing. *Communion Table:* with turned legs, plain stretchers, shaped framing and plain top; mid 17th century, now used as side-table in nave. *Font:* octagonal straight-sided Purbeck marble bowl with chamfered under-edge and two slightly sunk lancet-headed recesses to each face, on shaped octagonal stem with octagonal chamfered base; sockets for circular shafts in angles of base; bowl and base *c.* 1200, stem perhaps 15th century.

Monuments and *Floor-slabs. Monuments:* In N. aisle, (1) of William Box, rector, 1749, white marble wall-tablet, perhaps 19th century. In churchyard, N. of N. porch, (2) table-tomb, *c.* 1600, inscription obliterated. *Floor-slabs:* In nave, at E. end, (1) of Richard Basket, rector, 1684, and Ureth his wife, 1707, with arms of Basket. In N. aisle, (2) of John Keate, 1552, and his wife Marg[aret], 1554, Purbeck marble slab with black-letter inscription; (3) of Richard Samson, 1799. In S. aisle, (4) of Wm. Carpenter, 1786. *Niches:* In S. aisle, in E. wall, shallow recess with ogee septfoil head, plain shields in spandrels, 15th century. In N. porch, in E. wall, with cinquefoil head and stop-chamfered jambs, 15th century. Over N. porch entry, with four-centred cinquefoil head, chamfered side-standards and pedestal-corbel carved with leopard's head, 15th century. In S. porch, in E. wall, with four-centred hollow-chamfered head and continuous jambs, *c.* 1500. *Piscinae:* In chancel, in S. wall, with cinquefoil-headed opening and continuous chamfered jambs, moulded projecting bowl with hexagonal sinking, 15th century. In S. aisle, in S. wall, with four-centred head and chamfered jambs, round bowl with raised rim and fluted sinking, *c.* 1500. *Plate:* includes Elizabethan cup by Lawrence Stratford of Dorchester and cover-paten with engraved date 1574. *Pulpit:* octagonal, of oak, with six panelled sides in two heights with moulded framing, lower panels plain, upper panels fielded and with strapwork, *c.* 1630, stone base modern. *Screen:* In tower arch, of oak, centre opening and a bay on either side in two heights; lower height with plain panels, upper height divided into four lights with hollow-chamfered oak mullions, 16th century, made up with modern material. *Stair:* In W. tower, with solid oak steps on two heavy bearers, supported on modern stone corbel below W. window; with shaped newel, moulded handrail and plank fascia, late mediaeval; original steps cased in modern elm treads and risers. *Stoup:* In N. porch, in W. wall, rounded recess with mutilated projecting bowl, mediaeval. *Sundials:* Above S. porch arch, rectangular stone slab with Roman numerals, inscribed HC 1631 WM, with wrought-iron gnomon. On S. wall, scratch-dial. *Miscellanea:* In N. aisle, on sill of E. window, stone panel carved with achievement-of-arms of Kete, late 16th century with modern repainting. In N. aisle, on octagonal stone brackets on E. wall, two small stone *putti* with Italianate shields, 16th century. In S. porch, in niche, part of mediaeval gable-cross.

(2) LYSCOMBE CHAPEL (73660106), together with a cottage and a barn, stands in a remote place among the Downs, midway between Cerne Abbey and Milton Abbey and nearly 2 m. N.W. of Cheselbourne church

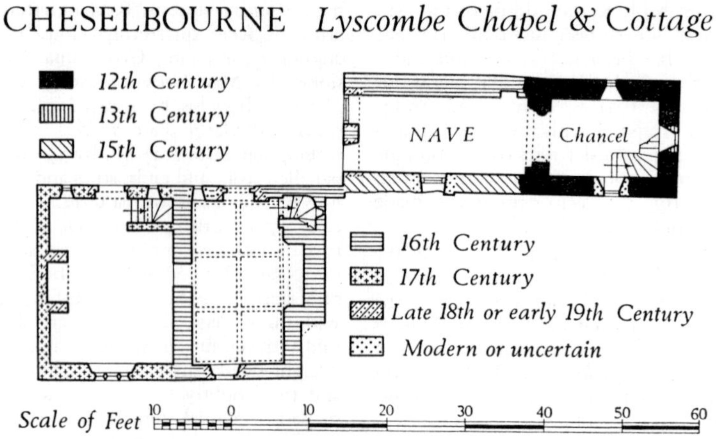

(Plate 130). The walls of the chapel are of flint with bonding-courses and dressings of rubble; there are also some later brick dressings. Until recently the roofs were thatched. The *Chancel* and chancel arch date from the late 12th century; the *Nave* was almost entirely rebuilt in the 15th and late 16th centuries; the chapel probably became a dwelling in the 17th century and it is now disused and protected only by a modern iron roof. The adjacent *Cottage* is of the early 16th century and no doubt was for the priest; in the 17th century it was doubled in size by an addition to the W., and the W. wall of the addition was repaired and refenestrated at the end of the 18th or early in the 19th century. The whole cottage is now derelict and in ruins. The *Barn*, some 70 yds. to the S.W., is substantially mediaeval; it is reported formerly to have borne an inscription 'L S 1638' but this was probably the date of some repair.

The three buildings form a small mediaeval group of considerable interest, but their history is obscure. Three and a half hides of land at Lyscombe formed part of the original endowment of Milton Abbey (*see* p. 183). The chapel (dedication unknown) is mentioned in 1311 together with the chapels of Woolland and Whitcombe.[1] It passed into lay hands when Henry VIII granted the abbey's possessions to Sir John Tregonwell in 1540.

Architectural Description—The *Chancel* (14 ft. by 9¾ ft.) has walls of flint. The original single-light E. window, with a round rear-arch and splayed ashlar jambs, was slightly widened in the 13th century and a chamfered trefoil head was inserted. The N. wall contains an original narrow window with a rebated round head and splayed reveals, the latter mutilated. In the S. wall the original window has been enlarged and fitted with a modern surround. The chancel arch is two-centred and of two plain orders on the W. side, with the remains of a moulded label; on the E. side it is flat. The responds have half-round shafts supporting the inner order, and smaller shafts under the outer order; the caps are scalloped and have moulded abaci continued as a string on the W.; the lower part of the N. respond and most of the S. respond have been destroyed and the capitals have been badly defaced. Floor beams and a stone stair were inserted in the chancel in the late 16th or early 17th century. The *Nave* (21¼ ft. by 9½ ft.) has walls of flint; the S. wall was rebuilt in the 15th century and the N. wall late in the 16th century. Part of the chamfered E. jamb of the S. doorway survives near the ground; above it is a window of uncertain date, now partly blocked and altered by the insertion of a second opening. The W. wall is of the late 16th century; the gable contains a window with chamfered jambs cut from a single stone; the opening is now square but it retains traces of two pointed lights and a central mullion. In the lower storey the W. wall has two 18th-century openings. A floor with stop-chamfered beams was inserted in the nave, as in the chancel.

The *Cottage* adjacent to the S.W. corner of the chapel is of one storey with an attic. The E. wall has a boldly projecting chimney-breast, the S. side of which is splayed above first-floor level and carried on a stone corbel. To the N., the chimney-breast incorporates a stone vice which has, in the E. side, a small loop consisting of a chamfered vertical slit with a circular widening at the centre; it overlooks the former S. doorway of the chapel. The other windows and doorways in the E. part of the cottage were altered and rebuilt in brick late in the 18th or early in the 19th century. A brick doorway on the N. side has a reset timber surround, perhaps of the 16th century, with a chamfered triangular head and chamfered jambs. The 17th-century western part of the S. wall contains a three-light stone-mullioned window. A scratch-dial occurs near the S.W. corner. The W. wall was repaired late in the 18th or early in the 19th century; it has two first-floor windows of this date with four-centred brick heads and jambs. In the gable are two reset 15th or early 16th-century fragments; part of a four-centred stone window head with trefoil-headed lights and a small stone panel with paired ogee-headed openings. Inside, the ground-floor room of the E. part of the cottage had, until recently, an original open timber ceiling divided into six panels by deeply chamfered intersecting beams and plates. To the E. is an open fireplace with a deep cambered and chamfered bressummer, and chamfered stone jambs with run-out stops. The entrance to the stone vice is through a doorway with a wooden lintel and a chamfered stone S. jamb with a run-out stop; at the head of the stair was a roughly wrought 16th-century oak door frame with a four-centred head. The W. part of the cottage has an open fireplace of the late 18th or early 19th century.

The *Barn* (92 ft. by 27 ft.) stands 100 yds. S.W. of the chapel;

[1] Cal. Pat. Rolls 1307–13, p. 389.

it is of flint with ashlar quoins and dressings and probably dates from the 16th century. The long axis lies N.–S. and there is a gabled transept to E. and W. in the middle of each long wall. The N. half of the W. side has been rebuilt but the other walls survive, at least in their lower parts. The S. half of the barn had a jointed-cruck roof until about 1950, when it collapsed; the whole structure has now been reroofed in modern materials. The original trusses were set at 10½ ft. centres and rose from ledges about half-way between the floor and the wall-head on the inner face of the side walls. Externally, the E. and S. walls have weathered two-stage buttresses of flint and ashlar, those on the E. side corresponding with the trusses; on the W. the rising ground obviates the need for buttresses. The gabled S. wall is pierced by a single slit ventilator outlined in ashlar, with chamfered jambs. The transept doorways, 11 ft. wide, are also of ashlar and chamfered.

SECULAR

(3) The Old Rectory (76209987), 300 yds. N. of the church, is two-storied and has walls of knapped flint banded with stone and brick, with ashlar quoins and dressings. The tiled roofs have stone-slate verges and the roof of the porch is entirely stone-slated. The original building, of the late 16th or early 17th century, had a plain rectangular plan of three bays, in which the central doorway led to a through-passage with one room on each side. About 1800 the original range was extended E., and a N. wing was added; the stairs are in the N. wing. Later in the 19th century a semi-octagonal two-storied porch with a hipped roof was built in the middle of the S. front, and at the same time the whole house was restored and the upper storey was largely rebuilt.

Above its chamfered plinth the S. front has been extensively refaced; the plat-band over the ground-floor window heads is probably an insertion; the two-light square-headed first-floor windows are original but reset, and the three-light ground-floor windows are modern. The window on the first floor of the porch is original but reset. The gabled E. and W. end walls have shaped kneelers, flat copings and chimneystacks at the apex; in the W. wall each storey has one original stone window of three lights with square heads and labels. The N. wall of the original range, where it is not concealed by the 19th-century extension, shows the remains of other stone windows, now blocked.

Inside, in the E. wall of the original building is a stone fireplace of *c.* 1600 with a rectangular head and jambs outlined by a heavy roll-mould; the deep lintel has remains of painted decoration in dark red depicting large fleurs-de-lis; in the N. jamb is the blocked opening to an oven. The drawing-room, to the W. of the through-passage, has a fireplace of *c.* 1600 with moulded jambs and a square head. A stone lintel over a blocked opening in the N. wall is crudely carved with a shield, a sun and a mask with leaves issuing from the mouth; it is perhaps of the 17th century but reset.

(4) Cheselbourne Manor (75650046), house, a little over ½ m. N.W. of the church, is of two storeys; the walls are of knapped flint with squared rubble bonding courses; the roofs have been reduced to a low pitch and are covered with modern slates. The house has an L-shaped plan with a small projecting stair-bay to the E.; it is of mid 16th-century origin but remodelled and modernised, and with a late 19th-century addition to the N. All window openings are modern although of 16th-century pattern. Inside, the stair-bay contains an original stone vice with a round newel rising from a chamfered base; the ground-floor entrance to the vice is a mid 16th-century stone doorway with a restored four-centred head in a square surround with carved spandrels; the moulded jambs have hollow-chamfered plinths and spur stops. A ground-floor fireplace, now rebuilt, retains traces of original painted decoration in red and black.

(5) Northfield Farm (75980014), is a two-storied house of cob and thatch, dating from the 17th century. The main range, facing S.E., has a central doorway which leads to a through-passage. A chimneystack emerges from the ridge a little to one side of the passage and another stack occurs at the apex of the S.W. gable. The eaves have been raised to accommodate the first-floor rooms on the S.E. front; on the N.W. side the house is single-storied.

Monuments (6–18)

The following 18th and early 19th-century cottages are dispersed in the village, on both sides of the road, from ¼ m. S.E. to ½ m. N.W. of the parish church. Unless otherwise described they have cob walls and thatched roofs and are of two storeys, or of one storey with dormer-windowed attics—(6) at 76509936; (7) at 76329965 is single-storied, without an attic; (8) at 76299973; (9) at 76199981 is single-storied, without an attic; (10) at 76149986; (11) at 76089998; (12) at 76099999, 10 yds. N.E. of the foregoing, has a modern tiled roof; (13) at 76030009; (14) at 76030013 is partly of banded brick and flint; (15) at 76080018; (16) at 76100020; (17) at 75790020; (18) at 75810028.

MEDIAEVAL AND LATER EARTHWORKS

(19) Settlement Remains (763995, 764994, 765991), formerly part of Cheselbourne village, lie around the church and also to the E. of West Farm and to the W. and S. of Waterside Farm. They consist of rectangular closes up to 80 yds. long and 30 yds. wide, bounded by low banks; there are no well-defined house sites.

(20) Cultivation Remains. The open fields of the parish were not finally enclosed until 1845 (Enclosure Award, D.C.R.O.) but it is clear from the Tithe Map of 1844 that the final arrangement of seven separate open fields, all W. and N.W. of the village, was only the last stage in a long process of enclosure and reorganisation. The only remains, four contour strip lynchets immediately N.W. of the church (761996), lie outside the area of the open fields.

ROMAN AND PREHISTORIC

(21) Occupation Debris, Romano-British, consisting of fragments of roof and flue tiles, was found in the stream bed S. of Lyscombe Farm (73680092–73710079), (C. Warne, *Ancient Dorset* (1872), 85; Dorset *Procs.* LXX (1948), 60). 'Castels' mentioned in a charter of 869 A.D. may indicate Roman buildings, while the name Streetway Lane also suggests Roman origin (Dorset *Procs.* LVI (1934), 124–7). For Roman coins in barrows, *see* below under *Round Barrows*.

'Celtic' Fields, *see* pp. 330–333, Groups (44–48).

Monuments (22–23), Cross-dykes

Two cross-dykes occur in the N.W. of the parish at altitudes between 600 ft. and 700 ft., on the spur which projects S.E. from Lyscombe Hill; they form part of a series discussed in 'Celtic' Field Group (44) (*see* p. 330).

(22) CROSS-DYKE, comprising two sections, probably connected. The first section (a) runs S.W.–N.E. (72960157–73070170) for 200 yds., from the crest of the spur on the parish boundary with Piddletrenthide, down a gentle slope, and ends well short of the shoulder of the spur. It consists of a main bank on the S.E. side with a ditch uphill and a slighter bank beyond. The main bank, 21 ft. across, increases in height downhill from 2 ft. to 10 ft. A later bank straddled by trees runs along its top. The ditch is 12 ft. wide, flat-bottomed and 2¾ ft. below the bank. The slighter bank on the N.W. is up to 20 ft. across. A gap near the centre may be original but the dyke appears to block a double-lynchet track associated with 'Celtic' fields. The increase in height of the main bank downhill indicates that it is built on a 'Celtic' field edge, and a 'Celtic' field continues its line N.E. to the shoulder of the spur. Air photographs suggest that the dyke formerly continued S.W. for some 50 yds. and then, making a right-angled turn N.W., joined the second section of the dyke (b) (72860160), which runs N.W. for 46 yds. across the head of a gulley. The bank, which is on the S.W. side, is 22 ft. wide and 5½ ft. high; the ditch, which is disturbed, is 27 ft. wide at the S.E. and narrows towards the N.W. There is a gap 24 ft. wide near the S. end.

(23) CROSS-DYKE, running S.W.–N.E. (73180124–73260137), some 400 yds. S.E. of (22), across the head of a gulley near the S.E. end of the spur, is 210 yds. long and has its ditch on the uphill side, beyond which is a very slight bank, probably a copse boundary. The bank is 30 ft. across, 8 ft. high on the S. and 3 ft. high above the ditch, which is 30 ft. across. The line of the dyke is continued N.E. on a different alignment by a slight bank on a scarp, while to the S.W. it is continued for 40 yds. as a lynchet with a slight bank on it, then as a scarp for 230 yds. to meet the angle of an enclosure, Piddletrenthide (65), now destroyed.

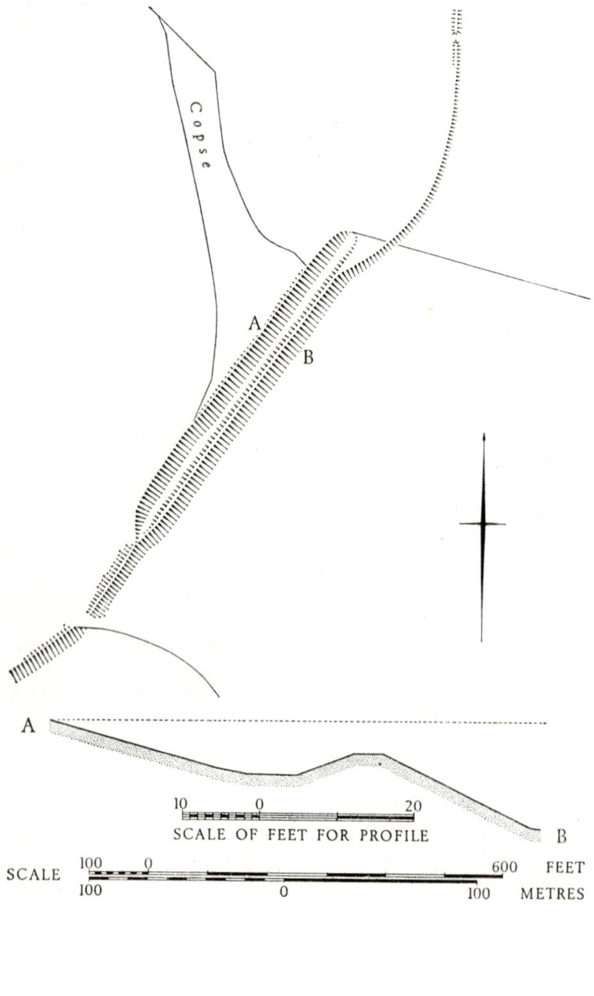

MONUMENTS (24–39), ROUND BARROWS

Of sixteen round barrows in the parish, Monuments (24–29) and (30–33) form two small groups on Cheselbourne West Down; the remainder are widely dispersed. Warne opened six barrows on Cheselbourne Down Hogleaze; they are probably among (24–29). His first barrow covered several cists cut into the natural chalk and filled with ashes; two others contained no interments and were apparently mere cenotaphs; the remainder yielded only ashes (*C.T.D. Pt. 1*, No. 9; *Archaeologia* XXX (1844), 334). C. Hall opened a small barrow, Rough Barrow, on Cheselbourne Common and found three urns, one of which appeared to contain bird bones (*Barrow Diggers*, 92); this is probably the barrow described by Warne (*C.T.D. Pt. 3*, No. 97) in which two urns were found in cists cut into the natural chalk and a coin of Diocletian was found just under the surface at the summit of the mound. A further barrow, destroyed in 1865, lay on the spur E. of Bramblecombe Farm. Some ten or twelve cinerary urns, some inverted, including one globular, were recovered from 'rude cists of flint' on the W. side of the mound. In addition, six coins (Domitian to Tetricus I) were found. An earlier cutting through the centre of the mound, probably by C. Hall, appears to have been unproductive (*Hutchins* IV, 352; *Arch. J.* CXIX (1962), 57).

Cheselbourne West Down Group 1 comprises six barrows which lie between 300 ft. and 400 ft. O.D., on a S.W. slope above a dry valley in the extreme S.W. of the parish. All have been reduced by ploughing.

(24) *Bowl* (74019850), at the foot of a slope; much ploughed; diam. about 60 ft., ht. 2 ft.

(25) *Bowl* (74049862), 135 yds. N.N.E. of (24), is now only an irregular mound cut away by ploughing; diam. about 30 ft., ht. 2½ ft.

(26) *Bowl* (74109865), 70 yds. N.E. of (25), is heavily ploughed; diam. about 30 ft., ht. 1 ft.

(27) *Bowl* (74039872), 110 yds. N.W. of (26); diam. 36 ft., ht. 1 ft.

(28) *Barrow* ? (74159887), 215 yds. N.E. of (27); much ploughed and somewhat irregular; diam. about 20 ft., ht. 1 ft.

(29) *Barrow* ? (74189886), 40 yds. E.S.E. of (28), is of similar form and dimensions to the foregoing.

Cheselbourne West Down Group 2 consists of the following four barrows which lie in arable on the spine of a ridge between 350 ft. and 400 ft. O.D., less than ½ m. N. of the previous group.

(30) *Bowl* (73969937), near the Piddletrenthide boundary, 600 yds. N.W. of (28); damaged by ploughing; diam. 56 ft., ht. 5 ft.

(31) *Bowl* (73869947), 155 yds. N.W. of (30); much damaged by ploughing; diam. about 42 ft., ht. 1½ ft.

(32) *Bowl* (73899947), 30 yds. E. of (31); a large hollow in the centre, full of flints, is probably the result of excavation; diam. 51 ft., ht. 5 ft.

(33) *Bowl* (73949956), 100 yds. N.E. of (32), is surmounted by a cylindrical stone column nearly 5 ft. high and probably of comparatively recent origin; there is a hollow in the centre of barrow; diam. 67 ft., ht. 6 ft.

(34) *Bowl* (74529999), 500 yds. S.E. of Kingcombe Farm on the W. slope of a ridge; much ploughed; diam. about 65 ft., ht. 1½ ft.

(35) *Bowl* (74549999), 25 yds E. of (34), is of similar dimensions, and contiguous with it; these two barrows lie at the angle of a 'Celtic' field.

(36) *Bowl* (73500031), 700 yds. W.N.W. of Kingcombe Farm on ground sloping S. and E., lies at the angle of a 'Celtic' field now almost destroyed by ploughing; diam. 50 ft., ht. 2 ft.

(37) *Bowl* (73460273), on Lyscombe Hill at the extreme N. of Cheselbourne parish, is thickly overgrown but appears to be joined to (38); diam. about 38 ft., ht. 5½ ft.

(38) *Bowl* (73470273), adjoining (37), with centre dug into; diam. 36 ft., ht. 5 ft.

(39) *Barrow* ? (77990039), 750 yds. S.E. of Bramblecombe Farm at about 400 ft. O.D., on a W.-facing slope, lies at the angle of a 'Celtic' field and has been much ploughed; diam. about 85 ft., ht. 2½ ft.

UNDATED

(40) Enclosure (75209860), now visible only as a crop mark on air photographs, lies across the parish boundary with Dewlish, at the head of a small valley (Plate 131). It is about 5 acres in area, roughly circular, and bounded by a ditch about 5 ft. across. No entrances or internal features are visible. It is probably Iron Age in date though a large concentration of Roman pottery has been found 300 yds. due E. (*see* Dewlish (10)). There is no demonstrable relationship between the enclosure and the adjacent 'Celtic' fields (Group 45).

The 'Earthworks' on Henning Hill, shown on O.S. maps (758012), are almost certainly remains of hollow-ways on a road line passing N.W. from the valley of the Devil's Brook to that of the Cheselbourne (*see* diagram on p. 320).

14 CHILD OKEFORD (8312)

(O.S. 6 ins. ST 81 SW)

Child Okeford is a parish of 1,570 acres on the E. bank of the R. Stour. The land is Upper and Lower Greensand, Gault and Kimmeridge Clay, with a tract of River Gravel close to the Stour. The greater part of the area undulates between 150 ft. and 300 ft. above sea-level, but to the E. the ground rises sharply to 623 ft. at the summit of Hambledon Hill, a detached outcrop of the Chalk escarpment. The village stands at the foot of the hill and near the centre of the parish. At the N. end of the parish is Fontmell Parva, a small settlement which seems to have had its own mediaeval open fields; although not recorded until the middle of the 14th century[1] it is almost certainly of earlier origin. The present manor house, however, is of the 17th century and the other dwellings are later. Between Child Okeford and Fontmell Parva lay a tract of common, much of it still unenclosed in 1840.[2] Land at Banbury Camp in Okeford Fitzpaine was formerly a detached part of Child Okeford.[3] The massively defended Iron Age hill-fort on Hambledon Hill, with its abundant occupation remains, is one of the major monuments of Dorset.

ECCLESIASTICAL

(1) The Parish Church of St. Nicholas, near the centre of the village and parish, was rebuilt in the last quarter of the 19th century except for the *West Tower*, which is of the late 15th or early 16th century.

Architectural Description—The *Tower* (12 ft. by 11 ft.) is of Greensand ashlar. It has two principal stages, and a moulded and weathered plinth and an embattled parapet; a weathered string divides the stages. At the N.W. and S.W. corners are diagonal four-stage buttresses; they have weathered offsets to each stage except at the foot of the top stage where the string-course continues around the buttress. At the N.E. corner is a similar square-set buttress and the S.E. corner is strengthened by the vice turret, which is of three stages, the lower stage corresponding with that of the tower. The turret parapet stands a little higher than the tower parapet. A little above plinth level the canted S.W. side of the vice turret rests on chamfered corbelling over a foliate base-stop; higher, the vice is lit by four loops. The two-centred tower arch is of two chamfered orders which die into square responds. The vice is entered through a two-centred doorway with chamfered jambs and head. The W. doorway has moulded jambs and a continuous four-centred head under a square label with foliate stops; the spandrels have trefoil panels and there is a small blank shield at the centre of the label. Above the doorway, the two-centred four-light W. window has a continuous casement-moulded surround; each light has a cinquefoil ogee head with vertical tracery above; the moulded label has square foliate stops. The hollow-chamfered mullions are embellished externally with rolls and internally with square standards; much of the tracery has been restored in Ham Hill stone. In the Greensand masonry over the W. window is a segmental relieving arch. In the lower part of the second stage, the S. wall has a small two-centred light, the E. wall has a square-headed loop and the W. wall has a clock in place of a former window. In the upper part of the second stage each side of the tower has a belfry window of two cinquefoil-headed lights in a square head with a moulded label. The parapet has a moulded string with gargoyles at the angles, except to the S.E. where the vice turret occurs; over each gargoyle is a pinnacle with a crocketed finial.

Fittings—*Book:* In case in N. aisle, The Bishops' Bible, 1568; parts of preface and two chapters of Genesis missing. *Chest:*

[1] Fägersten, 14.
[2] Tithe Map, 1840.
[3] See below, p. 206.

panelled, with guilloche and fluted ornament, mid 17th century. *Coffin-stools:* two, with turned legs, mid 17th century. *Font:* circular Purbeck bowl, coarsely tooled, with off-set rim and roll-moulded base, cylindrical stem and double roll-moulded, chamfered pedestal, 13th century. *Floor-slab:* of Roger Wood, late 17th century, reused as step outside S. porch. *Plate:* includes cup and cover-paten dated 1573 by hall-mark and inscription, also two late 18th-century secular dishes, plated, and a flagon, formerly gilt, presented 1783. *Miscellanea:* At base of tower, panel of lead removed from tower roof, embossed in Roman capitals E. CROWCH, T. ARNOLD, C.W., 1729. Lead cylindrical case inscribed 'Hanford Registers 1770'.

Font at Hanford Farm: *see* Monument (8).

SECULAR

(2) FONTMELL PARVA HOUSE (82701454) stands in a park 1¼ m. N. of the church. It is of brick with ashlar dressings and has two main storeys with basements and attics. The original parts of the roof are stone-slated with lead ridges. The house was probably built by Edward St. Loe of Knighton, who was buried in Child Okeford in 1686, (and not by his grandson, as stated in *Hutchins* IV, 80); it remained with his descendants until 1864 when it was bought by the Bower family. In the 19th century the house was enlarged to N., W. and S., but the original structure is seen in the five middle bays of the E. front (Plate 54).

The original façade is a pleasing example of Restoration architecture, probably of *c.* 1665; the original ground-floor rooms contain 18th-century panelling, partly of mahogany.

The centre bay of the E. front projects to form a two-storied porch, now crowned with a gabled attic window but originally hip-roofed. The basement storey is of coursed rubble capped by a chamfered ashlar plinth. Above, the walls are of small bricks laid in English bond, with stone quoins; a stone plat-band marks the level of the first floor and the eaves have a moulded stone cornice surmounted by a deep plaster cove. The cove formerly crossed the middle bay but was cut away when the gable was built, after 1864, as corbel-stones bearing the Bower crest indicate. The doorway, approached by a flight of stone steps flanked by parapets with ball finials, has a moulded stone architrave with a pulvinated frieze and a steep broken pediment; the central cartouche is of 1864 or later. The basement is lit by square-headed two-light hollow-chamfered mullioned windows which occur in the sides of the porch as well as on the four flanking bays of the E. front. The ground and first floors have two two-light windows on either side of the porch, with moulded ashlar architraves, central keystones and grooved and hollow-chamfered mullions; in both storeys the sides of the porch are pierced by small bull's-eye windows with moulded brick surrounds. A large brick chimneystack at the centre of the roof ridge has the sides decorated with arcaded panels of brickwork. On all sides other than the E. front the walls of the original house are concealed by the 19th-century additions.

Inside, the front doorway leads into a small vestibule, bounded to N. and S. by the side walls of the porch and to the W. by a panelled niche (Plate 79). Doors to N. and S. open into the hall and dining room. Hall, vestibule and dining room are lined with 18th-century panelling in which stiles, rails and cornices are of oak while the fielded panels, except in the dining room, are of Honduras mahogany which is supposed to have been imported by Admiral Edward St. Loe (d. 1729). The bedrooms over these rooms have 17th-century oak panelling.

The garden to the W. of the house is walled in brick, except on the E. side where there is an ornamental wrought-iron railing with a central gate embellished with the St. Loe arms (Plate 62).

(3) CHILD OKEFORD HOUSE (83381275), 170 yds. W. of the church, is two-storied with attics; the walls are partly of flint, partly of brick and partly rendered. It comprises an 18th-century N.–S. range with mid 19th-century additions and, to the E., a service range with walls that are of flint with ashlar dressings, probably of the 17th century.

The front doorway, in the S. end wall of the 18th-century range, has a round head with a moulded hood on scrolled brackets. The W. front has three sashed windows and a doorway on the ground floor, and five small sashed windows on the first floor; a late 19th-century bay projects W. at the N. end. The E. side of the range has 18th-century brickwork in the upper part, but below the brickwork the E. wall is of flint with occasional blocks of ashlar; it is probably of the 17th century. The re-entrant S.E. angle with the E. range is built with ashlar blocks and the S. wall of the E. range has a flint plinth capped with chamfered ashlar. Internally the house has been extensively altered; there are some moulded beams, and one room is lined with reset 17th-century oak panelling above an 18th-century dado. The drawing room fireplace has an 18th-century surround.

(4) MILLBROOK HOUSE (83151315), 600 yds. N. of the church, is in two parts. The main block, to the S.W., is three-storied and has rendered walls and a slated roof; this part is largely of the mid 19th century with modern additions but a moulded plinth and the hood moulds of blocked windows on the ground and first floors show that the N.E. wall is of the 17th century. Adjacent, to the N.E., is a two-storied 17th-century range, of rubble with ashlar dressings under a modern slated roof. The S.E. front of the 17th-century range has, on each floor, an original square-headed two-light window with chamfered and hollow-chamfered jambs and mullions; the labels have been renewed. The N.W. side of the range has a chamfered ashlar plinth; on the ground floor are two two-light windows with hood moulds, one of them converted into a doorway; and on the first floor are three two-light windows, one original and two modern. Adjoining the 17th-century wing to N. and E. is a former barn or outbuilding of the same date; its walls are of rubble with ashlar quoins and in the S.W. side is a three-light mullioned window with double-chamfered head and jambs. Inside the S.W. block the hall has some reset 17th-century panelling but all other rooms are of the early 20th century. S.E. of the house, at a distance of 120 yds., is a pair of ashlar gate piers with pine-cone finials and scroll-topped cheek walls.

(5) YEW TREE HOUSE (83621290) is two-storied with walls of brick, rubble and mathematical tiling; the roofs are tiled, with slate verges. The house was built at three periods; to the E. is a mid 18th-century range of three sash-windowed bays, with a rubble end-wall and tile revetment to the S. front. The central part of the house is a late 18th-century extension of the first, in brick. To the W. is a further extension of mid 19th-century date.

(6) MANOR FARM, house, 30 yds. E. of the church, is of two storeys with attics and is built partly of flint and rubble, partly of brick, and partly of clunch with mathematical tile revetment; the roofs are slated. The 18th-century W. range has a symmetrical W. front, in Flemish bond brickwork, with red stretchers and blue headers, with a round-headed doorway in the centre, sashed windows on each side, and three corresponding

sashed windows on the first floor. The S. wall is hung with mathematical tiles and high up in the middle of this wall is a stone inscribed 'W.T.D.T. Esq. 1841'. The E. wall is partly masked, but a wrought-iron casement with leaded glazing is visible on the first floor. An 18th-century *Barn* stands to the N.; the walls are brick-faced and clunch-lined and the roof is tiled; the doorways are in the E. and W. sides, the latter in a projecting bay.

(7) MONK'S YARD (83441274), house, facing S.S.E., 100 yds. W. of the church, is two-storied and has walls partly of rough Greensand ashlar, partly of brick and partly timber-framed; the roofs are thatched. The E. part of the building is now a separate tenement. The earliest parts of the timber-framed structure are probably of the first half of the 16th century. The plan does not have the usual characteristics of a dwelling-house and its original purpose is obscure.

CHILD OKEFORD *'Monk's Yard'*

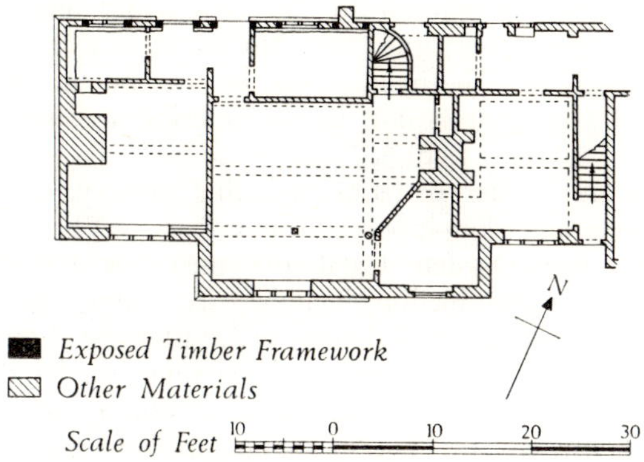

Above a rubble plinth the timber framework is exposed in the W. half of the N. wall. Two original wall posts, corresponding with roof trusses, have lightly moulded external corbels at the top; pegged to them is a chamfered overhanging wall-plate. Apart from these members most of the original framework in the N. wall was altered and heightened in the 17th century, when a square-headed chamfered timber doorway and two timber four-light windows with ovolo mouldings were inserted; at the same time the W. extremity of the N. front was slightly curtailed, the gabled W. wall being rebuilt in brick above a Greensand plinth. The S. front has four bays, the two middle bays projecting 5 ft. in front of the end bays. The W. bay is of brick above an ashlar plinth; of the middle bays that to the W. is faced with ashlar while the other is brick-faced; the E. bay is of brick. The E. end of the house and the eastern part of the N. wall are modern.

Inside, on the ground floor, the W. bay is spanned by two 16th-century beams with wide chamfers ending in roll-stops. A fireplace and oven against the W. wall must be later than the beams because the oven masonry partly encases the roll-stop chamfers; the beams are probably coeval with the original parts of the framed N. wall, while the fireplace was presumably built at the same time as the W. wall. The next room, corresponding with the stone-fronted bay of the S. front, is spanned by three 16th-century beams with roll-stops as before. To the W. these beams rest on a partition, presumably original, which separates the two rooms; to the E. they are supported on inserted members. The adjacent bay to the E. has been considerably altered and its original form is lost; at present it contains two back-to-back fireplaces and a large brick chimneystack. It is probable that the W. fireplace was originally much deeper and that its bressummer supported the ends of the ceiling beams in the second bay. In the E. bay the ceiling is supported on deep-chamfered beams that are probably of the 17th century. The stairs, in the N. part of the third bay, have no early features and the first floor is unremarkable. The roof rests on four trusses, that to the E. being set at a lower level than the others and retaining traces of smoke blackening; this suggests that the E. bay may have been single-storied until the 17th-century floor was inserted.

(8) HANFORD FARM (83941164), house, is a two-storied brick building of the late 18th or early 19th century. Until recent modernisation the symmetrical W. front was of three bays, with a central doorway with flanking sashed windows on the ground floor, and corresponding casement windows on the first floor.

The bowl of a 13th-century octagonal stone *Font* formerly stood in a scullery at the back of the farmhouse but it is now in the garden. The sides are vertical for about half the depth of the bowl and splayed inwards below that level. Each side is decorated with a roll-mould at the top and with a recessed trefoil-headed panel below; each angle has a moulded capital which presumably corresponded with a shaft worked on the stem, now missing.

(9) FONTMELL FARM (82961478), house, 380 yds. N.E. of (2), is an early 18th-century two-storied farmhouse, with brick walls with rubble plinths and ashlar quoins; the roof is mostly of stone-slates. The entrance, in the W. part of the six-bay S. front, has a 19th-century gabled brick porch with ashlar quoins and a chamfered elliptical stone head to the opening. The square-headed doorway inside the porch has a chamfered stone lintel and jambs. Traces of another doorway occur in the E. part of the S. front. The level of the first floor is marked by a brick plat-band.

MONUMENTS (10–15)

The following monuments are of the 17th or early 18th century and, unless otherwise described, are two-storied with thatched roofs.

(10) *Gold Hill Cottage* (83071327) retains the original flint and rubble walling at the back but was refronted in brickwork in the late 18th or early 19th century. The cottage has recently been remodelled.

(11) *Cottage* (83301304) has a modern slated roof and brick walls that were evidently refaced in the 19th century. The main ground-floor room has a six-panel ceiling with intersecting deep-chamfered beams and appears to be of the 17th century.

(12) *Cottage*, adjacent to the foregoing and perhaps a little later in date, has a brick front, but the rear and side walls are of rubble and flint.

(13) *Cottage* (83461254), originally of three ground-floor rooms but extended N. by another room in the 18th century, is built in its original parts of banded brick and flint. The ceiling beams are stop-chamfered.

(14) *Farmhouse* (83451239), with rendered brick and rubble walls, appears to be of the early 18th century. The original casement windows, three in each storey of the N. front, have tenoned and pegged timber frames. The N. doorway, walled up internally, has a heavy beaded oak frame and a plank door. Inside, the house has been greatly altered, but an open fireplace survives near the centre of the range. A lead rainwater head in the garden is dated 1798.

(15) *Cottage* (83681228), retains heavy intersecting chamfered ceiling beams and the remains of a plank-and-muntin partition.

Monuments (16–20)

The following monuments are of the later 18th century. All are two-storied and, unless otherwise described, have brick walls and thatched roofs.

(16) *Cottage* (83381298), one of a row, is earlier than the cottages on either side of it and was until recently distinguished by a somewhat massive chimneystack at the S. end.

(17) *Cottage*, adjacent to the foregoing on the S.

(18) *Inn* (83471276), with a symmetrical front of three bays. The widely spaced original sashed windows have been supplemented by modern openings; the eaves have a moulded plaster cove.

(19) *Cottages* (83481258), two adjoining, have walls of squared and coursed rubble; that to the N. is rendered.

(20) *House* (83521241) has slated roofs. In the 19th century the N.E. wing was rebuilt and another house was added to the S.

Early 19th-century buildings include a house, 50 yds. N.W. of the church, of two storeys with a symmetrical brick front and slated roofs; also a small cottage, subsequently enlarged, immediately N. of (18); also an inn (83471243); also two cottages 70 yds S.W. and the same distance W. of (4). A group of two-storied brick cottages at Gold Hill has the appearance of mid 19th-century development and is probably connected with the brickworks which formerly existed in that place.

MEDIAEVAL AND LATER EARTHWORKS

(21) Cultivation Remains. Little is known of the open fields of *Child Okeford.* Names on the Tithe Map of 1840 suggest former North and South Fields; enclosure probably went on over a long period of time since a number of isolated strips still existed in 1840. Ridge-and-furrow of these fields remains in a number of places, especially in Child Okeford Park (837125), where there are at least five interlocking furlongs with ridges 7 yds. to 9 yds. wide. Strip lynchets, probably marginal to the main open fields, remain in two places on Hambledon Hill: on the N.W. spur (842130) and on the S. spur (843121–845121).

Nothing is known of the date of enclosure of the open fields of *Fontmell Parva.* Near Fontmell Farm (828148, 833148) there are extensive remains of ridge-and-furrow, consisting of butting furlongs with reversed-S ridges up to 12 yds. wide.

ROMAN AND PREHISTORIC

(22) Hambledon Hill Iron Age Hill-fort (845125) is one of the most impressive earthworks in southern England (Plate 129); its multiple ramparts, enclosing an area of 31 acres, occupy the whole of the prominent N. spur of the hill between 460 ft. and 623 ft. above O.D. (*see* illustration on p. xxxix of the preface). The sequence of development and the abundant occupation remains within the fort are of particular interest, as is its close proximity to the even larger hill-fort on Hod Hill (Stourpaine (10)). No recent or extensive excavations have been made on the site, but in 1894 Edward Cunnington dug in the interior, apparently in the central section, and produced Romano-British and earlier material, including pottery, quern fragments and sling-stones (Dorset *Procs.* XVI, 1895, 156–7). The Durden Catalogue mentions Roman articles from Hambledon, including iron saws, bronze fibulae, knives and several coins of Constantine. Abundant Iron Age 'A' pottery has been found under the inner rampart near the N. entrance. Quarrying has partly destroyed this entrance but elsewhere the hill-fort has escaped serious damage. At the extreme N.

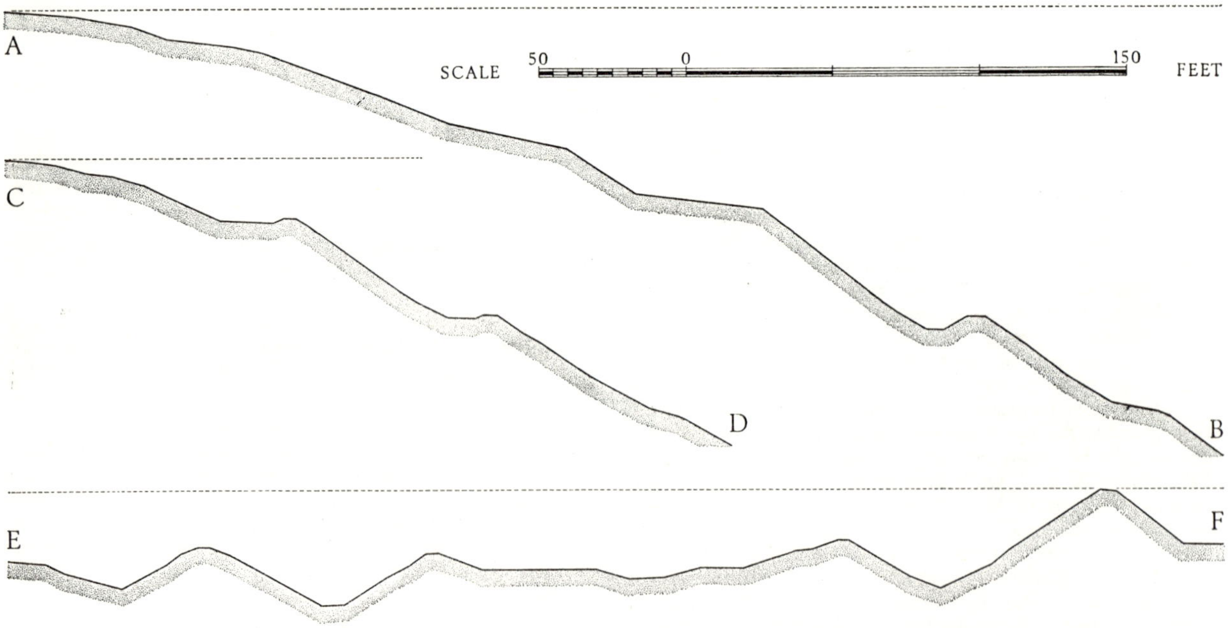

CHILD OKEFORD. (22) Hambledon Hill Iron Age Hill-fort. Profiles (*see* plan opposite).

HAMBLEDON HILL, IRON AGE HILL-FORT

CHILD OKEFORD

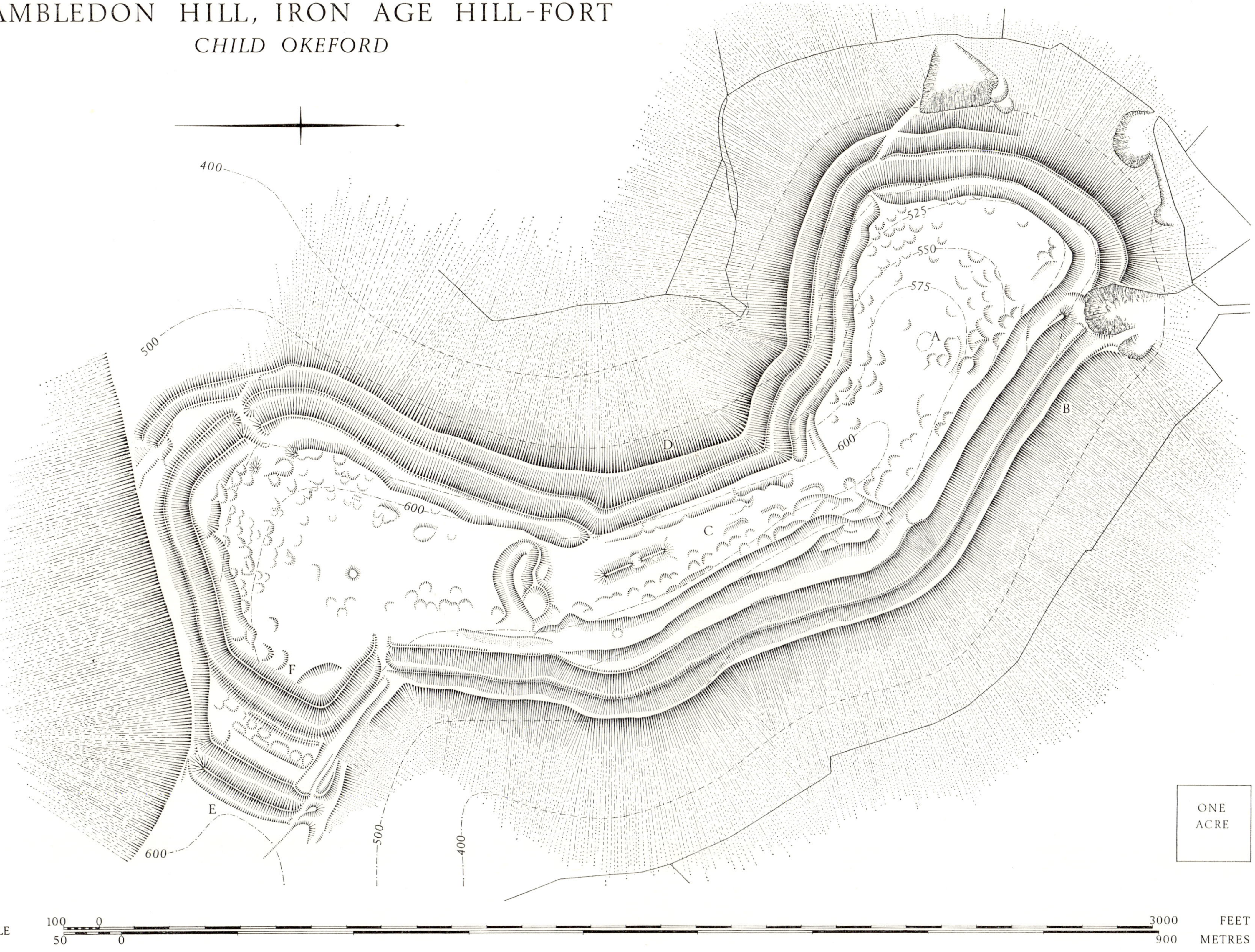

of the hill-fort 'Celtic' fields (Group (62)) protrude from under the defences. A full description of the earthworks appears in *Wessex from the Air*, by O. G. S. Crawford and A. Keiller (1928), pp. 44–55.

Topography has largely determined the bow-shape of the hill-fort, which adheres closely to changes in direction of the northern spur. The latter is level, but long, narrow and steep-sided, permitting expansion in one direction only, to the S. Successive enlargement has contributed to the present irregular shape of the fort, which falls clearly into three sections, northern, central and southern, marked by changes in the alignment of the ramparts and further emphasised by the remains of two earlier cross-ramparts within the interior. The fort measures 3,000 ft. overall from N. to S. but not more than 1,000 ft. from E. to W. and often much less. In consequence the proportion of rampart length to enclosed area, 2,300 yds. of inner rampart to 31 acres, is in marked contrast to Hod Hill where 2,050 yds. of rampart enclose 52 acres. With the exception of the flat spur top, at its broadest in the southern section, much of the interior of the fort is on a pronounced slope, particularly in the N. section.

The fort is defined by two main ramparts, with external ditches and with further scarping below the outer ditch for the greater part of its length. For much of their circuit the ramparts have been produced by scarping the steep natural slope, thus involving the minimum of building. The surviving crest of the rampart rarely exceeds 4 ft. in height on the inside, and whole stretches of the inner rampart are merely terraces, but from outside these ramparts present a formidable obstacle, measuring up to 70 ft. on the scarp. Immediately inside the inner rampart runs a continuous quarry area in the form of a terrace cut into the slope; this no doubt made movement easier within the interior and gave cover to the defenders as well as providing material for the rampart. At the S. end of the hill-fort, where slopes are gentler, the defences are of normal bank and ditch construction, the inner bank rising 30 ft. above its ditch bottom; here the internal quarry ditch is deeper and less regular. Beyond the counterscarp bank are massive outworks, comprising twin banks and ditches, crossing the neck of the spur where it joins the main mass of the hill, the most vulnerable point of the defences.

There are three entrances, differing in siting and form. The northern, now largely destroyed by a quarry, is sited below 500 ft. O.D. on a very steep slope; it appears never to have been more than a simple gap, the steep slope rendering it difficult of approach. The S.W. entrance is carefully sited on a local rise in ground level, the ramparts dipping away from it on either side. It is approached from the E. along the shoulder of the slope at the foot of the ramparts and consists of a terraced ramp within a hornwork 250 ft. long. It leads up a gentle slope before turning sharply to pass at a steeper slope through the middle and inner ramparts; the latter has a slight inturn. The S.E. entrance is not situated on the neck of the spur, facing the obvious line of approach from the S.E., but some distance to the N. where it faces into a steep combe. It consists of a simple gap through the middle and inner ramparts, the latter slightly inturned, and it is closely integrated with the outworks on the neck of the spur. Successive attempts to strengthen the defences have involved moving the approach way nearer to the shoulder of the slope, and eventually on to a ledge below the shoulder.

With the exception of a long barrow (23) and a round barrow (25), the interior features of the hill-fort consist mainly of hut platforms: 82 in the northern section, 45 in the central section, and 80 in the southern section. They are most clearly marked where the slopes are steep, but cover much of the interior. The most notable concentration of platforms is in the S.W. corner of the hill-fort. The platforms vary but little, except in size, floors ranging from 15 to 45 ft. across; basically they are areas levelled into the slope to provide sites for huts. Their curving rearward scarps naturally vary in height with the steepness of the slope. In certain cases the excavated material appears to have been used to level up the floor along the forward edge. The largest hut site is set into the southern cross-rampart and is notable for its high standard of finish. Another large platform stands immediately within the S.W. entrance.

It is obvious from the surface remains that there were at least three main structural phases. The first fortification occupied the most northerly part of the spur, extending as far as the northern cross-rampart. The latter consisted of a single bank and ditch but only shallow traces of the ditch survive. In addition to crossing the neck of the spur the fortification almost certainly enclosed the whole spur end, about 12 acres, on the line of the present inner rampart. In the very beginning, however, it may have been no more than a cross-dyke. During the second phase the defences were extended southwards on a different alignment as far as the southern cross-rampart, taking in a further 8 acres and including the long barrow. The rampart again consisted of a single bank and ditch separated by a narrow berm but this time of more massive proportions. The remaining fragments of bank and ditch have been much altered, the ditch is partly filled and a large hut platform has been inserted into the bank. An entrance may have existed E. of this feature.

In the final phase the hill-fort was extended to occupy the whole spur. The S.E. and S.W. entrances were constructed and on the western side of the central section the second phase ramparts were abandoned and others were built further down the slope. The second main rampart with its external ditch was also added, together with the S.E. outwork. The latter was modified at least once in an attempt to strengthen this weakest point of the hill-fort. At first it appears to have comprised only the inner bank, as far as the marked change in height and direction near its N.E. end; the entrance way would then have followed the approximate line of the present path. Subsequently, the outwork was strengthened by the extension of the inner bank north-eastward to the shoulder of the slope, and by the addition of the outer bank and ditch. Entry was then by means of a narrow ledge, still visible, along the steep slope below the end of the outwork.

NEOLITHIC CAUSEWAYED CAMP, *see* Iwerne Courtney (19).

(23) LONG BARROW (84531265), is prominently sited at 620 ft. Hambledon Hill, and lies within the ramparts of the Iron Age hill-fort. It is aligned almost due N.–S. (345°) by reason of the site and is strikingly regular in plan and profile, except for an undated gash across it just N. of centre. The parallel-sided mound, 240 ft. long and 55 ft. wide, is nearly 6 ft. high and fairly level along its length, with steep straight sides rising to a narrow flat top. The side ditches, extending the full length of the mound, are now visible only as slight depressions.

(24) LONG BARROW (84891207) on Hambledon Hill, at about 590 ft. O.D. on a gentle S.-facing slope, just below the highest part of the hill, lies within the earthworks of the Neolithic causewayed camp. Its N.–S. alignment (358°) does not appear to have been determined by topography. Short and parallel-sided, it is about 85 ft. long and 43 ft. wide, rising in height from 3½ ft. at its N. end to 7 ft. at its S. end, part of which has been quarried away. In cross profile it is steep and straight sided with a narrow top. There are traces of parallel side ditches, clear on the W. but much disturbed on the E. (Plate 132).

(25) BOWL BARROW (84521240) on Hambledon Hill, within the S. end of the hill-fort; centre disturbed; traces of ditch on S.; diam. 40 ft., ht. 1½ ft.

DEWLISH *The parish church of All Saints*

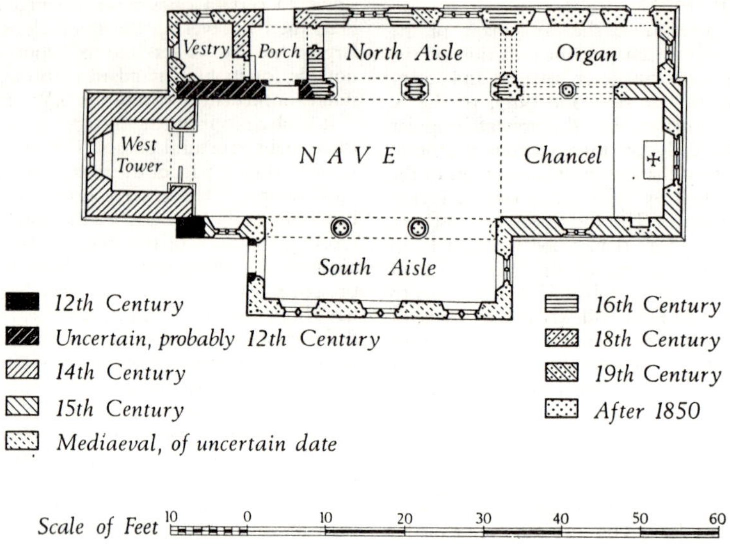

15 DEWLISH (7798)

(O.S. 6 ins. SY 79 NE)

Dewlish, with an area of a little over 2,100 acres, lies entirely on Chalk astride three parallel valleys which drain S. to the R. Piddle. The W. valley is drained by the Cheselbourne, the centre valley by the Devil's Brook, while the E. valley, Dennett's Bottom, is dry. The village is scattered over the W. slopes of the valley of the Devil's Brook, near the centre of the parish. The principal monuments are the Parish Church and Dewlish House. A triangular extension of the parish westwards beyond the Cheselbourne is presumably associated with Chebbard Farm which, from its location, appears to be an early settlement, but is undocumented.[1]

ECCLESIASTICAL

(1) The Parish Church of All Saints stands in the S. part of the village. The walls, except in the tower, are of knapped flint with bands of stone; the tower is of coursed rubble. The nave is roofed with Westmorland or Cornish slates and the other parts have stone-slated roofs. The main N. doorway and a doorway at the W. end of the S. Aisle have reused 12th-century chevron mouldings, probably from a single 12th-century doorway; the *Nave* therefore is probably of 12th-century origin. The *Tower* was built late in the 14th century. The *Chancel* is of the late 15th century and the *North Aisle* was added early in the 16th century. The *North Porch* is of the 18th century and the *Vestry* to the W. of the porch is of the 19th century. The *South Aisle* arcade is evidently a 19th-century insertion, presumably of 1872 when restorations are known to have taken place; however, a S. aisle was already in existence in the 18th century (Hutchins II, 612) and the surviving masonry appears to be mediaeval. The organ chamber was built in 1880.

Architectural Description—The *Chancel* (20½ ft. by 15 ft.) has a 19th-century E. window of three lights. In the N. wall two arches of 1880 open into the organ chamber; the S. wall has a late 15th-century window of two cinquefoil lights in a square head, below a moulded label with small square stops. A similar two-light window, reset in the E. wall of the organ chamber, presumably came from the N. side of the chancel. There is no chancel arch. The *Nave* (39½ ft. by 15¼ ft.) has an early 16th-century N. arcade of two bays in which the two-centred arches are outlined by continuous roll mouldings, and the jambs and soffits of the arches are decorated with two tiers of stone panelling with four-centred heads and sunk spandrels. The N. doorway has a segmental-pointed head composed of reset voussoirs with chevron ornament from a 12th-century arch, a label with nail-head enrichment, and head-stops representing a king and a queen, all reset. The wall containing the N. doorway is rendered on both faces and is of uncertain date, but it is likely to be of the 12th century. On the S. side of the nave, to the W. of the 19th-century arcade, is a 15th-century window of two cinquefoil-headed lights with vertical tracery. The S.E. corner of the nave appears to be of the 12th century.

The *North Aisle* (6¾ ft. wide) has a late 19th-century archway in the E. wall. The mid 19th-century eastern window in the N. wall cuts into the blocking of a 16th-century doorway with a four-centred head and chamfered jambs. The second window is of the 16th century and has three uncusped two-centred lights

[1] But *see* Fägersten, 173.

in a square head with a label. The plain square-headed doorway leading to the N. porch from the W. end of the aisle is of the 18th century. The *North Porch* ($7\frac{1}{2}$ ft. by $6\frac{3}{4}$ ft.) has a N. wall of banded brick and flint; the entrance has a plain round head. The *South Aisle* (29 ft. by 8 ft.) has windows of 1872 inserted in earlier walls of flint with occasional courses of roughly squared rubble. The W. doorway is made up with 12th-century voussoirs and jamb stones that are decorated on the fascia and reveal with roll-moulded chevron ornament; the segmental head has specially cut springers (Plate 11).

The *West Tower* ($7\frac{3}{4}$ ft by $8\frac{3}{4}$ ft.) is of two stages, with a moulded plinth, a weathered offset and an embattled parapet with a moulded string-course. The tower arch is segmental-pointed and has two wave-moulded orders; the inner order dies into the jambs, the outer order continues on the responds to terminate at rounded stops above a hollow-chamfered plinth. The two-centred 14th-century W. window has two trefoil-headed lights with cusped tracery above. High in the N. wall of the lower stage is a small rectangular window, now blocked with brickwork. Each face of the upper stage has a late 14th-century window of two cinquefoil lights with a central quatrefoil under a two-centred label.

The *Roof* of the chancel is concealed by a segmental plaster ceiling; in the nave a similar ceiling has recently been removed to disclose an arch-braced collar-beam roof in five bays, possibly of the 15th or 16th century.

Fittings—*Bells:* three; treble by W. K., 1724; 2nd by TP, 1663; tenor inscribed 'IW 1620 In God reioyce'. *Coffin-stool:* with turned legs, 17th century. *Communion-rails:* with moulded top and bottom rails and turned columns at ends, late 17th century, balusters replaced by modern uprights. *Communion table:* modern, standing on carved oak plinth enriched with foliate scroll-work and cherub heads, possibly fascia of an early 18th-century table. *Doors:* In porch entry, panelled oak gate, upper part with lattice of turned balusters, 18th century; in N. doorway, 18th-century plank door opening in two halves, with wrought-iron hinges and wooden box-lock from earlier door, perhaps 16th century. *Font:* of Ham Hill stone, with rounded bowl on circular stem with moulded capping, perhaps 13th century. *Inscriptions:* In base of tower, lead panel embossed ED LONG, SAM ADAMS, 1721, probably from former roof.

Monuments: In chancel, on S. wall, (1) of Elizabeth Moore, 1722, rectangular marble tablet with stone pediment, scrolled cheek-pieces and apron with consoles. In N. aisle, on W. wall, (2) of Emma Ann Churchill, 1842, marble tablet by Lester of Dorchester. In churchyard, N. of N. aisle, (3) of Thomas . . . , 17th-century table-tomb; (4) of Samuel Ademes, 1673, headstone; (5) of Mary Ademes, 1691, headstone; (6) of Charles Hall, 1791, headstone with inset lunette depicting an urn, signed Coade, London, 1792; S. of tower, (7) of Emma Ann Churchill, 1842, table-tomb by Marshall of Blandford. *Painting:* In nave, above N. arcade, late 17th-century cartouche containing text, Genesis XXVIII, 16, 17. *Panelling:* In chancel and N. aisle, 17th-century panelled dado with moulded framing and enriched frieze. Reset in organ chamber, similar dado with strapwork, guilloche ornament and carved panels; similar woodwork is used to make seating in chancel and a partition in N. arcade of nave. *Piscina:* In S. wall of chancel, chamfered trefoil-headed recess, mediaeval. *Plate:* includes an Elizabethan cup and cover-paten by Lawrence Stratford, the latter dated 1574 by inscription; a paten inscribed 'MR 1638' with date-letter for that year and maker's mark DW; also a brass almsdish with embossed representation of Caleb and Joshua carrying grapes, punched decoration on border, S. German, early 16th century. *Pulpit:* Of oak, hexagonal, with sides in two heights of panelling, upper panels arcaded, with enriched framing, early 17th century.

Sundial: On S. wall of tower, below belfry window, rectangular stone slab with Roman numerals and inscription 'AUT UMBRA SIC VITAR, 16.1'. *Miscellanea:* Against E. wall of chancel, fragment of stone coffin-lid with moulded edge and a foliate cross in low relief, late 13th-century.

SECULAR

(2) DEWLISH HOUSE (77109745), over $\frac{1}{2}$ m. S.S.W. of the church, is of two storeys with attics. According to Hutchins (II, 607) the house was built by Thomas Skinner in 1702. The main front, to the N.E., is of Purbeck stone; the S.E. end wall is of Ham Hill ashlar and the S.W. front is of brick, perhaps originally rendered; the N.W. end wall is modern, having been built since the removal of an 18th and 19th-century service wing which extended to the N.W. The roofs are slate-covered.

The house is a good example of domestic building of the period, with interesting archaism in the internal planning. It contains 18th-century fittings of good quality.

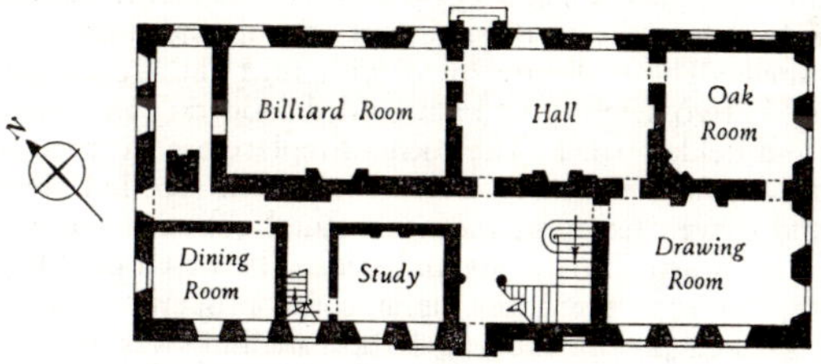

The N.E. front is symmetrical and of nine bays arranged as a central pavilion of three bays, single intermediate bays and terminal pavilions of two bays; the pavilions are emphasised by vertical quoins and the intermediate bays are slightly recessed (Plate 54). At the base is a moulded plinth, the first floor has a plat-band with a small moulding below it and the eaves have a modillion cornice. Over the greater part of the façade the eaves cornice has plain modillions and few mouldings and is probably of the early 19th century, but the centre pavilion (Plate 128) retains an original cornice with a high degree of enrichment and foliate modillions; above, the same mouldings are repeated in an elaborate curvilinear pediment. The central doorway is original and has a stone surround with attached Roman Doric side columns on pedestals. These support entablature blocks and a broken curved pediment, within which is a cartouche with the arms and crest of Skinner surrounded by bold mantling (Plate 68).

The S.W. front has neither plinth nor string-course and the modillion cornice is some 6 ins. lower than that of the N.E. and S.E. fronts, except over the pedimented central pavilion where it is rather higher. The centre pavilion has rusticated brick quoins and contains three bays; the flanking parts of the façade have ranges of four windows on each floor but the bays nearest the centre are set apart from the other three. The openings of the centre pavilion are of greater elaboration than the others; the doorway has a moulded architrave and a stepped keystone under a pediment on console brackets; it is linked by a stone panel with the window above, which has a round head and a plain stone architrave, with a keystone and moulded imposts; the windows on each side have stone keys and, on the first floor, stone aprons; there is a small window in the pediment. The other windows have gauged brick heads.

The S.E. end wall has a moulded plinth continuous with that of the N.E. front; also continuous is the 19th-century cornice and the Purbeck stone plat-band, the latter contrasting with the Ham Hill ashlar of the wall-face. The four plain window openings of each storey are arranged in pairs; those of the lower storey have been lowered both as to heads and sills, probably in the 19th century. The demolished kitchen wing to the N.W. was faced on the N.E. front with stone and had the centre part slightly recessed; several windows retained early 18th-century sashes with thick glazing bars. A stone cartouche-of-arms from this wing is now reset over a modern archway at the N. corner of the N.E. front; it is carved with the arms of Michel with a quarterly scutcheon of Bingham, Turberville, Chaldecott and Trenchard.

The interior of the house is so planned that the central doorway of the N.E. front leads into the end bay of the Hall, as in a mediaeval hall. The Hall contains an original fireplace with a square stone surround, a moulded architrave and console-brackets with shaped side-scrolls supporting a cornice with a broken pediment; the walls are lined with early 17th-century oak panelling, said to have been brought from Kingston Russell (*Dorset* I, 127). The Oak Room, in the E. corner of the house, has a plaster ceiling with a square centre panel enriched with guilloche, gadroon and egg-and-dart ornament, moulded side panels and, in the corners, baskets of fruit and flowers, and scallop shells. The walls are lined with mid 18th-century oak panelling, in two heights, with a moulded dado-rail, an enriched cornice and fielded panels. The corner fireplace has a carved oak surround and a pedimented overmantel with scrolled cheek-pieces and carved festoons; the overmantel contains a portrait by Thomas Beach, dated 1765 and said to be of Grace Michel (Plate 78). In 1756 the house became the property of David Robert Michel, her husband, and the panelling was probably installed by him. The Study is lined with original bolection-moulded fielded pine panelling, with large panels above and small panels below a moulded dado-rail; the fireplace has a marble surround in a moulded and enriched wood frame. The Billiard Room has a panelled dado made partly of reused 17th-century material, and a modern fireplace surround made up with old fragments, including part of a 15th-century traceried window which was recently discovered, presumably reset, in the upper storey of the house.

The principal Staircase is of *c.* 1760; it is of mahogany and has open strings with richly carved spandrels, spiral and straight-fluted Roman Doric colonette balusters arranged alternately, three to each tread, and a moulded hand-rail ending in a large horizontal curtail over a Doric newel-post (Plate 83). The second quarter-landing is carried on two Ionic columns of wood, perhaps insertions. The panelled dado is divided into bays by fluted pilasters.

On the first floor, the central N.E. bedroom has a dado-rail heavily enriched with egg-and-dart moulding, and a deep bed recess with a moulded elliptical head. The fireplace surround has a highly enriched foliate frieze, and consoles carved to represent eagles' heads holding pendant foliage; the consoles support an enriched and dentilled cornice-shelf; the overmantel contains a romantic landscape painting in an eared surround with key-pattern ornament, flanked by foliate cheek-pieces; the pediment has a pulvinated frieze of banded oak-leaves (Plate 78). Other bedrooms are lined with quadrant-moulded and fielded 18th-century panelling and have original fireplaces of simpler design in veined and coloured marbles; one has a late 18th-century fluted wooden fireplace surround with oval medallions in the frieze. Many of the doors are original, with bolection-moulded or fielded panels, and brass rim-locks.

The *Stables*, ¼ m. N.E. of the house, are two-storied with walls of brick with stone dressings, and tile-covered roofs. They were built on a U-shaped plan early in the 18th century. The coach-houses in the wings are now converted into cottages, the entrances being walled up and modern stone-mullioned windows of 17th-century pattern substituted. The stable range retains the original round-headed windows and arched central doorway.

(3) MANOR FARM HOUSE, immediately W. of the church, is of two storeys with attics; the walls are of banded flint and stone, with ashlar dressings; the roofs are slated. The house dates from the beginning of the 17th century and was probably built by Arthur Radford who acquired the manor from Lord Mordaunt (Hutchins II, 606). In the 19th century the roofs were renewed and altered and a new wing was built on the S.

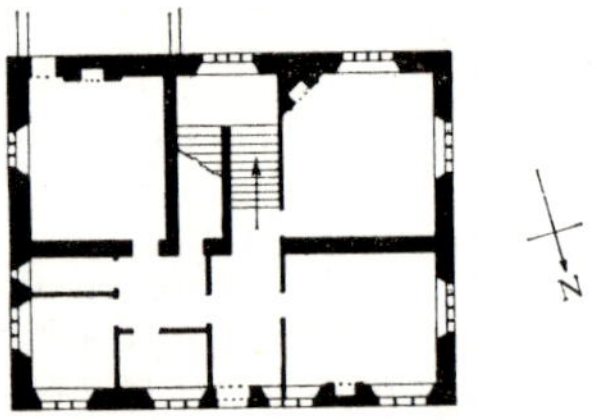

The N. front is symmetrical and of four bays with a central doorway. The windows of each storey are of three lights, with stone mullions and transoms and with moulded labels. At the top are two gables; the inward-facing slopes are steep and connected together by a horizontal parapet while the outer slopes are of shallower pitch and rest on shaped kneelers. The central doorway has a moulded lintel with a slightly raised centre forming a shallow four-centred arch with continuous moulded jambs; the wall above it is blank. Each gable contains a two-light attic window and has a chimneystack on the apex. In the W. front, which is of two bays, the upper part of the wall shows traces of rebuilding and there may originally have been two gables, as on the N. front.

Inside, several rooms are lined with plain 17th-century oak panelling with moulded beading; some have enriched friezes and one fireplace has a carved wood overmantel of three early 17th-century panels elaborately enriched with strapwork in gadrooned surrounds, with two guilloche-patterned tapering pilasters between them, all reset. A bedroom has a window flanked by Ionic pilasters carved with arabesque ornament and supporting consoles; another retains an original door with six small moulded panels below a larger panel enriched with gadrooning. The staircase has close strings, stout turned balusters, moulded handrails, and newels rising from floor to floor. Although some newels are modern others are of the 17th century and comprise stop-chamfered posts continuous with the turned balusters. The house is separated from the road on the N. by a garden which was formerly entered through a round-headed stone archway, wide enough for a carriage. The archway has been transferred to the opposite side of the road and is now incorporated in the buildings of an extensive model farm of the mid 19th century. Some 17th-century mullioned windows are reset in the same structure.

(4) DEWLISH HIGHER FARM, 300 yds. N.E. of the church, is a farmhouse of two storeys with attics, set out on a half-H plan

COURT CLOSE

DEWLISH (7)

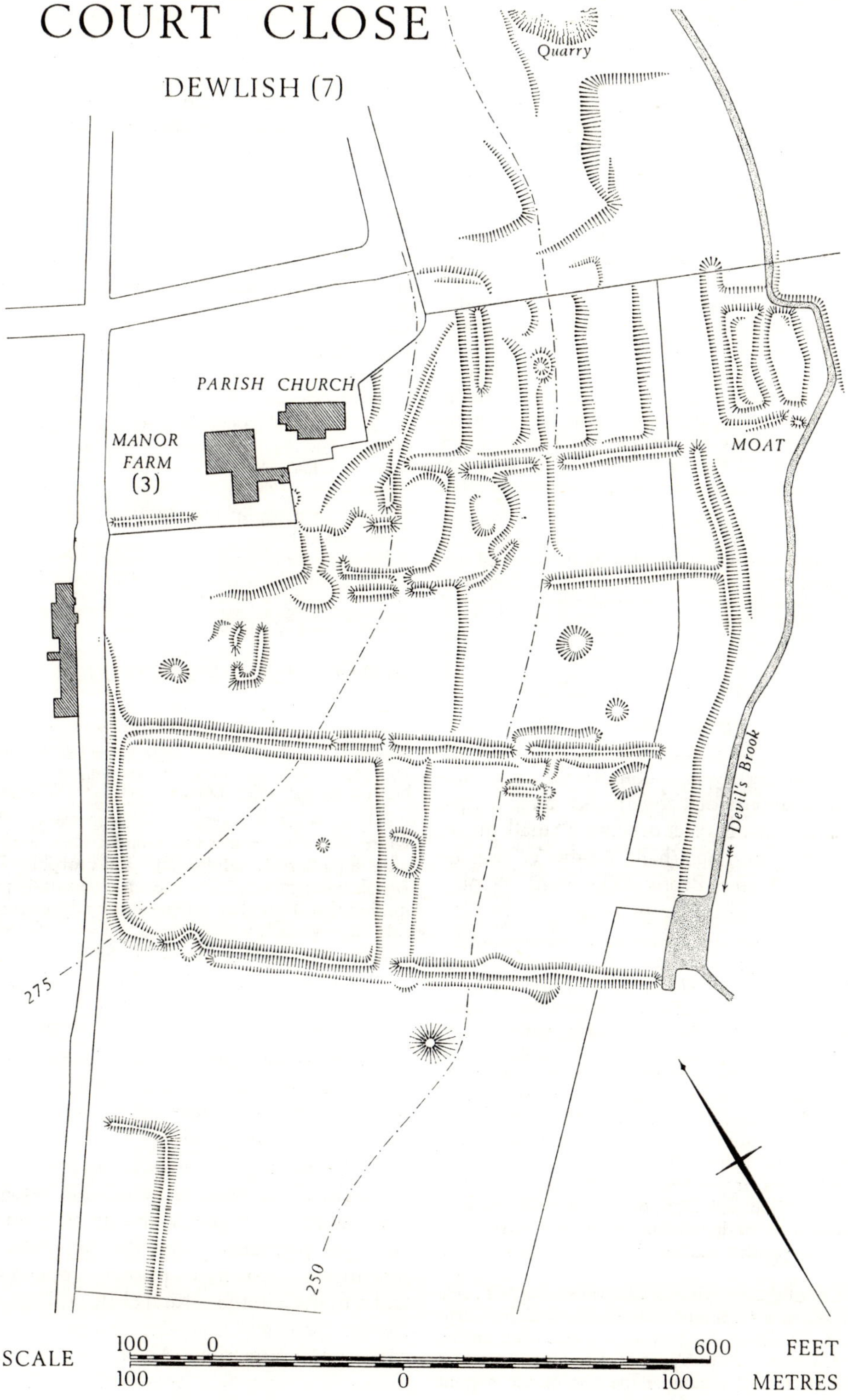

SCALE 100 0 600 FEET
100 0 100 METRES

with the opening to the small courtyard to the N. and the main front facing S. It is of the late 17th or early 18th century. The walls are principally of brick in English bond, with two stretcher courses to one of headers, but Flemish bond occurs at the S.E. corner; the W. and N. walls are of banded brick and flint up to the first floor. Where the walls are of brick they have plinths below, plat-bands at first-floor level, and coved plaster cornices at the eaves. The roofs are tiled, with stone-slates in the lower courses, and are hipped at every corner except at the W. end of the S. range, which is gabled and crowned by a large brick chimneystack. The S. front now has sashed windows but these are secondary; an original four-light casement with moulded wooden mullions is preserved on the N. side. A shallow round-headed recess occurs in the E. part of the S. front; it is outlined in stretcher bricks and embellished with brick imposts and a brick keystone; within the recess the wall is rendered. Internally no notable features are visible.

(5) COTTAGE, 100 yds. N.W. of the church, is two-storied with rendered walls and a slated roof; it probably dates from the beginning of the 18th century and has a plan with a cross-passage flanked on one side by a living room and on the other by two small rooms, one of them a pantry. The building was remodelled and the upper storey was rebuilt late in the 19th century.

(6) LOWER FARM (77179689), house, dates from the first half of the 19th century and is two-storied with walls of banded brick and flint and a hipped thatched roof. The symmetrical three-bay façade has wooden three-light casement windows with pointed 'Gothic' lights.

MEDIAEVAL AND LATER EARTHWORKS

(7) COURT CLOSE (775980), remains of former settlement, lies E., S. and S.W. of the church (*see* plan, p. 87 and Plate 130). The earthworks comprise a large embanked enclosure subdivided by banks and scarps, together with the remains of closes and a small moat; they cover some 17 acres, on Chalk, on the W. side of the valley of the Devil's Brook. The name 'Court Close' appears on the Tithe Map of 1844.

The greater part of the site is occupied by a large rectangular enclosure of 11 acres bounded by banks 25 ft. to 30 ft. wide and up to 5 ft. high, with external ditches on the N.E. and S.W. sides only. The enclosure is divided into two parts by a similar bank, with a ditch 2 ft. deep on the S.W. side, and is further subdivided by low scarps and banks which are secondary to the enclosure and the main dividing bank. The N. corner of the enclosure is much disturbed and appears to have been occupied by relatively recent buildings. The remainder of the interior of the enclosure is virtually featureless. Its purpose is unknown, but apart from its larger size it has close similarities in form and position with enclosures at Milborne St. Andrew (13) and Charminster (25). To the S.W. of the enclosure is an oval mound (77499796), 2 ft. high with no trace of a ditch. It is probably part of the earthworks to the N.E., rather than a barrow.

Immediately S.E. of the church and adjacent to the N.E. side of the enclosure are four rectangular closes bounded by scarps 2 ft. to 5 ft. high, overlying the ditch of the enclosure on the S.W. and bounded on the N.E. by an ill-defined hollow-way which runs N.W.–S.E. and continues the line of the present village street to N.W. To the N.E. of this hollow-way are further scarps, much disturbed by quarrying.

In the valley bottom immediately E. of the E. corner of the enclosure (77679812) is a small rectangular moat (Class A 1(a))[1] with ditches 30 ft. to 40 ft. wide and 3 ft. to 4 ft. deep. The Devil's Brook flows along the S.E. ditch and there is an internal bank 2 ft. to 3 ft. high along the S.W. side of the island. A ditch 25 ft. wide and 2 ft. to 3 ft. deep through the centre is probably associated with the water meadows which cover the valley floor. The moat probably encloses the site of a former manor house.

(8) EMBANKMENTS (77879940), parts of a former mill-pond dam, lie across the valley of the Devil's Brook, 100 yds. N. of Dewlish Mill. They comprise a massive earthen bank, 60 yds. long, 10 yds. to 15 yds. wide and 6 ft. to 8 ft. high; both ends have been destroyed. At the W. end, a large quarry scoop in the valley side and disturbed ground, through which the brook now flows, may be the site of the original mill; probably it was the one recorded in 1317 (P.R.O., Assize Roll No. 1375, m. 15).

(9) CULTIVATION REMAINS. Little is known of the open fields of the parish. There were certainly an East and a West Field (Tithe Map 1844) but most of the parish was already enclosed by 1819, when what little remained of the former West Field was finally enclosed (Award and Map, 1819, D.C.R.O.). Ridge-and-furrow, probably of the old West Field, remains in Dewlish Park (768972).

Evidence of temporary cultivation beyond the open fields is found in the form of ridge-and-furrow up to 6 yds. wide on Whitelands Down (767986) and from 7 yds to 9 yds. wide on South Down (781968).

ROMAN AND PREHISTORIC

(10) OCCUPATION DEBRIS, Romano-British, occurs near Chebbard Farm on a gentle S.E. slope at about 400 ft. O.D. (75459855). The debris includes samian and coarse pottery of the 1st to 3rd centuries A.D., and tile fragments. Some sherds may be of Iron Age date (Dorset *Procs.* LXXIV (1952), 88–9).

(11) ROMAN BUILDING, near Dewlish House. A black and white mosaic pavement was found *c.* 1740, and reopened *c.* 1790, on a slope S. of Dewlish House and probably W. of the Devil's Brook (near 770973). The measurement of 65 paces by 15 paces implies that more than one room was discovered. On the lower side the pavement was bordered by a gutter of red tiles. A coin of Faustina was found. (Hutchins II, 607.)

'CELTIC' FIELDS, *see* p. 331f., Groups (45), (47), (48), (63).

MONUMENTS (12–19), ROUND BARROWS

Eight round barrows survive and are widely dispersed, except for the small group on Lord's Down. That this group was formerly more numerous is evident from Warne's excavation of six barrows here, immediately before the Down was brought into cultivation (*C.T.D., Pt. 1*, Nos. 33 to 38). No. 33, probably (13), was 82 ft. in diameter and 12 ft. high, having been enlarged periodically for the reception of secondary interments. It covered a primary grave 6 ft. in diameter and 2 ft. deep in the natural chalk; this grave contained a Beaker (probably Long-Necked or Type A) but apparently no inhumation. Above this lay the secondary interments; first, on a layer of chalk rubble, the skeleton

[1] *See Cambridgeshire* I, lxi–lxiv.

of a child associated with Beaker fragments; second, in the top of the same layer, a cist with a small plain urn containing a cremation; third, above a layer of mould and in a further layer of chalk rubble, a cremation with ashes beneath an inverted ridged Food-vessel urn (*C.T.D.*, Pl. IV, No. 15; *Arch.J.* CXIX (1962), 65); fourth, in a cist cut into the same layer, an inverted biconical urn (*C.T.D.*, Pl. IV, No. 14; *Arch.J.*, CXIX (1962), 59); the bottom of the latter was smashed by, fifth, a further inverted biconical urn (*C.T.D.*, Pl. IV, No. 13; *Arch.J.*, CXIX (1962), 60). Just below the surface was an undated skeleton, probably intrusive. Nos. 34, 35 and 36 all adjoined No. 33 but are no longer visible. No. 34 contained a primary cremation with ashes in a small cist cut into the natural chalk; No. 35 had a skeleton 1½ ft. below the surface; No. 36 had a crouched interment, probably primary. No. 37, probably (12), contained a primary cremation within a central cist, 4 ft. long, 2 ft. wide and 2 ft. deep, at the base of the mound; in association were a crutch-headed bone pin, tweezers, a perforated whetstone and a bronze ogival dagger (Wessex grave-group 8, *P.P.S.* IV (1938), 102; *U.L.I.A. 10th Annual Rept.* (1954), 58). No. 38, probably (15), covered a primary cremation with a bronze ogival dagger in a cist cut in the natural chalk; within a cairn of flints covering the cist were the fragments of an urn (Wessex grave-group 11, *P.P.S.* IV (1938), 102; *U.L.I.A. 10th Annual Rept.* (1954), 58). A further barrow, almost certainly (14), was opened in 1882. At its centre, 10 ft. down and cut into the natural chalk, was a cist, 8 ft. long, 2 ft. wide and 1½ ft. deep, containing a bone pin and another bone object. Above the cist were the lower jaw of a pig and the foot bones of a calf (Dorset *Procs.* V (1883), 31). An unidentified barrow in Dewlish was opened by J. Brown in 1871. The mound was 4 ft. high and covered a primary cremation in a 'bucket' urn (*B.A.P.* ii, fig. 447) beneath a central flint cairn; a cremation in a globular urn was found near the margin of the mound (*Arch.J.* XXIX (1872), 286; CXIX (1962), 57). Another unidentified barrow opened by J. C. Mansel-Pleydell about 1881 lay on the N.W. side of Milborne Wood. It stood 10 ft. high and its lower half was composed of sand and gravel. A crude urn, containing a cremation and standing on a Purbeck slab, was probably secondary (Dorset *Procs.* V (1883), 30; *Ant.J.* XIII (1933), 445).

Lord's Down Group comprises the following four barrows which lie within the S. projection of the parish between 250 ft. and 300 ft. above O.D.

(12) *Bowl* (78479629), on the highest part of Lord's Down; much ploughed; diam. 53 ft., ht. 1½ ft.

(13) *Bowl* (78439632), 60 yds. N.W. of (12), much disturbed presumably by excavation on the N.W. side and heavily ploughed; diam. about 85 ft., ht. 2 ft.

(14) *Bowl* (78489635), 50 yds. E. of (13) on the parish boundary with Milborne, has an oval appearance, presumably the result of ploughing on either side, which is accentuated by the parish boundary bank running over it; diam. about 65 ft., ht. 7 ft.

(15) *Bowl* (78309654), 300 yds. N.W. of (14) immediately S. of the Milborne–Puddletown road, is heavily ploughed; diam. about 75 ft., ht. 2½ ft.

(16) *Bowl* (78629740), on a gentle S. slope above 350 ft. O.D. near Milborne Wood, is much ploughed; diam. about 50 ft., ht. 3 ft.

(17) *Bowl* (78859740), 250 yds. E. of (16) and severely ploughed; diam. about 35 ft., ht. 1 ft.

(18) *Barrow* ? (76799859), near the summit of Whitelands Down (S.) on a gentle N. slope, has been heavily ploughed and is now an irregular mound, apparently dug away on the E. side; two mounds are shown at this point on the 1811 O.S. map; diam. about 50 ft., ht. 2 ft.

(19) *Barrow* ? (76849962), in the N.W. angle of Whitelands Down (N.) and adjoining the parish boundary with Cheselbourne, lies at over 400 ft. O.D. on the ridge top; diam. about 40 ft., ht. 2 ft.

UNDATED

For ENCLOSURE across the parish boundary with Cheselbourne, *see* CHESELBOURNE (40).

16 DURWESTON (8508)

(O.S. 6 ins. ST 80 NE, ST 80 NW)

The parish of Durweston lies on the S.W. bank of the R. Stour and covers some 1,800 acres, rising from about 200 ft. above sea-level at the river to 600 ft. in the W.; the land is entirely Chalk. Before 1381 there were two parishes, Durweston and Knighton, and the division between the two is probably represented by the continuous line of field boundaries which bisects the parish from N.E. to S.W. The reason for combining the parishes is unknown, but it was certainly not due to desertion, since both settlements are still well populated. The present parish church was originally that of Knighton; the remains of Durweston church (Hutchins I, 266) are said to have existed near Durweston Mill (6), and a few moulded stones still lie there. The date of enclosure of the downland in the S.W. part of the parish is unknown, but cottages at Shepherd's Corner Farm indicate that this was done before the middle of the 19th century.

The principal monument is the church tower.

ECCLESIASTICAL

(1) THE PARISH CHURCH OF ST. NICHOLAS, standing in the S. part of the village, was largely rebuilt in 1846, the architect being P. C. Hardwick, and presents little

DURWESTON *The parish church of St. Nicholas*

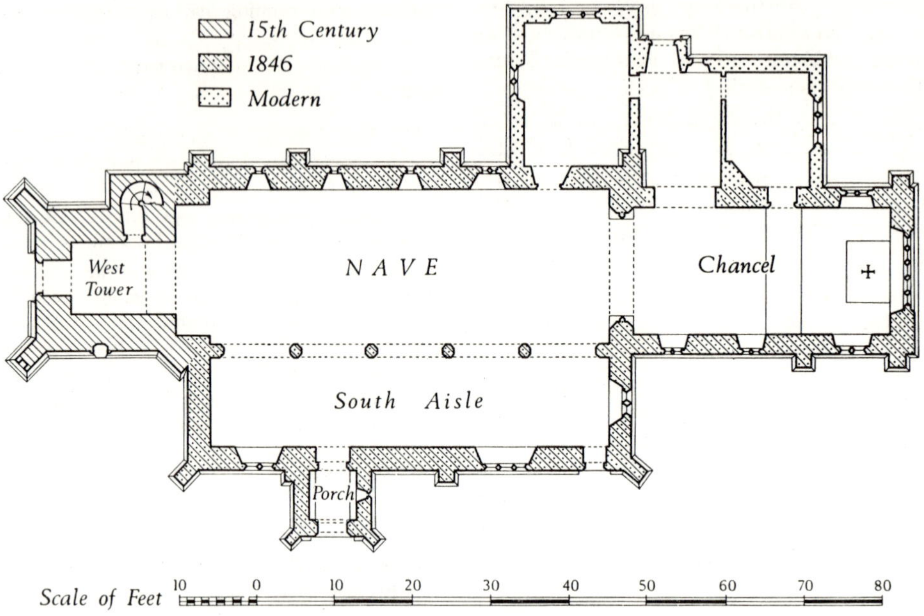

that is noteworthy apart from the 15th-century tower and a few reused fragments from the old building. The 19th-century Chancel, Nave, S. Aisle and S. Porch are faced with knapped flint chequered with blocks of ashlar. The S. doorway incorporates a reused 15th-century four-centred arch (Plate 49) inscribed with the epitaph of William Dounton, rector from 1442 to 1459, and another stone with the date 1455. The pillars of the nave arcade incorporate some mediaeval stones, and some of the moulded octagonal capitals are probably mediaeval although retooled.

Architectural Description—The *West Tower* (9½ ft. by 9 ft.) is built of coursed Greensand ashlar; it has three stages between the chamfered and moulded plinth and the embattled parapet (Plate 9). The top of the lower stage is marked by a weathered string-course and the upper stages have weathered and hollow-chamfered string-courses. The top string-course, at the base of the parapet, has a gargoyle at the centre of each face; above these and above the corners rise small crocketed pinnacles. The corners of the tower have diagonal buttresses; that at the N.E. corner springs from the roof of the vice a little below the top stage and the other three are each of six stages; a rough round-headed recess is cut into the lowest stage of the S.W. buttress. The rectangular vice turret is of two stages; its head is weathered back to the N. wall of the tower just below the top stage. The tower arch is two-centred and has two hollow-chamfered orders which die into the wall at the springing; there are no responds. The small doorway of the tower vice has a chamfered four-centred head and jambs. The W. doorway has a moulded four-centred head with continuous jambs and broach stops; the weathered and hollow-chamfered label ends in square foliate stops. The W. window, restored, has three cinquefoil lights and vertical upper tracery, in a two-centred casement-moulded head, and continuous jambs. The S. side of the tower is decorated externally on the lower stage with a tall niche carved in lighter and finer-grained Greensand. The projecting sill of the niche is supported on a moulded corbel; on either side, a buttress-shaped standard with a miniature corbel base continues up beyond the springing of the niche-head to a crocketed finial; above is a crocketed canopy, carved on the soffit to represent ribbed vaulting with a floral boss; the back of the recess retains traces of red pigment. In the second stage of the tower is another niche, similar to the first but with an ogee head and septfoil cusping in place of a canopy. A third niche, in the W. side of the second stage, is better preserved; it has an ogee head with trefoil cusping and sub-cusping. In the top stage, each face of the tower has a belfry window of two trefoil-headed lights with a blind quatrefoil in a two-centred head with a concentric label; the lights are fitted with pierced wooden shutters.

Fittings—*Bells:* six; 3rd, late 14th century, inscribed 'Sancta Maria', others recast. *Chests:* In S. aisle, small iron-bound chest with foliate escutcheon-plate and wrought iron handles, perhaps Flemish, 17th century. In vestry, 17th-century oak chest, 4¼ ft. long, with conventional leaf carving and moulded rails. *Door:* To tower vice, of planks with wrought iron strap hinges, heavily nail-studded, 16th century. *Font:* At W. end of S. aisle, with square base of Purbeck marble with mouldings for a round centre pedestal and four shafts, 12th century; stem modern; basin completely re-worked but possibly original. *Graffiti:* In S. arcade, incorporated in second column from E., inverted drum stone with late 17th and early 18th-century scratchings; on W. column, similar scratchings; presumably these stones survive from mediaeval fabric. Over S. doorway, reset four-centred chamfered arch with scratching of 1687 and several 18th-century scratchings (*see* also Inscription). *Image:* In S. aisle, reset above S. doorway, sculptured stone panel, 2 ft. high and with remains of red pigment, supposed to represent St. Eloi, patron saint of blacksmiths; discovered beneath E. window of old chancel during 19th-century restorations (Hutchins I, 266); 15th century (Plate 13). *Inscription:* On fascia of reset head of S. doorway, black-letter inscription in raised letters 2 ins. high in recessed concentric panel (Plate 49): "hic iacet sub tumilo downto will's humanis Rector erat ville durwesto' okefordie natus" and on W. impost of same doorway, in two horizontal lines of similar lettering, "Smpt. anno dni. mill'o cccclv".

Monuments: In S. aisle, above arcade, (1) of William Burtt, 1824, sarcophagus-shaped tablet by Hiscock of Blandford; (2) of Catherine Godwin, 1817, tablet by Hiscock; (3) of Thomas Keeping, 1840, sarcophagus-shaped tablet by Simmonds; on S. wall, (4) of Mary Ann Alford, 1839, tablet by Collins of Poole; (5) of William Dansey, 1800, white marble tablet with arms; on W. wall, (6) of Thomas Palmer, 1714, marble tablet in pedimented stone frame with scrolled side pieces and foliate apron. *Plate:* includes silver cup of 1837, paten of [1759] and set of cup, paten and flagon with hall-marks of 1764 and arms of Portman impaling Fitch (Plate 43); although dates do not quite agree this set is presumably the one noted by Nightingale (140) at Bryanston. *Sundial:* On S. side of tower at belfry level, square stone plate with incised radii and iron gnomon, probably 18th century.

SECULAR

(2) BRIDGE (86350863), over the R. Stour, is of Greensand ashlar in three main spans, the central arch being slightly higher than the others (Plate 51). Cutwaters at each end of the two piers are carried up to form refuges in the parapets. The semicircular archivolts, of plain ashlar voussoirs, die into the piers at the springing. Plat-bands mark the base of the parapet walls, which have rounded copings. At each end of the bridge the walls sweep out and terminate at ashlar piers. An inscription on the parapet records the building of the bridge by H. W. Portman in 1795, the architect being Joseph Towsey.

(3) KNIGHTON HOUSE (85920813) is a building of two storeys with rendered walls, a low-pitched slated roof and sashed windows. It was built about 1840 and is now a school.

(4) COTTAGE (85830846), 50 yds. S.W. of the church, is two-storied with a thatched roof and is of 17th-century origin. The walls, of knapped flint with stone dressings in the lower storey, include much repair in brickwork; part of the upper storey is timber-framed, elsewhere it is of brick. One ground-floor window on the N.E. side is of four lights with a chamfered and hollow-chamfered stone head and mullions; it has leaded glazing. The other windows are modern.

(5) HOUSE (85740884) is of two storeys with rendered walls and a partly thatched roof. The S.W. range may be of the late 17th or early 18th century.

(6) DURWESTON MILL HOUSE (85930890), of the late 18th century, is a two-storied English-bonded brick building with attics in a slated roof. A service wing to the S.W. was added in the 19th century. The symmetrical N.E. front has a central doorway, one large sashed window on each side, three smaller sashed windows on the first floor and two dormer windows above. The stairs have turned and moulded newel posts and lattice-work balustrades. A cast lead pump-head with the initials H.W.P. is dated 1776. Some moulded window stones in the garden are said to have come from old Durweston Church.

(7) KNIGHTON FARM HOUSE (85850858), 50 yds. N. of the church, has as its nucleus a two-storied late 18th-century brick house with slated roofs. It has a W. front of three bays, a central front doorway and casement windows. A brick plat-band occurs at first-floor level.

MONUMENTS (8–11)

The following cottages have walls of brick, flint and cob, often rendered, brick chimneystacks and thatched roofs; they are mostly single-storied with dormer-windowed attics. They are of the 18th century.

(8) *Cottage* (85850864), 110 yds. N. of the church, has heavy ashlar quoin stones in the S. corner, but these are now concealed by rendering.

(9) *Cottage* adjoining the N.E. side of the foregoing and facing S.E. is of the early 18th century.

(10) *Cottages*, row of four, face N.E., 40 yds. S. of the church. The most northerly has three sashed windows on the first floor and, on the ground floor, a door-hood which is supported on reused wooden consoles with foliate carving.

(11) *Cottage* (85880865) is of the late 18th century with a later extension to the W.

Buildings of the 19th century include the following—*Durweston Farm* (85740870), a two-storied farmhouse with rendered walls and tiled roofs; the original house, facing N.E., dates from about 1830; extensions to the N.W. and at the rear are of the middle of the century. A *House* (85950864), is two-storied with rendered walls and slated roofs. A *Range* of brick dwellings (85860869) is of the mid 19th century and were probably tenements of the Bryanston estate. The *Dairy House* (86090827) has as its nucleus a small 19th-century brick cottage, symmetrically windowed and perhaps originally a gate lodge of Bryanston House. *Shepherd's Corner Farm* (83550789), 1½ m. W. of the church, is of banded brick and flint with a tiled roof; it dates from *c.* 1840.

MEDIAEVAL AND LATER EARTHWORKS

(12) CULTIVATION REMAINS. It is probable that originally both Durweston and Knighton had separate open fields, but by 1580 there was only one system for both villages (map of Durweston *c.* 1580, copy in D.C.R.O.); enclosure took place some time after 1580, but before the 19th century.

E. and N. of Norton Wood (853089 and 849091) and S. of Norton Lane (853086) are three blocks of contour strip lynchets up to 400 yds. long and now ploughed down. To W. of Knighton House (854081) on both sides of a dry valley are well-preserved remains of fifteen contour and cross-contour strip lynchets, up to 250 yds. long. The upper three strip lynchets on the S. side of the valley run up to the hill top and fan out; on the resulting wide treads is ridge-and-furrow, 5 yds. to 7 yds. wide. The S.W. part of this group overlies 'Celtic' fields (Group (60)). S.W. of Four Acre Coppice (860074) are five fragmentary contour strip lynchets.

ROMAN AND PREHISTORIC

'CELTIC' FIELDS, *see* p. 341, Group (60).

BARROWS, two, W. of The Folly (842082) were opened by J. H. Austen *c.* 1860, but there is now no trace of them. One contained a central (? primary) inhumation surrounded by 'a walling of large flints', and an empty cist at a higher level; the other, a very small mound, contained only an empty cist, cut 4 ft. into the natural chalk (*C.T.D.*, *Pt. 2*, Nos. 28 and 29).

17 FIFEHEAD NEVILLE (7610)

(O.S. 6 ins. ST 70 NE, ST 71 SE)

The irregularly shaped parish covers 1,350 acres, undulating between 200 ft. and 300 ft. above sea-level. The land is drained by the R. Divelish in the E. and by a minor tributary of the R. Lydden in the W. Most of the parish is on Corallian Beds but there is a narrow strip of Kimmeridge Clay in the E. and S.E., and an area of Oxford Clay in the W. around Deadmoor Common. Until 1920 the parish was divided into two distinct parts, each with its own settlement; to the N. was Fifehead Neville, and to the S. was Lower Fifehead or Fifehead St. Quentin, a detached part of the former parish of Belchalwell. Each village presumably had its own mediaeval open fields. Woodrow, a later settlement on the edge of Deadmoor Common, is first recorded in the 14th century.

The most important monument in the parish is an extensive Roman Villa and its outbuildings.

ECCLESIASTICAL

(1) THE PARISH CHURCH OF ALL SAINTS, in the N. part of the village, has walls of rubble with ashlar dressings in local limestone and Greensand; the roofs are tiled. The 14th-century chancel arch indicates a *Chancel* and a *Nave* of that date. The *North Aisle* was added in *c.* 1500, and in 1736 new windows were inserted in the S. wall of the nave and in the N. wall of the aisle; the *Porch* also is of 1736. A former W. tower was demolished and the tower arch was blocked up, probably in the same year. The chancel was rebuilt in 1873.

Architectural Description—Above the apex of the 19th-century three-light E. window of the *Chancel* is a reset label-stop in the form of a bishop's head, probably a Gothic-revival work of the 18th century but of unknown provenance; above is the date stone of the 1873 reconstruction. Of the two windows in the N. wall, the W. includes elements of another 18th-century Gothic window; as restored it has two trefoil-headed lights and a central quatrefoil; over these is a hollow-chamfered label with head-stops representing a king and a bishop. The S. wall is entirely of 1873. The 14th-century chancel arch is two-centred and has two continuous chamfered orders; parts of both responds have been cut away on the W. side.

The *Nave* (27 ft. by 15 ft.) has a N. arcade of *c.* 1500, of three two-centred arches, each of two orders, the inner wave-moulded and the outer hollow-chamfered; these spring from moulded hollow-chamfered capitals enriched on the chamfer with leaf paterae and lozenges. The columns comprise four attached shafts and four hollow-chamfers. The E. respond is similar except that the capital is embellished with an angel, partly defaced; the W. respond has a corbelled shaft with a polygonal capital. The S. wall is of coursed rubble with ashlar dressings; at the S.E. corner is a two-stage buttress of *c.* 1500. On each side of the S. doorway is a round-headed 18th-century window with plain jambs and archivolt, projecting impost blocks and keystone; the leaded panes retain much original glass. The S. doorway, of *c.* 1500, has a chamfered four-centred head and continuous jambs; a large horizontal stone with faint traces of eliminated decoration, possibly a former cross-shaft, is built into the wall about 1 ft. above it. A weathered buttress of five stages at the S.W. corner of the nave is of the 18th century. The W. wall of the nave is rendered inside and out but shows traces of a blocked opening, which is presumably the arch of a former tower. The W. gable culminates in a small 18th or 19th-century bell-cote with one bell. The N. wall of the *North Aisle* (9 ft. wide) has two round-headed windows uniform with those of the nave. In the S.E. corner of the aisle, about 5 ft. above the floor, is a disused rood-loft doorway with a chamfered four-centred head. The *South Porch* ($5\frac{1}{2}$ ft. by $4\frac{1}{2}$ ft.) has a square-headed ashlar opening with a keystone on which is carved the date 1736.

FIFEHEAD NEVILLE
The parish church of All Saints

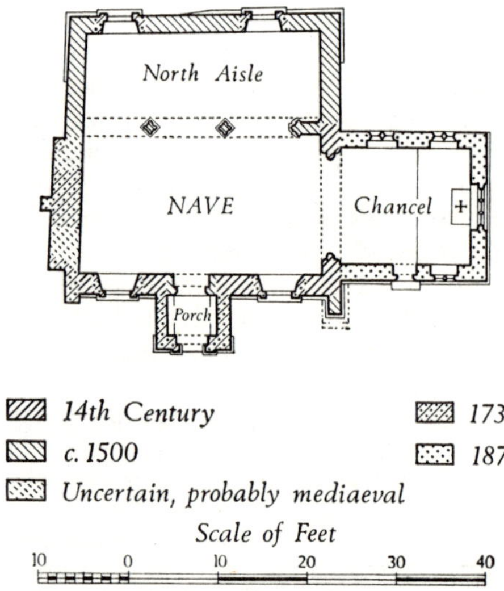

Fittings—*Benefactor's Table:* On W. wall, slate tablet in moulded stone surround recording benefaction of Roger Goodfellow, 1730. *Communion Rails:* with turned oak balusters, moulded rail and concealed centre gate, late 17th century. *Door:* In S. doorway, of oak, with vertical outside boards fastened with iron studs to horizontal inner boards; with iron strap hinges, early 16th century. *Font:* octagonal bowl of grey Purbeck stone chamfered underneath and resting on a pedestal of Greensand, square at base and octagonal above, with carved stops; 14th century, bowl retooled. *Glass:* Reset in tracery of E. window, quarry with date 1464.

Monuments and *Floor-slabs. Monuments:* In nave, on S. wall, (1) of William Salkeld, 1715, draped cartouche with Latin inscription and arms of Salkeld, with inescutcheon of Ryves; (2) of William Salkeld, 1782, marble tablet. In N. aisle, on N. wall, (3) of Robert Ryves, 1658, Anne Ryves, 1672, and their son Robert, 1673, marble tablet in painted clunch surround with arms of Ryves, erected *c.* 1673 (Plate 33); (4) probably of a member of the Rawles family and of the 17th century, illegible clunch tablet with pilasters, mask and strapwork decoration. In churchyard, N. of N. aisle, (5) mausoleum of Brune family in form of large table-tomb with inscriptions from 1707 to 1760, and arms of Brune impaling several others. *Floor-slabs:* In N. aisle, (1) of William Harbin, 1678; (2) of an infant son of John and Mary Ryves, 1681. *Panelling:* Nave and aisle lined to level of window-sills with 18th-century fielded oak panelling, probably reset woodwork of former box pews. *Plate:* includes silver cup and cover-paten of usual Elizabethan form with date-letter for 1571; also two pewter alms-dishes, 18th century. *Pulpit:* with fielded oak panels and moulded cornice and ledge, 18th century.

SECULAR

(2) FOOTBRIDGE (77181114), over the river Divelish, is probably mediaeval although much restored; it is of coursed rubble, 6 ft. wide, and spans 34 ft. The two pointed arches, practically straight-sided, rest on a central pier with a cut-water on the upstream side only (Plate 51). The kerb is of rubble stones set on edge.

(3) THE MANOR HOUSE, a few paces W. of the church, is two-storied, with rendered walls and slated roofs. It dates from the late 17th century but has been much altered and retains few features that are earlier than the 19th century. Some 18th-century wrought-iron casement-windows occur in the E. wall of the kitchen wing, and the dining-room contains a late 17th-century moulded and beaded plank-and-muntin partition. The *Stables* are of the late 18th century. A Roman *Column* set up in the garden is described below; *see* Monument (13).

(4) LOWER FIFEHEAD FARM (77291040), house, ½ m. S. of (2), is two-storied and of coursed rubble with slated roofs. The L-shaped plan incorporates a nucleus which appears to be of the late 16th or early 17th century. The N.W. front has, on the ground floor, a hollow-chamfered stone mullioned window of four lights with four-centred heads in an ogee-moulded surround with a moulded label. The first floor has two similar windows of three-centred lights below cable-moulded labels; another such window occurs on the ground floor of the S.E. front. All other windows and doorways are modern. Internally there are some stop-chamfered ceiling beams. The adjacent farm buildings are of the early 19th century and include a weather-boarded *Granary* on staddle stones and a rubble *Cowshed* with lunette windows.

(5) HOUSE (77171019), is now two-storied with rendered rubble walls, modern openings and a modern tiled roof, but it was until recently single-storied with attics. The plan comprises three rooms, perhaps originally with a through-passage. Stone-mullioned window frames and other 17th-century features were recently removed.

(6) FIFEHEAD FARM, house, 50 yds. E. of the church, has a late 17th or early 18th-century nucleus consisting of a single-storied rubble cottage of two rooms; it was extended W. in the later 19th century.

(7) COTTAGE, 90 yds. S.S.E. of the church, of one storey with rubble walls and dormer-windowed attics in a modern tiled roof, is of the late 17th or early 18th century.

MONUMENTS (8–11)

The following 18th and 19th-century buildings have rubble walls and are of two storeys, or of one storey with dormer-windowed attics; (8) has a tiled roof, the others are thatched.

(8) *Fifehead Mill* stands 100 yds. S.W. of (2). The mill-house dates from the early 18th century and has modern brick additions. The water mill, of rubble with an iron roof, now contains a turbine engine.

(9) *Cottages*, three, 30 yds. W. of (8), are now a single house. The middle tenement is of the 18th century and the two end ones are of the 19th century.

(10) *Cottage* (75961084), is of the 18th century. A room lies on each side of the central entrance passage and the chimneys are in the end walls.

(11) *Cottages* (75991090), two adjacent, are of the late 18th century.

MEDIAEVAL AND LATER EARTHWORKS

(12) CULTIVATION REMAINS. Nothing is known of the date of enclosure of the two former open field systems within the present parish. Traces of ridge-and-furrow, arranged in curving furlongs and corresponding neither with the existing nor with the Tithe Map field boundaries, can be seen on air photographs (R.A.F. CPE/UK 1974; 2179–84 and 3178–81); they lie S. of Lower Fifehead (774096). Ridge-and-furrow exists in old closes W. of the Manor House (765110); the ridges are 6 yds. to 8 yds. wide, with headlands 9 yds. wide.

ROMAN AND PREHISTORIC

(13) ROMAN VILLA. A mosaic pavement was found in 1881 about 90 ft. E. of the R. Divelish, N. of Fifehead Mill (77281121). It lay on Corallian limestone some 210 ft. above O.D. In 1902–5 this pavement was re-excavated, two more mosaics were exposed and a further wing of an extensive building was traced.

The wing containing the mosaics was orientated E. to W. and measured over 120 ft. by 50 ft., with rooms projecting to the S. at both ends.[1] The E. and W. extremities were apparently not fully cleared and the building probably continued further to the W. There appears to have been a range of five or more large rooms with corridors to the N. and S.; that to the S. was divided by three cross-walls and was 9 ft. wide.

At the W. end, the floor found in 1881 occupied a room measuring 13 ft. by 12 ft. The design (Plate 133) consisted of a two-handled chalice set in a circle within two concentric borders, the inner containing seven fish and the outer, wider band, four dolphins. The circle and borders were set in a square and the four triangular spaces at the corners were filled with patterns of stylised leaves. At the N. and S. were strips of dentil pattern and the whole was surrounded by a border of crowstep pattern in red and white within a plain edging of blue-grey tesserae. The colours of the main panel were red, brown and blue-grey on a white ground.

To the S. of this room was a rectangular plunge bath (9 ft. by 4 ft.) with sides of red cement and a bottom of large tiles. In it was found the limestone column which is now set up at the Manor House (3); it is 5 ft. 1½ ins. long, including the moulded capital and base (Plate 133). There was a lead outlet pipe 2¾ ins.

[1] Two plans exist, both drawn in 1904 but differing in details and measurements. One, by Miss M. E. Hartley, is preserved in the Dorset County Museum; the other, made for Messrs Rawlence and Squarey probably by J. E. Batchelor, is in the Digby Estate Office at Sherborne. The latter forms the basis of the accompanying plan. There are also two drawings of the best preserved mosaic, by Miss Hartley and by C. H. Goater, both in D.C.M.; the former is used for Plate 133, since a note by J. E. Acland and photographs suggest that it is the more accurate of the two.

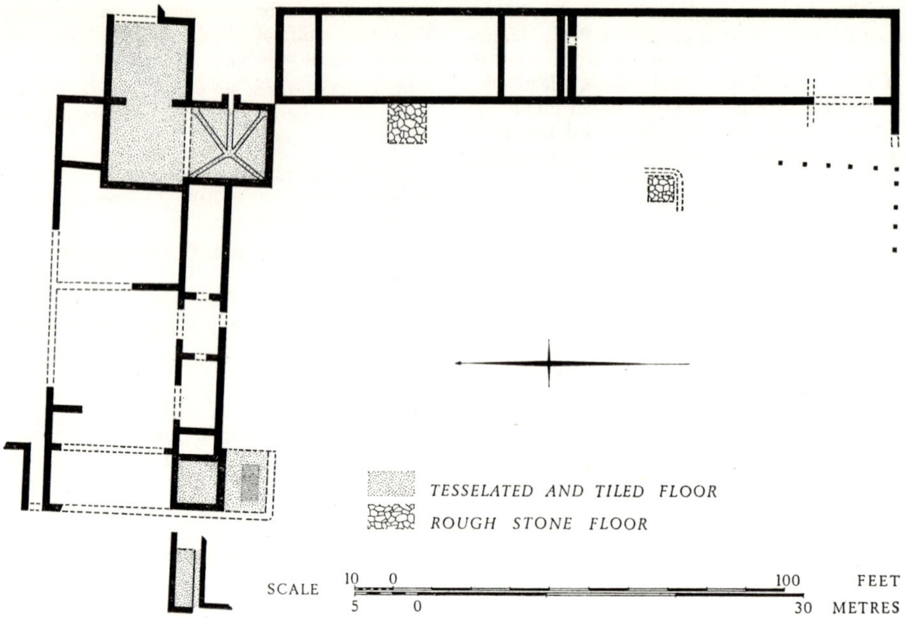

(13) Roman Villa at Fifehead Neville (after plan in Digby Estate Office).

in diameter at the bottom of the bath. To the W. of the first room were the pilae of a hypocaust system which had supported a white mosaic floor. A large column base was found in position some distance away.

The principal discoveries of 1902–5 were made at the E. end of the same block. The mosaic floor of a room 19½ ft. square had a design consisting of a central roundel containing a female bust with a staff or spear, surrounded by geometric designs (Plate 133). Some tesserae were of Kimmeridge shale. There was evidence for a concrete floor under the pavement, possibly of an earlier phase.

To the E. of this room another of similar size was reached through an opening 12 ft. wide. Only fragments of the mosaic pavement remained, including a circle with a palmette star and a border with a double pelta pattern, both designs being in red on white. A room to the S. measured 19 ft. by 17 ft. and its damaged mosaic floor, with a design of 'heads in a circle', was carried on a hypocaust with five channels radiating from the centre, four running to the angles of the room and the fifth to a stokehole in the E. wall.

To the S.E. of the main block, a building 160 ft. long by 24 ft. wide ran N. to S. This may be interpreted as two barns, of which the northern was divided into a central room 46 ft. long flanked by rooms 8 ft. and 12 ft. long. A series of post-holes, 5 ft. apart, continued the line of the S. wall of the S. barn and another series apparently ran parallel to the W. wall, 14 ft. from it. A ditch 3 ft. wide at the bottom with an outer scarp 6 ft. wide and 3 ft. high enclosed the buildings and court on the N., S. and E.

The finds included coins of Trajan and of Gallienus to Gratian. The principal discovery was a hoard, buried in the floor of a room at the W. end of the main block, consisting of two silver rings (*see* below), a silver necklace or girdle fastener, nine bronze bracelets and fragments of others. Each ring bore on the bezel a *Chi-Rho*, in one case below a dove and olive branches. Window glass, roofing tiles and stone roofing slabs, painted wall plaster with blue, white, green, black and red designs, brooches and shale beads were also found. Some of the finds survive, including five bracelets in the D.C.M. and roofing tiles in the B.M. (*P.S.A.* Ser. ii, VIII (1881), 543; IX (1882), 66; Dorset *Procs.* XXIV (1903), 172–7; L (1928), 92–6; also unpublished notes, plans and photographs in D.C.M. and Society of Antiquaries Library, London).

Fifehead Neville.
Bezels of silver rings.

18 GLANVILLE'S WOOTTON (6708)

(O.S. 6 ins. ST 60 NE)

The parish, covering 1,660 acres, rises gently from 250 ft. above sea-level at the Caundle Brook, which constitutes the N.W. boundary, to over 450 ft. in the S.E. The N. part of the parish lies on Oxford Clay; the central part is on Corallian Limestone and Gault Clay; the higher land on Dungeon Hill in the S.E. is Chalk, an outlier of the main escarpment. The land is drained by tributaries of the Caundle Brook, flowing N. and N.W.

The village, at the junction of the Oxford Clay and the Corallian Limestone, was probably once surrounded by open fields. Secondary settlements, Osehill and

Newlands, now Round Chimneys Farm,[1] lie N.W. and N. of the village. In the E. part of the parish is an area which also bears the name Newlands, but here the regularity of the fields indicates enclosure of a very late date; the fields are not shown on the Tithe Map of 1839 and houses at Over Newlands and Pitt's Farms are dated 1847 by inscription.

ECCLESIASTICAL

(1) THE PARISH CHURCH OF ST. MARY stands to the E. of the village. The oldest surviving part is the 14th-century *South Chapel*, which presumably corresponds with an endowment of 17 Oct. 1344 (*Cal. Patent Rolls*, 1343–1345, p. 343) wherein Sibyl de Glaunvyll alienates certain lands to a chaplain, who is to say mass daily at the altar of St. Mary in the parish church of Wootton Glanville. The *West Tower* is of *c.* 1400. The *Chancel* and *Nave* were of the 15th century but the chancel was rebuilt and the nave was extensively restored in 1876; drawings of the antecedent buildings are preserved in the faculty petition (Salisbury Diocesan Archives, 1875); the *South Porch* is of the 15th century, with some restoration. The South Chapel has walls of knapped flint with Ham Hill ashlar dressings and bonding courses, and a copper-covered roof; the rest of the church is of coursed rubble with ashlar dressings and is roofed with stone slates.

The South Chapel is a notable example of 14th-century architecture, well preserved and not greatly altered from its original form.

Architectural Description—The *Chancel* (22 ft. by 15 ft.) retains nothing original except a very large squint from the S. chapel; it has a segmental vault with three chamfered ribs resting to the E. on two original head-corbels and one original leaf-corbel; some of the ashlar lining of the squint is original but the N. front with embattled cresting is of 1876. The chancel arch has been entirely rebuilt.

The N. wall of the *Nave* (37 ft. by 17 ft.) was rebuilt in 1876 but following the lines of the former structure, which appears to have been of the 15th century. Over the N. doorway is a reset 15th-century head-stop; the western window has two similar head-stops. Except where it incorporates the N. side of the S. chapel, the S. wall of the nave is also of 15th-century origin, to some extent rebuilt in 1876. The S. doorway has a chamfered two-centred head and continuous jambs; the rear arch is triangular and surmounted by a rough relieving arch in rubble. W. of the S. doorway the nave has a square-headed two-light window of 1876.

The *South Chapel* (21½ ft. by 14 ft.) has, externally, a massive plinth of two stages, weathered below and with a moulded capping. The E. wall has a low-pitched gable parapet with a weathered ashlar coping and a cross-gabled apex stone with an original floriate cross-finial. The S.E. corner is strengthened by three-stage angle-buttresses with moulded and weathered offsets; the weathered plinth returns around the buttresses but the moulded upper plinth stops against them. At the N.E. corner the remains of another buttress are embedded in the chancel wall. The pointed E. window is of three lights with curvilinear tracery; externally the chamfered and hollow-chamfered head and continuous jambs are surmounted by a moulded label with head-stops; the tracery, chamfered inside and out, is restored but probably repeats the original. Of the three main lights the middle one is slightly wider than the other two and has a round head and cinquefoil cusping; the side lights have ogee heads and trefoil cusping. Internally the window has a splayed and ogee-moulded two-centred rear arch above square-set jambs which are decorated with half-round shafts with moulded caps and bases, the latter restored; splayed corbels carry the rear arch over the square-set jambs. The N. wall of the chapel has, at the E. end, the restored opening of the squint to the chancel. Further W. it is pierced by a large four-centred arch (Plate 138) which formerly spanned a tomb in the thickness of the wall; the arch was taken down and rebuilt in 1876 and the mouldings are of this period, but the chamfered and hollow-chamfered inner order rests to the E. on an original moulded corbel and to the W. on an attached half-shaft with a similar capital; parts of the label are also original.

[1] Hutchins III, 744; Fägersten, 208; C. W. Dale, *History of Glanville's Wootton* (1878), 8.

GLANVILLE'S WOOTTON *The parish church of St. Mary*

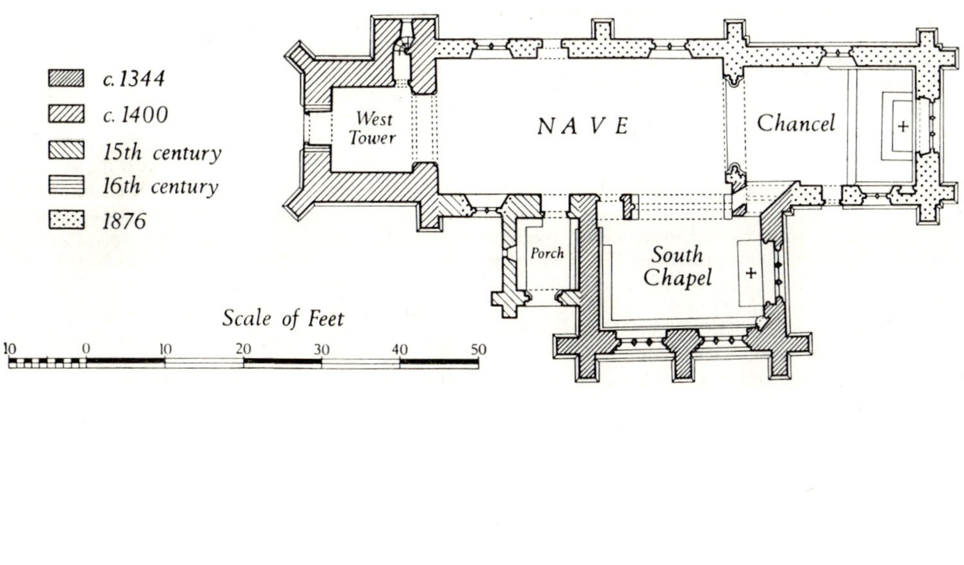

The doorway to the chapel, near the N.W. corner, has a hollow-chamfered two-centred head with continuous chamfered jambs; the rear arch is segmental-pointed and moulded.

The S. wall of the chapel has a square-set buttress corresponding with the angle-buttresses described; at the eaves is a hollow-chamfered ashlar string-course. The S. windows are of the 14th century, each having three cinquefoil-headed lights below tracery in a two-centred head, with internal mouldings like those of the E. window but externally with deeper reveals. The tracery of the window to the E. is geometric while that to the W. is curvilinear (Plate 140). Internally the windows have ogee-moulded two-centred rear arches above half-round jamb shafts with moulded capitals and bases, as in the E. window. The window-sills are moulded and continue from bay to bay, forming an internal string-course. Below them are two tomb recesses each with a moulded segmental head; the mouldings die into chamfered jambs which end in broach stops above the tomb tops. The latter extend forward and continue from side to side in the form of a wall bench. The S.W. corner has angle buttresses as described before and the W. wall of the chapel has a gabled coping like that to the E.; the plinth continues inside the 15th-century S. porch. Internally, the moulded string-course formed by the sill of the S. windows continues across the W. wall, as does the wall bench. The 19th-century timber roof is supported on a transverse beam which rests, to the N., on an original head-corbel of a woman in a wimple and to the S. on a male head-corbel.

The *West Tower* (10½ ft. by 10 ft.) is of two stages outside and of three storeys inside. In the lower stage, diagonal two-stage buttresses with weathered offsets strengthen the N.W. and S.W. corners and a square-set buttress stands at the S.E. corner; a square vice turret projects from the N.E. corner. At the base a moulded and chamfered plinth returns around the buttresses and turret; between the stages a hollow-chamfered string-course terminates against the buttresses just below their summit and a similar string-course with a gargoyle at each corner marks the foot of the parapet. The latter is embattled, with a continuous moulded coping, and each corner has a crocketed finial. The tower arch is of two two-centred orders, the inner chamfered and dying into the responds at the springing, the outer wave-moulded and continuing on the jambs. The vice doorway has a chamfered four-centred head with continuous jambs and run-out stops. The W. doorway is of the 16th century and has a chamfered four-centred head with continuous jambs and a chamfered segmental rear arch. Above it is a two-centred W. window of *c.* 1400 with two cinquefoil-headed lights below a quatrefoil; the label has square stops. In the lower stage, the S. wall of the tower has one small square-headed chamfered window, lighting the intermediate storey. In the top stage each face has a two-centred belfry window of two trefoil-headed lights below a quatrefoil; there are no labels. The windows are closed by latticed stone slabs with embattled tops, perhaps inserted later.

The *South Porch* (9 ft. by 8 ft.) is of the late 15th century and has a two-centred arch with double ogee mouldings, casement mouldings and hollow chamfers, uniform inside and out; the S.W. corner of the porch has small two-stage angle buttresses. In the W. wall is a narrow window with a chamfered trefoil head and sunk spandrels.

Fittings—*Altar:* In S. chapel, Purbeck marble slab (8 ft. by 3 ft.) with hollow-chamfered under-edge, 14th century, restored to embrasure of E. window and mounted on modern pedestals. *Bells:* four; 2nd, dated 1700, inscribed 'Thos. Knight, John Crake'; tenor, early 15th century, inscribed 'ave Maria' in Lombardic capitals; others modern. *Brackets:* In S. Chapel, N. of E. window, circular moulded corbel; S. of E. window, polygonal moulded corbel, both 14th century. *Chairs:* In chancel, of oak, one with turned and moulded front legs and arm uprights, scrolled arms, carved back-panel with arcading and fan ornament, arcaded rails and scroll cresting, early 17th century; another, similar, with moulded rails, arm uprights in form of columns, carved back-panel, top rail with scroll carving, and shaped cresting with rose at centre; mid 17th century. *Chest:* Of oak with moulded stiles and rails, panelled front and moulded edge to top; inside, locker with three locks, 18th century. *Door:* To tower vice, with vertical outer planks fastened to horizontal inner planks by iron studs, original strap hinges, late 15th century. *Font:* Octagonal Purbeck marble bowl, uniform with that of Cheselbourne (p. 75), on cylindrical Purbeck marble pedestal surrounded by eight detached cylindrical shafts; octagonal Purbeck marble base with chamfered edges; early 13th century. *Glass:* In S. windows of S. Chapel, tracery lights with small figures of angels, 15th century, also reset fragments, 15th and 16th century.

Monuments and *Floor-slabs. Monuments:* In chancel, reset on N. wall, (1) of Rev. Humphrey Evans, 1813, wall monument with urn and arms, by T. King of Bath; reset on S. wall, (2) of Thomas Mew, 1672, rector, plain stone slab with bold Roman lettering. In S. Chapel, below S.E. window, (3) tomb recess described above, with recumbent stone effigy of man clad in long military-like surcoat with short sleeves, tippet and hood (Plate 14); feet spurred and resting on dog or lion; at left side dagger and sword slung from belt buckled over the hips; late 13th century, face restored; before 1876 this effigy lay in archway in N. wall of S. Chapel. In S. Chapel on W. wall, (4) of Barbara Henley [1727], white marble monument with lozenge of arms (*dismantled*); (5) of John Every of Cothay, Somerset, 1679, and his mother Anne (Williams) Hurding [1670], large wall monument of painted clunch (Plate 35) with grey marble inscription tablet; console brackets flanking a panelled base with a scrolled apron support free-standing Corinthian columns on each side of the main panel, enclosed in a shaped surround with architrave mouldings; the columns support an entablature with masks, above which in an attic storey are two oval panels, one with a text, the other commemorating Anne Hurding; above, a broken curved pediment flanked by a male and a female kneeling figure in 17th-century dress has, at the centre, an achievement-of-arms of Every and Williams quarterly impaling Every and Trenchard paly; the crest is missing. In tower, on N. wall, (6) of James Dale, 1833, by Knight of Blandford; (7) of Anne Hurding [1670], painted stone panel with coarse scrollwork border and shaped apron, surmounted by four shields in strapwork cartouches: to left, (i) Hurding of Long Bredy; to right, (ii) Every; in middle, (iii) large shield with (i) impaling Williams; at top, (iv) small shield of Williams; (8) of Mary Williams [1654], round-headed wall monument of painted clunch with largely obliterated inscription on square panel in moulded border, with repainted shield-of-arms: quarterly (i) Williams, (ii) Delalynde, (iii) Herring, (iv) Syward, impaling quarterly Carent and Every; (9) of John Leigh, 1752, and Elizabeth Leigh, 1783, white marble tablet; on S. wall, (10) of [John Every, 1658], painted clunch tablet with obliterated inscription (Hutchins III, 747) in Corinthian architectural surround above which are the following arms: to left and right lozenges of Every and Williams; in centre, achievement of Every impaling Williams, with crest of Every; (11) of [George Williams, 1660], wall monument uniform with foregoing, with obliterated inscription (Hutchins, *l.c.*) and, at top, achievement-of-arms of Williams. In churchyard, 11 paces S. of tower, (12) of Mary Gillingham, 1737, table-tomb; 2 paces from N. doorway, (13) of Elizabeth Harben, 1746, and her mother Elizabeth, 1735, double headstone; 3 paces from vice turret, (14) of Mary Mayo, 1729, headstone. *Floor-slabs:* In chancel, underneath communion table, (1) of Margaret Allen, 1662, with additional inscription of Nicholas Rickard, rector,

From S.W.

Air view from N.E.

CHILD OKEFORD. (22) Hambledon Hill-fort. Iron Age

CHESELBOURNE. (2) Lyscombe Chapel and Cottage, from S. 12th-century and later

DEWLISH. (7) Court Close earthworks, from E. Mediaeval

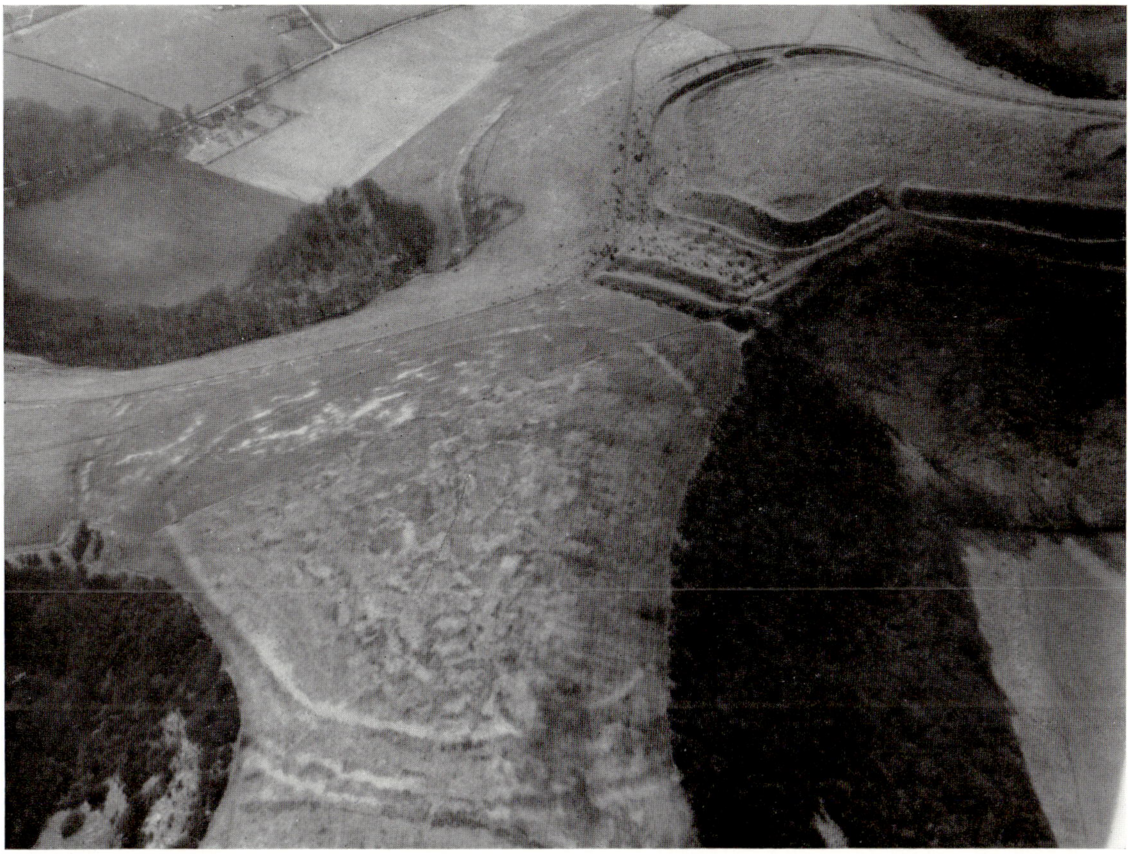

IWERNE COURTNEY. (19) Causewayed Camp. Neolithic

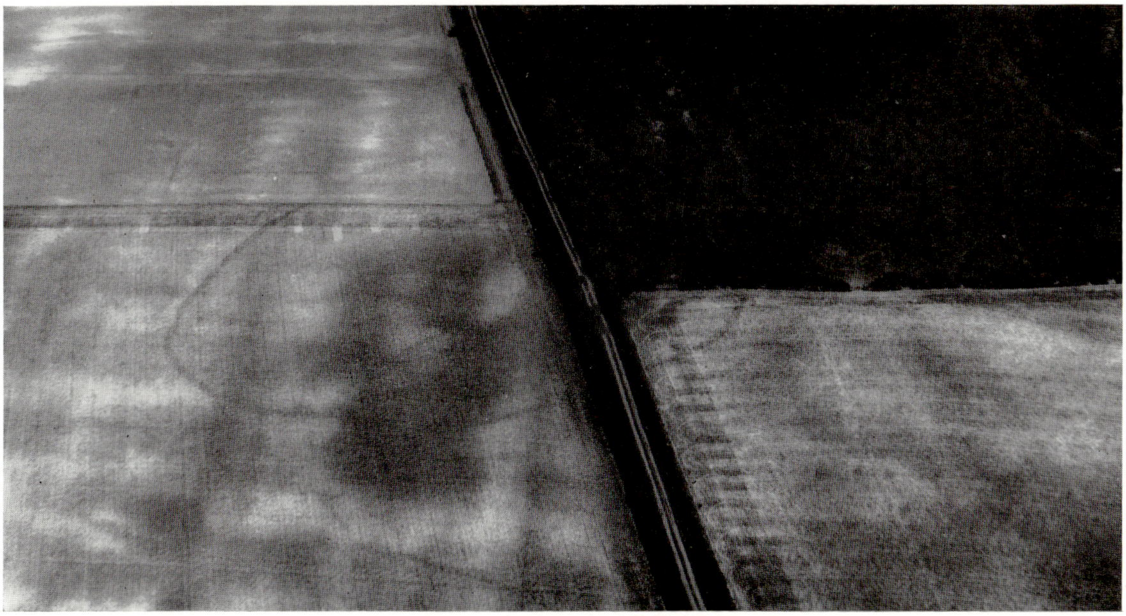

CHESELBOURNE. (40) Cropmark of Enclosure at parish boundary with Dewlish. Undated

CHILD OKEFORD. (24) Long Barrow on Hambledon Hill. Neolithic

MILBORNE ST. ANDREW. (30) Deverel Barrow at time of excavation (W. A. Miles, *op. cit.*). Bronze Age

Limestone column.

Painting of mosaic discovered in 1881.

Painting of mosaic pavement discovered in 1902-5.

FIFEHEAD NEVILLE. (13) Roman Villa. 4th-century

HAMMOON. (2) Manor House. S. Front.

16th-century

HANFORD. (2) Hanford House. N. Front.

Early 17th-century

HANFORD (2) Hanford House. Porch. Early 17th-century

PUDDLETOWN. (3) Waterston House. Porch. 17th-century

HAMMOON. (2) Manor House. Porch. *c.* 1560

1707, with incised architectural framework and arms of Coles impaling *six lions*. At foot of sanctuary steps, (2) of Elenor Williams, 1627. In centre of chancel, (3) of Katherine Williams, 1645, with incised architectural decoration. Under tower arch, (4) of Mary Williams, 1631. In tower, (5) of John Pine, 1643; (6) of Ursula Pine, 1639.

Piscinae: two; one reset in S. wall of chancel, with double-chamfered cinquefoil ogee head and quatrefoil basin with drain outlet, 14th century; another set obliquely across S.E. corner of S. chapel, with ovolo-moulded ogee head with trefoil cusping and continuous moulded jambs, trefoil basin on splayed bracket with male head corbel, stone shelf dividing recess at half height (Plate 24), 14th century. *Plate:* includes silver cup and cover-paten without hallmarks, inscribed 'Kiddle, 1689, Churchwarden'; also silver paten of 1704 with inscription of 1755. *Sundial:* On W. buttress of S. wall of S. Chapel, scratch-dial with iron gnomon. *Tiles:* In S. Chapel, near E. wall, and in W. tomb recess, 6 ins. square, with white slip decoration depicting: hart and huntsman with bow, arrow and dogs (*see* p. 98); shields-of-arms of England, of Eleanor of Castile, of *two keys in saltire* below 'deo grac', perhaps See of Exeter, and *vair* (*see* p. 317); two tiles from a set of four depicting a rose with 'deo gracias'; shield-of-arms of Clare, Earl of Gloucester; also tiles with foliage, griffins, etc. (*see* p. xx); all 14th century.

SECULAR

(2) BRIDGE (67160875) over the Caundle Brook, ⅔ m. N.W. of the church, is of the late 18th or early 19th century. It is of coursed rubble, with two semicircular arches and a central pier with a cutwater; the coping is of weathered ashlar.

(3) THE MANOR HOUSE (68150853), ¼ m. N. of the church, is of two storeys with attics and has walls of rubble with ashlar dressings and slated roofs. The main part of the house was built in 1804 as an addition to a smaller 17th-century house.

The 19th-century wing has a symmetrical three-bay S.W. front with large sashed windows, and a round-headed doorway sheltered by a later glazed porch. The mansard roof has three dormer windows behind a parapet with a moulded cornice and ashlar coping. The older wing, to the N.E., has a symmetrical two-storied N.W. front of three bays with a central doorway, which has a chamfered four-centred head and continuous jambs. The ground-floor windows are square-headed and of four lights with hollow-chamfered stone mullions and jambs; those of the first floor are of three lights. The N.E. gable has a mullioned two-light attic window with a label. Continuing the line of the N.W. elevation, a single-storied extension has a doorway with a moulded four-centred head with continuous jambs and run-out stops. Inside, the rooms of the 19th-century wing have moulded plaster cornices with acanthus enrichment, and the doorways and window openings have reeded architraves with angle paterae; the stairs have open strings, plain balusters and a moulded mahogany hand-rail. The 17th-century wing has, in the S.W. room, a chamfered ceiling beam, and an open fireplace with ashlar quoins, brick sides and back and a chamfered timber bressummer; the same room contains some reset 17th-century oak panelling and an 18th-century round-headed niche with fluted pilasters, coved head and shaped shelves.

(4) THE RECTORY, 100 yds. W. of the church, is of two storeys with attics and has rubble walls partly rendered, with ashlar dressings; the roofs are slated, with stone-slate verges. The L-shaped house was built at two periods; the N. range, now at the back, is of *c.* 1780 and the main S. range is of *c.* 1800. The symmetrical five-bay S. front of the later range has sashed windows and a round-headed central doorway with a moulded architrave and a delicate festooned metal fanlight. The windows have moulded stone architraves and the corners of the façade have rusticated stone quoins, but apart from these features the wall-face is rendered. The end walls of the S. range are of rubble with ashlar gable copings above shaped kneelers. The N. range, also of rubbel, and with the roof at a lower level, has one four-light casement window with square-section stone mullions and jambs on each storey of its E. front. An early 19th-century brick cottage continues the line of the N. range.

(5) CHURCH FARM, house, 100 yds. N.E. of the church, is two-storied and has walls of coursed rubble with ashlar quoins and dressings. The house was built in the 16th century but the S. front was remodelled in the 19th century and rendered and fitted with sashed windows; the slated roofs are modern. The W. wall has, on the ground floor near the S.W. corner, but perhaps reset, a blocked doorway with a hollow-chamfered four-centred head, continuous jambs with run-out stops, foliate spandrels and a casement-moulded square surround. On the first floor, near the N.W. corner, is a small blocked window of one light with a hollow-chamfered four-centred head, continuous jambs, sunk spandrels, and a chamfered surround; when open, this window lit the upper part of a rectangular projection on the N. side of the house, perhaps a stair turret. The N. front has the presumed stair turret to the W. and a projecting N. wing to the E., both with heavy ashlar quoins. On the ground floor, in the middle, is a square-headed two-light window with hollow-chamfered jambs and mullion, and on the first floor towards the E. is a window of two four-centred lights with double hollow-chamfers. A small single-light four-centred window opens on the first floor of the N. wing. (Entry to this interesting 16th-century building was denied.)

(6) ROUND CHIMNEYS FARMHOUSE (68200946), nearly ¾ m. N. of the parish church, is now of two storeys (Plate 56), but drawings reproduced by Hutchins (III, opp. 744) show that the main block formerly had a gabled and dormer-windowed third storey. The walls are of rubble with ashlar dressings, but are rendered on the S.E., S.W. and part of the N.E. fronts; the roofs are partly of stone-slate and partly tiled. Hutchins (III, 745) records that the date 159– was formerly seen.

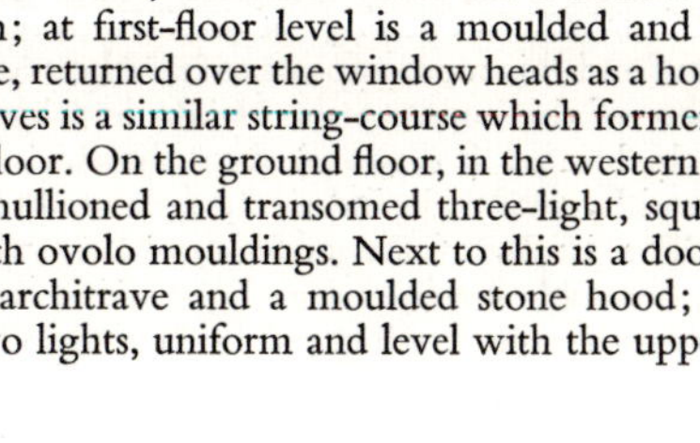

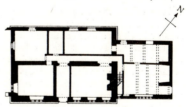

On the S.E. front, the main block has a hollow-chamfered ashlar plinth; at first-floor level is a moulded and weathered string-course, returned over the window heads as a hood-mould; under the eaves is a similar string-course which formerly marked the second floor. On the ground floor, in the western part of the front, is a mullioned and transomed three-light, square-headed window with ovolo mouldings. Next to this is a doorway with a moulded architrave and a moulded stone hood; above the hood are two lights, uniform and level with the upper lights of the adjacent three-light window. Next to the doorway is a two-light mullioned and transomed window uniform with the first; a precisely similar window occurs at the eastern end of the façade, and midway between these is a two-light window with no transom but with its flat head level with the transoms of the other openings. As one of the drawings in Hutchins shows, the last mentioned window and the doorway have been transposed and the S.E. façade originally had, from S.W. to N.E. on the ground floor, a three-light window, two two-light windows, a doorway and another two-light window; the windows were all transomed and of equal height; the doorway originally had no lights over it. All the first-floor windows are transomed; to the S.W. a three-light window corresponds with that of the ground floor and a two-light window opens above the present doorway; to the E. a similar three-light window opens above the place where the doorway originally was, but joints in the rendering show that it was formerly of five lights, as the drawing in Hutchins confirms. To the N.E., the S.E. front of the service wing is set back 2 ft. and although of two storeys it rises little higher than the first floor of the main block.

In the gabled N.E. wall of the service wing there is, on the ground floor, a doorway with moulded jambs and a shallow four-centred head; on the first floor, to the N.W., is a blocked three-light square-headed window, and in the attic are two blocked two-light windows, uniform with those of the S.E. front. The gable has a moulded coping above a shaped kneeler on the S.E. side and a cylindrical stone chimneystack at the apex; on the N.W. side the gable coping continues down to the level of the first floor. On the gabled N.E. wall of the main block, which stands higher than the service wing, the two string-courses of the S.E. front continue. The gable has a coping like that of the service wing and on the apex is a slightly smaller round chimneystack; it must have been transferred from one of the original gables when the second storey was removed; in Hutchins's drawings every gable culminates in a chimneystack. As with the service wing, the N.E. gable of the main block continues down on the N.W. side to the level of the first floor, the entire N.W. side of the house being single-storied. In the main block the N.W. wall is of rubble with a hollow-chamfered ashlar plinth at the base; to the S.W. is a square-headed doorway with moulded jambs and in the N.E. part are two casement windows. One of the drawings in Hutchins shows that this elevation was originally three-storied with irregularly disposed windows, including two lofty mezzanine windows which apparently lighted a staircase. In the N.W. wall of the service wing is a doorway with a shallow four-centred moulded head and continuous jambs.

The S.W. front of the main block is gabled like the N.E. front and again has a round chimneystack on the apex of the gable. The moulded string-courses continue from the S.E. front at both levels, but are cut away at the northern end. On the ground floor at the S.E. end is a mullioned and transomed two-light, square-headed window; to the N.W. is a two-light opening from which the mullion has been removed; the first floor has a single light near the N.W. end, with moulded head and jambs.

Inside, the original layout is obscure. A thick longitudinal wall divides the main block into two nearly equal parts, and a thick cross-wall defines a room in the south corner of the block. The four eastern openings of the S.E. front probably lit a single room and this room appears to have been closely linked with the part of the house to the N.W., in which a staircase was probably located (*see* above) since the thick longitudinal wall is pierced by two wide and richly decorated round-headed archways. The jambs of the archways have two orders of mouldings, a double ovolo and an ogee; these are capped by moulded imposts, above which are archivolts with the same mouldings as on the jambs; at the top are projecting keystones with pendant pyramidal soffits and fluted fronts.

Early and mid 19th-century monuments include the following—*Court Farm*, house, 400 yds. S. of the church, of one storey with attics, has rendered walls and a thatched roof and is of the early 19th century. *Wootton Glanville Farm*, house, 400 yds. W. of the church, is two-storied with coursed rubble walls and a tiled roof, and is of the mid 19th century; the openings of its symmetrical three-bay E. front have pointed heads. *Baskett's Farm*, house, 500 yds. N.W. of the church, is two-storied with rendered walls and a slated roof; it has a symmetrical three-bay S.E. front with large sashed windows and is of the mid 19th century. *Over Newland Farm* (69480845), house, *Pitt's Farm* (69220867), house, and *Blackmore Cottages* (68370959) are all two-storied, of coursed rubble with squared rubble dressings and slated roofs, and are similar to one another in constructional details.

MEDIAEVAL AND LATER EARTHWORKS

(7) CULTIVATION REMAINS. There is no evidence for open fields in the parish and they were certainly enclosed by 1770 (*see* two maps of Glanville's Wootton, by I. Taylor, 1770; copies in D.C.R.O.). Traces of ridge-and-furrow around the village can be seen on air photographs (R.A.F. CPE/UK 1974: 1190–94; 1975: 2043–6, 4042–6); where it remains, ridges are from 5 yds. to 7 yds. wide with headlands 6 yds. wide, all lying within existing field boundaries.

Tiles in Glanville's Wootton Church.

19 HAMMOON (8114)

(O.S. 6 ins. ST 81 SW)

The small parish of Hammoon, covering only 690 acres, lies in a bend of the R. Stour between Sturminster Newton and Shillingstone. It occupies a flat river terrace about 150 ft. above sea-level, except in the S. where it rises to 200 ft. on Kimmeridge Clay. The village stands at the edge of the river terrace. The open fields which formerly extended over most of the parish were enclosed before 1771.

ECCLESIASTICAL

(1) THE PARISH CHURCH OF ST. PAUL stands in the N. part of the village. It has walls of rubble with ashlar

dressings and the roofs are tiled, with stone-slate verges. The N. wall of the *Nave*, probably of the late 12th or early 13th century, is the only surviving part of the original church; it was aisleless certainly on the N. and it may have been a simple two-compartment building with chancel and nave both about 12 ft. wide. At an uncertain date a N. chapel was added, but this has long been demolished and only foundations survive. About the middle of the 13th century the *Chancel* was rebuilt on a larger scale than before, and a project to build a correspondingly larger nave was started; the S. wall of the nave was built, but the project was abandoned and the nave was left with its original N. wall, the axis thus falling about 4 ft. S. of that of the chancel. In the 15th century the old N. wall was provided with new windows and the nave was reroofed. In 1885 the chancel arch was rebuilt and the nave was extended to the W.

The church has a well-proportioned 13th-century E. window with good modern glass, and an interesting 15th-century nave roof. The communion rails, pulpit and reset reredos are noteworthy.

HAMMOON

The parish church of St. Paul

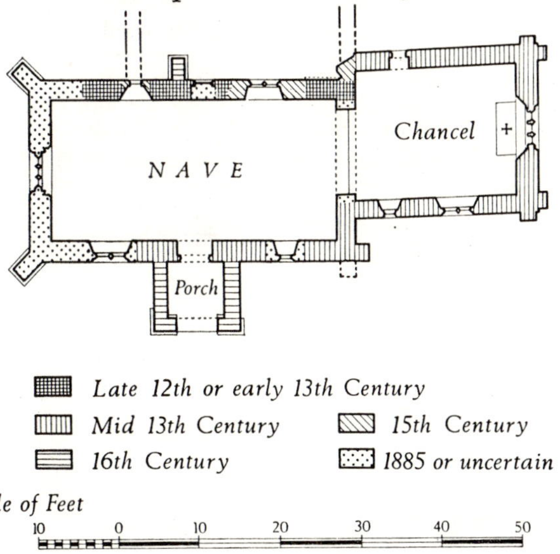

Architectural Description—The *Chancel* (20 ft. by 15¾ ft.) has single-stage angle-buttresses at the N.E. and S.E. corners. The E. window is of three gradated lancet lights under a chamfered two-centred head and a segmental-pointed rear-arch. Internally the lancet heads rest on shafts attached to the mullions and jambs, with roll-moulded caps but without base mouldings. The only opening in the N. wall is a narrow 13th-century doorway with a chamfered two-centred head; the upper part of the wall is restored. In the S. wall are two 13th-century trefoil-headed windows; that to the E. is of two lights with a quatrefoil above; it has chamfered jambs and a segmental-pointed rear-arch; the other is a single trefoil-headed light. The chancel floor was lowered to its 15th-century level in 1945, making it lower than the present nave floor.

The *Nave* (35½ ft. by 17 ft.) retains an original N. wall that is probably of the late 12th or early 13th century. At its junction with the chancel is an irregular mass of masonry, perhaps the remains of an inserted vice to a rood-loft; in the upper part it appears to retain the dressed reveal of a small window. Near it a weathered drip-course on the nave wall indicates the former existence of a low adjacent building, doubtless a N. chapel with a lean-to roof; a straight joint may indicate the E. jamb of an opening to it from the nave. Fragmentary footings of the E. and W. walls have recently been excavated. The eastern window of the N. wall of the nave is of the mid 15th century and has two cinquefoil-headed lights in a chamfered square-headed surround; adjacent is an original doorway of *c.* 1200, now blocked, with a chamfered two-centred head and continuous jambs. Beside the doorway is a 16th-century buttress of two weathered stages; further W. is a 15th-century window of one cinquefoil-headed light in wide splays which show that the opening itself is of the 12th or 13th century. The W. extremity of the N. wall is of the 19th century. The S. wall is of the mid 13th century; the S.E. corner has an original ashlar buttress running E. and traces of a corresponding buttress to the S., now cut back; adjacent is a late 19th-century window of one trefoil-headed light. The S. doorway is of the 12th or 13th century and has wide chamfered jambs; the monolithic segmental-pointed door-head is probably later. Further W. is a two-light window of 1885. The *South Porch* is of the 16th century and has a chamfered round-headed arch.

The timber *Roof* of the nave dates from the mid 15th century or perhaps a little later; it is supported on three trusses with moulded principals and cambered tie-beams. Main purlins lie half-way between the wall-plates and the ridge and are intersected at half length by moulded principal rafters. The square compartments so formed are sub-divided by secondary rafters and secondary purlins into four smaller rectangles so that each slope of the roof has thirty-two compartments; four additional compartments at the W. end were made in 1885. The principal intersections are decorated with wooden foliate bosses. Below the inclined members the wall-heads are decorated with embattled timber cornices at two levels.

Fittings—*Bells:* two; 1st, inscribed 'Maria' in Lombardic capitals, probably *c.* 1350; 2nd, with arms of Chertsey Abbey and ABCDEFG in black-letter, perhaps 16th century. *Brackets:* On N. wall of nave, 15th-century angel corbel. In porch, moulded square bracket with foliate terminal. *Chair:* of oak, with shaped front legs and arm-rests, moulded rails and conventional ornament on back rail; letters TE drilled on back panel, mid 17th century. *Chest:* of oak, with moulded lid, fluted top rail, and strap-hinges; early 17th century, restored 1913. *Communion Rails:* with stout oak balusters and beaded top rail, central gateway integral with balustrade, 17th century. *Door:* In S. doorway, with vertical oak boards outside and horizontal elm boards inside, nailed together and hung on strap-hinges with fleur-de-lis terminals; box lock (2½ ft. by ¾ ft.) out of a single block of oak; probably 15th century. *Font:* Octagonal bowl brought to square base by rounded stops; 14th century, on modern plinth.

Monuments and *Floor-slab. Monuments:* In nave, on S. wall, (1) of Henry Jenkins, 1826, plain marble slab with two-centred head, on painted back panel. In churchyard, S. of chancel, (2) of Mary Rideout, 1658, and Margaret Michel, 1659, table-tomb with panelled sides and moulded top; reset against porch, (3) of John Jenkins, 1814, and John Scutt, 1815, headstone with incised enrichment signed Robt. Domoney. *Floor-slab:* In chancel, to

S., of Mary Crowch, 1687, reset 1945. *Plate:* includes Elizabethan cup by the Gillingham silversmith, undated, and paten of 1830. *Pulpit:* Reassembly of oak panels with incised ornament of conventional foliage, guilloche and rosettes; panels in two heights separated by rails and styles enriched with cable pattern; cornice with conventional arcaded pattern; inscribed '1635 C.P.'. *Reredos:* of stone (5 ft. by 1¾ ft.) with seven pointed niches, the middle one cinquefoil-headed, the others trefoiled; central recess with Crucifixion, lateral recesses with figures of saints, spandrels with foliate enrichment; late 14th or early 15th century, purchased 1945, provenance unknown. *Stalls:* In chancel, incorporate fourteen early 16th-century oak panels carved with stylised fruit and foliage enclosed in ogee-headed borders (Plate 22). *Table:* In chancel, with roll-moulded rails and legs, early 18th century. *Miscellanea:* Set in wall close to pulpit, twisted wrought-iron hourglass-bracket, 17th century. Loose, sculptured head of cowled male figure lying in coffin (Plate 14), 14th century, removed from Hammoon Bridge in 1945. Reset in W. wall, fragments of glazed floor-tiles found in chancel in 1945, 13th century.

SECULAR

(2) THE MANOR HOUSE (81741460) is of two storeys with attics. The walls are of ashlar, rubble and timber-framing, the latter partly rendered and partly weather-boarded; the roofs are thatched. The S. range of the L-shaped plan is of the 16th century, the W. part being timber-framed and of the first half of the century while the E. part is of *c.* 1560; the later part is ashlar-fronted and appears to remain incomplete (Plate 134). The N.E. range was added in the 17th century.

The house retains interesting original joinery and the 16th-century ashlar front has good early Renaissance details. The continued use of thatch on so large a house is unusual.

The original S. range is of three bays. The S. front is rendered and may have been partly rebuilt but, to the W., some timber-framework has been discovered behind the rendering; the framework is set on a low plinth of rubble with a chamfered ashlar capping. At the W. end the framework terminates against a gabled end wall of squared rubble. The two-light and three-light mullioned windows of both storeys are of wood and of the 19th century. To the E., the S. wall butts against and is continued by the later 16th-century ashlar. This ashlar rises from a moulded plinth and is interrupted by a hollow-chamfered string-course below the first-floor window-sills. A polygonal angle-shaft defines the S.E. corner of the house and a corresponding shaft, some 20 ft. to the W., is partly concealed by the fabric of the porch. Presumably the intention was to build a gabled and pinnacled E. bay, outlined by ornamental angle-shafts, but it was never completed. A two-storey bay window is set midway between the angle-shafts; the stone mullions are recess-chamfered and the four-centred lights are set in square-headed casement-moulded surrounds. The ground-floor window has a hollow-chamfered label; in the upper storey the window is truncated by the eaves of the thatched roof immediately above the window-head. A sundial with black-letter numerals and a hole for a gnomon is incised on the E. angle-shaft, below the string course.

The two-storied S. porch (Plate 134) appears to have been added as an afterthought as its E. wall is built against and partly hides the W. angle-shaft, with a straight joint, although the mouldings of the plinth and string-course of the E. bay are repeated on it. The porch is crowned on the S. front with an ornamental gable, having curved and counter-curved moulded copings. The horizontal copings of the E. and W. sides are embellished with double scrolls surmounted by small obelisks. The entry to the porch is round-headed, with a plain archivolt culminating in a scrolled keystone enriched with acanthus ornament and half a Tudor rose. The archway is flanked by rusticated Tuscan half-columns standing on pedestals and supporting a horizontal entablature, the frieze of which consists of a series of embossed rectangles. Each spandrel is decorated with a circular wreath of gadroon, bead-and-reel and egg-and-dart

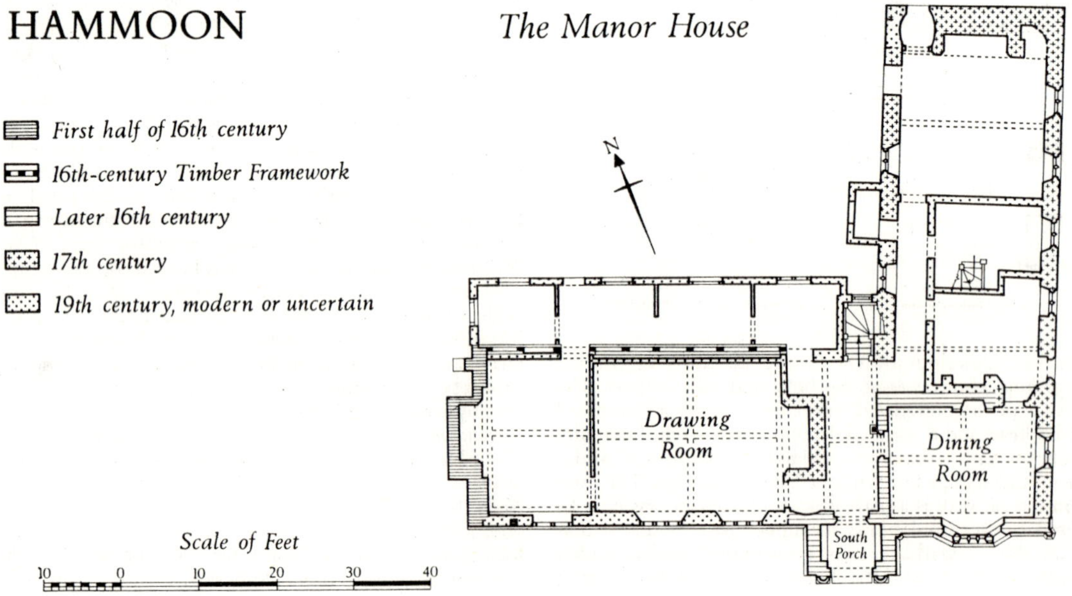

ornament; a scratched inscription reads I.R. 1687. The upper storey of the porch has a three-light window with details similar to the windows of the E. bay. The doorway inside the porch has a hollow-chamfered four-centred head in a square ogee-moulded surround with roses carved in the spandrels; the mouldings continue on the jambs and terminate at vase-shaped stops. The door is of oak with vertical planks nailed to horizontal inner planks, the vertical joints being covered with moulded fillets; the strap hinges are of wrought-iron.

In the E. elevation, the mid 16th-century ashlar masonry of the S.E. corner almost immediately gives way to rubble of a later period; a length of the 16th-century plinth moulding near the corner has been reset upside-down to provide a corbel on which the slightly thicker rubble-work rests. The casement-moulded square-headed two-light windows on each floor in the S. bay of the E. front are of the 16th century but reset; the lintel of the first-floor window formerly belonged to an opening with three four-centred lights. Further N. the two-light mullioned windows are square-headed; the ground-floor openings have stone dressings while the first-floor windows have timber surrounds. The doorway near the S. end of the E. front has a moulded four-centred head with continuous jambs. The N. gable of the N.E. range contains a small attic loop-light; lower down, the N. wall is masked by a modern lean-to addition. The W. side of the N.E. range is of ashlar and squared rubble. A doorway near the N. end has a four-centred head; it is blocked with masonry and is probably reset since it appears to occupy the position of a former oven. The ground-floor windows are square-headed with hollow-chamfered stone surrounds; the first-floor windows have timber surrounds.

The N. side of the S. range is partly obscured by a modern lean-to structure but portions of the original fabric can be seen above and inside. The wall is of timber-frame construction on a rubble plinth with a chamfered ashlar capping; the timber-framing is filled in with wattle-and-daub. The upper part of the wall is weather-boarded and has some original timber windows with chamfered mullions in the upper storey. The W. wall of the S. range is of rubble, with a large chimney-breast weathered back below roof-level. A projection to the N. of the chimney-breast is probably part of a former oven.

Inside, the porch doorway leads into a vestibule with, to the E., a stone doorway to the dining-room with a hollow-chamfered four-centred head with sunk spandrels. To the N. is a late 17th-century staircase with square newel-posts, ball-finials, vase-shaped balusters, close strings and moulded handrails; much of the woodwork has been restored. W. of the vestibule, the drawing-room has deeply chamfered intersecting beams dividing the ceiling into four panels. The fireplace, probably inserted in the 17th century, has an ogee-moulded timber head and moulded stone jambs; an iron fireback is dated 1579. The room W. of the drawing-room has a deeply chamfered ceiling beam. The W. fireplace is original and has moulded stone jambs and a deep moulded timber lintel, but the under side of the lintel has been cut away. The dining-room has deep-chamfered ceiling beams cased in plaster; the walls are lined with late 17th or early 18th-century panelling in four heights; the overmantel has linenfold panels. On the first floor the timber-framing of the N. wall of the S. range is exposed. The roof, seen in the attic, has five tie-beam trusses with cambered collars, principals tenoned together at the apex, a diagonally set ridge-piece and two purlins to each side; between the purlins are curved wind-braces. The tie-beams are seen below the first-floor ceilings and have curved angle-braces at each end, but several of the latter have been cut out. The W. chamber has a flat ceiling of four panels with deeply chamfered intersecting beams set level with the lower purlins; in the same room, the inclined bay of the roof to the N. of the flat ceiling is lined with boarding painted dark red and decorated with white stars; this is probably of the late 16th century.

(3) Hammoon Bridge (82031473) has a central pier and end abutments of rough ashlar, of uncertain date but possibly 17th century; they are cut down to provide support for steel girders.

(4) Farm House (81771441), is two-storied and of coursed rubble and ashlar, with much brick repair on the ground floor and entirely of brick on the first floor. The roof is thatched. Three of the ground-floor rooms retain elements of the original late 16th or early 17th-century house, the plan of which was L-shaped. One ground-floor room has moulded intersecting ceiling beams and moulded wall-plates, and a room on the first floor has a partition of 17th-century oak panelling in four heights with moulded rails and styles. One window retains part of a moulded stone frame but all other openings were renewed in the 19th century. (*Demolished.*)

(5) Cottage (81691448), 150 yds. S.W. of the church, now has two storeys and a tiled roof but was originally single-storied with an attic. The lower walls are of squared rubble, with repairs in brickwork. A fireplace at the N. end has a chamfered oak lintel and stone jambs. The cottage is of 17th-century origin but it has recently been completely modernised.

(6) Cross Base, 50 yds. S. of the church, is a socketed stone base block, 2¾ ft. square and 2 ft. high, chamfered at the top to form an octagon; it is probably of the 15th century. A vertical member with roll-moulded arrises cemented into the square central socket could be part of the original shaft. An inscription on one side records that the base was taken from nearer the church and set here in 1913.

MEDIAEVAL AND LATER EARTHWORKS

(7) Cultivation Remains. The open fields of the parish were enclosed before 1771 (Map of Hammoon, 1771, D.C.R.O.). Ridge-and-furrow 6 yds. to 10 yds. wide survives in the W. of the parish (807141); elsewhere extensive traces are visible on air photographs (R.A.F. CPE/UK 1974: 1158–61, 3158–60) which show straight and curved furlongs, generally end-to-end and up to 350 yds. long. All the remains are earlier than the field boundaries of 1771.

20 HANFORD (8411)

(O.S. 6 ins. ST 81 SW, ST 81 SE)

The small parish of Hanford, covering only 600 acres and with an irregular outline, lies across the Chalk saddle between Hambledon and Hod Hills, which reach altitudes of 600 ft. and 450 ft. respectively in the N. and S.E. extremities of the area. To W. and S. the parish is bounded by the R. Stour. The former village lay at the junction of the Chalk and the upper Greensand, overlooking the river; nothing is known of its open fields. The most important monument in the parish is Hanford House.

ECCLESIASTICAL

(1) The Parish Church of St. Michael and All Angels, some 50 yds. N. of Hanford House, has walls

of coursed ashlar and is roofed with stone-slates; the walls are probably of mediaeval origin but the church was largely rebuilt in the middle of the 17th century. The crypt is modern.

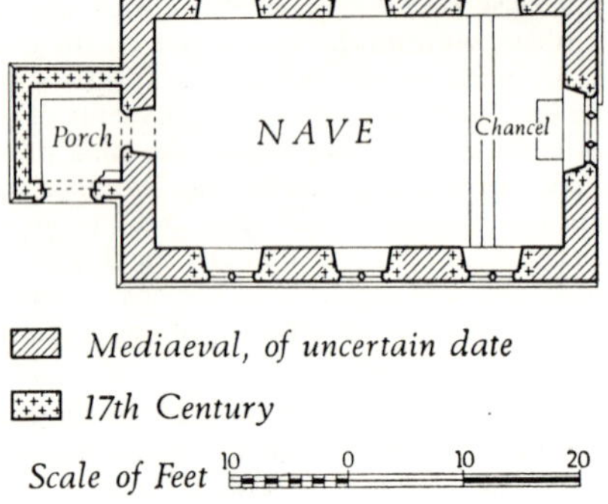

The *Nave* and *Chancel* (35 ft. by 19 ft.) are undivided. The 17th-century E. window (Plate 141) is of Gothic form and has three round-headed cinquefoil lights with vertical tracery in a two-centred head; the tracery has trefoil cusping at the top and bottom of each light. The N. and S. walls have each three 17th-century pointed windows of two lancet lights with a plain spandrel light above; the stone jambs and mullions are moulded externally and hollow-chamfered internally. The splayed reveals and rear arch of the central doorway in the W. wall probably survive from the mediaeval structure, but the elliptical door-head and continuous moulded jambs are of the 17th century. The W. gable is surmounted by an open stone bell-cote with a horizontal head resting on cyma-profiled imposts. The 17th-century *West Porch* (7 ft. square) is entered from the S. through an elliptical headed opening (Plate 141) with a moulded archivolt which springs from bold cyma cornices; these rest on pulvinated frieze-blocks, and jambs moulded to represent the vertical and horizontal members of an eared architrave, the horizontal mouldings of the lintel being returned on the reveals. The porch has a flat roof concealed by a parapet with a moulded string-course and capping. A reset stone in the parapet is inscribed ANNO DO. 1650.

Fittings—*Bell:* pear-shaped, without inscription, probably 13th century. *Door:* with incised fleur-de-lis wrought-iron hinges, mediaeval; woodwork 17th century. *Graffiti:* In W. porch, several 17th and 18th-century dates and initials. *Plate:* includes 19th-century reproduction of Elizabethan cup, also paten of 1721.

SECULAR

(2) HANFORD HOUSE (845111) is set on ground which falls away to S. and E. to the R. Stour, about $\frac{1}{4}$ m. away. The mansion has stone walls and is roofed with stone-slates; it has two principal storeys with attics and cellars and is planned around a square courtyard, on the model of an Italian palace. It was built for Sir Robert Seymer between 1604 and 1623. In the 18th century a staircase was renewed and a service wing was added on the W. Extensive remodelling of the interior took place in the 19th century, and in 1873 the courtyard was roofed over and a wooden gallery was inserted on the N., possibly in place of an earlier one. At the same time the leaded casements were removed from many of the mullioned windows and sashes were substituted.

Hanford House, distinguished as a well-preserved example of an early 17th-century country house, is also of importance for its plan. The Italian idea of a small enclosed courtyard is interpreted in a manner appropriate to a northern climate, large inward-looking windows on the ground and first floors taking the place of the open loggias of the south. The strict symmetry and the slightly ponderous grandeur of this medium-sized house well illustrate the attitude of English architects toward houses for the affluent in the early Jacobean period.

The North Front, of fine-jointed ashlar with traces of stucco rendering, presents a symmetrical composition comprising a two-storey, pedimented centrepiece, perhaps, a later 17th-century insertion, and two main flanking bays, all crowned by three equal gables (Plate 135). It has a hollow-chamfered plinth, continuous moulded string-courses at first and second floor levels and a continuous moulded coping to the gables and intervening parapets. All the windows have square heads and hollow-chamfered jambs and mullions. The classical centrepiece contains a round-headed gateway with a rusticated arch springing from moulded imposts and shafted jambs. The archway is flanked by Doric pilasters with an entablature. Superimposed Ionic pilasters on the first floor support a pedimented entablature and flank a transomed two-light window with a moulded architrave and a shaped apron. On the ground floor, transomed three-light windows open to each side of the central archway, and coupled pairs of transomed two-light windows are set axially in the gabled flanking bays. The same arrangement obtains on the first floor, and in each gable is a single four-light window, without transom, under a square label with returned stops. Two lead rainwater heads bear the Stuart royal arms and the date 1623.

The ashlar-faced East Front has string-courses returned from the N. front. The façade is crowned by four gables and at either end is a five-sided projection; that to the N. is central with the N. gable but the S. projection is set asymmetrically under the S. gable. Both projections are of two storeys with cellars and have hollow-chamfered transomed two-light windows in each side on each floor, the alternate windows being blind. Between the terminal projections and under the two central gables each principal storey has three transomed three-light windows, with mouldings as before. Doorways occur between the projections and the adjacent ground-floor windows. The doorway to the N. has a hollow-chamfered four-centred head in a square surround and a hollow-chamfered two-light stone window above it. The original oak door has twelve panels with moulded nail-studded ribs. The corresponding doorway to the S. has been renewed and slightly enlarged but the window above it is original. Each gable has a two-light attic window with a hood-mould and at the apex of each gable is a pair of cylindrical stone chimneys, united by a thin rectangular stone cornice. Of four lead rainwater heads three are embossed with the Seymer crest, a winged cap of estate; they discharge into a horizontal lead gutter decorated at intervals with embossed leopard masks.

The South Front is of coursed rubble; the plinth continues from the E. front but there are no string-courses. The fenestration is less regular than that already described and the windows, with and without transoms, are of two and three lights with moulded labels and returned stops. A doorway with a four-centred head is modern. On the W. side of the house the ground floor is masked by an ashlar-faced 18th-century service wing of one storey. Over this rises the three-gabled West Front, of coursed rubble with many irregularly disposed windows; a projection with a weathered stone roof originally contained garderobes.

The internal Courtyard, now roofed to form a hall, is entered from the N. gateway through a covered carriage-way with finely jointed ashlar walls containing eight paired niches with shell heads. A modern fireplace has been inserted on the E. side of the court, a gallery supported on columns has been added on the N. side and the lower storey has been lined with panelling; all these additions are probably of 1873, but several original windows have been retained. Facing the carriage-way on the S. side of the court is a two-storied Porch (Plate 136) with a hollow-chamfered plinth, and moulded string-courses at first and second floor levels. On the ground floor it has a round-headed archway with a plain keystone and moulded imposts, the mouldings of the head being continued on the jambs to terminate at run-out stops. Flanking the opening, fluted Ionic pilasters support an entablature with a strapwork frieze. Above the cornice and flanked by strapwork scrolls is a moulded square panel containing an achievement-of-arms of Seymer quartering Attwater and Lymbergh (Plate 48); the panel is surmounted by a modillion cornice on which is a couched lion in full relief. On the first floor the porch has a transomed three-light window and above, now hidden by the ceiling, is a gable with a three-light window. On each side of the porch are transomed three-light ground and first-floor windows. Similar windows occur on the other three sides of the court; originally each side probably had three openings on the ground and first floors, and a single attic window in a gable, but many of the windows have been suppressed.

The round-headed doorway from the porch into the South Range has a moulded head and jambs with run-out stops; on the W. jamb is scratched 'Jonathan Bartlett, July 2, 1677'. The nail-studded door has vertical outer planks and horizontal inner planks cut to a round head and hung on iron strap-hinges; the vertical joints are covered with hollow-chamfered ribs. The stairs in the hall to which this doorway leads are of the first half of the 18th century; they have cut strings, moulded and twisted balusters and a moulded handrail with a fist-shaped terminal scroll. In the East Range, the original dog-leg staircase (Plate 82) has square newel posts with reeded decoration; those at the main landings and half-landings have vase-shaped finials while the two intervening newels, where there are quarter-landings, run continuously between the floors, except at the top where they too have vase finials. The handrail is heavily moulded and intersects the close-string, which is decorated with fluting. Heavy turned balusters are spaced one to each tread.

The Drawing-room at the E. end of the N. range is entered

HANFORD HOUSE

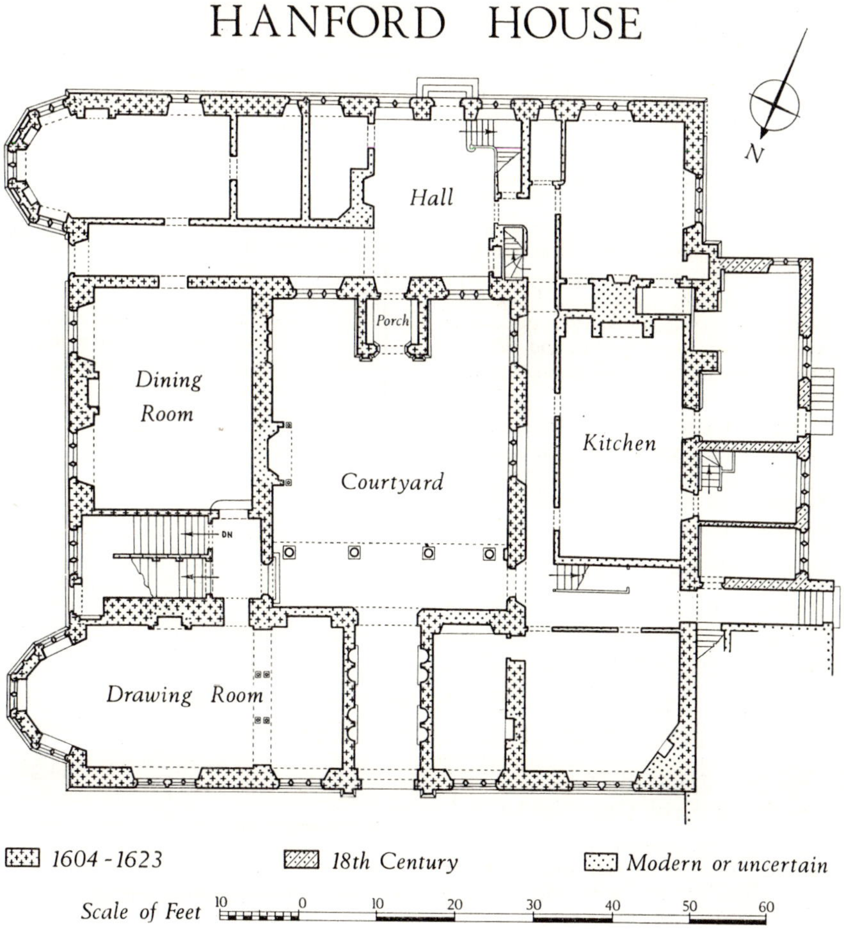

from the staircase hall through a mid 18th-century doorway with an eared and moulded architrave surmounted by a pulvinated laurel-leaf frieze and a pediment. The marble fireplace is of the late 18th century and has caryatid pilasters supporting a bacchic frieze. At the W. end, the room has been enlarged by removing the party-wall with the adjoining room and substituting slender cast-iron columns of *c.* 1870.

On the first floor, the chamber over the drawing-room contains an original carved stone fireplace surround and overmantel (Plate 74). Terminal figures rising from pilasters support an entablature with a heavy strapwork apron; strapwork also appears in the frieze, and the cornice has wave and leaf mouldings. Over this rises a colonnade of small Corinthian columns set in pairs to compose a central aedicule and smaller aedicules at each end; each aedicule contains a shell-headed niche. The two intercolumniations between these features contain half-length figures, in high relief, of soldiers wearing classical armour. The geometrical plaster ceiling (Plate 70) is contemporary; it is decorated with intersecting ribs which converge on pendant bosses, the polygonal panels enclosing conventionalised sprays of foliage. The cornice has a vine-scroll frieze. The adjoining chamber to the W. also has an early 17th-century ceiling with geometrical rib patterns enclosing arabesques, fleurs-de-lis, scrolled cartouches, cherub heads and roundels with male and female heads. The chamber at the centre of the E. range is lined on three sides with mid 17th-century panelling, and on part of the W. side with 18th-century panelling; that of the earlier period is in five heights with a frieze and a cornice and is divided into bays by pilasters. In the S. range a small doorway leading into the room over the porch has a four-centred head and an early 17th-century oak plank door. Stairs to the attics continue the line of the 18th-century S. staircase, but above first-floor level the 17th-century stairs survive; they have close strings and heavy turned balusters.

To the S. of the house a late 18th-century walled garden has a scrolled wrought-iron *Gate*, perhaps Italian and also of the 18th century.

The *Stables* to the W. of the house date from the late 16th century and were originally a barn. Above a deep chamfered plinth of ashlar and coursed rubble the walls are of brick with ashlar quoins and dressings; the tiled roofs have stone-slate verges. Wings, perhaps former porches, project E. and W. near the ends of the main range. All openings are modern and much of the brickwork has been renewed.

(3) Ice House (85361124), of brick, consists of a circular domed chamber (14 ft. diam.) sunk in the ground. The entrance is on the N. side. It is probably of the early 19th century and from its position appears likely to have served both Hanford House and Stepleton House (*see* p. 132).

MEDIAEVAL AND LATER EARTHWORKS

(4) Settlement Remains of the former hamlet of Hanford (845111) lie immediately N. of (1). A population of eight is recorded in 1086 (D.B. I, f. 79a) and the same number of taxpayers is listed in 1333. The tax paid in 1428 indicates by the terms of the Subsidy that there still were more than ten inhabitants (Feudal Aids, 1284–1431, II, 83). By 1650 Hanford House was the only inhabited building in the parish (Hutchins IV, 63).

The earthworks of the settlement, covering some four acres, include a hollow-way 80 yds. long, 20 ft. wide and 2 ft. deep, orientated N.E.–S.W. A mutilated scarp, 2 ft. to 3 ft. high, lies 30 yds. to the S.E. and parallel with the hollow-way. To the N.W. are three rectangular closes, 30 yds. long and 20 yds. wide, divided by low scarps, $\frac{1}{2}$ ft. to 2 ft. high and bounded on the N.W. by a bank 10 ft. wide and 3 ft. high. Beyond this are fragmentary traces of two other closes, up to 100 yds. long and 30 yds. wide, bounded by low banks.

Further W. is an area of irregular hollows, mounds and scarps which may also be part of the former settlement.

ROMAN AND PREHISTORIC

(5) Site of Romano-British Building (86051018), with occupation debris and inhumation burials, known locally as 'Great Bournes', was discovered in 1860 on the S.E. slopes of Hod Hill. The building had internal divisions indicating several rooms; stone roofing tiles were found and also the remains of a furnace with iron bars joined together like a grating, and a metallic mass of slag. Finds included shale bracelets and spindle whorls and 'amulets in coarse pottery', presumably loom weights. Higher up the hill were eight inhumations and Constantinian coins (Hutchins I, 309).

UNDATED

(6) Enclosure (855115), roughly circular and of 2 acres internally, lies between 450 ft. and 500 ft. O.D. near the tip of the S.E. spur of Hambledon Hill, on ground sloping S. and E. (*see* general plan on p. xxxix); it is now largely destroyed. Except for a gentle rise to the W. the ground falls fairly rapidly away on all sides. The enclosure is defined by a scarp, presumably once a bank, and an external ditch, best preserved on the N. where it reaches the spur top and crosses the parish boundary with Iwerne Courtney. Here the scarp is about 5 ft. high, the ditch about 30 ft. across and 1 ft. deep. S. of the parish boundary it has been severely reduced by ploughing and is visible only as a long low scarp, 3 ft. high, within the modern field angle. On the N.W.,

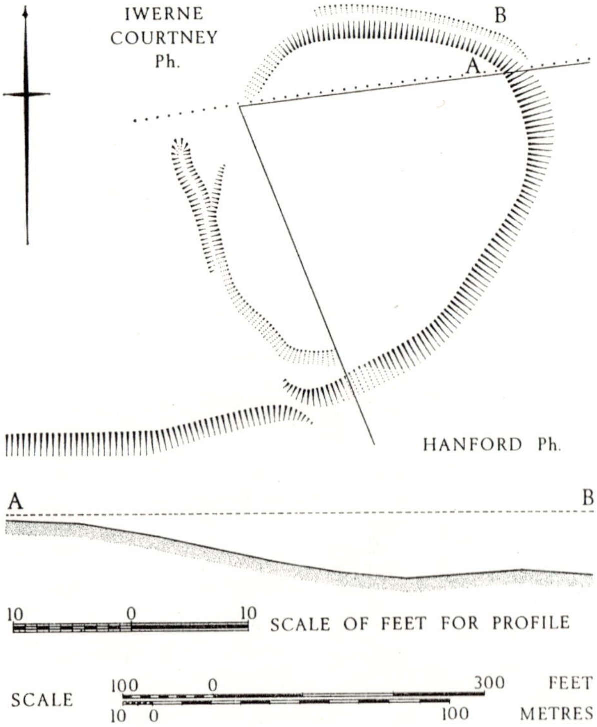

HILTON CHURCH. Painted panels, formerly at Milton Abbey. Late 15th-century

HAZELBURY BRYAN CHURCH. Interior, looking E. 15th-century

GLANVILLE'S WOOTTON CHURCH. Interior, looking S.E. from nave into S. chapel. *c.* 1344

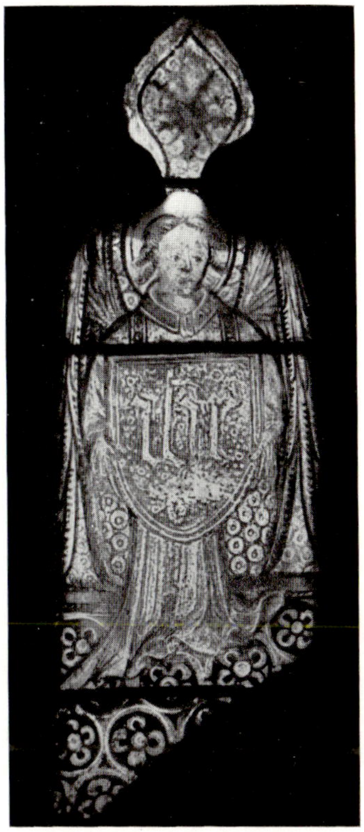

(a) Second window from E.

(b) Easternmost window.

(c) Second window from E.

(d) Third window from E.

(e) Third window from E.

(f) Second window from E.

HAZELBURY BRYAN CHURCH. Tracery lights of N. windows in N. aisle. 15th-century

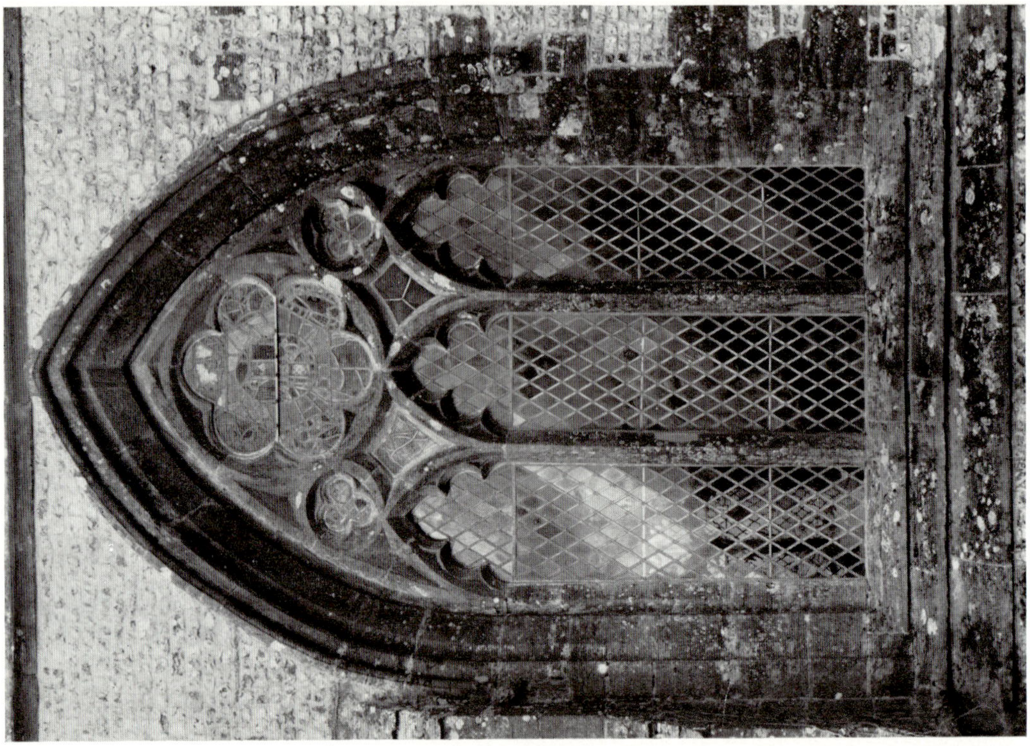

GLANVILLE'S WOOTTON CHURCH. Windows in S. wall of S. Chapel.

c. 1344

S. Doorway of Porch. 17th-century

E. Window. 17th-century

HANFORD CHURCH.

HILTON CHURCH. N. Aisle windows, probably from Milton Abbey. 15th-century

IWERNE COURTNEY CHURCH. Screen in N. Aisle. Early 17th-century

IBBERTON CHURCH. Glass in S. window of chancel; arms of Milton Abbey.
15th-century

LYDLINCH CHURCH. Glass in S. window of nave.
15th-century

where nearly 100 ft. of the scarp has been completely destroyed, the ditch swings outwards perhaps to form part of an original entrance-work. On the S. side, interpretation of the line of the enclosure is complicated by a low scarp, with a narrow terrace-way below it, running in to meet it from the W. This feature remains unexplained and is not certainly contemporary.

21 HAZELBURY BRYAN (7508)

(O.S. 6 ins. ST 70 NW, ST 70 NE, ST 71 SW)

Hazelbury Bryan is a large parish of 2,400 acres, undulating between 240 ft. and 300 ft. above sea-level and drained by several small streams which flow N. and N.W. to the R. Lydden, and N.E. to the R. Stour. A broad band of Corallian Limestone and Sand traverses the area from S.W. to N.E.; to N.W. the soil is Oxford Clay, to S.E. it is Kimmeridge Clay.

The somewhat scattered pattern of occupation seems to have developed from the three settlements of Droop, Wonston and Kingston, which all lie at about 300 ft. altitude on the Corallian Limestone. Whether each had a separate mediaeval open field system is not known; such fields as existed were partly enclosed by the middle of the 14th century,[1] and the map of the parish made in 1607 by Ralph Treswell[2] shows that they had been entirely enclosed by that date. On the other hand the hamlet of Woodrow seems to represent an extension of settlement into the waste area to the N.E. (where Treswell shows 'common closes'); monument (26) was probably built in consequence of this movement, while monuments (27) to (31) represent further encroachment on the waste between the early 17th century and 1858, when enclosure was completed.[3] The group of cottages at Park Gate is a 19th-century settlement on land which, as Treswell shows, was already enclosed by 1607; indeed this enclosure may even go back to the 14th century.[4]

The most important monument is the parish church.

ECCLESIASTICAL

(1) THE PARISH CHURCH OF ST. MARY AND ST. JAMES (Plate 5) is in the hamlet of Droop. It has walls of roughly coursed rubble with ashlar dressings; the nave and the N. aisle are roofed with stone-slates, the chancel is tiled and the other roofs are lead-covered. The entire building, comprising *Chancel*, *South Chapel*, *Nave*, *North* and *South Aisles*, *West Tower* and *South Porch*, dates from the second half of the 15th century. The chancel and tower appear to have been built first and the nave and other parts subsequently, and over a number of years since the S. arcade is stylistically about twenty years later than the N. arcade. The chancel was restored in 1827 and general restorations were undertaken in 1895.

The church is a good example of 15th-century architecture with few later alterations. The roofs are original and richly decorated and some interesting mediaeval glass is preserved. (For plan, *see* p. 106.)

Architectural Description—The *Chancel* (25½ ft. by 15½ ft.) has a casement-moulded 15th-century E. window of three two-centred lights with cinquefoil cusping and vertical tracery; the two-centred head has a hood-mould with head-stops. The N. wall, largely rebuilt in ashlar in 1827, has two restored windows each of two cinquefoil-headed lights with a quatrefoil above, under a main head of shallow triangular form with casement mouldings which continue on the jambs; above are hollow-chamfered hood-moulds with square leaf stops; the rear arches are stone slabs pitched together at the apex. The S. wall of the chancel has one window uniform with those of the N. wall. Further W. is a segmental-pointed archway to the S. Chapel; it is of three orders, comprising ogee mouldings on each side of a hollow-chamfer; the ogee mouldings spring from capitals enriched with conventional foliage. On the responds, the inner ogee is carried on attached shafts while the hollow-chamfer and the outer ogee are continuous; the moulded bases have hollow-chamfered polygonal plinths. Both in the arch and in the responds the continuous hollow-chamfer is decorated at intervals on the N. side with square foliate bosses. The chancel arch, partly rebuilt in the 19th century, is two-centred and of three orders. It resembles the archway to the S. Chapel except that the inner ogee is replaced by a roll-moulding and there are no foliate bosses. The mouldings continue on the responds but they are interrupted at the springing by horizontal fillets in place of capitals. The stairs to the former rood-loft are entered through a square-headed doorway in the S. face of the S. respond and a corbelled step appears on the W. face of the respond where the vice emerges at the top.

The *South Chapel* (17 ft. by 9 ft.) has a three-light E. window similar to that of the chancel; the hood-mould has square stops with flower centres. The S. wall contains a two-light window uniform with those in the side walls of the chancel, and a narorw doorway with a two-centred wave-moulded head, continuous jambs and broach stops. The S. and E. walls have embattled parapets with hollow-chamfered string-courses and moulded copings; a grotesque gargoyle is set in the string-course above the E. window. A diagonal buttress of two stages with weathered offsets strengthens the S.E. corner and a similar buttress is set square against the S. wall; it marks the W. end of the chapel but there is no internal feature, except a change in floor level, to distinguish the chapel from the S. aisle. Above each buttress a grotesque gargoyle protrudes from the string-course.

The *Nave* (41½ ft. by 16½ ft.) is flanked on the N. by an arcade of four bays with two-centred arches of three orders (Plate 138), similar to those of the archway to the S. Chapel, described above, but without foliate bosses. The piers consist of four attached shafts alternating with hollow-chamfers; the shafts have simple moulded capitals and moulded polygonal bases; at the level of the caps each hollow-chamfer is ornamented with a foliate boss. The responds are similar half-piers but part of the E. respond has been cut away, probably to make room for a former pulpit. The S. arcade corresponds with that on the N. in spacing, but the arches are slightly lower and the mouldings, particularly those of the capitals, are coarser.

---

1 Hutchins I, 275.
2 Photographic reproduction in D.C.R.O.
3 Enclosure award, D.C.R.O.
4 Fägersten, 55.

HAZELBURY BRYAN

The parish church of St. Mary & St. James

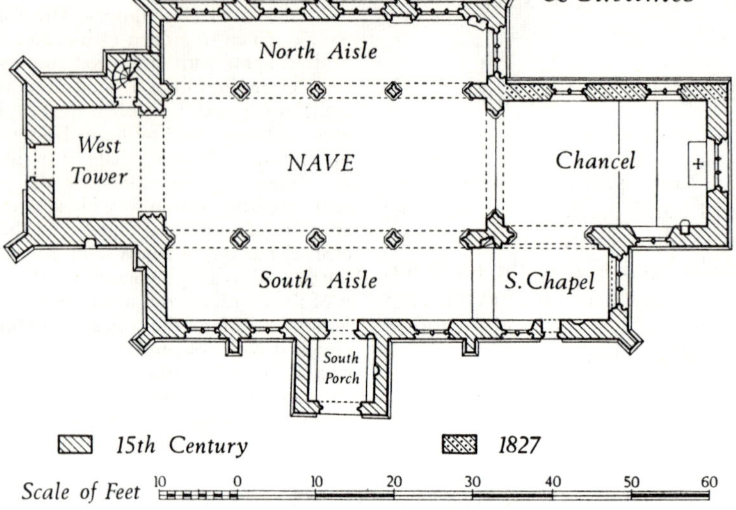

The *North Aisle* ($41\frac{3}{4}$ ft. by $7\frac{3}{4}$ ft.) must have been built after the W. tower because the profile of the vice turret appears internally on the W. The gabled E. wall has a weathered ashlar coping with a cross finial. The 15th-century E. window is of three cinquefoil-headed lights with vertical tracery and a casement-moulded two-centred outer head with continuous jambs; the rear arch is two-centred and hollow-chamfered. The N. wall has three square-set buttresses of two weathered stages and the N.E. and N.W. corners have similar buttresses set diagonally; between the buttresses are four three-light windows, uniform with the E. window of the aisle but set at a lower level.

The *South Aisle* (39 ft. by 9 ft.) has a S. wall continuous with that of the S. Chapel and with a continuous string-course and parapet mouldings, and similar buttresses. Gargoyles protrude from the string-course in correspondence with the buttresses, and chamfered standards above them are probably the bases of former pinnacles. A two-light window near the E. end of the S. wall is uniform with the adjacent window in the S. Chapel. The S. doorway has a two-centred moulded head of two orders, ogee and hollow-chamfered, with continuous jambs and moulded stops, and a rear arch composed of two chamfered stones pitched together at the apex. W. of the doorway the S. wall has buttresses as before described and two two-centred two-light windows with cinquefoil cusping and vertical tracery; the heads and continuous jambs are casement-moulded.

The *West Tower* (11 ft. by 14 ft.) is of rubble with occasional courses of roughly squared stone; it has four external stages between the moulded and chamfered plinth and the embattled parapet. Each stage is marked by a weathered string-course and a slight recession of the wall-face. Five-stage diagonal ashlar buttresses with weathered offsets strengthen the N.W. and S.W. corners, a similar buttress is set square at the E. end of the S. side and the N.E. corner is strengthened by the vice turret, which has three principal stages. The embattled parapet has a continuous moulded coping and a pinnacle with a crocketed finial at each corner; the vice turret stands a little higher than the main parapet and has similar terminal features. The tower arch is two-centred, with a panelled soffit and continuous jambs; the trefoil-headed panels are set in pairs, in four heights. The vice doorway has a chamfered four-centred head and continuous jambs. The W. doorway has a two-centred head with three orders of mouldings and continuous jambs; it is surmounted by a square label and the spandrels between the arch and the label have trefoil panels. Above, the two-centred W. window is of four cinquefoil ogee-headed lights with vertical tracery; the hoodmould is an extension of the lower string-course. In the lower stage the external face of the S. wall is decorated with a small niche, rectangular in plan, with an ogee canopied head flanked by crocketed finials. In the second stage two similar niches occur on either side of the W. window head. In the third stage is a square-headed N. window of two pointed lights with trefoil cusping. The fourth stage has in each face a casement-moulded belfry window of two transomed and trefoil-headed lights with a quatrefoil under a two-centred head with a hood-mould. The lights below the transoms are blocked with stone panels; those above are louvred.

The *South Porch* ($8\frac{1}{2}$ ft. by 8 ft.) has a string-course and an embattled parapet resembling those of the S. aisle but at a lower level; the string-course has a gargoyle at each corner. The porch entry has a two-centred arch with double ogee mouldings, continuous jambs and run-out stops; the hollow-chamfered label terminates in square stops with flower centres.

Roofs. The Chancel has a plaster barrel-vault of the 19th century divided into panels by moulded transverse and longitudinal ribs. At the springing are heavily-moulded wall-plates, and the intersections of the cross-ribs with the wall-plates are masked by painted shields, some with heraldic emblems, others with initials and one dated 1827. The Nave has a 15th-century wagon roof, four-centred in cross-section; the transverse members which were originally intended to be visible are moulded, and they are intersected by moulded longitudinal members to form panels; the panels must originally have been plastered but the plaster has now been removed to expose the intermediate timbers. The intersections of the moulded members are decorated with leaf-bosses. The transverse members spring from wall-plates with mouldings in two orders, decorated with carved bosses. The roof of the N. Aisle is of the same date and type as that of the Nave but narrower and more steeply pitched; blank shields decorate the wall-plates at the springing of the moulded transverse members. The S. Aisle and the S. Chapel have a continuous flat roof of twelve bays defined by heavily moulded transverse beams with slightly raised centres; the beams are intersected by a moulded longitudinal member and they rest on moulded wall-plates, thus forming square coffer-like panels (Plate 21); the panels are spanned alternately by joists set E.–W. and N.–S. Carved wooden leaf-bosses at the junctions of the main members are perhaps not original. The Porch has a similar roof of four panels with no bosses.

Fittings—*Bells:* six; 2nd inscribed 'Feare God IW 1613'; 3rd inscribed 'Ave gracia [pl]ena' in Lombardic letters, *c.* 1400; 4th inscribed 'Sancte Andrea' in floreated Lombardic letters, *c.*1400; 5th inscribed 'Remember thy end IW 1613'; others modern. *Benefactors' Tables:* In S. aisle, on W. wall, endowment record, 1709. In porch, endowment record, 1843; adjacent, matching table of kindred and affinity. *Brackets:* In chancel, below piscina, moulded polygonal stone bracket with angel head retaining traces of red pigment, 15th century. In nave, on E. respond of S. arcade, stone head-corbel with flat top, with traces of pigment, 15th century. *Chest:* of oak, with panelled front and sides, enriched styles and rails, 17th century. *Coffin-stools:* two, of oak, with square legs, 18th century. *Doors:* In S. doorway, of oak, with vertical external planks and internal battens, wrought iron strap-hinges, ring-handle, escutcheon-plate and lock, probably all 15th century; in tower vice doorway, with original planks and hinges, 15th century; in W. doorway, dated 1827. *Font:* of Purbeck marble; octagonal bowl decorated on each face with two shallow round-headed panels and with chamfered lower edge, cylindrical pedestal surrounded by eight smaller shafts on chamfered octagonal base, late 12th century. Font cover of oak, octagonal, with fretted cornice and tent-shaped head, 18th century, formerly part of pulpit sounding-board (*see* old photograph in church).

Glass: In chancel, in tracery of E. window, centre quatrefoil with blue Tudor rose with yellow rays, N. trefoil with shield-of-arms quarterly of Montagu and Monthermer, S. trefoil with shield-of-arms paly of Bryan and Bures; in lower tracery lights, in N. spandrel, leaf pattern, in adjacent cinquefoil, winged seraph in silver-stain, in next three cinquefoils, reset Tudor roses and sun, in S. spandrel, plain blue glass, all 15th or 16th century; in S. window, quatrefoil with leaf patterns and, in place of central roundel, fragment of glass with lettering, 15th century. In S. chapel, in E. window, tracery lozenge with fragment depicting tonsured head, 15th century; in centre light, reset fragment of canopy. In N. aisle, in E. window, in centre quatrefoil, inverted yellow and white crown; in two trefoil-headed tracery lights, lion and eagle symbols of Evangelists, each named on scroll; below, in two lights, fragments of crocketed canopies. In N. side of N. aisle, in easternmost window, rose in top quatrefoil and seraphs in three of four tracery lights (Plate 139, b), fragments of canopies in cinquefoil heads of main lights below; in second window, rose in top quatrefoil and angel bearing shield with monogram in each tracery light (Plate 139, a, c and f), also fragments of canopies below; in third window, angels holding shields with monograms and emblems in three tracery lights (Plate 139, d and e), also fragments of canopies below; in fourth window, small fragments; all 15th century. In tower, in W. window, another mediaeval fragment. *Inscriptions:* On plinth on S. face of tower, 'W.P. 1739'.

Monuments and *Floor-slabs. Monuments:* In chancel, on N. wall, (1) of Francis Reed, rector, 1821, marble tablet with arms, by Gray of Weymouth. In churchyard, against S.E. buttress of S. Chapel, (2) of Nicholas Kellaway, 1714, headstone with cherubs' heads (Plate 32); S. of S. porch, (3) of Mary Strange, 1840, 17th-century table-tomb reused. *Floor-slabs:* In nave, W. of chancel step, (1) of Richard Hill, 1764; adjacent, (2), (3) and (4) of Eliz. Woodrow, Elizabeth Hill Woodrow and . . . Woodrow, three worn 18th and 19th-century Purbeck slabs forming pavement; further W., (5) illegible, 1696, similar slab. *Niches:* In porch, on E. wall, (1) shallow niche with chamfered trefoil head; to E. of doorway to S. aisle, (2) roughly scooped round-headed niche. In N. aisle, in N.E. corner, (3) and (4), with shafted jambs, rib-vaulted canopies with rich crocketed cresting and angel-brackets, 15th century; on N. wall, (5) large reset niche, perhaps originally sedile, with grotesque-headed corbel, banded lateral shafts with crocketed finials, and ogee canopy with cusping and crockets; canopy flanked by quatrefoil spandrels with flower centres and surmounted by tall finial prolonged beyond square outer head, 15th century; niche now used as setting for modern sculpture. On S. and W. faces of W. tower, *see* Architectural Description. *Paintings:* On S. wall of nave, texts in two panels, that to E. with angel supporters; late 16th or early 17th century. *Piscinae:* In chancel, on S. side, lower part of piscina comprising bowl with central outlet and chamfered jambs of niche with broach-stops, 15th century; head of niche formed from fragment of window tracery, 14th century. In S. chapel, on S. wall, with chamfered round head and cut-back basin. *Plate:* includes silver cup with hallmark and inscription of 1630, paten of 1813, and candlesticks, pair, silver-plated, late 18th century. *Pulpit:* of oak, octagonal, inscribed 'Ben Lidford 1782', with later pedestal and stairs; above, sounding-board with inlaid soffit and fretted cornice, suspended by chain from nave roof, 18th century; for former head to sounding-board *see* font-cover. *Royal Arms:* At W. end of N. aisle, square panel painted with arms of Queen Anne, superscribed G.R. 1715. *Sundials:* On tower, on third stage of S.W. buttress, inserted rectangular stone slab with iron gnomon, 18th century. *Miscellanea:* Reset at N.E. and S.E. corners of S. chapel, two capitals, one with crowned monogram 'S T' in deeply undercut foliage surmounted by a moulded abacus (Plate 16), the other with foliage only, 14th century.

SECULAR

Droop

(2) Malthouse Farm (74990835) is a two-storied house with walls of squared rubble and slated roofs; it is of the late 17th century with 18th-century additions. A few windows have stone mullions and weathered hoodmoulds. A *Barn* to the W. is of the 18th century. Treswell's map shows a house in this position.

(3) Barn, 50 yds. S. of the church, is of the 16th century with later repairs. The walls are of coursed rubble and the roof is thatched. The E. wall contains a doorway 10 ft. wide located 20 ft. from the N. end, and what is probably the jamb of a second doorway 30 ft. further S.; beyond this the building has been rebuilt. The W. wall has one jamb of an original doorway opposite to the first but the N. and S. extremities of the wall are secondary. A cross wall half-way between the two E. doorways divides the original barn into two parts. The roof is supported on a series of jointed cruck trusses spanning E.–W. and set 10 ft. apart; the N. half retains three nearly complete trusses and the remains of a fourth; the truncated S. half retains two. The vertical members of each truss start at ground-level and stand 9 ft. high; they curve inwards at the top and are notched into the principals and fastened with pegs and free tenons. The principals are tenoned and pegged at the apex and support three purlins on each side; collar beams occur at the level of the middle purlins. Treswell's map shows a building in this position.

(4) Droop Farm, 200 yds. S. of the church, is a two-storied house of coursed rubble with a thatched roof. The S.W. front has four bays with sashed windows set at wide intervals; an old gable-line on the end wall shows that it has been heightened. A stone casement window in the S.E. wall has hollow-chamfered jambs and a square head. The house was probably built in the late 17th or early 18th century and remodelled in the 19th century.

(5) Cottage (75360805), perhaps of the late 16th or early 17th century, is built of rubble in two storeys with an iron roof. It contains elements of cruck trusses and an 18th-century plank-and-muntin partition.

(6) Cottage (75430797), of rubble, in one storey, with attics under a thatched roof, is probably of the late 17th or early 18th century. At the N.W. end is a later extension.

(7) Mount Pleasant Farm (77000837) is an L-shaped two-storied building with rubble walls with some brick dressings, and slated roofs. The oldest part, at the angle of the L, is an 18th-century cottage with wooden three-light casement windows; this was extended to the E. in the later part of the century, and to the S. in the 19th century.

Wonston

Monuments (8–25)

Unless otherwise described, the following monuments are of the 18th century and are two-storied, or single-storied with dormer-windowed attics; they have rubble walls, brick chimneys, thatched roofs and casement windows.

(8) *Cottage* (74420806), has some original leaded casement windows of the early 18th century. Inside, a large fireplace with a chamfered bressummer stands against the E. end wall and has the stairs beside it to the S.

(9) *Cottage* (74340807), 80 yds. W. of the foregoing, has a N. front of two bays with a central doorway. The fireplaces are in the end walls.

(10) *House*, immediately W. of the foregoing, is of rubble with brick dressings; it has two storeys with dormer-windowed attics under a tiled roof and is of the late 18th century.

(11) *House*, facing the foregoing on the N. side of the lane, is of brick and has gabled end walls with stone copings; the symmetrical three-bay S. front is patterned with blue headers.

(12) *Cottages* (74380808), four, stand in a row facing S.W. Treswell's map shows that cottages were set close together here in 1607, as is the case today, but none can be positively identified. The most southerly is two-storied, of coursed rubble with a slated roof, and is probably of the early 19th century. The next has brick walls on a high ashlar plinth and may go back to Treswell's time although the brick upper part, in English bond, was probably rebuilt early in the 18th century. The thatched roof continues over the next cottage to the N.W. which has similar brick walls and is probably contemporary. The next cottage is also contemporary with and in the same alignment as the foregoing; it has been heightened by the insertion of 19th-century semi-dormer attic windows.

(13) *Cottages*, two adjoining, continue the line of the foregoing towards the N.W. and are probably of the early 18th or possibly of the late 17th century. The S.W. fronts are rendered and the interior has been much altered in the conversion of the two dwellings into one.

(14) *House* (74280818), 100 yds. N.W. of the foregoing and on the opposite side of the road, is built of rubble to the height of the first-floor window-sills; above, it is of brick and the gabled S. end wall is patterned with blue headers. The roofs are slated and the windows are sashed. Presumably the original rubble house was heightened when the brick walls were built, and this work is probably dated by a stone plaque over the doorway, inscribed 'J.S.S. 1812'. The original building may date from the late 17th or early 18th century.

(15) *The Drum Inn* (74380815), 100 yds. E. of the foregoing, has rubble end walls and a three-bay brick S.E. front patterned with blue headers; the roof is slated.

(16) *Cottages* (74310821), two adjacent, were partly refronted and heightened in brickwork in the 19th century. Inside, the N. cottage has a stop-chamfered beam.

(17) *House* (74220837), perhaps originally of the late 17th century, was refronted with brick and divided into three tenements in the 19th century (date-stone 'WJM 1821'); it is now reconverted to a single house. Inside, the N. end room has a large fireplace, now blocked, with a wooden staircase beside it, and each of the other ground-floor rooms has a similar fireplace. One room has a chamfered beam.

(18) *Cottage* (74240840), has a large fireplace with stairs beside it against the N. end wall.

(19) *Cottage*, adjacent to the foregoing, to the N., may be of the late 17th century. The E. front is of two bays. The roof is slated.

(20) *Cottage* (74380870), has a rendered three-bay front, subsequently extended S. The roof is tiled.

(21) *Cottages* (74450877), four adjoining, are perhaps of the early 19th century; tiles, slates and thatch are used on the roofs. The two middle tenements are earlier than the end ones.

(22) *Cottage* (74730883), has rendered walls and may be of the late 17th century. A two-light casement window on the E. front has an ovolo-moulded wooden surround and mullion.

(23) *Cottage*, 100 yds. N.W. of the foregoing, has rendered walls; it may be of the late 17th century.

(24) *Farmhouse* (74660900), has rendered brick walls and tiled roofs and is of the late 18th or early 19th century, with a symmetrical three-bay S.E. front and sashed windows.

(25) *Inn*, 150 yds. S.W. of the foregoing, is a mid 18th-century building with walls of Flemish-bonded brickwork patterned with blue headers; the roofs are tiled. The symmetrical three-bay S. front has casement windows of three and two lights, and a plat-band at first-floor level. A rear wing at right-angles to the front range has walls of the same type of brickwork but with lower eaves. The E. room of the S. range has a corner fireplace, with an 18th-century stone surround with a fluted keystone and a moulded cornice. The room is lined with fielded oak panelling in two heights with a moulded dado rail.

Woodrow

(26) Farmhouse (74250953), 1 m. N.W. of the parish church, is two-storied and has cob walls and a thatched roof (Plate 59). A house is shown here on Treswell's map of 1607 and it is probable that this is the actual building; Treswell makes a distinction between houses with central fireplaces and those with the fireplaces against the end walls, and the building corresponds with the map in this respect as well as in location; thus the house may be assigned with some probability to the

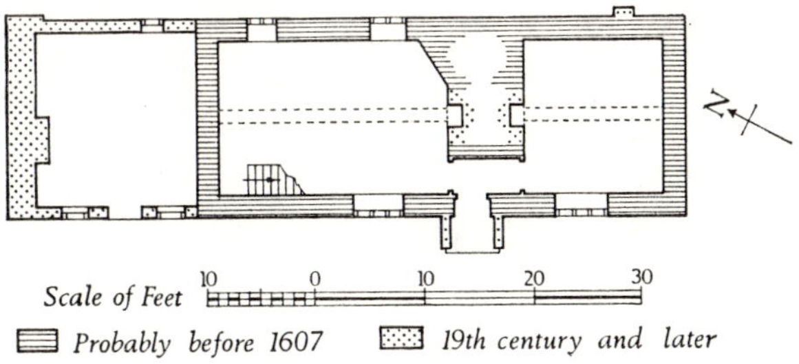

end of the 16th century. To the N. is a single-storied extension, probably of the 19th century, containing appliances for cider making. Inside, the former open fireplace and oven have been blocked. The stairs are modern. The first floor rests on rough stop-chamfered beams.

(27) High House Farm (73700949) has rendered walls and a tiled roof and probably dates from the first half of the 18th century; nevertheless there was a house here in 1607.

(28) Common Farm (73520960) is one-storied with attics, with rubble and brick walls and thatched roofs, and is of the 18th century. Inside, there are a stop-chamfered ceiling beam and a plank-and-muntin partition.

(29) Hazelbury Mill (73140975) is an 18th-century structure of rubble and brick in two storeys with tiled and stone-slated roofs. Later remodelling is attested by a stone inscribed 'WSA 1817'. A mill stood here in 1607.

(30) Cottage (72881039), of rendered rubble in two storeys with a tiled roof, is of the late 18th century.

(31) Cottages (73001020) are of rubble in two storeys with slated roofs. The S. cottage is of the late 18th or early 19th century; the other is a little later.

Kingston

(32) Farmhouse (74940987) consists of two parts, a front range facing E. and a rear range at right-angles; the latter was originally an independent cottage. Both ranges have thatched roofs. The E. range, of Flemish-bonded brickwork patterned with blue headers, is of the 18th century and has a symmetrical, two-storied front of five bays, with a central doorway and casement windows; the first floor is marked by a plat-band and there is a coved eaves cornice; the gabled end walls are surmounted by chimneystacks. The cottage at the rear is of the 17th century. It has one storey with an attic; the N. and S. walls are of coursed rubble and the gabled W. wall is of cob. A small three-light window on the N. side has chamfered wooden mullions. Internally, the original partitions of the cottage are lost but the ceiling is supported on large stop-chamfered beams, one transverse and one longitudinal. At the W. end is a large open fireplace and to the S. of the fireplace is space for a winding stair; both these openings are spanned by a continuous chamfered beam with splayed stops on which is carved the date 1666. A house is shown in this position on Treswell's map of 1607.

(33) Cottage, 50 yds. E. of the foregoing, is of rubble and brick in two storeys with thatched roofs. It is of 17th-century origin but was refronted in the late 18th or early 19th century.

(34) Farmhouse (74960971) is an 18th-century building of rubble and cob in one storey with attics.

(35) Cottage (75050972) is timber-framed and probably of the 16th century, but most of the original fabric was hidden or replaced by rubble walling in the 17th or 18th century. In the 19th century the walls were heightened in brickwork and the cottage now has two storeys. It is identifiable on Treswell's map.

(36) Cottage, 70 yds. S.W. of the foregoing, is of rubble and cob in two storeys. The original 18th-century walls were heightened in brickwork in the 19th century.

(37) House (75090976), of coursed rubble in two storeys with tiled roofs over thatch, dates from the early 19th century. The symmetrical three-bay S.W. front has a round-headed central doorway.

(38) Date Stone of 1679, from a cottage that was recently burned down, is preserved in a modern cottage on the same site, 30 yds. N. of (37).

(39) Cottage (75080980), 15 yds. N. of the foregoing, is two-storied and of coursed rubble with a tiled roof; it is of the early 18th century. The rendered S.E. front of the original range has a central doorway flanked by casement windows, and three corresponding windows on the first floor. The building was extended S.W. in the 19th century.

(40) Back Lane Farm (75250944) is a single-storied rubble and cob building with attics under a thatched roof; it is probably of the 17th century. The N.W. front is of two bays with a central doorway. Inside, at the N.E. end is an open fireplace with an oven; a second chimneystack occurs at the centre of the plan. Treswell's map of 1607 shows a house in this position.

Late 18th and early 19th-century monuments also include—*Almshouses*, immediately N. of the church, with a lengthy poem incised on two marble wall tablets by Marshall of Blandford; *Sunday School*, 275 yds. N.W. of the church, dated 1832; *House* (73950950); *Kingstag Bridge* (72711035), apparently a mid 19th-century structure although a bridge is shown on the plan of 1607; *Lyddon House* (73200974), with brick stables and barn; *Smithy* and *House* (75300996); two *Cottages* at Woodrow (74120962 and 30 yds. to the S.E.); *Cottages* at Park Gate, at the S. end of the parish; *Stockfield Farm* (75500902).

MEDIAEVAL AND LATER EARTHWORKS

(41) Cultivation Remains. Treswell's map shows that the open fields of the parish were already enclosed by 1607. Fragmentary remains of ridge-and-furrow occur in a few places, for example at 769084 and 769077; these and other traces that appear on air photographs (R.A.F. CPE/UK 1974: 1180–4, 3180–5) clearly antedate the field boundaries of 1607. The ridge-and-furrow was arranged in curving furlongs.

22 HILTON (7803)

(O.S. 6 ins. ST 70 SE, ST 70 NE)

Hilton covers an area of nearly 3,050 acres, straddling the summit of the Chalk escarpment, which at this point is considerably broken. The S.E. part of the parish, between 400 and 700 ft. above sea-level and mainly on Chalk, is drained by the headwaters of the Devil's Brook and the Milborne Brook. Except for the Chalk spur of Bulbarrow, the N.W. part of the parish is lower and lies on Greensand, Gault and Kimmeridge Clay; here the land is drained by streams flowing N. to the R. Lydden. The village of Hilton, in the S.E., is surrounded by extensive areas of strip fields (29, *a*). To W. and N.W. lie the hamlets of Lower and Higher

HILTON *The parish church of All Saints*

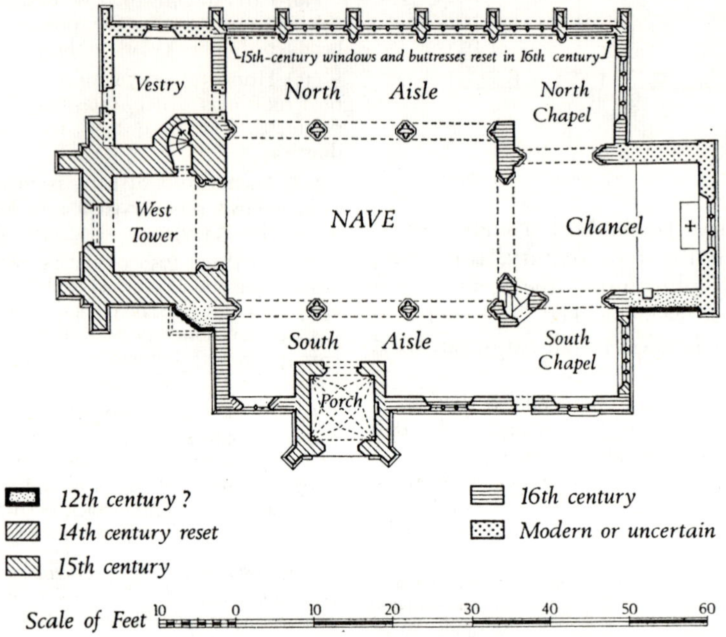

Ansty, perhaps secondary settlements and apparently without open fields. Further to the W. and N. lie the farmsteads of Cothayes, Hatherly and Rawlsbury; these are associated with old enclosed fields (29, *b*) and are more certainly secondary. Newton Farm at the S. extremity of the parish may have a similar origin.[1]

ECCLESIASTICAL

(1) THE PARISH CHURCH OF ALL SAINTS is built partly of squared rubble and partly of flint with bonding courses and dressings of ashlar. The roofs are covered with slate and with lead. That there was an early church on the site is attested by a late 12th-century font, by several detached fragments of 12th-century architectural ornament and by the anomalous position of the S. porch, which shows that the S. aisle was formerly narrower than at present; part of the S. wall of the chancel and the base of a ruined buttress at the S.E. corner of the tower may survive from this period. Capitals reset in the N. arcade of the nave suggest that an aisle was built in the 13th century, but little trace of it remains; the position of the porch shows that it was to the S. The *West Tower* and *South Porch* are of the late 15th century. The church took its present form in the 16th century when the *Nave*, *South Aisle* and *Chancel* were rebuilt and the *North Aisle* was added, the N. arcade probably being set on the foundations of the original N. wall. The N. Aisle extends E. to embrace part of the chancel, forming a *North Chapel* which is entered from the chancel through a side arch; the N. wall of the aisle includes a row of 15th-century windows and buttresses, almost certainly from Milton Abbey. In 1569 the S. Aisle was widened, without altering the position of the 15th-century porch, and a *South Chapel* was formed to correspond with that on the N., but separated from the aisle by a N.-S. wall in line with the chancel arch; this wall was not removed until the end of the 19th century and an old photograph preserved in the church shows that it was pierced by a small roundheaded window, suggesting that it may have been a 12th-century survival.

The church is of some architectural interest, particularly for the N. windows, and it has a fine tower. Painted wooden panels from Milton Abbey are noteworthy.

Architectural Description—The *Chancel* ($23\frac{1}{4}$ ft. by 16 ft.) has a 19th-century three-light E. window. The N. wall contains a four-centred 16th-century archway to the N. chapel, of two hollow-chamfered orders springing from responds with quarter and three-quarter shafts with moulded caps and plain plinths. The E. part of the S. wall may perhaps be of the 12th century, but it has been much restored. The opening to the S. chapel has a two-centred arch of three orders, the outer and inner orders ogee-moulded, the middle order hollow-chamfered; the arch springs from responds similar to those of the N. archway but slenderer and with subsequently recut capitals. An opening with a flattened triangular head in the S.W. corner of the chancel was

[1] Fägersten, 189, 190; Hutchins IV, 355, 356.

probably cut in the 16th century to give access to a pulpit; this opening intersects the former rood vice. The early 16th-century two-centred chancel arch has two ogee-moulded orders springing from attached shafts with moulded caps and plain plinths; the shafts are separated by hollow-chamfers decorated with leaf sprays at capital level. The rood-vice was entered through a four-centred doorway in the N.W. corner of the S. chapel and it ended at an ogee-headed doorway in the W. side of the S. abutment of the chancel arch, directly over the later pulpit opening.

The *Nave* (34¾ ft. by 20¼ ft.) has N. and S. arcades of three bays. In the N. arcade the arches are two-centred and of two moulded orders springing from piers and responds with attached shafts separated by hollow-chamfers; the shafts have moulded caps and the bases are set on octagonal plinths; the heads of the hollow-chamfers on the easternmost respond are carved with fleurs-de-lis and foliage. The moulded caps and part of the shafts of the second pier are reused 13th-century material, and similar material occurs in the W. respond. The S. arcade has segmental-pointed arches of three orders, the outer and inner orders moulded, the middle order hollow-chamfered and continuous on the piers and responds; the moulded orders spring from attached shafts with coarsely moulded caps and with bases on octagonal plinths.

The *North Chapel* (13 ft. by 13¾ ft.) and *North Aisle* (10¾ ft. wide) differ in width but have no other structural division. Externally the walls have chamfered moulded plinths in three heights, the topmost moulding forming the window-sill; above the windows is a parapet with two moulded strings. The E. wall contains a window of four cinquefoil-headed lights with vertical tracery in a four-centred head under a label; the surround is hollow-chamfered externally and moulded internally; at the apex of the moulded rear arch is a boss carved with oak leaves. The N. wall, almost certainly from Milton Abbey (*see* p. 184), is of six bays separated externally by buttresses of two weathered stages which continue up as standards to the parapet string-course and end at gargoyles: a beast's head, a man playing bagpipes, a winged beast, a devil swallowing a man, a grotesque man with a barrel (Plate 181). The E. and W. end bays are narrower than the others; they have two-centred blind arches with hollow-chamfered orders showing externally and internally; externally the chamfer dies into the responds, internally it is continued on the jambs. The windows of the intervening bays (Plate 142) are similar to that in the E. wall of the aisle and internally have carved apex bosses with foliage and the heads of a man and a woman. The mouldings of the rear arches spring from attached shafts with caps carved with conventional foliage. These are the lateral shafts of triple clusters in which the shafts are separated by hollow-chamfers; the central shafts originally supported vault-ribs but these have been omitted and their truncated springings have been notched to resemble small weathered buttresses. The moulded pedestals of the clusters project from the wall some 4 ft. above the aisle floor-level. Corresponding wall-shafts with similar capitals and truncated vaulting-ribs occur on the N. wall of the N. transept at Milton Abbey. The W. wall of the N. aisle contains a modern doorway to the vestry.

The *South Chapel* (13½ ft. by 11¼ ft.) and the *South Aisle* (10¼ ft. wide) are now without structural division but until late in the 19th century they were separated by a thick wall, as described above. The external walls have a moulded plinth and cornice. In the E. wall is a late 15th-century window with five ogee-headed cinquefoil lights and vertical tracery in a two-centred head; the reveals and rear arch are casement-moulded and the mouldings of the rear arch are continued on the jambs; the external label has square stops enclosing flowers. To the E. of the porch the S. wall has two square-headed windows each of three lights with four-centred heads under a square label and with a plain segmental rear arch; between them is a narrow doorway with a four-centred head, continuous chamfered jambs with shaped stops and a moulded label with a raised centre and a moulded and foliated corbel on the apex. In the ashlar above the windows are three sunk panels inscribed respectively 'T.I., AO 1569', 'W.F', and 'H.W., AO 1569'. The S. doorway, set inside the line of the 16th-century S. wall, is of the second half of the 15th century; it has a moulded two-centred head and continuous jambs with run-out stops. To the W. of the porch the S. wall is pierced by a window which incorporates late 14th-century elements, including two trefoil ogee-headed lights in a square head.

The *West Tower* (10¾ ft. by 12 ft.) is of the late 15th century. It has three stages, with a moulded plinth, weathered string-courses, square-set buttresses in four weathered stages, an embattled parapet and crocketed pinnacles rising from gargoyles at the corners of the parapet string-course; other parapet gargoyles occur at the centre of each side. The vice is in an octagonal turret projecting from the E. part of the N. face. The two-centred tower arch has a panelled soffit with two moulded ribs springing from attached jamb-shafts with moulded caps and chamfered plinths; the jambs contain two heights and the arch soffits one height of paired stone panels, rounded at head and foot. The doorway to the vice has a monolithic four-centred head and continuous chamfered jambs with shaped stops. The W. doorway has a moulded two-centred head with continuous jambs and shaped stops; inside is a monolithic hollow-chamfered rear arch with a raised centre. Over the W. doorway is a casement-moulded two-centred window of four transomed lights, with four-centred openings below the transom, two-centred cinquefoil openings above and vertical tracery in the head. The S.E. buttress of the tower incorporates a baulk of masonry that seems to survive from an earlier stage of development; much of the ashlar facing has broken away but the chamfered plinth is suggestive of the 12th century. In the second stage of the tower, the E. wall has a casement-moulded window of two trefoil ogee-headed lights with a quatrefoil in a two-centred head. The top stage has, in each face, a belfry window similar to that of the second stage but larger.

The *South Porch* (8 ft. square) projects some 4½ ft. into the S. aisle; it was built late in the 15th century and is of Ham Hill ashlar, with a moulded plinth. The entrance has a moulded two-centred head and continuous jambs. Inside, a stone fan vault springs from angle corbels, three with foliage and one carved with a human head. The vault has moulded ribs and trefoil-headed panels; the square centre compartment has four quatrefoil panels with bosses at the intersections; these are carved with foliage, a rose, and the arms of Milton and Abbotsbury Abbeys.

The very low-pitched lean-to *Roof* of the N. chapel and N. aisle is probably of the mid 16th century; it is of twelve bays and is divided into square coffers by heavily moulded transverse and longitudinal beams with foliate bosses at the intersections; moulded joists, four to each coffer, run from E. to W. The roof of the S. chapel and S. aisle is of twelve bays and has moulded transverse beams with slightly raised centres; these and similarly moulded longitudinal beams and wall-plates form coffers as in the N. aisle. Foliate bosses mask the intersections of the principal members. The joists in alternate coffers run E.–W. and N.–S.

Fittings—*Bells:* six; 3rd, from Salisbury foundry, inscribed in black-letter 'Non nobis Domine non nobis', 15th century; 4th, by Thomas Purdue, 1684; 5th, by Roger Purdue, 1637; 6th, by John Danton, 1626; others modern. *Brackets:* In chancel, in E.

wall, four octagonal stone brackets with hollow-chamfered under-edges, perhaps mediaeval. *Chairs:* pair, with high backs and scroll framing to cane panels, shaped octagonal legs with gadrooned knops, curved diagonal stretchers with turned finial at intersection, early 18th century, perhaps foreign. *Chests:* two; one with plain lid, panelled front and ends, moulded framing and three plain lock-plates, top rail inscribed MH ANNO DOMINI 1638; another, of oak, to contain bible, with sloping lid, and front enriched with guilloche ornament, 17th century. *Coffin-lid:* In churchyard, immediately S. of tower, tapering slab, 4¾ ft. long, with double hollow-chamfered edge and traces of cross, early 14th century, broken. *Coffin-stools:* two, with moulded tops, turned legs, moulded rails and stretchers, *c.* 1700. *Door:* In S. doorway, in two leaves, with nail-studded boards and double-hinged strap hinges with fleur-de-lis terminals; 15th century with modern repairs. *Font:* In tower, square Purbeck marble bowl with four round-headed panels on each side, *c.* 1200, stem and base modern. *Graffiti:* On tower vice doorway, 18th-century initials and dates; on porch arch, 17th-century scratchings; on S. doorway, RICHARD MICHEL 1625; on S. door, A.L. 1720.

Monument and *Floor-slabs. Monument:* In N. chapel, on E. wall, stone panel (28 ins. by 25 ins.) with moulded border surrounding shield-of-arms (*unidentified* 2), 17th century. *Floor-slabs:* At E. end of N. chapel, (1) illegible, 'MA . . .' perhaps mid 17th century; (2) anonymous, with crude skull and cross-bones; at W. end of N. chapel, (3) probably of a vicar of Hilton, 17th century, with later inscription mainly illegible. *Niches:* In S. porch, in E. wall, trefoil-headed recess in square surround with foliate cusps and spandrels, and ribbed vaulting with rosettes at intersections, early 16th century; externally, above entrance to porch, trefoil-headed recess with hollow-chamfered jambs, early 16th century. *Paintings:* In W. tower, twelve wooden panels (7¼ ft. by 1¼ ft.) depicting apostles, late 15th century in modern framing, removed from Milton Abbey (Hutchins, 2nd ed., IV, 230), (Plates 25, 137). *Piscina:* In chancel, plain recess with projecting sill and shallow circular bowl, date uncertain. *Plate:* includes silver cup of 1662, stand-paten of 1695 and alms-dish of 1778. *Pulpit:* of oak, polygonal, with three sides composed of late 16th-century panels carved with diaper pattern and foliate tracery between moulded stiles, fourth side with incised 17th-century line ornament, and fifth side with two heights of mid 17th-century plain panels in moulded stiles and rails; book-ledge and stone base modern. *Royal Arms:* Over S. doorway, arms of Victoria in painted cast-iron. *Stoup:* In N.E. corner of porch, remains of round bowl hollowed from a block of stone, with stop-chamfered outer edge, 15th century. *Sundials:* On top of S.E. corner of S. aisle, sculptured stone tablet dated 1690, with scrolled top carved with sun face from which projects fretted wrought-iron gnomon. High up on S. wall of S. aisle, towards E. end, scratch-dial, probably of 1569. *Miscellanea:* In W. wall of N. aisle, (1) reset hollow-chamfered stone panelling, perhaps from a parapet, consisting of diagonal squares, some cusped, with shields: (i) Earl of Cornwall, (ii) a device representing a nail threaded through a tau-cross and piercing a heart, (iii) Cerne Abbey, early 16th century. In external plinth of S. wall of S. chapel, (2) chamfered stone ledge, perhaps dole-stone. In S. aisle, high up at W. end of S. wall, (3) reset grotesque corbel with human head and winged beast body, 15th century; on W. wall, (4) angel corbel, 15th century. Detached, (5) various architectural fragments including cushion-capital and base of attached shaft, intermediate stone of attached shaft, and abacus with chevron ornament, all 12th century. In N. vestry, (6) two panels from lead roof with initials and dates 'I W, S F, 1722' and 'M A, I D, 1741'. In W. tower, (7) two pairs of cherub heads, carved wood, 18th century.

SECULAR

(2) VILLAGE HALL (76470313), at Lower Ansty, is of one storey and was originally a malthouse; it was built in 1777 by Charles Hall, reputedly with material from Higher Melcombe, Melcombe Horsey (3), *see* p. 168. The malthouse was remodelled and extensively rebuilt in 1948 when it was converted into a hall. The N. and part of the W. walls are original; the W. wall incorporates several transferred 17th-century features, including a doorway and parts of three two-light stone-mullioned windows.

MONUMENTS (3–27)

Unless otherwise described the following monuments are two-storied dwellings of the 18th century. In early examples the walls are of cob or, occasionally, rubble; later examples are of rubble and flint with brick bonding courses; the roofs are generally thatched. Many cottages have exposed ceiling-beams.

HILTON

(3) *Hilton Lower Farm* (78380286), house, has been more than doubled in size by 19th-century additions on the N. side. The original 18th-century dwelling, a two-bay cottage facing S., has brick walls in Flemish bond with vitrified headers. The 19th-century building is of flint with brick bonding-courses and has a small contemporary wrought-iron porch to the N. An open fireplace in the original kitchen has a heavy chamfered bressummer.

A nearby *Granary*, now demolished, was of brick with a tiled roof and was built late in the 18th century; it was raised above ground on an arcaded brick substructure.

(4) *Cottage* (78280298) is single-storied with an attic.

(5) *Cottage* (78300288), formerly the Crown Inn, incorporates an early 18th-century single-storied cob cottage.

(6) *Cottage* (78290289) is of the early 18th century.

(7)–(10) *Cottages* (78280295), (78240300), (78300306) and (78170310).

(11) *Cottages* (78050310), two adjacent; that to the E. is of squared rubble and dates from the 17th century; it has been extended to the W. in brick and flint at two periods.

HIGHER ANSTY

(12) *Range*, of three dwellings (76730398), is of the late 18th and early 19th century; the flint walls have brick bonding-courses and quoins.

(13) *Lower Farm* (76680395), house, is single-storied with dormer-windowed attics. The walls of the original range are of rubble with rough ashlar dressings; in the extensions they are of rubble, flint and brick; the roofs are thatched. The original range is of the early 16th century; in the 17th century it was extended to the S. and in the 18th century a pair of cottages was added to the N., at right-angles to the original range. On the W. side the 16th-century range has a square-headed stone doorway with a

HINTON ST. MARY. (20) Roman mosaic pavement. Detail. 4th-century

HINTON ST. MARY. (20) Roman mosaic pavement. General view. 4th-century

HINTON ST. MARY. (20) Roman mosaic pavement. Detail. 4th–century

hollow-chamfered and ogee-moulded surround; carved on the lintel is 'R.G. 1695'. The E. side retains a dormer window with a moulded wooden surround. Inside, the original range has a ground-floor room with a coffered ceiling of nine panels formed by intersecting beams and wall-plates, with ogee and hollow-chamfered mouldings.

(14) *Cottages* (76700400), two adjoining, have rubble walls with inserted brick dressings. The E. cottage probably dates from late in the 17th century and has an E. extension in cob; the W. cottage is of the 18th century.

(15) *Cottages*, two adjoining (76830398), are now united as a single house. The E. cottage is of the 16th century but it has an 18th-century façade with a plat-band and a coved cornice to the S. front; a stepped brick chimneystack projects from the gabled E. end wall. Inside, a ground-floor room has a six-panel ceiling with intersecting deep-chamfered beams. The W. cottage is of the 19th century.

(16) *Higher Ansty Farm* (76790399), house, has an 18th-century symmetrical three-bay S. front.

(17) *Pleck Farm* (76670417), house, was built late in the 17th or early in the 18th century. A lead pump in the garden is initialled and dated C.H.E. 1831.

Lower Ansty

(18) *House* (76520320), formerly several dwellings, is U-shaped in plan and has walls of banded flint and brick. The N. and W. ranges date from *c.* 1800; the S. range is modern.

(19)–(22) *Cottages*, are located as follows: (19) 76440308, (20) 76400296, (21) 76260282, (22) 76240278; the last comprises two adjoining three-bay cottages, that to the N. is of the early and that to the S. is of the late 18th century.

(23) *Post Office* (76270267), has an L-shaped plan and is built of cob. The date 1735 scratched on a piece of clunch that was found during recent alterations is probably the date of building. Two iron-framed casement windows with leaded lights are preserved.

(24)–(25) *Cottages* (76600314, 76650313) are of the 19th century; in its lower part (25) incorporates the walls of an earlier building.

(26) *Aller Farm* (76700302) probably originated in the 17th century but it was subsequently enlarged and may at one time have become several dwellings. Early in the 19th century the house was remodelled and no early features remain visible inside. Squared rubble quoins in the S.W. front provide evidence of earlier fenestration.

(27) *Cottages*, two (769029), one N. and one S. of the road, were built late in the 18th or early in the 19th century; they have walls of flint with brick quoins, and brick bonding-courses at intervals of approximately 1¼ ft.

MEDIAEVAL AND LATER EARTHWORKS

(28) Settlement Remains (784029) cover 7 acres on the S.E. side of Hilton village. The remains are all within an area that is bounded to N.E. and S.E. by a bank 2 ft. to 3 ft. high and 20 ft. wide; they consist of closes of various sizes and shapes, with sides up to 80 ft. long, bounded by low banks and scarps. Within the closes are platforms, probably of houses; they occur most conspicuously along the existing road to the S.W., where there are at least seven platforms up to 20 ft. by 60 ft. Many of the closes and the boundary bank were still in use in 1771 (Map by Wm. Woodward, 1771, see p. 183) although the house sites had been abandoned.

(29) Cultivation Remains: (*a*) A three-field system existed at Hilton in the 14th century (H. L. Gray, *English Field Systems*, 1915, appx. II, 461) but the date of enclosure is unknown. Strip lynchets of these fields cover about 60 acres around the village. Due W. of Manor Farm (776037) a particularly well-preserved set, of contour type with massive risers, appears in part to overlie 'Celtic' fields. On Thomas's Hill (793026) a series of narrow contour strip lynchets, in part cut by the Hilton–Milton Abbas road, curves E. round the spur and runs into and over 'Celtic' fields (*see* Group 52, p. 337). A more extensive group of contour strip lynchets E. of the village (789029) was formerly arranged in interlocking furlongs with run-out and ramped ends. At a subsequent period but before 1769 (*see* Woodward's map, 1771, and Tithe Map of Hilton, 1842) the area was divided into rectangular closes and the lower treads were reploughed; this has resulted in the treads having squared-off ends delimited by old hedge banks.

(*b*) In the N. of the parish around Rawlsbury Farm (765054) are extensive areas of ridge-and-furrow, 5 yds. to 7 yds. wide, confined within fields which appear to have been enclosed direct from the waste.

(*c*) In the S.W. of the parish (757030) are the massive risers of two cross-contour strip lynchets. These can only be explained as part of the former open fields of Melcombe Horsey (*see* p. 172), whence it appears that the parish boundary must have been changed at some period.

ROMAN AND PREHISTORIC

'Celtic' Fields, *see* pp. 333–7., Groups (48–52).

Rawlsbury Camp, *see* Stoke Wake (6), p. 259.

(30) Bowl Barrow (77730136), at the S. end of the parish, 350 yds. S.E. of Newton Farm, lies on a N.W. slope just off the top of a spur. The barrow was excavated in 1916 by Maj. C. Ashburnham and proved to be of two main periods. A primary crouched interment in a cist cut into the natural chalk lay under a flint cairn about 38 ft. in diameter and surrounded by a ditch. The cairn was later enlarged to its present diameter and a second ditch was cut. Numerous inhumations and one cremation, probably all secondary, were found in the mound, and two cremations, one with a small bronze awl, were found in ridged Food-vessel urns in the inner ditch (Dorset *Procs.* XXXVIII (1917), 74–80; *Arch.J.* CXIX (1962), 65, *s.v.* Bingham's Melcombe). A large hollow in the centre and an apparent berm on the W. are presumably the result of Maj. Ashburnham's excavation. Diam. 68 ft., ht. 8 ft.

(31) Bowl Barrow (78230490), 160 yds. W.N.W. of Hill Barn and 800 ft. above O.D., lies on the gentle S.W. slope of a broad ridge. Much ploughed. Diam. about 40 ft., ht. 1 ft.

UNDATED

(32) Valley Bottom Enclosure (777016), of 9 acres, lies in Coombe Bottom immediately E. of Newton Farm. The flat bottom of a narrow E.–W. dry valley is enclosed on the N., E. and S. sides by a bank, 10 ft. wide and 2 ft. high, with an outer, uphill, ditch 8 ft. wide and 2 ft. deep. The bank and ditch do not extend across the mouth of the valley. There is an entrance 20 ft. wide in the centre of the short E. side, at the head of the valley. In at least two places the enclosure bank lies over lynchets of 'Celtic' fields (Group 48).

23 HINTON ST. MARY (7816)

(O.S. 6 ins. ST 71 NE)

The parish covers 1,070 acres, nearly all of it on Corallian Beds. To the E. the land slopes gently down to Chiverick's Brook and to the W. it inclines a little more sharply down to the R. Stour, both streams being about 180 ft. above sea-level (Plate 2). The most important monument in the parish is the recently discovered Roman villa, with a fine quality mosaic pavement including a head with a *Chi-Rho* monogram. The Manor House incorporates a mediaeval hall, possibly of the 13th century, and there is also a large tithe barn.

ECCLESIASTICAL

(1) THE PARISH CHURCH OF ST. PETER stands on the S. side of the village. The *West Tower* dates from the second half of the 15th century but the rest of the church, consisting of *Chancel*, *Nave*, *North Vestry* and *South Porch*, was rebuilt in 1846; it is of ashlar and squared rubble, with stone-slated roofs. Some features from the earlier building are incorporated in the new fabric.

Architectural Description—The 19th-century *Chancel* has a two-centred E. window of three lights with vertical tracery, and similar two-light windows in the N. and S. walls; there is also a square-headed S. doorway. The chancel arch is of mediaeval origin but rebuilt in 1846; it is approximately semicircular and has two orders, the inner hollow-chamfered, the outer chamfered; the voussoirs may be of 12th or 13th-century origin but they were probably recut in the 15th century. The capitals are modern but the responds are probably refaced 15th-century material; they comprise a central attached shaft flanked by hollow-chamfers which in turn are bordered to E. and W. by ogee mouldings; the square plinths are modern. The N. and S. walls of the *Nave* are uniform, each having a centrally placed doorway with a chamfered two-centred head and continuous jambs, and two square-headed windows, each with three two-centred trefoil-headed lights below vertical tracery in casement-moulded surrounds with square labels; the two eastern windows retain some 15th-century stonework. The N. doorway opens into the *Vestry*; the S. doorway is sheltered by the *Porch*, which has a chamfered two-centred outer arch with a moulded label and return stops.

The *West Tower* (9 ft. square) is of two stages, with a chamfered plinth and an embattled parapet; the walls are of squared and coursed rubble with ashlar dressings; the stone is mostly Marnhull limestone but Greensand also occurs, especially near the base. The hollow-chamfered string-course between the stages is decorated at each corner with an angel bearing a blank shield. Above the angels each corner of the top stage has an angle pilaster, itself of two stages separated by a weathered offset. At the base of the parapet is a hollow-chamfered string-course with a gargoyle at each corner: a devil's mask swallowing a human body, a winged mask, a monkey, a human head; there is also a grotesque mask at the centre of the N. side. The parapet has a moulded coping and four crocketed pinnacles. The tower arch is segmental-pointed and of two chamfered orders which die into plain responds. In the upper part of the lower stage, on the N. side, is a small square-headed loop. The W. doorway has a two-centred head with a label, and two orders of ovolo mouldings which continue on the jambs to run-out stops. Over the W. doorway is a small two-centred two-light window, probably of 1846. In the upper stage each side of the tower has a 15th-century casement-moulded belfry window of two trefoil-headed lights with blind tracery in a two-centred head, and a hoodmould with carved head stops.

Fittings—*Bells:* two; treble 1842, tenor inscribed W P 1614, in old timber bell-cage. *Communion Table:* with arcaded supports, *c.* 1846. *Font:* of Purbeck marble, coarsely tooled; round bowl with tapering sides and lobed twelve-sided moulding underneath, stem cylindrical, base circular, coarsely moulded and much worn; bowl and base probably 13th century, bowl with later mediaeval recutting; stem modern. *Monuments* and *Floor-slab. Monuments:* In nave, on N. wall, (1) of Thomas Freke, 1642, black tablet with painted inscription in moulded stone surround with skull below, set between Corinthian columns on foliate brackets and surmounted by broken pediment with arms of Freke impaling Dodington; monument erected 1655 (Plate 33). In S. porch, on W. wall, (2) of John, 1769, William, 1792 and Anne Castleman, 1810, oval white marble tablet on shaped black background; (3) of Rachel Castleman, 1771, and others of same family, black painted stone tablet in rectangular moulded stone surround. *Floor-slab:* In nave, on S. side, of Samuell Rake, 1695, Purbeck marble slab with incised border of columns and arch. *Plate:* includes Elizabethan silver cup and cover-paten by the Gillingham silversmith, flagon of 1664 with maker's mark T L and arms of Freke impaling Dodington, and second paten with faint maker's mark TL. *Pulpit:* polygonal, of oak with mahogany veneer, each side having fielded and enriched panels in two heights below ledge supported on foliate brackets, 18th century; panelled pedestal later. *Royal Arms:* over chancel arch, of cast-iron, 19th century. *Tables of Creed and Decalogue:* incised on slate in traceried wooden surrounds, 19th century.

SECULAR

(2) THE MANOR HOUSE, immediately N.E. of the church, is a two-storied building of ashlar and squared rubble, with dormer-windowed attics under stone-slated roofs (Plate 53). The walls of a mediaeval hall are identifiable at the centre of the S.E. range but it has been chambered over, the roof has been renewed, the windows have been altered and it retains little of its original character. The remains of an opening with a chamfered two-centred head suggest that the hall may be of 13th-century origin. The rest of the house appears to be mainly of the 17th century, enlarged and altered in the 18th, 19th and 20th centuries, but the cross-wings to N.E. and S.W. of the hall may incorporate mediaeval elements.

The S.E. front has, as the central part, the S. wall of the original hall; it has a chamfered plinth and is now pierced on the ground floor by square-headed two-light and three-light transomed windows with hollow-chamfered surrounds; they are perhaps of the 17th century but restored and probably enlarged. Over them the inserted first-floor chambers have gabled semi-dormer windows of two large lights with square labels. To the S.W., the two-storied 17th-century porch has a modern outer doorway with a four-centred head; above is a three-light mullioned window with a label surmounted by a rectangular stone panel carved with an achievement-of-arms of Freke impaling Dodington (*c.* 1630–1642). To the east of the hall the S.E. front comprises the projecting gabled end wall of the N.E. wing, with a transomed three-light window on the ground floor and a modern three-light window in the gable. Beside the sill of the upper window is a date-stone inscribed 'E 1695'. S.W. of the porch is the gabled end wall of the S.W. wing; it is of two storeys with an attic; on the ground floor is a large three-light transomed window; the first and attic storeys have narrower three-light windows.

The S.W. elevation is mainly of the 17th century with a modern extension at the N.W. end. It is two-storied, with gabled dormer windows in the attics. The ground-floor rooms have low four-light windows with labels; the first floor has similar three-light windows and between two of them is a date-stone inscribed 'S.G.B. 1664'. A large two-light mullioned and transomed window lights the main staircase. The N.E. front has been rebuilt; it is of one storey with transomed three-light windows on the ground floor and modern dormer windows above.

Inside, in the passage which runs along the N.W. side of the former hall is a narrow opening, now a wall-niche, with a chamfered two-centred head and continuous jambs. The voussoirs of the head of a larger mediaeval opening in the same wall are visible from the first floor through a trap-door. A fireplace in the first-floor corridor which follows the inner face of the N.W. wall of the hall has a chamfered four-centred stone head and continuous jambs. On either side of the fireplace are shaped stone corbels, probably for the support of former roof trusses. At the S.W. end of the hall, on the ground floor, the doorway to the study is of the 16th century, with a four-centred ogee-moulded and hollow-chamfered head, with continuous jambs and carved stops. The dining-room, in the former hall, and the drawing-room to the N.E. are lined with reset 17th-century oak panelling; the fireplace of the intervening room has an 18th-century surround. The staircase has a 16th-century moulded plaster ceiling (Plate 71), recently brought from Fiddleford Mill, Sturminster Newton (4); it is decorated with curvilinear and straight ribbing interlaced to form geometric panels; these are

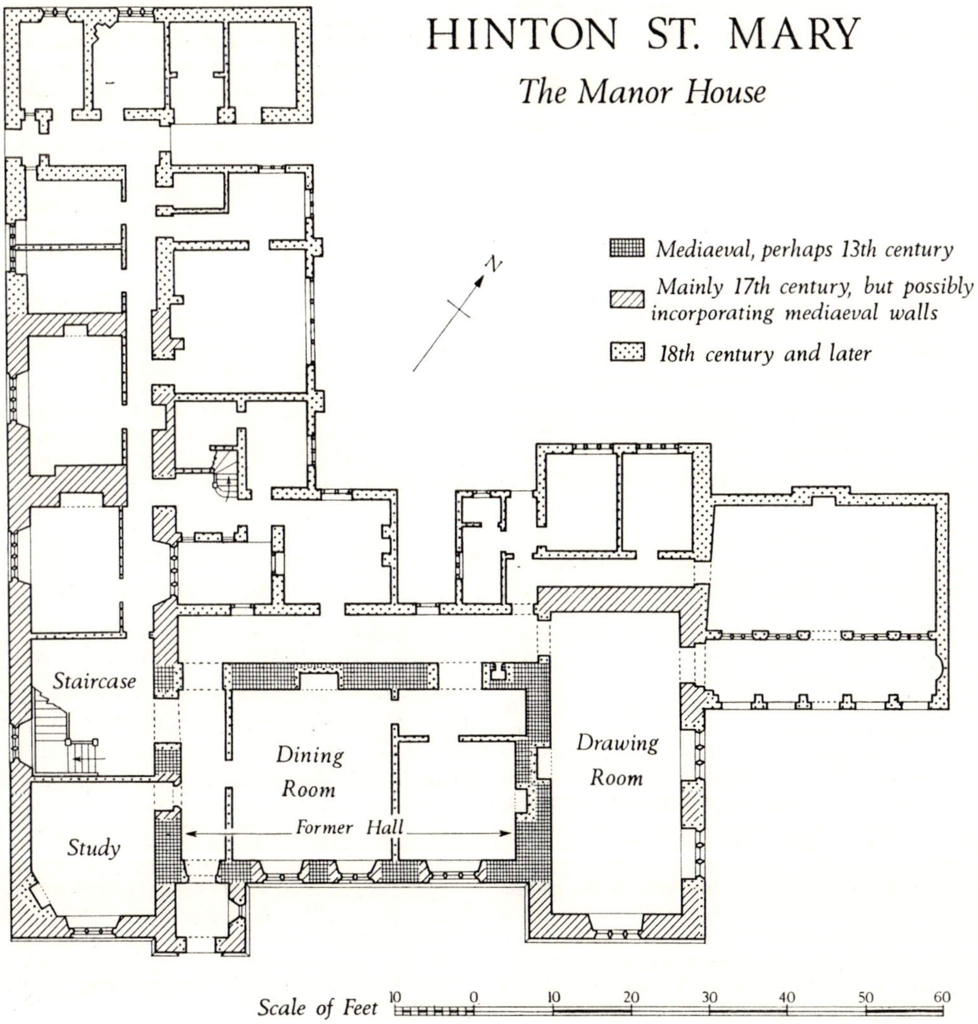

enriched at the intersections with foliate bosses and at the angles with fleurs-de-lis and other ornaments. One lozenge includes the initials A W, probably for Ann White of Fiddleford (*see* p. 272). The drawing-room contains a modern copy of the same ceiling.

The *Tithe Barn*, 100 yds. S. of the house, is of rubble and ashlar with a modern tiled roof and is probably of the late 15th or early 16th century. It is now used as an assembly hall. On the N.W. side are two transeptal entrance bays; the S.E. side has several two-stage buttresses with weathered offsets; between them modern entrances probably take the place of original barn doorways. Inside, the roof has been restored but some old timbers are preserved. The collar-braced trusses are supported on vertical wall-posts which rest on stone corbels; rough curved wind-braces occur between the purlins. A reset stone fireplace incorporates, as an overmantel, a 15th-century carved panel of Ham Hill stone which is said to have been originally the front of an altar in Cerne Abbey; it has three square panels of sub-cusped quatrefoils. At the centre of each panel is a foliate boss; two have sacred monograms and the third is carved with the letters 'I V' mitred, for John Vane, abbot 1458–1470.

Stables, 50 yds. S. of the church, are of coursed and squared rubble with heavy chamfered eaves cornices and a modern tiled roof; they are probably of the late 16th century. On the E. side are five original two-stage buttresses with weathered offsets; between some of these are reset and restored square-headed three-light windows with hollow-chamfered mullions and jambs, and square labels; in the wall above are several chamfered rectangular loops. The W. side has nine similar buttresses and a number of similar loops.

(3) Burt's Farm (78691621), 130 yds. N. of the church, is a two-storied 17th-century farmhouse, built partly of ashlar and partly of coursed rubble, with a thatched roof. The plan is L-shaped with the re-entrant angle to the E. and the main doorway in this corner. Adjacent, on the ground floor, the N.E. front of the S.E. wing has a stone window of four square-headed lights with a moulded label; at attic level in the gable of the N.E. wing is a single stone light, now blocked; all other openings have later wooden surrounds. An open fireplace at the S.E. end of the S.E. wing has a chamfered oak bressummer, and the ceiling beam in the S.E. room has cyma mouldings and shaped stops. In the upper flight of the stairs the handrails are supported on baluster-profiled slats.

(4) Dalton's Farm (78691628), 190 yds. N. of the church, is of the 18th century. It is of two storeys with attics and its walls are mainly of coursed rubble, but the E. front is of ashlar and the chimneystacks are of brick; the roof is covered with Welsh slates. The E. front is symmetrical and of five bays. The central doorway has a moulded stone architrave with a keystone and a segmental broken pediment on console brackets; the sashed windows, uniform in each storey, have unmoulded architraves with plain keystones and moulded window-sills. A plat-band marks the first floor, and the eaves have a coved stone cornice. Inside, the staircase balustrade is of the Tuscan-column pattern but each newel-post is composed of three vase-shaped balusters conjoined. The N.W. ground-floor room has fielded panelling in two heights, with bolection mouldings.

(5) Nicholson's Farm (78531617), 160 yds. N.W. of the church, is of two storeys, with walls of coursed rubble and a thatched roof. A date-stone in the N.E. front is inscribed C.W.M. 1728 but interior fittings show that the house is of the 16th century. Apart from a modern extension at the S.E. end, the house has a simple rectangular plan consisting of two ground-floor rooms separated by a central through-passage. An open fireplace between the S. room and the through-passage has a chamfered and cambered oak bressummer supported on inclined timber jambs with chamfered edges and shaped base stops. A carved wooden console bracket attached to the bressummer supports a deeply chamfered ceiling beam. Within the fireplace, on the N.E. side, is a small recess with a two-centred head; to the S.W. of the fireplace is a 17th-century plank-and-muntin partition.

(6) House (78581620), 160 yds. N.W. of (1), is of two storeys, with walls of squared rubble and ashlar, and a thatched roof; the rear wall has been rebuilt in brick. The house is of 17th-century origin but it has been much altered and is now derelict. The E. front has, on the ground floor, one square-headed four-light window with hollow-chamfered stone mullions and a weathered and hollow-chamfered label; on the first floor is a similar window of three lights. Two other bays to the N. appear to have been rebuilt in the 18th century and two blocked doorways indicate that the range was at one time divided into three tenements.

(7) House (78721633), of two storeys with ashlar walls and a thatched roof, dates from the end of the 17th century. The S. front is of three bays; to the W. of the central doorway is a five-light stone window and to the E. is a similar window of two lights. On the first floor the W. bay contains a stone-mullioned four-light window, and similar two-light windows occur above the doorway and to the E. Another mullioned window occurs on the N. front.

(8) Castleman's Farm (78531632) is of two storeys with coursed rubble walls and squared rubble dressings; the walls have been largely rebuilt in recent years. A date-stone inscribed C.I.E. 1685 has been reset in the masonry. The roof is thatched.

(9) Cottage (78511622) is of one storey with an attic; the lower walls are of coursed rubble but the dormer-windowed attic is of timber-framing and brick; the roof is thatched. It was probably built early in the 18th century.

(10) House (78651620), 130 yds. N. of (1), was almost entirely rebuilt in the 19th century but it retains the chamfered plinth of an earlier building. Reset in the S.E. front is a date-stone inscribed T.F. 1675.

Monuments (11–18)

The following are 18th-century cottages of two storeys with rubble walls and thatched roofs. The plans consist of simple ranges divided by cross partitions into two or three rooms on each floor, with fireplaces in the end walls and with service rooms in lean-to annexes at the back. Windows are plain wooden casements.

(11) *Cottage* (78741633) has a symmetrical N.W. front of three bays.

(12) *Cottage* (78551634) was originally of one storey with attics but now has an upper storey. One room has a stop-chamfered beam.

(13) *Cottages* (78601611), two adjacent, 70 yds. N.W. of the church.

(14) *Cottages* (78551625), two adjacent.

(15) *Cottage* (78381618) was originally of one storey but now has a semi-dormered attic.

(16) *Cottage* (78431606), 270 yds. W. of (1).

(17) *Cottage* (78491607), 180 yds. W. of (1).

(18) *Cottage* (78731625), 170 yds. N. of (1), has two chamfered beams with run-out stops.

Early 19th-century buildings include the *Inn*, 100 yds. N.W. of the church, with coursed rubble walls, a stone-slate roof and wooden casement windows; *Cut Mill* (77631655), partly of coursed rubble and partly of brick, with a slated roof; also eight cottages, one immediately W. of the church, and others dispersed in the W. part of the village.

MEDIAEVAL AND LATER EARTHWORKS

(19) CULTIVATION REMAINS. There were formerly three open fields in the parish, but the small acreages recorded in the 16th century indicate that a great deal of enclosure had already taken place (H. L. Gray: *English Field Systems*, 1915, Appx. II, 442; and Dorset *Procs.*, Vol. LXXIII, 1951, 117). Ridge-and-furrow can be seen on air photographs (R.A.F. CPE/UK 1974: 2161–4 and 2018, 3213–7, 4190–4) in a number of places in the parish (*e.g.* 780169 and 791158–793163); it all appears to have lain within the existing fields.

ROMAN AND PREHISTORIC

(20) ROMAN VILLA (78451602), on the edge of the present village and W. of the road to Marnhull, lies at 260 ft. above O.D. on a terrace of Corallian limestone which slopes gently W. to the R. Stour, ½ m. away. Mosaic pavements were found in 1963 and 1964. The date of the villa is uncertain, but the mosaics are definitely of the 4th century; most of the coins and pottery found are also of the 4th century.

The principal pavement (Plate 146), excavated by H. S. L. Dewar and R. N. R. Peers and now relaid in the British Museum, forms a rectangle 28⅓ ft. E. to W., by 19½ ft.; it was divided by wall footings into an E. portion 17½ ft. long and a W. portion 10½ ft. long, with an opening 10½ ft. wide and 2¾ ft. deep between them. The design of the larger portion is a square, flanked on N. and S. by a strip of double plait pattern; it contains a central roundel surrounded by four semicircular panels, each with its chord along a side of the square, and four quarter-round panels in the angles of the square. All panels are edged by guilloche borders; the semicircles have in addition fret borders and the roundel has three concentric circular borders of wave, single plait and fret patterns. Between the main panels are four pairs of boat-shaped panels, each containing a floral scroll.

In the central roundel is the bust of a yellow-haired, clean-shaven man with dark eyes and a slightly cleft chin (Plate 147). He is heavily draped in a pinkish under-tunic and a white outer garment with a thick purple fold on the left shoulder; the *Chi-Rho* monogram in yellow appears behind his head and a pomegranate lies on either side. The roundel is meant to be viewed from the E. and on this side the semicircle contains a spreading blue-green tree. In each of the other semicircles a dog with a collar chases or confronts a stag or doe in a setting of trees. Each quarter-circle contains a male bust facing outwards. Each bust has red hair with three or four upstanding wind-blown locks on the crown of the head, and each wears a red cloak fastened by a round brooch on the right shoulder, leaving the right arm exposed. The two E. busts have rosette-like flowers on either side of the head and the other two have pomegranates in the same position. The bust in the N.W. quadrant is smaller than the others and inferior in quality.

The panel linking the two portions of the pavement has a running pelta pattern in red on white. The W. portion is rectangular with a central square flanked by two rectangles, all with guilloche borders (Plate 145). In the square, a roundel, meant to be viewed from the W., with a wide border of floral scroll, contains the scene of Bellerophon mounted on Pegasus spearing the Chimaera, both facing to the S. The upper part of the figure has been obliterated by damage extending E. and roughly patched with roofing slabs. Bellerophon wears a red cloak and his spear has a blue-grey point. Pegasus has a flowing mane and a feathery tail; there is no sign of wings, but they may have been in the damaged area. The mane of the Chimaera is patterned in alternate lozenges of red and yellow. In each corner of the square is a two-handled chalice flanked by tendrils. In the N. rectangular side panel a collared hound chases a stag among trees and in the S. panel a similar hound pursues a stag and a doe.

The double room containing these pavements resembles a *triclinium*. Excavations by K. S. Painter in 1964–5 provided evidence of the way the mosaics were laid, and suggested that other rooms lay to the W. in a range at least 150 ft. long and 32 ft. wide, but none to the S. To the W. was a room containing a damaged mosaic with guilloche patterns and a border of widely-spaced triangles. Finds of roof and flue tiles, roofing slabs, painted wall plaster, a complete iron window grille 21½ ins. by 24 ins., coarse pottery and decorated bone fragments, probably from a casket, show that this was a substantial building. There is also a fragment of a curved stone table carved with rosettes, as at Rockbourne (*J.R.S.*, LII (1962), p. 185 and Pl. XXIV).

The bust with the *Chi-Rho* has been tentatively interpreted by J. M. C. Toynbee as a representation of Christ, and the four corner figures as Evangelists in the guise of wind-gods. The tree could be a tree of life, the Bellerophon and Chimaera could represent the triumph of good over evil, and the hunting scenes could represent the life of paradise, or Christians threatened by evil. The beardless figure with the *Chi-Rho* behind the head is best paralleled in a mosaic at San Lorenzo, Milan. Parallels in detail between these mosaics and those at Frampton (*Dorset* I, 150), Fifehead Neville (above p. 93) and Hemsworth (*Dorset* V) suggest that a single school of craftsmen was responsible. (Dorset *Procs.*, LXXXV (1963), 116–21; LXXXVI (1964), 150–4; *J.R.S.*, LIV (1964), 7–14; S. & D. N. & Q., XXVIII (1964), 161–4.)

24 HOLWELL (7011)

(O.S. 6 ins. ST 61 SE, ST 71 SW)

The parish of Holwell covers some 2,400 acres at an altitude of 200 ft. to 300 ft. above sea-level; until 1844 it was a detached part of Somerset. The undulating land, almost entirely Oxford Clay, is drained by small streams flowing N. to the Caundle Brook, which constitutes the N. and W. boundaries of the parish. As the accompanying plan shows, the nucleus of the village stands near the centre of the N. boundary and the open fields (19) lay around it to E., S. and W. Secondary settlements such as Buckshaw, the Manor House, Westrow, Pleck and Woodbridge, each with its enclosures, were established beyond the perimeter of the open fields at unknown dates. The S. quarter of the parish, beyond Holwell Drove and Pleck, was enclosed in 1797; since then, 19th-century and later dwellings have been built along the edges of this area.

The most important monuments are the parish church and Naish Farm (14); the latter is an interesting specimen of mediaeval domestic architecture.

ECCLESIASTICAL

(1) The Parish Church of St. Laurence (Plate 4) stands in a hollow, 50 yds. S. of the Caundle Brook. It is built of coursed limestone rubble with ashlar dressings of the same material, probably from the Marnhull quarries. The *Chancel* was rebuilt in 1770 and again in 1885, when the organ chamber was added,

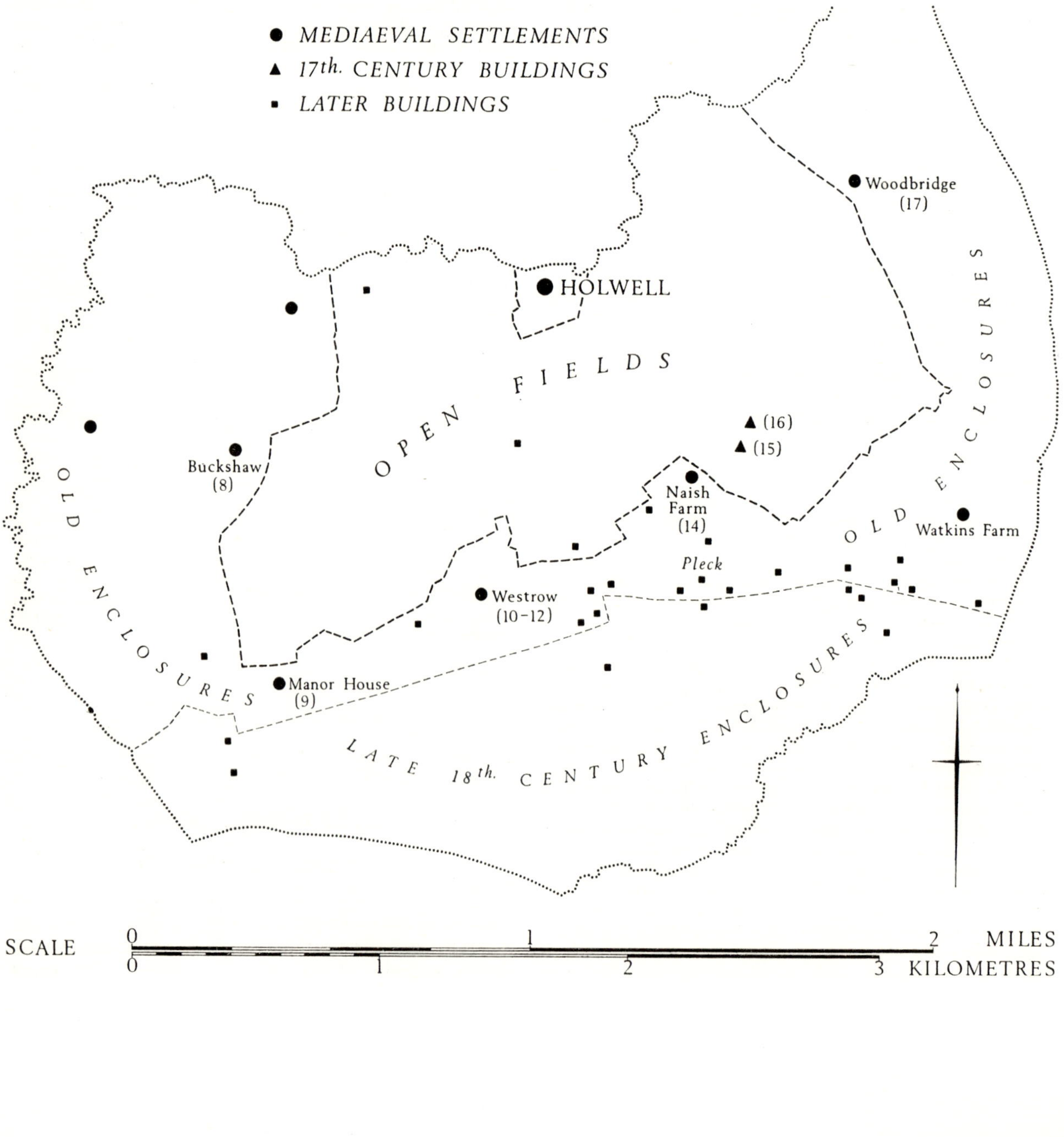

HOLWELL *The parish church of St. Laurence*

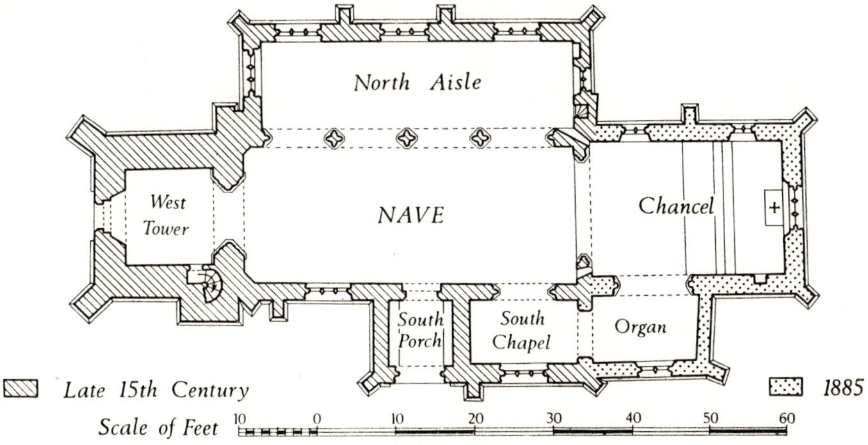

but the *Nave, North Aisle, South Chapel, West Tower* and *South Porch* are uniformly of the late 15th century. The jointing of the masonry shows that the tower was built before the nave, but it can be only a few years older.

The church is well preserved and has suffered few alterations except in the chancel; the carved capitals of the nave arcade and the timber roof of the N. aisle are noteworthy.

Architectural Description—The 19th-century chancel (25 ft. by 17 ft.) is entered through a 15th-century *Chancel Arch*, two-centred and comprising an ogee moulding and a wide hollow-chamfer. The ogee moulding springs from three-quarter respond shafts with simply moulded caps; on the W. face the hollow-chamfer continues on the responds but on the E. face its width is reduced to allow for square-headed squints to N. and S. Above each squint the wide hollow-chamfer is supported on a carved head corbel, integral with the masonry of the respond and therefore almost certainly of the 15th century although the style of the sculpture is suggestive of the 12th century. The springing of a small arch at right-angles to the chancel arch projects eastwards from the N. abutment.

The *Nave* (42 ft. by 17 ft.) has, on the N., a four-bay arcade in which the arches are of three orders: an inner ogee moulding, a central hollow-chamfer and an outer ogee; these spring from piers composed of four attached shafts and four hollow-chamfers, the latter continuous with those of the arches; the responds are similar (Plate 7). The piers and responds have polygonal base mouldings and the attached shafts have carved capitals representing winged angels bearing scrolls which continue from angel to angel; the sculpture retains traces of gilt and pigment but the heads of all the angels except for one on the S. side of the E. respond are modern replacements. The three angels of the E. respond have scrolls inscribed with Latin texts such as BEATI O[MN]ES Q[UI] TIME[N]T D[OMI]NU[M] in black-letter, in relief. The four angels of the E. pier hold pens and have blank scrolls interrupted by emblems of the Evangelists; the angels of the middle pier bear more texts in black-letter in relief; those of the W. pier have blank scrolls except for that on the W. which has a text; the W. respond has an angel bearing a blank shield in the centre, and blank shields only on the N. and S. sides; that to the S. is broken. Above the original angel-head on the S. side of the E. respond is a stone corbel which probably supported the rood beam; the sill of the opening at the head of the rood vice lies just below it. The S. side of the nave has, at the E. end, an archway to the S. chapel; it is two-centred and has mouldings similar to the N. arcade. Each respond has an attached central shaft with a moulded cap and base, continuous hollow chamfers and outer ogee-mouldings with plain capitals at springing level. The S. doorway has a moulded two-centred head with continuous jambs, below a square label which terminates in square stops at the level of the springing; the spandrels are decorated with foliate carving; the rear arch has a raised centre. The nave wall W. of the porch has a moulded plinth and a hollow-chamfered roll-moulded string-course below an embattled parapet. At the W. end the wall dies into the diagonal S.E. buttress of the tower; adjacent, a square-set buttress to the nave wall has two weathered offsets and terminates below a large gargoyle projecting from the string-course. Between the buttress and the porch is a casement-moulded two-centred window of three lights with cinquefoil heads and vertical tracery; the hoodmould is hollow-chamfered with square stops; the rear arch is two-centred.

In the *South Chapel* (13½ ft. by 8 ft.) the E. wall contains an opening to the 19th-century organ chamber. At the S.E. corner is a diagonal buttress of two weathered stages. The string-course and embattled parapet of the S. wall are uniform with those of the nave; at the S.E. corner is a grotesque gargoyle. The S. wall is continuous with that of the porch and is only separated from it by a square-set buttress, similar to that of the S.E. corner and also surmounted by a string-course gargoyle. In the S. wall is a window uniform with that in the S. wall of the nave.

The *North Aisle* (39½ ft. by 11 ft.) has, on the E., N. and W. sides, moulded plinths and hollow-chamfered and moulded string-courses, with embattled parapets and moulded copings, as in the S. chapel. Diagonal buttresses as before described strengthen the N.E. and N.W. corners, and two similar square-set buttresses occur on the N. wall; the E. bay is wider than the others. In correspondence with each buttress a grotesque gargoyle protrudes from the string-course and another, in the form of a human head with flowing hair, occurs above the easternmost

N. window. At the S. extremity of the E. wall a square turret containing the rood-loft vice is capped with weathered stonework. Adjacent is a small, square-headed casement-moulded E. window of two cinquefoil two-centred lights below a hollow-chamfered label. Internally the window is spanned by a segmental rear arch and to the S. it is flanked by the rood vice doorway, which is two-centred and rebated for a door. The N. wall of the aisle has three three-light windows similar to the window of the S. chapel. The W. wall contains a reset window which is richer and perhaps earlier than the others in the church; it may come from the original chancel. It is casement-moulded externally and internally and has three ogee-headed cinquefoil lights, and intersecting tracery in a two-centred head. The jambs and head are bordered internally by a continuous double-ogee moulding.

The *West Tower* (11½ ft. by 12 ft.) is of coursed rubble with ashlar dressings and has three external stages defined by weathered string-courses, that between the second and third stage being also hollow-chamfered. At the base is a moulded plinth; at the top, a deep hollow-chamfered and moulded string-course is surmounted by an embattled parapet with a continuous moulded coping. At each corner of the parapet string-course is a grotesque gargoyle; above are 18th-century corner pinnacles with fluted sides and crocketed finials. Each corner of the tower has a diagonal buttress with weathered offsets; those to N.W. and S.W. are of five stages, those to the N.E. and S.E. are truncated below by the Nave and N. Aisle walls. The two top stages of each buttress, corresponding with the top stage of the tower, are narrower than in the lower stages and have weathered offsets just above the string-course. Square-set buttresses in the E. part of the N. and S. sides of the two lower stages provide abutment for the tower arch; that to the S. is incorporated in the vice turret, which is of rectangular section, with a gabled roof of weathered ashlar; it contains two chamfered loops. The tower arch is two-centred and of three orders, the two inner orders wave-moulded and the outer order an ogee. The inner order rests on attached shafts with moulded caps and polygonal bases; the middle order is continuous, and the outer ogee is repeated on the responds below moulded capitals. The W. doorway has a two-centred chamfered and hollow-chamfered head, continuous jambs and a concentric hoodmould. Above, the two-centred W. window continues into the second stage, the string-course outlining the head, as a hood-mould; the window is of two lights with cinquefoil cusping in two-centred heads below vertical tracery. In the S. wall of the tower, internally, the vice doorway has a two-centred head and chamfered jambs. A little way up the vice is a blocked doorway which must formerly have given access to a gallery. Near the top of the second stage of the tower, on the S. side, is a small trefoil-headed light. In the third stage each face has a uniform belfry window of two transomed lights with two-centred trefoil heads (cinquefoil on the S. side) and vertical tracery in a two-centred casement-moulded outer head with a hood-mould; the lights have perforated wooden shutters.

The *South Porch* has plinth, string-course and embattled parapet continuous with those of the Nave and S. Chapel. The S.W. corner has a diagonal two-stage buttress with weathered offsets and, in the string-course above, an angle gargoyle. The two-centred S. archway has continuous jambs and moulded stops; the arch profile, uniform inside and out, consists of double ogee mouldings, a deep casement moulding and a hollow-chamfer; externally there is a moulded label.

Roofs: The nave has a late 15th-century wagon roof rising above treble hollow-chamfered cornices at wall-plate level. The cornices have square leaf bosses at intervals in each order of chamfering, and an embattled moulding at the top. The roof is divided into panels by moulded transverse and longitudinal ribs which protrude below the plaster ceiling and form six bays, each with four rectangular panels; at the intersections are carved wooden bosses. The S. Chapel has a modern flat roof but some of the head-corbels on which it rests are probably original; on the N. side they represent a woman, a bishop and two bearded men; on the S. side are four male heads. The flat roof of the N. Aisle is original; it has heavily moulded transverse beams, with raised centres, intersecting three similarly moulded longitudinal members and moulded wall-plates to form thirteen bays of coffering, each bay four coffers in width (Plate 21). Every coffer is subdivided into four panels by smaller intersecting cross-beams. Every main intersection is decorated with a carved wooden flower boss with leaves masking the mitre of the mouldings; the intersections of the cross-beams are similarly decorated but on a smaller scale. On the N. side of the aisle the transverse members rest on curved timber brackets which are morticed into vertical wall-posts; of these the three easternmost are shaped like columns and two of them rest on roughly carved stone head-corbels. The four easternmost bays of the roof are set at a slightly higher level than the others and have transverse members that are deeper than the longitudinal ones; the rafter bosses in this part of the roof are richer, and the points where the smaller cross-beams meet the main beams are additionally enriched with leaf-shaped covers. The distinction implies that an altar formerly stood beneath these bays. In the S. Porch, carved head-corbels at the four corners probably indicate the level of a former roof.

Fittings—*Bier:* with turned legs, moulded rails and turned sliding shafts, late 17th century. *Bracket:* Over S. door, with hollow-chamfered sides. *Chests:* Two, of oak, one 4 ft. by 1⅓ ft. by 1⅝ ft. high, with panelled front, carved initials 'T.E.' and date AD 1712; another 3½ ft. by 1¼ ft. by 1½ ft. high, with flush panels, late 18th century. *Doors:* In S. doorway, of oak, with vertical outer and horizontal inner planks fastened with wrought-iron nails; jointing of external planks covered with chamfered vertical fillets, shaped at top to form pointed tracery in two-centred door-head; 15th century, with wrought-iron latch and escutcheon, probably later. In tower vice doorway, of oak, with chamfered fillets to outline of two-centred head, and wrought-iron hinges; probably 15th century. *Graffiti:* In N. aisle roof, wall-plate on S. side in second bay from E. inscribed in black paint 'Jon London', perhaps signature of joiner. On leaden tower roof, on jambs of S. porch and on W. jamb of tower vice doorway, 18th-century dates and initials. *Hour-glass:* Mahogany frame and glass, 18th century, in wrought-iron bracket protruding from wall over pulpit, perhaps 15th century.

Monuments and *Floor-slabs. Monuments:* In organ chamber, reset on E. wall, (1) of Thomas Hobson, 1777, and his wife, 1779, oval tablet with pediment, by Thomas of Sherborne; reset on S. wall, (2) of Samuel Fitzherbert, 1832, tablet by G. Crawford of Sherborne. In churchyard, E. of chancel, (3) of Robert Bridgis, 1607, table-tomb. *Floor-slabs:* At foot of chancel step, (1) of John Pullen, 1718, Purbeck stone. In S. Chapel, (2) of Mrs. Francis Jeanes, 1646, Purbeck slab with arms of Willoughby (Coker, 132). *Niche:* In E. wall of N. aisle, roughly cut recess with four-centred inner head retaining red pigment. *Panelling:* At entry to chancel, fielded oak panelling in one height with moulded plinth and cornice, probably transferred from former gallery; other sections of similar panelling reused in S. Chapel; 18th century. *Piscina:* In S.E. corner of N. aisle, with chamfered four-centred head below sunk spandrels, also remains of bowl and outlet, 15th century. *Plate:* includes late 17th-century cup and cover-paten, also paten with date-mark for 1724, and pewter alms-dish of *c.* 1800. *Pulpit:* oak, with five panelled sides in two heights; lower height reeded, upper height with frets, both heights with enriched beading; late 17th century, moulded base and cornice modern. *Royal Arms:* Above tower arch, wooden panel with eared architrave, painted with arms of George III and inscribed 'The gift of Henry D'Aubeny Esqr., Anno Domini 1804'. *Sundials:* On parapet above porch arch, square stone dial with incised degrees, perhaps 18th century; on buttress to E. of porch entry, two scratch-dials, mediaeval. *Miscellanea:* Built into N. wall of chancel, miscellaneous architectural fragments including two head-corbels, perhaps 12th century, also fragments of foliate enrichment and portions of chamfered and cusped 15th-century tracery. In Porch, incomplete piscina with mason's setting-out lines, carved head at one corner, 13th century.

SECULAR

In the neighbourhood of the church the original nucleus of the village, known as 'The Borough', contains the following monuments:

(2) Bridge (69931202), across the Caundle Brook about 50 yds. N. of the church, is of rubble. It was originally of two spans but it now has three, the former S. abutment being separated from the bank by a secondary channel. The massive centre pier has cut-waters at each end; the N. abutment is joined to it by a segmental arch of rough stone voussoirs, probably of the 18th or 19th century; the two intervals to the S. of the centre pier are spanned by iron girders. The massiveness of the centre pier and abutments suggest that the bridge is of mediaeval origin.

(3) The Rectory (69931190), 100 yds. S. of the church, is an early 18th-century building of two storeys, with rendered walls and a hipped tiled roof with stone-slate verges. The eaves have moulded plaster coves. The windows are sashed. The S. façade has three bays, the central bay recessed; the N. side has five symmetrical bays. Inside, several rooms have carved wooden fireplace surrounds and overmantels and other mid 18th-century joinery of good quality. A reset stone in a 19th-century outbuilding is dated 1678.

(4) Stocks, with renewed woodwork but with iron fittings which are probably of the 18th century, stand outside the churchyard wall about 20 yds. S. of the church porch.

(5)–(7) Cottages, three, of two storeys with rubble walls and thatched or tiled roofs, stand respectively 30 yds., 75 yds. and 100 yds. S. of the church: (5) is of the early 18th century and has only one room on each floor; it is now the outhouse of a later dwelling; (6) comprises two original rooms of the late 17th century and an 18th-century extension to the N.; (7) is of the 18th century and has three three-light casement windows in each storey.

The following monuments are scattered in the outlying parts of the parish to W., S. and E. of The Borough:

(8) Buckshaw House (68731133) is a mid 18th-century building with extensive late 19th-century additions. The walls are rendered and of ashlar; the roofs are slated. Except for the E. front, little of the 18th-century house remains visible. It is two-storied and of seven bays, having a central doorway and two flanking bays in a central pavilion, and other bays arranged symmetrically, two on either side. All the windows are sashed and of equal size, but the window above the doorway is enriched with scrolled cheek-pieces. Rusticated ashlar quoins define the central pavilion and the extremities of the front; a lightly moulded plat-band marks the first floor. Presumably there was originally an eaves cornice above the first-floor windows, but it was destroyed when a pedimented attic storey was added in 1894. The doorway has an ashlar architrave and reeded consoles supporting a segmental pediment. Inside, all details appear to be of the late 19th century.

(9) The Manor House (68931040) is two-storied with attics and has walls of squared and coursed rubble, and a stone-slated roof. Though of 16th-century origin it was to a large extent rebuilt in 1889. In the W. front, to the N. of the end wall of the 19th-century S. range, is an original doorway with a moulded four-centred head and continuous jambs, surmounted by a small rectangular window with a moulded label. To the N. of the doorway is a 16th-century window of two square-headed lights with casement and hollow-chamfered mouldings, and with a label which is continuous with the moulded capping of the high plinth. The first floor of the W. front has two three-light windows with similar mouldings and square labels; the other windows of the W. front and a projecting chimneystack to the N. are modern, but the stack includes a reset head corbel which is perhaps mediaeval. A mediaeval carved stone figure of a long-haired woman in flowing robes is set into the S. side of a 19th-century bow window at attic level in the W. end wall of the S. range. Inside, a first-floor room at the W. end of the S. range has a 16th-century plaster frieze with acanthus and griffin-headed knots above a band of vine-scroll ornament.

The house is surrounded on three sides by the remains of a rectangular *Moat* (class A 3)[1]; it is almost certainly mediaeval in origin and it probably represents the site of a farm that was established in the waste beyond the open fields in the 12th or 13th century. Until late in the 19th century the moat was a normal mediaeval homestead moat and the Tithe Map of 1841 (D.C.R.O.) shows the site as a rectangular island completely surrounded by a wet ditch, with the house in the S.E. corner and extensive farm buildings outside it to S. and S.E. The ditch now remains only on the N., W. and S. sides, where it is 15 ft. to 20 ft. wide and up to 4 ft. deep. At the S.W. corner it has been turned into a water-garden with ponds, waterfalls and sluices, and at the E. end of the S. side the ditch has a rectangular projection to the S., crossed by the present drive to the house. The construction of the water-garden and the S. projection, together with the destruction of the E. side of the moat and the removal of the farm buildings, probably occurred in 1889.

(10) Westrow House (69471064) is an early 19th-century house of two storeys with rendered walls and a tiled roof. The three-bay S. front, with sashed windows, is sheltered on the ground floor by a wrought-iron verandah.

(11) Westrow Cottage E. (69721077) is an L-shaped house of two storeys in coursed rubble with a tiled roof. Although originally of the early 17th century it has been modernised and all openings are new. The gable of the W. wing has moulded kneelers and it formerly culminated in a moulded ashlar chimneystack, fragments of which are found in the garden. A head-corbel resembling those on the chancel arch in the church is also in the garden. Inside, there are open fireplaces at the N. end of the N. wing and at the W. end of the W. wing; the rooms are spanned by moulded and chamfered beams. The W. bedroom contains a moulded stone fireplace surround with a square head and shaped stops.

(12) Westrow Cottages W. (69691075), two adjacent, have rubble walls and thatched roofs. A date-stone of 1707 is set in the S. wall. The stairs in the W. tenement have an oak balustrade

[1] *See Cambridgeshire* I, lxi–lxiv.

with chamfered knops to the newel posts, and baluster-shaped slats.

(13) THE FOX INN (70171078) is a two-storied L-shaped house of the late 18th century, with coursed rubble walls, sashed windows and a thatched roof. A small cottage of slightly later date was added at the S. end. (*Demolished.*)

(14) NAISH FARM (70561123), externally an undistinguished two-storied dwelling with rubble walls and a thatched roof, nevertheless retains many original features of a 15th-century farmhouse. It comprises a single-storied hall of three bays, with a solar and undercroft at the N.E. end and service rooms at the S.W. end. In the 16th century the hall was chambered over and a large open fireplace was built; at the same time the N.E. wall was rebuilt, and the service rooms were enlarged. The house, still fulfilling its original purpose, is a well-preserved specimen of its class and period. Although the small farmyard and ranges of buildings to N. and W. have no ancient features, they probably occupy the site of original buildings and combine with the house to illustrate the lay-out of a mediaeval farmstead.

HOLWELL *Naish Farm*

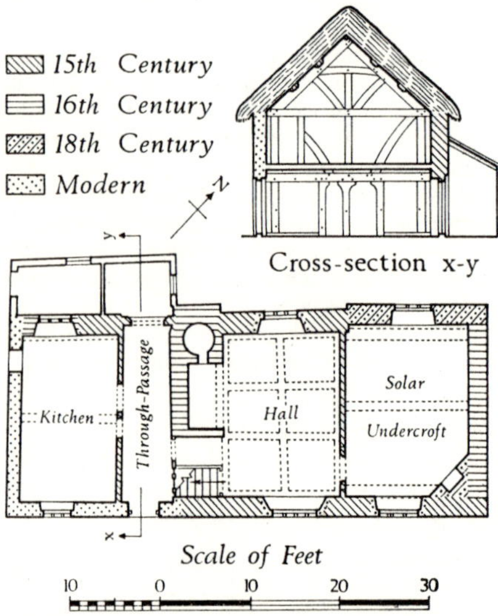

A modern doorway in the S.E. side of the house opens into a through-passage. The original 15th-century N.W. doorway still exists at the opposite end of the same passage and gives access to a wash-room that has been built outside; it has a massive oak surround with a chamfered two-centred head and jambs and a large elm plank door hung on wrought-iron strap hinges. The S.W. wall of the passage is an original timber-framed partition, the central third of which contains two doorways set side-by-side, that to the N.W. being wider than the other. The two service rooms to which they originally led have now been combined as a kitchen. The oak posts are chamfered and shouldered and the common door-head, chamfered over the openings, continues unchamfered to right and left as far as the side walls of the house. The N.E. side of the passage is largely composed of the chimney-breast at the back of the hall fireplace, which was inserted in the 16th century; S.E. of the chimney-breast it is defined by a stud partition and a doorway with a chamfered and shouldered oak surround. The hall is divided into two storeys by a 16th-century ceiling with deeply-chamfered intersecting beams and wall-plates. The large 16th-century fireplace, spanned by a chamfered lintel, has an oven on the N. side. An original 15th-century doorway in the N.E. wall of the hall leads to the solar undercroft; it has a chamfered oak surround with a two-centred head, now modified to receive a square-headed door. The undercroft has chamfered wall-plates to N.W. and S.E. and a chamfered beam near the centre. The gap of several inches between the wall-plates and the walls is probably due to movement of the masonry; the N.W. wall was probably rebuilt in the 18th century, but the S.E. wall is at least in part original. The underside of these wall-plates is exposed to view and the absence of mortices and peg-holes indicates that the house never had timber-framed outside walls. The corner fireplace is probably an 18th-century addition.

The first floor repeats the plan of the ground floor. In the N.E. wall of the solar, somewhat N. of the centre-line, is a fireplace with a chamfered four-centred wooden head and stop-chamfered stone jambs; probably it was inserted in the 16th century. The middle room, originally the upper part of the hall, is open to the roof. Altogether there are six transverse oak trusses in the length of the house; the second and fifth, counting from the S.W., are framed partition-trusses with tie-beams, collar-beams, side and centre studs, and braces; the others, except the most westerly, are jointed-cruck arch-braced collar trusses. The S.W. truss is also a jointed cruck, but it must be a later insertion because the original trusses have carpenter's tally-marks *I* to *V* in sequence from S.W. to N.E., while that which spans the chamber over the kitchen has no tally-marks and stands S.W. of the truss marked *I*. Presumably the kitchen was originally only the width of one roof-bay and then was enlarged to two bays in the 16th century. The inserted jointed cruck is now represented by the principals alone; they are notched to receive the elbowed lower members which were each fastened with two pegs. The framed partition-truss marked *I* rises above the S.W. side of the through-passage and forms the upper part of the S.W. wall of the hall. Trusses *II* and *III*, spanning the hall, are chamfered arch-braced collar trusses. Truss *IV*, similar to *I*, is the original partition between the hall and the solar; truss *V*, arch-braced, spans the solar. All these trusses carry two purlins on each side of the ridge and are braced by curved wind-braces set diagonally and paired, two above and two below each lower purlin.

(15) HOUSE (70761134), 250 yds. N.E. of the foregoing, is of coursed rubble in two storeys, with a thatched hipped roof; it dates from the second half of the 17th century. The plan is a long rectangle containing two rooms, with a single central chimneystack serving back-to-back fireplaces. A small entrance vestibule lies on one side of the stack, the staircase on the other. The N.E. front is symmetrically designed with four three-light wood-framed casement windows to each storey, two on each side of a projecting two-storied porch; the latter is rendered and possibly timber-framed; it has a two-light window on the first floor. Inside, some ceiling beams are chamfered and moulded. The two ground-floor rooms contain 18th-century fielded panelling, and the stairs have an 18th-century balustrade. (*Demolished.*)

(16) HOUSE (70791139), of coursed rubble in two storeys with a modern roof, has the fireplaces and chimneystacks in the gabled end walls. It probably dates from the late 17th century.

(17) WOODBRIDGE FARM (71221235), house, is T-shaped in plan and is of two storeys with thatched roofs. The head of the T has a symmetrical S.W. front of three bays, rendered, and of the early 19th century; the gabled end walls are of rubble and are surmounted by chimneystacks. Behind, the rear wing of the 19th-century house is prolonged by a two-storied brick structure, now a store, which dates probably from the first half of the 18th century; this is likely to have been an earlier farmhouse. A plat-band decorates each side wall at first-floor level, and the eaves have simple brick cornices. On the S.E. side there were originally five evenly spaced and uniform rectangular first-floor windows, and there are traces of two corresponding ground-floor openings with segmental heads. The N.W. side had four openings on each floor, with segmental heads on the ground floor and with flat lintels on the first floor.

(18) ELM TREE FARM (70871084) probably dates from the beginning of the 18th century. It is of brick in two storeys with dormer-windowed attics under a tiled roof. The symmetrical five-bay front is patterned with blue header bricks and is traversed, above the ground-floor window heads, by a weathered and moulded stone string-course. The two-light casement windows, uniform on ground and first floors, have stone surrounds and mullions with beaded margins. The central doorway has a moulded stone surround with a shallow four-centred head.

Early and mid 19th-century buildings in the parish include *Lower Buckshaw Farm* (680112), *Crouch Hill Farm* (701106), *Cottages* in Crouch Lane (70111095) and (69821142), and *Middle Piccadilly Farm* (716110).

MEDIAEVAL AND LATER EARTHWORKS

(19) CULTIVATION REMAINS. The date of enclosure of the open fields of Holwell is unknown. Field names on the Tithe Map of 1839 suggest former North, Brook, West and Birds Fields. Ridge-and-furrow in the former North Field can be seen on air photographs (R.A.F. CPE/UK 1974: 2189–94, 3187–92) underlying existing field boundaries, E. and S. of the village. To the N. and N.E. of the Manor House ridge-and-furrow, 8 yds. to 10 yds. wide, occurs in four butting furlongs.

Traces of ridge-and-furrow, lying within fields which were enclosed from the 'waste', exist or can be seen on air photographs in a number of places, *e.g.* around Lower Buckshaw (680113–682110), where four irregularly-shaped fields contain ridges 6 yds. to 8 yds. wide, with headlands 8 yds. wide.

For the MOAT at the Manor House, *see* Monument (9).

ROMAN AND PREHISTORIC

(20) INHUMATION BURIALS found at Westrow (approx. 696112 and 696115) while draining fields in 1866 and 1868 were accompanied by pottery, probably Roman, including a samian bowl (Dorset *Procs.* LXXVII (1955), 146; LXXXVI (1964), 119).

Roman coarse pottery has been found near Hill Street, around 70821184 and 70791149 (Dorset *Procs.* LXXII (1950), 78).

25 IBBERTON (7807)

(O.S. 6 ins. ST 70 NE, ST 80 NW)

The parish extends over nearly 1,400 acres and straddles the main Chalk escarpment which at this point stands 300 ft. high. The E. half of the area is a broad dry valley draining E. down the dip-slope of the Chalk from 700 ft. to 500 ft. above sea-level. The W. half, below the escarpment, undulates gently between 300 ft. and 400 ft. on Gault and Kimmeridge Clay. The village lies on the spring line at the foot of the escarpment, at the junction of the Greensand and Gault. Marsh Farm and Leigh Farm seem to be secondary settlements; the former is first recorded in the 14th century.[1]

ECCLESIASTICAL

(1) THE PARISH CHURCH OF ST. EUSTACE stands above the village, on the steep hillside to the S. It has walls of banded rubble and flint, with ashlar dressings, except for the tower which is of squared rubble and ashlar; the roofs are tiled. The building was in an advanced state of decay at the end of the 19th century and extensive restorations were effected *c.* 1903, but the main fabric is of the middle of the 15th century. It consisted originally of a *Chancel* and *Nave*; the *North Chapel* and the *West Tower* were early additions, and the nave arcade and the *North Aisle* were built in the first half of the 16th century.

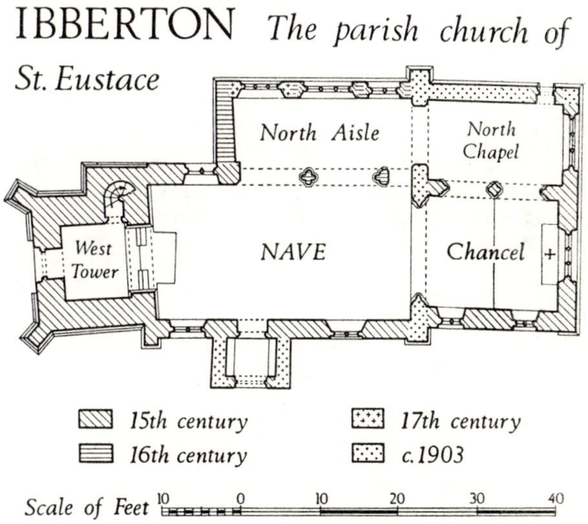

Architectural Description—The *Chancel* (16½ ft. by 13½ ft.) has a 15th-century E. window of three cinquefoil-headed lights with outer casement mouldings; it was originally square-headed but was provided with a pointed head and intersecting tracery *c.* 1903, the original square head being retained as a transom. In the N. wall is a two-bay arcade to the N. chapel; the two-centred arches have been retooled but the masonry is substantially of the 15th century. The arches consist of two ogee-moulded orders separated by a hollow-chamfer which continues on the responds

[1] Fägersten, 190.

and central column. The inner order is carried on attached shafts while the outer orders have shafts on the column but continue as ogees on the responds; the shafts have plain conical caps and polygonal bases. In the S. wall are two square-headed windows, each of two cinquefoil-headed lights with hood-moulds; that to the E. has a segmental rear arch and a sill about 1 ft. higher than that to the W. The chancel arch is of *c.* 1903.

The *North Chapel* (17 ft. by 10 ft.) has a gabled E. wall continuous with that of the chancel; in it is a restored three-light E. window similar to that of the chancel, but square-headed. The N. wall, rebuilt *c.* 1903, includes a reset late 15th-century doorway with a four-centred hollow-chamfered and casement-moulded head, continuous jambs and a square label. On the W. side of the chapel an archway of *c.* 1903 leads into the N. aisle.

The *Nave* (32¾ ft. by 16½ ft.) has, on the N. side, a 16th-century arcade of two bays augmented to the E. by a small modern archway cut through the respond. The arcade has segmental-pointed arches composed of two chamfered orders. The same orders continue in the form of polygonal shafts with chamfered and wave-moulded capitals on the E. respond and central column, but the W. respond, which is formed from the original N. wall, has the outer chamfer of the arch repeated on its S. face only; a wave-moulded corbel supports the inner order. W. of the arcade the N. wall is pierced by a square-headed 15th-century window of two cinquefoil lights with a square label with head-stops: to the E. a woman wearing a head-dress, to the W. a man in a cap. The S. wall of the nave has a square-headed window of two cinquefoil lights on each side of the doorway; that to the E. has an ogee-moulded external surround while that to the W. has casement mouldings; both windows have restored labels with square stops. The S. doorway has a two-centred chamfered head with continuous jambs and a hollow-chamfered segmental-pointed rear arch.

In the *North Aisle* (22¾ ft. by 8½ ft.) the lower courses of the N. wall are built with heavy ashlar blocks, forming a chamfered plinth. A modern two-stage buttress marks the junction of the aisle and the N. chapel. In the E. part of the aisle wall is a reset 15th-century window of two cinquefoil-headed lights in a square-headed casement-moulded surround, with no label. Near the middle is another reset 15th-century window of three cinquefoil ogee-headed lights with a chamfered square-headed surround with no label; this window is said to come from Milton Abbey. Further W. is a 17th-century window of three square-headed lights. The gabled W. wall of the N. aisle has no openings.

The *West Tower* (9¼ ft. by 8½ ft.) is of two stages with an embattled parapet. At the base is a moulded plinth; the stages are divided by a weathered string-course and the parapet has a roll-moulded and hollow-chamfered string-course. The string-courses continue around the vice turret, which has three main stages; it stands at the N.E. corner and its embattled parapet is slightly higher than that of the tower. The lower stage of the tower has diagonal N.W. and S.W. buttresses of three weathered stages, and a similar square-set buttress at the S.E. corner. The tower arch is two-centred and of two wave-moulded orders; the outer moulding continues on the responds and ends in shaped stops; the inner moulding dies into the responds at the springing. The vice doorway has a chamfered segmental-pointed head. The W. doorway has a casement-moulded segmental-pointed head with continuous jambs and a segmental-pointed rear-arch. Above it, the W. window has three cinquefoil-headed lights under a two-centred head with vertical tracery, a casement-moulded surround and a hollow-chamfered hood-mould; the rear-arch is two-centred and hollow-chamfered. In the upper stage of the tower each side has a belfry window of two cinquefoil-headed lights under a square head and label.

The *South Porch* is largely rebuilt, but the two-centred hollow-chamfered arch with continuous jambs has original plinths and includes portions of original voussoirs, one scratched '1636'.

Fittings—*Bells:* four; treble inscribed 'Joseph Daubeny Esqr. 1799, Thomas Mears of London fecit'; 2nd inscribed 'TP. RR. TA. CW. ANNO DOMINI 1656'; 3rd inscribed 'Richard Rogens, Allen Hayne, Churchwardens, 1641, W.P.'; tenor by James Wells of Aldebourne, 1813. *Book:* Chained, leather-bound book of homilies, 1673. *Brass:* In floor near N. respond of chancel arch, to Joseph D'aubeny, 1817. *Chair:* In chancel, with turned legs, shaped arms, carved back panel and frame, 17th century. *Coffin Stools:* Two, with beaded uprights and stiles, late 18th century. *Communion Table:* In N. Chapel, with turned legs and fluted front and side rails, early 17th century; top modern. *Font:* Octagonal stone bowl with vertical sides, and chamfered and undercut mouldings below, each side with a trefoil-headed panel, much worn, on octagonal stem and moulded octagonal base; 15th century. *Glass:* In chancel, in E. window, reassembled fragments and two roundels; in S. window, shield-of-arms of Milton Abbey (Plate 144), with letters I and T in border, perhaps for John Towninge, rector 1452–1478, and in cusping, a rose and a sun. In N. aisle, in N.E. window, oval panel of strapwork enclosing shield with Tudor rose and letters E.R., 16th century; in adjacent light, larger panel displaying royal achievement-of-arms of Elizabeth I, 16th century (Plate 44); in N.W. window, three quarries, one inscribed 1588, one with three battle-axes, one with a shield with three stars, probably late 16th century. In nave, in N. window, crowns, roses and other fragments; in S.W. window, a sun; probably 15th or 16th century. In tower, in W. window, tracery lights with tops of scrolls, probably 15th or 16th century.

Monuments: In chancel, on S. wall, (1) of Richard Daubeney, rector, 1802, wall-tablet of variegated marbles with pediment. In N. chapel, on N. wall, (2) of Richard Applin, 1792, marble tablet; (3) of Richard Seymer, 1785, marble tablet; (4) of Mary Galton, 1758, marble wall monument with vase in broken pediment, and cherub-head on shaped apron, also later inscription commemorating donor, C. Elswood, 1774, rector. In nave, on S. wall, (5) of Elizabeth Davis, 1842, marble tablet by 'Patent Works, Esher St. West'r'. *Piscina:* On S. side of chancel, with cinquefoil cusping in hollow-chamfered two-centred head with continuous jambs and broach stops, three-sided projection to bowl; 15th century. *Plate:* includes a heavy and plain silver cup with straight-sided conical bowl and tapering stem on domed base; date-letters of 1632, churchwardens' initials and date 1686. *Royal Arms:* Above E. window of N. chapel, arms of George III on shaped panel inscribed 'Jos. D'aubeny Esqr. 1801'. *Screen:* In tower arch, early 17th-century panelled oak screen, 6 ft. high, in three heights; upper height comprising turned balustrade. *Tables of Decalogue:* In tower, incised on two stone panels, late 18th or early 19th century. *Tiles:* In pavement of S. porch, slip tiles with various patterns, much abraded; 15th century.

SECULAR

(2) THE MANOR HOUSE (78940774), 200 yds. N. of the church, is a mid 17th-century farmhouse of two storeys with walls of banded flint and ashlar and a modern slated roof. The plan consists of one room on each side of a central entrance passage, with a service wing behind; the fireplaces are in the end walls. A 19th-century addition, recently refaced, extends the original range westwards.

The original S. front is of three bays, having a doorway flanked symmetrically by four-light casement windows with square heads and hollow-chamfered stone surrounds, and three similar three-light windows above. The central doorway has a hollow-chamfered and ogee-moulded four-centred head, continuous jambs and roll stops; it is sheltered by a gabled ashlar and rubble porch with a round-headed archway. A reset stone in the porch bears the dates 1666 and 1686. The E. wall of the house is banded like the S. front but the chimneystack on the gable has been rebuilt in brick; the original W. wall is hidden by the 19th-century extension. The 17th-century nail-studded front door is of two layers of oak planks, vertical outside and horizontal inside, hung on wrought-iron strap-hinges. The central passage is separated from the ground-floor rooms by plank-and-muntin partitions with chamfered bottom rails and moulded top rails. The ground and first-floor rooms in the original range have ceiling beams with double roll-mouldings. One room has 18th-century fielded panelling.

(3) Cottage, 50 yds. W. of (2), is of rubble, mainly rendered, and has two storeys and a thatched roof; it is of 17th-century origin but has been extensively restored. The doorway and one casement window in the N.E. front retain original chamfered oak surrounds. The entrance passage is flanked by plank-and-muntin partitions.

(4) Barn (78760796), 300 yds. N.W. of (2), is of banded flint and rubble and dates from the late 17th or early 18th century.

(5) Cottages, range of four (78770778), with walls of rubble and brick and with thatched roofs, are of 18th-century origin. They were formerly single-storied with attics but an upper storey was added, probably in the 19th century. (*Demolished.*)

(6) Inn (78780777), originally two cottages, is of the early 19th century but incorporates a late 17th-century door, of elm planks in two thicknesses fastened together with wrought-iron studs.

(7) Cottage (78740780) is of brick in two storeys with a thatched roof and dates from the late 18th century. The symmetrical three-bay E. front has a recessed panel over the doorway and blue-brick *chaînage* at each corner.

(8) Cottage, 100 yds. N. of (7), of one storey with an attic, is of the 18th century.

(9) Cottages, pair, at Leigh Farm (78370869), are one-storied with dormer-windowed attics and have rendered rubble walls and thatched roofs; they date from the middle of the 18th century but the upper floors have been rebuilt.

Early 19th-century monuments in the parish include the house at Leigh Farm (78390871) and three two-storied cottages with brick walls and thatched roofs, dispersed in the village.

MEDIAEVAL AND LATER EARTHWORKS

(10) Cultivation Remains. Nothing is known about the open fields of the parish but, upon the evidence of the remains of strip fields, indented modern field boundaries and the situation of apparently secondary settlements, they must have been in two separate areas. Some lay around the village, at the foot of and on the Chalk scarp, while others were on the dip-slope in Coombe Bottom a mile to the S.E.

On the steep Chalk scarp immediately N.E. of the church a group of eight contour strip lynchets covers about 22 acres (791077). Originally the strips were up to 400 yds. long with risers up to 18 ft. high, but extensive alterations were made to the group before 1840, as a result of enclosure. Two of the fields, 'Cross Lands' on the Tithe Map of 1840, are laid out across the risers of the original strips, and subsequent ploughing in these fields has produced secondary risers cutting obliquely across the older treads. Some 500 yds. S.E. of the church, also on the scarp slope, further contour strip lynchets overlie 'Celtic' fields (*see* Group 54).

In Coombe Bottom (801071 and 804071) at least five fragmentary contour strip lynchets lie within an area which, to judge by the shape of the existing boundaries, was once an open field. N. and N.W. of these, on the steep hill-side (803074), are very slight contour strip lynchets with low risers, apparently outside the permanent open fields.

ROMAN AND PREHISTORIC

(11) Settlement, Romano-British, on South Down (80530692), has been destroyed by ploughing. It lay at 625 ft. above O.D., overlooking a dry valley, on the N. shoulder of a spur dropping eastward from the main Chalk escarpment. The site, already ploughed when investigated, included a small group of platforms, three certain and two probable, levelled into the slope; they measured about 20 ft. across and were backed by curving scarps. About 90 yds. E. of the platforms and probably associated with them was a small enclosure of ⅛ acre, with four unequal sides, rounded corners and an entrance on the S. It was defined by a low bank up to 2 ft. high and 15 ft. across, with an external ditch, most clearly marked on the S. Coarse Romano-British pottery and a few samian fragments were found in the platforms but none was found in the enclosure. 'Celtic' fields which surround the settlement site are directly related to the enclosure.

'Celtic' Fields, *see* p. 339, Group (54).

(12), (13) Cross-dykes, two, lie across the ridge top at the summit of the Chalk escarpment. The first runs W.N.W.–E.S.E. (78800643–79080638) slightly obliquely across the ridge between Chitcombe Down and a combe to the E. It is univallate and about 325 yds. long, with a ditch on the S. side, but it is now almost completely ploughed out. At the E. end, about 30 yds. remain; the low bank is 20 ft. across and the ditch is 15 ft. across and 1 ft. deep. A possible break N. of centre is suggested by air photographs (R.A.F. CPE/UK 1934 2172–3).

The second dyke, 1 m. N.E. of the first, runs N.W. to S.E. (79590807–79760787) at about 800 ft. above O.D. across the ridge top, on ground falling S.W. from Bell Hill; the dyke faces the higher ground to the N.E. It is about 315 yds. long, with a bank some 22 ft. across and 3 ft. to 4 ft. high, and a ditch of about the same width and depth. Except towards the ends, a low counterscarp bank is visible; it is nowhere more than 1 ft. high and 5 ft. wide. There are three differently aligned lengths; at the N.W. end, where the dyke runs out on the steepening slope, a length of 165 yds. extends S.E.; a central length of about 33 yds. is aligned N.–S.; to the S. is a length of some 116 yds. running N.N.W.–S.S.E. and fading out on the well-marked shoulder of a S.-facing slope, along which runs a track. The abrupt change of alignment where the present ridgeway track passes obliquely through the central length suggests an original entrance. The parish boundary with Okeford Fitzpaine is marked by a bank about 3 ft. wide and 1 ft. to 2 ft. high which runs along the ditch of the N. length, and continues down the hill.

(14) Barrow ? (79200723), on Ibberton Hill at about 750 ft. above O.D., on a N.W. slope near the spine of a ridge, is now roughly D-shaped on plan, probably owing to destruction by a trackway on the S.E. There appears to have been digging at the centre. Diam. (S.W.–N.E.) 54 ft., ht. 3½ ft.

IWERNE COURTNEY *The parish church of St. Mary*

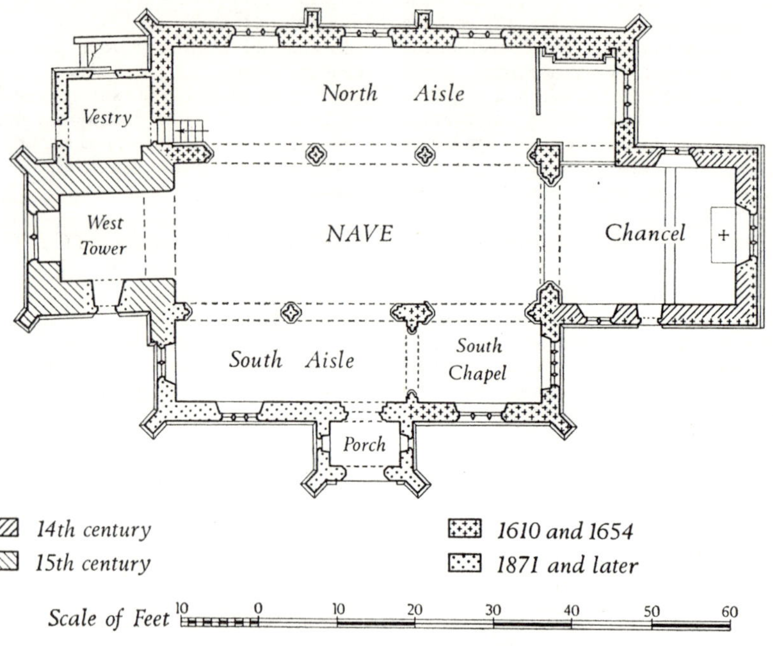

26 IWERNE COURTNEY or SHROTON (8512)

(O.S. 6 ins. ST 81 SE, ST 81 SW, ST 81 NW)

The parish, covering an L-shaped area of nearly 2,000 acres, lies on both sides of the R. Iwerne to N. and E. of Hambledon Hill. The E. part straddles the Chalk escarpment and rises from about 200 ft. above sea-level, near the river, to over 500 ft. in the E.; the W. part undulates between 150 ft. and 250 ft. on Greensand, Gault and Kimmeridge Clay, except in the S.W. where Hambledon Hill, a detached outcrop of the Chalk escarpment, rises to over 600 ft. The unusual shape of the parish results from the combination of three settlements, each of which had its own open fields: Farrington in the N.W., Iwerne Courtney at the centre, and Ranston to the E. of the R. Iwerne.[1] Except for the manor house (3), Ranston is now deserted. The most important monument is the parish church.

ECCLESIASTICAL

(1) THE PARISH CHURCH OF ST. MARY stands near the S. end of Iwerne Courtney village. The walls are partly of squared and coursed rubble and partly of ashlar; the roofs were stone-slated until recently but are now tiled. The *Chancel* is of 14th-century origin but was extensively remodelled in the 17th century; the *West Tower* is of the 15th century with 17th-century alterations. The *Nave*, *North Aisle* and *South Chapel* were built in 1610 by Sir Thomas Freke (Coker, 103, and epitaph on Freke monument; *see* Hutchins IV, 99), the nave presumably replacing an earlier one. The *South Aisle* and *South Porch* were built in 1871, and the interior of the chancel was remodelled in 1872. The *Vestry* to the N. of the tower is modern.

The church illustrates the continuation of mediaeval architectural forms in the 17th century and it also contains a very noteworthy Renaissance oak screen, of the early 17th century, and an important wall monument of 1654.

Architectural Description—The *Chancel* (22½ ft. by 17 ft.) has a gabled E. wall with inclined copings surmounted by a cross; at the foot of the gable are two crocketed finials, that to the N. carved with the date 1610. The walls are faced with ashlar and have ogee and roll-moulded plinths which continue throughout the N. aisle and S. chapel. The E. window is of three cinquefoil-headed lights under a pointed head with rose tracery and a hoodmould; it appears to be of the 19th century and the level of the sill has been raised, possibly in 1872. The N. wall has a moulded eaves cornice and a 14th-century window of two ogee trefoil-headed lights with an ogee quatrefoil above, in a two-centred head with a moulded label; the rear-arch is segmental-pointed and the wide splays suggest that the wall is substantially mediaeval, although refaced externally in the 17th century. To the W. of the window the wall is pierced by an unmoulded two-centred archway which opens into the E. end of the N. aisle. The S. wall has a restored 14th-century doorway

[1] Dorset *Procs.*, LXIX (1947), 49.

with a roll-moulded two-centred head and continuous jambs, an external hoodmould and a segmental-pointed rear-arch. Further W. is a two-light window uniform with that in the N. wall. Although the chancel arch is stylistically of the early 16th century the sources named above show that it really is of 1610; this also applies to the N. nave arcade and the archway to the S. chapel (*see* below). The chancel arch is two-centred and has two ogee moulded orders separated by a wide hollow chamfer; the latter is continuous but the ogee mouldings are carried on attached shafts with moulded capitals and chamfered bases. On the W. side the arch is outlined by an ovolo moulding.

The *Nave* (47 ft. by 17½ ft.) is flanked on the N. by an arcade of three segmental-pointed arches with mouldings and responds similar to those of the chancel arch; each pier has four attached shafts with moulded caps and polygonal bases; between the shafts are continuous hollow chamfers. To the S., the archway opening into the S. chapel is uniform with those of the N. arcade; further W. the arcade to the S. aisle is of 1871. The *North Aisle* (56½ ft. by 12 ft.) extends eastwards to embrace part of the N. wall of the chancel, forming a chapel in which stands the memorial of Sir Thomas Freke. The walls are faced externally with ashlar and have a moulded plinth, buttresses of two weathered stages, and a moulded eaves cornice on the N. The E. gable has a moulded coping with pyramidal finials at the base and a fretted finial at the apex. The E. window and the three N. windows are uniform, each being of three gradated hollow-chamfered lancet lights in a two-centred casement-moulded head with continuous jambs and a moulded label; internally the two-centred rear-arches are continuous with the splays. The *South Chapel* (16 ft. by 10 ft.) has E. and S. windows uniform with those of the N. aisle; the W. archway, communicating with the S. aisle, is of 1871.

The *West Tower* (11 ft. square) is of three stages between a chamfered plinth and an embattled parapet; the stages are defined by weathered string-courses. There is no tower vice. Diagonal buttresses of two weathered stages strengthen the N.W. and S.W. corners of the bottom stage and a square-set buttress at the S.E. corner is partly incorporated in the fabric of the S. aisle. The top stage, which was probably remodelled in the 17th century, is decorated at each corner with a square pilaster. The weathered and hollow-chamfered parapet string-course returns around the pilasters and is interrupted on each face by two symmetrically spaced gargoyles. The embattled parapet has a continuous moulded coping and at each corner the pilasters of the third stage continue upwards to terminate in crocketed finials. The two-centred tower arch has three chamfered orders, the outer chamfer continuing on the jambs while the inner orders die into flat responds. In the W. wall of the lower stage is a 15th-century window of two trefoil-headed lights below a quatrefoil in a two-centred head, with a moulded label and a two-centred rear arch; the S. wall has a small doorway with a moulded two-centred head and continuous jambs, probably of the 19th century but inserted in the position of an earlier doorway. The middle stage has square-headed single-light windows on the N. and S. sides. The third stage has in each wall a louvred belfry window uniform with the W. window of the lower stage. The *South Porch* is of 1871; until recently it incorporated an embattled parapet which may have been part of a former porch, but the parapet has now been removed.

Fittings—*Bells:* four; 1st blank, 2nd dated 1631, 3rd by John Wallis, inscribed 'Geve thanks to God I W 1590', 4th inscribed 'Santa Maria' in black-letter. *Font:* of Purbeck marble with slightly tapering octagonal bowl, each facet with round-headed panel, rim encircled by chamfered horizontal fillet, under-edge of bowl chamfered; cylindrical Purbeck marble stem with roughly shaped mouldings at top and bottom; bowl and stem perhaps late 12th-century but bowl entirely refaced. *Glass:* In N. window of chancel, two fragments, probably 15th or 16th century. *Helm:* In N. aisle, on bracket on S. wall, with skull combed and roped at ridge and reinforced over forehead by shaped frontal piece, lower edge of sight and rim of vantail roped, vantail turning on faceted pins and resting on similar pin to right of chin; above, Freke crest, a bull's head collared or; skull, sights, vantail and chin probably *c.* 1560, gorget plates Cromwellian.

Monuments and *Floor-slabs. Monuments:* In N. aisle, near E. end of N. wall, (1) of Sir Thomas Freke Kt., 1633, and Elizabeth (Talor) his wife, 1641, stone and slate monument erected by their sons in 1654 (Plate 36); at top, achievement-of-arms of Freke impaling Talor enclosed in broken segmental pediment, surmounted by putti and dove bearing inscribed scrolls; epitaph painted on slate panel within moulded stone surround; on each side five numbered shields, each with shield-of-arms of Freke impaled by or impaling another, corresponding with names of children listed, with alliances, in lower part of panel (*see* Hutchins IV, 99); below, sculptured podium with angels with wreaths and trumpets, and large central panel containing swag of fruit and flowers below winged angel bust. In N. aisle, near centre of N. wall, (2) of Frederick Ryves, 1826, Catherine Elizabeth Ryves, 1803, and Anna Maria Ryves, 1815, marble tablet by Hiscock; (3) of [Elizabeth Ryves, 1755, and her daughter Charlotte, 1785,] grey and white marble monument with urn and arms. In S. chapel, on S. wall, (4) of Wellington Baker and William Baker, both 1847, white marble tablet by Reeves of Bath; (5) of Sir E. Baker Baker Bt., 1825, white marble tablet in form of sarcophagus surmounted by urn, backed by grey marble obelisk; over W. arch, (6) of Peter William Baker, 1815, and his wife Jane, 1816, marble tablet with urn, angel heads and crossed swords. In tower, on N. wall, (7) of J. Stubbs, 1755, and his wife Mary, 1798, white and variegated marble tablet. In churchyard, N.E. of N. aisle, (8) of Agnis Mew, 1670, stone table-tomb. *Floor-slabs:* In nave, to N.E., (1) of George [Ryves, 1689], worn Purbeck marble slab; (2) of Mary Ryves, 1697, similar slab with Latin inscription; (3) of George Ryves [1666], Purbeck marble slab with boldly carved cartouche-of-arms of Ryves.

Plate: includes silver cup and cover-paten and two flagons, all date-marked 1667, cup inscribed 'Ex dono Johannis Ryves de Ranston Armiger qui obiit tertio die Maii 1667'. *Screens:* Across E. end of N. aisle and in archway from aisle to chancel, thus enclosing Freke monument, but probably intended at first to surround Freke family pew, oak screens (Plate 143) in two heights of panelling surmounted by a height of colonettes and ornamental latticework enclosing crests of Freke; above, entablature with masks and tendrils on frieze, enriched cornice, and strapwork cresting with fretted pinnacles and central coats-of-arms of Freke and Talor; early 17th century. *Miscellanea:* Fragments of architectural sculpture some 50 yds. S.W. of church, (1) reset in churchyard wall, stone panel, 2 ft. by 2 ft., with mouldings forming four triangular panels, each containing cusped circlet; (2) octagonal finial, *c.* 2 ft. diameter, with embattled moulding; (3) drum of Purbeck marble shafting; (4) fragment of coarse crocketed finial.

(2) THE CHURCH OF ST. PETER, FARRINGTON (84151507), at the N. end of the parish and 2 m. N.W. of the parish church, was extensively rebuilt in 1856 and was again restored in 1899. It is a rectangular building of Greensand, with rough ashlar walls and finer ashlar dressings, roofed with stone-slates and tiles. The walls have chamfered double plinths. Weathered diagonal

buttresses stand at the corners and a square-set buttress in the middle of each side. The W. gable culminates in a stone bell-cote dated 1839. The font is of the 12th century, but nothing remains identifiable of the mediaeval building.

Fittings—*Bell:* probably of 1839. *Communion Tables:* In chancel, oak table with turned and moulded legs, arcaded decoration on top rails, scrolled spandrel pieces; 17th century. In nave, with turned and moulded legs and carved top rails; early 17th century, top board modern. *Font:* (Plate 26) of stone, tub-shaped, 2⅓ ft. high and of equal diameter, upper part crudely reeded above two horizontal roll mouldings; tapering lower part plain; shallow rebate in rim with fragments of iron cover fastenings; circular basin with deep square sinking at bottom; 12th century, with modern base. *Plate:* includes silver cup of *c.* 1575 without marks.

SECULAR

(3) Ranston (86291220), a country house of medium size, stands in a park 400 yds. S.E. of the parish church and a short distance from the E. bank of the R. Iwerne. The estate belonged to the Ryves family from 1545 to 1781, after which it was bought by Peter William Baker, whose heirs still own it. The house has been wholly rebuilt in recent years except for the graceful 18th-century W. front, but many original 18th-century fittings have been reset in the new structure. It is of two principal storeys with basements; the walls are rendered, except for plinths, quoins and architectural features, which are of ashlar; the roofs are slated. A brick wall that formed part of the W. side of a 17th-century range was found underground during the recent rebuilding and is incorporated in the present basement; it includes the lower part of two two-light windows with chamfered stone jambs. A scrolled wrought-iron weather-vane dated 1653, which formerly decorated a gable on the N. side of the house, probably belonged to the same building as the two windows. In 1753 the 17th-century house was enlarged to the W., a staircase, drawing-rooms and principal bedrooms being added; the new range was fronted by the formal W. façade which still exists. W. Watts (*The Seats of the Nobility and Gentry*, 1779, pl. VIII) states that the W. front was built in 1758, but the dated staircase (*see* below) shows that the alterations had been started at least five years earlier. In the 19th century further additions were made to N. and S. of the original range, but these extensions have now been demolished.

The W. front is of five bays (Plate 148); the three middle bays are emphasised by four Corinthian pilasters and a pediment, executed in Portland stone. At the foot of the pilasters a double flight of balustraded steps leads up to the central ground-floor opening; the original steps were removed in the 19th century but the feature has recently been restored on the basis of an 18th-century painting preserved in the house. Inside, the 18th-century staircase (Plate 85) which was originally at the centre of the N. side of the main block has now been transferred to the centre of the modern E. front. The steps are of stone, the balustrades are of scrolled wrought-iron and the moulded hand-rail is of figured walnut veneer. The scrolled ironwork of the landing balustrade encloses the Ryves crest, on the reverse of which is engraved 'Thos. Ryves 1753'. An original Palladian staircase window and rich rococo plaster-work on the walls and ceiling of the stair hall have also been transferred and restored; an oval canvas by Casali forms the central panel of the ceiling. Another oval canvas by the same painter, formerly in the drawing-room ceiling, has been reset in the ceiling of the first-floor hall.

An *Ornamental Bridge* of the mid 18th century, crossing the river 300 yds. S.W. of the house, is of Greensand ashlar, with three semicircular arches moulded on the N. side only and with plain keystones (Plate 64). Above a plat-band are balustrades with vase-shaped balusters similar to those of the stairs on the W. front of the house. At each end, where the abutments curve out to join the banks of the river, the balustrades are replaced by solid parapets. The bridge conceals a dam.

The *Stables*, some 40 yds. S. of the house, are of one storey with lofts, and have brick walls and slated roofs. The L-shaped plan bounds the stable yard to the S. and W. The W. wing has, at the centre of the E. wall, an entrance with a semicircular brick head and a keystone bearing the initials P.W.B., for Peter William Baker, and the date 1785, presumably the date of construction; on each side of the archway the ground-floor has three round-headed windows lighting the stalls and loose-boxes and over it is a circular window to the loft. The S. wing contains four coach-houses, each with a separate entrance with an elliptical brick head and an ashlar keystone and impost blocks. Extending the wing to the E. is another stable, but this was originally an open shelter of two bays with elliptical arches uniform with those of the coach-house entrances; the arches are now bricked up and furnished with semicircular windows. A cast lead pump-head is inscribed 'E.B.B. 1844'.

(4) Shroton House (85741300), 700 yds. N. of (1), is of two storeys with attics and cellars, and has walls of brick, largely rendered, and slated roofs. It dates from the first half of the 18th century and incorporates date-stones inscribed 'William Jeanes, 1728' and 'William and Anne Jeanes 1736'. The original plan comprised a long range facing S. and a shorter E. range at right-angles; subsequently the E. range was extended N., the S. range was extended W. and other additions were made to N. and W. in the re-entrant angle between the two original ranges.

The S. front, of seven bays, has at the centre a large 19th-century two-storied bow with three sashed windows on each floor; to the E. of the bow is a single-storied late 19th-century porch. Flanking these features are giant Doric pilasters, and similar pilasters mark the E. and W. extremities of the elevation; between the western pair of pilasters are three two-storied bays of sashed windows while the eastern pair have two similar bays between them. The two E. pilasters are surmounted by the S. gable of the E. range.

Inside, the entrance hall has 18th-century pine panelling in two heights, with a moulded dado rail, fielded panels and a moulded cornice. The dining-room, at the S. end of the E. range, has late 19th-century decorations. The study, to the N. of the dining-room, has 19th-century panelling but sashed windows with heavy glazing bars of the 18th century. The stairs adjacent to the study are of oak and of the 18th century; they have open strings, scrolled spandrels, column newel-posts, turned balusters and moulded handrails; the staircase walls have raking dados. A sitting-room on the N. side of the S. range has 18th-century pine panelling in two heights, and a panelled overmantel with Greek-key enrichment. The chamber above the dining-room is lined with 18th-century fielded panelling in two heights, with a moulded dado rail and a cornice with consoles alternating with lozenges; the fireplace has a moulded stone surround and brackets supporting a cornice; above is a fielded overmantel in an eared architrave with a broken pediment.

(5) WILLIS'S SHROTON FARM (85701294), 60 yds. S.W. of the foregoing, is of two and three storeys with a cellar, and has walls of brick and rubble, and slated roofs. The W. part of the farmhouse is of the first half of the 18th century and the three-storied E. range was added *c.* 1800. The original W. range is two-storied with an attic; on the ground floor it has a large kitchen to the N.W. and an office, perhaps originally a parlour, to the N.E. To the S. of these rooms are a scullery, a store-room and a staircase. The E. range consists of a N. and a S. room with a narrow passage between them. The E. front is of brick but the N. and S. side-walls are rendered, the rendering returning on the E. front in the guise of rusticated quoins. The E. front is symmetrical and of three bays, with a round-headed doorway on the ground floor, square-headed sashed windows on each side, and three similar windows in each of the two upper storeys.

A *Cottage* immediately S.W. of the farmhouse is two-storied with English-bond brick walls and a thatched roof. It appears to be of the mid 18th century and incorporates a date-stone marked 'W.J. 1758'; it was originally a dairy with a small dwelling to the E. Blocked ventilation loops occur in the N. and S. walls and in the N. wall are traces of a wide doorway, also blocked, with large ashlar guard-stones at the foot of each jamb.

(6) COTTAGE (85801293), on the S. side of the lane, 100 yds. S.E. of (4), is of one storey with attics. It dates from the 17th century and has walls of clunch, rubble, timber-framing and brick, and a thatched roof. At the centre of the N. front is a small three-sided two-storied bay window of squared clunch blocks with jambs and mullions of wood. The E. part of the N. wall is of rubble; the W. part has been rebuilt in brick. Internally, the ground floor has three rooms and a through-passage; the middle room and that to the W. have back-to-back fireplaces; the E. room has a fireplace in the gabled end wall, with a winding stair beside it.

(7) SHROTON COTTAGE (85941293), 530 yds. N. of the church, is of two storeys, with rubble walls and a thatched roof. Although much rebuilt and restored the nucleus is probably of the 17th or early 18th century.

(8) SHROTON FARM (85991254), house, 150 yds. N. of the church, is mainly of the early 19th century, but it incorporates a 17th-century wing. The 19th-century part is two-storied, with brick walls, a tiled roof and a symmetrical E. front of three bays. The 17th-century wing, which projects forward from the N. end of the E. front, has the E. wall of squared clunch blocks and in this wall are vestiges of a stone window with a moulded label. Internally the 17th-century wing has stop-chamfered beams.

The *Barn*, 80 yds. S. of the farmhouse, is of the 18th century; it has rubble walls with ashlar quoins and dressings, and a thatched roof; internally the walls are lined with roughly squared clunch. The plan is a long rectangle with wings projecting N. at each end and a central projecting bay to the S. The main entrance is a wide doorway in the centre of the N. side while the S. bay has a similar doorway opposite. Many dates are scratched on the clunch walls, the earliest noted being 1731. A 17th-century *Pigeon House*, 15 yds. S.W. of the barn, is rectangular on plan. The walls are of ashlar and the roof is tiled. The walls have a chamfered plinth and on the S. side is a blocked doorway with a four-centred stone head and chamfered jambs. Internally the structure is built in courses of thin stone slabs alternating with courses of square blocks, the latter spaced so that each interstice forms a nesting-box. A *Granary*, 30 yds. S.E. of the barn, has brick walls raised on an arcaded substructure with stone impost blocks of sufficient overhang to defeat the agility of rats; the granary is lined with elm planks. The granary and an adjacent *Stable* are of the late 18th or early 19th century.

(9) THE RECTORY (86041255), 100 yds. N.E. of the church, is two-storied with attics and cellars and has ashlar walls and slated roofs. It was built in 1812.

(10) COTTAGES, three adjacent, 50 yds. S.E. of the church, are of rubble and ashlar in two storeys, with attics in a tiled roof. A triple gable on the N. side and the symmetrically spaced windows of both storeys are evidently secondary. The structure is likely to date from the 17th century.

(11) TRAY TOWN (86521198), 750 yds. S.E. of the church, is an early 19th-century *cottage orné* of one storey, with squared rubble walls and a thatched roof (Plate 60). The windows of the W. front have pointed heads. The plan is square and the pyramidal roof culminates in a central chimneystack; reset at the base of the stack is an 18th-century keystone with a grotesque mask.

(12) FARRINGTON BRIDGE (84091558), crossing the Fontmell Brook at the N. extremity of the parish, is of coursed rubble and ashlar with segmental arches in two spans; it is dated 1830.

(13) FARRINGTON HOUSE (84151523), a 17th-century farmhouse of two storeys with attics, has walls of coursed rubble with ashlar dressings and a thatched roof; a brick wing to the N. is probably of the 18th century. The doorway in the N. wall of the original range is now blocked; it has a four-centred head and chamfered jambs. On the ground floor the gabled W. wall has two square-headed four-light windows with chamfered stone mullions and moulded labels; symmetrically placed above them is a three-light first-floor window with similar details; the attic has a similar two-light window. The S. front of the original range and the later N. range have wooden casement windows. Internally there are exposed stop-chamfered ceiling beams.

(14) 'MEADOW GATE' (84241500), 300 yds. S.E. of the foregoing, is mainly of brick with some rubble and flint, and has a thatched roof; it dates from the late 18th or early 19th century.

(15) CHURCH FARM (84201505), 50 yds. N. of the foregoing, is a 17th-century farmhouse of one storey with attics; the S.W. front is of ashlar and the N.W. end wall is of banded flint and rubble; the roofs are thatched (Plate 60). The S.E. end of the house is modern. The original S.W. front has, on the ground floor, two windows of three and four lights with ovolo-moulded stone surrounds, square heads and weathered labels; above, in gabled stone dormers, are two corresponding three-light windows and above these, in each gable, is a chamfered loop. Inside, a fireplace has a chamfered stone surround with a three-centred head; some exposed ceiling beams are stop-chamfered.

MEDIAEVAL AND LATER EARTHWORKS

(16) SETTLEMENT REMAINS (863120) of the former village of *Ranston* lie in Ranston Park on the E. side of the R. Iwerne.

The settlement was one of the Iwernes in Domesday Book and has been identified by Eyton (p. 137) as the three-hide manor of Robert, son of Gerald (D.B. Vol. I, f. 80b); this manor had a recorded population of nine. By 1274 five free tenants and ten

CAUSEWAYED CAMP, HAMBLEDON HILL

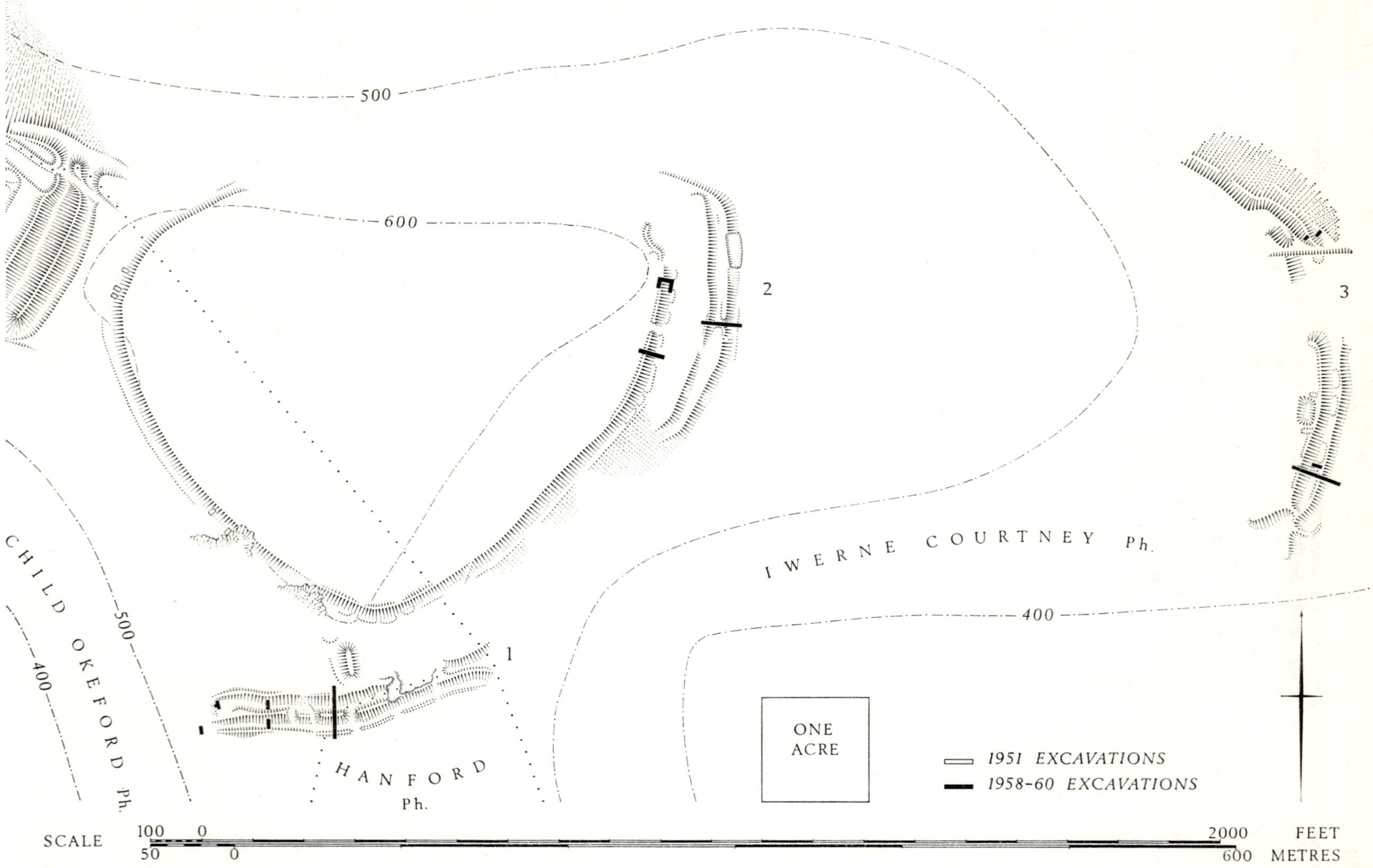

villeins were listed (Dorset *Procs.* Vol. LXIX, 49). The settlement is not recorded separately in the mid 14th-century Subsidy Rolls but it is possible that it was included with Iwerne Stepleton. After this date there is no record of population until 1662, when nothing but Ranston House remained (Meeking, p. 67, s.v. 'Steepleton'). Any surviving dwellings were probably destroyed when the 17th-century house was built.

The remains cover about 6 acres and are mainly indeterminate banks and scarps, up to 3 ft. high and distributed around an almost square enclosure with sides 30 yds. long. The enclosure is bounded on the S. and E. by a low bank with an outer ditch and on the N. and W. by a scarp 1 ft. high. Inside the enclosure is a platform 60 ft. long, 30 ft. wide and 1 ft. high, orientated E.–W.; it is marked on O.S. maps as the site of a chapel.

(17) BULL PIT (88831348) lies in Bull Pit Coppice, 2 m. E.N.E. of the village and immediately W. of the Shaftesbury–Blandford Road. Its date and purpose are unknown but it could have been a pit for bull-baiting. The remains consist of a circular pit 90 ft. in diameter and 7 ft. deep, with a flat bottom 65 ft. across. A ditch or hollow-way 25 ft. wide and 2½ ft. deep runs around the outside of the pit from the S.W. and turns, on the N.E., into a ramped entrance to the pit, 30 ft. wide.

(18) CULTIVATION REMAINS. The open fields of *Iwerne Courtney* were enclosed by agreement in 1548 (Hutchins IV, 89). Ridge-and-furrow of these fields remains due W. of Park House Farm Buildings (852136); it consists of two rectangular butting furlongs with ridges 6 yds. to 8 yds. wide.

Nothing is known of the date of enclosure of the open fields of *Farrington*. Around Church Farm (15) some 50 acres of ridge-and-furrow, in end-on and butting furlongs of curved or reversed-S ridges, 7 yds. to 9 yds. wide, remain or can be seen on air photographs (R.A.F. CPE/UK 1944: 4329–30).

ROMAN AND PREHISTORIC

IRON AGE HILL-FORT, *see* Child Okeford (22).

(19) NEOLITHIC CAUSEWAYED CAMP, on Hambledon Hill (849122), consists of a single enclosure of nearly 20 acres embracing the domed central summit of the hill, here reaching 640 ft. above O.D., and three multiple cross-dykes situated on spurs radiating to the S. and E. (*see* also plan on p. xxxix and Plate 131). The earthworks have been much disturbed in the past by tracks and diggings for flint gravel, particularly the interior of the enclosure, and recently they have been almost completely destroyed by ploughing. The site was first fully described in Crawford and Keiller *Wessex from the Air* (1928), 44–7. The enclosure was examined in a test excavation by G. de G. Sieveking in 1951 (Dorset *Procs.* LXXIII (1951), 105–6) and the cross-dykes were investigated by this Commission in 1958–60. A radiocarbon date of 2790 B.C.±90 was provided by a carbon sample from the bottom of the inner ditch of cross-dyke 1.

In plan the enclosure is a rounded triangle, up to 1,000 ft. across and surrounding the hilltop at about 600 ft., although scarcely taking full advantage of the contours in the way that a hill-fort might. Before destruction it was defined by a scarp, varying in height from 2 ft. to 6 ft., surmounted by a low bank, 15 ft. across and 6 ins. high, visible only on the S. and E. sides. Outside was a causewayed or interrupted ditch, but this, due to silting, appeared for much of its length as a terrace about 10 ft. across. On the N. side soil creep and thick scrub masked the line of the enclosure. The whole of the interior was pocked by numerous pits and hollows, the result of flint digging for road-metal over many years.

Cross-dyke 1 lies on gently sloping ground 40 yds. S. of the enclosure and facing outwards from it. It comprises a double line of banks and ditches, 600 ft. long and extending in a gentle curve across the neck of the S. spur from shoulder to shoulder. It has been disfigured by tracks and flint digging but the interrupted nature of the inner ditch is still visible. The banks, now little more than scarps, still stand over 5 ft. above the ditch bottoms.

Cross-dyke 2, of similar length and construction, lies across the neck of the E. spur, within 100 ft. of the enclosure and following its curve. It is now almost almost completely destroyed.

Cross-dyke 3 lies further down the E. spur, ¼ m. away from the enclosure and at a point where the slope steepens; it extends for nearly 1,000 ft. in a broad convex curve from shoulder to shoulder. A 100 ft. gap half-way along it is almost certainly not original. To the S. of the gap the dyke is a single bank and ditch, but N. of it, where the natural slope is very steep, it is certainly double.

Excavation showed that, owing to weathering, very little of the original banks remained, at most 6 ins. All the ditches were comparatively small, fairly steep-sided and, with the exception of the outer ditch of cross-dyke 1, clearly flat-bottomed; the exception was more V-shaped. The ditches varied in width between 11 ft. and 14 ft., except in cross-dyke 2 where they were both 7 ft. In depth they varied between 3 ft. and 7 ft., except the enclosure ditch which shallowed to a mere scrape on the steeper slope; here the effect of a bank was produced by scarping and a quarry ditch for material was hardly necessary.

Neolithic pottery of simple form, akin to that from Maiden Castle, was found scattered throughout the filling of the ditches and was the only pottery from the lower filling; it included a very degenerate example of a trumpet-lug. Other finds included chipped and polished flint axes, leaf-shaped arrowheads, large coarse scrapers, a bone chisel or gouge, animal bones, chiefly of cattle, and two human skulls from the ditch bottoms of cross-dyke 2. Within the upper part of the ditch fillings occasional abraded 'B' beaker and rusticated sherds appeared; they were abundant in the shallow inner ditch of cross-dyke 2, where a Beaker pit had been cut into the earlier filling.

(20) OCCUPATION SITE (890132), of Mesolithic date, lies at 500 ft. above O.D. on the summit of the Chalk escarpment, which is here capped with Clay-with-flints. The site is in the extreme E. of the parish and is generally known by the name of the adjacent parish, Iwerne Minster. The site, covering some two acres, has been ploughed and has yielded a considerable number of surface finds of flint tools, including cores, tranchet picks, flake axes and microliths (*P.P.S.*, VII (1941), 145–6; Dorset *Procs.*, LXXXIII (1961), 92–4, 97).

UNDATED

(21) ENCLOSURE (88701335), in Ditchey Coppice, lies at just over 500 ft. above O.D. on the ridge top, E. of the R. Iwerne. It consists of a rectangular enclosure about 100 ft. square, bounded by a low bank with an outer ditch. The interior is divided into two unequal parts by a low bank, orientated E.–W., which continues for 240 ft. W. of the enclosure. An entrance on the E., 4 yds. wide, gives access to the S. part; in the S.W. corner of this part is a rectangular depression 60 ft. long, 12 ft. wide and 6 ins. deep, orientated E.–W. and probably the site of a building. The appearance of the enclosure suggests that it is of mediaeval or later date.

27 IWERNE STEPLETON (8611)

(O.S. 6 ins. ST 81 SE)

The narrow strip-like parish, little more than 800 acres in extent, lies on the E. side of the R. Iwerne, entirely on Chalk. The parish occupies a broad dry valley and rises from 150 ft. above sea-level at the river bank to over 500 ft. at the E. boundary. The church dates from about the end of the 11th century and the village almost certainly stood near by, but it was deserted by 1662 and no traces of earlier habitation remain visible. The site is now occupied by Stepleton House and its gardens, in which the church stands. The house is the principal monument.

ECCLESIASTICAL

(1) THE PARISH CHURCH OF ST. MARY stands at the W. end of the parish and close to the R. Iwerne, which at this point is dammed up to form a lake. The walls are mainly rendered, but the N. wall of the nave has been exposed during recent repairs, showing it to be of flint and rubble with squared rubble dressings; the roofs are stone-slated and tiled. The *Chancel* and *Nave* are of the late 11th or early 12th century; from the thickness of the walls it appears probable that the chancel was originally surmounted by a tower. A blocked archway in the E. wall of the chancel presumably opened into a sanctuary, now demolished; according to Hutchins (I, 300) the foundations of a compartment to the E. were exposed at some time by excavation, but no details are known. Hutchins also refers to the discovery of eight narrow windows in the nave; one of them, a round-headed loop, has recently been rediscovered.

IWERNE STEPLETON

The parish church of St. Mary

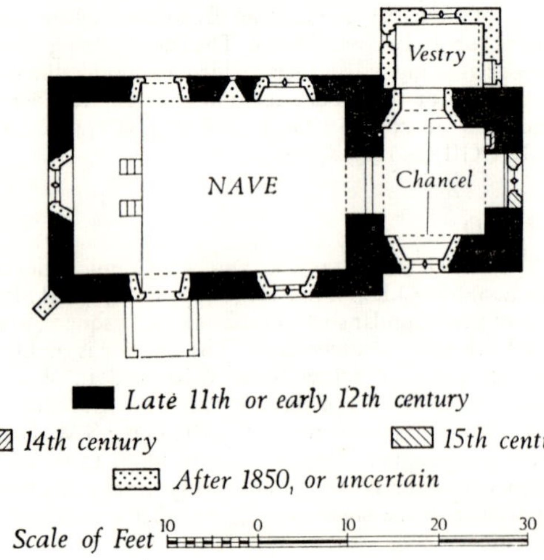

Architectural Description—The *Chancel* (11½ ft. square) has in the E. wall a round-headed recess which was presumably the original sanctuary archway. The arch has a single order of plain voussoirs springing from chamfered imposts which are enriched with a pattern of small rectangles enclosing diagonal crosses and pearls. The decoration is original only on the imposts in the reveals of the archway; elsewhere it is of the 19th century, as is the similarly decorated label which outlines the arch. The ashlar responds are square and undecorated. The wall which closes the archway contains a restored 15th-century window of two cinquefoil-headed lights with a quatrefoil in a two-centred head. To the N. a round-headed opening with splayed reveals gives access to a modern vestry; to the S. is a modern two-light window with a splayed round-headed rear-arch; to the W. is a round-headed archway from the nave; all three openings are rendered. The *Nave* (30½ ft. by 18½ ft.) has an original round-headed loop set high up near the middle of the N. wall; to the E. is a 19th-century two-light window and to the W. is a 19th-century doorway with a four-centred head. The S. wall has similar 19th-century openings; any original openings that may survive are concealed by rendering. The W. wall has a 19th-century two-light window and, high up, a round-headed opening of uncertain date, now used as a bell-cote.

Fittings—*Bell:* one, dated 1809. *Monuments:* In nave, in vertical E. side of raised platform at W. end, four plain slabs of white marble; (1) with inscription 'P.B. sibi et suis MDCCCIX', (2) of Marcia Louisa Pitt, 1850, and George Horace Pitt, 1850, (3) of William Horace, third Lord Rivers, 1831, (4) of Peter Beckford, 1811. *Niche:* In chancel, in N. respond of former E. archway, square recess with cusped two-centred head and stop-chamfered jambs, 14th century. *Piscina:* In chancel, on S. side, with hollow-chamfered cinquefoil ogee-headed opening in square casement-moulded head, and mutilated polygonal basin with hollow-chamfered rim; early 15th century. *Plate:* includes silver cup (Plate 42) with hall-mark of 1649 and cover-paten with hall-mark of 1638, the latter engraved with arms of Pitt impaling Cadbury; also silver almsdish with hall-mark of 1770.

SECULAR

(2) STEPLETON HOUSE (86331129), 50 yds. N.E. of the church, has ashlar walls of Greensand and limestone, and stone-slated roofs with lead ridges (Plate 148). A rectangular central block of two main storeys with basement and attics is symmetrically flanked to E. and W. by smaller two-storied pavilions, isolated but joined to the main block by linking passages of one storey. In conformity with the fall of the land the W. pavilion has also a basement storey, and on the W. front of the main block the basement stands wholly above ground. The central block dates substantially from the first quarter of the 17th century. It is nearly square in plan and originally had a small central courtyard; the main entrance was probably on the E. From 1654 to 1745 the house belonged to the Fownes family who made numerous improvements, including the transfer of the main entrance from the E. front to the S. front, and the building of pedimented central features on those two fronts. In 1745 Julines Beckford acquired the house and soon afterwards the courtyard was roofed over to accommodate a new staircase and vestibule. The flanking

STEPLETON HOUSE

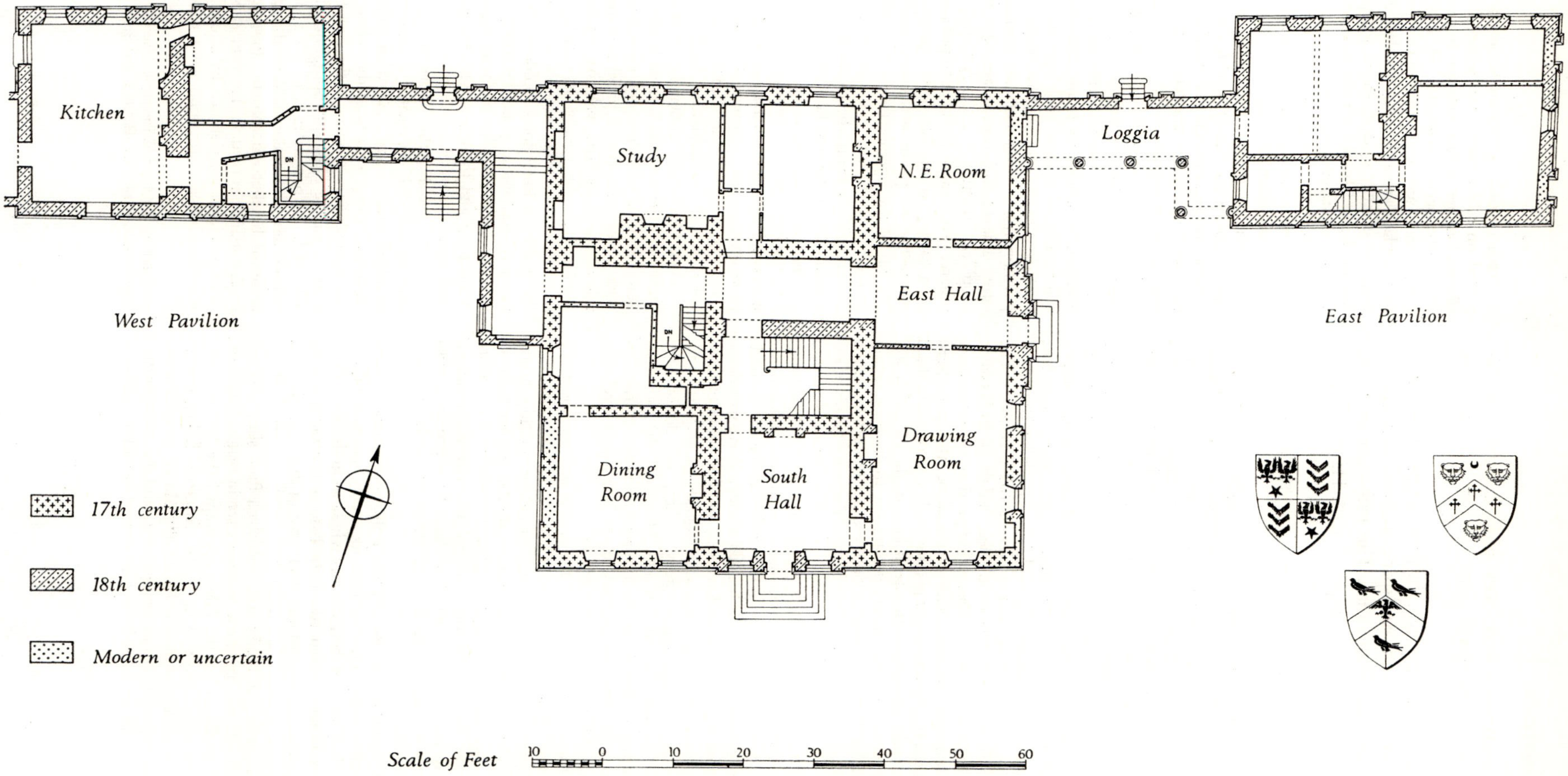

Kitchen
Study
N. E. Room
Loggia
East Hall
West Pavilion
East Pavilion
Dining Room
South Hall
Drawing Room
DN
17th century
18th century
Modern or uncertain
Scale of Feet
10
0
10
20
30
40
50
60

pavilions appear to have been built in 1758, the date inscribed with Beckford's crest on the lead rainwater heads.

Although of two periods, the house in its present form is a harmonious and well-proportioned example of English domestic architecture. The 17th-century building is of interest when compared with Hanford House (p. 102), which is nearly contemporary and similar in ground-plan; the cylindrical chimneystacks also find parallels at Hanford.

The S. front of the main block has six regularly spaced bays with sashed windows in the two principal storeys and three dormer windows in the hipped roof. The windows of the two middle bays are set in a slightly projecting centrepiece, added in the 18th century when the front doorway was inserted between the two middle ground-floor windows and this became the principal front. A niche over the doorway and a pediment at the top of the centrepiece successfully convert the former side elevation of six equal bays into an axial main front. Above window-sill level the lower storey of the centrepiece is rusticated; the central doorway is square-headed with a triple keystone, and above it is a flat stone hood supported on scrolled consoles. The two first-floor windows of the centrepiece and the niche between them are flanked by Ionic pilasters supporting an entablature which continues in the concavity of the niche, the niche-head rising into the tympanum of the pediment. The heavily moulded cornice extends across the four lateral bays of the elevation and effectively binds the 18th-century centrepiece to the pre-existing façade; similar cornices continue on the other three sides of the building. In the lateral bays of the S. front the main details of the original 17th-century elevation are preserved. At the base is a plinth of Greensand ashlar, with a hollow-chamfered capping; above, the walls are of limestone and a weathered and hollow-chamfered string-course occurs a few inches above the ground-floor window heads. The square-headed windows have weathered sills flush with the wall-face, and recessed and hollow-chamfered jambs and heads; these openings are evidently of the early 17th century with inserted 18th-century sashes; no doubt they originally had mullions and transoms. However, the two first-floor windows to the E. of the centrepiece were entirely remodelled in the 18th century; they are set at a lower level than the others and have classical architraves.

The E. front is of five bays and the central bay is embellished with another added centrepiece (Plate 149) consisting of a rusticated doorway, a round-headed first-floor window and a pediment. The two bays on each side retain the original hollow-chamfered plinth, which is 1½ ft. higher than that of the S. front but otherwise similar, and also a string-course that is continuous with that to the S.; all the windows have been provided with 18th-century architraves. As in the S. front, the attic has three dormer windows.

The N. front retains its original hollow-chamfered plinth and weathered string-course and has six evenly spaced windows on each main floor, and three dormer windows in the attic; there are also six square-headed two-light basement windows with sills a few inches above ground-level; two of them are blocked. All except the dormer windows have 17th-century hollow-chamfered jambs and heads, and weathered flush sills, as noted on the S. front; the basement windows retain original hollow-chamfered mullions but the other openings have 18th-century sashes, as described before. On the W. front the falling terrain causes the basement storey to be wholly above ground level. The 17th-century plinth and string-course, and the 18th-century cornice are continuous, as before. A service corridor, added in the 18th century, partly masks the principal storey; it is supported on ashlar piers with square impost blocks and shallow elliptical arches with keystones. In the basement elevation, seen below the service corridor, is a wide square-headed 17th-century doorway with a deeply chamfered stone surround and an oak plank door, heavily studded. Adjacent is a 17th-century window of two square-headed lights with hollow-chamfered surrounds, and further to the S. is a smaller two-light opening with a chamfered surround. The ground and first floors have 17th-century windows, some of them blocked and others with 18th-century sashes, except where the 18th-century service corridor supervenes.

The chimneystacks of the main block are of ashlar and terminate above roof level in cylindrical brick flues, grouped in batteries of from two to six. At the top the flues are united by rectangular slabs of terracotta with moulded edges, continuous over a whole battery.

The mid 18th-century pavilions to E. and W. of the main block have walls of Greensand ashlar, with plat-bands at first-floor level corresponding with the string-courses of the original house. The hipped roofs are stone-slated with lead flats at the centre; instead of eaves they have parapet walls above modillion cornices. On the ground floor, at the centre of the N. front each pavilion has a rusticated and pedimented false doorway; on either side of this feature are two tall sashed windows with moulded architraves and keystones; five similar windows of squarer proportions light the upper storey. On the E., S. and W. sides each pavilion has three openings in each storey, except where the W. pavilion is partly masked by a lean-to addition. Several of the openings are false and have imitation windows painted on the blocking. On the S. side, the central openings are accentuated by round heads on the ground floor and by eared architraves on the first floor. At the middle of the roof of each pavilion is a square brick chimneystack. The single-storied ranges which join the pavilions to the main block have, to the N., doorways with moulded architraves and keystones, set between pairs of rusticated pilasters. The W. range is a corridor, with windows to the S.; the E. range is an open loggia with Ionic columns and an entablature; both ranges have flat lead roofs.

Inside, the fittings generally are of the mid 18th century. The central doorway in the S. front of the main block opens into the South Hall, where there is a carved wooden fireplace surround with a sun-mask centre panel and rococo scrollwork on either side of the head. The walls have a dado of fielded panels. The moulded plaster ceiling is enriched with rococo arabesques surrounding an octagonal centre panel. In the Dining Room, the dado has bolection-moulded panels and the plaster ceiling has a round central panel enclosing, among floral arabesques, two scrolled cartouches, one with the arms of Fownes quartering Armstrong and the other with the arms of Fitch[1]; the Fownes eagle crest decorates each corner of the ceiling. In the Drawing Room to the E., the doorways have eared architraves and entablatures with pulvinated acanthus friezes; the fireplace has a moulded marble surround with a cross-lugged wooden architrave and a dentil cornice; the ceiling has an oval centre panel and a modillion cornice. In the East Hall are doorways similar to those of the drawing room, but with pediments in addition. The N.E. corner room also has a pedimented doorway; the ceiling has an octagonal central panel with Greek-key and acanthus bracket enrichment; the fireplace has a 19th-century reeded marble surround. The central N. room has pine panelling in two heights surmounted by a moulded wooden cornice; the wooden fireplace surround has scrolled cheek-pieces, a carved

[1] Meliora Fitch of Wimborne Minster married Thomas Fownes of Stepleton in 1728 (D.C.R.O., f. 4021).

IWERNE STEPLETON. (2) Stepleton House. Exterior, from S.E. 17th and 18th-century

IWERNE COURTNEY. (3) Ranston. W. front. 1753

IWERNE STEPLETON. (2) Stepleton House. Detail of E. front. 18th-century central panel and a cornice supported on shaped brackets with acanthus enrichment. The Study is lined with early 17th-century oak panelling in five heights, with moulded rails and stiles; it has probably been reset and is made up with some modern work; the fireplace is flanked by Ionic pilasters in two heights, one standing directly on top of the other, with conventional scroll-foliage carving on the shafts; above the pilasters is a strapwork frieze. The moulded plaster ceiling is a modern reproduction of the 17th-century ceiling in the dining-room at Bingham's Melcombe, Melcombe Horsey (2).

The main Staircase, inserted in the former courtyard, has stone steps with shaped soffits and moulded nosing; the scrolled wrought-iron balustrade supports a moulded and veneered wooden handrail (Plate 85). The fascia of the first-floor landing is decorated with a Greek-key frieze which continues as a string-course around the stair well; the soffit below the landing has rococo ornament. On the first floor, the stair well is flanked to the N. by an arcade of three elliptical-headed arches with panelled soffits and piers. The staircase ceiling has a deep cove surrounding a skylight. The back stairs are of the early 17th century and have close strings, stout turned balusters and square handrails; in the top flight the balusters are vase-shaped. The flight of stairs which leads down to the basement has a 17th-century balustrade with a moulded handrail, large turned balusters and a moulded close string; it is possible that these elements belonged to an early main staircase and were transfered to the basement in the mid 18th century, when the present main staircase was inserted.

In the basement, a room in the N.W. corner of the main block has a large open fireplace with brick jambs and a chamfered elliptical head; presumably this was the former kitchen, before the building of the W. pavilion, where the kitchen is now situated. To the E., in a position which corresponds with the W. side of the East Hall, a thick wall in the basement is pierced by a square-headed doorway with a chamfered surround, similar to that of the W. front; the doorway suggests that the E. front of the house may originally have been in this position, but the evidence is inconclusive. The cellars to the E. of the doorway have groined brick vaults; those to the W. have wooden beams.

On the first floor, the chamber above the South Hall has a plain dado, and a carved wooden fireplace surround with a foliate pulvinated frieze, a centre panel with rococo ornament in high relief, and carved enrichment at the sides; the ceiling has moulded panels. A large chamber over the Drawing Room is lined with fielded and enriched panelling in two heights below a wooden dentil cornice. The chamber over the Dining Room has a dado with fielded panelling, and a fireplace surround of carved wood with scrolled cheek-pieces, a frieze in high relief representing a festoon of flowers, and a pedimented cornice; these are of the 18th century, but the pictorial wallpaper is a modern reprint from early 19th-century blocks. The N.E. bedroom has fielded panelling in two heights. A bedroom at the centre of the N. front has a richly carved wood fireplace surround with rococo cheek-pieces and a flower frieze; the mantelshelf rests on brackets with acanthus and scale decoration. The plaster ceiling of this room has a sun-mask at the centre and a guilloche outer moulding enriched at the corners with arabesques.

The detached pavilion to the E. has a plain stone staircase and, on the first floor, a large room with a coved ceiling with a moulded cornice; the other rooms have no architectural decoration. The W. pavilion contains the kitchen and other service rooms; the kitchen has elliptical-headed recesses to the E.

(3) STABLES (Plate 63), 30 yds. W. of Stepleton House, date probably from the second quarter of the 18th century. The building is of one storey with lofts and has walls of brick with ashlar dressings; the roofs are partly tiled and partly stone-slated. The N. façade has a pedimented centre bay defined by quoins, with a rusticated arch at the centre; the brickwork of the centre bay is entirely of headers. These details are closely paralleled in the stables at Bryanston (p. 47) and it is probable that the same architect was employed. On each side extend symmetrical wings, each with three round-headed sashed windows. The pediment is crowned by a wooden clock turret and bell-cote with an ogival lead cupola; this too is closely paralleled in the turret on the Portman Chapel at Bryanston.

(4) KENNELS (86041134), built about 1770 for Peter Beckford's hounds, have now been converted into cottages; an upper floor has been inserted, with casement windows under the eaves. The walls are of Flemish-bonded brickwork and the roofs are tiled. Original openings are identifiable by surviving segmental heads and keystones, although many openings have been walled up and others have been made. The original building closely resembled Beckford's drawing (*Thoughts on Hunting*, Letter II), except that the plan is a little smaller, the 'lodging room' windows have segmental instead of round heads, and the roofs have gables to N. and S. instead of being hipped.

MEDIAEVAL AND LATER EARTHWORKS

(5) CULTIVATION REMAINS. Nothing is known of the open fields of the parish although it has been suggested that there once was a two-field system, Dorset *Procs.*, LXIX (1947), 48); about 40 acres of strip lynchets and ridge-and-furrow remain. N.E. of Everley Farm (871118) are faint traces of two strip lynchets. In Stepleton Park (868115, 865115 and 865112), ten contour strip lynchets are arranged in three-furlong blocks, up to 300 yds. long. Also in the park (863114) are faint traces of almost straight ridge-and-furrow, 6 yds. to 9 yds. wide.

28 LYDLINCH (7413)

(O.S. 6 ins. ST 71 SW, ST 71 SE)

The parish has an area of about 3,400 acres and is divided into two parts, distinct from one another both geologically and historically. The W. part is roughly square and lies entirely on Oxford Clay at a general altitude of 200 ft. to 250 ft., except where a slight eminence near the centre rises to 300 ft. The other part is a narrow tongue of land stretching out to the E.; it lies on Corallian Beds and has an altitude of 200 ft. to 300 ft. The W. area is drained by the R. Lydden and the Caundle Brook, the latter forming the N. boundary; the tip of the E. tongue drains into the R. Divelish.

The parish probably contains three original settlements: Lydlinch, Stock Gaylard and Plumber. The western square was divided between the first two while Plumber occupied the eastern tongue. Stock Gaylard, in the N.W. corner of the area, continued to be a separate parish until the 19th century; its territory extended over the S. part of the area although separated from the village by ground belonging to Lydlinch.[1] Today Stock Gaylard village is represented only by its church (2) and manor house (5). Lydlinch village consists of

[1] Tithe Map of Stock Gaylard, 1841.

the parish church (1) and about twenty houses in the N.E. quarter of the western square. Plumber is a single farm (6). Stock Gaylard and Plumber are both named in Domesday Book, but Lydlinch is not, although it was almost certainly in existence. Lydlinch and Stock Gaylard both had open fields, but there is no evidence of them at Plumber.

Secondary settlements such as Hydes, Stroud Farm, Ramsbury (which is probably Berry Farm), Blackrow and Holebrook Green led, by the 14th century at the latest, to the formation of enclosures beyond the open fields.[1] Enclosure of the waste and consequent formation of new farms continued in the post-mediaeval period; for instance the late 16th-century Haydon Farm (9) is likely to have come into existence in consequence of the enclosure of part of Haydon Common, and the date of Little Rodmore Farm (20) confirms the implication of the geometrical field layout, that the S.W. corner of the parish was enclosed in the 18th century. Ridge Farm (18), also with geometrical fields, reflects later 18th-century enclosure in the S. part of the parish.

The strung-out hamlet of Kingstag in the S.W. corner of the parish is probably another late 18th-century development. The monuments noted there are not earlier than the 19th century, but buildings are shown on the O.S. map of 1811, and it must be presumed that several existing late 19th-century cottages replace others of somewhat earlier date.

Enclosure of the common lands continued into the middle of the 19th century[2], and even today some 80 acres of Lydlinch Common remain unenclosed.

[1] Fägersten, 217 f.
[2] Enclosure map and award, Haydon Common, 1867, (D.C.R.O.).

The principal monuments are the parish church and Stock Gaylard House. The parish is notable for the large number of 17th-century farmhouses to survive.

ECCLESIASTICAL

(1) THE PARISH CHURCH OF ST. THOMAS À BECKET stands on the W. side of Lydlinch village. Its walls are of rubble with ashlar dressings; the roofs are covered with Welsh slates, except in the chancel which has stone slates and the tower which is leaded. The *Chancel* and *Nave* appear to be of 15th-century origin but with much restoration and alteration; the *West Tower* is of the early 15th century; the *North Aisle* and *South Porch* are of the 16th century. In the first half of the 19th century the nave walls were heightened, the chancel arch was restored, a new N. arcade was inserted and a new low-pitched nave roof was provided; the *North Vestry* was probably added at this period. The chancel was re-roofed in 1875.

A passage in Hutchins (2nd ed. IV, 62), describing the church as it was before restoration, mentions two round-headed arches; these might have been of the 12th century but they have now gone and the font is the only remaining evidence for a building of that period.

Architectural Description—The walls of the *Chancel* (20½ ft. by 16¼ ft.) rise from chamfered plinths. The gabled E. wall has a restored 15th-century window of three ogee-headed trefoil lights below vertical tracery; the two-centred head has a moulded label with square stops. In the N. wall are two square-headed 15th-century windows, each of two ogee-headed cinquefoil lights; between the windows is a 19th-century doorway to the vestry with a moulded four-centred head and continuous jambs. The S. wall has two windows uniform with those

LYDLINCH *The parish church of St. Thomas à Becket*

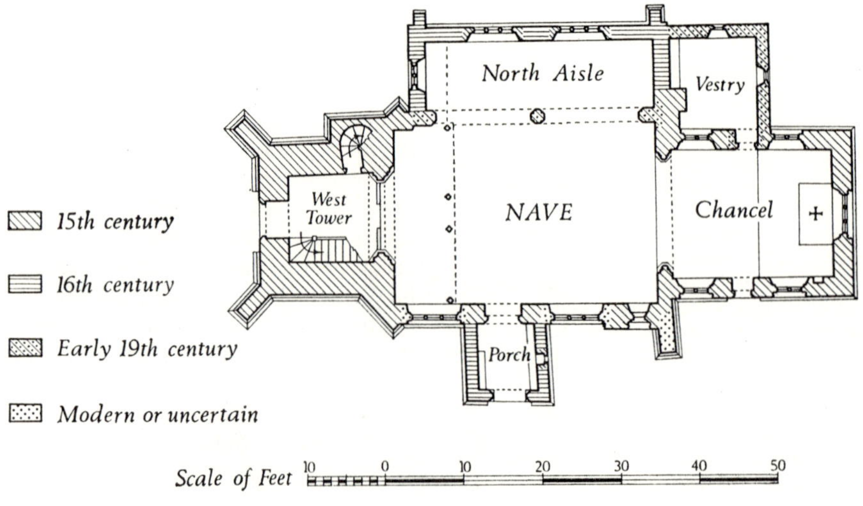

of the N. wall and between them is a S. doorway with a moulded four-centred head and continuous jambs, original but largely restored. The chancel arch is segmental-pointed and of two orders, the outer with a hollow-chamfer, the inner with an ogee moulding; these mouldings are continuous on the responds but the inner order is interrupted at the springing by shaped brackets of the late 19th century on which rests a modern rood-beam. A projection from the W. wall of the *Vestry* probably represents a former rood-loft vice turret.

The *Nave* (33½ ft. by 22½ ft.) has, to the N., an early 19th-century two-bay arcade with boldly chamfered four-centred arches, continuous chamfered responds and an octagonal centre pier. At the S.E. corner is a two-stage buttress, apparently modern. W. of the buttress a short length of the S. wall is thicker than elsewhere, the thickness terminating at a weathered capping some 3 ft. below the eaves; presumably this is a vestige of the nave wall as it was before being rebuilt and heightened early in the 19th century. In the thick part of the wall is a single-light window with a cinquefoil ogee head and blind spandrels in a square-headed casement-moulded surround. The S. doorway is flanked symmetrically by two 19th-century windows uniform with the E. window of the chancel, but somewhat taller. The doorway is of the late 15th century and has a moulded four-centred head with continuous jambs.

In the *North Aisle* (29 ft. by 8½ ft.) the N. wall has a chamfered plinth and small square-set buttresses of three weathered stages. Between the buttresses are two square-headed windows, each of three cinquefoil-headed lights; they appear to be of the late 15th century and are presumably reset. Hutchins describes two-light windows in this position, possibly in error. In the W. wall is a 16th-century window of two four-centred lights under a square head.

The *West Tower* (11 ft. square) has a double chamfered plinth and is divided into three stages by hollow-chamfered and moulded string-courses. At the top is an embattled parapet with a continuous moulded coping. At each corner is a diagonal buttress around which the string-courses are continuous. The buttresses are of four stages, with moulded and weathered offsets about half way up each of the tower stages. Above the buttresses, diagonally-set pinnacles mark the four corners of the embattled parapet and terminate in obelisk-shaped finials. At the centre of each parapet a smaller pinnacle rises from a gargoyle in the parapet string-course and ends in a moulded capping at battlement level; above is an obelisk slightly smaller than those at the corners. The tower arch is two-centred and has two hollow-chamfered orders with continuous responds and square plinths. In the E. part of the N. side is a projecting vice turret with two small loop lights, the upper one with radial tracery. The vice doorway has a chamfered four-centred head with continuous jambs. The W. doorway has a four-centred hollow-chamfered and ogee-moulded head with continuous jambs. Above, the two-centred casement-moulded W. window contains three trefoil ogee-headed lights with vertical tracery above, and a moulded label with square stops. In the second stage the E. wall is divided at about half height by a weathered offset, above which the wall is set back about 1 ft.; the outline of a former nave roof, steeper than the present roof, can be traced immediately below the offset. The vice turret terminates in a weathered stone capping at about the same level as the E. offset. Internally the vice newel ends at a roll-moulded and hollow-chamfered capital; the doorway at the top of the vice is square-headed. The W. wall of the second stage of the tower has a small window with a two-centred head and continuous jambs. In the third stage, each side has a two-centred belfry window of two cinquefoil-headed lights with a blind quatrefoil above; each window has a moulded label with return stops; on the E. and N. sides the window heads are partly masked by modern clock-faces. S. of the eastern clock-face is a small loop.

The *South Porch* (7½ ft. by 8½ ft.) has an archway with a moulded four-centred head and continuous jambs ending at run-out stops. A churchwardens' inscription dated 1753, over the opening, probably refers to repairs; the archway appears to be of the 16th century. At the apex of the gable is an 18th-century finial with a sundial attached to the S. face. Reset low down in the E. wall is a small 15th-century quatrefoil loop.

The mid 19th-century *Roof* of the nave is of four bays and has three tie-beam trusses filled in with trefoil-headed vertical tracery in wood; the trusses rest on coved and moulded wall-plates.

Fittings—*Bells:* five, by Thomas Purdue; treble recast 1908; 2nd with initials CB, NR, CW, TP and date 1681; 3rd recast 1908; 4th with initials C B, N R, C W, date 1681 and inscription 'Three bells were caste and hey made fowre They all here hangs now in this tower'; 5th with initials C B, N R, T P, date 1681 and inscription 'First second fowrth and tennur tells They were the fowre made of three bells'. *Brass:* In N. aisle, reset on N. wall, shaped brass plate inscribed 'Good Sr. for Jesus sake forbear to move the bodies that rest here. R.B.P. 1767'. *Doors:* three; S. door with vertical external planks and horizontal internal planks, with original wrought-iron studs and strap-hinges and wooden lock-case, 16th century, with 19th-century cover-fillets; door to tower vice with chamfered ribs terminating in four-centred head, 16th century; at head of tower vice, similar door, square-headed. *Font:* (Plate 26) comprising square Purbeck marble bowl with splayed angles and chamfered under-edge, vertical sides of bowl decorated with round-headed flush panels in grooved outline, bowl rests on large central shaft with four small corner shafts, all standing on chamfered base; late 12th century. *Gallery:* At W. end of nave, supported on wooden uprights shaped as hollow-chamfered columns with attached shafts; front of gallery with carved panelling in which the panel-heads are of cast-iron; 19th century. A section of same parapet, perhaps originally from W. end of N. aisle, now forms dado on N. side of chancel. *Glass:* In nave, reset in E. window of S. wall, formerly in chancel (Hutchins IV, 191), four panels depicting winged angels with feathered bodies, two headless (Plate 144), 15th century. In W. window of tower, in tracery lights, five 15th-century fragments. *Hatchments:* In chancel, on S. wall, (1) wooden lozenge (Plate 44) with cartouche-of-arms tierced in pale, Brune, Dennis, Collier quartering Williams, presumably for Charles Brune, *c.* 1650, who married Margaret Dennis and Jane Collier. In nave, on N. wall, (2) lozenge of wood and canvas with arms of Fane impaling Flint, 19th century; on W. wall, (3) wooden lozenge with arms probably of Jeffery. *Graffiti:* On S. doorway, 17th-century scratched initials and dates; on stone seats in porch, 18th and 19th-century initials and dates.

Monuments and *Floor-slabs. Monuments:* In nave, on E. wall, (1) of Nicholas Romayne, 1702, baroque white marble wall-monument with shield-of-arms of Romayne, flower-swags and drapery, surmounted by metal crest. In N. aisle, on E. wall, (2) of John Combe, 1745, grey and white marble wall-monument with black slate panel and brackets, erected 1746; on N. wall, (3) of Philip Henville, 1803, white marble tablet with gadrooned head on black back-plate with arms, by Reeves of Bath; (4) of Francis William Fane, 1844, tablet by White of Bath. In churchyard, E. of chancel, (5) of John Bugg, 1781, headstone; (6) of Richard Crocker, 1806, headstone; N. of chancel, (7) of Levi Bewsey, 1831, headstone; S.E. of chancel, (8) of Elizabeth, 1653, and of Richard [Tr]ime ?, 1654, table-tomb; S. of chancel, (9) of Thomas Forward, 1609, table-tomb with Latin inscription; (10) of Robert Fill, 1640, table-tomb with inscription on fascia of top slab, further inscription on plinth defaced; S. of S. porch,

(11) of an anonymous lady, a benefactor of the church, table-tomb, probably 18th century. *Floor-slabs:* In nave, (1) of Nicholas Fill, 1662, and Ann Fill, 1668, grey Purbeck stone with incised decoration and inscription; (2) of Joseph and Nicholas Romayn, both 1668, grey Purbeck stone with incised decoration and inscription; (3) of Joseph Romayn, 1661, grey Purbeck slab with incised decoration and inscription. In N. vestry, reset headstones from churchyard, (4) of John Williams, stone slab with pointed head and partly defaced inscription; (5) of Samuel and Thomas Lambert, 1803, 1810, stone slab with shaped head; (6) of Mary Lambert, 1811, similar slab carved in two oval panels, with drapery.

Piscina: In chancel, in S. wall, with two-centred head and cinquefoil cusping, 15th century. *Plate:* includes cup and cover-paten of silver, both with date-marks of 1573 and maker's initials I P, cover-paten inscribed 1574; another paten without hall-marks inscribed 1717. *Pulpit:* of oak, now forming three sides of hexagon, with fretted decoration of cusped arcading below cornice, stem similarly decorated; early 19th century, originally free-standing. *Royal Arms:* In tower, on S. wall, painted wood lozenge with arms of James II, dated 1686. *Screen:* In tower arch, of wood with fielded panels, upper part of door with balustraded openwork, late 18th century. *Sundials:* On apex of porch gable, square stone with iron gnomon, probably 18th century; on S.W. buttress of tower at top of second stage, stone plate with Roman numerals, much worn; on S.E. buttress of tower, traces of similar sundial. *Miscellanea:* In gable of porch, square stone inscribed '. . . Romayn [C]hurch [W]ardens, 1753'. Reset in E. wall of porch, small fragment of 12th-century carved stone. In vestry, plans of church lands dated 1711 and 1720. In ringing chamber of tower, painted inscription—

Rules to be observ'd by Ringers.

Put off your Hats, your Belts & Spur's,
And when you ring make no Demurs,
Sound out the Bells well if you can,
(Silence is best for evry Man,)
But if a Bell you overthrow,
Six Pence unto the Clerk you owe.

John Hopps & John Young. Church Wardens 1746.

(2) THE CHURCH (of unknown dedication) at Stock Gaylard (72241298) stands near the N.W. corner of the parish, in the park of (5), and is no longer associated with a village. The walls are of squared rubble with ashlar dressings and the roofs are stone-slated. The building comprises *Chancel*, *Nave*, *South Porch* and *North Vestry*; it was almost completely rebuilt in 1884. Among various mediaeval features included in the rebuilt church are a well-preserved 13th-century tomb effigy and a bell that probably is of about the same date.

The *Chancel* has, in the S. wall, a restored mediaeval doorway with a chamfered two-centred head and continuous jambs. To the W. is a window of one light with a chamfered two-centred head and trefoil cusping, perhaps old but restored. In the *Nave* the N. wall has a reset 16th-century window of two segmental-headed lights in a square-headed casement-moulded surround; a similar window is reset in the S. wall. The mediaeval S. doorway has a two-centred ovolo-moulded head with recut chamfered jambs and broach stops. At the centre of the gabled W. wall is a restored square-headed window, perhaps originally of the 15th century, with two hollow-chamfered lights with four-centred heads below blind spandrels. The *South Porch* has an archway with a chamfered two-centred head, probably of the 16th century.

Fittings—*Bells:* two, in bell-cote over W. gable; 1st perhaps 13th century with narrow pear-shaped form; 2nd probably 15th century with Lombardic inscription, AVE GRACIA GABBRALA AVE. *Communion Table:* In chancel, with stone slab (6 ft. by 2½ ft. by 5½ ins.), perhaps originally from a table-tomb, roll-moulded and hollow-chamfered on N., W. and S. edges, E. edge hidden; slab rests on reset Purbeck marble table-tomb, 1¾ ft. high, with moulded and chamfered corners, decorated on exposed faces with retooled, cusped and subcusped hollow-chamfered tracery forming square quatrefoil panels alternating with narrow cinquefoil-headed panels, each quatrefoil with blank shield at centre; below, moulded plinth with square quatrefoil panels. Stone slab, probably 14th century, discovered in church during restorations; table-tomb, 15th century, brought from Canford Magna (Dorset *Procs.*, XLVI, 25). *Font:* Octagonal stone bowl with vertical sides and hollow-chamfered under-edge, vertical faces with quatrefoil panels enclosing flowers, hollow-chamfered under-edge with coarse foliate carving, octagonal panelled stone pedestal and chamfered base; 15th century. *Glass:* In S. window of chancel, roundel depicting Crucifixion (8½ ins. diam.), early 16th century, Flemish; in nave, reset in S. window, two panels representing St. James and St. John, mid 19th century.

Monuments: In nave, in S. wall, reset in 19th-century cinquefoil-headed recess, (1) recumbent effigy (said to be of Sir Ingelramus de Walys) in mail armour (Plate 14), with plain heater-shaped shield hanging from left shoulder, legs crossed and right hand resting on pommel of sword, spurred feet on couched lion; Ham Hill stone, second half of 13th century. On S. wall, W. of S. doorway, marble tablets: (2) of Rev. John Yeatman, 1819; (3) of Emma Yeatman, 1842; (4) of Rev. Harry Yeatman, 1796; (5) of members of Lewys family, 1749, tablet with arms; (6) of Theophila Burland, 1802, tablet with arms, by T. King, Bath; (7) of John Farr, 1773, and his wife Mary, 1783; (8) of James, 1811, and Bridget Wolcott, 1835; (9) of Louisa Moilliet, 1844, white marble monument by Osmond of Sarum. In vestry, (10) of Anna [(Freeke) Stevens, 17]20, painted wooden panel with mitred surround, painted scroll-work and shield-of-arms, now indecipherable. Externally, on N. wall of chancel, (11) of Richard Stevens, rector, 1728, stone cartouche with scrolled surround. *Painting:* In vestry, oak panel 4 ft. high by 1½ ft. wide representing apostle, perhaps St. John, probably part of rood-screen, early 16th century. *Piscina:* In chancel, in E. wall, with chamfered two-centred head and corbelled bowl, perhaps mediaeval. *Plate:* includes silver cup with hallmark of 1732, maker's initials I.W. and inscription 'Deo et Ecclesiae de Stock Gaylard', and matching silver flagon with hallmark of 1750 and similar maker's mark, inscribed 'The gift of Mrs. Braithwaite'; also silver almsdish with hallmark of 1791, maker's initials R.S., dedicatory inscription of Berkeley Burland and arms of Burland impaling Lewys; also pewter almsdish, perhaps mid 18th century. *Miscellanea:* Refixed on modern S. door, oak box lock, perhaps early 17th century.

(3) MISSION ROOM (72531123), 1 m. S. of (2), is of one storey, with walls of coursed rubble with ashlar dressings, and with a thatched roof; it was built probably in 1836. In the W. front the entrance doorway has a moulded and hollow-chamfered round head and continuous jambs; to the S. is a square-headed window of two round-headed lights with mouldings as on the doorway; to the N. are two windows uniform with the first. An iron strip in the threshold is dated 1836. Internally there is a single room with a raised platform at the S. end. A lean-to kitchen has been added on the E.

SECULAR

(4) TWOFORDS BRIDGE (75071375), ½ m. N.E. of the

parish church, carries the main road from Sherborne to Blandford across the R. Lydden and appears to be of the 18th century. It is of coursed rubble with ashlar dressings and has two segmental arches. The central pier has semicircular cut-waters with rounded tops. The parapets have rounded ashlar copings and there is an ashlar plat-band at road level. The causeway to the E. was raised on three land arches in 1825 (Agreement of 25th August 1825, D.C.R.O.).

(5) STOCK GAYLARD HOUSE (72231330), 1¼ m. S.W. of Lydlinch church and some 30 yds. N. of (2), is of two storeys with cellars and attics; the walls are of rubble, in most cases rendered externally, and the roofs are stone-slated. The house appears to date from early in the 18th century. Towards the end of the same century the principal rooms were remodelled and the house was enlarged westwards, probably by John Berkeley Burland whose wife Theophila (Farr) inherited the estate in 1773. The original W. walls are to some extent indicated by old plinths, now seen indoors. Further additions are of the 19th century.

The E. front is symmetrical, with a pedimented centre pavilion of three bays and two flanking bays on each side. The windows are sashed and have moulded stone architraves; the central doorway has stone pilasters and a pediment; at the eaves is a moulded stone cornice. The N. front is of five bays, in general with sashed windows as on the E. In the two eastern bays a three-light sashed window of *c.* 1800 takes the place of the original ground-floor windows. In the two western bays the ground-floor windows have casements with moulded stone surrounds, mullions and transoms of the late 18th century; the attic has been developed into a third storey by raising the old cornice and substituting low-pitched slates for the former stone-slates. The S. front is of five bays, with sashed windows somewhat higher than those on the E.; the three eastern bays are more closely spaced than those to the W. and a straight joint in the stone plinth indicates the original extent of the range. The W. wall of the S. range has late 18th-century casement windows with moulded stone surrounds, as at the western end of the N. front.

On the W. of the principal building and perhaps originally isolated, the late 18th-century kitchen range is single-storied with an attic and has walls of rubble and of ashlar; it is roofed with stone-slates; the windows are casements, with stone mullions and transoms as before described.

Inside, the entrance hall has a fireplace surround with a frieze of foliate swags, and mutules below the mantelshelf; above is a portrait medallion of John Berkeley Burland. The drawing room was redecorated late in the 18th century, presumably by Burland, and the ceiling level was raised at the expense of the chambers above; the fireplace surround is of wood with *carton-pierre* enrichments depicting wreathed musical instruments and other emblems; the doorcase has an entablature with inverted swags and paterae. In the dining room the sideboard recess is flanked by classical columns. The stairs have open strings, scrolled spandrels, mahogany newel posts in the form of slender Doric columns, and moulded mahogany handrails. The bedrooms over the heightened drawing room are approached by flights of steps and have deep coved ceilings rising into the former attics.

In the garden to the W. of the house is a circular *Pigeon Cote*

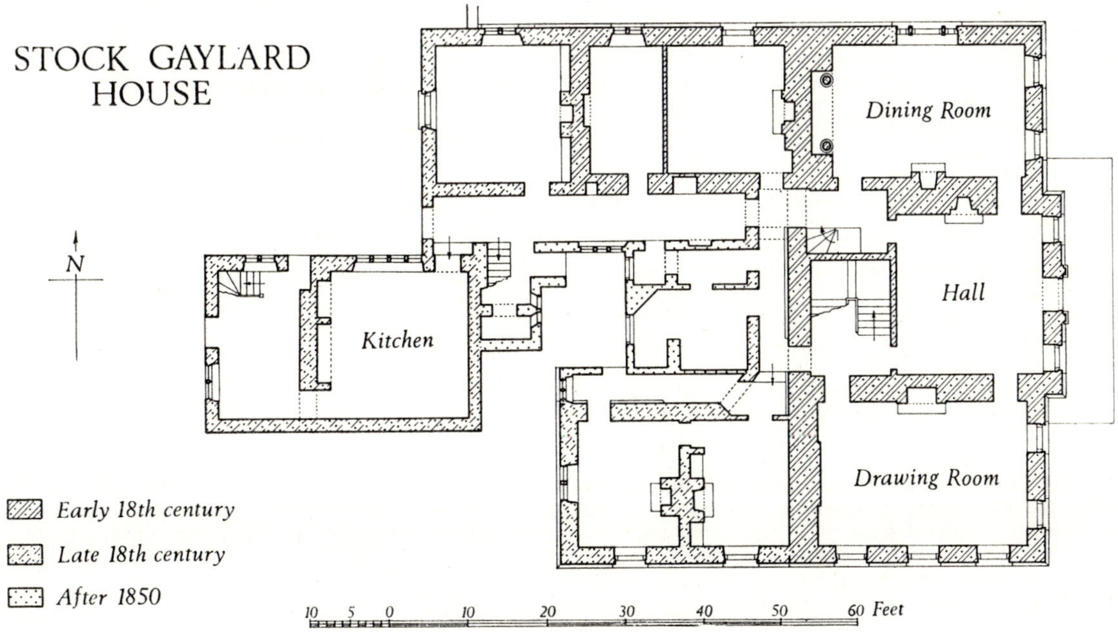

with rubble walls, and a tiled roof partly hidden by a parapet. The cote appears to have been remodelled as a summer-house in the 19th century, with the reuse of earlier elements from elsewhere. To the S. are an upper and a lower doorway and small windows flanking the lower doorway; all these openings have segmental-pointed heads and are of the 19th century; the lower doorway has a brick head while the other openings have heads and jambs of moulded ashlar. Over the upper doorway is a lozenge shaped stone panel carved with the arms of Lewys (Plate 48). Small windows similar to those already described open to E. and W. in the upper storey. On the N. side is a ground-floor window of two lights with two-centred heads and continuous hollow-chamfered jambs; in the upper storey a single-light window is blocked by a clock which is probably of the late 18th or early 19th century. A cast-lead rainwater head has the shield of Lewys and the date 1675. A scrolled wrought-iron weather-vane caps the conical roof.

The *Stables*, to the W., are of one storey with rendered walls and slated roofs; they are of the late 18th or early 19th century.

(6) PLUMBER MANOR (77181179), 2 m. S.E. of (1) and at the E. extremity of the parish, is of two storeys with attics and is built partly of rubble and partly of brick, with ashlar dressings. The roofs are slated. Although extensively remodelled, the house incorporates a considerable part of the 17th and 18th-century mansion illustrated by Hutchins (IV, facing 189).

The S. range has a S. front of coursed rubble with a chamfered plinth and a coved eaves cornice. All openings are modern replicas in the 17th-century style and probably replace those depicted by Hutchins in the right hand part of his engraving. The E. wall of the wing is of rubble below and of ashlar above the first floor. In the upper storey, to the N., is a square-headed two-light window with chamfered and hollow-chamfered jambs and mullions. The N. elevation of the S. range is of English-bonded brickwork with a chamfered plinth of rubble and quoins of ashlar. On the ground floor are two two-light windows with restored stone jambs and heads; the first-floor openings are modern. Near the W. end of the N. elevation, at right-angles and thus facing E., is a gabled 17th-century stone bay with an attic window of two square-headed lights and the remains of a moulded label; below, the bay is masked by modern additions. The roof of the S. range is modern but the E. chimneystack, of brick, in two separate parts united at the top by an arch, is as depicted by Hutchins and presumably is of the 18th century.

The large W. range seen in Hutchins's engraving has been demolished. The W. end of the S. range repeats the plinth and cornice of the S. front and is probably a modern rebuilding. N. of this, the W. front is set at an angle for a short stretch and this too is modern. Reset in this part of the wall is a chamfered four-centred 17th-century door head, now spanning a window. Further N. the masonry appears to be old, although repointed and pierced by modern openings; it is probably the E. wall of the demolished W. range, reused inside-out; in the upper storey is a blocked stone window of one light, probably reset. At the N. end of the W. front the old masonry returns and is incorporated in the S. front of a modern N. range; in it is a reset doorway with a chamfered square head and jambs; beside the doorway is an old pump with a cast-lead head bearing the letter B and four rosettes. Internally, the house has been entirely rebuilt and an 18th-century wooden staircase has been brought from elsewhere.

To the S., a large block of *Farm Buildings* of squared and coursed rubble is perhaps of the late 18th or early 19th century; the roofs are modern. The walled inner *Garden* depicted in Hutchins's engraving lies to the N. of the house but all the other garden walls and pavilions depicted have gone. Some 75 yds. S. of the house, a small late 18th or early 19th-century *Bridge* spans the R. Divelish with three round-headed brick arches with ashlar keystones.

(7) LYDLINCH OLD RECTORY (74351330), 150 yds. S.E. of the parish church, is of two storeys with rendered walls and slated roofs; it is of the mid 19th century. To the N. an L-shaped range of outbuildings and a barn have rubble walls with slated roofs and are probably of the 18th century. At the N. end of the barn is a two-storied cottage with rubble walls and a tiled roof; it also is of the 18th century.

(8) STOCK GAYLARD OLD RECTORY (72071240), 650 yds. S.W. of (2), is two-storied with rubble walls, partly rendered, and with tiled roofs. The main part of the house is of the early or mid 19th century; it has a three-bay S.E. front with sashed windows and a central doorway. The lower rear wing probably dates from the 18th century; in its original form it may have been single-storied.

(9) HAYDON FARM (76301159), house, has an L-shaped plan and is of two storeys with rubble walls, in part rendered, and with tiled roofs; it dates from the late 16th century. All windows are modern, but the S.W. doorway has a moulded stone architrave with a square head, above which is a moulded hood supported on scrolled stone brackets. On the N.E. front a square-headed doorway, nearly opposite the first, has a heavy moulded oak frame and a door made of vertical and horizontal planks fastened with iron studs. Inside, the parlour in the projecting N.E. wing has a four-panel ceiling with richly moulded cross-beams and wall-plates. The original fireplace in the N.E.

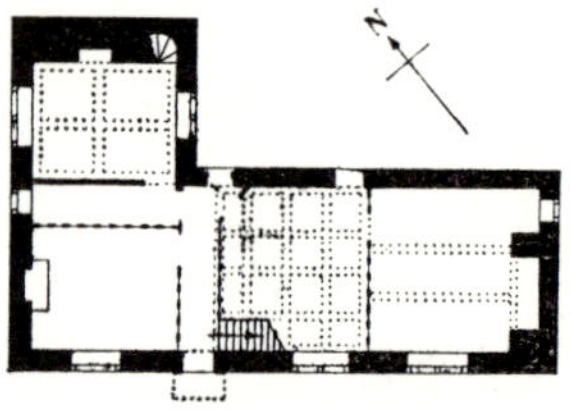

wall is blocked up; beside it is a newel staircase to the first floor. The S.W. wall of the adjacent passage is of plank-and-muntin construction, as are both sides of the through-passage which connects the N.E. and S.W. doorways; in the through-passage the muntins have moulded edges. The room to the S.E. of the through-passage has a ceiling of sixteen square panels formed by the intersection of six elaborately moulded beams, three each way, and corresponding wall-plates. The S.E. room, separated from the middle room by another plank-and-muntin partition, has two unmoulded ceiling beams and an open fireplace. Other plank-and-muntin partitions occur on the first floor.

MONUMENTS (10–16)

Except as otherwise noted the following monuments are 17th-century farmhouses of two storeys, with rubble walls, thatched roofs and casement windows.

(10) *Manor Farm* (74331324), house, 130 yds. S.E. of the parish church, is an early 18th-century farmhouse with walls of coursed rubble, brick chimneystacks and stone-slated roofs. A small two-storied extension to the W. is of brick with a tiled roof. The main part of the house has a symmetrical N. front

of three bays (Plate 58). The central doorway is sheltered by a small gabled porch with an arched entry; on either side is a casement window of three square-headed lights with chamfered and hollow-chamfered stone jambs and heads, and hollow-chamfered labels with return stops. Corresponding with these openings, on the first floor, are three similar two-light windows. All these windows are leaded and in each light the top row of panes is arcaded. The S. elevation is rendered and the casement windows are modern.

(11) *Coombe Farm* (74351350), house, 200 yds. N.E. of the parish church, has roofs which appear formerly to have been thatched although they now are covered with asbestos tiles. The house dates from the 17th century and is of one build except for the E. wing, which appears to be a little later than the main range. The casement windows are of wood and are nearly all modern; however, the E. elevation has, on the ground floor near the N. end, a window of one light with an oak frame with pegged joints, perhaps original, and a similar two-light window on the first floor. To the S. of the projecting E. wing the E. elevation has an original doorway with a square-headed chamfered oak surround, and a door of nail-studded planks hung on wrought-iron strap hinges with triple poppy-head finials. On the first floor in this part of the E. elevation a stretch of disused wall-plate indicates a former roof level.

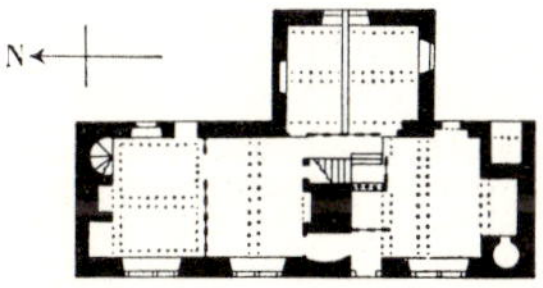

Inside, the original ground plan of the house is only partly preserved. The central stairs and chimneystack are probably insertions, and a plank-and-muntin partition that originally traversed the house to the S. of the W. doorway has been partly reset. In the N. room the open fireplace has been modified; to the E. of the chimney breast is an original spiral staircase with solid wooden treads. The ceiling has moulded wall-plates and a moulded cross-beam supporting heavy joists of square cross-section. The S. wall of this room is a plank-and-muntin partition in which the muntins are beaded on the N. and ogee-moulded on the S.; the doorway through the partition has an ogee head and a nail-studded plank door. The central room has a stop-chamfered beam and exposed ceiling joists; the fireplace has a chamfered bressummer, one chamfered jamb and one moulded jamb, both of wood but mounted on stone plinths. On the W. side of the fireplace the entrance passage is closed with a nail-studded plank door. To the E., the doorway into the E. wing has an ogee-headed surround set in a length of reset plank-and-muntin partition. The S. room has a stop-chamfered ceiling beam and, in the S. wall, an open fireplace with a chamfered bressummer; to the W. is an oven. The N. side of this room retains part of an original plank-and-muntin partition, and mortices for the continuation of the same partition are seen in the transverse beam. Associated with the inserted stairs is an open partition composed of two heights of turned oak balusters, presumably reset. The E. wing has a stop-chamfered ceiling beam and wall-plates. On the first floor, the N. and middle rooms have stone fireplace surrounds with four-centred heads and continuous jambs, that of the N. room is moulded and that of the middle room is chamfered. There are various lengths of plank-and-muntin partition on the first floor, and several doorways have nail-studded plank doors.

(12) *Rodmore Farm* (72491208), house, nearly 1½ m. S.W. of the parish church, is of the 17th century but with a modern slated roof. The plan of the original house is L-shaped, with the re-entrant angle to the S.E. The W. front is of three bays and has, to the N., a stone window of three square-headed lights; at the centre is a similar but slightly lower two-light window and to the S. is another, now blocked; the latter has a hollow-chamfered label with return stops. On the first floor, the N. bay has a four-light window, the middle bay has a two-light window and the S. bay is blank. Although the pitched roof of the W. range stops at a gabled N. wall with a brick chimneystack at the apex, the W. front continues beyond the line of this gable to form a single-storied N. extension with a lean-to roof against the N. gable; the masonry of the extension is continuous with that of the W. front. In the attic storey of the extension is a blocked square-headed single-light window with a chamfered and hollow-chamfered stone surround. On the E. front, the lean-to N. extension has a two-light stone window on the ground floor and another in the attic; the former retains part of a moulded label. The E. gable of the E. wing has, at the apex, a cylindrical stone chimneystack with a moulded square capping (cf. Glanville's Wooton (6)). Internal inspection was not allowed.

(13) *Blackrow Farm* (72731197), house, 1¼ m. S.W. of the parish church, has an L-shaped plan with the main range facing N.W., and a S.E. wing at the back; it appears to be of the late 17th or early 18th century. The N.W. front has four bays; the two to N.E. have, in each storey, uniform stone windows of three square-headed lights with chamfered and hollow-chamfered surrounds; the ground-floor windows have hollow-chamfered labels, those above are without labels. The third bay of the N.W. front contains the doorway, sheltered by a modern porch; above it on the first floor is an oval bull's-eye window with a moulded ashlar surround. The fourth bay is uniform with the first two. Inside, few original features remain. Some rooms have chamfered ceiling beams and there are some plank-and-muntin partitions, notably between the N. and central rooms, where the muntins have beaded edges. One fireplace has a head with a raised centre.

(14) *Holebrook Green Farm* (74721196), house, nearly 1 m. S. of the parish church, is a mid 17th-century farmhouse with an L-shaped plan. Originally it was of one storey with attics in a thatched roof, but the rubble walls have been heightened in brickwork to provide an upper storey and a new roof of corrugated iron has been substituted. The S. front, of four bays, retains one original stone window of three lights with chamfered and hollow-chamfered surrounds, and a hollow-chamfered label with return stops; the other openings are modern. Inside, a central through-passage has, on one side, a plank-and-muntin partition in which an ogee-headed doorway leads to the E. room. Here the ceiling rests on two chamfered beams and the open fireplace has a chamfered bressummer with a raised centre. In the W. room, chamfered wall-plates and intersecting beams form a panelled ceiling, and the fireplace has another chamfered bressummer.

(15) *Stroud Farm* (72871357), house, nearly 1 m. W. of the church, is a late 17th-century farmhouse with an L-plan in which the S. wing is two-storied and the W. wing is one storied with an attic; to the S. is a two-storied late 18th-century extension. The original part of the house has recently been reroofed. Internally there are no noteworthy features; the ceiling beams are rough-hewn and all old fireplace openings have been blocked up.

(16) *Hydes Farm* (73241234), cottage, nearly 1 m. S.W. of the church, is of one storey with attics. The farmhouse evolved in three stages: at the centre is a small 17th-century rubble cottage

of one storey with an attic; in the 18th century the cottage was extended to the S. in brickwork; to the N. is another addition, perhaps a little later, of light timber framework with brick nogging. N.E. of the cottage are large farm buildings, substantially built in rubble.

Monuments (17–22)

The following houses are of the 18th century and, except as otherwise noted, are of two storeys with rubble walls and casement windows.

(17) *Blackmore Farm* (74381369), house, 400 yds. N.E. of the parish church, has walls of rubble and of brick, partly rendered, and tiled roofs. The windows are modern wooden casements. The oldest part of the house faces S. and is of four bays. The E. bay has a three-light ground-floor window and a two-light first-floor window. Next is the front doorway with a moulded timber frame and a tiled hood on wooden brackets; over it on the first floor is a round bull's-eye window. The third and fourth bays are uniform with the first. The E. gable wall is of rubble and there is a blocked window on the first floor. To the rear, in line with the E. gable, projects a two-storied N. wing, of rubble on the ground floor and of brick above. At the W. end of the S. front a two-storied addition extends the range for one more bay and then turns S. in an L-shaped plan; this wing contains stables and lofts. Inside the house, the W. room of the original range is lined with 18th-century fielded panelling in two heights with moulded skirting, dado rail and cornice. The stairs, opposite the front doorway, are of oak, with close strings, turned newels and balusters, and moulded handrails. The ground-floor room in the W. extension has a chamfered beam and an open fireplace with a cambered and chamfered bressummer.

(18) *Ridge Farm* (72971075), house, 1¾ m. S.W. of the parish church, is of two storeys with dormer-windowed attics. The walls are of rubble in the lower storey and of cob above; the roofs are thatched. The W. front, of three bays, has a central doorway flanked symmetrically by original four-light casement windows above which, on the first floor, are three uniform three-light windows; the jambs, mullions and heads are of oak, and the casements are of wrought-iron with leaded glazing. Internally, some ceilings have chamfered beams; there is an open fireplace, now blocked.

(19) *Berry Farm* (73751149), house, 1¼ m. S. of the parish church, has walls of rendered rubble and tiled roofs. The plan is oblong, with a lean-to addition along the whole length of the rear N. side. Inside, are chamfered beams and large fireplaces, now blocked.

(20) *Little Rodmore Farm* (72061113), house, nearly 2 m. S.W. of the parish church, is of early 18th-century origin and formerly was of one storey with a dormer-windowed attic; it had rubble walls and a thatched roof. In recent years the attic has been removed, the lower storey has been reroofed with asbestos and the walls have been incorporated in a range of farm buildings.

(21) *The Three Boars' Heads Inn* (74591373), 600 yds. N.E. of the parish church, has brick walls, in part rendered, and a tiled roof. The symmetrical three-bay S. front has sashed windows and a central doorway. It is probably of the late 18th century.

(22) *Cottage* (74481368), ¼ m. N.E. of the parish church, is of one storey with a dormer-windowed attic; some walls are of rendered brick and others are of timber-framing with cob infilling; the roof is thatched. The leaded casement windows have wooden mullions and heads. Inside, there is a plank-and-muntin partition with beaded muntins, and some chamfered ceiling beams.

(23) *Cottage* (74321332), 80 yds. S.E. of the church, has a tiled roof and appears to have been much restored. Inside, the S. room has an open fireplace with a moulded timber bressummer with a raised centre; on the N. side of the room is a chamfered plank-and-muntin partition. Certain older fittings have recently been brought from elsewhere.

Early 19th-century buildings in the parish include the following: *House*, 330 yds. N. of the church, is of two storeys with rendered walls and low-pitched slated roofs; it has a symmetrical three-bay S. elevation with sashed windows and a central doorway with a metal hood on trellised iron uprights. *Cottages*, two, 220 yds. S.E. of the church, are two-storied, with rubble and brick walls and slated roofs, the E. cottage perhaps being of the 18th century. *Cottages*, three, at Kingstag (72491095), (72521095) and (72521101), are two-storied with walls of brick and cob, and with thatched roofs.

MEDIAEVAL AND LATER EARTHWORKS

(24) Settlement Remains (723130), formerly part of the village of Stock Gaylard, lie immediately E. of (5). The village is probably the 'Stoches', belonging to William of Eu in 1086 (D.B. Vol. I, f. 82a), which had a recorded population of 11. The church was not taxed in 1291 (Hutchins III, 690). By 1304 only two people are listed as belonging to the manor (*Cal. I.P.M.*, Vol. 4, 144), and only three are listed in the 1327 and 1333 Subsidy Rolls; thereafter there is no record of population.

The remains, covering about 2 acres, consist of a roughly rectangular area bounded to N., E. and S. by a low bank or scarp 1 ft. to 2 ft. high, and by the garden of Stock Gaylard House on the W. The interior is disturbed by later drainage channels but there are remains of closes bounded by low scarps, and at least two well-defined building platforms.

(25) Cultivation Remains. In the mid 14th century a three field system was in operation at *Lydlinch* (Dorset *I.P.M.*, Vol. I (1916), 438); the fields appear to have been gradually enclosed over a long period of time and a small fragment still remained in the present century (*S. & D.N. & Q.*, XXIII (1939–42), 62). Traces of ridge-and-furrow of these fields can be seen on air photographs (R.A.F. CPE/UK 1974: 1168, 2183–4) in a number of places around the village (*e.g.* 741124, 744123 and 753133); they consist of gently curving furlongs underlying existing field boundaries.

Nothing is known of the date of enclosure of the open fields of *Stock Gaylard* but it had taken place before the 18th century, when the park at Stock Gaylard House was laid out. Ridge-and-furrow of these fields remains in the park (*e.g.* at 721132) and further traces can be seen on air photographs; the ridges are 6 yds. to 8 yds. wide and are arranged in butting furlongs.

Ridge-and-furrow within old enclosures beyond the former open fields remains on the ground or can be seen on air photographs in a number of places; for example N. of Hallow Hill Plantation in an area enclosed from Lydlinch Common (732135), also N. of Little Rodmore Farm (721111) and S.W. of Haydon Farm (762115). These remains all lie within the existing fields and have ridges 7 yds. to 9 yds. wide and headlands 10 yds. wide.

Dd. 132468 K24